SIXTH EDITION

# Fundamental Statistics for the Behavioral Sciences

## David C. Howell

THOMSON
™
WADSWORTH

Australia • Brazil • Canada • Mexico • Singapore • Spain • United Kingdom • United States

# THOMSON

## WADSWORTH

**Fundamental Statistics for the Behavioral Sciences, Sixth Edition**
*David C. Howell*

Editor: *Erik Evans*
Assistant Editor: *Gina Kessler*
Editorial Assistant: *Christina Ganim*
Technology Project Managers: *Bessie Weiss, Lauren Keyes*
Marketing Manager: *Karin Sandberg*
Marketing Assistant: *Natasha Coats*
Marketing Communications Manager: *Linda Yip*
Project Manager, Editorial Production: *Mary Noel*
Creative Director: *Rob Hugel*
Art Director: *Vernon Boes*

Print Buyer: *Rebecca Cross*
Permissions Editor: *Bob Kauser*
Production Service: *Sonia Taneja, ICC Macmillan Inc.*
Copy Editor: *Michelle Gaudreau*
Cover Designer: *Lisa Langhoff*
Compositor: *ICC Macmillan Inc.*
Printer: *R.R. Donnelley/Crawfordsville*

Printed in the United States of America
1 2 3 4 5 6 7 11 10 09 08 07

**Thomson Higher Education**
**10 Davis Drive**
**Belmont, CA 94002-3098**
**USA**

For more information about our products, contact us at:
**Thomson Learning Academic Resource Center**
**1-800-423-0563**
For permission to use material from this text or product, submit a request online at
**http://www.thomsonrights.com.**
Any additional questions about permissions can be submitted by e-mail to **thomsonrights@thomson.com.**

Library of Congress Control Number: 2006937605

Student Edition:
ISBN-13: 978-0-495-09900-0
ISBN-10: 0-495-09900-7

# Preface

## Why Statistics?

Those of us who teach in this area hate to admit it, but statistics is seldom listed as the most sought-after course on campus. A high percentage of students enroll because the faculty have made this a required course. Under these conditions students have a right to ask "why?" and there are at least two good answers to that question. The traditional answer is that we want our students to learn a specific set of skills about data analysis (including formulae and procedures) so that they can understand the experimental literature and conduct analyses on their own data. The broader answer, and one that applies to perhaps a larger number of students, is that some more general facility with numbers and data in general is an important skill that has lifelong and career-related value. Most of us, and not only those who do experimental work, frequently come across numerical data as part of our jobs, and some broad understanding of how to deal with those data is an important and marketable skill. It is my experience that students who have taken a course in statistics, even if they think that they have forgotten every technique they ever learned, have an understanding of numerical data that puts them ahead of their colleagues. And in a world increasingly dominated by quantitative data, that skill is more and more in demand. Some of my former students have told me that they were assigned an important task because they were the only one in their office who wasn't afraid of data.

Statistics is not really about numbers; it is about understanding our world. Certainly an important activity for statisticians is to answer such questions as whether cocaine taken in a novel context has more of an effect than cocaine taken in a familiar context. But let's not forget that what we are talking about here is drug addiction or the effect of the environment on learning and memory. The results of our experiment have a life beyond the somewhat limited world of the cognitive or social scientist. And let's also remember that the numbers that most people see do not relate to tightly controlled experiments, but to the implications of a traffic study for the development of a shopping center, the density of residential housing and its impact on the local school budget, and a marketing survey for a new product. All of these examples involve many of the basic statistical concepts covered in this book.

## Why This Text?

Enough preaching on the value of a course in statistics. Presumably the instructor was convinced before he or she started reading, and I hope that students have become at least a bit more open minded. But the question remains, why should you

use this book instead of another of the many available texts? Part of the answer comes down to the matter of style. I have deliberately set out to make this book both interesting and useful for students and instructors. It is written in an informal style, every example is put in the context of an investigation that one might reasonably conduct, and almost all of the examples are taken from the published literature. It does not make much sense to ask people to learn a series of statistical procedures without supplying examples of situations in which those techniques would actually be applied.

This text is designed for an introductory statistics course in psychology, education, and other behavioral sciences. It does not presuppose a background in mathematics beyond high school algebra, and it emphasizes the *logic* of statistical procedures rather than their derivation.

Over the past twenty years the world of data analysis has changed dramatically. Whereas we once sat down with a calculator and entered data by hand to solve equations, we are now much more likely to use a statistical package running on a desktop computer. As the mechanics of doing statistics have changed, so too must our approach to teaching statistical procedures. While we cannot, and should not, forego all reference to formulae and computations, it is time that we relaxed our emphasis on them. And by relaxing the emphasis on computation, we free up the time to increase the emphasis on interpretation. That is what this book tries to do. It moves away from simply declaring group differences to be significant or not significant and toward an explanation of what such differences mean relative to the purpose behind the experiment. I like to think of it as moving toward an analysis of *data* and away from an analysis of numbers. It becomes less important to concentrate on whether there is a difference between two groups than to understand what that difference means.

In the process of moving away from a calculator toward a computer, I have altered my approach to formulae. In the past I often gave a definitional formula, but then immediately jumped to a computational one. But if I have to worry less about computation, and more about understanding, then I am able to revert to the use of definitional formulae. It is my hope that this will make students' lives a bit easier.

## Unique Features

Several features of this book set it apart from other books written for the same audience. One of these was just noted: the use of examples from the research literature. I have attempted to choose studies that address problems of interest to students. Examples include the effect of context on heroin overdose, the relationship between daily stress and psychological symptoms, variables influencing course evaluations, the effect of early parental death on children's feelings of vulnerability, and factors underlying homophobic behavior. I want students to have some involvement in the questions being asked, and I want to illustrate that statistical analyses involve more than just applying a few equations.

In most chapters a section is devoted to an example based on one of the major data analysis computer packages. Readers have suggested that I concentrate most on SPSS, which is probably the most widely used package, and I have done so in

this edition. My purpose is to familiarize students with the form of computer printouts and the kinds of information they contain. I am not trying to teach students how to use a particular statistical package, but I want them to get a feel for what is available.

Data files for all of the examples and exercises used in the text are available on a Web site that I maintain for this book. The basic URL for that site is http://www.uvm.edu/~dhowell/fundamentals/index.html. The first link at that site will take you to the data. You can also reach the site through www.thomsonedu.com/psychology/howell. These files are formatted in ASCII, so that they can be read by virtually any statistical program. The variable names appear on the first line and can be directly imported to your software. The data can be saved to your computer simply by selecting your browser's "Save" option. The availability of these files makes it easy for students and instructors to incorporate any statistical package with the text.

A *Student Manual* is also available at the Web site referred to above. It provides complete solutions for half the exercises. I have included answers only to the odd-numbered questions because many instructors prefer to assign problems (or exam questions) on material that does not have an answer in the back of the book or in the *Student Manual*. (I am very much aware that this does annoy students, from whom I sometimes receive unhappy email messages, but it is a balance between the needs of students and instructors.)

The book includes over 350 homework exercises and answers to half of them. Approximately half of these exercises involve direct calculation, and the others require students to think about the whole process of data analysis. A number of homework problems have been added to the book over the years, with a particular emphasis on problems that require students to think about the material. In addition, the last chapter includes a set of examples of actual research studies. For these studies, students are asked to decide upon the appropriate method of analysis. This is an area in which many people have difficulty, and these exercises are intended to help overcome this difficulty.

I have also included many links to other sites, where you can find good examples, small programs to demonstrate statistical techniques, a more extensive glossary, and so on. People have devoted a great deal of time to making material available over the Internet, and it is very worthwhile to use that material.

An Instructor's Manual with Test Bank is also available to assist instructors with preparation for their statistics course. This helpful resource features answers to all the book exercises, lecture suggestions, additional examples, and web links, plus approximately 1500 test items. These test items are also available for download or as ExamView computerized test bank files.

## New to This Edition

This book differs in several ways from the first five editions. I have benefited greatly from the feedback from instructors and students who have used earlier editions. Not only has that feedback been gratifying in terms of what people like about the book, but also it has pointed out important areas that could be made clearer.

I have made two important additions to this edition. In the first place I have greatly increased the discussion of measures of effect size. This is in line with trends in the field, but it is also important because it causes the student, and the researcher, to think carefully about what a result means. In presenting effect size measures I have tried to convey the idea that the writer is trying to tell the reader what the study found, and there are different ways of accomplishing that goal. In some situations it is sufficient to simply talk about the difference between means or proportions. In other situations a standardized measure, such as Cohen's $\hat{d}$, is helpful. I have stayed away from correlation-based measures as much as I reasonably can because I don't think that they tell the reader much of what he or she wants to know.

The other change that I have consistently made is to show the student how they should prepare a written summary of the results. These summaries are by necessity brief, but they show the kinds of information that needs to be included and how to present test statistics. I did a bit of this in the fifth edition, but I have extended it to all of the chapters in the last half of the book.

I have maintained from the fifth edition a section labeled "Seeing Statistics." These sections are built around a set of Java applets, written by Gary McClelland at the University of Colorado. These allow the students to illustrate for themselves many of the concepts that are discussed in the book. The student can open these applets, change parameters, and see what happens to the result. A nice example of this is the applet illustrating the influence of heterogeneous subsamples in a correlation problem. See Chapter 9, pp. 203. In the past, these applets were made available on a CD bound with the book, but in this edition they are available directly from my Web site referred to earlier.

In addition to the features already described, the Web site linked to this book contains a number of other elements that should be helpful to students. There are links to multiple resources, a review of basic arithmetic, and links to other examples and additional material. More helpful features, including interactive flash cards, statistics workshops, and chapter-by-chapter self-quizzes, are available on the publisher's Web site at http://www.thomsonedu.com/psychology/howell.

## Organization and Coverage

This section is meant primarily for instructors, because frequent reference is made to terms that students cannot yet be expected to know. Students may wish to skip to the next section.

- The first seven chapters of the book are devoted to standard descriptive statistics, including ways of displaying data, measures of central tendency and variability, the normal distribution, and those aspects of probability that are directly applicable to material in the rest of the book.

- Chapter 8 on hypothesis testing and sampling distributions serves as a nontechnical introduction to inferential statistics. That chapter was

specifically designed to allow students to examine the underlying logic of hypothesis testing without simultaneously being concerned with learning a set of formulae and the intricacies of a statistical test.

- Chapters 9, 10, and 11 deal with correlation and regression, including multiple regression.

- Chapters 12–14 are devoted to tests on means, primarily *t* tests.

- Chapter 15 is concerned with power and its calculation and serves as an easily understood and practical approach to that topic.

- Chapters 16–18 are concerned with the analysis of variance. I have included material on simple repeated-measures designs, but have stopped short of covering mixed designs. These chapters include consideration of basic multiple comparison procedures by way of Fisher's protected *t*, which not only is an easily understood statistic but has also been shown to be well behaved, under limited conditions, with respect to both power and error rates. At the request of several users of the earlier editions, I have included treatment of the Bonferroni test, which does a very commendable job of controlling error rates, while not sacrificing much in the way of power when used judiciously. Also included are measures of magnitude of effect and effect size, a fairly extensive coverage of interactions, and procedures for testing simple effects. The effect size material, in particular, is considerably expanded from earlier editions.

- Chapter 19 deals with the chi-square test, although that material could very easily be covered at an earlier point if desired.

- Chapter 20 covers the most prominent distribution-free tests.

- Chapter 21 offers the student practice in deciding upon the most appropriate statistical procedure for use with a given experimental design.

Not every course would be expected to cover all these chapters, and several (most notably multiple regression, power, and distribution-free statistical methods) can be omitted or reordered without disrupting the flow of the material. (I cover chi-square early in my courses, but I took the advice of reviewers , and placed it late in the text.)

## Acknowledgments

Many people have played an important role in the development of this book. My editor, Vicki Knight, was extremely supportive of this revision, offering numerous suggestions for my consideration. Michelle Gaudreau did an excellent job of editing of the manuscript and was always supportive on those few occasions when I insisted that quaint spellings and my positioning of prepositions were better than the ones preferred by style manuals. My daughter, Lynda (University of Texas Health Sciences Center), did extensive work on aligning and formatting the Instructor and Student manuals and spotting the occasional error.

A number of reviewers made many helpful suggestions in earlier editions, especially Dr. Kevin J. Apple (Ohio University), Eryl Bassett (University of Kent at Canterbury), Drake Bradley (Bates College), Deborah M. Clauson (Catholic University of America), Jose M. Cortina (Michigan State University), Gary B. Forbach (Washburn University), Edward Johnson (University of North Carolina), Dennis Jowaisas (Oklahoma City University), David J. Mostofsky (Boston University), Maureen Powers (Vanderbilt University), David R. Owen (Brooklyn College CUNY), Dennis Roberts (Pennsylvania State University), Steven Rogelberg (Bowling Green State University), Deborah J. Runsey (Kansas State University), Robert Schutz (University of British Columbia), N. Clayton Silver (University of Nevada), Patrick A. Vitale (University of South Dakota), Bruce H. Wade (Spelman College), Robert Williams (Gallaudet University), Eleanor Willemsen (Santa Clara University), Pamela Zappardino (University of Rhode Island), and Dominic Zerbolio (University of Missouri-St. Louis). For years Dr. Karl Wuensch (East Carolina University) has filled pages with suggestions, disagreements, and valuable advice. He deserves special recognition, as does Dr. Kathleen Bloom (University of Waterloo) and Joan Foster (Simon Fraser University). Gary McClelland, at the University of Colorado, graciously allowed me to use some of his Java applets, and was willing to modify them when necessary to meet my needs.

The reviewers for this edition include Dr. Natalie Ciarocco Belenky (Florida Atlantic University: TCC), Dr. Tamara Bond (Boston College), Dr. James Bruning (Ohio University), Dr. Justin Buckingham (Towson University), Dr. Kristopher Preacher (University of North Carolina), Dr. David Schwebel (University of Alabama at Birmingham), and Dr. Howard Wainer (Wharton School at the University of Pennsylvania).

I want to thank all of those users (instructors and students alike) who have written me with suggestions and who have pointed out errors. I don't have the space to thank them individually, but many are listed along with the errors they found, on the Web pages labeled "Errata."

I owe thanks to my past colleagues at the University of Vermont. I retired from there in May of 2002, but still consider the University to be my intellectual home. I most certainly want to thank colleagues at the University of Bristol, England, where part of a sabbatical leave was devoted to completing the first edition of the book. Most of all, however, I owe a debt to all of my students who, over the years, have helped me to see where problems lie and how they can best be approached. Their encouragement has been invaluable. Finally, I want to thank the Biometrika trustees for permission to reproduce the table of Wilcoxon's $W$ statistic.

*David C. Howell*
Steamboat Springs, CO
November, 2006
Internet: David.Howell@uvm.edu

# 1

# Introduction

**QUESTIONS**

- What do you think will be covered in a course like this?

- What are the relationships between statistics and mathematics?

- Why do we need statistical procedures?

- How is all this stuff organized?

- Do I really have to know how to use a computer to do statistical analyses?

In the past, when I was asked at parties and other social situations what I did for a living, I would answer that I was a psychologist. After years of receiving the remarks and weird looks that this admission produced, I finally changed tactics and started telling people that I taught statistics—an answer that is also perfectly true. That answer solved one problem—people no longer look at me with blatant suspicion—but it created another. Now they tell me how terrible they are in math and how successful they were in avoiding ever taking a statistics course—not a very tactful remark to make to someone who spent his professional life teaching that subject.

Let's begin by asking what the field of statistics is all about. After all, you are about to invest a semester in studying statistical methods, so it might be handy to know

what you are studying. The word *statistics* is used in at least three different ways. As used in the title of this book, *statistics* refers to a set of procedures and rules (not always computational or mathematical) for reducing large masses of data to manageable proportions and for allowing us to draw conclusions from those data. That is essentially what this book is all about.

A second, and very common, meaning of the term is expressed by such statements as "statistics show that the number of people applying for unemployment benefits has fallen for the third month in a row." In this case *statistics* is used in place of the much better word *data*. For our purposes *statistics* will never be used in this sense.

A third meaning of the term is in reference to the result of some arithmetic or algebraic manipulation applied to data. Thus the mean (average) of a set of numbers is a statistic. This perfectly legitimate usage of *statistics* will occur repeatedly throughout this book.

We thus have two proper uses of the term: (1) a set of procedures and rules and (2) the outcome of the application of those rules and procedures to samples of data. You will always be able to tell from the context which of the two meanings is intended.

The term *statistics* usually elicits some level of math phobia among many students, but mathematics and mathematical manipulation do not need to, and often don't, play a leading role in the lives of people who work with statistics. (Indeed, Jacob Cohen, one of the clearest and most influential writers on statistical issues in the social sciences, suggested that he had been so successful in explaining concepts to others precisely because his knowledge of mathematical statistics was so inadequate.) Certainly you can't understand any statistical text without learning a few formulae and understanding many more. But the required level of mathematics is not great. You learned more than enough in high school. Those who are still concerned should spend a few minutes going over Appendix A, "Arithmetic Review." It lays out some very simple rules of mathematics that you may have forgotten, and a small investment of your time will be more than repaid in making the rest of this book easier to follow. I know—when I was a student I probably wouldn't have looked at it either, *but you really should!* A more complete review of arithmetic, which is perhaps more fun to read, can be found at

 http://www.uvm.edu/~dhowell/fundamentals/ArithmeticReview/review_of_arithmetic_revised.html

(The capitalization in that URL is critical, as it will be in all of the links that I give in this book.)

Something far more important than worrying about algebra and learning to apply equations is thinking of statistical methods and procedures as ways to tie the results of some experiment to the hypothesis that led to that experiment. In revising this book I have made a major effort to remove as much mathematical material as possible when that material would not contribute significantly to your understanding of data analysis. In its place, however, I am asking you to think a bit more about the logic of what you are doing. I don't mean just the logic of a hypothesis test. I mean the logic behind the way you approach a problem. It doesn't do any good to be able to ask if two groups have different means (averages) if a difference in means has

nothing to say about the real question you hoped to ask. One reviewer whose work I respect has complained that I am trying to teach critical thinking skills along with statistics. The reviewer is right, and I enthusiastically plead guilty. You will never be asked to derive a formula, but you will be asked to think. I leave it to you to decide which skill is harder.

Another concern that some students have, and I may have contributed to that concern in the preceding paragraph, is the belief that the only reason to take a course in statistics is to be able to analyze the results of experimental research. Certainly your instructor hopes many of you will use statistical procedures for that purpose, but those procedures and, more important, the ways of thinking that go with them have a life beyond standard experimental research. This is my plea to get the attention of those, like myself, who believe in a liberal education. Much of the material we will cover here will be applicable to whatever you do when you finish college. People who work for large corporations or small family-owned businesses have to work with data. People who serve on a town planning commission have to be able to ask how various changes in the town plan will lead to changes in residential and business development. They will have to ask how those changes will in turn lead to changes in school populations and the resulting level of school budgets, and on and on. Those people may not need to run an analysis of variance (Chapters 16 through 18), though some acquaintance with regression models (Chapters 9 through 11) may be helpful. Keep in mind, however, that the logical approach to data required in the analysis of variance is also required for dealing with town planning. (And if you mess up town planning, you have everybody mad at you.)

A course in statistics is not something you take because it is required and then promptly forget. (Well, that probably is why many of you are taking it, but I hope you expect to come away with more than just three credits on your transcript.) If learned well, knowledge of statistics is a job skill you can use (and market). That is largely why I have tried to downplay the mathematical foundations of the field. Those foundations are important, but they are not what will stay with you and what will be important later. Being able to think through the logic and the interpretation of an experiment or a set of data is an important skill that will stay with you; being able to derive the elements of a regression equation is not. That is why most of the examples used in this book relate to work that people actually do. Work of that type requires thought. It may be easier to understand an example that starts out, "Suppose we had three groups labeled A, B, and C" than it is to understand an actual experiment. But the former is boring and doesn't teach you much. A real-life example is more interesting and has far more to offer.

## 1.1  The Importance of Context

Drug use and abuse is a major problem in our society. Heroin addicts die every day from overdoses. Psychologists should have something to contribute to understanding the problem of drug overdoses, and, in fact, we do. I will take the time to describe an important line of research in this area because a study that derives from

that line of research can be used to illustrate a number of important concepts in this chapter and the next. Some of you may know someone who is involved with heroin, and because heroin is a morphine derivative, this example may have particular meaning to you.

Morphine is a drug commonly used to alleviate pain, and you may know that repeated administrations of morphine lead to morphine tolerance, in which a fixed dose has less and less of an effect (pain reduction) over time. Patients suffering from extreme pain are very familiar with these tolerance effects. A common experimental task demonstrating morphine tolerance involves placing a mouse on a warm surface. When the heat becomes too uncomfortable, the mouse will lick its paws, and the latency of the paw-lick is used as a measure of the mouse's sensitivity to pain. Mice injected with morphine are less sensitive to pain and show longer paw-lick latencies than noninjected mice. But as tolerance develops over repeated administrations, the morphine has less effect and the paw-lick latencies shorten.

Here's where psychology enters the picture. In 1975 a psychologist at McMaster University, Shepard Siegel, hypothesized that tolerance develops because the cues associated with the context in which morphine is administered (room, cage, and surroundings) come to elicit in the mouse a learned compensatory mechanism that counteracts the effect of the drug. It is as if the mouse, seeing the stimuli associated with morphine administration in the past, has learned to turn off the brain receptors through which morphine works, making the morphine less effective at blocking pain. As this compensatory mechanism develops over a series of trials, an animal requires larger and larger doses of morphine to have the same pain-killing effect. But suppose you give that larger dose of morphine in an entirely different context. Because the context is different, the animal doesn't internally compensate for the morphine because it doesn't recognize that the drug is coming. Without the counterbalancing effects, the animal should now experience the full effect of that larger dose of the drug. In that case it should take a long time for the animal to feel the need to lick its paws, because it has received the larger dose of morphine required by the increased tolerance without the compensating mechanism elicited by the usual context.

But what do mice on a warm surface have to do with drug overdose? First, heroin is a derivative of morphine. Second, heroin addicts show clear tolerance effects with repeated use and, as a result, often increase the amount of each injection. By Siegel's theory they are protected from the dangerous effects of the large (and to you and me, lethal) dose of heroin by the learned compensatory mechanism associated with the context in which they take the drug. But if they take what has come to be their standard dose in an entirely new setting, they would not benefit from that protective compensatory mechanism, and what had previously been a safe dose could now be fatal. In fact, Siegel noted that many drug overdose cases occur when an individual injects heroin in a novel environment. Novelty, to a heroin user, can be deadly!

If Siegel is right, his theory has important implications for the problem of drug overdose. One test of Siegel's theory, which is a simplification of studies he actually ran, is to take two groups of mice who have developed tolerance to

morphine and whose standard dosage has been increased above normal levels. One group is tested in the same environment in which they previously have received the drug. The second group is treated exactly the same, except that they are tested in an entirely new environment. If Siegel is correct, the animals tested in the new environment will show a much greater pain threshold (the morphine will have more of an effect) than the animals injected in their usual environment. This is the basic study we will build on.

Our example of drug tolerance illustrates a number of important statistical concepts. It also will form a useful example in later chapters of this book. Be sure you understand what the experiment demonstrates. It will help if you think about what events in your own life or the lives of people around you illustrate the phenomenon of tolerance. What effect has tolerance had on behavior as you (or they) developed tolerance? Why is it likely that you probably feel more comfortable with comments related to sexual behavior than do your parents? Would language that you have come to ignore have that same effect if you heard it in a commencement speech?

You may think that an experiment conducted 30 years ago, which is before most of the readers of this book were born, is too old to be interesting. But a quick search of Google™ will reveal a great many recent studies that have derived directly from Siegel's early work. A particularly interesting one by Mann-Jones, Ettinger, Baisden, and Baisden, has shown that the drug dextromethorphan can counteract morphine tolerance. That becomes interesting when you learn that dextromethorphan is an important ingredient in cough syrup. This suggests that heroin addicts don't want to be taking cough syrup any more than they want to be administering heroin in novel environments. The study can be found at

 http://www.eou.edu/psych/re/morphinetolerance.doc

## 1.2  Basic Terminology

Statistical procedures can be separated into roughly two overlapping areas: descriptive statistics and inferential statistics. The first several chapters of this book will cover descriptive statistics, and the remaining chapters will examine inferential statistics. We will use the simplified version of Siegel's morphine study to illustrate the differences between these two terms.

### Descriptive Statistics

Whenever your purpose is merely to *describe* a set of data, you are employing descriptive statistics. A statement about the average length of time it takes a normal mouse to lick its paw when placed on a warm surface would be a descriptive statistic, as would be the time it takes a morphine-injected mouse to do the same thing. Similarly, the amount of change in the latency of paw-licks once morphine has been administered and the variability of change among mice would be other

descriptive statistics. Here we are simply reporting measures that describe average latency scores or their variability. Examples from other situations might include an examination of dieting scores on the Eating Restraint Scale, crime rates as reported by the Department of Justice, and certain summary information concerning examination grades in a particular course. Notice that in each of these examples we are just describing what the data have to say about some phenomenon.

## Inferential Statistics

All of us at some time or another have been guilty of making unreasonable generalizations on the basis of limited data. If, for example, one mouse showed shorter latencies the second time it received morphine than it did the first, we might try to claim clear evidence of morphine tolerance. But even if there were no morphine tolerance, there would still be a 50-50 chance that the second trial's latency would be shorter than that of the first, assuming that we rule out tied scores. Or you might hear or read that tall people tend to be more graceful than short people, and conclude that that is true because you once had a very tall roommate who was particularly graceful. You conveniently forget about the 6′4″ klutz down the hall who couldn't even put on his pants standing up without tripping over them. Similarly, the man who says that girls develop motor skills earlier than boys because his daughter walked at 10 months and his son didn't walk until 14 months is guilty of the same kind of error: generalizing from single (or too limited) observations.

Small samples or single observations may be fine when we want to study something that has very little variability. If we want to know how many legs a cow has, we can find a cow and count its legs. We don't need a whole herd—one will do. However, when what we want to measure varies from one individual to another, such as the length of cows' tails or the change in response latencies with morphine injections in different contexts, we can't get by with only one cow or one mouse. We need a bunch. Here you've just seen an important principle in statistics—variability. The difference between how we determine the number of legs on a cow, versus the lengths of cows' tails, depends critically on the degree of variability in the thing we want to measure. Variability will follow you throughout this course.

When the property in question varies from animal to animal or trial to trial, we need to take multiple measurements. However, we can't make an unlimited number of observations. If we want to know whether morphine injected in a new context has a greater effect, how long a typical cow's tail is, or when girls usually start to walk, we must look at more than one mouse, one cow, or one girl. But we cannot possibly look at all mice, cows, or girls. We must do something in between—we must draw a *sample* from a *population*.

---

**Definition**   **Population:** Complete set of events in which you are interested.

---

POPULATIONS, SAMPLES, PARAMETERS, AND STATISTICS   A **population** can be defined as the *entire* collection of events in which you are interested (e.g., the scores of all morphine-injected mice, the lengths of the tails of all the cows in the country, the ages

at which every girl first began to walk). Thus if we were interested in the stress levels of all adolescent Americans, then the collection of *all* adolescent Americans' stress scores would form a population, in this case a population of more than 50 million numbers. If, on the other hand, we were interested only in the stress scores of the sophomore class in Fairfax, Vermont (a town of approximately 2,300 inhabitants), the population would contain about 60 numbers and could be obtained quite easily in its entirety. If we were interested in paw-lick latencies of mice, we could always run another mouse. In this sense the population of scores theoretically would be infinite. (Mathematicians prefer the word *uncountable*, but *infinite* will do.)

The point is that a population can range from a relatively small set of numbers, which is easily collected, to an infinitely large set of numbers, which can never be completely collected. The populations in which we are interested are usually quite large. The practical consequence is that we can seldom, if ever, collect data on entire populations. Instead, we are forced to draw a **sample** of observations from a population and to use that sample to infer something about the characteristics of the population.

When we draw a sample of observations, we normally compute numerical values (such as averages) that summarize the data in that sample. When such values are based on the sample, they are called **statistics**. The corresponding values in the population (e.g., population averages) are called **parameters**. The major purpose of inferential statistics is to draw inferences about parameters (characteristics of populations) from statistics (characteristics of samples).[1]

---

**Definition**

**Sample:** Set of actual observations; subset of a population.

**Statistics:** Numerical values summarizing sample data.

**Parameters:** Numerical values summarizing population data.

**Random Sample:** A sample in which each member of the population has an equal chance of inclusion.

---

We usually assume that a sample is a truly **random sample**, meaning that each and every element of the population has an equal chance of being included in the sample. If we have a true random sample, not only can we estimate parameters of the population, but we also can have a very good idea of the accuracy of our estimates. To the extent that a sample is not a random sample, our estimates may be meaningless, because the sample may not accurately reflect the entire population. In fact, we rarely take truly random samples because that is impractical in most settings. We usually take samples of convenience (volunteers from Introductory

---

[1]The word *inference* as used by statisticians means very much what it means in normal English usage—a conclusion based on logical reasoning. If three-fourths of the people at a picnic suddenly fall ill, I am likely to draw the (possibly incorrect) inference that something is wrong with the food. Similarly, if the average social sensitivity score of a random sample of fifth-grade children is very low, I am likely to draw the inference that fifth graders in general have much to learn about social sensitivity. Statistical inference is generally more precise than everyday inference, but the basic idea is the same.

Psychology) and hope that their results reflect what we would have obtained in a truly random sample.

Let's clear up one point that tends to confuse many people. The problem is that one person's sample might be another person's population. For example, if I were to conduct a study into the effectiveness of this book as a teaching instrument, the scores of one class on an exam might be considered by me to be a sample, though a nonrandom one, of the population of scores for all students who are or might be using this book. The class instructor, on the other hand, cares only about her own students and would regard the same set of scores as a population. In turn, someone interested in the teaching of statistics might regard my population (the scores of everyone using this book) as a nonrandom sample from a larger population (the scores of everyone using *any* textbook in statistics). Thus the definition of a population depends on what you are interested in studying. Notice also that when we speak about populations, we speak about populations of *scores*, not populations of *people* or *things*.

The fact that I have used nonrandom samples here to make a point should not lead the reader to think that randomness is not important. On the contrary, it is the cornerstone of much statistical inference. As a matter of fact, one could define the relevant population as the collection of numbers from which the sample has been *randomly* drawn.

INFERENCE    We previously defined inferential statistics as the branch of statistics that deals with inferring characteristics of populations from characteristics of samples. This statement is inadequate by itself because it leaves the reader with the impression that all we care about is determining population parameters such as the average paw-lick latency of mice under the influence of morphine. There are, of course, times when we care about the exact value of population parameters. For example, we often read about the incredible number of hours per day the average child spends in front of a television set, and that is a number that is meaningful in its own right. But if that were all there were to inferential statistics, it would be a pretty dreary subject, and the strange looks I get at parties when I admit to teaching statistics would be justified.

In our example of morphine tolerance in mice, we don't really care what the average paw-lick latency of mice is. But we do care whether the average paw-lick latency of morphine-injected mice tested in a novel context is greater or less than the average paw-lick latency of morphine-injected mice tested in the same context in which they had received previous injections. Thus in many cases inferential statistics is a tool used to estimate parameters of two or more populations, more for the purpose of finding if those parameters are different than for the purpose of determining the actual numerical values of the parameters.

Notice that in the previous paragraph it was the population parameters, not the sample statistics, that I cared about. It is a pretty good bet that if I took two different *samples* of mice and tested them, one sample mean (average) would be larger than another. (It's hard to believe that they would come out absolutely equal.) But the real question concerns the population means. Does the fact that the sample mean of the mice tested in a novel context—is sufficiently longer than

the sample mean of mice tested in a familiar context—lead me to conclude that the corresponding *population* means are also different?

And don't lose sight of the fact that we really don't care very much about drug addiction in mice. What we do care about are heroin addicts. But we probably wouldn't be very popular if we gave heroin addicts overdoses in novel settings to see what would happen. So we have to make a second inferential leap. We have to make the *statistical* inference from the sample of mice to a population of mice, and then we have to make the *logical* inference from mice to heroin addicts. Both inferences are critical if we want to learn anything useful to reduce the incidence of heroin overdose.

## 1.3 Selection among Statistical Procedures

As we have just seen, there is an important distinction between descriptive statistics and inferential statistics. The first part of this book will be concerned with descriptive statistics because we must describe a set of data before we can use it to draw inferences. When we come to inferential statistics, however, we need to make several additional distinctions to help us focus the choice of an appropriate statistical procedure. On the inside cover of this book is what is known as a **decision tree**, a device used for selecting among the available statistical procedures to be presented in this book. This decision tree not only represents a rough outline of the organization of the latter part of the text, it also points up some fundamental issues that we should address at the outset. In considering these issues, keep in mind that at this time we are not concerned with which statistical test is used for which purpose. That will come later. Rather, we are concerned with the kinds of questions that come into play when we try to do anything statistically with data, whether we are talking about descriptive or inferential procedures. These issues are listed at the various branching points of the tree. I will discuss the first three of these briefly now and leave the rest for a more appropriate time.

Definition **Decision tree:** Graphical representation of decisions involved in the choice of statistical procedures.

**Measurement data (quantitative data):** Data obtained by measuring objects or events.

### Types of Data

Numerical data generally come in two kinds; there are measurement data and categorical data. By **measurement data** (sometimes called **quantitative data**) we mean the result of any sort of measurement, for example, a score on a measure of stress, a person's weight, the speed at which a person can read this page, or an individual's score on a scale of authoritarianism. In each case some sort of instrument (in its broadest sense) has been used to measure something.

**Categorical data** (also known as **frequency data** or **count data**) consist of statements such as, "Seventy-eight students reported coming from a one-parent family, while 112 reported coming from two-parent families" or "There were 238 votes for the new curriculum and 118 against it." Here we are counting things, and our data consist of totals or frequencies for each category (hence the name categorical data). Several hundred members of the faculty might vote on a proposed curriculum, but the results (data) would consist of only two numbers—the number of votes for, and the number of votes against, the proposal. Measurement data, on the other hand, might record the paw-lick latencies of dozens of mice, one latency for each mouse.

---

Definition    Categorical data (frequency data, count data): Data representing counts or number of observations in each category.

---

Sometimes we can measure the same general variable to produce either measurement data or categorical data. Thus, in our experiment we could obtain a latency score for each mouse (measurement data), or we could classify the mice as showing long, medium, or short latencies and then count the number in each category (categorical data).

The two kinds of data are treated in two quite different ways. In Chapter 19 we will examine categorical data to see how we can determine whether there are reliable differences among the tumor rejection rates of rats living under three different levels of stress. In Chapters 9 through 14, 16 through 18, and 20 we are going to be concerned chiefly with measurement data. But in using measurement data we have to make a second distinction, not in terms of the type of data, but in terms of whether we are concerned with examining differences among groups of subjects or with studying the relationship among variables.

## Differences versus Relationships

Most statistical questions fall into two overlapping categories, differences and relationships. For example, one experimenter might be interested primarily in whether there is a difference between smokers and nonsmokers in terms of their performance on a given task. A second experimenter might be interested in whether there is a relationship between the number of cigarettes smoked per day and the scores on that same task. Or we could be interested in whether pain sensitivity increases with the number of previous morphine injections (a relationship) or whether there is a difference in pain sensitivity between those who have had previous injections of morphine and those who have not. Although questions of differences and relationships obviously overlap, they are treated by what appear, on the surface, to be quite different methods. Chapters 12 through 14 and 16 through 18 will be concerned primarily with those cases in which we ask if there are differences between two or more groups, whereas Chapters 9 through 11 will deal with cases in which we are interested in examining relationships between two or more variables. These seemingly different statistical techniques turn out to be basically the same fundamental procedure, although they ask somewhat different questions and phrase their answers in distinctly different ways.

## Number of Groups or Variables

As you will see in subsequent chapters, an obvious distinction between statistical techniques concerns the number of groups or the number of variables to which these techniques apply. For example, you will see that what is generally referred to as an independent *t* test is restricted to the case of data from two groups of subjects. The analysis of variance, on the other hand, is applicable to any number of groups, not just two. The third decision in our tree, then, concerns the number of groups or variables involved.

The three decisions we have been discussing (type of data, differences versus relationships, and number of groups or variables) are fundamental to the way we look at data and the statistical procedures we use to help us interpret those data. One further criterion that some textbooks use for creating categories of tests and ways of describing and manipulating data involves the scale of measurement that applies to the data. We will discuss this topic further in the next chapter because it is an important concept that any student should be familiar with.

## 1.4 Using Computers

In the not too distant past, most statistical analyses were done on calculators, and textbooks were written accordingly. Methods have changed, and most calculations are now done by computers, either large mainframes or, more likely, desktop microcomputers. (In fact, the distinction between mainframes and microcomputers has become almost irrelevant.) In addition to performing statistical analyses, computers now provide access to an enormous amount of information via the World Wide Web. We will make use of some of this information in this book.

This book deals with the increased availability of computer software by incorporating it into the discussion. The level of computer involvement increases as the book proceeds and as computations become more laborious. It is not necessary that you work the problems on a computer (and many students won't), but I have used computer printouts in almost every chapter to give you a sense of what the results would look like. For the simpler procedures, the formulae are important in defining the concept. For example, the formula for a standard deviation or a *t* test defines and makes meaningful what a standard deviation or a *t* test actually is. In those cases hand calculation is included even though examples of computer solutions also are given. Later in the book, when, for example, we discuss multiple regression, the formulae become less informative. The formula for computing regression coefficients with five predictors would not be expected to add anything to your understanding of the material. In that case I have omitted the formulae completely and relied on computer solutions for the answers.

Many statistical software packages are currently available to the researcher or student conducting statistical analyses. Three of the most important large statistical packages, which will carry out nearly every analysis that statisticians have invented, are Minitab™, SAS™, and SPSS™. These are highly reliable and

relatively easy-to-use packages, and one or more of them generally are available in any college or university computing center. In this edition I have focused on SPSS, because it is the most commonly available package for students. Each package has its own set of supporters, and they are all excellent. Choosing among them hinges on subtle differences and/or personal preferences.

I do not expect, with this book, to teach anyone to use any specific statistical package. That is much too large a task. I do, however, want you to have some appreciation of what a computer printout looks like for any given problem and how it is to be read, whether or not you have access to that particular package.

One of the great advances in the past few years has been the spread of the World Wide Web. This has meant that many additional resources are available to expand on the material to be found in any text. On the Web you will find demonstrations of points made in this book, material that expands or illustrates what I have covered, software to illustrate specific techniques, and a wealth of other information. I will make frequent reference to Web sites throughout this book, and I encourage you to check out those sites for what they have to offer. I have created a site specifically for this book, and I encourage you to make use of it. It contains all of the data used in this book, answers to odd-numbered exercises (instructors generally want some answers to be unavailable), two primers on using SPSS, computer applets that illustrate important concepts, and a host of other things. The site can be found at

 http://www.uvm.edu/~dhowell/fundamentals/fundweb.html

(Capitalize exactly as given here.)

My Web site even contains a list of typographical errors for this book (yes, I'm sure there will be some), which will expand as I, or other people, find them.

A dozen years ago very few students would have had any idea about how to gain access to the World Wide Web; in fact, most people had never heard of it. Today most people have had experience with the Web, and they link to Web pages on a regular basis. If you have not used the Web, but have either a network connection or a modem, simply ask a friend to show you how to connect. You can learn in about five minutes. Even if you don't want to work with Web pages for this course, there is such a world of information out there that you owe it to yourself to become familiar with Internet resources. (Remember: Whenever you are confused on a point, Google is your friend. Just type in your question and you are bound to get an answer.)

## 1.5 Summary

We began this chapter by considering an example that illustrates the kinds of procedures we will use and the questions we will address. We then went on to discuss the two major branches of statistics, descriptive and inferential. After that, we covered the distinction between populations and samples and defined the concept of a

random sample. Finally, we dealt with several dimensions along which various statistical procedures could be distinguished. The point to keep in mind, above all else, is that there is a huge difference between statistics and mathematics. They both use numbers and formulae, but statistics does not need to be seen as a mathematical science, and many of the most important issues in statistics have very little to do with mathematics.

Some important terms in this chapter are

| | |
|---|---|
| Population, 6 | Decision tree, 9 |
| Sample, 7 | Measurement data (quantitative data), 9 |
| Statistics, 7 | |
| Parameters, 7 | Categorical data (frequency data, count data), 10 |
| Random sample, 7 | |

## 1.6 Exercises

**1.1** To better understand the morphine example that we have been using, think of an example in your own life in which you can see the role played by tolerance and context. How would you go about testing to see whether context plays a role?

**1.2** In testing the effects of context in the example you developed in Exercise 1.1, to what would the words "population" and "sample" refer?

**1.3** Think of an example in everyday life wherein context affects behavior.

For Exercises 1.4–1.6: Suppose that we are designing a study that involves following heroin addicts around and noting both the context within which they inject themselves and the kind of reaction that results.

**1.4** In this hypothetical study, what would the population of interest be?

**1.5** In this study, how would we define our sample?

**1.6** For the heroin study, identify both a parameter and a statistic in which we might be interested.

**1.7** Why would choosing names from a local telephone book not produce a random sample of the residents of that city? Who would be underrepresented and who would be overrepresented?

**1.8** Suggest ways in which we might be able to produce a random (or nearly random) sample of people from a small city.

**1.9** Give an example of a study in which we don't care about the actual numerical value of a population average, but in which we would want to know whether the average of one population is greater than the average of a different population.

**1.10**  I mentioned the fact that variability is a concept that will run throughout the book. I said that you need only one cow to find out how many legs cows have, whereas you need many more to estimate the average lengths of their tales. How would you expect that variability would contribute to the size of the sample you would need? What would you have to do if you suspected that some varieties of cows had relatively short tails, while other varieties had relatively long ones?

**1.11**  To better understand the role of "context" in the morphine study, what would you expect to happen if you put decaf in your mother's early morning cup of coffee?

**1.12**  Give three examples of categorical data.

**1.13**  Give three examples of measurement data.

**1.14**  In the past the Mars Candy Company actually kept track of the number of red, blue, yellow, etc. M&Ms™ there are in each batch. These make wonderful examples for discussions of sampling. An example of the use of M&Ms to illustrate statistical concepts can be found at

 http://www.maa.org/mathland/mathland_3_10.html

(a) This is an example of _____ data.
(b) How do the words "population," "sample," "parameter," and "statistic" apply to the example at this link?

**1.15**  Give two examples of studies in which our primary interest is in looking at relationships between variables.

**1.16**  Give two examples of studies in which our primary interest is in looking at group differences.

**1.17**  How might you redesign our study of morphine tolerance to involve three groups of mice to provide more information on the role of context in the development of morphine tolerance?

**1.18**  Connect to

 http://www.uvm.edu/~dhowell/StatPages/index.html

and navigate to the "Lecture and lab ideas" page. What kinds of material can you find there that you want to remember to come back to later as you work through the book?

**1.19**  Connect to any "search engine" on the Internet, such as Google

 http://www.google.com

and search for the word "statistics."
(a) What kind of uses of that term do you find?
(b) One of your "hits" will likely be a statistics department. Follow one of those links and note the kinds of things that you find there.
(c) Many statistics departments have links to statistics-related pages. What kinds of things do you find on those pages?
(d) I found a link to something called the "Statistics Homepage," supported by a company named StatSoft. See if you can find that and notice the kinds of things that it can help you with.

**1.20**   An interesting Web source contains a collection of Web pages known as "SurfStat," maintained by Keith Dear at the Australian National University. The address is

 http://www.anu.edu.au/nceph/surfstat/surfstat-home/surfstat.html

Go to these pages and note which kinds are likely to be useful to you in this course. (I know that this text isn't in his list of favorites, but I'm sure that was just an oversight, and so I will forgive him.) (**Note:** I will check all addresses carefully just before this book goes to press, but addresses do change, and it is very possible that an address that I have given you will no longer work when you try it. One trick is to progressively shorten the address by deleting elements from the right, trying the link after each deletion. You may then be able to work your way through a set of links to what you were originally seeking. Or you could do what I just did when I found the old address didn't work. I entered "surfstat" in Google, and the first response was what I wanted. One final trick is to select the name of the file you want [e.g., the file "surfstat.html"] and enter that name into Google. Some sites just disappear off the face of the earth, but more commonly they move to a new location.)

# 2

# Basic Concepts

**QUESTIONS**

- What are the different kinds of scales of measurement that we will use?

- What is a variable?

- How do independent variables differ from dependent variables?

- What is the difference between random sampling and random assignment?

- Do I have to worry about all those subscripts and superscripts?

In the preceding chapter we dealt with a number of statistical terms (e.g., parameter, statistic, population, sample, and random sample) that are fundamental to understanding the statistical analysis of data. In this chapter we will consider some additional concepts that you need. We will start with the concepts of measurement and measurement scales, because in statistics everything we do begins with the measurement of whatever it is we want to study.

**Measurement** is frequently defined as the assignment of numbers to objects, with the words *numbers* and *objects* being interpreted loosely. That looks like a definition that only a theoretician could love, but actually it describes what we mean quite

# Contents

# Brief Contents

*To my wife, Donna, who has tolerated*
*"I can't do that now, I am working on my book"*
*for far too long.*

accurately. When, for example, we use paw-lick latency as a measure of pain sensitivity, we are measuring sensitivity by assigning a number (a time) to an object (a mouse) to assess the sensitivity of that mouse. Similarly, when we use one of the most popular measures of depression, the Beck Depression Inventory (Beck, Ward, Mendelson, Mock, & Erbaugh, 1961) to obtain a depression score for a person, we are measuring that characteristic by assigning a number (a score) to an object (a person). Depending on what we are measuring and how we measure it, the numbers we obtain may have different properties, and those different properties of numbers often are discussed under the specific topic of scales of measurement.

| | |
|---|---|
| Definition | **Measurement:** The assignment of numbers to objects. |

## 2.1  Scales of Measurement

**Scales of measurement** is a topic that some writers think is crucial and others think is irrelevant. Although this book tends to side with the latter group, it is important that you have some familiarity with the general issue. (You do not have to agree with something to think that it is worth studying. After all, evangelists claim to know a great deal about sin, but they certainly don't endorse it.) An additional benefit of this discussion is that you will begin to realize that statistics as a subject is not merely a cut-and-dried set of facts but rather a set of facts put together with a variety of interpretations and opinions.

| | |
|---|---|
| Definition | **Scales of measurement:** Characteristics of relations among numbers assigned to objects. |

Probably the foremost leader of those who see scales of measurement as crucially important to the choice of statistical procedures was S. S. Stevens.[1] Basically, Stevens defined four types of scales: nominal, ordinal, interval, and ratio. These scales are distinguished on the basis of the relationships assumed to exist between objects having different scale values. Later scales in this series have all the properties of earlier scales and additional properties as well. Zumbo and Zimmerman (2000) have discussed measurement scales at considerable length and remind us that Stevens's system has to be seen in its historical context. In the 1940s and 1950s, Stevens was attempting to defend psychological research against those in the "hard sciences" who had a restricted view of scientific measurement. He was trying to make psychology "respectable." Stevens spent much of his very distinguished professional career developing measurement scales for the field of

---

[1]Chapter 1 in Stevens' *Handbook of Experimental Psychology* (1951) is an excellent reference for anyone who wants to go further into the substantial mathematical issues underlying his position.

psychophysics and made important contributions. However, outside of that field there has been little effort in psychology to develop the kinds of scales that Stevens pursued, nor has there been much real interest. The criticisms that so threatened Stevens have largely evaporated, and with them much of the belief that measurement scales critically influence the statistical procedures that are appropriate. But debates over measurement have certainly not disappeared.

## Nominal Scales

In a sense a **nominal scale** is not really a scale at all, because it does not scale items along any dimension, but rather labels items. The classic example of a nominal scale is the set of numbers assigned to football players. Frequently these numbers have no meaning whatsoever other than as convenient labels that distinguish the players, or their positions, from one another. We could just as easily use letters or pictures of animals. In fact, gender is a nominal scale that uses words (male and female) in place of numbers, although when we code gender in a data set we often use 1 = male and 2 = female. Nominal scales generally are used for the purpose of *classification*. Categorical data, which we discussed briefly in Chapter 1, are measured on a nominal scale because we merely assign category labels (e.g., Male or Female, Same context group or Different context group) to observations. Quantitative (measurement) data are measured on the other three types of scales.

---

Definition

**Nominal scale:** Numbers used only to distinguish among objects.

**Ordinal scale:** Numbers used only to place objects in order.

---

## Ordinal Scales

The simplest true scale is an **ordinal scale**, which orders people, objects, or events along some continuum. An example of an ordinal scale might be the class standings of people graduating from high school. Here the scale tells us who in the class had the highest average, who had the second-highest average, and so on. Another example would be the Holmes and Rahe (1967) scale of life stress. Using this scale you simply count up (sometimes with differential weightings) the number of changes in the past six months of a person's life (marriage, moving, new job, etc.). A person with a score of 20 is presumed to have experienced more stress than someone with a score of 15, who is presumed to have experienced more stress than someone with a score of 10. Thus we order people, in terms of stress, by the changes in their lives.

Notice that these two examples of ordinal scales differ in the numbers that are assigned. In the first case we assigned the ranks 1, 2, 3, . . . , whereas in the second case the scores represented the number of changes rather than ranks. Both are examples of ordinal scales, however, because no information is given about the *differences* between points on the scale. This is an important characteristic of ordinal scales. We do not assume, for example, that the difference between 10 and 15 life changes represents the same increase in stress as the difference between 15 and 20 life changes. Distinctions of that sort must be left to the next type of scale.

## Interval Scales

An **interval scale** is a scale of measurement about which we can speak legitimately of differences between scale points. A common example is the Fahrenheit scale of temperature, in which a 10-point difference has the same meaning anywhere along the scale. Thus, the difference in temperature between 10°F and 20°F is the same as the difference between 80°F and 90°F. Notice that this scale also satisfies the properties of the two preceding scales. What we do not have with an interval scale, however, is the ability to speak meaningfully about ratios. Thus we cannot say, for example, that 40°F is one-half as hot as 80°F or twice as hot as 20°F, because the zero point on the scale is arbitrary. For example, 20°F and 40°F correspond roughly to −7° and 4° on the Celsius scale, respectively, and the two sets of ratios are obviously quite different and arbitrary. The Kelvin scale of temperature *is* a ratio scale, but few of us would ever think of using it to describe the weather.

Definition    **Interval scale:** Scale on which equal intervals between objects represent equal differences—differences are meaningful.

**Ratio scale:** A scale with a true zero point—ratios are meaningful.

The measurement of pain sensitivity is a good example of something that is probably measured on an interval scale. It seems reasonable to assume that a difference of 10 seconds in paw-lick latency may represent the same difference in sensitivity across most, but not all, of the scale.

Notice that I said that our measure can *probably* be taken as an interval measure. This is another way of suggesting that it is rare that you would find a true and unambiguous example of any particular kind of scale. I can think of several reasons why I might argue that paw-lick latencies are not absolutely interval scales, but I would be willing to go along with considering them to be that for purposes of discussion. (I might have considerable reluctance about saying that the scale is interval at its extremes, but in our experiment we would not work with a surface that is extremely hot or one that is at room temperature.)

I would be very reluctant, however, to suggest that an animal that takes 25 seconds to lick its paw is *twice* as sensitive as one that takes 50 seconds. To be able to make those types of statements (statements about ratios), we need to go beyond the interval scale to the ratio scale.

## Ratio Scales

A **ratio scale** is one that has a true zero point. Notice that the zero point must be a *true* zero point, and not an arbitrary one, such as 0°F or 0°C. A true zero point is the point that corresponds to the absence of the thing being measured. (Because 0°F and 0°C do not represent the absence of electron movement, they are not true zero points. However, 0° Kelvin is taken as a true zero point, because it represents, at least in theory, the absence of molecular motion, and thus heat.) Examples of ratio scales are the common physical ones of length, volume, time, and so on. With these scales not only do we have the properties of the preceding scales, but we can also speak about ratios. We can say that in physical terms 10 seconds is twice as long as 5 seconds, 100 lbs is one-third as heavy as 300 lbs, and so on.

One might think that the kind of scale with which we are working would be obvious to everyone who thought about it. Unfortunately, especially with the kinds of measures that we collect in the social sciences, this is rarely the case. Consider for a moment the temperature of the room you are in right now. I just told you that temperature, measured in degrees Celsius or Fahrenheit, is a clear case of an interval scale. Well, it is and it isn't. There is no doubt that to a physicist the difference between 62° and 64° is exactly the same as the difference between 72° and 74°. But if we are measuring temperature as an index of comfort rather than as an index of molecular activity, the same numbers no longer form an interval scale. To a person sitting in a room at 62°F, a jump to 64°F would be distinctly noticeable and probably welcome. The same cannot be said about the difference in room temperature between 82°F and 84°F. This points up the important fact that it is the underlying variable being measured (e.g., comfort), not the numbers themselves, that define the scale.

Because there is usually no unanimous agreement concerning the scale of measurement employed, it's up to you, as an individual user of statistical procedures, to make the best decision you can about the nature of the data. All that can be asked of you is that you think about the problem carefully before coming to a decision and not simply assume that the standard answer is necessarily the best answer. It seems a bit unfair to dump that problem on you, but there really is no alternative.

## The Role of Measurement Scales

I made the statement earlier that there is a difference of opinion as to the importance assigned to scales of measurement. Some authors have ignored the problem totally, but others have organized whole textbooks around the different scales. It seems to me that the central issue is the absolute necessity of separating in our minds the numbers we collect from the objects or events to which they refer. If one participant in a memory study recalled 20 items and another participant recalled 10 items, the number of words recalled was twice as large for the first participant. However, we might not be willing to say that the first participant remembered twice as much about the material studied.

A similar argument was made for the example of room temperature, wherein the scale (interval or ordinal) depended on whether we were interested in measuring some physical attribute of temperature or its effect on people. A difference of 2°F is the same *physically* anywhere along the scale, but a difference of 2°F when a room is already warm may not *feel* as large as a difference of 2°F when a room is relatively cool. In other words, we have an interval scale of the physical units, but no more than an ordinal scale of comfort. (In fact, it gets worse, because where molecular activity continues to increase as temperature increases, comfort at first rises as the temperature rises, levels off briefly, and then starts to fall. In other words, the relationship is shaped like an inverted U.)

Because statistical tests use numbers without considering the objects or events to which those numbers refer, we can carry out standard mathematical operations (addition, multiplication, etc.) regardless of the nature of the underlying scale. An excellent and highly recommended reference on this point is an entertaining paper by Lord (1953) entitled "On the Statistical Treatment of Football Numbers." Lord argues that you can treat these numbers in any way you like. His often quoted statement on this issue is "The numbers do not remember where they came from." You don't need a course in statistics to know that the average of 8 and 15 is 11.5, regardless of whether that average has any sensible interpretation in terms of what we are measuring.

The problem comes when it is time to interpret the results of some form of statistical manipulation. At that point we must ask if the statistical results bear any meaningful relationship to the objects or events in question. Here we are no longer dealing with a statistical issue, but with a methodological one. No statistical procedure can tell us whether the fact that one group received higher grades than another on a history examination reveals anything about group differences in knowledge of the subject matter. (Perhaps they received specific coaching on how to take multiple-choice exams.) Moreover, to be satisfied because the examination provides grades that form a ratio scale of correct items (50 correct items is twice as many as 25 correct items) is to lose sight of the fact that we set out to measure knowledge of history, which may not increase in any orderly way with increases in scores. Statistical tests can be applied only to the numbers we obtain, and the validity of statements about the objects or events that we think we are measuring hinges primarily on our knowledge of those objects or events, not on the scale of measurement. We do our best to ensure that our measures bear as close a relationship as possible to what we want to measure, but our results are ultimately only the numbers we obtain and our faith in the *relationship* between those numbers and the underlying objects or events.

To return for a moment to the problem of heroin overdose, notice that in addressing this problem we have had to move several steps away from the heroin addict sticking a needle in his arm under a bridge. Because we can't use actual addicts, we have used mice. We assume that pain tolerance under morphine is a good analogue to the tolerance we see in drug addicts, and it probably is. But then to measure pain tolerance we measure changes in sensitivity to pain, and to measure sensitivity we measure paw-lick latency. And finally, to measure changes in sensitivity, we measure changes in paw-lick latencies. All these assumptions seem reasonable, but they are assumptions nonetheless. When we worry about the scale of measurement, we need to think about the relationships among these steps. That does not mean that paw-lick latency needs to be an interval measure of heroin tolerance in addicts—that wouldn't make any sense. But it does mean that we need to think about the whole system and not just one of its parts.

## 2.2 Variables

Properties of objects or events that can take on different values are referred to as **variables**. Hair color, for example, is a variable because it is a property of an object (hair) that can take on different values (brown, yellow, red, and, in recent years, blue, green, and purple). Properties such as height, length, and speed are variables for the same reason. We can further discriminate between **discrete variables** (such as gender, marital status, and the number of television sets in a private home), in which the variable can take on only a relatively few possible values; and **continuous variables** (such as speed, paw-lick latency, length of a cow's tail, and so on), in which the variable could assume—at least in theory—any value between the lowest and highest points on the scale. (Note that nominal variables cannot be continuous.) As you will see later in this book, the distinction between discrete and continuous variables plays a role in some of our procedures.

---

Definition  **Variables:** Properties of objects or events that can take on different values.

**Discrete variables:** Variables that take on a small set of possible values.

**Continuous variables:** Variables that take on any value.

**Independent variables:** Those variables controlled by the experimenter.

**Dependent variables:** The variables being measured; the data or score.

---

In statistics we also distinguish between different kinds of variables in an additional way. We speak of **independent variables** (those that are manipulated by the experimenter) and **dependent variables** (those that are not under the experimenter's control—the data).[2] In psychological research the experimenter is interested in measuring the effects of independent variables on dependent variables. Common examples of independent variables in psychology are schedules of reinforcement, forms of therapy, placement of stimulating electrodes, methods of treatment, and the distance of the stimulus from the observer. Common examples of dependent variables are running speeds, depression scores, behavioral response of a subject, number of aggressive behaviors, and apparent size of an object. Basically what the study is all about is the independent variable, and the results of the study (the data) are measurements of the dependent variable. For example, a psychologist may measure the number of aggressive behaviors in depressed and nondepressed adolescents. Here the state of depression is the independent variable, and the number of aggressive acts is the dependent variable. Independent variables can be either qualitative (e.g., a comparison of three different forms of psychotherapy)

---

[2]Some readers have pointed out that some independent variables are not "manipulated" by the experimenter. For example, we cannot manipulate the subject's gender or, generally, the school that he or she attends. However, we do manipulate those variables in the sense that we *choose* which schools to compare or we *choose* to compare males and females. In that sense we do manipulate the independent variable; that is, it is under our control.

or quantitative (performance following one, three, or five units of caffeine), but dependent variables are generally—but certainly not always—quantitative.[3] What are the independent and dependent variables in our study of morphine tolerance in mice?

## 2.3 Random Sampling

In the first chapter I said that a sample is a random sample if each and every element of the population has an equal chance of being included in the sample. I further stated that the concept of a random sample is fundamental to the process of using statistics calculated on a sample to infer the values of parameters of a population. It should be obvious that we would be foolish to try to estimate the average level of sexual activity of all high school students on the basis of data on a group of ninth graders who happen to have a study hall at the same time. We would all agree (I hope) that the data would underestimate the average value that would have been obtained from a truly random sample of the entire population of high school students.

There are a number of ways of obtaining random samples from fairly small populations. We could assign every person a number and then use a table of random numbers to select the numbers of those who will be included in our sample. Or, if we would be satisfied with a nearly random sample, we could put names into a hat and draw blindly. The point is that every score in the population should have an equal chance of being included.

It is often helpful to have a table of random numbers to use for drawing random samples, assigning subjects to groups, and other tasks. Such a table can be found in Appendix D (Table D.9). This table is a list of uniform random numbers. The adjective *uniform* is used to indicate that every number is equally (uniformly) likely to occur. (For example, if you counted the occurrences of the digits 1, 5, and 8 in this table, you would find that they all occur about equally often.)

Table D.9 is quite easy to use. For example, if you wanted to draw random numbers between 0 and 9, you would simply close your eyes and put your finger on the table. You would then read down the column (after opening your eyes), recording the digits as they come. When you came to the bottom of the column, you would go to the next column and continue the process until you had as many numbers as you needed. If you wanted numbers between 0 and 99, you would do the same thing, except that you would read off pairs of digits. If you wanted random numbers between 1 and 65, you again would read off pairs of digits, but ignore 00 and any number greater than 65.

If, instead of collecting a set of random data, you wanted to use the random-number table to assign subjects to two treatment groups, you could start at any place in the table and assign a participant to Group I if the random number was odd

---

[3]Hint: The next time you come across the independent/dependent-variable distinction on a test, just remember that *dependent* and *data* both start with a d. You can figure out the rest from there.

and to Group II if it was even. Common sense extrapolations of this procedure will allow you to randomly assign participants to any number of groups.

With large populations most standard techniques for ensuring randomness are no longer appropriate. We cannot put the names of all U.S. women between 21 and 30 into a hat (even a very big hat). Nor could we assign all U.S. women a number and then choose women by matching numbers against a random-number table. Such a procedure would be totally impractical. Unless we have substantial resources, about the best we can do is to eliminate as many potential sources of bias as possible (e.g., don't estimate level of sexual behavior solely on the basis of a sample of people who visit Planned Parenthood), restrict our conclusions on the basis of those sources of bias that we could not feasibly control (e.g., acknowledge that the data came only from people who were willing to complete our questionnaire), and then hope a lot. Any biases that remain will limit the degree to which the results can be generalized to the population as a whole. A large body of literature is concerned with sampling methods designed to ensure representative samples, such as techniques used in conducting the decennial census, but such methods are beyond the scope of this book.

Random numbers don't always look as random as you and I might expect. Try writing down the results you think might be reasonable from five coin flips—e.g., H T H H H. Then go to the July 1997 issue of *Chance News* on the Internet for an interesting discussion of randomness (Item 13). The address is

http://www.dartmouth.edu/~chance/chance_news/recent_news/
chance_news_6.07.html

This could form the basis of an interesting class discussion. (If you have a minute, snoop around at this site. They have all sorts of cool things.)

Two paragraphs back I spoke about using random numbers to assign subjects to groups. This is called **random assignment**, and I would argue that it is even more important than random sampling. We like to have a random sample because it gives us confidence that our results apply to a larger population. You aren't going to draw a truly random sample from the population of all college sophomores in the U.S., and no one would fault you for that. But you certainly wouldn't want to compare two methods of teaching general survival skills by applying one method in a large urban school and the other in a small rural school. Regardless of the effectiveness of the teaching methods themselves, preexisting differences between the two samples would greatly influence the results, though they are not what we intended to study. Random sampling is a consideration primarily in the generalizability from the sample to the population. Random assignment, on the other hand, is necessary to ensure that the differences between the groups reflect the differences in the experimental treatments, and nothing more. Where possible, you should always aim for random assignment.

Definition     **Random assignment:** The allocation or assignment of participants to groups by a random process.

## 2.4 Notation

Any discussion of statistical techniques requires a notational system for expressing mathematical operations. It is thus perhaps surprising that no standard notational system has been adopted. Although there have been several attempts to formulate a general policy, the fact remains that textbooks do not use exactly the same notation.

The notational systems that we do have range from the very complex to the very simple. The more complex systems gain precision at the loss of easy intelligibility, and the simpler systems gain intelligibility at the loss of some precision. Because the loss of precision is usually trivial when compared with the gain in comprehension, this book will use an extremely simple system of notation.

### Notation for Variables

The general rule for our purposes is that a variable will be represented by an uppercase letter, often $X$ or $Y$. An individual value of that variable will be represented by the letter and a subscript. Suppose, for example, that we have the following five scores on the length of time (in seconds) that third-grade children can sit absolutely still:

$$45 \quad 42 \quad 35 \quad 23 \quad 52$$

This set of scores will be referred to as $X$. The first number of this set (45) can be referred to as $X_1$, the second (42) as $X_2$, and so on. To refer to a single score without specifying which one, we will refer to $X_i$, where $i$ can take on any value between 1 and 5. The use of subscripts is essential to the precise description of statistical procedures. In practice, however, the use of subscripts is often more of a distraction than an aid.

### Summation Notation

One of the most common symbols in statistics is the uppercase Greek letter **sigma** ($\Sigma$), the standard notation for summation, which is readily translated as "add up, or sum, what follows." Thus, $\Sigma X_i$ is read "Sum the $X_i$s." To be perfectly precise, the notation for summing all $N$ values of $X$ is

$$\sum_{1}^{N} X_i$$

which translates to, "Sum all the $X_i$s from $i = 1$ to $i = N$." There is seldom any need in practice to specify what is to be done in such detail; $\Sigma X_i$, or even $\Sigma X$, will do. In most cases in this book subscripts will be dropped, and the notation for the sum of the values of $X$ will be simply $\Sigma X$.

---

Definition    **Sigma ($\Sigma$):** Symbol indicating summation.

---

Several extensions of the simple case of $\Sigma X$ must be noted, and you need to understand them. One of these is $\Sigma X^2$, which is read, "Sum the squared values of X" (i.e., $45^2 + 42^2 + 35^2 + 23^2 + 52^2$). Another common expression is $\Sigma XY$, which means, "Sum the products of the corresponding values of X and Y." The use of these terms is illustrated in the following example.

EXAMPLE:    Imagine a simple experiment in which we record the number of life events (major and minor) in an adolescent's life, as well as a measure of adolescent behavior problems. For the sake of our example, we will use only five adolescents. The data and simple summation operations on them are illustrated in Table 2.1. Some of these operations have been discussed already; others will be discussed in the next few chapters. Examination of Table 2.1 reveals another set of operations involving parentheses, such as $(\Sigma X)^2$. *The general rule that always applies is to perform operations within parentheses before performing operations outside parentheses.* Thus for $(\Sigma X)^2$ we would sum the values of X and *then* square the result, as opposed to $\Sigma X^2$, in which we would square the Xs *before* we sum. You should confirm that $\Sigma X^2$ is not equal to $(\Sigma X)^2$ by using simple numbers such as 2, 3, and 4.    ■

**Table 2.1**
Illustration of Operations Involving Summation Notation

|  | Life Events X | Behavior Problems Y | $X^2$ | $Y^2$ | $X - Y$ | $XY$ |
|---|---|---|---|---|---|---|
|  | 10 | 3 | 100 | 9 | 7 | 30 |
|  | 15 | 4 | 225 | 16 | 11 | 60 |
|  | 12 | 1 | 144 | 1 | 11 | 12 |
|  | 9 | 1 | 81 | 1 | 8 | 9 |
|  | 10 | 3 | 100 | 9 | 7 | 30 |
| Sum | 56 | 12 | 650 | 36 | 44 | 141 |

$$\Sigma X = (10 + 15 + 12 + 9 + 10) = 56$$
$$\Sigma Y = (3 + 4 + 1 + 1 + 3) = 12$$
$$\Sigma X^2 = (10^2 + 15^2 + 12^2 + 9^2 + 10^2) = 650$$
$$\Sigma Y^2 = (3^2 + 4^2 + 1^2 + 1^2 + 3^2) = 36$$
$$\Sigma(X - Y) = (7 + 11 + 11 + 8 + 7) = 44$$
$$\Sigma XY = (10*3 + 15*4 + 12*1 + 9*1 + 10*3) = 141$$
$$(\Sigma X)^2 = 56^2 = 3136$$
$$(\Sigma Y)^2 = 12^2 = 144$$
$$(\Sigma(X - Y))^2 = 44^2 = 1936$$
$$(\Sigma X)(\Sigma Y) = 56*12 = 672$$

A thorough understanding of notation is essential if you are to learn even the most elementary statistical techniques. Demonstration of the following rules of summation is left to you, inasmuch as their application can be illustrated with very simple examples.

---

### Rules of Summation

1. $\Sigma(X - Y) = \Sigma X - \Sigma Y$.
2. $\Sigma CX = C\Sigma X$. The notation $\Sigma CX$ means to multiply every value of $X$ by the constant $C$ and then sum the results. A **constant** is any number that does not change its value in a given situation (as opposed to a variable, which does). Constants are most often represented by the letters $C$ and $k$, but other symbols may be used.
3. $\Sigma(X + C) = \Sigma X + NC$. where $N$ represents the number of items that are being summed.

---

Definition   **Constant:** A number that does not change in value in a given situation.

---

## 2.5 Summary

In this chapter we examined briefly the concept of measurement and considered four different levels, or scales, of measurement. We also discussed variables, the different types of variables, the importance of random sampling and random assignment, and the system of notation that will be used throughout this book. At this point you have the basic terminology you will need to begin looking at data. Now we can get started.

Some important terms in this chapter are

| | |
|---|---|
| Measurement, *17* | Discrete variables, *22* |
| Scales of measurement, *17* | Continuous variables, *22* |
| Nominal scale, *18* | Independent variables, *22* |
| Ordinal scale, *18* | Dependent variables, *22* |
| Interval scale, *19* | Random assignment, *24* |
| Ratio scale, *20* | Sigma ($\Sigma$), *25* |
| Variables, *22* | Constant, *27* |

## 2.6 Exercises

**2.1**  Give one example each of a nominal, ordinal, interval, and ratio measure.

**2.2**  Give an example of a scale that might be said to use a ratio scale for some purposes and an interval or ordinal scale for other purposes.

**2.3**  We trained rats to run a straight-alley maze for food reinforcement. All of a sudden, one of the rats lay down and went to sleep halfway through the maze. What does this say about the scale of measurement when speed is used as an index of learning?

**2.4**  What does Exercise 2.3 say about speed used as an index of motivation?

**2.5**  In Section 2.1 I talked about the chain of assumptions that take us from a heroin addict under a bridge to a mouse on a warm surface. List those assumptions.

**2.6**  Write a sentence describing the morphine tolerance experiment in terms of an independent variable and a dependent variable.

Exercises 2.7–2.10 relate to a study conducted by Pliner and Chaiken (1990). In their study about the social desirability of behavior, they examined the amount of food eaten by male and female participants in the presence of a person of either the same gender or opposite gender.

**2.7**  What are the independent variables in the study just described?

**2.8**  What is the dependent variable in that study?

**2.9**  Experiments like this are always done with some hypothesis in mind. What would you expect was the experimenter's hypothesis?

**2.10**  Describe the chain of assumptions underlying the measurement issues in this study.

**2.11**  Give three examples of continuous variables.

**2.12**  Give three examples of discrete variables.

**2.13**  Most people assume that random numbers are actually more orderly than they really are. For example, they assume that if you draw 50 random numbers, nature will somehow almost ensure that you have 25 even numbers and 25 odd ones, or very close to that. Draw 50 random numbers from Table D.9 in Appendix D and calculate the proportion of even numbers. Then do this two more times and record the proportion of even numbers that you obtained each time. Do these data look the way you would expect them to look?

**2.14**  To follow up on the question of randomness, as well as anticipate some material that will appear later, assume that you have drawn 18 one-digit (0 included) random numbers and the number 7 has yet to appear. How likely is it that you will get a 7 on the next draw? What kinds of information/ideas went into your answer?

**2.15**  In a study of the moon illusion that we will discuss in Chapter 5, Kaufman and Rock (1962) tested an earlier hypothesis by Holway and Boring (1940) about reasons for the moon illusion. Kaufman and Rock compared how subjects performed when they were able to first look at the moon with their eyes level, and then look again with their eyes elevated. The data for the Eyes Level condition follow:

$$1.65 \quad 1.00 \quad 2.03 \quad 1.25 \quad 1.05 \quad 1.02 \quad 1.67 \quad 1.86 \quad 1.56 \quad 1.73$$

Using $X$ to represent this variable,
(a) What are $X_3$, $X_5$, and $X_8$?
(b) Calculate $\Sigma X$.
(c) Write the summation notation for (b) in its most complex form.

**2.16**  With reference to Exercise 2.15, the data for the Eyes Elevated condition are

$$1.73 \quad 1.06 \quad 2.03 \quad 1.40 \quad 0.95 \quad 1.13 \quad 1.41 \quad 1.73 \quad 1.63 \quad 1.56$$

Using $Y$ for this variable,
(a) What are $Y_1$ and $Y_{10}$?
(b) Calculate $\Sigma Y$.

**2.17**  Using the data from Exercise 2.15,
(a) Calculate $(\Sigma X)^2$ and $\Sigma X^2$.
(b) Calculate $\Sigma X / N$, where $N$ = the number of scores.
(c) What do you call what you just calculated?

**2.18**  Using the data from Exercise 2.16,
(a) Calculate $(\Sigma Y)^2$ and $\Sigma Y^2$.
(b) Given the answers to (a), calculate

$$\frac{\Sigma Y^2 - \dfrac{(\Sigma Y)^2}{N}}{N - 1}$$

(c) Calculate the square root of the answer to (b). (You will come across these calculations again in Chapter 5.)

**2.19**  The data from Exercises 2.15 and 2.16 come from the same 10 ($N$) subjects. In other words, the same person had a score of 1.65 in the Eyes Level condition and a score of 1.73 in the Eyes Elevated condition. Therefore the data form pairs of scores.
(a) Multiply the scores in each pair together to get a variable called $XY$.
(b) Calculate $\Sigma XY$.
(c) Calculate $\Sigma X \Sigma Y$.
(d) Do $\Sigma XY$ and $\Sigma X \Sigma Y$ differ, and would you normally expect them to?
(e) Calculate

$$\frac{\Sigma XY - \dfrac{\Sigma X \Sigma Y}{N}}{N - 1}$$

(You will come across these calculations again in Chapter 9. The result is called the covariance. Very few of the calculations in this book will be any more complex than this one.)

**2.20**    Use the previous data to show that
(a) $\Sigma(X + Y) = \Sigma X + \Sigma Y$
(b) $\Sigma XY \neq \Sigma X \Sigma Y$
(c) $\Sigma CX = C\Sigma X$
(d) $\Sigma X^2 \neq (\Sigma X)^2$

**2.21**    Make up five data points and show that $\Sigma(X + C) = \Sigma X + NC$, where $C$ is any constant (e.g., 4) and $N$ is the number of data points.

**2.22**    I have been (correctly) criticized for using "the number of hairs on a goat" as an example of a continuous variable in an earlier edition of this book. Why is this really a discrete variable?

**2.23**    Can an ordinal variable be measured on a continuous scale?

**2.24**    I have argued that paw-lick latencies can reasonably be taken to be an interval scale of pain sensitivity in mice. Suppose that someone else felt that the square root of paw-lick latency was more appropriate. How might we decide between these two competing measures?

**2.25**    The *Chicago Tribune* of July 21, 1995 reported on a study by a fourth-grade student named Beth Peres. In the process of collecting evidence in support of her campaign for a higher allowance, she polled her classmates on what they received as an allowance. She was surprised to discover that the 11 girls who responded reported an average allowance of $2.63 per week, but the 7 boys reported an average of $3.18, 21% more than for the girls. At the same time, the boys had to do fewer chores to earn their allowance than did the girls. The story had a considerable national prominence and raised the question of whether the income disparity for adult women relative to adult men may actually have its start very early in life.
(a) What are the dependent and independent variables in this study, and how are they measured?
(b) What kind of a sample are we dealing with here?
(c) How could the characteristics of the sample influence the results Beth obtained?
(d) How might she go about "random sampling"? How would she go about "random assignment"?
(e) If random assignment is not possible in this study, does that have negative implications for the validity of the study?
(f) What are some of the variables that might influence the outcome of this study—separate, that is, from any true population differences between boys' and girls' income?
(g) Distinguish clearly between the descriptive and inferential statistical features of this example.

**2.26**    The *Journal of Public Health* published data on the relationship between smoking and health (see Landwehr and Watkins [1987]). They reported the cigarette consumption per adult for 21 mostly western and developed countries, along with the coronary heart disease rate for each country. The data clearly show that coronary heart disease is highest in those countries with the highest cigarette consumption.
(a) Why might the sampling in this study have been limited to western and developed countries?
(b) How would you characterize the two variables in terms of what we have labeled "scales of measurement"?
(c) If our goal is to study the health effects of smoking, how do these data relate to that overall question?
(d) What other variables might need to be taken into consideration in such a study?

(e) It has been reported that tobacco companies are making a massive advertising effort in Asia. A few years ago only 7% of Chinese women smoked (compared to 61% of Chinese men). How would a health psychologist go about studying the health effects of likely changes in the incidence of smoking among Chinese women?

(f) Do a search of the Internet using Google to find articles relating secondhand smoke to coronary heart disease. What do these articles suggest?

**2.27** A list of Frequently Asked Questions that I found on the Internet at

 http://www.powerball.com/pb_faq.asp#drawing

explains the process that the Powerball lottery goes through to ensure that the draws are random. It is quoted below:

> We work very hard to ensure that the numbers are truly random. Besides making sure that the balls are equal in size, weight, and density, we also randomly rotate between four ball sets (a total of eight sets for the two colors) and two draw machines for each color. We chart the results of the drawings and the pre- and post-draw tests to watch for any behavior that falls outside of statistical expectations. If a ball set does fall outside of our very unreasonable standards for randomness, we pull it and test it with a greater number of ball drops to ensure it is random. In addition, each ball set is put through very precise measurement by a government lab and is X-rayed at least annually.

In 1996 the winning numbers in Connecticut had the following distribution. The winning number (grouped into intervals of 5) is shown along the X axis, and the frequency with which each number interval came up is shown on the Y axis to the left. Do the results look random to you? What would you expect produced the particular pattern you see here?

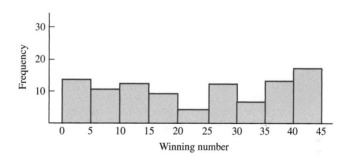

**2.28** Go to the Internet link at

 http://www.stat.ucla.edu/cases/yale/

and read the very short case study there. Answer the questions on sampling and compare your answer with the explanation given in an accompanying link.

# 3

## Displaying Data

### QUESTIONS

- Why should we bother to plot data rather than just look at the numbers?

- What can histograms show us and how do we create them?

- Are there other ways of displaying data?

- How is all this stuff organized?

**A** collection of raw data, taken by itself, is no more exciting or informative than junk mail before election day. Whether you have neatly arranged the data in rows on a data collection form or scribbled them on the back of an out-of-date announcement you tore from the bulletin board, a collection of numbers is still just a collection of numbers. To be interpretable, they first must be organized in some sort of logical order.

How do human beings process information that is stored in their short-term memory? If I asked you to tell me if the number "6" was included as one of a set of five digits that you just saw presented on a screen, do you use *sequential processing* to search your short-term memory of the screen and say "Nope, it wasn't the first one; nope, it wasn't the second," and so on? Or do you use *parallel processing* to compare the digit "6" with your memory of all the previous digits at the same time?

Obviously in this case the latter approach would be faster and more efficient, but human beings don't always do things in the fastest and most efficient manner. How do *you* think that you do it? How do you search back through your memory and identify the person who just walked in as Lynda? Do you compare her one at a time with all the women her age whom you have met, or do you make comparisons in parallel? (This second example uses long-term memory rather than short-term memory, but the questions are analogous, though perhaps with different answers.)

Over thirty years ago Saul Sternberg at Bell Labs (1966) ran a simple but important study that examined how people recall data from short-term memory. On a screen in front of the subject he briefly presented a *comparison* set of one, three, or five digits. Shortly after each presentation he flashed a single test digit on the screen and required the subject to push one button (the positive button) if the test digit had been included in the comparison set or another button (the negative button) if the test digit had not been part of the comparison set. For example, the two stimuli might look like this:

| Comparison | 2 | 7 | 4 | 8 | 1 |
|------------|---|---|---|---|---|
| Test       |   |   | 5 |   |   |

(Remember, the two lines of stimuli were presented one after the other, not simultaneously.) Since the numeral "5" was not part of the comparison set, the subject should have responded by pressing the negative button. Sternberg then measured the time, in 100ths of a second, that the subject took to respond. This process was repeated over many randomly organized trials. Because Sternberg was interested in how people process information, he was interested in how reaction times varied as a function of the number of digits in the comparison set and as a function of whether the test digit was a positive or negative instance for that set. (If you make comparisons sequentially, the time to make a decision should increase as the number of digits in the comparison set increases. If you make comparisons in parallel, the number of digits in the comparison set shouldn't matter.)

Although Sternberg's primary aim was to compare data for the different conditions, we can gain an immediate impression of our data by taking the full set of reaction times, regardless of the stimulus condition. We will come back and compare the different conditions later. The data in Table 3.1 were collected in an experiment similar to Sternberg's but with only one subject—myself. No correction of responses was allowed, and the data presented here come only from correct trials.

## 3.1  Plotting Data

As you can see, there are simply too many numbers in Table 3.1 for us to be able to interpret them at a glance. One of the simplest methods for reorganizing data to make them more intelligible is to plot them in some sort of graphical form. Data

**Table 3.1**
Reaction-Time Data from the Digit-Identification Experiment

| Comparison Stimuli* | Reaction Times, in 100ths of a Second |
|---|---|
| 1Y | 40 41 47 38 40 37 38 47 45 61 54 67 49 43 52 39 46 47 45<br>43 39 49 50 44 53 46 64 51 40 41 44 48 50 42 90 51 55 60<br>47 45 41 42 72 36 43 94 45 51 46 52 |
| 1N | 52 45 74 56 53 59 43 46 51 40 48 47 57   54 44   56 47 62<br>44 53 48 50 58 52 57 66 49 59 56 71 76   54 71 104 44 67<br>45 79 46 57 58 47 73 67 46 57 52 61 72 104 |
| 3Y | 73 83 55 59 51 65 61 64 63 86 42 65 62 62 51 62 72 55 58<br>46 67 56 52 46 62 51 51 61 60 75 53 59 56 50 43 58 67 52<br>56 80 53 72 62 59 47 62 53 52 46 60 |
| 3N | 73 47 63 63 56 66 72 58 60 69 74 51 49 69 51 60 52 72 58<br>74 59 63 60 66 59 61 50 67 63 61 80 63 60 64 64 57 59 58<br>59 60 62 63 67 78 61 52 51 56 95 54 |
| 5Y | 39 65 53 46 78 60 71 58 87 77 62 94 81 46 49 62 55 59 88<br>56 77 67 79 54 83 75 67 60 65 62 62 62 60 58 67 48 51 67<br>98 64 57 67 55 55 66 60 57 54 78 69 |
| 5N | 66 53 61 74 76 69 82 56 66 63 69 76 71 65 67   67 55 65<br>58 64 65 81 69 69 63 68 70 80 68 63 74 61 85 125 59 61<br>74 76 62 83 58 72 65 61 95 58 64 66 66 72 |

\* 1, 3, and 5 refer to the number of digits in the comparison stimuli, and Y and N refer to whether the test digit was included in the comparison set (Y) or not (N).

can be represented graphically in several common ways. Some of these methods are frequency distributions, histograms, and stem-and-leaf displays, which we will discuss in turn.

## Frequency Distributions

As a first step we can make a **frequency distribution** of the data as a way of organizing them in some sort of logical order. For our example of reaction times, we would count the number of times that each possible reaction time occurred. For example, the subject responded in 50/100 of a second five times and in 51/100 of a second twelve times. On one occasion he became confused and took 1.25 seconds (125/100 of a second) to respond. The frequency distribution for these data is presented in Table 3.2, which reports how often each time occurred. The data are plotted in Figure 3.1.

Definition | **Frequency distribution:** A distribution in which the values of the dependent variable are tabled or plotted against their frequency of occurrence.

**Table 3.2**
Frequency Distribution of Reaction Times

| Reaction Time | Frequency | Reaction Time | Frequency | Reaction Time | Frequency |
|---|---|---|---|---|---|
| 36 | 1 | 61 | 11 | 86 | 1 |
| 37 | 1 | 62 | 14 | 87 | 1 |
| 38 | 2 | 63 | 10 | 88 | 1 |
| 39 | 3 | 64 | 7 | 89 | 0 |
| 40 | 4 | 65 | 8 | 90 | 1 |
| 41 | 3 | 66 | 8 | 91 | 0 |
| 42 | 3 | 67 | 14 | 92 | 0 |
| 43 | 5 | 68 | 2 | 93 | 0 |
| 44 | 5 | 69 | 7 | 94 | 2 |
| 45 | 6 | 70 | 1 | 95 | 2 |
| 46 | 11 | 71 | 4 | 96 | 0 |
| 47 | 9 | 72 | 8 | 97 | 0 |
| 48 | 4 | 73 | 3 | 98 | 1 |
| 49 | 5 | 74 | 6 | 99 | 0 |
| 50 | 5 | 75 | 2 | 100 | 0 |
| 51 | 12 | 76 | 4 | 101 | 0 |
| 52 | 10 | 77 | 2 | 102 | 0 |
| 53 | 8 | 78 | 3 | 103 | 0 |
| 54 | 6 | 79 | 2 | 104 | 2 |
| 55 | 7 | 80 | 3 | 105 | 0 |
| 56 | 10 | 81 | 2 | .. | .. |
| 57 | 7 | 82 | 1 | .. | .. |
| 58 | 12 | 83 | 3 | .. | .. |
| 59 | 11 | 84 | 0 | 125 | 1 |
| 60 | 12 | 85 | 1 | .. | .. |

From the distribution shown in Table 3.2, and a plot of the data in Figure 3.1, it is clear that there is a wide distribution of reaction times, with times as low as 36/100 second and as high as 125/100 seconds. The data tend to cluster around about 60/100, with most of the scores between 40/100 and 90/100. This tendency was not apparent from the unorganized data shown in Table 3.1.

## 3.2 Stem-and-Leaf Displays

A frequency distribution tells you how many times each value occurs, and the associated graph gives you a visual representation of the data. A very nice way of retaining both the individual values and the frequency of those values is by creating a **stem-and-leaf display**.

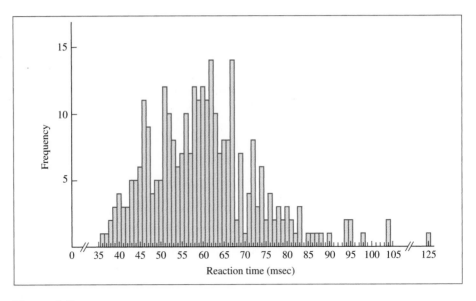

**Figure 3.1**
Plot of reaction times against frequency

| Definition | **Stem-and-leaf display:** Graphical display presenting original data arranged into a histogram. |
|---|---|

**Exploratory data analysis (EDA):** A set of techniques developed by Tukey for presenting data in visually meaningful ways.

**Leading digits (most significant digits):** Leftmost digits of a number.

John Tukey (1977), as part of his general approach to data analysis, known as **exploratory data analysis (EDA)**, developed a variety of methods for displaying data in visually meaningful ways. One of the simplest of these methods is a stem-and-leaf display. I can't start with the reaction-time data here because, due to the large number of observations, that would require a slightly more sophisticated display. Instead, I'll use a real set of data on the number of intrusive thoughts experienced by newly diagnosed breast cancer patients (Epping-Jordan, Compas, & Howell, 1994). As you might expect, some of these women are troubled a great deal by thoughts that keep coming to mind about their cancer. On the other hand, some women report very few such thoughts.

The raw data are given in Figure 3.2. On the left side of the figure are the raw data, and on the right is the complete stem-and-leaf display that results.

From the raw data in Figure 3.2, you can see that there are several scores below 10, many scores in the teens, some in the 20s, and three in the 30s. We refer to the tens' digits—here 0, 1, 2, and 3—as the **leading digits** (sometimes called the **most significant digits**) for these scores. These leading digits form the **stem,** or

| Raw Data | Stem | Leaf |
|---|---|---|
| 0 1 1 2 2 3 4 4 4 5 5 5 6 6 7 7 7 7<br>8 8 9 9 | 0<br>1 | 0112234445556677778899<br>01112223333344455555556666666666<br>6777888899 |
| | 2 | 00112233444455667889 |
| 10 11 11 11 12 12 12 13 13 13 13<br>13 14 14 14 15 15 15 15 15 15 16<br>16 16 16 16 16 16 16 16 16 17 17<br>17 18 18 18 18 19 19 | 3 | 005 |
| 20 20 21 21 22 22 23 23 24 24 24<br>24 25 25 26 26 27 28 28 29 | | |
| 30 30 35 | | |

**Figure 3.2**
Stem-and-leaf display of data on intrusive thoughts

vertical axis, of our display. Within the set of 32 scores that were in the 20s, you can see that there were two 20s, two 21s, two 22s, two 23s, four 24s, two 25s, two 26s, one 27, two 28s, and one 29. The units' digits 0, 1, 2, 3, 4, and so on, are called the **trailing digits** (or **less significant digits**). They form the **leaves**—the horizontal elements—of our display.[1]

Definition  **Stem:** Vertical axis of display containing the leading digits.

**Trailing digits (less significant digits):** Digits to the right of the leading digits.

**Leaves:** Horizontal axis of display containing the trailing digits.

On the right side of Figure 3.2 you can see that next to the stem entry of 2 you have two 0s, two 1s, two 2s, two 3s, four 4s, two 5s, two 6s, one 7, two 8s, and one 9. These leaf values correspond to the units' digits in the raw data. Similarly, note how the leaves opposite the stem value of 1 correspond to the units' digits of all responses in the teens. From the stem-and-leaf display you could completely regenerate the raw data that went into that display. For example, you can tell that one person reported no intrusive thoughts, two people each reported one intrusive thought, and so on. Moreover, the shape of the display looks just like a sideways histogram, giving you all of the benefits of that method of graphing data as well.

One apparent drawback of this simple stem-and-leaf display is that for some data sets it will lead to a grouping that is too coarse for our purposes. In fact, that is

---

[1]It is not always true that the tens' digits form the stem and the units' digits the leaves. For example, if the data ranged from 100 to 1,000, the hundreds' digits would form the stem, the tens' digits the leaves, and we would ignore the units' digits.

why I needed to move away from the reaction time example temporarily. When I tried to use the reaction time data, I found that the stem for 50 (i.e., 5) had 88 leaves opposite it, which was a little silly. Not to worry; Tukey was there before us and figured out a clever way around this problem.

If we have a problem when we try to lump together everything between 50 and 59, perhaps what we should be doing is breaking that interval into smaller intervals. We *could* try using the intervals 50–54, 55–59, and so on. But then we couldn't just use 5 as the stem, because it would not distinguish between the two intervals. Tukey suggested using "5*" to represent 50–54, and "5." to represent 55–59. But that won't solve our problem here, because the categories still are too coarse. So Tukey suggested an alternative scheme whereby "5*" represents 50–51, "5t" represents 52–53, "5f" represents 54–55, "5s" represents 56–57, and "5." represents 58–59. (You might wonder why he chose those particular letters, but "two" and "three" both start with "t," and you can figure out the rest.) If we apply this scheme to the data on reaction times, we obtain the results shown in Figure 3.3. In Figure 3.3 I have presented only some of the raw data for purposes of illustration, but the complete stem-and-leaf display is there, allowing you to reproduce the original data set. (In deciding on the number of stems to use, the problem is similar to one we will soon face in selecting the number of categories in a histogram. You want to do something that makes sense and that conveys information in a meaningful way. The one restriction is that the stems should be the same width. You would not let one stem be 50–54, and another 60–69.)

Notice that in Figure 3.3 I did not list the extreme values as I did the others. I used the word *High* in place of the stem and then inserted the actual values. I did this to highlight the presence of extreme values, as well as to conserve space. I would have done a similar thing if there had been unusually low values.

### Back-to-Back Stem-and-Leaf Displays

Do you attend class reliably? Does it matter? I think it matters, and the data to support that belief can best be presented by plotting two distributions on opposite sides of the stem in a stem-and-leaf display. In a course that I once taught we asked the laboratory assistants, at the end of the course, to indicate which of their students came to class regularly (3), occasionally (2), or rarely (1)[2]. We will ignore those who came occasionally, leaving us with the data on two groups. Figure 3.4 shows the actual distribution of total points in the course for the two groups. These are actual data. Notice the code at the bottom of the table that indicates how entries translate to raw scores. This particular code says that | 25 | 6 represents 256, not 25.6 or 2560. Finally, notice that the figure nicely illustrates the difference in performance between those students who attend class regularly and those who came when they couldn't think of anything better to do. A few got away with it, but most people who skipped got into trouble. (The folks who came to class sporadically fell in the middle in terms of total points.)

---

[2]The laboratory assistants came to each lecture and were in a position to make an informed judgment on attendance.

| Raw Data (partial) | Stem | Leaf |
|---|---|---|
| 36 37 38 38 39 39 39 40 | 3s | 67 |
| 40 40 40 41 41 41 42 42 | 3. | 88999 |
| 42 43 43 43 43 43 44 44 | 4* | 0000111 |
| 44 44 44 45 45 45 45 45 | 4t | 22233333 |
| 45 46 46 46 46 46 46 46 | 4f | 44444555555 |
| 46 46 46 46 47 47 47 47 | 4s | 6666666666677777777 |
| 47 47 47 47 47 48 48 48 | 4. | 888899999 |
| 48 49 49 49 49 49 50 50 | 5* | 0000011111111111 |
| 50 50 50 51 51 51 51 51 | 5t | 222222222233333333 |
| 51 51 51 51 51 51 51 52 | 5f | 4444445555555 |
| 52 52 52 52 52 52 52 52 | 5s | 66666666667777777 |
| 52 53 53 53 53 53 53 53 | 5. | 88888888888899999999999 |
| 53 54 54 54 54 54 54 55 | 6* | 0000000000000011111111111 |
| 55 55 55 55 55 55 | 6t | 2222222222222223333333333 |
| | 6f | 444444455555555 |
| | 6s | 666666667777777777777 |
| | 6. | 889999999 |
| | 7* | 01111 |
| | 7t | 22222222333 |
| | 7f | 44444455 |
| | 7s | 666677 |
| | 7. | 88899 |
| | 8* | 00011 |
| | 8t | 2333 |
| | 8f | 5 |
| | 8s | 67 |
| | 8. | 8 |
| | 9* | 0 |
| | 9t | |
| | 9f | 4455 |
| | 9s | |
| | 9. | 8 |
| | High | 104; 104; 125 |

**Figure 3.3**
Stem-and-leaf display for reaction-time data

## 3.3 Histograms

In the earlier discussion of frequency distributions (Table 3.2) I plotted the frequency of the individual values of reaction time. But when we are dealing with a variable, such as this one on reaction times, that has many different values, each individual value often occurs with low frequency, and there is often substantial

| Missed Class Often | Stem | Attended Regularly |
|---:|:---:|:---|
| 8 | 18 | |
| 5 5 | 19 | |
| | 20 | |
| | 21 | |
| 8 5 | 22 | |
| 9 7 3 2 | 23 | |
| 0 | 24 | 1 3 6 9 |
| 6 6 6 0 | 25 | 0 2 4 4 5 6 |
| 8 4 4 1 | 26 | 1 2 3 4 4 4 5 7 7 |
| 7 4 4 0 0 | 27 | 0 1 2 3 6 6 7 8 8 |
| | 28 | 0 1 2 4 8 8 |
| | 29 | 0 1 1 2 3 4 6 6 7 8 |
| 8 | 30 | |
| | 31 | 0 |
| | 32 | 0 1 8 |
| Code | 25 | 6 = 256 | | |

**Figure 3.4**

Total points in an actual course on psychological methods plotted separately for those who missed class often or attended regularly

fluctuation of the frequencies in adjacent intervals. Notice in Figure 3.3, for example, that there are fourteen 67s, but only two 68s. In situations such as this it makes more sense to group adjacent values together into a **histogram**. Doing so obscures some of the random "noise" that is not likely to be meaningful, but preserves important trends in the data. We might, for example, group the data into blocks of 5/100 of a second, combining the frequencies for all outcomes between 35 and 39, between 40 and 44, and so on. An example of such a distribution is shown in Table 3.3.

Definition    **Histogram:** Graph in which a rectangle is used to represent frequencies of observations within each interval.

**Real lower limit:** The point halfway between the bottom of one interval and the top of the one below it.

**Real upper limit:** The point halfway between the top of one interval and the bottom of the one above it.

In Table 3.3 I have reported the upper and lower boundaries of the intervals as whole integers, for the simple reason that it makes the table easier to read. However, you should realize that the true limits of the interval (known as the real lower limit and the real upper limit) are decimal values that fall halfway between the top of one interval and the bottom of the next. The **real lower limit** of an interval is the smallest value that would be classed as falling into that interval. Similarly, an

**Table 3.3**
Grouped Frequency Distribution

| Interval | Midpoint | Frequency | Cumulative Frequency | Interval | Midpoint | Frequency | Cumulative Frequency |
|---|---|---|---|---|---|---|---|
| 35–39 | 37 | 7 | 7 | 85–89 | 87 | 4 | 291 |
| 40–44 | 42 | 20 | 27 | 90–94 | 92 | 3 | 294 |
| 45–49 | 47 | 35 | 62 | 95–99 | 97 | 3 | 297 |
| 50–54 | 52 | 41 | 103 | 100–104 | 102 | 2 | 299 |
| 55–59 | 57 | 47 | 150 | 105–109 | 107 | 0 | 299 |
| 60–64 | 62 | 54 | 204 | 110–114 | 112 | 0 | 299 |
| 65–69 | 67 | 39 | 243 | 115–119 | 117 | 0 | 299 |
| 70–74 | 72 | 22 | 265 | 120–124 | 122 | 0 | 299 |
| 75–79 | 77 | 13 | 278 | 125–129 | 127 | 1 | 300 |
| 80–84 | 82 | 9 | 287 | | | | |

interval's **real upper limit** is the largest value that would be classed as being in that interval. For example, had we recorded reaction times to the nearest thousandth of a second, rather than to the nearest hundredth, the interval 35–39 would include all values between 34.5 and 39.5, because values falling between those points would be rounded up or down into that interval. (People often become terribly worried about what we would do if a person had a score of exactly 39.50000000 and therefore sat right on the breakpoint between two intervals. Don't worry about it. First, it is unlikely to happen. Second, you can always flip a coin. Third, there are many more important things to worry about. This is one of those nonissues that make people think the study of statistics is confusing, boring, or both.) The **midpoints** listed in Table 3.3 are the averages of the upper and lower limits and are presented for convenience.

---

Definition | **Midpoint:** Center of the interval; average of the upper and lower limits.

---

Table 3.3 lists the frequencies with which scores fell into each interval. For example, there were seven reaction times between 35/100 and 39/100 of a second. The distribution in Table 3.3 is shown as a histogram in Figure 3.5.

People often ask about the optimal number of intervals to use when grouping data. Although there is no right answer to this question, somewhere around 10 intervals is usually reasonable.[3] In this example I used 19 intervals because the numbers naturally broke that way, and because I had a lot of observations. In general and when practical it is best to use natural breaks in the number system (e.g., 0–9, 10–19, . . . or 100–119, 120–139) rather than to break up the range into exactly

---

[3]One interesting scheme for choosing an optimal number of intervals is to set it equal to the integer closest to $\sqrt{N}$, where $N$ is the number of observations. Applying that suggestion here would leave us with $\sqrt{300} = 17.32 = 17$ intervals, which is close to the 19 that I actually used.

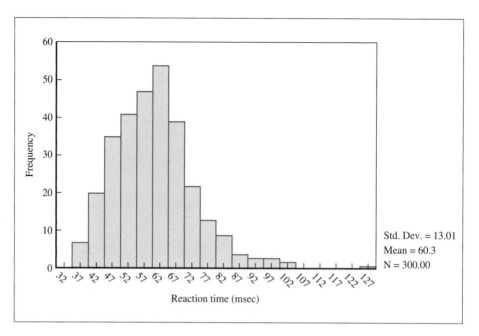

**Figure 3.5**
Grouped distribution of reaction times

10 arbitrarily defined intervals. However, if another kind of limit makes the data more interpretable, then use those limits. Remember that you are trying to make the data meaningful—don't try to follow a rigid set of rules made up by someone who has never seen your problem.

In Figure 3.5 the reaction time data are generally centered between 50/100 and 70/100 second, the distribution rises and falls fairly regularly, and the distribution trails off to the right. We would expect such times to trail off to the right (referred to as being positively skewed) because there is some limit on how *quickly* the subject can respond, but really no limit on how *slowly* he can respond. Notice also the extreme value of 125 hundredths. This value is called an **outlier** because it is widely separated from the rest of the data. Outliers frequently represent errors in recording data, but in this particular case it was just a trial in which the subject became flustered and couldn't make up his mind which button to push.

Definition | **Outlier:** An extreme point that stands out from the rest of the distribution.

## 3.4 Reading Graphs

In recent years I have heard more and more comments from my colleagues to the effect that students are having trouble understanding graphs. It is hard to tell whether this is just an example of the fact that my colleagues are getting older and

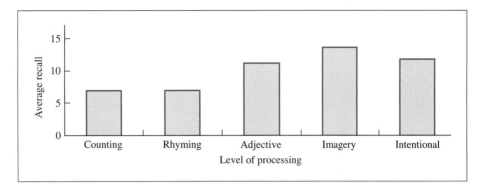

**Figure 3.6**
Average recall as a function of level of processing

"students aren't like they were in my day," or if interpretation of graphs has become more difficult for students. This section is my attempt at addressing the problem.

One difficulty stems from the fact that we can't make any nice dogmatic statement about whether the dependent variable goes on the Y axis or the X axis, and so on. Clear rules make life so much simpler, but they don't apply here. If you take the histograms that we have been looking at, you will see that the dependent variable (e.g., Reaction time) is placed along the X axis, and the frequency with which each value occurred is on the Y axis. That is true for any histogram that I can think of. On the other hand, consider the graph shown in Figure 3.6. This is a graph showing the average level of recall of verbal material (words) for groups that differed in the level of processing that they applied to those words during training. (We will examine this study in detail in Chapter 16.) In this graph the level of processing required by the participants increases as we go from Counting to Intentional.

Notice that the independent variable (levels of processing) is presented on the X axis, and the dependent variable (average level of recall) is on the Y axis. It is apparent from the graph that as participants process information more completely, their level of recall generally increases. However the increase is not completely consistent, because it drops a trivial amount between Counting and Rhyming, and between Imagery and Intentional. The general trend, however, is upward.

A second graph with Time on the X axis, is shown in Figure 3.7. Here we see the trend in life expectancy of white females from 1920 to 1990.

In creating this graph I have connected the data points with a line, making it a **line graph**, rather than bars, which would be a **bar graph**. I did this because it seems appropriate, given the continuous nature of the independent variable. Notice that this graph nicely illustrates the increase over time in life expectancy.

Definition  Line graph: A graph in which the Y values corresponding to different values of X are connected by a line.

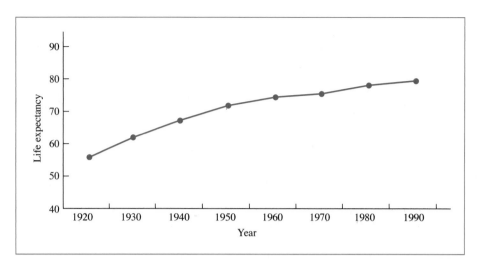

**Figure 3.7**
Life expectancy of white females as a function of year

---

Definition    **Bar graph:** A graph in which the frequency of occurrence of different values of X is represented by the height of a bar.

---

It may seem rather obvious to say so, but the most important thing in making sense of a graph is to first identify what is plotted on each axis. Then identify the dependent and independent variables, and finally, look for patterns in the data. In histograms we are looking for the shape of the distribution, and usually hoping to see that it is at least highest toward the center. For bar graphs (Figure 3.6) and line graphs (Figure 3.7) we are generally looking for differences between groups and/or trends in the data. Often the choice between a bar graph and a line graph is a matter of preference, though there are many people with strongly held views on this topic. If one of them is your instructor, you should pay close attention.

## 3.5 Alternative Methods of Plotting Data

The previous sections dealt with only a few ways of plotting data. Data can be represented in an almost unlimited number of other ways, some of which are quite ingenious and informative. A few examples are shown in Figures 3.8 and 3.9. These examples were chosen because they illustrate how displays can be used to reveal interesting features of data.

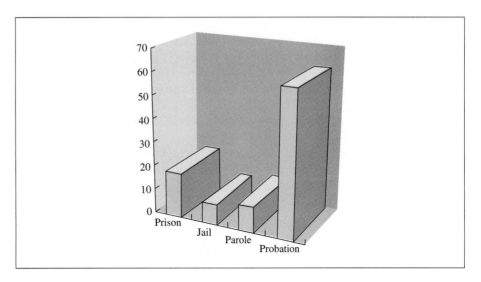

**Figure 3.8**
Disposition of those under correctional supervision

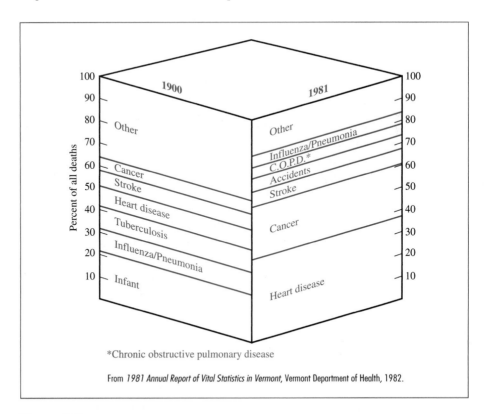

*Chronic obstructive pulmonary disease

From *1981 Annual Report of Vital Statistics in Vermont*, Vermont Department of Health, 1982.

**Figure 3.9**
Major causes of death in Vermont, 1900 and 1981

Two comments are in order about how we plot data. First, the point of representing data graphically is to communicate to an audience. If there is a better way to communicate, then use it. Rules of graphical presentation are intended as guides to clearer presentation, not as prescriptive rules that may never be broken. This point was made earlier in the discussion about the number of intervals that should be used for a histogram, but it goes beyond histograms. So the first "rule" is this: *If it aids understanding, do it; if it doesn't, don't.*

The second rule is to keep things simple. Generally, the worst graphics are those that include irrelevant features that only add to the confusion. Tufte (1983) calls such material "chart junk," and you should avoid it. Perhaps the worst sin, in the opinion of many, is plotting something in three dimensions that could be better plotted in two. There are legitimate reasons for three-dimensional plots (Figure 3.9 may be one), but three dimensions are more likely to confuse the issue than to clarify it. Unfortunately, most graphics packages written for corporate users (often called "presentation graphics") encourage the addition of unnecessary dimensions. Graphics should look utilitarian, neat and orderly; they should rarely look "pretty." If you think you need three dimensions to represent the material, ask yourself if the reader is going to be able to understand what you're trying to show. Often the third dimension either makes the figure visually uninterpretable, or it adds a level of complication that many of us are not prepared to handle. If you have taken a psychology course on perception, you will know that the eye is great at handling three-dimensional objects in three-dimensional space. But our eyes (and brains) play tricks on us when they try to handle three-dimensional objects in two-dimensional space. (See, psychology has something—often a lot—to say to statistics, just as statistics has something to say to psychology.) Figure 3.8 is a poorly constructed version of a graph you will see in Chapter 6. It purports to show the disposition of people under correctional supervision. Can you tell whether there are more people in jail than on parole? What percentage of those in the correctional system are on parole? Glance ahead to Figure 6.2 to see a much clearer way of presenting these data.

Figure 3.9 is a comparison of the causes of death of Vermont residents in 1900 and 1981. Notice that the various causes have been ordered from bottom to top in terms of decreasing order of magnitude. From this figure it is immediately apparent that, whereas almost one-third of the deaths in 1900 were attributable to a high rate of infant mortality and to tuberculosis, neither of those sources contributed noticeably to death rates in 1981. On the other hand, cancer and heart disease, which together accounted for 60% of all deaths in 1981, played a much-reduced role in 1900, accounting for less than 15% of all deaths. Do these data make sense from what you know about changes in health care? You can compare these results to the 2000 data (for all of the U.S.) by going to

http://www.cdc.gov/nchs/fastats/lcod.htm

Some really interesting data can be found at

http://www.infoplease.com/ipa/A0922292.html

Life's risks have certainly changed in the last 100 years.

Figure 3.10 is the distribution, by age and gender, of the populations of Mexico, Spain, the United States, and Sweden. This figure clearly portrays differences between countries in terms of their age distributions. (Compare Mexico and Sweden, for example.) By having males and females plotted back to back, we can also see the effects of gender differences in life expectancy. The older age groups in three countries contain more females than males. In Mexico it appears that men begin to outnumber women in their early twenties. This type of distribution was common in the past when many women died in childbirth, and we might start looking there for an explanation. The purpose in presenting graphs such as these is to illustrate that very simple graphs can tell a very compelling story.

## 3.6 Describing Distributions

The distributions of scores illustrated in Figures 3.1 and 3.2 were more or less regularly shaped distributions, rising to a maximum and then dropping away smoothly. Not all distributions are like that, however (see the stem-and-leaf display in Figure 3.5), and it is important to understand the terms used to describe different distributions. Consider the two distributions shown in Figure 3.11(a) and (b). These plots are of data that were computer generated to come from populations with specific shapes. These plots, and the other two in Figure 3.11, are based on samples of 1000 observations, and the slight irregularities are just random variability. The distributions in Figure 3.11(a) and (b) are called **symmetric** because they have the same shape on both sides of the center. The distribution shown in Figure 3.11(a) came from what we will later refer to as a normal distribution. The distribution in Figure 3.11(b) is referred to as **bimodal**, because it has two peaks. The term *bimodal* is used to refer to any distribution that has two predominant peaks, whether or not those peaks are of exactly the same height. If a distribution has only one major peak, it is called **unimodal**. The term used to refer to the number of major peaks in a distribution is **modality**.

Definition    **Symmetric:** Having the same shape on both sides of the center.

**Bimodal:** A distribution having two distinct peaks.

**Unimodal:** A distribution having one distinct peak.

**Modality:** The number of meaningful peaks in a frequency distribution of the data.

**Negatively skewed:** A distribution that trails off to the left.

**Positively skewed:** A distribution that trails off to the right.

Next consider Figure 3.11(c) and (d). These two distributions obviously are not symmetric. The distribution in Figure 3.11(c) has a tail going out to the left, whereas that in Figure 3.11(d) has a tail going out to the right. We say that the former is **negatively skewed** and the latter **positively skewed**. (*Hint:* To help

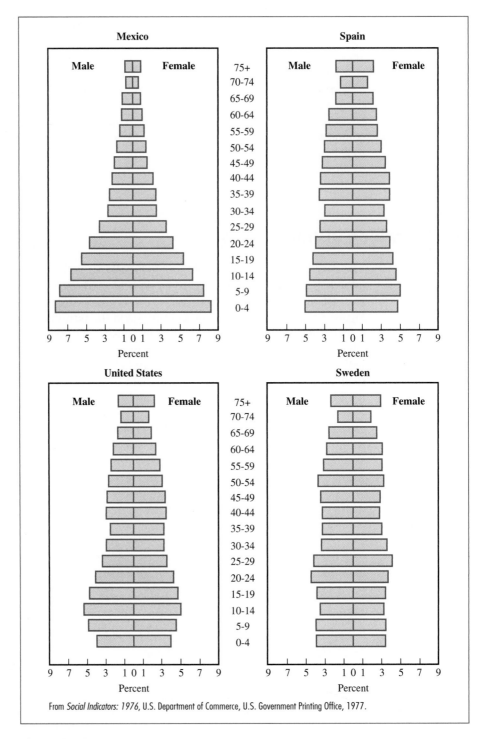

**Figure 3.10**

Population for selected countries by sex and age, 1970

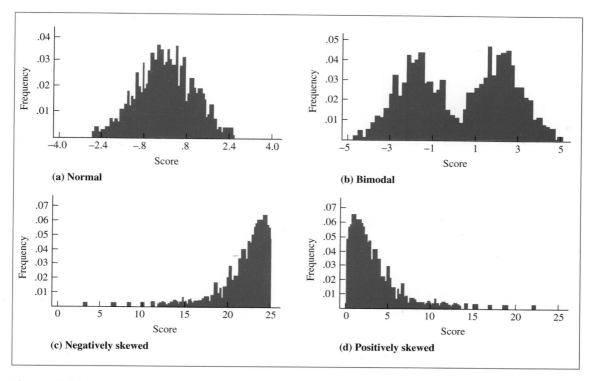

**Figure 3.11**
Shapes of frequency distributions: (a) Normal; (b) Bimodal; (c) Negatively skewed; (d) Positively skewed

you remember which is which, notice that negatively skewed distributions point to the negative, or small, numbers, and that positively skewed distributions point to the positive end of the scale.) There are statistical measures of the degree of asymmetry, or **skewness**, but they are not commonly used in the social sciences.

---

Definition | **Skewness:** A measure of the degree to which a distribution is asymmetrical.

---

An interesting real-life example of a positively skewed bimodal distribution is shown in Figure 3.12. These data were generated by Bradley (1963), who instructed subjects to press a button as quickly as possible whenever a small light came on. Most of the data points are smoothly distributed between roughly 7 and 17 hundredths of a second, but a small but noticeable cluster of points lies between 30 and 70 hundredths, trailing off to the right. This second cluster of points was obtained primarily from trials on which the subject missed the button on the first try and had to try again. Their inclusion in the data significantly affects the distribution's shape. An experimenter who had such a collection of data might seriously consider separately treating times greater than some maximum, on the grounds that those

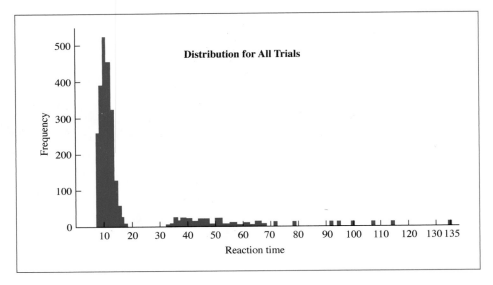

**Figure 3.12**
Frequency distribution of Bradley's reaction-time data

times were more a reflection of the *accuracy* of a psychomotor response than a measure of the *speed* of that response.

It is important to consider the difference between Bradley's data, shown in Figure 3.12, and the data that I generated, shown in Figure 3.1. Both distributions are positively skewed, but my data generally show longer reaction times without the second cluster of points. One difference was that I was making a decision on *which* button to press, whereas Bradley's subjects had to press only a single button whenever the light came on. (This may remind some of you of the older literature on time required to make decisions.) In addition, the program I was using to present stimuli recorded data only from *correct* responses, not from errors. There was no chance to correct and hence nothing equivalent to missing the button on the first try and having to press it again. I point out these differences to illustrate that differences in the way in which data are collected can have noticeable effects on the kinds of data we see and what we are actually measuring.

Nearly every textbook author feels the need to discuss another measure of the shape of a distribution, called its kurtosis. But very few people know what it really measures, and even fewer have ever used it. So I'm going to break with tradition and not even discuss it. In return for not having to memorize four new terms, you can go to the World Wide Web, link to

 http://www.geom.umn.edu/docs/education/chance/chance_news/
current_news/current.html

or

http://www.helsinki.fi/~jpuranen/links.html

and explore material having nothing to do with kurtosis. You'll learn far more there than in any discussion of kurtosis (and you can call it a study break).

It is important to recognize that relatively large samples of data are needed before we can have a good idea about the shape of a distribution. With sample sizes of around 30, the best we can reasonably expect to see is whether the data tend to pile up in the center of the distribution or are markedly skewed in one direction or another.

## 3.7 Using Computer Programs to Display Data

As I said earlier, almost all statistics texts once assumed that simple data analyses will be carried out by hand with the help of a standard calculator. This may be the best approach to teaching, though I don't think so, but today computer programs carry out more and more analyses. Thus you need to know how to read and interpret the results of computer printouts. Most chapters in this book will include samples of computer solutions for examples previously analyzed by hand. I will focus primarily on a statistical package named SPSS because it is the most commonly available and most requested by instructors. This package will carry out almost any standard analysis you can think of. However anything I do here can be done with any program you can get your hands on, with the possible exception of some of the graphical stuff.

Figure 3.13 shows a histogram and a stem-and-leaf display produced by SPSS for the data on intrusive thoughts shown in Figure 3.2. (In SPSS the stem-and-leaf plot is found under **Analyze/Descriptives/Explore.**) These plots are somewhat different from the ones that we obtained earlier, owing to the amount of grouping that was done.

So far in our discussion, almost no mention has been made of the numbers themselves. We have seen how data can be organized and presented in the form of distributions, and we have discussed a number of ways in which distributions can be characterized: symmetry or its lack (skewness), and modality. As useful as this information might be in certain situations, it is inadequate in others. We still do not know the average speed of a simple decision reaction time nor how alike or dissimilar are the reaction times for individual trials. Nor do we know the mean scores for students who did, and who did not, attend my class regularly. To obtain this knowledge, we must reduce the data to a set of measures that carry the information we need. The questions to be asked refer to the location, or central tendency, and to the dispersion, or variability, of the distributions along the underlying scale. Measures of these characteristics will be considered in the next two chapters.

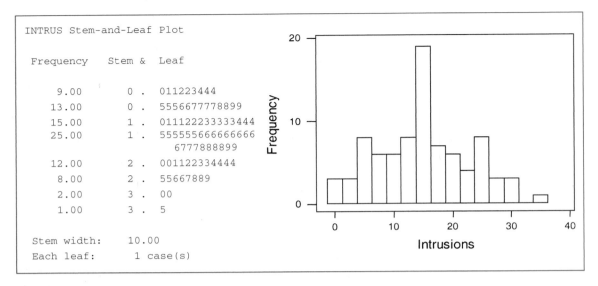

**Figure 3.13**
SPSS stem-and-leaf and histogram of intrusion data

## 3.8 Summary

In this chapter we discussed ways of describing distributions. All the techniques discussed here are intended primarily to organize and reduce the information contained in large sets of data to manageable proportions and to readily communicate some of that information to other people. In examining these techniques we also looked briefly at stem-and-leaf displays (one small part of Tukey's exploratory data analysis) and examined a number of terms that are useful in characterizing the shapes of distributions.

Some important terms in this chapter are

| | |
|---|---|
| Frequency distribution, *34* | Trailing digits (less significant digits), *37* |
| Stem-and-leaf display, *36* | |
| Exploratory data analysis (EDA), *36* | Leaves, *37* |
| Leading digits (most significant digits), *36* | Histogram, *40* |
| | Real lower limit, *40* |
| Stem, *37* | Real upper limit, *40* |

Midpoint, *41*                        Unimodal, *47*

Outlier, *42*                         Modality, *47*

Line graph, *43*                      Negatively skewed, *47*

Bar graph, *44*                       Positively skewed, *47*

Symmetric, *47*                       Skewness, *49*

Bimodal, *47*

## 3.9 Exercises

**3.1**   Have you ever wondered how you would do on the Scholastic Aptitude Test (SAT) if you didn't even bother to read the passage you were asked about?[4] Katz, Lautenschlager, Blackburn, and Harris (1990) asked students to answer SAT-type questions without seeing the passage on which the questions were based. This was called the NoPassage group. Data closely resembling what they obtained follow, where the dependent variable was the individual's score on the test.

54   52   51   50   36   55   44   46   57   44   43   52   38   46

55   34   44   39   43   36   55   57   36   46   49   46   49   47

(a) Plot an ungrouped frequency distribution for these data.
(b) What is the general shape of the distribution?

**3.2**   Make a histogram for the data in Exercise 3.1 using a reasonable number of intervals.

**3.3**   What kind of stems would you need for a stem-and-leaf display of the data in Exercise 3.1?

**3.4**   If students had just guessed in the Katz et al. study, they would have been expected to earn a score of approximately 20. Do these students appear to do better than chance even when they haven't read the passage?

**3.5**   As part of the study described in Exercise 3.1, the experimenters obtained the same kind of data from a smaller group who had read the passage before answering the questions (called the Passage group). Their data follow.

66   75   72   71   55   56   72   93   73   72   72   73   91   66   71   56   59

(a) What can you tell just by looking at these numbers? Do students do better when they have read the passage?
(b) Plot these data on one side of a stem-and-leaf display and the NoPassage data on the other side of the same stem-and-leaf display.

---

[4]For those readers outside the U.S., SAT exams are exams taken by many, though by no means all, students seeking admission to American universities. Scores typically range from 200 to 800, with an average somewhere around 500. I will refer to SAT scores occasionally throughout this book.

(c) What can you see by looking at this stem-and-leaf display?

(d) A further discussion of this example can be found at

http://www.uvm.edu/~dhowell/fundamentals/Katzfolder/katz.html

although that link also covers material that we will discuss later in this book.

**3.6** Create a positively skewed set of data and plot it.

**3.7** Create a bimodal set of data that represents some actual phenomenon and plot it. Why would you expect the data to be bimodal for this phenomenon?

**3.8** What would you predict to be the shape (e.g., skewness and modality) of the distribution of the number of cigarettes smoked per day for the next 200 people you meet?

The next two exercises refer to data that can be downloaded from the Web at

http://www.uvm.edu/~dhowell/fundamentals/DataFiles/Add.dat

These data come from a research study by Howell and Huessy (1985). We will refer to them throughout the book

**3.9** Using the Web link shown in Exercise 3.8, look at the data for GPA. Create a histogram for the data, using reasonable intervals.

**3.10** Create a stem-and-leaf display for the ADDSC score in Add.dat.

**3.11** What three interesting facts about the populations of Mexico and Spain can be seen in Figure 3.10?

**3.12** In some stem-and-leaf displays with one or two low values, the last stem is often written as LOW with the complete values in the leaf section. Why and when might we do this?

**3.13** How would you describe the distributions of the grades of students who did, and did not, attend class in Figure 3.4? Why would you have expected this kind of distribution even before you saw the data?

**3.14** In Table 3.1 the reaction-time data are broken down separately by the number of digits in the comparison stimulus. Create three side-by-side stem-and-leaf displays, one for each set of data. (Ignore the distinction between positive and negative instances.) What kinds of differences do you see between the reaction times under the three conditions? These data can also be found on the Web at

http://www.uvm.edu/~dhowell/fundamentals/DataFiles/Rxtime.dat

**3.15** Sternberg ran his original study (the one that is replicated in Table 3.1) to investigate whether people process information simultaneously or sequentially. He reasoned that if they process information simultaneously, they would compare the test stimulus against all digits in the comparison stimulus at the same time, and the time to decide whether a digit was part of the comparison set would not depend on how many digits were in the comparison. If people process information sequentially, the time to come to a decision would increase with the number of digits in the comparison. Which hypothesis do you think the figures you created in Exercise 3.14 support?

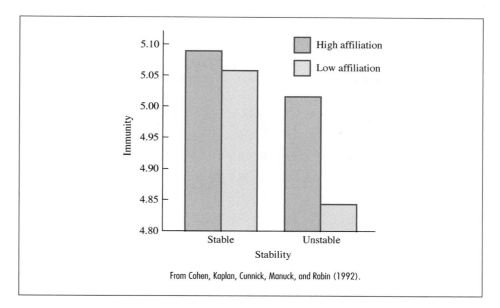

From Cohen, Kaplan, Cunnick, Manuck, and Rabin (1992).

**Figure 3.14**
From Cohen, Kaplan, et al. (1992)

**3.16**  In addition to comparing the three distributions of reaction times, as in Exercise 3.15, how else could you use the data from Table 3.1 to investigate how people process information?

**3.17**  One frequent assumption in statistical analyses is that observations are independent of one another. (Knowing one response tells you nothing about the magnitude of another response.) How would you characterize the reaction time data in Table 3.1, just based on what you know about how it was collected? (A lack of independence would not invalidate anything we have done with these data in this chapter, though it might have an effect on more complex analyses.)

**3.18**  Figure 3.14 is adapted from a paper by Cohen, Kaplan, Cunnick, Manuck, and Rabin (1992), which examined the immune response of nonhuman primates raised in stable and unstable social groups. In each group, animals were classed as high or low in affiliation, measured in terms of the amount of time they spent in close physical proximity to other animals. Higher scores on the immunity measure represent greater immunity to disease. Write two or three sentences describing what these results would seem to suggest.

**3.19**  Rogers and Prentice-Dunn (1981) had 96 white male undergraduates deliver shock to their fellow subjects as part of a biofeedback study. They recorded the amount of shock that the subjects delivered to white participants and black participants when the subjects had and had not been insulted by the experimenter. Their results are shown in Figure 3.15. Interpret these results.

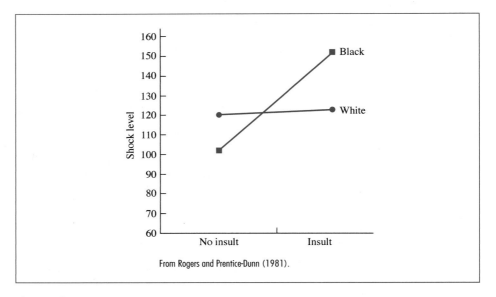

From Rogers and Prentice-Dunn (1981).

**Figure 3.15**
From Rogers and Prentice-Dunn (1981)

**3.20**    The following data represent U.S. college enrollments by census categories as measured in 1982 and 1991. Plot the data in a form that represents the changing ethnic distribution of college students in the United States. (The data entries are in 1,000s.)

| Ethnic Group | 1982 | 1991 |
|---|---|---|
| White | 9,997 | 10,990 |
| Black | 1,101 | 1,335 |
| Native American | 88 | 114 |
| Hispanic | 519 | 867 |
| Asian | 351 | 637 |
| Foreign | 331 | 416 |

**3.21**    Data can be found at

    http://www.sfaf.org/documents/2005_4th_qtr_stats.pdf

showing the changes in AIDS statistics from 1983 to 2004. Describe what those data would appear to show.

**3.22**    The following data represent the total number of U.S. households, the number of households headed by women, and family size from 1960 to 1990. Present these data in a way that reveals any changes in U.S. demographics. What do the data suggest about how a social scientist might look at the problems facing the United States? (Households are given in 1,000s.)

| Year | Total Households | Households Headed by Women | Family Size |
|------|------|------|------|
| 1960 | 52,799 | 4,507 | 3.33 |
| 1970 | 63,401 | 5,591 | 3.14 |
| 1975 | 71,120 | 7,242 | 2.94 |
| 1980 | 80,776 | 8,705 | 2.76 |
| 1985 | 86,789 | 10,129 | 2.69 |
| 1987 | 89,479 | 10,445 | 2.66 |
| 1988 | 91,066 | 10,608 | 2.64 |
| 1989 | 92,830 | 10,890 | 2.62 |
| 1990 | 92,347 | 10,890 | 2.63 |

**3.23**  Moran (1974) presented data on the relationship, for Australian births, between maternal age and Down's syndrome (a serious handicapping condition that psychologists have studied extensively). The data follow, though, in a form that may require some minor calculations on your part to be meaningful. What can you conclude from these results?

| Age of Mother | Total Number of Births | Number of Births with Down's Syndrome |
|------|------|------|
| 20 or less | 35,555 | 15 |
| 20–24 | 207,931 | 128 |
| 25–29 | 253,450 | 208 |
| 30–34 | 170,970 | 194 |
| 35–39 | 86,046 | 197 |
| 40–44 | 24,498 | 240 |
| 45 or more | 1,707 | 37 |

**3.24**  Does the month in which you were born relate to your later mental health? Fombonne (1989) took all children referred to a psychiatric clinic in Paris with a diagnosis of psychosis and sorted them by birth month. (There were 208 such children.) He had a control group of 1050 children referred with other problems. The data are given below, along with the percentage in the general population born in that month.

| | Jan | Feb | Mar | Apr | May | Jun | Jul | Aug | Sep | Oct | Nov | Dec | Total |
|------|------|------|------|------|------|------|------|------|------|------|------|------|------|
| **Psychosis** | 13 | 12 | 16 | 18 | 21 | 18 | 15 | 14 | 13 | 19 | 21 | 28 | 208 |
| **Control** | 83 | 71 | 88 | 114 | 86 | 93 | 87 | 70 | 83 | 80 | 97 | 88 | 1040 |
| **% General Population** | 8.4 | 7.8 | 8.7 | 8.6 | 9.1 | 8.5 | 8.7 | 8.3 | 8.1 | 8.1 | 7.6 | 8.0 | |

(a) How will you adjust (transform) the Psychosis and Control groups' data so that all three data sets can fit on the same graph?

(b) How will you plot the data?

(c) Plot the data.

(d) Do those diagnosed with psychosis appear to differ from the general population?

(e) What purpose does the Control group play?

(f) What do you conclude?

**3.25** Psychologists concerned about self-injurious behaviors (smoking, eating fatty diets, drug abuse, etc.) worry about the effects of maternal smoking on the incidents of low birth-weight babies, who are known to be at risk for developmental problems. The Centers for Disease Control has published statistics relating maternal smoking to low birth weight. The data follow in terms of the percentage of birth weights <2,500 grams. Find a way to present these data that illustrates this relationship clearly. Why is this relationship not likely to be a statistical fluke?

|            | 1989   | 1990  | 1991  | 1992  | 1993  |
|------------|--------|-------|-------|-------|-------|
| Smokers    | 11.36% | 11.25 | 11.41 | 11.49 | 11.84 |
| Nonsmokers | 6.02   | 6.14  | 6.36  | 6.35  | 6.56  |

**3.26** The *Journal of Statistics Education* maintains a fairly extensive collection of data on a wide variety of topics. Each data set is accompanied by a description of the data and how they might be used. These data are available at

http://www.amstat.org/publications/jse/jse_data_archive.html

Go to this Internet link, find a set of data that interests you, and display those data in a way that makes their meaning clear. For most of these data sets you will want to use some sort of computer software, although that is not a requirement. There are many things that could be done with the data that we have not yet covered, but displaying the data will reveal much that is of interest.

**3.27** In Section 3.4 we saw a graph illustrating changes in life expectancy among white females. The following graph adds the data on black females. What conclusions would you draw from this graph?

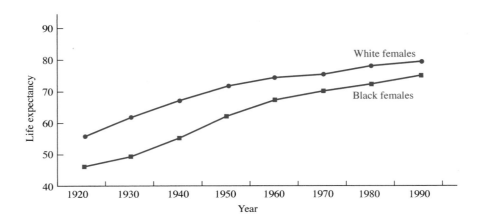

**3.28**  In 1970, at the height of the Vietnam War, the U.S. government held a lottery to determine which individuals would be drafted. Balls representing the 366 possible birthdays were drawn from an urn, and the order in which the days were drawn represented the order in which young males would be drafted. (If your birthday were one of those selected early, you would have a low selection number and a very high probability of being drafted, and if it were one of those with a high selection number, you probably would not be called.) That particular lottery received considerable criticism because people born late in the year appeared much more likely to receive a low number. (The average selection number for those born in December was 121.5, while the average selection number for those born in January was 201.2.)

The results appear below. Graph these data and draw appropriate conclusions. There is every reason to believe that those that carried out the lottery tried to be fair, but if you were one of those eligible to be drafted, would you be satisfied with the result? How might you explain these results? More complete data are available at

 http://www.amstat.org/publications/jse/v5n2/datasets.starr.html

| Jan | Feb | Mar | Apr | May | June | July | Aug | Sept | Oct | Nov | Dec |
|-----|-----|-----|-----|-----|------|------|-----|------|-----|-----|-----|
| 201.2 | 203.0 | 225.8 | 203.7 | 208.0 | 195.7 | 181.5 | 173.5 | 157.3 | 182.5 | 148.7 | 121.5 |

# 4

# Measures of Central Tendency

## QUESTIONS

- What do we mean by a measure of central tendency?
- How can we measure central tendency?
- Is one measure better than another?
- Do I have to do this by hand?
- Can you give me a real-life example?

In Chapter 3 you saw how to display data in ways that allow us to begin to draw some conclusions about what the data have to say. Plotting data shows the general shape of the distribution and gives a visual sense of the general magnitude of the numbers involved. Some of the graphs in Chapter 3 had "averages" plotted on the Y axis, and those averages play a central role in this chapter.

In this chapter you will see several statistics that can be used to represent the "center" of the distribution. These statistics are called **measures of central tendency.** In the next chapter we will go a step further and look at measures that deal with how the observations are scattered around that central tendency, but first we must address identifying the center of the distribution.

Definition   **Measures of central tendency:** Numerical values that refer to the center of the distribution.

The three common measures of central tendency are the mode, the median, and the mean, and they will be discussed in turn. We will begin with what is probably the least used (and least useful) measure, the mode.

## 4.1 The Mode

The **mode (Mo)** can be defined simply as the most common score; that is, the score obtained from the largest number of subjects. Thus the mode is that value of X that corresponds to the highest point on the distribution. In the example in Chapter 3 that dealt with reaction times in a simple short-term memory task (see Table 3.2), the values of 62 and 67 are tied for this honor, because more trials (fourteen) had a reaction time of 62 (or 67) hundredths of a second than had any other time.

Definition   **Mode (Mo):** The most commonly occurring score.

If two *adjacent* times occur with equal (and greatest) frequency, a common convention is to take an average of the two values and call that the mode. If, on the other hand, two *nonadjacent* reaction times occur with equal (or nearly equal) frequency, we say that the distribution is bimodal and would most likely report both modes. The data plotted in Figure 3.1 raise an interesting issue. When we plot the individual values, the histogram would tell us that we have a bimodal distribution, because both 62 and 67 have 14 observations. However, when we combine the data into a grouped histogram, which eliminates much of the "noise" in the plot, we have a unimodal distribution with a mode in the 60s. I don't want to get involved in a discussion of whether we are talking about a bimodal or a unimodal distribution here, because I see no future in such a discussion. Perhaps the closest I would come is to say that when we are speaking of "bimodal" distribution, we are speaking of prominent characteristics of the distribution, not the results of minor fluctuations in the sample.

## 4.2 The Median

The **median (Mdn)** is most easily defined as the middle score in an ordered set or data. By this definition the median is also called the 50th percentile.[1] For example, consider the numbers (5 8 3 7 15). If the numbers are arranged in numerical

---

[1]The specific percentile is defined as the point on a scale at or below which a specified percentage of the scores fall.

order (3 5 7 8 15), the middle score is 7, and it would be called the median. Suppose, however, that there were an even number of scores, for example, (5 11 3 7 15 14). Rearranging, we get (3 5 7 11 14 15), and there is no middle score. That point actually falls between the 7 and the 11. In such a case the average (9) of the two middle scores (7 and 11) is commonly taken as the median.[2]

---

Definition    **Median (Mdn):** The score corresponding to the point having 50% of the observations below it when the observations are arranged in numerical order.

**Median location:** The location of the median in an ordered series.

---

A term that we will need shortly is the **median location**. The median location of N numbers is defined as

$$\text{Median location} = (N + 1)/2$$

Thus for five numbers the median location $= (5 + 1)/2 = 3$, which simply means that the median is the third number in an ordered series. For 12 numbers the median location $= (12 + 1)/2 = 6.5$; the median falls between, and is the average of, the sixth and seventh numbers.

For the data on reaction times in Table 3.2, the median location $= (300 + 1)/2 = 150.5$. When the data are arranged in order, both the 150th and 151st times are 60 hundredths of a second, which is the median. You can calculate this for yourself from Table 3.2. For the data on intrusive thoughts in breast cancer patients there are 85 scores, and the median location is $(85+1)/2 = 43$. We can tell from the stem-and-leaf display in Figure 3.2 that the 43rd score is 15, so the median would be 15.

## 4.3 The Mean

The most common measure of central tendency is the mean, or what people generally have in mind when they use the word *average*. The **mean** $(\overline{X})$ is the sum of the scores divided by the number of scores and is usually designated $\overline{X}$ (read "X bar"). It is defined (using the summation notation given in Chapter 2) as

---

Definition    **Mean ($\overline{X}$):** The sum of the scores divided by the number of scores.

---

[2]The definition of the median is another one of those things over which statisticians love to argue. The definition given here, in which the median is defined as a *point* on a distribution of numbers, is the one most critics prefer. It is also in line with the statement that the median is the 50th percentile. On the other hand, there are many who are perfectly happy to say that the median is either the middle *number* in an ordered series (if N is odd) or the average of the two middle *numbers* (if N is even). Reading these arguments is a bit like going to a faculty meeting when there is nothing terribly important on the agenda. The less important the issue, the more there is to say about it.

$$\overline{X} = \frac{\Sigma X}{N}$$

where $\Sigma X$ is the sum of all values of $X$, and $N$ is the number of $X$ values. Therefore the mean of the numbers 3, 5, 12, and 5 is

$$(3 + 5 + 12 + 5)/4 = 25/4 = 6.25$$

For the reaction time data in Table 3.2, the sum of the observations is 18,078. When we divide that by $N = 300$, we get $18,078/300 = 60.26$. Notice that this answer agrees well with the median, which we found to be 60. It also agrees reasonably well with the modal interval (60–64). The mean and the median will be close whenever the distribution is nearly symmetric (as defined in Chapter 3). When the distribution is nearly symmetric and unimodal, the mode will also be in general agreement with the mean and median. But for nonsymmetric distributions, the mean, median, and mode can all be quite different from one another.

We could calculate the mean for the intrusive-thoughts data by obtaining the raw data values from the stem-and-leaf display in Figure 3.2, summing those values, and dividing by 85. For that example, the mean would be $1298/85 = 15.27$. Later in this chapter you will see how to use SPSS to save yourself considerable work in calculating the mean for large data sets.

## 4.4   Relative Advantages and Disadvantages of the Mode, the Median, and the Mean

Only when the distribution is symmetric will the mean and the median be equal, and only when the distribution is symmetric and unimodal will all three measures be the same. In all other cases—including almost all situations that we will deal with—some measure of central tendency must be chosen. A set of rules governing when to use a particular measure of central tendency would be convenient, but there are no such rules. Some idea of the strengths and weaknesses of each statistic is required to make intelligent choices among the three measures.

### The Mode

The mode is the most commonly occurring score. By definition, then, it is a score that actually occurred, whereas the mean and sometimes the median may be values that never appear in the data. The mode also has the obvious advantage of representing the largest number of people having the same score. Someone who is running a small store would do well to concentrate on the mode. If 80% of your customers want the giant economy family size and 20% want the teeny-weeny, single-person size, it wouldn't seem particularly wise to aim for the mean or median and stock only the regular size.

Related to these two advantages is the fact that, by definition, the probability that an observation drawn at random ($X_i$) will be equal to the mode is greater than the probability that it will be equal to any other specific score. Expressing this algebraically, we can say

$$p(X_i = \text{mode}) > p(X_i = \text{any other score})$$

Finally, the mode has the advantage of being applicable to nominal data, which is obviously not true of the median or the mean.

The mode has its disadvantages, however. We have already seen that the mode depends on how we group our data. Moreover, it may not be particularly representative of the entire collection of numbers. This is especially true when the modal value is 0, such as would occur if we calculated the number of cigarettes each person in a group smokes in a day. Here the mode would be 0 because of the preponderance of nonsmokers, but it would tell us nothing about the behavior of smokers. (Note that the mean or median would be a lot more informative, but they, too, would be biased by the nonsmokers.)

## The Median

The major advantage of the median, which it often shares with the mode, is the fact that it is unaffected by extreme scores. Thus the medians of both (5 8 9 15 16) and (0 8 9 15 206) are 9. Many experimenters find this characteristic to be useful in studies in which extreme scores occasionally occur but have no particular significance. For example, the average trained rat can run down a short runway in approximately 1 to 2 seconds. Every once in a while this same rat will inexplicably stop halfway down, scratch himself, poke his nose at the photocells, and lie down to sleep. In that instance it is of no practical significance whether he takes 30 seconds or 10 minutes to get to the other end of the runway. It may even depend on when the experimenter gives up and pokes him with a pencil. If we ran a rat through three trials on a given day and his times were (1.2, 1.3, and 20 seconds), that would have the same meaning to us—in terms of what it tells us about the rat's knowledge of the task—as if his times were (1.2, 1.3, and 136.4 seconds). In both cases the median would be 1.3. Obviously, however, his daily *mean* would be quite different in the two cases (7.5 versus 46.3 seconds). In situations like this, experimenters often work with the median score over a block of trials. Similarly, we often use the median salary and the median cost of a home in place of the corresponding means.

The median has another point in its favor, when contrasted with the mean, which those writers who get excited over scales of measurement like to point out. The calculation of the median does not require any assumptions about the interval properties of the scale. With the numbers (5, 8, and 11), the object represented by the number 8 is in the middle, no matter how close or distant it is from objects represented by 5 and 11. When we say that the *mean* is 8, however, we, or our readers, may be making the implicit assumption that the underlying distance between objects 5 and 8 is the same as the underlying distance between objects 8 and 11. Whether or not this assumption is reasonable is up to the experimenter to determine. I prefer to work on the principle that if it is an absurdly unreasonable assumption, we will realize that and take appropriate steps. If it is not absurdly unreasonable, then its practical effect on the results most likely will be negligible. (This problem of scales of measurement was discussed in more detail in Chapter 2.)

A major disadvantage of the median is that it does not enter readily into equations and is thus more difficult to work with than the mean. It is also not as stable from sample to sample as is the mean, as we will see in the next chapter, and this often presents problems when we use the sample statistics to estimate parameters.

## The Mean

Of the three principal measures of central tendency, the mean is by far the most common. It would not be too much of an exaggeration to say that for many people statistics is (unfortunately) nearly synonymous with the study of the mean.

As we have already seen, certain disadvantages are associated with the mean. It is influenced by extreme scores, its value may not actually exist in the data, and its interpretation in terms of the underlying variable being measured requires at least some faith in the interval properties of the data. You might be inclined to politely suggest that if the mean has all the disadvantages I have just ascribed to it, then maybe it should be quietly forgotten and allowed to slip into oblivion along with statistics like the "critical ratio," a statistical concept that hasn't been heard of in years. The mean, however, is made of sterner stuff.

The mean has several important advantages that far outweigh its disadvantages. Probably the most important of these from a historical point of view (though not necessarily from your point of view) is that the mean can be manipulated algebraically. In other words, we can use the mean in an equation and manipulate it through the normal rules of algebra, specifically because we can write an equation that defines the mean. Since you cannot write a standard equation for the mode or the median, you have no real way of manipulating those statistics using standard algebra. Whatever the mean's faults, this accounts in some part for its widespread application. The second important advantage of the mean is that it has several desirable properties with respect to its use as an estimate of the population mean. In particular, if we drew many samples from some population, the sample means that resulted would be more stable (less variable) estimates of the central tendency of that population than would the sample medians or modes. The fact that the sample mean is in general a better estimate of the population mean than is the mode or the median is a major reason why it is so widely used by statisticians.

## Trimmed Means

We are going to go back for a moment and look at an old idea that has recently started to take on new life. When I discussed the mean I said that one of our criteria for selecting a good statistic was how well it estimated the population parameter. Although the sample mean is generally a good estimate of the population mean, there are times when it doesn't do as well as we would like. Suppose we have a badly skewed distribution, for example, or a heavy tailed distribution—one with an unusual number of large and small values. Repeated samples from that population would have sample means that vary a great deal with regard to one another, giving quite different estimates of the population mean. One way around this problem is to use what are called **trimmed means**. To calculate a trimmed mean we take one or more of the largest and smallest values in the sample, set them aside, and take the mean of what remains. For a 10% trimmed mean, for example, we would set aside the largest 10% of the observations and the lowest 10% of the observations. The mean of what remained would be the 10% trimmed mean.

Definition    **Trimmed mean:** The mean that results from trimming away (or discarding) a fixed percentage of the extreme observations.

A number of people (e.g., Wilcox, 2003) have argued that we should make more use of trimmed means. They claim that doing so would overcome some of the problems of overly wide populations and improve the conclusions we draw from experiments. I will return to this problem later in the book and illustrate an advantage of trimmed means. For now all you need to know is what a trimmed mean is.

# 4.5 Obtaining Measures of Central Tendency Using SPSS

For small sets of data it is perfectly reasonable to compute measures of central tendency by hand. With larger sample sizes or data sets with many variables, however, it is much simpler to let a computer program do the work. SPSS is ideally suited to this purpose since it is easy to use, versatile, and widely available.

We will take the data from the Katz et al. study (see Exercise 3.1) on the performance of students who were asked to answer multiple-choice questions about a passage they had not read. These data are illustrated in Figure 4.1. We can obtain the mean and the median directly, but to get the mode we need to produce a histogram (or a stem-and-leaf display) and then look for the most frequently appearing interval.

From the figure you can see that the mean (46.6), the median (46), and the mode (44) are approximately equal, and that the distribution is fairly smooth. We don't really have enough data to talk about skewness. We can also see from the histogram that there is variability in the scores of our 28 subjects. This dispersion on either side of the mean is discussed in the next chapter.

```
Raw Data:   54  52  51  50  36  55  44  46  57  44  43  52  38  46
            55  34  44  39  43  36  55  57  36  46  49  46  49  47
```

**Descriptives**

| | | Statistic | Std. Error |
|---|---|---|---|
| Score for nonpassage group | Mean | 46.5714 | 1.29041 |
| | 95% Confidence Interval for Mean | | |
| |    Lower Bound | 43.9237 | |
| |    Upper Bound | 49.2191 | |
| | 5% Trimmed Mean | 46.6587 | |
| | Median | 46.0000 | |
| | Variance | 46.624 | |
| | Std. Deviation | 6.82820 | |
| | Minimum | 34.00 | |
| | Maximum | 57.00 | |
| | Range | 23.00 | |
| | Interquartile Range | 9.0000 | |
| | Skewness | -.224 | .441 |
| | Kurtosis | -.901 | .858 |

**Scores for Group not Reading Passage**

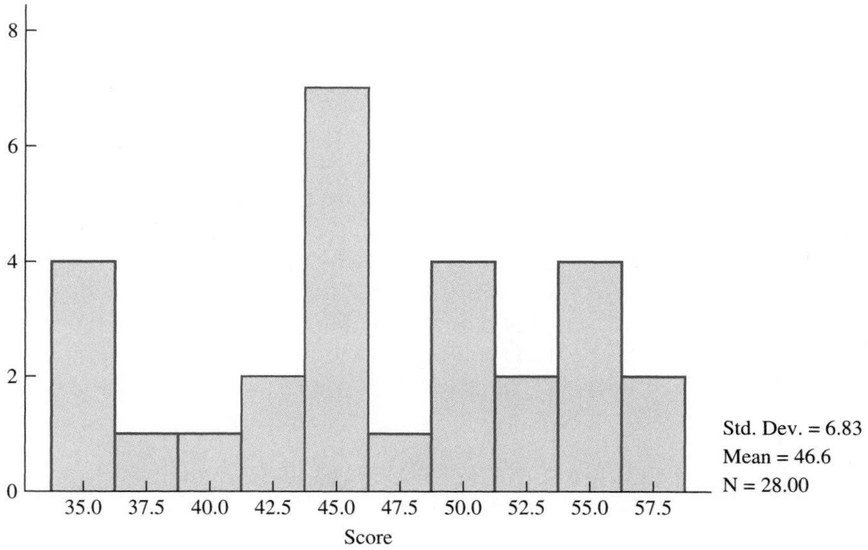

Std. Dev. = 6.83
Mean = 46.6
N = 28.00

**Figure 4.1**
Score on items when passage not read

## 4.6 A Simple Demonstration—Seeing Statistics

Before we end this chapter, I think that you will find it interesting to make use of a small computer program (called a Java applet) produced by Gary McClelland at the University of Colorado. Dr. McClelland has produced a large number of applets and packaged them under the title *Seeing Statistics*. An overview can be found at

 http://www.seeingstatistics.com

though you would need to subscribe to view all of the applets. Many of those applets have been included on the Web site established for this book and are available free. Simply go to

 http://www.uvm.edu/~dhowell/fundamentals/
SeeingStatisticsApplets/Applets.html

We will refer to them many times throughout the text.

The purpose of using these applets is to give you an opportunity to play an active role in learning this material, and to allow you to illustrate for yourself many of the concepts that are discussed in the text. For example, when we come to the *t* test in later chapters, I will tell you what a *t* distribution would look like under certain conditions. But the associated applet will allow you to vary those conditions and actually see what that does to the distribution of *t*. I suspect that you will learn far more from what you do than from what I tell you.

It is my expectation that the applets will also assist you in preparing for exams. Having worked through the short activities associated with each applet, you will have access to yet another way of retrieving information you have stored. The more methods of access, the better the retrieval.

The first applet we will use produces a set of meaningful data and illustrates an important principle of visual perception. To see this applet, simply go to

 http://www.uvm.edu/~dhowell/fundamentals/
SeeingStatisticsApplets/Applets.html

and follow the instructions. The applet you want is named Brightness Matching. (Be sure to read the instructions on the opening page about Java applets. You may need to download free software [but probably won't], and sometimes the applets take a bit of time to load.)

This Brightness Matching applet allows you to manipulate the brightness of a gray circle centered within a larger circle of a lighter or darker color. An example is shown in the accompanying figure. Your task is to adjust the center of the circle on the right to be the same shade of gray as the center of the circle on the left.

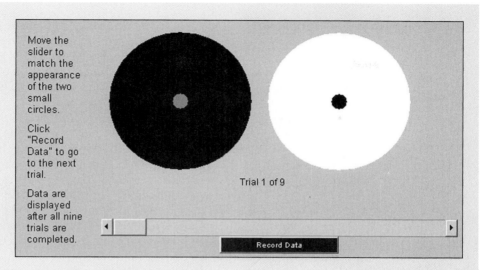

As you move the slider to the right, the center of the right circle will lighten. When you think that you have a match, click on the button labeled "Record Data." At this point another set of circles will appear and you will repeat the process. When you have made nine settings, the applet will present your data, showing you how accurate you were. (Write these data down or print them out, because you can't retrieve them once you move on.)

When I performed that task, I produced the following data.

| Move the | Trial | BG1 | BG2 | FG1 | Match | Diff |
|---|---|---|---|---|---|---|
| slider to | 1 | 1.0 | 0.0 | 0.5 | 0.43 | 0.07 |
| match the | | | | | | |
| appearance | 2 | 0.25 | 0.75 | 0.4 | 0.7 | -0.3 |
| of the two | | | | | | |
| small | 3 | 0.5 | 0.5 | 0.6 | 0.62 | -0.02 |
| circles. | 4 | 0.75 | 0.25 | 0.5 | 0.37 | 0.13 |
| | 5 | 0.0 | 1.0 | 0.6 | 0.78 | -0.18 |
| Click | 6 | 0.25 | 0.75 | 0.6 | 0.74 | -0.14 |
| "Record | | | | | | |
| Data" to go | 7 | 0.0 | 0.0 | 0.4 | 0.5 | -0.1 |
| to the next | | | | | | |
| trial. | 8 | 1.0 | 0.0 | 0.4 | 0.31 | 0.09 |
| | 9 | 1.0 | 1.0 | 0.5 | 0.53 | -0.03 |
| Data are | | | | | | |
| displayed | | | | | | |
| after all | | | | | Record Data | |
| nine trials | | | | | | |
| are | | | | | | |
| completed. | | | | | | |

The headings "BG1" and "BG2" refer to the grayness of the left and right backgrounds (0 = white, 1 = black). "FG1" refers to the grayness of the foreground (the center dot) on the left. "Match" refers to my setting for the dot on the right, and "Diff" is the difference in the setting for the two dots. A positive difference means that my setting was less gray than it should have been to match the dot on the left.

A general principle of human visual perception is that a dark background will cause a spot in the center to appear lighter than it actually is. Thus, in the example shown on page 69, we would expect you to err by setting the center spot at the right lighter than it really should be. This means that the *difference* in brightness between the two center dots will be positive. This would apply to trials 1, 4, and 8. The reverse should happen on trials 2, 5, and 6, where the background on the left is lighter than the one on the right—here the differences should be negative. Finally, trials 3, 7, and 9 were control conditions, where the two backgrounds were the same, and we would expect most accurate settings, and relatively small (positive or negative) differences.

For your own data, calculate the mean and median differences under each of the three conditions described above. Create a table similar to Table 4.1

- What do your data show with respect to the hypothesis outlined above?

- Would you have a preference for the mean over the median as the important statistic here?

- Why would the mode not be a useful measure?

- Why do you suppose that the three differences within any one line are not all the same? (This will be a very important point later when we refer to this variability of scores obtained under similar conditions as "random error.")

I chose to use this applet here because it serves several purposes. First, it gives you something active to do, rather than just to plod through what I have written. Second, it gives you a chance to collect real data on a real phenomenon. Third, it will allow you to examine those data in light of a set of reasonable

**Table 4.1**
Results of Nine Trials of Color Matching

| Left Background | Trials | Differences | Mean | Median |
|---|---|---|---|---|
| Lighter | 2, 5, 6 | −.30, −.18. −.14 | −.21 | −.18 |
| Darker | 1, 4, 8 | .07, .13, .09 | .10 | .09 |
| Equal | 3, 7, 9 | −.02, −.10, −.03 | −.05 | −.03 |

hypotheses about human perceptions. Finally, although there are too few data points to get you too excited about the actual measures of central tendency, you can make some interesting observations about the role of the mean and median, although the actual observations you make will depend, at least in part, on your personal data.

## 4.7 Summary

In this chapter we considered several measures used to describe the center of a distribution. Each measure has its own particular strengths and weaknesses. One of these, the mean, forms the basis for much of the material discussed in the remainder of this book. Another (the trimmed mean) is not covered in many texts and is very likely to play an important role in data analysis in the future.

Some important terms in this chapter are

| | |
|---|---|
| Measures of central tendency, *61* | Median location, *62* |
| Mode (Mo), *61* | Mean ($\overline{X}$), *62* |
| Median (Mdn), *62* | Trimmed mean, *66* |

## 4.8 Exercises

**4.1**   As part of the Katz et al. (1990) study described earlier in the text, the experimenters obtained the same kind of data from a smaller group of students who had read the passage (called the Passage group). Their data follow.

   66   75   72   71   55   56   72   93   73   72   72   73   91   66   71   56   59

Calculate the mode, median, and mean for these data.

**4.2**   The measures of central tendency for the data on students in Katz's study who did not read the passages were given in the SPSS printout in Figure 4.1. Compare those answers with the answers to Exercise 4.1. What do they tell you about the value of reading the passage on which questions are based?

**4.3**   If a student in Katz's study simply responded at random (even without reading the questions), she would be expected to get 20 items correct. How does this compare to the measures we found in Section 4.5?

**4.4**   Make up a set of data for which the mean is greater than the median.

**4.5** Make up a positively skewed set of data. Does the mean fall above or below the median?

**4.6** How can you make up a unimodal set of data wherein the mean and median are equal but different from the mode?

**4.7** A group of 15 rats running a straight-alley maze required the following number of trials to perform to a predetermined criterion. The frequency distribution follows.

| Trials to reach criterion | 18 | 19 | 20 | 21 | 22 | 23 | 24 |
|---|---|---|---|---|---|---|---|
| Number of rats (frequency) | 1 | 0 | 4 | 3 | 3 | 3 | 1 |

Calculate the mean and median number of trials to criterion for this group.

**4.8** Given the following set of data, demonstrate that subtracting a constant (e.g., 5) from every score reduces all measures of central tendency by that amount.

8  7  12  14  3  7

**4.9** Given the following data, show that multiplying each score by a constant multiplies all measures of central tendency by that constant.

8  3  5  5  6  2

**4.10** Create a sample of ten numbers that has a mean of 8.6. Notice carefully how you do this—it will help you later to understand the concept of degrees of freedom.

**4.11** Calculate the measures of central tendency for the data on ADDSC and GPA that is available at the book's Web site:

http://www.uvm.edu/~dhowell/fundamentals/DataFiles/Add.dat

**4.12** Using the link in Exercise 4.11, go to the book's Web site and look at the data on SEX and ENGL. Why would it not make any sense to calculate the mean for SEX or ENGL? If we did go ahead and compute the mean for SEX, what would the value of $(\overline{X} - 1)$ really represent?

**4.13** Why is the mode an acceptable measure for nominal data? Why are the mean and the median not acceptable measures for nominal data?

**4.14** In Table 3.1 the reaction time data are broken down separately by the number of digits in the comparison stimulus. Calculate the three main measures of central tendency for each set of data differing in the number of stimuli. Ignore the distinction between positive and negative instances. How well do these measures agree within each data set?

**4.15** With reference to Exercise 4.14, if people process information in short-term memory in parallel, the mean reaction time should not depend on the number of digits in the comparison stimulus, whereas if we process information sequentially, reaction times should increase with increasing size of the comparison stimulus. What do the answers to Exercise 4.14 suggest about how we process information?

**4.16** In the exercises for Chapter 2 we considered the study by a fourth-grade girl who examined the average allowance of her classmates. You may recall that 7 boys reported an average allowance of $3.18, while 11 girls reported an average allowance of $2.63. These data raise some interesting statistical issues. This fourth-grade student did a meaningful study (well, it was better than I would have done in fourth grade), but let's look at the data more closely.

The paper reported that the highest allowance for a boy was $10, while the highest for a girl was $9. It also reported that the two lowest girls' allowances were $0.50 and $0.51, while the lowest reported allowance for a boy was $3.00.

(a) Create a set of data for boys and girls that would produce these results. (No, I didn't make an error.)

(b) What is the most appropriate measure of central tendency to report in this situation?

(c) What does the available information suggest to you about the distribution of allowances for the two genders?

(d) What do the data suggest about the truthfulness of little boys?

**4.17** What are the mean and median scores of students who did, and did not, attend class on a regular basis in Figure 3.4? (The data are reproduced here for convenience.) What do they suggest about the value of attending class?

| Attended class | 241 | 243 | 246 | 249 | 250 | 252 | 254 | 254 | 255 | 256 |
|---|---|---|---|---|---|---|---|---|---|---|
| | 261 | 262 | 263 | 264 | 264 | 264 | 265 | 267 | 267 | 270 |
| | 271 | 272 | 273 | 276 | 276 | 277 | 278 | 278 | 280 | 281 |
| | 282 | 284 | 288 | 288 | 290 | 291 | 291 | 292 | 293 | 294 |
| | 296 | 296 | 297 | 298 | 310 | 320 | 321 | 328 | | |
| Skipped class | 188 | 195 | 195 | 225 | 228 | 232 | 233 | 237 | 239 | 240 |
| | 250 | 256 | 256 | 256 | 261 | 264 | 264 | 268 | 270 | 270 |
| | 274 | 274 | 277 | 308 | | | | | | |

**4.18** Why do you think that I did not ask you to calculate the mode? (*Hint*: If you calculate the mode for those who skipped class frequently, you should see the problem.)

**4.19** Search the Internet for data on smoking among teenagers. How do you think we can best characterize the age at which people start smoking? (This will require some thought.) If someone is going to smoke before the age of 20, when would you say they are most likely to start?

**4.20** What kinds of things did you have to consider in Exercise 4.19?

**4.21** (a) Calculate the 10% trimmed mean for the data on test performance in Figure 4.1. (Remember that 10% trimming means removing the 10% of the scores at *each* end of the distribution.)

(b) Assume that you collected the following data on the number of errors that participants made in reading a passage under distracting conditions.

10 10 10 15 15 20 20 20 20 25 25 26 27 30 32 37 39 42 68 77

Calculate the 10% trimmed mean for these data.

(c) Trimming made more of a difference in (b) than it did in (a). Can you explain why this might be?

**4.22** Seligman, Nolen-Hecksema, Thornton, and Thornton (1990) classified participants in their study (who were members of a university swim team) as Optimists or Pessimists. They then asked them to swim their best event, and in each case they reported times that were longer than the swimmer actually earned. Half an hour later they asked them to repeat the event again. The dependent variable was $Time_1/Time_2$, so a ratio greater than 1.0 indicates faster times on the second trial. The data follow.

**Optimists**

| 0.986 | 1.108 | 1.080 | 0.952 | 0.998 | 1.017 | 1.080 | 1.026 | 1.045 | 0.996 |
| 0.923 | 1.000 | 1.003 | 0.934 | 1.009 | 1.065 | 1.053 | 1.108 | 0.985 | 1.001 |
| 0.924 | 0.968 | 1.048 | 1.027 | 1.004 | 0.936 | 1.040 | | | |

**Pessimists**

| 0.983 | 0.947 | 0.932 | 1.078 | 0.914 | 0.955 | 0.962 | 0.944 | 0.941 | 0.831 |
| 0.936 | 0.995 | 0.872 | 0.997 | 0.983 | 1.105 | 1.116 | 0.997 | 0.960 | 1.045 |
| 1.095 | 0.944 | 1.069 | 0.927 | 0.988 | 1.015 | 1.045 | 0.864 | 0.982 | 0.915 |
| 1.047 | | | | | | | | | |

Calculate the mean for each group. Seligman et al. thought that optimists would try harder after being disappointed. Does it look as if they were correct?

**4.23** The study described in Exercise 4.22 did not show much difference between the women who were Optimists and those who were Pessimists. The first 17 scores in the Optimist group are for men and the first 13 scores in the Pessimist group are for men. What differences do you find for men?

# 5

# Measures of Variability

## QUESTIONS

- What do we mean by variability?

- Why is variability such a central concept in statistics?

- How many different ways can we find to measure variability, and why are some better than others?

- What makes a good estimator of variability?

- How can we represent variability graphically?

- Are you sure that the divisor for the variance should be $N - 1$?

In Chapter 3 we looked at ways to characterize and display the shape of a distribution. In Chapter 4 we considered several measures related to the center of a distribution. However, the shape and average value for a distribution (whether it be the mode, the median, or the mean) fail to give the whole story. We need some additional measure (or measures) to indicate the degree to which individual observations are clustered about or, equivalently, deviate from that average value. The average may reflect the general location of most of the scores, or the scores may be distributed over a wide range of values, and the "average" may not be very representative of the observations.

Probably everyone has had experience with examinations on which all students received approximately the same grade and with examinations on which the scores ranged from excellent to dreadful. Measures that refer to the differences between these two types of situations are what we have in mind when we speak of **dispersion**, or **variability**, around the median, the mode, or any other point we wish. In general we will refer specifically to dispersion around the mean.

---

Definition    **Dispersion (Variability):** The degree to which individual data points are distributed around the mean.

---

As an example of a situation in which we might expect differences in variability from one group to another, consider the example in the previous chapter wherein some students answered questions about passages they had read, and other students answered questions about the same passages, but without reading them. It could be that for those who did not read the passage, they simply guessed wildly, and their performance would differ from each other only by chance—some people who guessed were luckier in their guesses than others. But for those who read the passage there might be more substantial differences among people. Not only would there be chance differences, depending on how lucky they were when they didn't know the answer, but there would be real differences reflecting how much more of the passage one person understood than did another. Here the means of the two groups would most likely differ, but that is irrelevant. The difference in variability is our focus. The groups could have different levels of variability even if their means were comparable. Do my hypotheses correspond with your experience? If not, what would you expect to happen? Does your expectation lead to differences in means, variances, both, or neither?

For another illustration we will take some interesting data collected by Langlois and Roggman (1990) on the perceived attractiveness of faces. Think for a moment about some of the faces you consider attractive. Do they tend to have unusual features (e.g., prominent noses or unusual eyebrows), or are the features rather ordinary? Langlois and Roggman were interested in investigating what makes faces attractive. Toward that end they presented students with computer-generated pictures of faces. Some of these pictures had been created by averaging together actual snapshots of four different people to create a composite. We will label these photographs Set 4. Other pictures (Set 32) were created by averaging across snapshots of 32 different people. As you might suspect, when you average across four people, there is still room for individuality in the composite. For example, some composites show thin faces, while others show round ones. However, averaging across 32 people usually gives results that are very "average." Noses are neither too long nor too short, ears don't stick out too far nor sit too close to the head, and so on. Students were asked to examine the resulting pictures and rate each one on a 5-point scale of attractiveness. The authors were primarily interested in determining whether the *mean* rating of the faces in Set 4 was less than the mean rating of the faces in Set 32. The data came out as expected, suggesting that faces with distinctive characteristics are judged as

**Table 5.1**

Data from Langlois and Roggman

| | Set 4 | | Set 32 | |
|---|---|---|---|---|
| Picture | Composite of 4 Faces | Picture | Composite of 32 Faces |
| 1 | 1.20 | 21 | 3.13 |
| 2 | 1.82 | 22 | 3.17 |
| 3 | 1.93 | 23 | 3.19 |
| 4 | 2.04 | 24 | 3.19 |
| 5 | 2.30 | 25 | 3.20 |
| 6 | 2.33 | 26 | 3.20 |
| 7 | 2.34 | 27 | 3.22 |
| 8 | 2.47 | 28 | 3.23 |
| 9 | 2.51 | 29 | 3.25 |
| 10 | 2.55 | 30 | 3.26 |
| 11 | 2.64 | 31 | 3.27 |
| 12 | 2.76 | 32 | 3.29 |
| 13 | 2.77 | 33 | 3.29 |
| 14 | 2.90 | 34 | 3.30 |
| 15 | 2.91 | 35 | 3.31 |
| 16 | 3.20 | 36 | 3.31 |
| 17 | 3.22 | 37 | 3.34 |
| 18 | 3.39 | 38 | 3.34 |
| 19 | 3.59 | 39 | 3.36 |
| 20 | 4.02 | 40 | 3.38 |
| | Mean = 2.64 | | Mean = 3.26 |

less attractive than more ordinary faces. In this chapter, however, we are more interested in the degree of *similarity* in the ratings of faces than in the mean. We expect that composites of 32 faces will be more homogeneous, and thus would be rated more similarly, than composites of four faces.

The data are shown in Table 5.1, where the scores are the consensus across several judges rating the images on a 5-point scale, with "5" as the most attractive.[1] From the table you can see that Langlois and Roggman were correct in predicting that Set 32 faces would be rated as more attractive than Set 4 faces. (The means were 3.26 and 2.64, respectively.) But notice also that the ratings for the composites of 32 faces are considerably more homogeneous than the ratings of the

---

[1] These data are not the actual numbers that Langlois and Roggman collected, but they have been generated to have exactly the same mean and standard deviation as the original data. Langlois and Roggman used six composite photographs per set. I have used 20 photographs per set to make the data more applicable to my purposes in this chapter. The conclusions that you would draw from these data, however, are exactly the same as the conclusions you would draw from theirs.

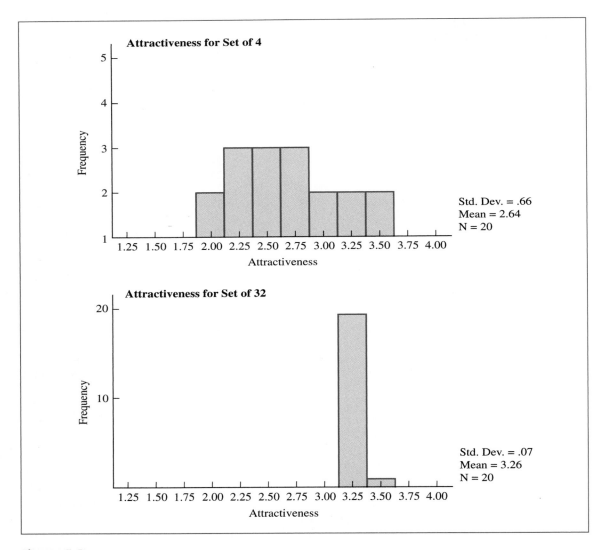

**Figure 5.1**
Distribution of scores for attractiveness of composite

composites of four faces. We can plot these two sets of data as standard histograms, as in Figure 5.1.

Although it is apparent from Figure 5.1 that there is much greater variability in the rating of composites of four photographs than in the rating of composites of 32 photographs, some sort of measure is needed to reflect this difference in variability. A number of measures could be used, and they will be discussed in turn, starting with the simplest.

## 5.1 Range

The **range** is a measure of distance, namely the distance from the lowest to the highest score. For our data the range for Set 4 is $(4.02 - 1.20) = 2.82$ units; for Set 32 it is $(3.38 - 3.13) = .25$ unit. The range is an exceedingly common measure and is illustrated in everyday life by such statements as, "The price of green peppers fluctuates over a $2 range from $0.99 to $2.99 per pound." The range suffers, however, from a total reliance on extreme values, or, if the values are *unusually* extreme, on what are called outliers. As a result, the range may give a distorted picture of the variability. One really unusual value could change the range drastically.

Definition | **Range:** The distance from the lowest to the highest score.

## 5.2 Interquartile Range and Other Range Statistics

The **interquartile range** (which is closely related to something we will soon call the *H*-Spread) represents an attempt to circumvent the problem of the range being heavily dependent on extreme scores. An interquartile range is obtained by discarding the upper and lower 25% of the distribution and taking the range of what remains. As such, it is the range of the middle 50% of the observations, or the difference between the 75th percentile and the 25th percentile. We can calculate the interquartile range for the data on attractiveness of faces by omitting the lowest five scores and the highest five scores and determining the range of the remainder. In this case the interquartile range for Set 4 would be .58 and the interquartile range for Set 32 would be only .11.

Definition | **Interquartile range:** The range of the middle 50% of the observations.

The interquartile range plays an important role in a useful graphical method known as a boxplot. This method will be discussed in Section 5.8.

In many ways the interquartile range suffers from problems that are just the opposite of those found with the range. Specifically, it discards too much of the data. This may make it a good estimate of the mean, but not a very good estimate of overall variability. If we want to know if one set of photographs is judged more variable than another, it does not make much sense to toss out the half of those scores that are most extreme and thus vary the most from the mean.

There is nothing sacred about eliminating the upper and lower 25% of the distribution before calculating the range. In fact we could eliminate any percentage we wanted as long as we could justify that number to ourselves and to others. What we really want to do is eliminate those scores that are likely to be accidents or errors without eliminating the variability that we seek to study. Samples that have had a certain percentage (e.g., 10%) of the values in each tail removed are called **trimmed samples**, and statistics calculated on such samples are called **trimmed statistics** (e.g., trimmed means or trimmed ranges). We discussed trimmed means briefly in the last chapter. Statisticians seem to like trimmed samples a lot more than psychologists do. That is unfortunate because trimmed samples, and their associated trimmed statistics, have a lot to offer, and can make our analyses more meaningful. As I said earlier, trimmed samples are beginning to make a comeback, though it will take time.

Definition | **Trimmed samples:** Samples with a percentage of the extreme scores removed.
**Trimmed statistics:** Statistics calculated on trimmed samples.

## 5.3 The Average Deviation

At first glance it would seem that if we want to measure how scores are dispersed around the mean (i.e., deviate from the mean) the most logical thing to do would be to obtain all the deviations (i.e., $X_i - \overline{X}$) and average them. The more widely the scores are dispersed, the greater the deviations and therefore the greater the average of the deviations—at least that is what you might think. However, common sense has led you astray here. If you calculate the deviations from the mean, some scores will be above the mean and have a positive deviation, while others will be below the mean and have negative deviations. In the end the positive and negative deviations will balance each other out, and the sum of the deviations will be zero. This will not get us very far.

## 5.4 The Variance

One way to eliminate the problem of the positive and negative deviations balancing each other out would be to use absolute deviations, where we simply eliminate the sign. Although that produces a legitimate measure of variability (the **mean absolute deviation, m.a.d.**), that measure is seldom used, and so we will not say more about it here. The measure that we will consider in this section, the **sample variance ($s^2$)**, represents a different approach to the problem that the deviations themselves average to zero. (When we are referring to the **population variance**, we use $\sigma^2$ [sigma squared] as the symbol.) In the case of the variance, we take advantage of the fact that the square of a negative number is positive. Thus we sum the *squared* deviations rather than the deviations themselves. Because we want an average, we next divide that sum by a function of $N$, the number of scores. Although you might reasonably expect that we would divide by $N$, we actually divide by $(N - 1)$. We use $(N - 1)$ as a divisor *only for the sample variance* because, as we will see shortly, it leaves us with a sample variance that is a better estimate of the corresponding population variance. (The population variance is calculated by dividing the sum of the squared deviations, for each value in the population, by $N$ rather than $(N - 1)$). However, we only rarely calculate a population variance. (Other than in writing textbooks, I don't think that I can recall a time that I calculated a *population* variance, though there are countless times when I have estimated them with a *sample* variance.) If it is important to specify more precisely the variable to which $s^2$ refers, we can subscript it with a letter representing the variable. Thus if we denote the data in Set 4 as $X$, the variance could be denoted as $s_x^2$ (You could refer to $s_{Set\ 4}^2$, but long subscripts are usually awkward. In general we label variables with simple letters like $X$ and $Y$.)

---

Definition

**Mean absolute deviation (m.a.d.):** The average of the absolute values of the deviations from the mean.

**Sample variance ($s^2$):** Sum of the squared deviations about the mean divided by $N - 1$.

**Population variance ($\sigma^2$):** Variance of a population; usually estimate, rarely computed.

---

For our example we can calculate the sample variances of Set 4 and Set 32 as follows:[2]

Set 4 $(X)$

$$s_X^2 = \frac{\Sigma(X - \overline{X})^2}{N - 1}$$

$$= \frac{(1.20 - 2.64)^2 + (1.82 - 2.64)^2 + \cdots + (4.02 - 2.64)^2}{20 - 1}$$

$$= \frac{8.1567}{19} = .4293$$

Set 32 $(Y)$

$$s_Y^2 = \frac{\Sigma(Y - \overline{Y})^2}{N - 1}$$

$$= \frac{(3.13 - 3.26)^2 + (3.17 - 3.26)^2 + \cdots + (3.38 - 3.26)^2}{20 - 1}$$

$$= \frac{.0902}{19} = .0048$$

---

[2] In these calculations and others throughout the book, my answers may differ slightly from those that you obtain for the same data. If so, the difference is most likely due to rounding. If you repeat my calculations and arrive at a similar answer, that is sufficient.

From these calculations we see that the difference in variances reflects the differences we see in the distributions.

Although the variance is an exceptionally important concept and one of the most commonly used statistics, it does not have the direct intuitive interpretation we would like. Because it is based on *squared* deviations, the result is in terms of squared units. Thus Set 4 has a mean attractiveness rating of 2.64 and a variance of .4293 *squared* unit. But squared units are awkward things to talk about and have little intuitive meaning with respect to the data. Fortunately, the solution to this problem is simple: Take the square root of the variance.

## 5.5 The Standard Deviation

The **standard deviation ($s$ or $\sigma$)** is defined as the positive square root of the variance and, for a sample, is symbolized as $s$ (with a subscript identifying the variable if necessary) or, occasionally, as SD. (The notation $\sigma$ is used in reference to a *population* standard deviation.) The following formula defines the standard deviation:

$$s_X = \sqrt{\frac{\Sigma(X - \overline{X})^2}{N - 1}}$$

For our example,

$$s_X = \sqrt{s_X^2} = \sqrt{.4293} = .6552$$
$$s_Y = \sqrt{s_Y^2} = \sqrt{.0048} = .0693$$

For convenience I will round these answers to .66 and .07, respectively.

---

Definition   **Standard deviation ($s$ or $\sigma$):** The square root of the variance.

---

If you look at the formula, you will see that the standard deviation, like the mean absolute deviation, is basically a measure of the average of the deviations of each score from the mean. Granted, these deviations have been squared, summed, and so on, but at heart they are still deviations. And even though we have divided by $(N - 1)$ instead of $N$, we still have obtained something very much like a mean or an "average" of these deviations. Thus we can say without too much distortion that attractiveness ratings for Set 4 deviated positively or negatively, on the average, .66 unit from the mean, whereas attractiveness ratings for Set 32 deviated, on the average, only .07 unit from the mean. This rather loose way of thinking about the standard deviation as a sort of average deviation goes a long way toward giving it meaning without doing serious injustice to the concept.

These results tell us two interesting things about attractiveness. The fact that computer averaging of many faces produces similar composites would be reflected in the fact that ratings of pictures in Set 32 do not show much variability—all those images are judged to be pretty much alike. Second, the fact that those ratings have a higher mean than the ratings of faces in Set 4 reveals that averaging over many faces produces composites that seem more attractive. Does this conform to your everyday experience? I, for one, would have expected that faces judged attractive would be those with distinctive features, but I would have been wrong. Go back and think again about those faces you class as attractive. Are they really distinctive? If so, do you have an additional hypothesis to explain the findings?

We can also look at the standard deviation in terms of how many scores fall no more than a standard deviation above or below the mean. For a wide variety of reasonably symmetric and mound-shaped distributions, we can say that approximately two-thirds of the observations lie within one standard deviation of the mean (for a normal distribution, which will be discussed in Chapter 6, it is almost exactly two-thirds). Although there certainly are exceptions, especially for badly skewed distributions, this rule is still useful. If I told you that for traditional jobs the mean starting salary for college graduates this year is expected to be $33,000 with a standard deviation of $4,000, you probably would not be far off to conclude that about two-thirds of graduates who take these jobs will earn between $29,000 and $37,000.

A third characteristic of the standard deviation is that it is usually about one-fifth or one-sixth of the range. Although this is not a particularly useful way of interpreting the standard deviation, it is a handy way of checking your work. If a glance at the data shows that the range is about 20 units, and you have just calculated $s_X = 15$, I would strongly suggest that you redo your arithmetic. You may be right, but I doubt it. On the other hand, if you find that $s_X = 3.8$, your answer is at least reasonable.

## 5.6 Computational Formulae for the Variance and the Standard Deviation

The previous expressions for the variance and the standard deviation, although perfectly correct, are unwieldy if you are doing the calculations by hand for any reasonable amount of data. They are also prone to rounding errors, since they usually involve squaring fractional deviations. They are excellent definitional formulae, but we will now consider a more practical set of calculational formulae. These formulae are algebraically equivalent to the ones we have seen, so they will give the same answers but with much less effort. (Interestingly, in earlier editions of this book I emphasized the computational formulae that I'm about to produce over the definitional ones. But as people rely more and more on computers, and less and less on calculators, I find myself swinging more in the direction of definitional formulae.)

The definitional formula for the sample variance was given as

$$s_X^2 = \frac{\Sigma(X - \overline{X})^2}{N - 1}$$

A more practical computational formula, which is algebraically equivalent, is

$$s_X^2 = \frac{\sum X^2 - \dfrac{(\sum X)^2}{N}}{N - 1}$$

Similarly, for the sample standard deviation

$$s_X = \sqrt{\frac{\sum (X - \overline{X})^2}{N - 1}}$$

$$= \sqrt{\frac{\sum X^2 - \dfrac{(\sum X)^2}{N}}{N - 1}}$$

It would be an excellent idea for you to memorize these formulae, because these equations, or parts of them, will recur throughout this book and crop up in unexpected places. (There are very few times in this book where I will even hint that memorization of a formula is a good thing. This is one of those rare exceptions.) Applying the computational formula for the sample variance for Set 4, we obtain

$$s_X^2 = \frac{\sum X^2 - \dfrac{(\sum X)^2}{N}}{N - 1}$$

$$= \frac{1.20^2 + 1.82^2 + \cdots + 4.02^2 - \dfrac{52.89^2}{20}}{19}$$

$$= \frac{148.0241 - \dfrac{52.89^2}{20}}{19} = .4293$$

Note that the answer we obtained here is exactly the same as the answer we obtained by the definitional formula. Note also, as pointed out in Chapter 2, that $\sum X^2 = 148.0241$ is quite different from $(\sum X)^2 = 52.89^2 = 2797.35$. I leave the calculation of the standard deviation for Set 32 to you, but the answer is .0689.

You might be somewhat reassured that the level of mathematics required for the previous calculations is about as much as you will need anywhere in this book. (I told you that you learned it all in high school.)

## 5.7 The Mean and the Variance as Estimators

Mention was made in Chapter 1 of the fact that we generally calculate measures such as the mean and the variance as *estimates* of the corresponding values in the populations. Characteristics of samples are called *statistics* and are designated by

Roman letters (e.g., $\overline{X}$). Characteristics of populations, on the other hand, are called *parameters* and are designated by Greek letters. Thus the population mean is symbolized by $\mu$ (lowercase mu) and the population standard deviation as $\sigma$ (lower case sigma). In general, then, we use statistics as estimates of parameters.

If the purpose of obtaining a statistic is to use it as an estimator of a parameter, it should come as no surprise that our choice of a statistic (and even how we define it) is partly a function of how well that statistic functions as an estimator of the parameter in question. In fact, the mean is usually preferred over other measures of central tendency precisely because of its performance as an estimator of $\mu$. The variance ($s^2$) is defined as it is specifically because of the advantages that accrue when $s^2$ is used to estimate the population variance, signified by $\sigma^2$.

## The Sample Variance as an Estimator of the Population Variance

The sample variance offers an excellent example of a property of estimators known as **bias**. A biased statistic is one whose long-range average is not equal to the parameter it is supposed to estimate. An unbiased statistic, as you might guess, is one whose long-range average is equal to the parameter it estimates. Unbiased statistics, like unbiased people, are nicer to have around. If you calculate the sample variance in the right way, it is unbiased.

Definition
|**Bias:** A property of a statistic whose long-range average is not equal to the parameter it estimates.

You may recall that I earlier sneaked in the divisor of ($N - 1$) instead of $N$ for the calculation of the variance and the standard deviation. Now is the time to explain why. You need to have a general sense of the issues involved, but you do not need to worry about the specifics. Whenever you see a variance or a standard deviation, it will have been computed with ($N - 1$) in the denominator. You can say "It's probably because of some obscure statistical argument," and skip this section, or you can read this section and see that ($N - 1$) makes a good deal of sense.

The reason why sample variances require ($N - 1$) as the denominator can be explained in a number of ways. Perhaps the simplest is in terms of what has been said already about the sample variance ($s^2$) as an unbiased estimate of the population variance ($\sigma^2$). Assume for the moment that we had an infinite number of samples (each containing $N$ observations) from one population and that we knew the population variance. Suppose further that we were foolish enough to calculate sample variances as $\Sigma(X - \overline{X})^2/N$ (note the denominator). If we took the average of these sample variances, we would find

$$average\left(\frac{\Sigma(X - \overline{X})^2}{N}\right) = E\left(\frac{\Sigma(X - \overline{X})^2}{N}\right) = \frac{(N - 1)\sigma^2}{N}$$

where $E(\ )$ is read as "the **expected value** of" whatever is in parentheses. Here we see that the expected value of the variance, when calculated with $N$ in the denominator, is not equal to $\sigma^2$, but to $(N - 1)/N$ times $\sigma^2$.

| Definition | **Expected Value, $E(\ )$:** The long-range average of a statistic over repeated samples. |
|---|---|

Let's take a simple example. Suppose we had a population that consisted of only the numbers 1, 2, and 3. Because this is the entire population, we can calculate $\mu$ and $\sigma^2$ exactly: $\mu = 2$ and $\sigma^2 = .667$. (Remember that if, *and only if,* we have the entire population instead of a sample, $\sigma^2 = \Sigma(X - \overline{X})^2/N$.) Suppose further that we estimate the population variance on the basis of a sample of two observations. Only nine *different* samples of $N = 2$ could possibly be drawn from this population, and it is a simple matter in this case to list them all and to compute the mean and the variance of each sample. For our example we will calculate $s^2$ using both $N$ and $(N - 1)$ as the denominator. The data and the calculations are presented in Table 5.2.

Notice that, as predicted, the mean of the sample means is exactly equal to $\mu$, and the mean of the sample variances, using $(N - 1)$ as the denominator, is exactly equal to $\sigma^2$. Furthermore, the average of $\Sigma(X - \overline{X})^2/N$ (the biased statistic) is

$$average\left(\frac{\Sigma(X - \overline{X})^2}{N}\right) = \frac{(N - 1)\sigma^2}{N} = \frac{1}{2}\sigma^2 = \frac{1}{2}(.667) = .333$$

Thus the expected value of $\Sigma(X - \overline{X})^2/N$ is not $\sigma^2$, which is what we had hoped to estimate, but instead $\sigma^2(N - 1)/N$, as we saw a few paragraphs back. When we use $N$ in the denominator, we are estimating the wrong thing and have a biased

**Table 5.2**
The Results of Sampling from a Very Small Population

| Sample | | $\overline{X}$ | $s^2$ Using $(N-1)$ | $s^2$ Using $N$ |
|---|---|---|---|---|
| 1 | 1 | 1.0 | .00 | .00 |
| 1 | 2 | 1.5 | .50 | .25 |
| 1 | 3 | 2.0 | 2.00 | 1.00 |
| 2 | 1 | 1.5 | .50 | .25 |
| 2 | 2 | 2.0 | .00 | .00 |
| 2 | 3 | 2.5 | .50 | .25 |
| 3 | 1 | 2.0 | 2.00 | 1.00 |
| 3 | 2 | 2.5 | .50 | .25 |
| 3 | 3 | 3.0 | .00 | .00 |
| Average | | 2.0 | .667 | .333 |

estimate of $\sigma^2$. This result does, however, provide us with a basis for getting an unbiased estimate $\sigma^2$. If

$$E\left(\frac{\Sigma(X - \overline{X})^2}{N}\right) = \frac{(N - 1)\sigma^2}{N}$$

then simple algebra will show that

$$E\left(\frac{\Sigma(X - \overline{X})^2}{N}\right) \times \left(\frac{N}{N - 1}\right) = \sigma^2$$

and thus

$$E\left(\frac{\Sigma(X - \overline{X})^2}{N - 1}\right) = \sigma^2$$

This last formula is our standard definitional formula for the variance. It shows us not only how to find the estimate of $\sigma^2$, but also that this estimate is unbiased.

## 5.8 Boxplots: Graphical Representations of Dispersion and Extreme Scores

In Chapter 3 you saw how stem-and-leaf displays can represent data in several meaningful ways at the same time. Such displays combine data into something very much like a histogram, while retaining the individual values of the observations. In addition to the stem-and-leaf display, John Tukey developed other ways of looking at data, one of which gives greater prominence to the dispersion of the data. This method is known as a **boxplot**, or sometimes, **box-and-whisker plot**. Tukey's method of calculating the ingredients of a boxplot are more complicated than they really need to be, and in recent years most people have adopted a somewhat simpler approach that produces nearly the same plot with more easily understood steps. That is the approach that I will adopt for this edition.

Definition   **Boxplot:**  A graphical representation of the dispersion of a sample.

**Box-and-whisker plot:**  A graphical representation of the dispersion of a sample.

The data and the accompanying stem-and-leaf display in Table 5.3 were taken from normal- and low-birthweight infants participating in a study at the University of Vermont and represent preliminary data on the length of hospitalization of 38 normal-birthweight infants. Data on three infants are missing for this particular variable and are represented by an asterisk (*). (They are included to emphasize that we should not just ignore missing data.) Because the data vary from 1 to 10, with two exceptions, all the leaves are zero. The zeros really just fill in space

**Table 5.3**
Data and Stem-and-Leaf Display on Length of Hospitalization for
Full-Term Newborn Infants (in days)

| Data | | | Stem-and-Leaf | |
|---|---|---|---|---|
| 2 | 1 | 7 | 1 | 000 |
| 1 | 33 | 2 | 2 | 000000000 |
| 2 | 3 | 4 | 3 | 00000000000 |
| 3 | * | 4 | 4 | 0000000 |
| 3 | 3 | 10 | 5 | 00 |
| 9 | 2 | 5 | 6 | 0 |
| 4 | 3 | 3 | 7 | 0 |
| 20 | 6 | 2 | 8 | |
| 4 | 5 | 2 | 9 | 0 |
| 1 | * | * | 10 | 0 |
| 3 | 3 | 4 | HI | 20, 33 |
| 2 | 3 | 4 | | |
| 3 | 2 | 3 | Missing = 3 | |
| 2 | 4 | | | |

to produce a histogram-like distribution. Examination of the data as plotted in the stem-and-leaf display reveals that the distribution is positively skewed with a median stay of three days. Near the bottom of the stem you will see the entry HI and the values 20 and 33. These are extreme values, or outliers, and are set off in this way to highlight their existence. Whether they are large enough to make us suspicious is one of the questions a boxplot is designed to address. The last line of the stem-and-leaf display indicates the number of missing observations.

To help understand the next few points, I have presented the boxplot of the data listed in Table 5.3. This is shown in Figure 5.2. It was constructed using a programming language/statistical package called R, but looks similar to boxplots produced by other software. I will discuss each part of that figure in turn.

To understand how a boxplot is constructed, we need to invoke a number of concepts we have already discussed and then add a few more. In Chapter 4 we defined the median location of a set of $N$ scores as $(N + 1)/2$. When the median location is a whole number, as it will be when $N$ is odd, then the median is simply the value that occupies that location in an ordered arrangement of data. When the median location is a decimal number (i.e., when $N$ is even), the median is the average of the two values on either side of that location. For the data in Table 5.3 the median location is $(38 + 1)/2 = 19.5$, and the median is 3. Notice that the horizontal line in the middle of the small box in Figure 5.2 is drawn at the median. The next step in constructing a boxplot is to take what amounts to the medians of each half of the ordered distribution. These are the locations of the first and third quartiles, which are also referred to as the **hinges**. To calculate the quartiles (or hinges), we first need to obtain the **quartile location**, sometimes called the hinge location, which is defined as

$$\text{Quartile location} = \frac{\text{Median location} + 1}{2}$$

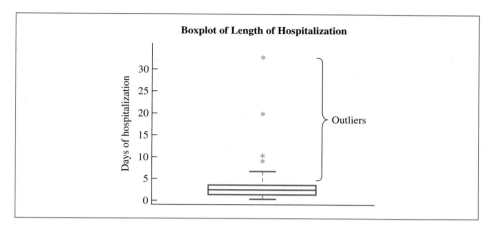

**Figure 5.2**
Boxplot of data on length of hospitalization from Table 5.3

---

Definition

**Hinges (quartiles):** Those points that cut off the bottom and top quarter of a distribution.

**Quartile location:** The location of the quartile in an ordered series.

*H*-spread: The range between the two hinges (also the interquartile range).

**Whisker:** Line from top and bottom of the box to the farthest point that is no more than 1.5 times the *H*-spread from the box.

---

If the median location is a fractional value, the fraction should be dropped from the numerator before you compute the quartile location. The quartile location is to a quartile what the median location is to the median. It tells us where, in an ordered series, the quartile values are to be found. For the data on hospital stay, the quartile location is $(19 + 1)/2 = 10$. Thus the quartiles are going to be the tenth scores from the bottom and from the top. These values are 2 and 4, respectively. For data sets without tied scores, or for large samples, the hinges will bracket the middle 50% of the scores. Notice that the top and bottom of the box in Figure 5.2 are at 2 and 4, and correspond to the first and third quartiles.

The next concept we need is that of the **H-spread**, which is simply the range between the two quartiles, and is what we have elsewhere called the interquartile range. For our data the *H*-spread is $4 - 2 = 2$. The next step in drawing the box-plot, then, is to draw a line (**whisker**) from the top and bottom of the box to the farthest point that is *no more than* $1.5 \times$ the *H*-spread from the top and bottom of the box. Because the *H*-spread is 2 for our data, the whisker will be no farther than three units out from the box. (It won't be a full three units unless there is an obtained value at that point. Otherwise it will go as far as the most extreme value that is not more than three units from the box.) Three units below the box would

### Table 5.4
Calculation for Boxplots for Data from Table 5.3

| | |
|---|---|
| Median location | $(N + 1)/2 = (38+1)/2 = 19.5$ |
| Median | 3 |
| Quartile location | (Median location[†] $+ 1)/2 = (19 + 1)/2 = 10$ |
| Lower quartile | 10th lowest score $= 2$ |
| Upper quartile | 10th highest score $= 4$ |
| $H$-spread | Upper hinge $-$ Lower hinge $= 4 - 2 = 2$ |
| $H$-spread $\times$ 1.5 | $2 \times 1.5 = 3$ |
| Maximum lower whisker | First quartile $- 1.5(H\text{-spread}) = 2 - 3 = -1$ |
| Maximum upper whisker | Third quartile $+ 1.5(H\text{-spread}) = 4 + 3 = 7$ |
| End lower whisker | Smallest value $\geq -1 = 1$ |
| End upper whisker | Largest value $\leq 7 = 7$ |

[†]Drop any fractional value

be at $2 - 3 = -1$, but the smallest value in the data is 1, so we will draw the whisker to 1. Three units above the box would be at $4 + 3 = 7$. There is a 7 in the data, so we will draw that whisker to 7. The calculations for all the terms we have just defined are shown in Table 5.4.

The steps above were all illustrated in Figure 5.2. The only question is "Where did those asterisks come from?" The asterisks in that plot represent values that are so extreme that they lie outside the whiskers. They are outliers. They could be honest values that are just extreme, or they could be errors. The nice thing about that boxplot is that it at least directs our attention to those values. I will come back to them in just a minute.

From Figure 5.2 we can see several important things. First, the central portion of the distribution is reasonably symmetric. This is indicated by the fact that the median lies in the center of the box and was apparent from the stem-and-leaf display. We can also see that the distribution is positively skewed, because the whisker on the top is substantially longer than the one on the bottom. This also was apparent from the stem-and-leaf display, although not so clearly. Finally, we see that we have four outliers, where an outlier is defined here as any value more extreme than the whiskers. The stem-and-leaf display did not show the position of the outliers nearly so graphically as does the boxplot.

Outliers deserve special attention. An outlier could represent an error in measurement, in data recording, or in data entry, or it could represent a legitimate value that just happens to be extreme. For example, our data represent length of hospitalization, and a full-term infant might have been born with a physical defect that required extended hospitalization. Because these are actual data, it was possible to go back to hospital records and look more closely at the four extreme cases. On examination, it turned out that the two most extreme scores were attributable to errors in data entry and were readily correctable. The other two extreme scores were caused by physical problems of the infants. Here a decision was required by the project director as to whether the problems were sufficiently severe to cause the infants to be dropped from the study (both were retained). The two corrected

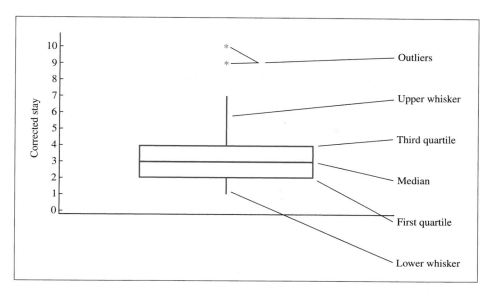

**Figure 5.3**
Corrected boxplot

values were 3 and 5 instead of 33 and 20, respectively, and a new boxplot on the corrected data is shown in Figure 5.3. This boxplot is identical to the one shown in Figure 5.2 except for the spacing and the two largest values. (You should verify for yourself that the corrected data set would indeed yield this boxplot.) These data look more like we would like them to look.

From what has been said, it should be evident that boxplots are extremely useful tools for examining data with respect to dispersion. I find them particularly useful for screening data for errors and for highlighting potential problems before subsequent analyses are carried out. Boxplots are presented often in the remainder of this book as visual guides to the data.

### For People in a Hurry
A boxplot really doesn't take all that long to draw, but some people just don't have any patience. Assuming that you have a large number of scores, you can set aside the largest 2.5% and the smallest 2.5% and draw the whiskers to the largest and smallest values that remain. Then put those extreme values in as outliers. In fact, some computer programs look as if that's exactly the way they construct boxplots.

## 5.9 A Return to Trimming

As you should recall from Chapter 4, one technique for dealing with outliers that distort the mean is to trim the sample, meaning that we lop off a certain number of values at each end of the distribution. We then find the mean of the observations that remain. You might logically think that we should do the same thing when examining the variance or standard deviation of that sample. But, instead, we are going to modify the procedure slightly.

## Winsorized Variance

For a 20% trimmed mean we set aside the 20% of the highest and lowest values and find the mean of what remains. Instead of simply omitting the extreme observations in a sample, we often create what is called a **Winsorized sample**. In a Winsorized sample we replace the extreme observations with the highest (and lowest) value remaining after trimming. The **Winsorized mean**, then, is the mean of a Winsorized sample. For example, suppose that we had the following observations:

12 14 19 21 21 22 24 24 26 27 27 27 28 29 30 31 32 45 50 52

With 20 values, 20% trimming would remove the lowest and highest four observations, giving us

21 22 24 24 26 27 27 27 28 29 30 31

which gives a trimmed mean of 316/12 = 26.33. (The original mean was 28.05.)

---

Definition   **Winsorized sample:** A sample in which trimmed observations are replaced with the highest (and lowest) remaining values.
**Winsorized mean:** The mean of a Winsorized sample.

---

When we Winsorize the data we replace the lowest scores that we have eliminated with 21 (the lowest value remaining), and replace the highest scores that we have eliminated with 31 (the highest value remaining). This gives us

21 21 21 21 21 22 24 24 26 27 27 27 28 29 30 31 31 31 31 31

Therefore, the Winsorized mean would be 524/20 = 26.2, which is actually quite close to the trimmed mean.

For technical reasons that I won't elaborate, we rarely use the Winsorized mean, but use the trimmed mean instead. However, when it comes to calculating a variance or standard deviation, we do fall back on Winsorizing. When we work with a trimmed mean we find that the **Winsorized variance** or **Winsorized standard deviation** is a more useful statistic than the traditional variance or standard deviation. And to compute a Winsorized variance we simply compute the variance of the Winsorized sample. So we want the variance of

21 21 21 21 21 22 24 24 26 27 27 27 28 29 30 31 31 31 31 31

which is 16.02. (The variance of the trimmed sample would have been only 9.52.)

Definition   Winsorized variance: The variance of a Winsorized sample.

Winsorized standard deviation: The standard deviation of a Winsorized sample.

We will return to Winsorized variance and standard deviations later in the book, but for now you simply need to understand what they are. And if you know that, you will be ahead of most people around you.

## 5.10  Obtaining Measures of Dispersion Using SPSS

We will use SPSS to calculate measures of dispersion on the reaction time data discussed in Chapter 3 (see page 51). I calculated the output using **Descriptive Statistics/Explore**. Figure 5.4a shows the measures of central tendency and dispersion for the complete data set of 300 observations. SPSS also prints a histogram, a boxplot, and a stem-and-leaf display for these data, but I have omitted those because we have already seen examples for this variable. In Figure 5.4b you can see the descriptive statistics calculated separately by the number of stimuli flashed on the screen, followed by the corresponding boxplots.

You should recall from Chapter 3 that if we process information sequentially, our reaction times would be expected to increase as the number of digits in the

**Descriptives**

|  |  | Statistic | Std. Error |
|---|---|---|---|
| RXTIME | Mean | 60.260 | .7512 |
|  | 95% Confidence Interval for Mean |  |  |
|  | Lower Bound | 58.782 |  |
|  | Upper Bound | 61.738 |  |
|  | 5% Trimmed Mean | 59.541 |  |
|  | Median | 59.500 |  |
|  | Variance | 169.277 |  |
|  | Std. Deviation | 13.0106 |  |
|  | Minimum | 36 |  |
|  | Maximum | 125 |  |
|  | Range | 89 |  |
|  | Interquartile Range | 16.000 |  |
|  | Skewness | .978 | .141 |
|  | Kurtosis | 2.213 | .281 |

**Figure 5.4a**
Distribution and measures of central tendency and dispersion on complete reaction time data set

**Descriptives**

|  |  | Statistic |  |  |
|---|---|---|---|---|
|  |  | NSTIM | | |
|  |  | 1 | 3 | 5 |
| RXTIME | Mean | 53.270 | 60.650 | 66.860 |
|  | 95% Confidence Interval for Mean | | | |
|  |     Lower Bound | 50.620 | 58.783 | 64.423 |
|  |     Upper Bound | 55.920 | 62.517 | 69.297 |
|  | 5% Trimmed Mean | 51.867 | 60.200 | 66.200 |
|  | Median | 50.000 | 60.000 | 65.000 |
|  | Variance | 178.381 | 88.513 | 150.849 |
|  | Std. Deviation | 13.3559 | 9.4081 | 12.2821 |
|  | Minimum | 36 | 42 | 39 |
|  | Maximum | ** | 95 | ** |
|  | Range | 68 | 53 | 86 |
|  | Interquartile Range | 12.750 | 11.500 | 14.250 |
|  | Skewness | 1.752 | .807 | 1.330 |
|  | Kurtosis | 3.715 | 1.344 | 4.453 |

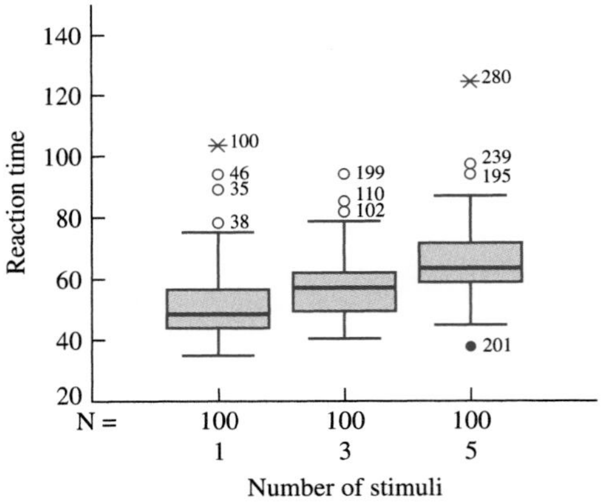

**Figure 5.4b**
Measures displayed separately by number of digits in comparison set

comparison set increases. On the other hand, if we engage in parallel processing, reaction times would not be expected to increase with a larger number of digits. What would you conclude from the output in Figure 5.4b? What, if anything, would you conclude from the fact that dispersion remained nearly constant as the number of digits increased?

## 5.11  A Final Worked Example

Why does the moon appear to be so much larger when it is near the horizon than when it is directly overhead? This simple question has produced a wide variety of theories from psychologists. Kaufman and Rock (1962) carried out a very complete series of studies. They proposed that the moon illusion is caused by the greater *apparent distance* of the moon when it is at the horizon than when it is at its zenith (something along the idea that "if it is really that far away, it must be really big").[3] When we discuss the *t* test in Chapters 12 through 14, we will examine Kaufman and Rock's data in more detail, but first we have to ask if the apparatus they used really produced a moon illusion in the first place. Table 5.5 gives measures of the moon illusion collected by Kaufman and Rock. For these data a score of 1.73, for example, means that the moon appeared to the subject to be 1.73 times larger when on the horizon than when overhead. Ratios greater than 1.00 are what we would expect if the apparatus works correctly (producing an illusion). Ratios close to one would indicate little or no illusion. Moreover, we hope that if the task given the subjects is a good one, there would not be much variability in the scores.

For the data in Table 5.5 we can calculate the following statistics:
Mean:

$$\overline{X} = \frac{\Sigma X}{N} = \frac{14.63}{10} = 1.463$$

### Table 5.5
Moon Illusion Data

| Illusion (X) | X² |
|:---:|:---:|
| 1.73 | 2.9929 |
| 1.06 | 1.1236 |
| 2.03 | 4.1209 |
| 1.40 | 1.9600 |
| .95 | .9025 |
| 1.13 | 1.2769 |
| 1.41 | 1.9881 |
| 1.73 | 2.9929 |
| 1.63 | 2.6569 |
| 1.56 | 2.4336 |
| $\Sigma X = 14.63$ | $\Sigma X^2 = 22.4483$ |

---

[3]For an interesting discussion of the recent work by Lloyd Kaufman and his son James Kaufman, go to

 http://www.xs4all.nl/~carlkop/moonillu.html

The brief historical section near the end of that Web page is interesting, and shows that the moon illusion has been around for a very long time, as has what has now come to be the dominant theory used to explain it.

Variance:

$$s^2 = \frac{\Sigma X^2 - \dfrac{(\Sigma X)^2}{N}}{N-1} = \frac{22.4483 - \dfrac{(14.63)^2}{10}}{9} = .1161$$

Standard deviation:

$$s = \sqrt{.1161} = .3407$$

Boxplots:

First rearrange the observations in ascending order:

.95  1.06  1.13  1.40  1.41  1.56  1.63  1.73  1.73  2.03

Median location = $(N+1)/2 = 11/2 = 5.5$

Median = $(1.41 + 1.56)/2 = 1.485$

Quartile location = (Median location + 1)/2 = (5 + 1)/2 = 3

(Drop any fraction from median location.)

Quartiles = The third observations from the top and the bottom of the ordered series = 1.13 and 1.73

H-spread = Distance between third and first quartiles = $1.73 - 1.13 = .60$

$1.5 \times$ H-spread = 1.5(.60) = .90

Maximum whisker length = Quartiles $\pm$ 1.5(H-spread)

Maximum of upper whisker = $1.73 + .90 = 2.63$

Maximum of lower whisker = $1.13 - .90 = .23$

Values closest to *but not exceeding* whisker lengths:

Lower whisker end = .95

Upper whisker end = 2.03

Resulting boxplot:

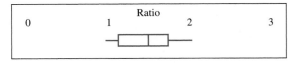

From these results we can see that the average moon illusion is well above 1.00; in fact only one measurement was less than 1. With a mean of 1.46, we can say that, on average, the horizon moon appears to be about half again as large (46% more) as the zenith moon. More important for our purposes here, the variability of the illusion is reasonably small ($s = .34$), meaning that the measurements are in pretty good agreement with one another, and there are no outliers. It looks as if Kaufman and Rock's apparatus works well for their purpose.

## 5.12 Seeing Statistics

Earlier I told you that we use the divisor of $N - 1$ in calculating the variance and standard deviation because it leads to a less biased estimate of the population variance. Although I used a small demonstration in Table 5.2, I largely left it to you to accept my statement on faith. However, using one of McClelland's applets from *Seeing Statistics*, you can illustrate this for yourself. You will see that while $N - 1$ does not *always* produce the better estimate, it certainly does on average.

The applet can be found at

 www.uvm.edu/~dhowell/fundamentals/SeeingStatisticsApplets/Applets.html

and is named "Why divide by $N - 1$?" In this applet we have created a population consisting of each of the numbers between 0 and 100. Because we have the whole population, we know that the true mean is $\mu = 50$, and the variance is $\sigma^2 = 853$. The true standard deviation ($\sigma$) is thus 29.2. (You could calculate those for yourself if you are compulsive.) The applet itself, before any samples have been collected, looks like the one shown.

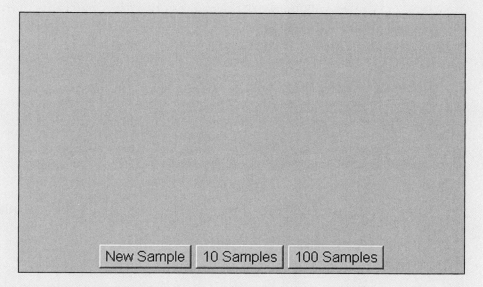

You can draw individual samples of size 3 from this population, and display the results using both $N$ and $N - 1$ as the denominator by clicking on the New Sample button. First, draw individual samples and note how they vary. Note that sometimes one denominator produces the closer estimate, and sometimes the other denominator does so. Now click on the "10 samples" button. This will draw 10 samples of $N = 3$ at once and will give you the average values for these 10 samples. Such a display is illustrated next.

```
Results displayed for last 10 samples of size3
St. Dev. when dividing by n-1
    31.7 26.4 22.1 24.8 26.1 18.4 4.9 20.2 23.0 8.5
St. Dev. when dividing by n
    25.8 21.5 18.1 20.2 21.3 15.0 4.0 16.5 18.8 6.9
Averages of St. Dev. from all 10 samples:
    when dividing by n-1 : 22.0
    when dividing by n   : 18.0



                New Sample | 10 Samples | 100 Samples
```

Usually, though not always, with 10 samples you can see that the divisor of $N - 1$ produces the better average estimate. (Remember that the true population standard deviation is 29.2.) For this example, I have drawn 10 samples. The display shows you the estimated standard deviations for those 10 samples, as computed by using both $(N - 1)$ and $N$ as the denominator. It also shows you the averages of the 10 values for each of those two estimates.

If you keep clicking on this button you will be adding 10 new samples to your collection each time. Clicking on the next button will add 100 samples at a time. I drew a total of 500 samples. Using $(N - 1)$ as the denominator, our average estimate was 31.8, which is too high by 2.6 units. Using $N$ as the denominator, we were off, on average, by $29.2 - 26 = 3.2$ units. Clearly $(N - 1)$ was more accurate.

Click on the "100 Samples" button until you have accumulated about 5000 samples. What is your average estimate of the population standard deviation using the two different divisors?

It should be evident that as $N$, the size of an individual sample, increases, the relative difference between $N$ and $N - 1$ will decrease. This should mean that there will be less of a difference between the two estimates. In addition, with larger sample sizes, the average sample standard deviation will more closely approximate $\sigma$. The second applet on your screen allows you to repeat the process above, but to use a sample size of 15. What effect does this have on your results?

## 5.13 Summary

In this chapter we considered a number of measures of the degree to which scores are distributed around the mean. Of these measures, the standard deviation and the variance are the most important and will play a major role in the remainder of the text. We also examined how to use boxplots to highlight the shape of the distribution and to help in identifying outliers.

Some important terms in this chapter are

| | |
|---|---|
| Dispersion (variability), 76 | Boxplot, 87 |
| Range, 79 | Box-and-whisker plot, 87 |
| Interquartile range, 79 | Hinges, 89 |
| Trimmed samples, 80 | Quartile location, 89 |
| Trimmed statistics, 80 | $H$-spread, 89 |
| Mean absolute deviation (m.a.d.), 81 | Whisker, 89 |
| Sample variance ($s^2$), 81 | Winsorized sample, 92 |
| Population variance ($\sigma^2$), 81 | Winsorized mean, 92 |
| Standard deviation ($s$ or $\sigma$), 82 | Winsorized variance, 93 |
| Bias, 85 | Winsorized standard deviation, 93 |
| Expected value, $E(\ )$, 86 | |

## 5.14 Exercises

**5.1**  Calculate the range, the variance, and the standard deviation for the Katz et al. data (see Figure 4.1) on the SAT performance of participants who did not read the passage. The data follow.

54  52  51  50  36  55  44  46  57  44  43  52

38  46  55  34  44  39  43  36  55  57  36  46

49  46  49  47

**5.2**  Calculate the range, the variance, and the standard deviation for the Katz et al. data (below) on the SAT performance of participants who did read the passage.

66  75  72  71  55  56  72  93  73  72  72  73

91  66  71  56  59

**5.3**   Compare the answers to Exercises 5.1 and 5.2. Is the standard deviation for performance when people do not read the passage different from the standard deviation when people do read the passage?

**5.4**   In Exercise 5.1 what percentage of the scores fall within two standard deviations from the mean?

**5.5**   In Exercise 5.2 what percentage of the scores fall within two standard deviations from the mean?

**5.6**   Create a small data set of about seven scores and demonstrate that adding or subtracting a constant to each score does not change the standard deviation. What happens to the *mean* when a constant is added or subtracted?

**5.7**   Given the data you created in Exercise 5.6, show that multiplying or dividing by a constant multiplies or divides the standard deviation by that constant. How does this relate to what happens to the *mean* under similar circumstances?

**5.8**   Using what you have learned from Exercises 5.6 and 5.7, transform the following set of data to a new set with a standard deviation of 1.00.

   5   8   3   8   6   9   9   7

**5.9**   Use the answers to Exercises 5.6 and 5.7 to modify the answer to Exercise 5.8 to have a mean of 0 and a standard deviation of 1.00. (*Note:* The solution to Exercises 5.8 and 5.9 will be important in Chapter 6.)

**5.10**   Create two sets of scores with equal ranges but different variances.

**5.11**   Create a boxplot for the data in Exercise 5.1.

**5.12**   Create a boxplot for the data in Exercise 5.2.

**5.13**   Create a boxplot for the variable ADDSC in the data file at

 http://www.uvm.edu/~dhowell/fundamentals/DataFiles/Add.dat

**5.14**   Using the data for ENGG in the data file referred to in Exercise 5.13,
   (a) Calculate the variance and the standard deviation for ENGG.
   (b) These measures should be greater than the corresponding measures on GPA. Can you explain why this should be? (We will come back to this in Chapter 12, but see if you can figure it out.)

**5.15**   The mean of the data used in Exercise 5.1 is 46.57. Suppose that we had an additional participant who had a score of 46.57. Recalculate the variance for these data. (You can build on the intermediate steps used in Exercise 5.1.) What effect does this score have on the answers to Exercise 5.1?

**5.16**   Instead of adding a score equal to the mean (as in Exercise 5.15), add a score of 40 to the data used in Exercise 5.1. How does this score affect the answers to Exercise 5.1?

**5.17**   Repeat the computations used to generate Table 5.2, but this time let the population consist of the numbers 1, 2, 3, 4, and 5 and draw all possible samples of $N = 3$. (*Hint:* There are 125 possible samples, so this problem is best done by those who have access to a spreadsheet program such as Excel.)

**5.18**  Given the following data:

1  3  3  5  8  8  9  12  13  16  17  17  18  20  21  30

(a) Draw a boxplot.
(b) Calculate the standard deviation of these data and divide every score by the standard deviation.
(c) Draw a boxplot for the data in (b).
(d) Compare the two boxplots.

**5.19**  The following graph came from the JMP statistical package applied to the data in Table 5.3 on length of hospitalization. Notice the boxplot on the top of the figure. How does that boxplot compare with the ones we have been using? (*Hint:* The mean is 4.66.)

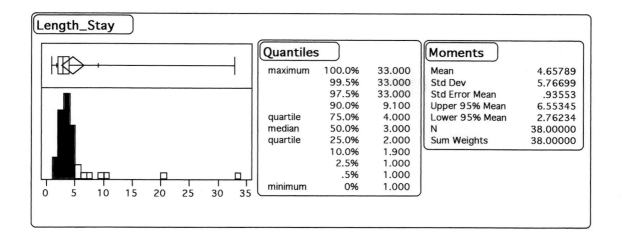

**5.20**  In Section 5.9 statistics were computed from the reaction time data in Chapter 3. What would you conclude from these data about how we process information in short-term memory?

**5.21**  Everitt, as reported in Hand et al. (1994), presented data on the amount of weight gained by 72 anorexic girls under one of three treatment conditions. The conditions were Cognitive Behavior Therapy, Family Therapy, and a Control group who received no treatment. The data follow:

| Cog. | 1.7 | .7 | −.1 | −.7 | −3.5 | 14.9 | 3.5 | 17.1 | −7.6 | 1.6 | 11.7 | 6.1 | 1.1 |
|------|-----|-----|-----|-----|------|------|------|------|------|-----|------|-----|-----|
| Behav. | −4.0 | 20.9 | −9.1 | 2.1 | −1.4 | 1.4 | −.3 | −3.7 | −.8 | 2.4 | 12.6 | 1.9 | 3.9 |
|  | .1 | 15.4 | −.7 | | | | | | | | | | |

| Family | 11.4 | 11.0 | 5.5 | 9.4 | 13.6 | −2.9 | −.1 | 7.4 | 21.5 | −5.3 | −3.8 | 13.4 | 13.1 |
|--------|------|------|-----|-----|------|------|-----|-----|------|------|------|------|------|
|  | 9.0 | 3.9 | 5.7 | 10.7 | | | | | | | | | |

| Control | −.5 | −9.3 | −5.4 | 12.3 | −2.0 | −10.2 | −12.2 | 11.6 | −7.1 | 6.2 | −.2 | −9.2 | 8.3 |
|---------|-----|------|------|------|------|-------|-------|------|------|-----|-----|------|-----|
|  | 3.3 | 11.3 | .0 | −1.0 | −10.6 | −4.6 | −6.7 | 2.8 | .3 | 1.8 | 3.7 | 15.9 | −10.2 |

(a) What would you hypothesize about central tendency and variability?

(b) Calculate the relevant descriptive statistics and graphics.

(c) What kind of conclusions would you feel comfortable drawing, and why? (We haven't covered hypothesis testing, but you are doing an elementary hypothesis test here. Think carefully about how you are doing it. This may help you in Chapter 8.)

**5.22**  Compare the mean, standard deviation, and variance for the data in Exercise 5.1 with their trimmed and Winsorized counterparts.

**5.23**  Compare the mean, standard deviation, and variance for the data from the Cognitive Behavior condition in Exercise 5.21 with their 20% trimmed and Winsorized counterparts. Why is the Winsorized variance noticeably smaller than the traditional variance?

# The Normal Distribution

**QUESTIONS**

- What's so normal about the normal distribution?

- There are an unlimited number of different normal distributions, so how do we work with all of them?

- Can we predict what kinds of values we will obtain?

- What about all those other things, like *T* scores?

- How do I use *Seeing Statistics* to illustrate concepts?

**F**rom the preceding chapters it should be apparent that we are going to be very much concerned with distributions—distributions of data, hypothetical distributions of populations, and sampling distributions. Of all the possible forms that distributions can take, the class known as the **normal distribution** is by far the most important for our purposes.

| | |
|---|---|
| Definition | **Normal Distribution:** A specific distribution having a characteristic bell-shaped form. |

Before elaborating on the normal distribution, however, it is worth a short digression to explain just why we are so interested in distributions in general. The critical factor is that there is an important link between distributions and probabilities. If we know something about the distribution of events (or of sample statistics), we know something about the probability that one of those events (or statistics) is likely to occur. To see the issue in its simplest form, take the lowly pie chart. (This is the only time you will see a pie chart in this book. I am one of those people who stand too long in cafeteria lines, trying to figure out which slice of pie is the largest, and afraid that I'll make the wrong choice. We shouldn't be using graphics whose message isn't obvious.)

The pie chart shown in Figure 6.1 is taken from a U.S. Department of Justice report on probation and parole. It shows the status of all individuals convicted of a criminal offense. From this figure you can see that 9% were in jail, 19% were in prison, 61% were on probation, and the remaining 11% were on parole. You can also see that the percentages in each category are directly reflected in the percentage of the area of the pie that each wedge occupies. The area taken up by each segment is directly proportional to the percentage of individuals in that segment. Moreover, if we declare that the total area of the pie is 1.00 unit, the area of each segment is equal to the proportion of observations falling within that segment.[1]

It is easy to go from speaking about areas to speaking about probabilities. The concept of probability will be elaborated in Chapter 7, but even without a precise

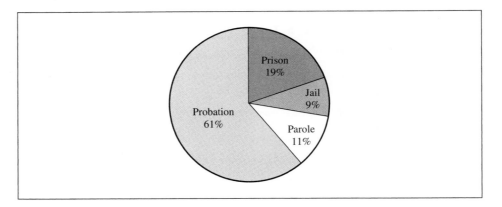

**Figure 6.1**
Pie chart showing persons under correctional supervision, by type of supervision in 1982[2]

---

[1] Some students think that it is rather cavalier to just decide on your own that the area of the pie is 1.0 unit. If you have that problem, just imagine redrawing the pie chart, to scale, so that its total area is one square inch. Then a slice of the pie that represents 25% of the incarcerations, will actually measure .25 square inch.

[2] For 2004, the figures were: Jail = 10%, Prison = 20%, Probation = 60% and Parole = 10%. What does this tell us about changes in how we deal with convictions? A search of the Internet under the words "correctional supervision" reveals all sorts of interesting statistics, which seem to vary with the politics of the person reporting them. In particular, you might try

 http://www.ojp.usdoj.gov/bjs/glance/corr2.htm

(Just double-click on the graphic on that Web site to see the raw data.) The alarming thing is that the percentages haven't changed all that much, but the total numbers have gone up drastically.

definition of probability we can make an important point about areas of a pie chart. For now simply think of probability in its common everyday usage, referring to the likelihood that some event will occur. From this perspective it is logical to conclude that, because 19% of those convicted of a federal crime are currently in prison, if we were to randomly draw the name of one person from a list of convicted individuals, the probability is .19 that the individual would be in prison. To put this in slightly different terms, if 19% of the area of the pie is allocated to prison, then the probability that a randomly chosen person would fall into that segment is .19.

This pie chart also allows us to explore the addition of areas. It should be clear that if 19% are in prison and 9% are in jail, 19 + 9 = 28% are incarcerated. In other words, we can find the percentage of individuals in one of several categories just by adding the percentages for each category. The same thing holds in terms of areas, in the sense that we can find the percentage of incarcerated individuals by adding the areas devoted to prison and to jail. And finally, if we can find percentages by adding areas, we can also find probabilities by adding areas. Thus the probability of being incarcerated is the probability of being in one of the two segments associated with incarceration, which we can get by summing the two areas (or their associated probabilities). I hope that I haven't really told you anything that you didn't already know. I'm just setting the stage for what follows.

There are other ways to present data besides pie charts. Two of the simplest are a bar chart and its closely related cousin, the histogram (discussed in Chapter 3). Figure 6.2 is a redrawing of Figure 6.1 in the form of a bar chart. Although this figure does not contain any new information, it has two advantages over the pie chart. First, it is easier to compare categories because the only thing we need to look at is the height of the bar, rather than trying to compare the lengths of two different arcs in different orientations. The second advantage is that the bar chart is visually more like the common distributions we will deal with, in that the various levels or categories (the independent variable) are spread out along the horizontal dimension, and the percentages in each category (the dependent variable) are shown along the vertical dimension. Here again you can see that the various areas of the distribution are related to probabilities. Further, you can see that we can meaningfully sum areas in exactly the same way that we did in the pie chart. When we move to more common distributions,

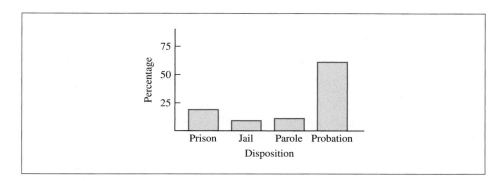

**Figure 6.2**
Bar chart showing persons under correctional supervision, by type of supervision

particularly the normal distribution, the principles of areas, percentages, probabilities, and the addition of areas or probabilities carry over almost without change.

## 6.1 The Normal Distribution

Now let's move closer to the normal distribution. I stated earlier that the normal distribution is one of the most important distributions we will encounter. There are several reasons for this:

1. Many of the dependent variables we deal with are commonly assumed to be normally distributed in the population. That is to say, we frequently assume that if we were to obtain the whole population of observations, the resulting distribution would closely resemble the normal distribution.

2. If we can assume that a variable is at least approximately normally distributed, then the techniques that are discussed in this chapter allow us to make a number of inferences (either exact or approximate) about values of that variable.

3. The theoretical distribution of the hypothetical set of sample means obtained by drawing an infinite number of samples from a specified population can be shown to be approximately normal under a wide variety of conditions. Such a distribution is called the sampling distribution of the mean and is discussed and used extensively throughout the remainder of this book.

4. Most of the statistical procedures we will employ have, somewhere in their derivation, an assumption that a variable is normally distributed.

To introduce the normal distribution, we will look at one additional data set that is approximately normal (and would be closer to normal if we had more observations). The data we are going to look at were collected using the Achenbach Youth Self-Report form (Achenbach, 1991). This is a frequently used measure of behavior problems that produces scores on a number of different dimensions. The one we are going to look at is the dimension of Total Behavior Problems, which represents the total number of behavior problems reported by the child's parent (weighted by the severity of the problem). (Examples of Behavior Problem categories are "Argues," "Impulsive," "Shows off," and "Teases.") Figure 6.3 is a histogram of data from 289 junior high school students. A higher score represents more behavior problems. You can see that this distribution has a center very near 50 and is fairly symmetrically distributed on either side of that value, with the scores ranging between about 25 and 75. The standard deviation of this distribution is approximately 10. The distribution is not perfectly even—it has some bumps and valleys—but overall it is fairly smooth, rising in the center and falling off at the ends. (The actual mean and standard deviation for this particular sample are 49.13 and 10.56, respectively.)

One thing that you might note from this distribution is that if you add the frequencies of subjects falling into the intervals 52–53, 54–55, and 56–57, you will

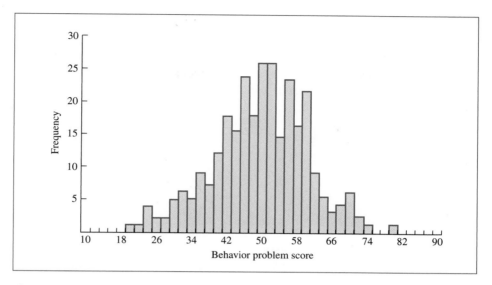

**Figure 6.3**

Histogram showing distribution of total behavior problem scores

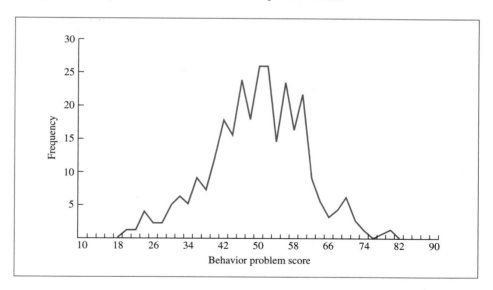

**Figure 6.4**

Frequency polygon showing distribution of total behavior problem scores

find that 64 students obtained scores between 52 and 56. Because there are 289 observations in this sample, $64/289 = 22\%$ of the observations fell in this interval. This illustrates the comments made earlier on the addition of areas.

If we take this same set of data and represent it by a line graph rather than a histogram, we obtain Figure 6.4. There is absolutely no information in this figure that was not in Figure 6.3. I merely connected the tops of the bars in the histogram

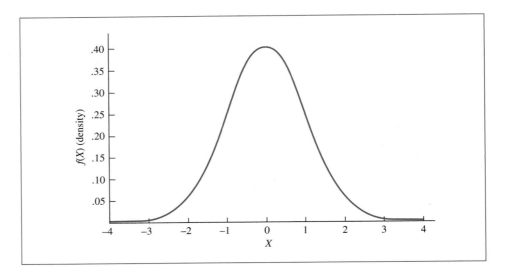

**Figure 6.5**

A characteristic normal distribution with values of X on the abscissa and density on the ordinate

and then erased the bars themselves. Why, then, waste an artist's time by putting in a figure that has nothing new to offer? The reason is simply that I want to get people to see the transition from a histogram, which you see nearly every time you open a newspaper or a magazine, to a line graph. The next transition from there to the smoothed curves you will often see in the rest of the book (e.g., Figure 6.5) is straightforward. The major difference between the line graph (frequency polygon) and the smoothed curve is that the latter is a stylized version that leaves out the bumps and valleys. If you would prefer, you can always think of the smoothed curve as sitting on top of an invisible histogram (with very narrow bars).

Now we are ready to go to the normal distribution. First, we will consider it in the abstract, and then we will take a concrete example, making use of the Achenbach Youth Self-Report Total Behavior Problem scores that we saw in Figure 6.3 and Figure 6.4.

The distribution shown in Figure 6.5 is a characteristic normal distribution. It is a symmetric, unimodal distribution, frequently referred to as "bell shaped," and has limits of $\pm\infty$. The **abscissa**, or horizontal axis, represents different possible values of X, while the **ordinate**, or vertical axis, is referred to as the **density** and is related to (but not the same as) the frequency or probability of occurrence of X. The concept of density is discussed in further detail in the next chapter.

Definition    **Abscissa:** Horizontal (X) axis.

**Ordinate:** Vertical (Y) axis.

**Density:** Height of the curve for a given value of X; closely related to the probability of an observation falling in an interval around X.

The normal distribution has a long history. It was originally investigated by DeMoivre (1667–1754), who was interested in its use to describe the results of games of chance (gambling). The distribution was defined precisely by Pierre-Simon Laplace (1749–1827) and put in its more usual form by Carl Friedrich Gauss (1777–1855), both of whom were interested in the distribution of errors in astronomical observations. In fact, the normal distribution often is referred to as the Gaussian distribution and as the "normal law of error." Adolph Quetelet (1796–1874), a Belgian astronomer, was the first to apply the distribution to social and biological data. He collected chest measurements of Scottish soldiers and heights of French soldiers. (I can't imagine why—he must have had too much time on his hands.) He found that both sets of measurements were approximately normally distributed. Quetelet interpreted the data to indicate that the mean of this distribution was the ideal at which nature was aiming, and observations to either side of the mean represented error (a deviation from nature's ideal). (For 5′8″ males like myself, it is somehow comforting to think of all those bigger guys as nature's errors, although I don't imagine they think of themselves that way.) Although we no longer think of the mean as nature's ideal, this is a useful way to conceptualize variability around the mean. In fact, we still use the word *error* to refer to deviations from the mean. Francis Galton (1822–1911) carried Quetelet's ideas further and gave the normal distribution a central role in psychological theory, especially the theory of mental abilities. Some would insist that Galton was *too* successful in this endeavor, and that we tend to assume that measures are normally distributed even when they are not. I won't argue the issue here, but it is very much a point of debate among statisticians.

Mathematically the normal distribution is defined as

$$f(X) = \frac{1}{\sigma \sqrt{2\pi}}(e)^{-(X-\mu)^2/2\sigma^2}$$

where $\pi$ and $e$ are constants ($\pi = 3.1416$ and $e = 2.7183$), and $\mu$ and $\sigma$ are the mean and the standard deviation, respectively, of the distribution. Given that $\mu$ and $\sigma$ are known, $f(X)$, the height of the curve, or ordinate, for any value of $X$ is obtained simply by substituting the appropriate values for $\mu$, $\sigma$, and $X$ and solving the equation. This is not nearly as difficult as it looks, but in practice you will probably never to have to make the calculations. The cumulative form of this distribution is tabled, and we can simply read the information we need from the table.

Those of you who have had a course in calculus may recognize that the area under the curve between any two values of $X$ (say, $X_1$ and $X_2$), and thus the probability that a randomly drawn score will fall within that interval, could be found by integrating the function over the range from $X_1$ to $X_2$—although that is not a simple task. Those of you who have not had such a course can take comfort from the fact that tables are readily available in which this work has already been done for us or by use of which we can easily do the work ourselves. Such a table appears in Appendix D (Table D.10), and an abbreviated version of that table is shown in Table 6.1. For those who think that paper-and-pencil tables and calculations went out in the very dim past before instant messaging and the iPod, you can go to the Web and find sites that will do the calculations for you. My favorite is maintained

**Table 6.1**
The Normal Distribution (Abbreviated Version of Table D. 10)

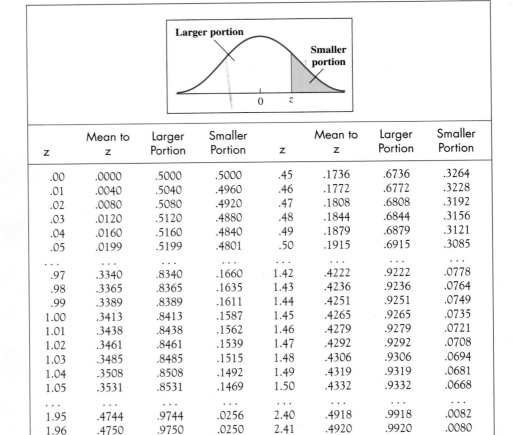

| z | Mean to z | Larger Portion | Smaller Portion | z | Mean to z | Larger Portion | Smaller Portion |
|---|---|---|---|---|---|---|---|
| .00 | .0000 | .5000 | .5000 | .45 | .1736 | .6736 | .3264 |
| .01 | .0040 | .5040 | .4960 | .46 | .1772 | .6772 | .3228 |
| .02 | .0080 | .5080 | .4920 | .47 | .1808 | .6808 | .3192 |
| .03 | .0120 | .5120 | .4880 | .48 | .1844 | .6844 | .3156 |
| .04 | .0160 | .5160 | .4840 | .49 | .1879 | .6879 | .3121 |
| .05 | .0199 | .5199 | .4801 | .50 | .1915 | .6915 | .3085 |
| ... | ... | ... | ... | ... | ... | ... | ... |
| .97 | .3340 | .8340 | .1660 | 1.42 | .4222 | .9222 | .0778 |
| .98 | .3365 | .8365 | .1635 | 1.43 | .4236 | .9236 | .0764 |
| .99 | .3389 | .8389 | .1611 | 1.44 | .4251 | .9251 | .0749 |
| 1.00 | .3413 | .8413 | .1587 | 1.45 | .4265 | .9265 | .0735 |
| 1.01 | .3438 | .8438 | .1562 | 1.46 | .4279 | .9279 | .0721 |
| 1.02 | .3461 | .8461 | .1539 | 1.47 | .4292 | .9292 | .0708 |
| 1.03 | .3485 | .8485 | .1515 | 1.48 | .4306 | .9306 | .0694 |
| 1.04 | .3508 | .8508 | .1492 | 1.49 | .4319 | .9319 | .0681 |
| 1.05 | .3531 | .8531 | .1469 | 1.50 | .4332 | .9332 | .0668 |
| ... | ... | ... | ... | ... | ... | ... | ... |
| 1.95 | .4744 | .9744 | .0256 | 2.40 | .4918 | .9918 | .0082 |
| 1.96 | .4750 | .9750 | .0250 | 2.41 | .4920 | .9920 | .0080 |
| 1.97 | .4756 | .9756 | .0244 | 2.42 | .4922 | .9922 | .0078 |
| 1.98 | .4761 | .9761 | .0239 | 2.43 | .4925 | .9925 | .0075 |
| 1.99 | .4767 | .9767 | .0233 | 2.44 | .4927 | .9927 | .0073 |
| 2.00 | .4772 | .9772 | .0228 | 2.45 | .4929 | .9929 | .0071 |
| 2.01 | .4778 | .9778 | .0222 | 2.46 | .4931 | .9931 | .0069 |
| 2.02 | .4783 | .9783 | .0217 | 2.47 | .4932 | .9932 | .0068 |
| 2.03 | .4788 | .9788 | .0212 | 2.48 | .4934 | .9934 | .0066 |
| 2.04 | .4793 | .9793 | .0207 | 2.49 | .4936 | .9936 | .0064 |
| 2.05 | .4798 | .9798 | .0202 | 2.50 | .4938 | .9938 | .0062 |

by the Statistics Department at the University of California at Los Angeles (UCLA) and can be found at

 http://calculators.stat.ucla.edu/cdf/

It's fun to play with.

You might be excused at this point for wondering why anyone would want to table such a distribution in the first place. Just because a distribution is common (or at least commonly assumed) doesn't automatically suggest a reason for having an appendix that tells all about it. The reason is quite simple. By using Table D.10, we can readily calculate the probability that a score drawn at random from the population will have a value lying between any two specified points ($X_1$ and $X_2$). Thus by using statistical tables we can make probability statements in answer to a variety of questions. You will see examples of such questions in the rest of this chapter. They will also appear in many other chapters throughout the book.

## 6.2 The Standard Normal Distribution

A problem arises when we try to table the normal distribution, because the distribution depends on the values of the mean and the standard deviation ($\mu$ and $\sigma$) of the distribution. To do the job right, we would have to make up a different table for every possible combination of the values of $\mu$ and $\sigma$, which certainly is not practical. What we actually have in the table is what is called the **standard normal distribution**, which has a mean of 0 and a standard deviation, and variance, of 1. Such a distribution is often designated as $N(0, 1)$, where $N$ refers to the fact that it is normal, 0 is the value of $\mu$, and 1 is the value of $\sigma^2$. ($N(\mu, \sigma^2)$ is the more general expression.) Given the standard normal distribution in the appendix and a set of rules for transforming any normal distribution to standard form and vice versa, we can use Table D.10 to find the areas under any normal distribution.

| Definition | **Standard normal distribution:** A normal distribution with a mean equal to 0 and a standard deviation equal to 1; denoted as $N(0,1)$. |
| --- | --- |

Consider the distribution shown in Figure 6.6, with a mean of 50 and a standard deviation of 10 (variance of 100). It represents the distribution of *an entire population* of Total Behavior Problem scores from the Achenbach Youth Self-Report form, of which the data in Figure 6.3 and Figure 6.4 are a sample. If we knew something about the areas under the curve in Figure 6.6, we could say something about the probability of various values of Behavior Problem scores and could identify, for example, those scores that are so high that they are obtained by only 5% or 10% of the population.

The only tables of the normal distribution that are readily available are those of the *standard* normal distribution. Therefore, before we can answer questions about the probability that an individual will get a score above some particular value, we must first transform the distribution in Figure 6.6 (or at least specific points along it) to a standard normal distribution. That is, we want to be able to say that a score of $X_i$ from a normal distribution with a mean of 50 and a variance of 100—often denoted $N(50,100)$—is comparable to a score of $z_i$ from a distribution

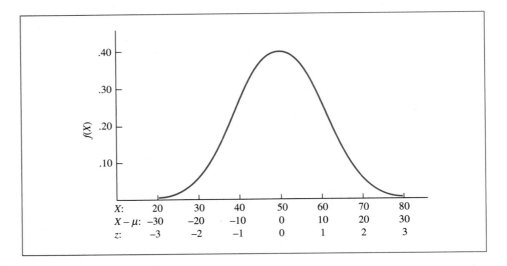

**Figure 6.6**
A normal distribution with various transformations on the abscissa

with a mean of 0 and a variance, and standard deviation, of 1—denoted $N(0,1)$. Then anything that is true of $z_i$ is also true of $X_i$, and $z$ and $X$ are comparable variables.

From Exercise 5.6 we know that subtracting a constant from each score in a set of scores reduces the mean of the set by that constant. Thus if we subtract 50 (the mean) from all the values for $X$, the new mean will be $50 - 50 = 0$. (More generally, the distribution of $(X - \mu)$ has a mean of 0.) The effect of this transformation is shown in the second set of values for the abscissa in Figure 6.6. We are halfway there, because we now have the mean down to 0, although the standard deviation (s) is still 10. We also know from Exercise 5.7 that if we divide all values of a variable by a constant (e.g., 10), we divide the standard deviation by that constant. Thus the standard deviation will now be $10/10 = 1$, which is just what we wanted.[3] We will call this transformed distribution $z$ and define it, on the basis of what we have done, as

$$z = \frac{X - \mu}{\sigma}$$

Notice that we subtract the mean before we divide by the standard deviation. For our particular case, where $\mu = 50$ and $\sigma = 10$,

$$z = \frac{X - \mu}{\sigma} = \frac{X - 50}{10}$$

---

[3]We won't change the mean when we divide by 10 because the mean was already 0 and $0/10 = 0$.

The third set of values (labeled $z$) for the abscissa in Figure 6.6 shows the effect of this transformation. Note that aside from a **linear transformation**[4] of the numerical values, the data have not been changed in any way. The distribution has the same shape and the observations continue to stand in the same relation to each other as they did before the transformation. It should not come as a great surprise that changing the unit of measurement does not change the shape of the distribution or the relative standing of observations. Whether we measure the quantity of alcohol that people consume per week in ounces or in milliliters really makes no difference in the relative standing of people. It just changes the numerical values on the abscissa. (The town drunk is still the town drunk, even if now his liquor is measured in milliliters.) It is important to realize exactly what converting $X$ to $z$ has accomplished. A score that used to be 60 is now 1. That is, a score that used to be one standard deviation (10 points) above the mean remains one standard deviation above the mean, but now is given a new value of 1. A score of 45, which was .5 standard deviation *below* the mean, now is given the value of $-.5$, and so on. In other words, a **$z$ score** represents the number of standard deviations that $X_i$ is above or below the mean—a positive $z$ score being above the mean and a negative $z$ score being below the mean.

Definition

**Linear transformation:** A transformation involving addition, subtraction, multiplication, or division of or by a constant.

**$z$ score:** Number of standard deviations above or below the mean.

The equation for $z$ is completely general. We can transform any distribution to a distribution of $z$ scores simply by applying this equation. Keep in mind, however, the point that was just made. The *shape* of the distribution is unaffected by the transformation. That means that *if the distribution was not normal before it was transformed, it will not be normal afterward.* Some people believe that they can "normalize" (in the sense of producing a normal distribution) their data by transforming them to $z$. It just won't work.

You can see what happens when you draw random samples from a population that is normal by going to

http://www.anu.edu.au/nceph/surfstat/surfstat-home/surfstat.html

and clicking on "Hotlist for Java Applets" Just click on the histogram and it will come up with another page that contains a histogram that you can modify in various ways. By repeatedly clicking "start" without clearing, you can add cases to the sample. It is useful to see how the distribution approaches a normal distribution as the number of observations increases.

---

[4]A linear transformation involves only multiplication (or division) of $X$ by a constant and/or adding or subtracting a constant to or from $X$. Such a transformation leaves the relationship among the values unaffected. In other words, it does not distort values at one part of the scale more than values at another part. Changing units from inches to centimeters is a good example of a linear transformation.

## Using the Tables of the Standard Normal Distribution

As I have mentioned, the standard normal distribution is extensively tabled. Such a table can be found in Table D.10, part of which is reproduced in Table 6.1.[5] To see how we can make use of this table, consider the normal distribution represented in Figure 6.7. This might represent the standardized distribution of the Behavior Problem scores as seen in Figure 6.6. Suppose we want to know how much of the area under the curve is above one standard deviation from the mean if the total area under the curve is taken to be 1.00. (We care about areas because they translate directly to probabilities.) We already have seen that $z$ scores represent standard deviations from the mean, and thus we know that we want to find the area above $z = 1$.

Only the positive half of the normal distribution is tabled. Because the distribution is symmetric, any information given about a positive value of $z$ applies equally to the corresponding negative value of $z$. From Table 6.1 (or Table D.10) we find the row corresponding to $z = 1.00$. Reading across that row, we can see that the area from the *mean to* $z = 1$ is .3413, the area in the *larger portion* is .8413, and the area in the *smaller portion* is .1587. (If you visualize the distribution being divided into the segment below $z = 1$ [the unshaded part of Figure 6.7] and the segment above $z = 1$ [the shaded part], the meanings of the terms *larger portion* and *smaller portion* become obvious.) Thus the answer to our original question is .1587. Because we already have equated the terms *area* and *probability* (see Chapter 3), we

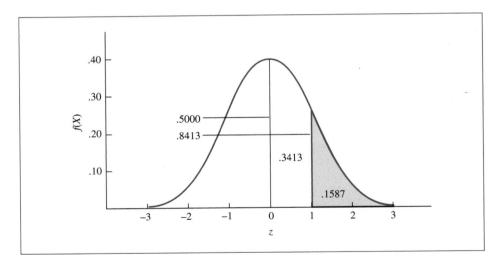

**Figure 6.7**
Illustrative areas under the normal distribution

---

[5]An online video displaying properties of the normal distribution is available at

 http://huizen.dds.nl/~berrie/normal.html

Later in this chapter we will use McClelland's *Seeing Statistics* applets to explore the normal distribution further.

now can say that if we sample a child at random from the population of children, and if Behavior Problem scores are normally distributed, then the probability that the child will score more than one standard deviation above the mean of the population (i.e., above 60) is .1587. Because the distribution is symmetric, we also know that the probability that a child will score more than one standard deviation *below* the mean of the population is also .1587.

Now suppose that we want the probability that the child will be more than one standard deviation (10 points) from the mean *in either direction*. This is a simple matter of the summation of areas. Because we know that the normal distribution is symmetric, then the area below $z = -1$ will be the same as the area above $z = +1$. This is why the table does not contain negative values of $z$—they are not needed. We already know that the areas in which we are interested are each .1587. Then the total area outside $z = \pm 1$ must be .1587 + .1587 = .3174. The converse is also true. If the area outside $z = \pm 1$ is .3174, then the area between $z = +1$ and $z = -1$ is equal to $1 - .3174 = .6826$. Thus the probability that a child will score between 40 and 60 is .6826.

To extend this procedure, consider the situation in which we want to know the probability that a score will be between 30 and 40. A little arithmetic will show that this is simply the probability of falling between 1.0 standard deviation below the mean and 2.0 standard deviations below the mean. This situation is diagrammed in Figure 6.8. (*Hint:* It is always wise to draw simple diagrams such as Figure 6.8. They eliminate many errors and make clear the area(s) you are looking for.)

From Table D.10 we know that the area from the mean to $z = -2.0$ is .4772 and from the mean to $z = -1.0$ is .3413. The difference in these two areas must represent the area between $z = -2.0$ and $z = -1.0$. This area is $.4772 - .3413 = .1359$. Thus the probability that Behavior Problem scores drawn at random from a normally distributed population will be between 30 and 40 is .1359.

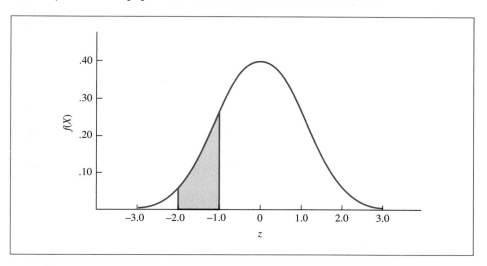

**Figure 6.8**
Areas between 1.0 and 2.0 standard deviations below the mean

## 6.3 Setting Probable Limits on an Observation

For a final example consider the situation in which we want to identify limits within which we have some specified degree of confidence that a child sampled at random will fall. In other words, we want to make a statement of the form, "If I draw a child at random from this population, 95% of the time her score will lie between _____ and _____." From Figure 6.9 you can see the limits we want—the limits that include 95% of the scores in the population.

If we are looking for the limits within which 95% of the scores fall, we also are looking for the limits beyond which the remaining 5% of the scores fall. To rule out this remaining 5%, we want to find that value of $z$ that cuts off 2.5% at each end, or "tail," of the distribution. (We do not need to use symmetric limits, but we typically do because they usually make the most sense and produce the shortest interval.) From Table D.10 we see that these values are $z \pm 1.96$. Thus we can say that 95% of the time a child's score sampled at random will fall between 1.96 standard deviations above the mean and 1.96 standard deviations below the mean.

Because we generally want to express our answers in terms of raw Behavior Problem scores, rather than $z$ scores, we must do a little more work. To obtain the raw score limits, we simply work the formula for $z$ backward, solving for X instead of $z$. Thus if we want to state the limits within which 95% of the population falls, we want to find those scores that are 1.96 standard deviations above or below the mean of the population. This can be written as

$$z = \frac{X - \mu}{\sigma}$$

$$\pm 1.96 = \frac{X - \mu}{\sigma}$$

$$X - \mu = \pm 1.96\sigma$$

$$X = \mu \pm 1.96\sigma$$

where the values of X corresponding to $(\mu + 1.96\sigma)$ and $(\mu - 1.96\sigma)$ represent the limits we seek. For our example the limits will be

$$\text{Limits} = 50 \pm (1.96)(10) = 50 \pm 19.6 = 30.4 \text{ and } 69.6$$

So the probability is .95 that a child's score (X) chosen at random would be between 30.4 and 69.6. We may not be interested in low scores because they don't represent behavior problems. But anyone with a score of 69.6 or higher is a problem to someone. Only 2.5% of children score that high.

What we have just discussed is closely related to, but not quite the same as, what we will later consider under the heading of confidence limits. The major difference is that here we knew the population mean and were trying to estimate where a single observation (X) would fall. When we discuss confidence limits, we will have a sample mean (or some other statistic) and will want to set limits using a procedure that has a .95 probability of bracketing the population mean (or some

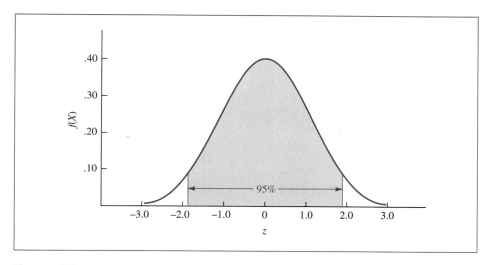

**Figure 6.9**
Values of z that enclose 95% of the behavior problem scores

other relevant parameter). You do not need to know anything at all about confidence limits at this point. I simply mention the issue to forestall any confusion in the future.

## 6.4 Measures Related to z

We already have seen that the z formula given earlier can be used to convert a distribution with any mean and variance to a distribution with a mean of 0 and a standard deviation (and variance) of 1. We frequently refer to such transformed scores as **standard scores**. Every day people use other transformational scoring systems with particular properties without realizing what they are.

Definition | **Standard scores:** Scores with a predetermined mean and standard deviation.
**Percentile:** The point below which a specified percentage of the observations fall.

A good example of such a scoring system is the common IQ. Raw scores from an IQ test are routinely transformed to a distribution with a mean of 100 and a standard deviation of 15 (or 16 in the case of the Binet). Knowing this, you can readily convert an individual's IQ (e.g., 120) to his or her position in terms of standard deviations above or below the mean (i.e., you can calculate the z score). Because IQ scores are more or less normally distributed, you can then convert z into a percentage measure by use of Table D.10. (In this example, a score of 120 would be 1.33 standard deviations above the mean, and would have approximately 91% of the scores below it. This is known as the 91st **percentile**.)

Another common example is a nationally administered examination such as the SAT. The raw scores are transformed by the producer of the test and reported as coming from a distribution with a mean of 500 and a standard deviation of 100 (at least when the tests were first developed—the mean and standard deviation are no longer exactly those values). Such a scoring system is easy to devise. We start by converting raw scores to $z$ scores (on the basis of the raw score mean and standard deviation). We then convert the $z$ scores to the particular scoring system we have in mind. Thus

New score = New S.D.$(z)$ + New mean

where $z$ represents the $z$ score corresponding to the individual's raw score. For the SAT,

New score = $100(z)$ + 500

Scoring systems such as the one used on Achenbach's Youth Self-Report checklist, which have a mean set at 50 and a standard deviation set at 10, are called **T scores** (the $T$ is always capitalized). These tests are useful in psychological measurement because they have a common frame of reference. For example, people become used to seeing a cutoff score of 63 as identifying the highest 10% of the subjects. (The true cutoff would be 62.8, but the test scores come as integers.)

---

Definition | **T scores:**  A set of scores with a mean of 50 and a standard deviation of 10.

---

## 6.5 Seeing Statistics

When you open the applet named Normal Distribution from

  www.uvm.edu/~dhowell/fundamentals/SeeingStatisticsApplets/Applets.html

and click on the applet for this chapter, you will see a display that looks like the display in Figure 6.10.

This applet will allow you to explore the normal distribution by changing values of the mean, the standard deviation, the observation, or $z$ itself, and examining the areas under the curve. When you change any value, you must press the Enter (or Return) key to have that value take effect.

On the left of the display are the definitions of the way the different tails of the distribution can be displayed. Make selections from the box that is currently labeled "Two-Tailed" to illustrate these various choices.

Next change the entry in the box labeled "prob:" to .01. Notice that the entry in the box for "$z$" changes accordingly, and is the two-tailed critical value for $z$ to cut off the extreme 1% of the distribution.

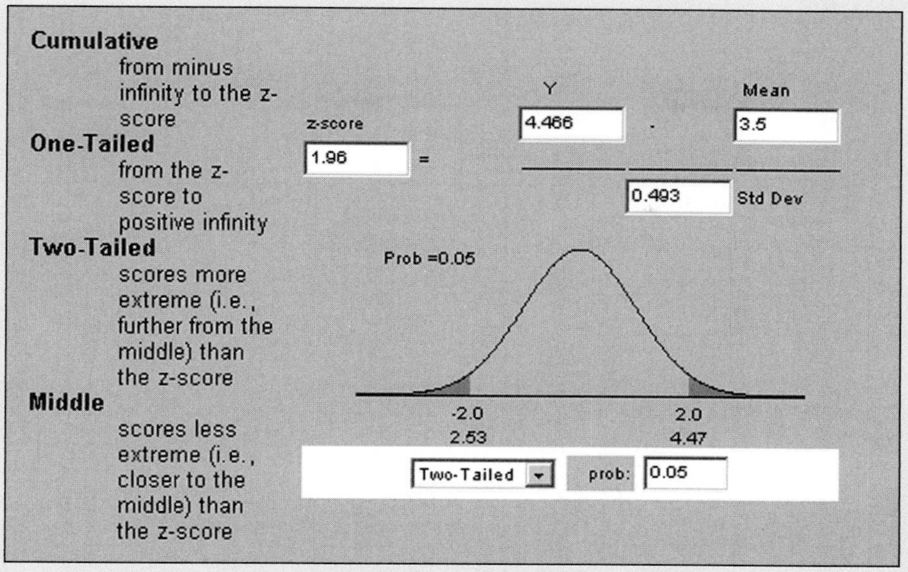

**Figure 6.10**
An applet illustrating various aspects of the normal distribution and $z$ scores

In Exercise 6.14 I give an example of a year in which the mean Graduate Record Exam score was 489 and the standard deviation was 126. Use this display to calculate the percentage of students who would be expected to have a score of 500 or higher. (You simply enter the appropriate numbers in the boxes and press the Return key after each entry.) What about the percentage expected to score over 700? (Be sure that you select the proper tail of the distribution in computing your percentages.)

## 6.6 Summary

In this chapter we examined the normal distribution. I discussed how to use the tables of the standard normal distribution to obtain areas under any normal distribution, and we saw that areas are directly related to probabilities. We also examined how to use the normal distribution to calculate percentages.

Some important terms in this chapter are

| | |
|---|---|
| Normal distribution, *103* | Ordinate, *108* |
| Abscissa, *108* | Density, *108* |

| | |
|---|---|
| Standard normal distribution, *111* | Standard scores, *117* |
| Linear transformation, *113* | Percentile, *117* |
| z score, *113* | T scores, *118* |

## 6.7 Exercises

**6.1**   Assuming that the following data represent a population of X values with $\mu = 4$ and $\sigma = 1.58$:

$$X = 1 \quad 2 \quad 2 \quad 3 \quad 3 \quad 3 \quad 4 \quad 4 \quad 4 \quad 4 \quad 5 \quad 5 \quad 5 \quad 6 \quad 6 \quad 7$$

(a)  Plot the distribution as given.
(b)  Convert the distribution in (a) to a distribution of $X - \mu$.
(c)  Go the next step and convert the distribution in (b) to a distribution of z.

**6.2**   Using the distribution in Exercise 6.1, calculate z scores for X = 2.5, 6.2, and 9. Interpret these results.

**6.3**   Most of you have had experience with exam scores that were rescaled so that the instructor could "grade on a curve." Assume that a large Psychology 1 class has just taken an exam with 300 four-choice multiple-choice questions. (That's the kind of Psych 1 exam I took when I was but a lad, and I had to get there over the snow banks.) Assume that the distribution of grades is normal with a mean of 195 and a standard deviation of 30.
(a)  What percentage of the counts will lie between 165 and 225?
(b)  What percentage of the counts will lie below 195?
(c)  What percentage of the counts will lie below 225?

**6.4**   Using the example from Exercise 6.3:
(a)  What two values of X (the count) would encompass the middle 50% of the results?
(b)  75% of the counts would be less than _____.
(c)  95% of the counts would be between _____ and _____.

**6.5**   Remember the earlier study by Katz et al. that had students answer SAT-type questions without first reading the passage? Suppose that we gave out the answer sheets for our Psychology 1 exam mentioned in Exercise 6.3 but forgot to hand out the questions. If students just guessed at random, they would be expected to have a mean of 75 and a standard deviation of 7.5. The exam was taken by 100 students.
(a)  Among those who guessed randomly, what would be the cutoff score for the top 10 students?
(b)  What would be the cutoff score for the top 25% of the students?
(c)  We would expect only 5% of the students to score below _____.
(d)  What would you think if 25% of the students got more than 225 questions correct?

**6.6**   Students taking a multiple-choice exam rarely guess randomly. They usually can rule out some answers as preposterous and identify others as good candidates. Moreover, even students who have never taken Psychology 1 would probably know who Pavlov was, or what

we mean by sibling rivalry. Use the Psychology 1 example in Exercise 6.5 and assume that each question had four alternative choices.
(a) What would you conclude if the student got a score of 70?
(b) How high a score would the student have to get so that you were 95% confident that the student wasn't just guessing at random?

**6.7** A set of reading scores for fourth-grade children has a mean of 25 and a standard deviation of 5. A set of scores for ninth-grade children has a mean of 30 and a standard deviation of 10. Assume that the distributions are normal.
(a) Draw a rough sketch of these data, putting both groups in the same figure.
(b) What percentage of fourth graders score better than the average ninth grader?
(c) What percentage of the ninth graders score worse than the average fourth grader? (We will come back to the idea behind these calculations when we study power in Chapter 15.)

**6.8** Under what conditions would the answers to (b) and (c) of Exercise 6.7 be equal?

**6.9** Many diagnostic tests are indicative of problems only if a child scores in the upper 10 percent of those taking the test (at or above the 90th percentile). Many of these tests are scaled to produce $T$ scores, with a mean of 50 and a standard deviation of 10. What would be the diagnostically meaningful cutoff?

**6.10** A dean must distribute salary raises to her faculty for next year. She has decided that the mean raise is to be $2,000, the standard deviation of raises is to be $400, and the distribution is to be normal. She will attempt to distribute these raises on the basis of merit, meaning that people whose performance is better get better raises.
(a) The most productive 10% of the faculty will have a raise equal to or greater than $_____.
(b) The 5% of the faculty who have done nothing useful in years will receive no more than $_____ each.

**6.11** We have sent out everyone in a large introductory course to check whether people use seat belts. Each student has been told to look at 100 cars and count the number of people wearing seat belts. The number found by any given student is considered that student's score. The mean score for the class is 44, with a standard deviation of 7.
(a) Diagram this distribution, assuming that the counts are normally distributed.
(b) A student who has done very little work all year has reported finding 62 seat belt users out of 100. Do we have reason to suspect that the student just made up a number rather than actually counting?

**6.12** Several years ago a friend of mine in the communication sciences department produced a diagnostic test of language problems that is still widely used. A score on her scale is obtained simply by counting the number of language constructions (e.g., plural, negative, passive) that the child produces correctly in response to specific prompts from the person administering the test. The test has a mean of 48 and a standard deviation of 7. Parents have trouble understanding the meaning of a score on this scale, and my friend wanted to convert the scores to a mean of 80 and a standard deviation of 10 (to make them more like the kinds of grades parents are used to). How could she have gone about her task?

**6.13** Unfortunately the whole world is not built on the principle of a normal distribution. In the preceding example the real distribution is badly skewed because most children do not have language problems and therefore produce all constructions correctly.
(a) Diagram how this distribution might look.
(b) How would you go about finding the cutoff for the bottom 10% if the distribution is not normal?

**6.14** A number of years ago the mean and the standard deviation on the Graduate Record Exam (GRE) for all people taking the exam were 489 and 126, respectively. What percentage of students would you expect to have a score of 600 or less? (This is called the percentile rank of 600.)

**6.15** In Exercise 6.14 what score would be equal to or greater than 75% of the scores on the exam? (This score is called the 75th percentile.)

**6.16** For all seniors and nonenrolled college graduates taking the GRE referred to in Exercise 6.14, the mean and the standard deviation were 507 and 118, respectively. How does this change the answers to Exercises 6.14 and 6.15?

**6.17** What does the answer to Exercise 6.15 suggest about the importance of reference groups?

**6.18** The data available at

www.uvm.edu/~dhowell/fundamentals/DataFiles/Add.dat

are actual data on students from local schools. What is the 75th percentile for GPA in these data? (This is the point below which 75% of the observations are expected to fall.)

**6.19** Assuming that the Behavior Problem scores discussed in this chapter come from a population with a mean of 50 and a standard deviation of 10, what would be a diagnostically meaningful cutoff if you wanted to identify those children who score in the highest 2% of the population? (Diagnostic cutoffs like this are a major reason for converting raw scores to $T$ scores on such tests.)

**6.20** In Section 6.4 I said that $T$ scores are designed to have a mean of 50 and a standard deviation of 10 and that the Achenbach Youth Self-Report measure produces $T$ scores. The data in Figure 6.3 do not have a mean and standard deviation of exactly 50 and 10. Why do you suppose that this is so?

**6.21** On December 13, 2001, the Associated Press reported a story entitled "Study: American kids getting fatter at disturbing rate."

> By 1998, nearly 22 percent of black children ages 4 to 12 were overweight, as were 22 percent of Hispanic youngsters and 12 percent of whites. . . . In 1986, the same survey showed that about 8 percent of black children, 10 percent of Hispanic youngsters and 8 percent of whites were significantly overweight. . . . Overweight was defined as having a body-mass index higher than 95 percent of youngsters of the same age and sex, based on growth charts from the 1960s to 1980s. . . . Disturbing trends also were seen in the number of children who had a body-mass index higher than 85 percent of their peers. In 1986, about 20 percent of blacks, Hispanics and whites alike were in that category. By 1998, those figures had risen to about 38 percent of blacks and Hispanics alike and nearly 29 percent of whites.

This report drew a lot of attention from a statistics list server that is populated by statisticians. Why do you think that a group of professional statisticians would be so excited and annoyed by what they read here? Do these data seem reasonable?

**6.22** You can use SPSS to create normally distributed variables (as well as variables having a number of other shapes). Start SPSS, and under **Data/Go To Case**, tell it to go to case 1,000 and then enter any value in that cell. (That just sets the size of the data set to 1,000.) Then click on **Transform/Compute** and create a variable named X with the formula rv.normal(15, 3). That will sample from a normally distributed population with mean = 15 and standard deviation = 3. Then plot the histogram, instructing the software to superimpose a normal distribution. Experiment with other means and standard deviations. Then use the **Functions** menu on the **Transform/Compute** dialog box to try other distributions.

**6.23**  Suppose that we are collecting a large set of data on emotional reactivity in adults. Assume that for most adults emotional reactivity is normally distributed with a mean of 100 and a standard deviation of 10. But for people diagnosed with bipolar disorder their scores are all over the place. Some are temporarily depressed and they have low reactivity scores. Others are temporarily in a manic phase and their scores are quite high. As a group they still have a mean of 100, but they have a standard deviation of 30. Assume that 10% of the population is bipolar. (The actual percentage is closer to 1%, but 10% will lead to a better example.) This is a case of what is called a mixed normal distribution. Sketch what you think that this distribution might look like. What would happen if we made the means very different?

# 7

# Basic Concepts of Probability

## QUESTIONS

- I hate probability—why do I have to read this chapter?

- OK, what is the minimum I have to know?

- You mean I have to learn different things depending on the kinds of variables I have?

- What do we mean by a probability distribution?

In Chapter 6 we began to make use of the concept of probability. For example, we saw that about 68% of children have Behavior Problem scores between 40 and 60, and we thus concluded that if we choose a child at random, the probability that he or she would score between 40 and 60 is .68. When we begin concentrating on inferential statistics in Chapter 8, we will rely heavily on statements of probability. There we will be making statements of the form, "If this hypothesis were true, the probability is only .015 that we would have obtained a result as extreme as the one we actually obtained." If we are to rely on statements of probability, it is important to understand what we mean by probability and to understand a few basic rules for computing and manipulating probabilities. That is the purpose of this chapter.

My colleagues will probably chastise me for saying it, but probability is not one of those topics that students rank high in their list of favorite things to study.

Probability is scary to many, and it can be confusing to even more. Add to this the fact that most instructors, myself included, have a weak background in probability, and you have a bad situation. However, just because people are anxious about a topic doesn't constitute grounds for avoiding all mention of it. There are some things you just have to know, whether you want to or not. To avoid slurping your soup in a restaurant is one, and probability is another. But soup can be good even if eaten properly, and probability can be manageable, even if you hated it in high school.

The material covered in this chapter has been selected for two reasons. First, it is directly applicable to an understanding of the material presented in the remainder of the book. Second, it is intended to allow you to make simple calculations of probabilities that are likely to be useful to you. Material that does not satisfy either of these qualifications has been deliberately omitted. For example, we will not consider such things as the probability of drawing the queen of hearts, given that 14 cards, including four hearts, have already been drawn. Nor will we consider the probability that your desk light will burn out in the next 25 hours of use, given that it has already lasted 250 hours. Both of those topics may be important in some situations, but you can go miles in statistics and have a good understanding of the methods of the behavioral sciences without having the slightest idea about either of those probability questions.

## 7.1 Probability

The concept of probability can be viewed in several different ways. There is not even general agreement as to what we mean by the word *probability*. The oldest and most common definition of a probability is what is called the **analytic view**. Let's take an example that I have used through many editions of two books. (It once was a true example, but regrettably I have improved my health habits over the years.[1]) I have a bag of caramels hidden in the drawer of my desk. The bag contains 85 of the light caramels, which I like, and 15 of the dark ones, which I save for candy-grubbing colleagues. Being hungry, I reach into the bag and grab a caramel at random. What is the probability that I will pull out a light-colored caramel? Most of you could answer this without knowing anything more about probability. Because 85 of the 100 caramels are light, and because I am sampling at random, the

---

[1]For those of you who would like to try examples similar to this one, but don't have bags of caramels handy, I strongly recommend M&Ms™. They are readily available, and we actually know quite a bit about them. They are such a popular example for statistics courses, that the Mars company even set up their own Web page. You can find the distribution of the various colors, for the various varieties, from links given at

 http://www.m-ms.com/us/about/products/milkchocolate/

And when you're done, you can eat them.

probability ($p$) of drawing a light caramel is 85/100 = .85. This example illustrates one definition of probability:

> **Analytic view of probability:** If an event can occur in $A$ ways and can fail to occur in $B$ ways, and if all possible ways are equally likely (e.g., each caramel has an equal chance of being drawn), then the probability of its occurrence is $A/(A + B)$, and the probability of its failing to occur is $B/(A + B)$.

Definition   **Analytic view:** Definition of probability in terms of an analysis of possible outcomes.

**Relative frequency view:** Definition of probability in terms of past performance.

**Sample with replacement:** Sampling in which the item drawn on trial $N$ is replaced before the next draw.

**Subjective probability:** Definition of probability in terms of personal subjective belief in the likelihood of an outcome.

That is a rather pompous and formal way of saying something rather simple. There are 85 ways to draw a light caramel, because there are 85 light caramels. And there are 15 ways *not* to draw a light caramel, because 15 of the caramels are not light. Then the probability of drawing a light caramel is $85/(85 + 15) = .85$. Notice that all ways of drawing the caramels have to be equally likely. If the dark ones oozed out of the wrapper and stuck to the bottom of the bag, the system would fail and you would be disproportionately likely to get a light caramel. This is called the analytic view of probability because it is based on an analysis of the system.

An alternative view of probability is the **relative frequency view**. Suppose that we keep drawing caramels from the bag, noting the color on each draw. In conducting this sampling study we **sample with replacement**, meaning that each caramel is replaced before the next one is drawn. If we made a very large number of draws, we would find that (approximately) 85% of the draws would result in a light caramel. Thus we might define probability as the limit[2] of the relative frequency of occurrence of the desired event that we approach as the number of draws increases. Notice that there is no particular analysis of the problem here—we base our probability on the relative frequency with which light caramels appear. We don't have to know how many caramels are in the bag or how many are light. We base our estimate solely on the results of repeated samples.

Yet a third concept of probability is advocated by a number of theorists. That is the concept of **subjective probability**. By this definition probability represents an individual's subjective belief in the likelihood of the occurrence of an event. For

---

[2]The word *limit* refers to the fact that as we sample more and more caramels, the proportion of light caramels will get closer and closer to some value. After 100 draws, the proportion might be .83; after 1000 draws it might be .852; after 10,000 draws it might be .8496, and so on. Notice that the answer is coming closer and closer to $p = .8500000. . .$ The value that is being approached is called the limit.

example, the statement, "I'm pretty sure that tomorrow will be a good day," is a subjective statement of degree of belief, which probably has very little to do with the long-range relative frequency of the occurrence of good days, and in fact may have no mathematical basis whatsoever. This is not to say that such a view of probability has no legitimate claim for our attention. Subjective probabilities play an extremely important role in human decision making and govern all aspects of our behavior. Just think of the number of decisions you make based on subjective beliefs in the likelihood of certain outcomes. You order pasta for dinner because it is probably better than the mystery meat special; you plan to go skiing tomorrow because the weather forecaster says that there is an 80% chance of snow overnight; you bet your money on a horse because you think that the odds of its winning are better than the 6:1 odds the bookies are offering. Statistical decisions as we will make them here generally will be stated with more mathematical approaches, although even so the *interpretation* of those probabilities has a strong subjective component.

Although the particular definition that you or I prefer may be important to each of us, any of the definitions will lead to essentially the same result in terms of hypothesis testing, the discussion of which will begin in Chapter 8 and run through the rest of the book. (It should be said that those who favor subjective probabilities often disagree with the general hypothesis-testing orientation.) In actual fact most people use the different approaches interchangeably. When we say that the probability of losing at Russian roulette is 1/6, we are referring to the fact that one of the gun's six cylinders has a bullet in it. When we buy a particular car because *Consumer Reports* said it has a good repair record, we are responding to the fact that a high proportion of these cars have been relatively trouble-free. When we say that the probability of the Boston Red Sox winning the World Series is high, we are stating our subjective belief in the likelihood of that event (in the face of years of disappointments and one year of success). But when we reject some hypothesis because there is a very low probability that the actual data would have been obtained if the hypothesis had been true, it may not be important which view of probability we hold.

## 7.2 Basic Terminology and Rules

Here's where you have to start learning some probability stuff. There isn't much, and it isn't hard or painful, but you have to learn it.

---

Definition | **Event:** The outcome of a trial.

---

The basic bit of data for a probability theorist is called an **event**. The word *event* is a term that statisticians use to cover just about anything. An event can be the occurrence of a king when we deal from a deck of cards, a score of 36 on a scale of likeability, a classification of "female" for the next person appointed to the Supreme

Court, or the mean of a sample. Whenever you speak of the probability of something, the "something" is called an event. When we are dealing with a process as simple as flipping a coin, the event is the outcome of that flip—either heads or tails. When we draw caramels out of a bag, the possible events are light and dark. When we speak of a grade in a course, the possible events are the letters A, B, C, D, and F.

Two events are said to be **independent events** when the occurrence or nonoccurrence of one has no effect on the occurrence or nonoccurrence of the other. The voting behaviors of two randomly chosen citizens normally would be assumed to be independent, especially with a secret ballot, because how one person votes could not be expected to influence how the other will vote. However, the voting behaviors of two members of the same family probably would not be independent events, because those people share many of the same beliefs and attitudes. The events would probably not be independent even if each of those two people were careful not to let the other see their ballot.

Definition

---

**Independent events:** Events are independent when the occurrence of one has no effect on the probability of the occurrence of the other.

**Mutually exclusive:** Two events are mutually exclusive when the occurrence of one precludes the occurrence of the other.

**Exhaustive:** A set of events that represents all possible outcomes.

---

Two events are said to be **mutually exclusive** if the occurrence of one event precludes the occurrence of the other. For example, the standard college classes (under the U.S. university system) of freshman, sophomore, junior, and senior are mutually exclusive because one person cannot be a member of more than one class. A set of events is said to be **exhaustive** if it includes all possible outcomes. Thus the four college classes in the previous example are exhaustive with respect to full-time undergraduates, who have to fall into one or another of those categories—if only to please the registrar's office. At the same time, they are not exhaustive with respect to total university enrollments, which include graduate students, medical students, nonmatriculated students, hangers-on, and so forth.

As you already know—or could deduce from our definitions of probability—probabilities range between .00 and 1.00. If some event has a probability of 1.00, then it *must* occur. (Very few things have a probability of 1.00, including the probability that I will be able to keep typing until I reach the end of this paragraph.) If some event has a probability of .00, it is certain *not* to occur. The closer the probability comes to either extreme, the more likely or unlikely is the occurrence of the event.

## Basic Laws of Probability

Two important theorems are central to any discussion of probability. (If my use of the word *theorems* makes you nervous, substitute the word *rules*.) They are often referred to as the additive and multiplicative rules.

THE ADDITIVE RULE   To illustrate the additive rule, we will complicate the caramel example by eating many of the light candies and replacing them with wooden cubes. We now have 30 light caramels, 15 dark caramels, and 55 rather tasteless wooden cubes. Given these frequencies, we know from the analytic definition of probability that $p$(light) = 30/100 = .30, $p$(dark) = 15/100 = .15, and $p$(wooden) = 55/100 = .55. But what is the probability that I will draw a caramel, either light or dark, instead of a piece of wood? Here we need the **additive law of probability**.

> **Additive law of probability:** Given a set of *mutually exclusive* events, the probability of the occurrence of one event *or* another is equal to the sum of their separate probabilities.

Thus $p$(light or dark) = $p$(light) + $p$(dark) = .30 + .15 = .45. Notice that we have imposed the restriction that the events must be mutually exclusive, meaning that the occurrence of one event precludes the occurrence of the other. If a caramel is light, it can't be dark. This requirement is important. About one-quarter of the students in a given university are sophomores, and about one-half of the students are female. But the probability that a person chosen at random will be a sophomore *or* will be female is obviously not .25 + .50 = .75. Here the two events are *not* mutually exclusive. However, the probability that a female student will be a sophomore or a junior is .25 + .25 = .50. Here the classes are mutually exclusive because you can't be both a sophomore and a junior.

Definition  **Additive law of probability:** The rule giving the probability of the occurrence of one or more mutually exclusive events.

**Multiplicative law of probability:** The rule giving the probability of the joint occurrence of independent events.

THE MULTIPLICATIVE RULE   Let's continue with the bag of caramels in which $p$(light) = .30, $p$(dark) = .15, and $p$(wooden) = .55. Suppose I draw two caramels, replacing the first before drawing the second. What is the probability that I will draw a light caramel on the first trial *and* a light one on the second? Here we need to invoke the **multiplicative law of probability**.

> **Multiplicative law of probability:** The probability of the joint occurrence of two or more independent events is the product of their individual probabilities.

Thus $p$(light, light) = $p$(light) $\times$ $p$(light) = .30 $\times$ .30 = .09. Similarly, the probability of a light caramel followed by a dark one is $p$(light, dark) = $p$(light) $\times$ $p$(dark) = .30 $\times$ .15 = .045. Notice that we have restricted ourselves to independent events, meaning the occurrence of one event has no effect on the occurrence or nonoccurrence of the other. Because gender and college class are independent, it would be correct to state that $p$(female, sophomore) $= .50 \times .25 = .125$. But it would be wrong to state that $p$(senior and over 21) $= .25 \times .20 = .05$, because there is a strong relationship between a student's age and his or her year in college.

In Chapter 19 we will use the multiplicative law to answer questions about the independence of two variables. An example from that chapter will help illustrate a specific use of this law. In a study to be discussed in that chapter, Geller, Witmer, and Orebaugh (1976) wanted to test the hypothesis that what someone did with a supermarket flier depended on whether the flier contained a request not to litter. Geller et al. distributed fliers to people entering the store. Approximately half of these fliers included the request not to litter, and half did not. At the end of the day they searched the store to find where the fliers had been left. Testing their hypothesis involves, in part, calculating the probability that a flier would contain a message about littering *and* would be found in a trash can. We need to calculate what this probability would be if the two events (contains message about littering and flier in trash) are independent. They would be independent if the recipient didn't even look at the message or looked at it but totally ignored it. *If we assume that these two events are independent, the multiplicative law tells us that $p$(message, trash) $= p$(message) $\times p$(trash). In their study 49% of the fliers contained a message, so the probability that a flier chosen at random would contain the message is .49. Similarly, 6.8% of the fliers were later found in the trash, giving $p$(trash) $= .068$. Therefore, if the two events are independent, $p$(message, trash) $= .49 \times .068 = .033$, and we would expect 3.3% of the fliers with the message would be in the trash. (In fact, 4.5% of the fliers with messages were found in the trash, which is a bit higher than we would expect if the ultimate disposal of the flier were independent of the message. Assuming that this small difference between 3.3% and 4.5% is reliable, what does this suggest to you about the effectiveness of the message?)

Finally, we can take a simple example that illustrates both the additive and the multiplicative laws. What is the probability that over two trials (sampling with replacement) I will draw one light caramel and one dark one, *ignoring the order in which they are drawn*? First, we use the multiplicative rule to calculate

$$p(\text{light, dark}) = .30 \times .15 = .045$$
$$p(\text{dark, light}) = .15 \times .30 = .045$$

Because these two outcomes satisfy our requirement (and because they are the only ones that do), we now need to know the probability that one *or the other* of these outcomes will occur. Here we apply the additive rule:

$$p(\text{light, dark}) + p(\text{dark, light}) = .045 + .045 = .09$$

Thus the probability of obtaining one caramel of each color over two draws is .09—that is, it will occur a little less than one-tenth of the time.

Students sometimes get confused over the additive and multiplicative laws because they almost sound the same when you read them quickly. One useful idea is to realize the difference between the situations in which the rules apply. In those situations where you use the additive rule, you know that you are worrying about *one* outcome. A caramel that you draw may be dark or light, but there is going to be only one of them. In the multiplicative case, we are speaking about at least *two* outcomes (e.g., the probability that we will get one dark caramel *and* one light one). For single independent outcomes we add probabilities; for multiple independent outcomes we multiply them.

## Joint and Conditional Probabilities

Two types of probabilities play an important role in discussions of probability: joint probabilities and conditional probabilities.

A **joint probability** is defined simply as the probability of the co-occurrence of two or more events. For example, in Geller's study of supermarket fliers, the probability that a flier would *both* contain a message about littering *and* be found in the trash is a joint probability, as is the probability that a flier would both contain a message about littering and be found stuffed down behind the Raisin Bran. Given two events, their joint probability is denoted as $p(A, B)$, just as we have used $p(\text{light, dark})$ or $p(\text{message, trash})$. *If those two events are independent,* then the probability of their joint occurrence can be found by using the multiplicative law, as we have just seen. If they are *not* independent, the probability of their joint occurrence is more complicated to compute. We won't compute that probability here.

---

**Definition**

**Joint probability:** The probability of the co-occurrence of two or more events.

**Conditional probability:** The probability that one event will occur *given* the occurrence of some other event.

---

A **conditional probability** is the probability that one event will occur, *given* that some other event has occurred. The probability that a person will contract AIDS, given that he or she is an intravenous drug user, is a conditional probability. The probability that an advertising flier will be thrown into the trash, given that it contains a message about littering, is another example. A third example is a phrase that occurs repeatedly throughout this book: "If the null hypothesis is true, the probability of obtaining a result such as this is. . . ." Here I have substituted the word *if* for *given*, but the meaning is the same. (I'll define the phrase *null hypothesis* in Chapter 8.)

With two events, A and B, the conditional probability of A, given B, is denoted by use of a vertical bar, as $p(A \mid B)$, for example, $p(\text{AIDS} \mid \text{drug user})$ or $p(\text{trash} \mid \text{message})$.

## 7.3 The Application of Probability to Controversial Issues

A number of studies have looked at the imposition of the death sentence in the U.S. as a function of the race of the defendant and the victim. (Data on the role of the victim will be presented in the exercises at the end of this chapter.) A report on the influence of the race of the defendant was compiled by Dieter (1998) and can be found at

 http://www.deathpenaltyinfo.org/article.php?scid=45&did=539

To oversimplify the issue, but not to distort the findings, we can look at the breakdown of death sentence by race of defendant. The data are shown in Table 7.1.

The row percentages are computed by dividing the frequency of "Yes" or "No" by the number of cases in that row. The column percentages are calculated by dividing Black or Nonblack by the column totals. The cell percentages are simply the number of observations in that cell divided by the total sample size (667).

The information in Table 7.1 allows us to calculate the simple, joint, and conditional probabilities. The simple probability that a defendant will be given the death penalty is 114/667 = .171, the proportion of the total cases that receive that sentence. The probability that a defendant is black is 520/667 = .780. The joint probability that a person is black and is sentenced to death is .142, the proportion of the total observations that fell in the Black/Yes cell.

Most interesting in this table are the conditional probabilities. The probability that a defendant will be sentenced to death *given* that they are black is 95/520 = .183. The conditional probability that a defendant will be

**Table 7.1**
The Relationship Between Death Sentence and Race of the Defendant

| Defendant's Race | Death Sentence | | Total |
| --- | --- | --- | --- |
| | Yes | No | |
| Black | 95 | 425 | 520 |
| Row % | 18.3% | 76.8% | 78.0% |
| Col. % | 36.8% | 81.7% | |
| Cell % | 14.2% | 63.7% | |
| Nonblack | 19 | 128 | 147 |
| Row % | 12.9% | 23.1% | 22.0% |
| Col. % | 16.7% | 87.1% | |
| Cell % | 2.8% | 19.2% | |
| Total | 114 | 553 | 667 |
| Col. % | 17.1% | 82.9% | |

sentenced to death given that they are nonblack is 19/147 = .129. That is a considerable disparity between the sentencing of black and nonblack defendants. The death sentence rate for black defendants is nearly 50% higher than for nonblacks.

You might ask why I didn't calculate the joint probability of being black and receiving a death sentence here by multiplying the appropriate simple probabilities, as I did in the previous section. The reason is that the use of the multiplicative law requires that Race and Penalty be independent. In this example they are not, because the data show that the death penalties are disproportionately assigned to black defendants. (If I had assumed independence, I would have predicted the joint probability to be .780 × .171 = .133, which is less than the actual obtained joint probability of .142.)

To take another example, the probability that you have been drinking alcoholic beverages *and* that you have an accident is a joint probability. This probability is not very high, because relatively few people are drinking at any one time and relatively few people have accidents. However, the probability that you have an accident *given* that you have been drinking, and the probability that you have been drinking *given* that you have an accident, are both much higher. At night the conditional probability of $p$(drinking | accident) exceeds .50, since over half of all automobile accidents at night in the United States involve alcohol. (If you have ever wondered why they have all those "If you drink, don't drive" signs out there, now you know. Who says probability theory can't come up with something worth thinking about?) I don't know the conditional probability of $p$(accident | drinking), but I do know that it is much higher than the **unconditional probability** of an accident, that is, $p$(accident).

---

**Definition**

**Unconditional probability:** The probability of one event *ignoring* the occurrence or nonoccurrence of some other event.

**Risk:** The number of occurrences on one event divided by the total number of occurrences of events—a probability.

**Risk ratio:** The ratio of two risks.

---

## Odds and Risk

This is a good place to introduce a few terms that you need to know and be able to work with. Even if you did not need them for a statistics course, you would need to know them in everyday life. Unfortunately they are easily confused and often used incorrectly.

I will start with **risk**, which is simply the probability that something will happen. For a black defendant in the previous example, the risk of being sentenced to death was 95/520 = .183. For a nonblack defendant the risk of a death sentence was 19/147 = .129, which we also saw before. But we can go one step further and compute what is called the **risk ratio**, which is just the ratio of the two risks. In this case that is .183/.129 = 1.42. This tells us that the risk of being sentenced to death is 1.42 times greater for black than for nonblack participants. That's quite a difference.

Now lets move to **odds**. On the surface they look almost like risks, but here we take the number of black defendants who were sentenced to death divided by *the number who were not*. Notice that the denominator has changed from the total number of blacks to the number of blacks that did not receive a death sentence. In this case the odds are 95/425 = .224. For nonblacks the odds are 19/128 = .148. Just as we did with the risk ratio, we can create an **odds ratio**, as the ratio of the two odds. In this case the odds ratio is .224/.148 = 1.51, which is a bit higher than the risk ratio. We would interpret this to say that your odds of being sentenced to death are 1.51 times higher if you are black.

---

Definition | **Odds:** The number of occurrences of an event divided by the number of nonoccurrences.
**Odds ratio:** The ratio of two odds.

---

You might wonder which of these is the more useful ratio and ask why we need both. One answer is that many people feel more comfortable speaking in terms of odds, and the ratio of odds, rather than risks and the ratio of risks. (I am not one of those people, but I can dimly see their reasoning.) For others, risk seems like a more reasonable statistic, because it speaks directly to the probability that a person will fall in one category or another. When it comes to the ratios, there is a very good technical reason for using odds ratios. Depending on how the study was designed, there are many situations where it is not possible to compute a risk ratio. But we can always compute an odds ratio, and when we are speaking of unlikely events (e.g., being diagnosed with tuberculosis), the odds ratio is an excellent estimate of what the risk ratio would be if we could derive it for our sample.

We are not going to return to odds, risks, and their ratios for a while, but it is important to understand the distinction. For risks we divide by the total row frequency, whereas for odds we divide by the number of observations in the other cell of that row.

## 7.4 Writing Up the Results

Throughout the remainder of this book I will insert sections on how to write up the results of a statistical analysis. The write-ups will be quite brief, but they will show the kinds of things that you need to cover. In this chapter we have not seen a full-blown experiment with tests of statistical hypotheses, but I can at least write up the results of the study on the death penalty as if I had shown that the differences were reliable. (They actually are.)

I will start by listing the things that need to go into such a report. We want to say something about what the problem is, where and how we collected the data, and how many observations were involved. Then we would want to mention the important unconditional probabilities, such as the overall probability that a person will be sentenced to death, and perhaps the probabilities for each race. The conditional probabilities, and/or odds, are also important, and then we need to create and report the risk or odds ratio. Finally we need to draw conclusions and put the study in a context of other work that has been done on the topic. To include all of this I would write

The Death Penalty Information Center issued a report edited by Dieter (1998) on the application of the death penalty as a function of race. The report examined the outcomes of cases in Philadelphia between 1983 and 1993. The fundamental purpose was to ask whether the death penalty was applied evenly for defendants of different races. The authors surveyed 667 instances when a defendant faced the possibility of the death penalty, and broke the data down by the race of the defendant and the sentence that was given.

The results revealed that in 17.1% of the cases the defendant was sentenced to death. However, sentencing was statistically related to race. When the defendant was black the risk of being sentenced to death was .183, whereas for nonblack defendants the risk was only .129. This produces a risk ratio of 1.42, indicating that blacks are approximately 40% more likely to be sentenced to death than nonblacks. This disparity held even when the data were split on the basis of the severity of the offense. There would appear to be racial bias in the assignment of death penalties.

These are data from the period 1983–1993, and it is possible that the results would be different if more current data were used. However that question deserves separate study. The results were a replication of very similar results by Radelet and Pierce (1991). Work published as recently as 2001 has come to very similar conclusions.

## 7.5 Discrete versus Continuous Variables

We have covered several terms that are used with probability, and have looked at two rules that allow us to calculate probabilities in simple, but very real and common, situations. Now we need to go a bit further and look at the variables to which these probabilities apply. It turns out that we do different things, depending on the kind of variable we have.

In Chapter 2, I made a distinction between discrete and continuous variables. As mathematicians view things, a discrete variable is one that can take on a countable number of different values, whereas a continuous variable is one that can take on an infinite number of different values. For example, the number of people participating in an experiment on interpersonal space is a discrete variable because we literally can count the number of people in the experiment, and there is no such thing as a fractional person. However, the distance between two people in a study of personal space is a continuous variable because the distance could be 2′, or 2.8′, or 2.8173754814′. Although the distinction given here is technically correct, common usage is somewhat different.

In practice when we speak of a discrete variable, we *usually* mean a variable that takes on one of a relatively small number of possible values (e.g., a five-point scale of socioeconomic status, or a three-point scale of preference [like, neutral, or dislike]). A variable that can take on one of many possible values is generally treated as a continuous variable if the values represent at least an ordinal scale. Thus we usually think of an IQ score as a continuous variable, even though we recognize that IQ scores come in whole units and we will not find someone with an IQ of 105.317.

The distinction between discrete and continuous variables is reintroduced here because the *distributions* of the two kinds of variables are treated somewhat differently in probability theory. With discrete variables we can speak of the probability of a specific outcome. With continuous variables, on the other hand, we need to speak of the probability of obtaining a value that falls within a specific *interval*.

## 7.6 Probability Distributions for Discrete Variables

An interesting example of a discrete probability distribution is seen in Figure 7.1. The data plotted in this figure come from a study by Campbell, Converse, and Rodgers (1976), in which they asked 2164 respondents to rate on a 1–5 scale the importance they attach to various aspects of their lives (1 = extremely important, 5 = not at all important). Figure 7.1 presents the distribution of responses for

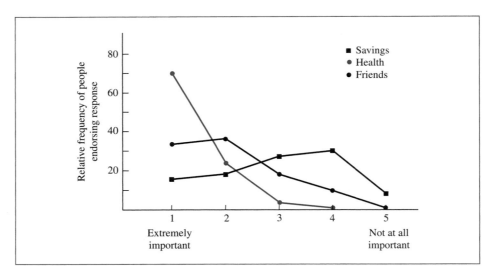

**Figure 7.1**
Distribution of importance ratings of three aspects of life

several of these aspects. The possible values of X (the rating) are presented on the abscissa, and the relative frequency (or proportion) of people choosing that response is plotted on the ordinate. From the figure you can see that the distributions of responses to questions concerning health, friends, and savings are quite different. Proportions translate directly to probabilities for the sample, and the probability that a person chosen at random will consider his or her health to be extremely important is .70. On the other hand, the probability that the same person will consider a large bank account to be extremely important is only .16. (So much for the stereotypical American Dream.) Campbell et al. collected their data in the mid-1970s. Would you expect to find similar results today? How might they differ?

## 7.7 Probability Distributions for Continuous Variables

When we move from discrete to continuous probability distributions, things become more complicated. We dealt with a continuous distribution when we considered the normal distribution in Chapter 6. You may recall that in that chapter we labeled the ordinate of the distribution "density." We also spoke in terms of intervals rather than in terms of specific outcomes. Now we need to elaborate somewhat on those points.

EXAMPLE:
When
Children First
Learn to Crawl

Figure 7.2 shows the approximate distribution of the age at which children first learn to crawl, based on data from Benson (1993). The mean is approximately 35 weeks, the standard deviation is approximately three weeks, and the distribution is slightly negatively skewed. You will notice that in this figure the ordinate is labeled "density," whereas in Figure 7.1 it was labeled "relative frequency." Density is not synonymous with probability, and it is probably best thought of as merely the height of the curve at different values of X. At the same time, the fact that the curve is higher near 35 weeks than it is near 28 weeks tells us that children are more likely to crawl at around 35 weeks than at about 6½ months. The reason for changing the label on the ordinate is that we now are dealing with a continuous distribution

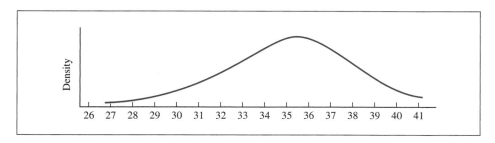

**Figure 7.2**
Age at which child first crawls

rather than a discrete one. If you think about it for a moment, you will realize that although the highest point of the curve is at 35 weeks, the probability that a child picked at random will first crawl at *exactly* 35 weeks (i.e., 35.00000000 weeks) is infinitely small— statisticians would argue that it is in fact 0. Similarly, the probability of first crawling at 35.00000001 weeks also is infinitely small. This suggests that it does not make any sense to speak of the probability of any *specific* outcome, although that is just what we did with discrete distributions.

On the other hand, we know that many children start crawling at *approximately* 35 weeks, and it does make considerable sense to speak of the probability of obtaining a score that falls within some specified *interval*. For example, we might be interested in the probability that an infant will start crawling at 35 weeks plus or minus one week. Such an interval is shown in Figure 7.3. If we arbitrarily define the total area under the curve to be 1.00, then the shaded area in Figure 7.3 between points 34 and 36 weeks will be equal to the probability that an infant chosen at random will begin crawling at this time. Those of you who have had calculus will probably recognize that if we knew the form of the equation that describes this distribution (i.e., if we knew the equation for the curve), we would simply need to integrate the function over the interval from 34 to 36. But you don't need calculus to solve this problem, because the distributions with which we will work are adequately approximated by other distributions that have already been tabled. In this book we will never integrate functions, but we will often refer to tables of distributions. You have already had experience with this procedure with regard to the normal distribution in Chapter 6.

We have just considered the area of Figure 7.3 between 34 and 36 weeks, which is centered on the mean. However, the same things could be said for any interval. In Figure 7.3 you can also see the area that corresponds to the period that is one week on either side of 30 weeks (denoted as the shaded area between 29 and 31 weeks). Although there is not enough information in this example for us to calculate actual probabilities, it should be clear by inspection of Figure 7.3 that the 2-week interval around 35 weeks has a higher probability (greater shaded area) than the 2-week interval around 30 weeks.

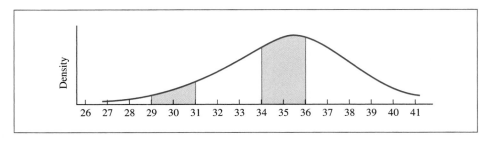

**Figure 7.3**
Probability of crawling within one week of 35 weeks

A good way to get a feel for areas under a curve is to take a piece of transparent graph paper and lay it on top of the figure (or use a regular sheet of graph paper and hold the two up to a light). If you count the number of squares that fall within a specified interval and divide by the total number of squares under the whole curve, you will approximate the probability that a randomly drawn score will fall within that interval. It should be obvious that the smaller the size of the individual squares on the graph paper, the more accurate the approximation.

## 7.8 Summary

In this chapter we examined the various definitions of the term *probability* and a number of fundamental concepts and rules of probability theory. We also considered the differences between discrete and continuous variables and their distributions. Some important terms in this chapter are

| | |
|---|---|
| Analytic view, *126* | Multiplicative law of probability, *129* |
| Relative frequency view, *126* | |
| Sample with replacement, *126* | Joint probability, *131* |
| Subjective probability, *126* | Conditional probability, *131* |
| Event, *127* | Unconditional probability, *133* |
| Independent events, *128* | Risk, *133* |
| Mutually exclusive, *128* | Risk ratio, *133* |
| Exhaustive, *128* | Odds, *134* |
| Additive law of probability, *129* | Odds ratio, *134* |

## 7.9 Exercises

**7.1** Give one example each of an analytic, a relative frequency, and a subjective view of probability.

**7.2** Suppose one of the neighborhood soccer players is selling raffle tickets for $500 worth of groceries at a local store, and you bought a $1 ticket for yourself and one for your mother. The children eventually sold 1000 tickets.
(a) What is the probability that you will win?

(b) What is the probability that your mother will win?

(c) What is the probability that you *or* your mother will win?

**7.3**   Now suppose that because of the high level of ticket sales, an additional $250 prize will also be awarded.

(a) Given that you don't win first prize, what is the probability that you will win second prize? (The first-prize ticket is not put back into the hopper before the second-prize ticket is drawn.)

(b) What is the probability that your mother will come in first and you will come in second?

(c) What is the probability that you will come in first and she will come in second?

(d) What is the probability that the two of you will take first and second place?

**7.4**   Which parts of Exercise 7.3 dealt with joint probabilities?

**7.5**   Which parts of Exercise 7.3 dealt with conditional probabilities?

**7.6**   Make up a simple example of a situation in which you are interested in joint probabilities.

**7.7**   Make up a simple example of a situation in which you are interested in conditional probabilities. Frame the issue in terms of a research hypothesis.

**7.8**   In some homes a mother's behavior seems to be independent of her baby's and vice versa. If the mother looks at her child a total of two hours each day, and if the baby looks at the mother a total of three hours each day, and if they really do behave independently, what is the probability that they will look at each other at the same time?

**7.9**   In Exercise 7.8 assume that both mother and child sleep from 8:00 p.m. to 7:00 a.m. What would be the probability now?

**7.10**   I said that the probability of alcohol involvement, given an accident at night, was approximately .50, but I don't know the probability of an accident, given that you had been drinking. How would you go about finding the answer to that question if you had sufficient resources?

**7.11**   In the example dealing with what happens to supermarket fliers, we found that the probability that a flier carrying a "do not litter" message would end up in the trash, *if what people do with fliers is independent of the message that is on them*, was .033. I also said that 4.5% of those messages actually ended up in the trash. What does this tell you about the effectiveness of messages?

**7.12**   Give an example of a common continuous distribution for which we have some real interest in the probability that an observation will fall within some specified interval.

**7.13**   Give an example of a continuous variable that we routinely treat as if it were discrete.

**7.14**   Give two examples of discrete variables.

**7.15**   A graduate admissions committee has finally come to realize that it cannot make valid distinctions among the top applicants. This year the committee rated all 500 applicants and randomly chose 10 from those at or above the 80th percentile. (The 80th percentile is the point at or below which 80 percent of the scores fall.) What is the probability that any particular applicant will be admitted (assuming you have no knowledge of her rating)?

**7.16** With respect to Exercise 7.15, determine the conditional probability that the person will be admitted, given the following:
(a) That she has the highest rating
(b) That she has the lowest rating

**7.17** In the Add.dat dataset on the Web site, what is the probability that a person drawn at random will have an ADDSC score greater than 50?

**7.18** For the data in Exercise 7.17, what is the probability that a male will have an ADDSC score greater than 50?

**7.19** For the data in Exercise 7.17, what is the probability that a person will drop out of school, given that he or she has an ADDSC score of at least 60?

**7.20** How might you use conditional probabilities to determine if an ADDSC cutoff score of 66 (see dataset Add.dat on the Web site) is predictive of whether or not a person will drop out of school?

**7.21** Compare the conditional probability from Exercise 7.20 with the unconditional probability of dropping out of school.

**7.22** People who sell cars are often accused of treating male and female customers differently. Make up a series of statements to illustrate simple, joint, and conditional probabilities with respect to such behavior. How might we begin to determine if those accusations are true?

**7.23** Assume you are a member of a local human rights organization. How might you use what you know about probability to examine discrimination in housing?

**7.24** A paper by Fell (1995) has many interesting statistics on the relationship between alcohol, drugs, and automobile accidents in the U.S. The paper is available at

 http://raru.adelaide.edu.au/T95/paper/s14p1.html

With the author's permission, I have made a copy of the paper in case the original site becomes unavailable. The copy can be found at

 http://www.uvm.edu/~dhowell/StatPages/More_Stuff/Fell.html

From the statistics in this paper, create several questions illustrating the principles discussed in this chapter. (These might make good exam questions if collected by the instructor.)

**7.25** In 2000 the U.S. Department of Justice released a study of the death penalty from 1995 to 2000, a period during which U.S. Attorneys were required to submit to the Justice Department for review and approval all cases in which they sought the death sentence. The report can be found at

 http://www.usdoj.gov/dag/pubdoc/_dp_survey_final.pdf

The data were broken down by whether or not the U.S. attorney recommended seeking the death penalty and by the race of the *victim* (not the defendant). These data are summarized below.

**Death Sentence Recommendation**

| Victim's race | Yes | No | Total |
|---|---|---|---|
| Nonwhite | 388 | 228 | 616 |
| Row proportion | .630 | .370 | 1.000 |
| White | 202 | 76 | 278 |
| Row proportion | .726 | .274 | 1.000 |
| Total | 590 | 304 | 894 |
| Col. % | .660 | .340 | |

What would you conclude from looking at this table?

**7.26** Using the data from Exercise 7.25, compute the risk and odds ratios of punishment as a function of race.

# 8

# Sampling Distributions and Hypothesis Testing

### QUESTIONS

■ Do people really treat folks who drive nice cars with more politeness?

■ What do we mean when we talk about hypothesis testing?

■ What do sampling distributions have to do with hypothesis testing?

■ What are sampling distributions, anyway?

■ What is a null hypothesis, and why would we ever care?

■ What does it mean to reject a null hypothesis, and what do I know if I do?

■ Do I really need to memorize more technical terms?

■ How does this all go together to tell me anything about an experiment?

**M**y wife is one of those people who believes strongly in birth order effects, in which people assert that firstborn children are more independent, middle children are more laid-back (unless they're fighting for attention), and later children are more whatever. Well, you're not going to see data on that phenomenon here, because despite all her urging, I can't get excited about it. (But if you are interested, a search of the Internet for the key words "birth order" will result in many sources, though I can't speak to their quality.) However, imagine that I did care, and imagine that I had lots of data on the independence of first-, middle-, and later-born children. How would I go about asking if firstborn children really are different from the others? Asking questions of this nature is the subject of much of the rest of this book, and this chapter lays out the basic groundwork for asking those questions. Put much too extremely, this chapter discusses how to frame the question, what kinds of things to think about, and how to evaluate the answer, whereas the rest of the book discusses the specific logical and computational approaches that apply to certain kinds of data.

This is a transitional chapter. In the preceding chapters we examined a number of different statistics and how they might be used to describe a set of data or present the probability of the occurrence of some event. You now have covered the groundwork that underlies the more interesting questions that statisticians are asked to answer. Starting in the next chapter we will begin to look at specific statistical techniques and their application. Although the description of data is important and fundamental to any analysis, it is not sufficient to answer many of the most interesting problems we encounter. And although it is nice to be able to compute various statistical tests, we need to know what to do with those tests once we have done the arithmetic. In this chapter we are going to examine the general procedure for going from sample statistics to conclusions about population parameters.

In a typical experiment we might treat one group in a special way and then see if their scores differ from the scores of people in general. Descriptive statistics will not tell us, for example, whether the difference between a sample mean and a hypothesized population mean, or between two obtained sample means, is small enough to be explained on the basis of chance alone or represents a true difference that might be attributable to the effect of our experimental treatment(s). Nor will descriptive statistics tell us whether the difference in rates at which prosecutors seek the death penalty is reliably tied to race. (It is.) And as we will see in Chapters 9–11, descriptive statistics will not tell us if an apparent relationship between two or more variables is real or just a chance occurrence that would be difficult to reproduce on a second try.

Statisticians frequently use phrases such as "differ by chance" and "sampling error" and assume you know what they mean. But this terminology and the ideas behind it are so central to the rest of the book that if you aren't sure about the concepts you will be in trouble. So we need to take a minute to be clear about chance and error.

In Chapter 6 we considered the distribution of Total Behavior Problem scores from the Achenbach Youth Self-Report form. Total Behavior Problem scores are approximately normally distributed in the population (i.e., the complete population of such scores would be normally distributed) with a population mean ($\mu$) of 50 and a population standard deviation ($\sigma$) of 10. We know that different children show different levels of problem behaviors and therefore have different scores. Similarly, different samples of children are not likely to have exactly the same mean. We also know that if we took a sample of children, their mean would probably not equal exactly 50. One sample of children might have a mean of 49.1, while a second sample might have a mean of 53.3. The actual sample means would depend on the particular children who happened to be included in the sample. This expected variability that we see from sample to sample is what is meant when we speak of "variability due to chance." We are referring to the fact that statistics (in this case, means) obtained from samples naturally vary from one sample to another.

Along the same lines, the term **sampling error** often is used in this context as a synonym for variability due to chance. It indicates that the value of a sample statistic probably will be in error (i.e., will deviate from the parameter it is estimating) as a result of the particular observations that are included in the sample. In this context "error" does not imply carelessness or mistakes. In the case of behavior problems, one random sample might just happen to include an unusually obnoxious child, whereas another sample might happen to include an unusual number of relatively well-behaved children. Please remember that in statistics "error" does not usually mean what it means in standard English; it simply means random variability.

| Definition | **Sampling error:** Variability of a statistic from sample to sample due to chance. |
|---|---|

I can illustrate this concept of sampling error by drawing samples from a population with a mean of 50 and a standard deviation of 10. (This population will represent the population of behavior problem scores.) If I draw 15 scores at a time and compute their mean, and then do it again, the second mean will probably not be exactly equal to the first. Nor will a third mean likely be exactly equal to the first two. I repeated this process 5000 times and obtained the results shown in Figure 8.1. We will have more to say about such distributions shortly, but for now all that I want you

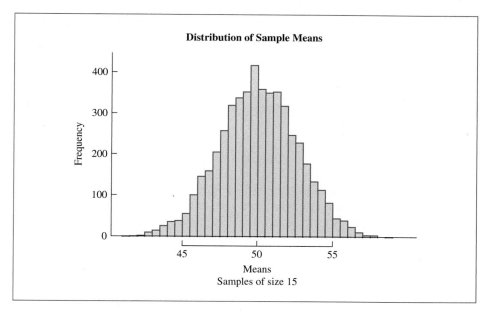

**Figure 8.1**
Distribution of sample means drawn from a population with $\mu = 50$, $\sigma = 10$, and $N = 15$. This distribution illustrates what we mean by sampling error.

to see is that sampling error represents differences from one sample statistic (in this case a mean) and another. Notice how a few means are way down in the 40s and some are in the upper 50s, but most fall pretty much in the middle.

# 8.1 Two Simple Examples Involving Course Evaluations and Rude Motorists

EXAMPLE:
Course
Evaluations

One example that we will investigate near the end of the next chapter looks at the relationship between how students evaluate a course and the grade they expect to receive in that course. This is a topic that many faculty feel strongly about, because even the best instructors turn to the semiannual course evaluation forms with some trepidation—perhaps the same amount of trepidation with which many students open their grade report form. Some faculty think that a course is good or bad independently of how well a student feels he or she will do in terms of a grade. Others feel that a student who seldom came to class and who will do poorly as a result will also (unfairly?) rate the course as poor. Finally, there are those who argue that students who do well and experience success take something away from the course other than just a grade and that those students will generally rate the course highly. But the relationship between course ratings and student performance is an empirical question and, as such, can be answered by looking at relevant data. Suppose that in a random sample of fifty courses we find a general trend—in those courses where students expect to do well, they tend to rate the course highly; and in those courses where students expect to do poorly, they tend to rate the overall quality of the course as low. How do we tell whether this trend in our small data set is representative of a trend among students in general or just a fluke that would disappear if we ran the study over? (For your own interest, make your prediction of what kind of results we will find. We will return to this issue in the next chapter.) ∎

EXAMPLE:
Rode Motorists

A second example comes from a study by Doob and Gross (1968), who investigated the influence of perceived social status. They found that if an old, beat-up (low-status) car failed to start when a traffic light turned green, 84% of the time the driver of the car behind it honked the horn. However, when the stopped car was an expensive, high-status car, only 50% of the time did the following driver honk.[1] These results could be explained in one of two ways:

- The difference between 84% in one sample and 50% in a second sample is simply attributable to sampling error (random variability

---

[1]There was recently a report in the literature (Ruback & Juieng, 1997) showing that a driver would spend longer to back out of a parking space if someone else was waiting for it. (I agree that sounds childish, but adults often behave childishly.) An interesting class project would be to hang around parking lots and surreptitiously record the time it takes someone to leave a parking space when someone else is, or is not, waiting.

among samples); therefore, we cannot conclude that perceived social status influences horn-honking behavior.

■ The difference between 84% and 50% is large. The difference is not just sampling error; therefore, people are less likely to honk at drivers of high-status cars.

Although the statistical calculations required to answer this question are different from those used to answer the one about course evaluations (because the first deals with relationships and the second deals with proportions), the underlying logic is fundamentally the same.    ■

These examples of course evaluations and horn honking are two kinds of questions that fall under the heading of **hypothesis testing**. This chapter is intended to present the theory of hypothesis testing in as general a way as possible, without going into the specific techniques or properties of any particular test. I will focus largely on the situation involving differences instead of the situation involving relationships, but the logic is basically the same. You will see additional material on examining relationships in the next chapter.

| Definition | **Hypothesis testing:** A process by which decisions are made concerning the value of parameters. |
|---|---|

The theory of hypothesis testing is so important in all that follows that a thorough understanding of it is essential. Many students who have had one or more courses in statistics and who know how to run a number of different statistical tests still do not have a basic knowledge of what it is they are doing. As a result they have difficulty interpreting statistical tables and must learn every new procedure in a step-by-step, rote fashion. This chapter is designed to avoid that difficulty by presenting the theory in its most general sense, without the use of any formulae. You can learn the formulae later, after you understand *why* you might want to use them. Professional statisticians might fuss over the looseness of the definitions, but that will be set right in subsequent chapters. Others may object that we are considering hypothesis testing before we consider the statistical procedures that produce the test. That is precisely the intent. The material covered here cuts across all statistical tests and can be discussed independently of them. By separating the material in this way, you are free to concentrate on the underlying principles without worrying about the mechanics of calculation.

The important issue in hypothesis testing is to find some way of deciding whether we are looking at a small chance fluctuation in differences between the horn-honking rates for low- and high-status cars or at a difference that is sufficiently large for us to believe that people are much less likely to honk at those they consider higher in status.

## 8.2 Sampling Distributions

The next example is one that affects a large number of children in our society. Consider the situation in which we have five students from recently divorced households. These five children have a mean of 56 on the Achenbach Youth Self-Report scale of Total Behavior Problems. This mean is over half a standard deviation above the mean (50) in the general population, and we want to know if this finding is sufficiently deviant for us to conclude that the stress associated with divorce tends to elicit behavior problems in children at higher than normal levels. Perhaps we just came up with a peculiar sample, and another sample of children from divorced households would show normal levels of behavior. Or perhaps divorce is a sufficiently stressful event in children's lives to produce serious behavior problems. There certainly is a lot of information in the literature that suggests that divorce is even more stressful on children than it is on their parents. To answer this kind of question, we have to use what are called **sampling distributions**, which tell us specifically what degree of sample-to-sample variability we can expect by chance as a function of sampling error.

---

Definition   **Sampling distribution:** The variability of a statistic over repeated sampling from a specified population.

**Standard error:** The standard deviation of a sampling distribution.

---

*The most basic concept underlying all statistical tests is the sampling distribution of a statistic.* It is fair to say that if we did not have sampling distributions, we would not have any statistical tests. Roughly speaking, sampling distributions tell us what values we might (or might not) expect to obtain for a particular statistic under a set of predefined conditions (e.g., what the obtained mean of five children might be *if* the true mean of the population from which those children come is 50). Notice that I'm talking about a conditional probability here: the probability of something happening *if* something else is true.

We not only need to know what kind of value to expect for a mean Total Behavior Problem score, but we also have to know something about how variable those mean values might be if we had several of them. The standard deviation of the distribution of sample means (known as the "**standard error**" of the distribution) reflects the variability that we would expect to find in the values of that statistic over repeated trials. Sampling distributions provide the opportunity to evaluate the likelihood of an obtained sample statistic, given that such predefined conditions actually exist.

Basically, the sampling distribution of a statistic can be thought of as the distribution of values obtained for that statistic over repeated sampling (i.e., running the experiment, or drawing samples, an unlimited number of times). Although sampling distributions are almost always derived mathematically, it is easier to understand what they represent if we consider how they could, in theory, be derived empirically with a simple sampling experiment.

Definition   **Sampling distribution of the mean:** The distribution of sample means over repeated sampling from one population.

We will take as an illustration the **sampling distribution of the mean**, because it is the most easily understood and relates directly to the example of behavior problems. The sampling distribution of the mean is nothing more than the distribution of means of an infinite number of random samples drawn under certain specified conditions (e.g., under the condition that the true mean of our population is 50 and the standard deviation is 10). You have already seen a sampling distribution of the mean in Figure 8.1, although I did not label it as that at the time. There we took a population with a known mean ($\mu = 50$) and standard deviation ($\sigma = 10$). We then drew a very large number (theoretically an infinite number) of random samples from this population, each sample consisting of fifteen scores. For each sample we calculated its mean, and when we finish drawing all the samples, we plotted the distribution of these *means*. Such a distribution is a sampling distribution of the mean and would look like the one presented in Figure 8.1. A second example can be seen in Figure 8.2, although this time I drew samples of size 5, rather than size 15. (To obtain this figure, I used SPSS to generate 5000 samples of random data, wherein each observation was the mean of 5 random

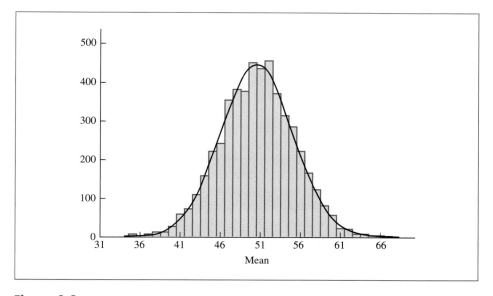

**Figure 8.2**
Distribution of sample means of behavior problems, each based on $n = 5$ scores

observations from a $N(50,100)$ population. I further had SPSS superimpose a normal distribution on top of the histogram. Notice how well it fits. Notice also that the distribution in Figure 8.1 is less spread out than the one in Figure 8.2. That is because means based on more scores are more consistent.)

We can see from Figure 8.2 that sample means between 46 and 56, for example, are quite likely to occur when we sample five children at random. We also can see that it is extremely unlikely that we would draw from this population a sample of five observations with a sample mean as low as 35, although there is some (very, very small) probability of doing so. The fact that we know the kinds of values to expect for the mean of a sample drawn from this population is going to allow us to turn the question around and ask if an obtained sample mean can be taken as evidence in favor of the hypothesis that we actually are sampling from this population.

## 8.3 Hypothesis Testing

We do not go around obtaining sampling distributions, either mathematically or empirically, simply because they are interesting to look at. We have important reasons for doing so. The usual reason is that we want to test some hypothesis. Let's go back to the random sample of five highly stressed children with a mean behavior problem score of 56. We want to test the hypothesis that such a sample mean could reasonably have arisen had we drawn our sample from a population in which $\mu = 50$. This is another way of saying that we want to know whether the mean of stressed children is different from the mean of normal children. The only way we can test such a hypothesis is to have some idea of the probability of obtaining a sample mean as extreme as 56 *if* we actually sampled observations from a population in which the children are normal ($\mu = 50$). The answer to this question is precisely what a sampling distribution is designed to provide.

Suppose we obtained (constructed) the sampling distribution of the mean for samples of five children from a population whose mean ($\mu$) is 50 (the distribution plotted in Figure 8.2). Suppose further that we then determined from that distribution the probability of a sample mean of 56 or higher. For the sake of argument, suppose this probability is .09. Our reasoning could then go as follows: "If we did sample from a population with $\mu = 50$, the probability of obtaining a sample mean as high as 56 is .09—a reasonably likely event. Because a sample mean that high is obtained about 9% of the time from a population with a mean of 50, we don't have a very good reason to doubt that this sample came from such a population."

Alternatively, suppose we obtained a sample mean of 62 and calculated from the sampling distribution that the probability of a sample mean as high as 62 was only .0037. Our argument could then go like this: "*If* we did sample from a population with $\mu = 50$, the probability of obtaining a sample mean as high as 62 is only .0037—an unlikely event. Because a sample mean that high is unlikely to be obtained from such a population, it would be reasonable to conclude that this sample probably came from some other population (one whose mean is higher than 50)."

It is important to realize what we have done in this example, because the logic is typical of most tests of hypotheses. The actual test consisted of several stages:

1. We wanted to test the hypothesis, often called the **research hypothesis,** that children under the stress of divorce are more likely than normal children to exhibit behavior problems.

2. We set up the hypothesis (called the **null hypothesis, $H_0$**) that the sample was actually drawn from a population whose mean, denoted $\mu_0$, equals 50. This is the hypothesis that stressed children do not differ from normal children in terms of behavior problems.

3. We obtained a random sample of children under stress.

4. We then obtained the sampling distribution of the mean under the assumption that $H_0$ (the null hypothesis) is true (i.e., we obtained the sampling distribution of the mean from a population with $\mu_0 = 50$).

5. Given the sampling distribution, we calculated the probability of a mean *at least as large* as our actual sample mean.

6. On the basis of that probability, we made a decision: either to reject or fail to reject $H_0$. Because $H_0$ states that $\mu = 50$, rejection of $H_0$ represents a belief that $\mu > 50$, although the actual value of $\mu$ remains unspecified.

---

**Definition**

**Research hypothesis:** The hypothesis that the experiment was designed to investigate.

**Null hypothesis ($H_0$):** The statistical hypothesis tested by the statistical procedure; usually a hypothesis of no difference or no relationship.

---

The preceding discussion is oversimplified in the sense that we generally would prefer to test the research hypothesis that children under stress are *different from* (rather than just *higher than*) other children, but we will return to that point shortly. It is also oversimplified in the sense that in practice we also would need to take into account (either directly or by estimation) the value of $\sigma^2$, the population variance, and $N$, the sample size. But again, those are specifics we can deal with when the time comes. The logic of the approach is representative of the logic of most, if not all, statistical tests. In each case we follow the same steps: (1) specify a research hypothesis, (2) set up the null hypothesis, (3) collect some data, (4) construct the sampling distribution of the particular statistic on the assumption that $H_0$ is true, (5) compare the sample statistic to that distribution, and find the probability of exceeding the observed statistic's value, and (6) reject or retain $H_0$, depending on the probability, under $H_0$, of a sample statistic as extreme as the one we have obtained.

## 8.4 The Null Hypothesis

As we have seen, the concept of the null hypothesis plays a crucial role in the testing of hypotheses. People frequently are puzzled by the fact that we set up a hypothesis that is directly counter to what we hope to show. For example, if we hope to demonstrate the research hypothesis that college students do not come from a population with a mean self-confidence score of 100, we immediately set up the null hypothesis that they do. Or if we hope to demonstrate the validity of a research hypothesis that the means ($\mu_1$ and $\mu_2$) of the populations from which two samples are drawn are different, we state the null hypothesis that the population means are the same (or, equivalently, $\mu_1 - \mu_2 = 0$). (The term "null hypothesis" is most easily seen in this second example, in which it refers to the hypothesis that the difference between the two population means is zero, or *null*.) We use the null hypothesis for several reasons. The philosophical argument, put forth by Fisher when he first introduced the concept, is that we can never prove something to be true, but we can prove something to be false. Observing 3,000 cows with only one head does not prove the statement "Every cow has only one head." However, finding one cow with two heads does disprove the original statement beyond any shadow of a doubt. While one might argue with Fisher's basic position—and many people have—the null hypothesis retains its dominant place in statistics. You might also draw the parallel between the null hypothesis that we usually test, and the idea that someone is innocent until proven guilty, which is the basis for our system of justice. We begin with the idea that the defendant is innocent and agree to convict only if the data are sufficiently inconsistent with that belief. You can't push that idea very far, but it has considerable similarity with the way we test hypotheses.

A second and more practical reason for employing the null hypothesis is that it provides us with the starting point for any statistical test. Consider the case in which you want to show that the mean self-confidence score of college students is greater than 100. Suppose further that you were granted the privilege of proving the truth of some hypothesis. What hypothesis are you going to test? Should you test the hypothesis that $\mu = 101$, or maybe the hypothesis that $\mu = 112$, or how about $\mu = 113$? The point is that we do not have a *specific* alternative (research) hypothesis in mind (and I can't recall any experiment that did), and without one we cannot construct the sampling distribution we need. However, if we start off by assuming $H_0: \mu = 100$, we can immediately set about obtaining the sampling distribution for $\mu = 100$ and then, with luck, reject that hypothesis and conclude that the mean score of college students is greater than 100, which is what we wanted to show in the first place.

## 8.5 Test Statistics and Their Sampling Distributions

We have been discussing the sampling distribution of the mean, but the discussion would have been essentially the same had we dealt instead with the median, the variance, the range, the correlation coefficient (as in our course evaluation example), proportions (as in our horn honking example), or any other statistic you care to consider. (Technically the shape of these distributions would be different, but I am deliberately ignoring such issues in this chapter.) The statistics just mentioned usually are referred to as **sample statistics** because they describe samples. A whole different class of statistics called **test statistics**, are associated with specific statistical procedures and have their own sampling distributions. Test statistics are statistics such as $t$, $F$, $\chi^2$, which you may have run across in the past. If you are not familiar with them, don't worry—we will consider them separately in later chapters. This is not the place to go into a detailed explanation of any test statistic (I put this chapter where it is because I didn't want readers to think that they were supposed to worry about technical issues.) This chapter is the place, however, to point out that the sampling distributions for test statistics are obtained and used in essentially the same way as the sampling distribution of the mean.

---

**Definition**

**Sample statistics:** Statistics calculated from a sample and used primarily to describe a sample.

**Test statistics:** The results of a statistical test.

---

As an illustration, consider the sampling distribution of the statistic $t$, which will be discussed in Chapters 12 through 14. For those who have never heard of the $t$ test, it is sufficient to say that the $t$ test is often used, among other things, to determine whether two samples were drawn from populations with the same means. Suppose that $\mu_1$ and $\mu_2$ represent the means of the populations from which the two samples were drawn. The null hypothesis is the hypothesis that the two population means are equal, in other words, $H_0: \mu_1 = \mu_2$ (or $\mu_1 - \mu_2 = 0$). If we were extremely patient, we could empirically obtain the sampling distribution of $t$ when $H_0$ is true by drawing an infinite number of pairs of samples, all from one population, calculating $t$ for each pair of samples (by methods to be discussed later), and plotting the resulting values of $t$. In that case $H_0$ must be true because the samples came from the same population. The resulting distribution is the sampling distribution of $t$ when $H_0$ is true. If we had a sample with two groups that produced a particular value of $t$, we would test the null hypothesis by comparing that sample $t$ to the sampling distribution of $t$. We would reject the null hypothesis if our obtained $t$ did not look like the kinds of $t$ values that the sampling distribution told us to expect when the null hypothesis is true.

I could rewrite the preceding paragraph substituting $\chi^2$, or $F$, or any other test statistic in place of $t$, with only minor changes dealing with how the statistic is calculated. Thus you can see that all sampling distributions can be obtained in basically the same way (calculate and plot an infinite number of statistics by sampling from a known population). Once you understand that fact, much of the remainder of the book is an elaboration of methods for calculating the desired statistic and a description of characteristics of the appropriate sampling distribution.

Keep in mind the analogy that I used to our legal system. The null hypothesis is roughly analogous to the idea that someone is innocent until proven guilty.

The idea of rejecting the null hypothesis is analogous to the idea that we convict someone when we believe him or her to be guilty "beyond a reasonable doubt." We don't have to "prove" that the null hypothesis is true; we have to conclude only that the test of "reasonable doubt" fails in this instance.

## 8.6 Using the Normal Distribution to Test Hypotheses

Much of the discussion so far has dealt with statistical procedures that you do not yet know how to use. I did this deliberately to emphasize the point that the logic and the calculations behind a test are two separate issues. You now know quite a bit about how hypothesis tests are conducted, even if you don't have the slightest idea how to do the arithmetic. However, we now can use what you already know about the normal distribution to test some simple hypotheses. In the process we can deal with several fundamental issues that are more easily seen by use of a concrete example.

An important use of the normal distribution is to test hypotheses, either about individual observations or about sample statistics such as the mean. In this chapter we will deal with individual observations, leaving the question of testing sample statistics until later chapters. Note, however, that in the general case we test hypotheses about sample statistics such as the mean rather than about individual observations. I am starting with an example of an individual observation because the explanation is somewhat clearer. Since we are dealing with only single observations, the sampling distribution invoked here will be the distribution of individual scores (rather than the distribution of means). The basic logic is the same, and we are using an example of individual scores only because it simplifies the explanation and is something with which you have had experience.

For a simple example assume that we are concerned with the rate at which people can tap their fingers. That may seem like an odd thing to worry about, but medical psychologists and neurologists frequently use finger tapping as a diagnostic tool. We will assume that we know that the mean rate of finger tapping of normal healthy adults is 100 taps in 20 seconds, with a standard deviation of 20, and that tapping speeds are normally distributed in the population. Assume further that we know that the tapping rate is slower among people with certain neurological problems. (In fact, the difference in rates between left and right hands is more important than the absolute rate of either hand, but one-handed tapping is easier to talk about.) Finally, suppose that an individual has just been sent to us who taps at a rate of 70 taps in 20 seconds. Is his score sufficiently below the mean for us to assume that he did not come from a population of neurologically healthy people? This situation is diagrammed in Figure 8.3, in which the arrow indicates the location of our piece of data (the person's score).

The logic of the solution to this problem is the same as the logic of hypothesis testing in general. We begin by assuming that the individual's score does come from the population of healthy scores. This is the null hypothesis ($H_0$). If $H_0$ is true, we automatically know the mean and the standard deviation of the population

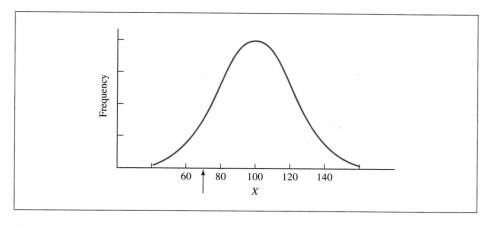

**Figure 8.3**
Location of a person's tapping score on a distribution of scores of neurologically
healthy people

from which he was supposedly drawn (100 and 20, respectively). With this information we are in a position to calculate the probability that a score *as low as* his would be obtained from this population. If the probability is very low, we can reject $H_0$ and conclude that he did not come from the healthy population. Conversely, if the probability is not particularly low, then the data represent a reasonable result under $H_0$, and we would have no reason to doubt its validity and thus no reason to doubt that the person is healthy. Keep in mind that we are not interested in the probability of a score *equal* to 70 (which, because the distribution is continuous, would be infinitely small) but rather in the probability that the score would be at least as low as (i.e., less than or equal to) 70.

The individual had a score of 70. We want to know the probability of obtaining a score *at least as low as* 70 if $H_0$ is true. We already know how to find this—it is the area below 70 in Figure 8.3. All we have to do is convert 70 to a $z$ score and then refer to Table D.10.

$$z = \frac{X - \mu}{\sigma} = \frac{70 - 100}{20} = \frac{-30}{20} = -1.5$$

From Table D.10 we can see that the probability of a $z$ score of $-1.5$ or below is .0668. (Locate $z = 1.50$ in the table and then read across to the column headed "Smaller Portion." Remember that the distribution is symmetric, so the probability of $z \leq -1.50$ is the same as the probability of $z \geq +1.50$.)

At this point we have to become involved in the **decision-making** aspects of hypothesis testing. We must decide if an event with a probability of .0668 is sufficiently unlikely to cause us to reject $H_0$. Here we will fall back on arbitrary conventions that have been established over the years. The rationale for these conventions will become clearer as we go along, but for the time being keep in mind that they are merely conventions. One convention calls for rejecting $H_0$ if the probability under $H_0$ is less than or equal to .05 ($p \leq .05$), while another convention calls for rejecting $H_0$ whenever the probability under $H_0$ is less than or equal to .01. The latter convention is more conservative with respect to the probability of rejecting $H_0$. These values of .05 and .01 are often referred to as the **rejection level**, or **significance level**, of the test. Whenever the probability obtained under $H_0$ is less than or equal to our predetermined significance level, we will reject $H_0$. Another way of stating this is to say that any outcome whose probability under $H_0$ is less than or equal to the significance level (i.e., the probability provides "more than a reasonable doubt"), falls into the **rejection region**, since such an outcome leads us to reject $H_0$. In this book we will use the .05 level of significance, keeping in mind that some people would consider this level to be too lenient.[2] For our particular example we have obtained a probability value of .0668, which obviously is greater than .05. Because we have specified that we will not reject $H_0$ unless the probability of the data under $H_0$ is less than .05, we must conclude that we have no reason to decide that the person did not come from a population of healthy people. More specifically, we conclude that a finger-tapping rate of 70 reasonably could have come from a population of scores with a mean equal to 100 and a standard deviation equal to 20. It is important to note that we have not shown that this person is healthy, but only that we have insufficient reason to conclude that he is not. It may be that he is just acquiring the disease and therefore is not quite as different from normal as is usual for his condition. Or maybe he has the disease at an advanced stage but just happens to be an unusually fast tapper. Remember that we can never say that we have proved the null hypothesis. We can conclude only that this person does not tap sufficiently slowly for an illness, if any, to be statistically detectable.

Definition

**Decision making:** A procedure for making logical decisions on the basis of sample data.

**Rejection level:** The probability with which we are willing to reject $H_0$ when it is, in fact, correct.

**Significance level:** The probability with which we are willing to reject $H_0$ when it is, in fact, correct.

**Rejection region:** The set of outcomes of an experiment that will lead to rejection of $H_0$.

[2]The particular view of hypothesis testing described here is the classical one that a null hypothesis is rejected if its probability is less than the predefined significance level, and not rejected if its probability is greater than the significance level. Currently a substantial body of opinion holds that such cut-and-dried rules are inappropriate and that more attention should be paid to the probability value itself. In other words, the classical approach (using a .05 rejection level) would declare $p = .051$ and $p = .150$ to be (equally) "nonsignificant" and $p = .048$ and $p = .0003$ to be (equally) "significant." The alternative view would think of $p = .051$ as "nearly significant" and $p = .0003$ as "very significant." While this view has much to recommend it, it will not be wholeheartedly adopted here. Most computer programs do print out exact probability levels, and those values, when interpreted judiciously, can be useful. The difficulty comes in defining what is meant by "interpreted judiciously."

Definition | **Alternative hypothesis ($H_1$):** The hypothesis that is adopted when $H_0$ is rejected; usually the same as the research hypothesis.

The theory of significance testing as just outlined was popularized by R. A. Fisher in the first third of the 20th century. The theory was expanded and cast in more of a decision framework by Jerzy Neyman and Egon Pearson between 1928 and 1938, often against the loud and abusive objections of Fisher. Current statistical practice more closely follows the Neyman-Pearson approach, which emphasizes more than did Fisher the fact that we also have an **alternative hypothesis ($H_1$)** that is contradictory to the null hypothesis $(H_0)$[3]. Thus if the null hypothesis is

$$H_0: \mu = 100$$

then the alternative hypothesis could be

$$H_1: \mu \neq 100$$

or

$$H_1: \mu > 100$$

or

$$H_1: \mu < 100$$

We will discuss alternative hypotheses in more detail shortly.

## 8.7 Type I and Type II Errors

Whenever we reach a decision with a statistical test, there is always a chance that our decision is the wrong one. While this is true of almost all decisions, statistical or otherwise, the statistician has one point in her favor that other decision makers normally lack. She not only makes a decision by some rational process, but she can also specify the conditional probabilities of a decision's being in error. In everyday life we make decisions with only subjective feelings about what is probably the right choice. The statistician, however, can state quite precisely the probability that she erroneously rejected $H_0$ in favor of the alternative $(H_1)$. This ability to specify the probability of error follows directly from the logic of hypothesis testing.

---

[3]A recent theoretical approach by Jones and Tukey (2000) goes even more in the direction of the alternative hypothesis and away from the null hypothesis. Their position is an appealing one, but it would add too much confusion to elaborate on it here.

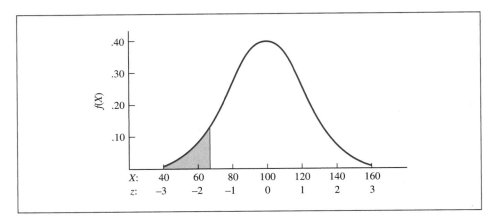

**Figure 8.4**
Lowest 5% of scores from clinically healthy people

Consider the finger-tapping example, this time ignoring the score of the individual sent to us. The situation is diagrammed in Figure 8.4, in which the distribution is the distribution of scores from healthy subjects, and the shaded portion represents the lowest 5% of the distribution. The actual score that cuts off the lowest 5% is called the **critical value**. Critical values are those values of $X$ (the variable), or a test statistic, that describe the boundary or boundaries of the rejection region(s). For this particular example the critical value is 67.

---

Definition    **Critical value:** The value of a test statistic at or beyond which we will reject $H_0$.

**Type I error:** The error of rejecting $H_0$ when it is true.

**$\alpha$(alpha):** The probability of a Type I error.

---

If we have a decision rule that says to reject $H_0$ whenever an outcome falls in the lowest 5% of the distribution, we will reject $H_0$ whenever an individual's score falls into the shaded area; that is, whenever a score as low as his has a probability of .05 or less of coming from the population of healthy scores. Yet by the very nature of our procedure, 5% of the scores from perfectly healthy people will themselves fall into the shaded portion. Thus if we actually have sampled a person who is healthy, we stand a 5% chance of his score being in the shaded tail of the distribution, causing us erroneously to reject the null hypothesis. This kind of error (rejecting $H_0$ when, in fact, it is true) is called a **Type I error**, and its conditional probability (the probability of rejecting the null hypothesis given that it is true) is designated as $\alpha$ **(alpha)**, the size of the rejection region. In the future, whenever we represent a probability by $\alpha$, we will be referring to the probability of a Type I error.

Keep in mind the "conditional" nature of the probability of a Type I error. I know that sounds like jargon, but what it means is that you should be sure you understand that when we speak of a Type I error, we mean the probability of rejecting

$H_0$, *given that it is true*. We are not saying that we will reject $H_0$ on 5% of the hypotheses we test. We would hope to run experiments on important and meaningful variables and, therefore, to reject $H_0$ often. But when we speak of a Type I error, we are speaking only about rejecting $H_0$ in those situations in which the null hypothesis happens to be true.

You might feel that a 5% chance of making an error is too great a risk to take and suggest that we make our criterion much more stringent, by rejecting, for example, only the lowest 1% of the distribution. This procedure is perfectly legitimate, but you need to realize that the more stringent you make your criterion, the more likely you are to make another kind of error—failing to reject $H_0$ when it is actually false and $H_1$ is true. This type of error is called a **Type II error**, and its probability is symbolized by **$\beta$ (beta)**.

Definition

---

**Type II error:** The error of not rejecting $H_0$ when it is false.

**$\beta$ (beta):** The probability of a Type II error.

---

The major difficulty in terms of Type II errors stems from the fact that if $H_0$ is false, we almost never know what the true distribution (the distribution under $H_1$) would look like for the population from which our data came. We know only the distribution of scores under $H_0$. Put in the present context, we know the distribution of scores from healthy people but not from unhealthy people.[4] It may be that people suffering from some neurological disease tap, on average, considerably more slowly than healthy people, or it may be that they tap, on average, only a little more slowly. This situation is illustrated in Figure 8.5, in which the distribution labeled $H_0$ represents the distribution of scores from healthy people (the set of observations expected under the null hypothesis), and the distribution labeled $H_1$ represents our hypothetical distribution of scores from unhealthy people (the distribution under $H_1$). Remember that the curve labeled $H_1$ is only hypothetical. We really do not know the location of the unhealthy distribution, other than that it is lower (slower speeds) than the distribution of $H_0$. (I have arbitrarily drawn that distribution with a mean of 80 and a standard deviation of 20.)

The darkly shaded portion in the top half of Figure 8.5 represents the rejection region. Any observation falling into that area (i.e., to the left of about 67) would lead to rejection of the null hypothesis. If the null hypothesis is true, we know that our observation will fall into this area 5% of the time. Thus we will make a Type I error 5% of the time.

The lightly shaded portion in the bottom half of Figure 8.5 represents the probability ($\beta$) of a Type II error. This is the situation of a person who was actually

---

[4]I bet that some of you are about to say, "Well, go out and get some sick people and make them tap." Well, how sick would you like them to be? Very sick, with very slow speeds, or just a little sick, with slightly slow speeds? We aren't so much interested in classifying people as very sick or a little sick. We want to classify them as healthy or not healthy, and in that situation the only thing we can do is to compare a patient against healthy people.

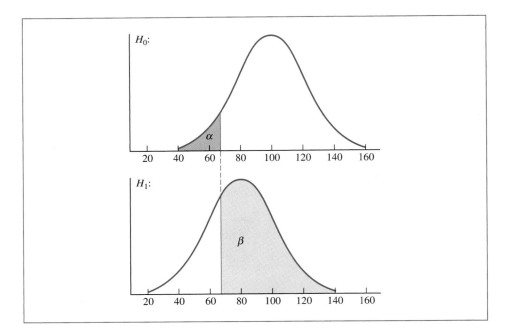

**Figure 8.5**
Areas corresponding to $\alpha$ and $\beta$ for tapping speed example

drawn from the unhealthy population but whose score was not sufficiently low to cause us to reject $H_0$.

In the particular situation illustrated in Figure 8.5, we can, in fact, calculate $\beta$ by using the normal distribution to calculate the probability of obtaining a score *greater than* 67 (the critical value) if $\mu = 80$ and $\sigma = 20$. The actual calculation is not important for your understanding of $\beta$; this chapter was designed specifically to avoid calculation. I will simply state that this probability (i.e., the area labeled $\beta$) is .74. Thus for this example, 74% of the time when we have a person who is actually unhealthy (i.e., $H_1$ is actually true), we will make a Type II error by failing to reject $H_0$ when it is false (as medical diagnosticians, we leave a lot to be desired).

From Figure 8.5 you can see that if we were to reduce the level of $\alpha$ (the probability of a Type I error) from .05 to .01 by moving the rejection region to the left, it would reduce the probability of Type I errors but would increase the probability of Type II errors. Setting $\alpha$ at .01 would mean that $\beta = .908$. Obviously there is room for debate over what level of significance to use. The decision rests primarily on your opinion concerning the relative seriousness of Type I and Type II errors for the kind of study you are conducting. If it is important to avoid Type I errors (such as telling someone that he has a disease when he does not), then you would set a stringent (i.e., small) level of $\alpha$. If, on the other hand, you want to avoid Type II errors (telling someone to go home and take an aspirin when, in fact, he needs immediate treatment), you might set a fairly high level of $\alpha$. (Setting $\alpha = .20$ in

**Table 8.1**
Possible Outcomes of the Decision-Making Process

| Decision | True State of the World | |
|---|---|---|
| | $H_0$ True | $H_0$ False |
| **Reject $H_0$** | Type I error $p = \alpha$ | Correct decision $p = 1 - \beta$ = Power |
| **Fail to Reject $H_0$** | Correct decision $p = 1 - \alpha$ | Type II error $p = \beta$ |

this example would reduce $\beta$ to .44.) Unfortunately, in practice most people choose an arbitrary level of $\alpha$, such as .05 or .01, and simply ignore $\beta$. In many cases this may be all you can do. (In fact, you will probably use the alpha level that your instructor recommends.) In other cases, however, there is much more you can do, as you will see in Chapter 15.

I should stress again that Figure 8.5 is purely hypothetical. I was able to draw the figure only because I arbitrarily decided that the tapping speeds of unhealthy people were normally distributed with a mean of 80 and a standard deviation of 20. In most everyday situations we do not know the mean and the standard deviation of that distribution and can make only educated guesses, thus providing only crude estimates of $\beta$. In practice we can select a value of $\mu$ under $H_1$ that represents the *minimum* difference we would like to be able to detect, since larger differences will have even smaller $\beta$s.

From this discussion of Type I and Type II errors we can summarize the decision-making process with a simple table. Table 8.1 presents the four possible outcomes of an experiment. The items in this table should be self-explanatory, but there is one concept—power—that we have not yet discussed. The **power** of a test is the probability of rejecting $H_0$ when it is actually false. Because the probability of *failing* to reject a false $H_0$ is $\beta$, then power must equal $1 - \beta$. Those who want to know more about power and its calculation will find the material in Chapter 15 relevant.

---

Definition | **Power:** The probability of correctly rejecting a false null hypothesis.

---

## 8.8 One- and Two-Tailed Tests

The preceding discussion brings us to a consideration of one- and two-tailed tests. In our tapping example we knew that unhealthy subjects tapped more slowly than healthy subjects; therefore, we decided to reject $H_0$ only if a subject tapped too slowly. However, suppose our subject had tapped 180 times in 20 seconds. Although this is an exceedingly unlikely event to observe from a healthy subject, it would not fall into the rejection region, which consists *solely* of low rates. As a result we find ourselves in the unenviable position of not rejecting $H_0$ in the face of a piece of data that is very unlikely, but not in the direction expected.

The question then arises as to how we can protect ourselves against this type of situation (if protection is thought necessary). The answer is to specify before we run the experiment that we are going to reject a given percentage (say 5%) of the *extreme* outcomes, both those that are extremely high and those that are extremely low. But if we reject the lowest 5% and the highest 5%, then we would, in fact, reject $H_0$ a total of 10% of the time when it is actually true; that is, $\alpha = .10$. We are rarely willing to work with $\alpha$ as high as .10 and prefer to see it set no higher than .05. The only way to accomplish our goal is to reject the lowest 2.5% and the highest 2.5%, making a total of 5%.

The situation in which we reject $H_0$ for only the lowest (or only the highest) tapping speeds is referred to as a **one-tailed**, or **directional, test**. We make a prediction of the direction in which the individual will differ from the mean and our rejection region is located in only one tail of the distribution. When we reject extremes in both tails, we have what is called a **two-tailed**, or **nondirectional, test**. It is important to keep in mind that while we gain something with a two-tailed test (the ability to reject the null hypothesis for extreme scores in either direction), we also lose something. A score that would fall into the 5% rejection region of a one-tailed test may not fall into the rejection region of the corresponding two-tailed test, because now we reject only 2.5% in each tail.

Definition

---

**One-tailed test:** A test that rejects extreme outcomes in one specified tail of the distribution.

**Directional test:** Another name for a one-tailed test.

**Two-tailed test:** A test that rejects extreme outcomes in either tail of the distribution.

**Nondirectional test:** Another name for a two-tailed test.

---

In the finger-tapping example, the decision between a one- and a two-tailed test might seem reasonably clear-cut. We know that people with a given disease tap more slowly; therefore we care only about rejecting $H_0$ for low scores—high scores have no diagnostic importance. In other situations, however, we do not know which tail of the distribution is important (or if both are), and we need to guard against extremes in either tail. The situation might arise when we are considering a campaign to persuade young people not to smoke. We might find that the campaign leads to a decrease in the rate of smoking. Or, we might find that the campaign actually is taken by young adults as a challenge, making smoking look more attractive instead of less. (In fact, there is some evidence that this is exactly what happens.) In either case we would want to reject $H_0$.

In general, two-tailed tests are far more common than one-tailed tests for several reasons. One reason for this is because the investigator may have no idea what the data will look like and therefore has to be prepared for any eventuality. Although this situation is rare, it does occur in some exploratory work.

Another common reason for preferring two-tailed tests is that the investigators are reasonably sure the data will come out one way but want to cover themselves in the event that they are wrong. This type of situation arises more often than you might think. (Carefully formed hypotheses have an annoying habit of being phrased in the wrong direction, for reasons that seem so obvious after the event.) A frequent question that arises when the data may come out the other way around is, "Why not plan to run a one-tailed test and then, if the data come out the other way, just change the test to a two-tailed test?" I hear that question frequently, and it comes from people who have no intention of being devious but who are struggling with the logic of hypothesis testing. If you start an experiment with the extreme 5% of the left-hand tail as your rejection region and then turn around and reject any outcome that happens to fall into the extreme 2.5% of the right-hand tail, you are working at the 7.5% level. In that situation you will reject 5% of the outcomes in one direction (assuming that the data fall into the desired tail), and you are willing also to reject 2.5% of the outcomes in the other direction (when the data are in the unexpected direction). There is no denying that 5% + 2.5% = 7.5%. To put it another way, would you be willing to flip a coin for an ice cream cone if I choose "heads" but also reserve the right to switch to "tails" after I see how the coin lands? Or would you think it fair of me to shout, "Two out of three!" when the coin toss comes up in your favor? You would object to both of these strategies, and you should. For the same reason the choice between a one-tailed test and a two-tailed one is made *before* the data are collected. It is also one of the reasons that two-tailed tests are usually chosen.

Although the preceding discussion argues in favor of two-tailed tests, and although in this book we generally confine ourselves to such procedures, there are no hard and fast rules. The final decision depends on what you already know about the relative severity of different kinds of errors. It is important to keep in mind that with respect to a given tail of a distribution, the difference between a one-tailed test and a two-tailed test is that the latter just uses a different cutoff. A two-tailed test at $\alpha = .05$ is more liberal than a one-tailed test at $\alpha = .01$.[5]

---

[5]One of the reviewers of an earlier edition of this book made the case for two-tailed tests even more strongly: "It is my (minority) belief that what an investigator *expects to be true* has absolutely no bearing *whatsoever* on the issue of one- versus two-tailed tests. Nature couldn't care less what psychologists' theories predict, and will often show patterns/trends in the opposite direction. Since our goal is to know the truth (not to prove we are astute at predicting), our tests must always allow for testing *both* directions. I say *always* do two-tailed tests, and if you are worried about $\beta$, jack the sample size up a bit to offset the loss in power" (D. Bradley, personal communication, 1983). I am personally inclined toward this point of view. Nature is notoriously fickle, or else we are notoriously inept at prediction. On the other hand, a second reviewer (J. Rodgers, personal communication, 1986) takes exception to this position. While acknowledging that Bradley's point is well considered, Rodgers argues, "To generate a theory about how the world works that implies an expected direction of an effect, but then to hedge one's bet by putting some (up to 1/2) of the rejection region in the tail other than that predicted by the theory, strikes me as both scientifically dumb and slightly unethical. . . . Theory generation and theory testing are much closer to the proper goal of science than truth searching, and running one-tailed tests is quite consistent with those goals." Neither Bradley nor I would accept the judgment of being "scientifically dumb and slightly unethical" (Bradley is certainly neither of those, and has done more work than most people on these issues), but I presented the two views in juxtaposition because doing so gives you a flavor of the debate. Obviously there is room for disagreement on this issue, and Rodgers's opinion is not without its supporters.

If you have a sound grasp of the logic of testing hypotheses by use of sampling distributions, the remainder of this course will be relatively simple. For any new statistic you encounter, you will need to ask only two basic questions.

**1.** How and with which assumptions is the statistic calculated?

**2.** What does the statistic's sampling distribution look like under $H_0$?

If you know the answers to these two questions, your test is accomplished by calculating the test statistic for the data at hand and comparing the statistic to the sampling distribution. Because the relevant sampling distributions are tabled in the appendices, all you really need to know is which test is appropriate for a particular situation and how to calculate its test statistic. (Keep in mind, however, there is a great deal more to understanding the field of statistics than how to calculate, and evaluate, a specific statistical test.)

## 8.9 Seeing Statistics

You can easily practice manipulating probabilities, one- and two-tailed tests, and the null hypothesis by opening SeeingStatistics at

 www.uvm.edu/~dhowell/fundamentals/SeeingStatisticsApplets/Applets.html

and going to the applets for Chapter 8. Because this applet allows you to change any values within a problem, and to choose between one- and two-tailed tests, you can reproduce the statistics behind the discussion of finger tapping in Section 8.6. The output of the applet is shown here.

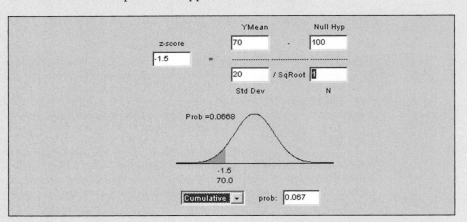

Remember that we are working with individual observations, not sample means, so we can enter "YMean" as our individual score of 70. The null hypothesis is given by the problem, as is the standard deviation. The sample size ($N$) is one because this is a single observation.

You can see that in my example the probability came out to be .067, which is the answer I received earlier. You should now try varying the observed score, and note how the probability, and the shaded portion of the graphic, change. You can select a two-tailed test by clicking on the box in the lower left and choosing "two-tailed." You may be surprised by what happens if you select "one-tailed" in that box. Why is the right half of the curve shaded rather than the left half? Finally, read the next section (Section 8.10), and use the applet to reproduce the values found there. Again, remember that we are substituting a single observation for a mean, and the sample size is 1.

## 8.10   A Final Worked Example

A number of years ago the mean on the verbal section of the Graduate Record Exam (GRE) was 489 with a standard deviation of 126. The statistics were based on all students taking the exam in that year, the vast majority of whom were native speakers of English. Suppose we have an application from an individual with a Chinese name who scored particularly low (e.g., 220). If this individual is a native speaker of English, that score would be sufficiently low for us to question his suitability for graduate school unless the rest of the documentation is considerably better. If, however, this student is not a native speaker of English, we would probably disregard the low score entirely, on the grounds that it is a poor reflection of his abilities.

We have two possible choices here, namely that the individual (1) *is* or (2) *is not* a native speaker of English. If he is a native speaker, we know the mean and the standard deviation of the population from which his score was sampled: 489 and 126, respectively. If he is not a native speaker, we have no idea what the mean and the standard deviation are for the population from which his score was sampled, but we don't need them. To help us to draw a reasonable conclusion about this person's status, we will set up the null hypothesis that this individual is a native speaker, or, more precisely, $H_0: \mu = 489$. We will identify $H_1$ with the hypothesis that the individual is not a native speaker ($\mu \neq 489$).

We now need to choose between a one-tailed and a two-tailed test. In this particular case we will choose a one-tailed test on the grounds that the GRE is given in English, and it is difficult to imagine that a population of nonnative speakers would have a mean higher than the mean of native speakers of English on a test that is given in English. (*Note:* This does not mean that non-English speakers may not, singly or as a population, outscore English speakers on a fairly administered test. It just means that they are unlikely to do so, especially as a population, when both groups take the test in English.) Because we have chosen a one-tailed test, we have set up the alternative hypothesis as $H_1$: $\mu < 489$.

Before we can apply our statistical procedures to the data at hand, we must make one additional decision. We have to decide on a level of significance for our test. In this case I have chosen to run the test at the 5% level because I am using $\alpha = .05$ as a standard for this book and also because I am more worried about a Type II error than I am about a Type I error. If I make a Type I error and erroneously conclude that the student is not a native speaker when, in fact, he is, it is very likely that the rest of his credentials will exclude him from further consideration anyway. If I make a Type II error and do not identify him as a nonnative speaker, I am doing him a real injustice.

Next we need to calculate the probability of a student receiving a score *at least as low as* 220 when $H_0$: $\mu = 489$ is true. We first calculate the $z$ score corresponding to a raw score of 220:

$$z = \frac{X - \mu}{\sigma} = \frac{220 - 489}{126} = \frac{-269}{126} = -2.13$$

We then go to tables of $z$ to calculate the probability that we would obtain a $z$ value less than or equal to $-2.13$. From Table D.10 we find that this probability is .017. Because this probability is less than the 5% significance level we chose to work with, we will reject the null hypothesis on the grounds that it is too unlikely that we would obtain a score as low as 220 if we had sampled an observation from a population of native speakers of English who had taken the GRE. Instead we will conclude that we have an observation from an individual who is not a native speaker of English.

It is important to note that in rejecting the null hypothesis we could have made a Type I error. We know that if we do sample speakers of English, 1.7% of them will score this low. It is possible that our applicant was a native speaker who just did poorly. All we are saying is that such an event is sufficiently unlikely that we will place our bets with the alternative hypothesis.

## 8.11 Back to Course Evaluations and Rude Motorists

We started this chapter with a discussion of the relationship between how students evaluate a course and the grade they expect to receive in that course. Our second example looked at the probability of motorists honking their horns at low- and high-status cars that did not move when a traffic light changed to green. As you will see in the next chapter, the first example uses a correlation coefficient to represent the degree of relationship. The second example simply compares two proportions. Both examples can be dealt with using the techniques discussed in this chapter. In the first case, if there is no relationship between the two variables, we would expect that the true correlation in the population of students is .00. We simply set up the null hypothesis that the population correlation is .00 and then ask about the probability that a sample of 15 observations would produce a correlation as large as the one we obtained. In the second case we set up the null hypothesis that there is no difference between the proportions of motorists *in the population* who honk at low- and high-status cars. Then we ask, "What is the probability of obtaining a difference in sample proportions as large as the one we obtained (in our case .34) if the null hypothesis is true?" I do not expect you to be able to run these tests now, but you should have a general sense of the way we will set up the problem when we do learn to run them.

## 8.12 Summary

The purpose of this chapter has been to examine the general theory of hypothesis testing without becoming involved in the specific calculations required to actually carry out a test. We first considered the concept of the sampling distribution of a statistic, which is the distribution that the statistic in question would have if it were computed repeatedly from an infinite number of samples under certain specified conditions. The sampling distribution basically tells us what kinds of values are reasonable to expect for the statistic if the conditions under which the distribution was derived are met. We then examined the null hypothesis and the role it plays in hypothesis testing. We saw that we can test any null hypothesis by asking what the sampling distribution of the relevant statistic would look like if the null hypothesis were true and then comparing our particular statistic to the distribution. We next saw how a simple hypothesis actually could be tested using what we already know about the normal distribution. Finally, we considered Type I and Type II errors and one- and two-tailed tests.

Some important terms in this chapter are

| | |
|---|---|
| Sampling error, *145* | Decision making, *156* |
| Hypothesis testing, *147* | Rejection level (significance level), *156* |
| Sampling distribution, *148* | |
| Standard error, *148* | Rejection region, *156* |
| Sampling distribution of the mean, *149* | Alternative hypothesis ($H_1$), *157* |
| | Critical value, *158* |
| Research hypothesis, *151* | Type I error, *158* |
| Null hypothesis ($H_0$), *151* | $\alpha$ (alpha), *158* |
| Sample statistics, *153* | Type II error, *159* |
| Test statistics, *153* | $\beta$ (beta), *159* |

<table>
<tr><td>Power, 161</td><td>Two-tailed test, 162</td></tr>
<tr><td>One-tailed test, 162</td><td>Nondirectional test, 162</td></tr>
<tr><td>Directional test, 162</td><td></td></tr>
</table>

## 8.13 Exercises

**8.1** Suppose I told you that last night's NHL hockey game resulted in a score of 26 to 13. You would probably decide that I had misread the paper and was discussing something other than a hockey score. In effect you have just tested and rejected a null hypothesis.
(a) What was the null hypothesis?
(b) Outline the hypothesis-testing procedure that you have just applied.

**8.2** For the past year I have spent about $4.00 a day for lunch, give or take a quarter or so.
(a) Draw a rough sketch of this distribution of daily expenditures.
(b) If, without looking at the bill, I paid for my lunch with a $5 bill and received $.75 in change, should I worry that I was overcharged?
(c) Explain the logic involved in your answer to (b).

**8.3** What would be a Type I error in Exercise 8.2?

**8.4** What would be a Type II error in Exercise 8.2?

**8.5** Using the example in Exercise 8.2, describe what we mean by the rejection region and the critical value.

**8.6** Why might I want to adopt a one-tailed test in Exercise 8.2, and which tail should I choose? What would happen if I chose the wrong tail?

**8.7** Imagine that you have just invented a statistical test called the Mode Test to determine whether the mode of a population is some value (e.g., 100). The statistic (M) is calculated as

$$M = \text{Sample mode/Sample range}$$

Describe how you could obtain the sampling distribution of M. (*Note:* This is a purely fictitious statistic.)

**8.8** In Exercise 8.7 what would we call M in the terminology of this chapter?

**8.9** Describe a situation in daily life in which we routinely test hypotheses without realizing it.

**8.10** Define "sampling error."

**8.11** What is the difference between a "distribution" and a "sampling distribution"?

**8.12** How would decreasing $\alpha$ affect the probabilities given in Table 8.1?

**8.13** Give two examples of research hypotheses and state the corresponding null hypotheses.

**8.14** For the distribution in Figure 8.4, I said that the probability of a Type II error ($\beta$) is .74. Show how this probability was obtained.

**8.15** Rerun the calculations in Exercise 8.14 for $\alpha = .01$.

**8.16** In the example in Section 8.10, how would the test have differed if we had chosen to run a two-tailed test?

**8.17** Describe the steps you would go through to flesh out the example given in this chapter about the course evaluations. In other words, how might you go about determining if there truly is a relationship between grades and course evaluations?

**8.18** Describe the steps you would go through to test the hypothesis that motorists are ruder to fellow drivers who drive low-status cars than to those who drive high-status cars.

**8.19** In the exercises in Chapter 2 we discussed a study of allowances in fourth-grade children. We considered that study again in Chapter 4, where you generated data that might have been found in such a study.
(a) Consider how you would go about testing the research hypothesis that boys receive more allowance than girls. What would be the null hypothesis?
(b) Would you use a one-tailed or a two-tailed test?
(c) What results might lead you to reject the null hypothesis, and what might lead you to retain it?
(d) What might you do to make this study more convincing?

**8.20** Simon and Bruce (1991), in demonstrating a different approach to statistics called "resampling statistics," [6] tested the null hypothesis that the price of liquor (in 1961) for the 16 "monopoly" states, where the state owned the liquor stores, was different from the mean price in the 26 "private" states where liquor stores were privately owned. (The means were $4.35 and $4.84, respectively, giving you some hint at the effects of inflation.) For technical reasons several states don't conform to this scheme and could not be analyzed.
(a) What is the null hypothesis that we are actually testing?
(b) What label would you apply to $4.35 and $4.84?
(c) If these are the only states that qualify for our consideration, why are we testing a null hypothesis in the first place?
(d) Identify a situation in which it does make sense to test a null hypothesis here.

**8.21** Several times in this chapter I have drawn a parallel between hypothesis testing and our judicial system. How would you describe the workings of our judicial system in terms of Type I and Type II errors, and in terms of power?

---

[6]The home page containing information on this approach is available at

 http://www.statistics.com/

# Correlation

## QUESTIONS

- How can we plot the relationship between two variables in a way that makes sense of the data?

- How can we measure the degree of relationship quantitatively using the covariance?

- Why is Pearson's Product-Moment Correlation Coefficient ($r$) a better measure of the relationship than was the covariance?

- What do we do if our data are just a bunch of rankings?

- What factors can confuse our interpretation of a correlation?

- How can we tell if a correlation between two variables is really reliably different from zero?

- How do we present correlations if we have more than two variables?

- What are some of the other correlation coefficients we could use?

- What does the printout from standard computer software look like?

**T**he previous chapters have dealt in one way or another with describing data on a single variable. We have discussed the distribution of a variable and how to find its mean and standard deviation. However, some studies are designed to deal with not one dependent variable, but with two or more. In such cases we often are interested in knowing the relationship between two variables, rather than what each variable looks like on its own. To illustrate the kinds of studies that might involve two variables (denoted $X$ and $Y$), consider the following research questions:

- Does the incidence of breast cancer ($Y$) vary with the amount of sunlight ($X$) in a particular location?

- Does life expectancy ($Y$) for individual countries vary as a function of the per capita consumption of alcohol ($X$)?

- Does the rating of an individual's "likability" ($Y$) have anything to do with physical attractiveness ($X$)?

- Does degree of hoarding behavior in hamsters ($Y$) vary as a function of level of deprivation ($X$) during development?

- Does the accuracy of performance ($Y$) decrease as speed of response ($X$) increases?

- Does the average life span ($Y$) in a given country increase as the country's per capita health expenditure ($X$) increases?

In each case we are asking if one variable ($Y$) is related to another variable ($X$). When we are dealing with the relationship between two variables, we are concerned with **correlation**, and our measure of the degree or strength of this relationship is represented by a **correlation coefficient**. We can use a number of different correlation coefficients, depending primarily on the underlying nature of the measurements, but we will see later that in many cases the distinctions among these different coefficients are more apparent than real. For the present we will be concerned with the most common correlation coefficient—the **Pearson product-moment correlation coefficient ($r$)**.

Definition   **Correlation:** Relationship between variables.

**Correlation coefficient:** A measure of the relationship between variables.

**Pearson product-moment correlation coefficient ($r$):** The most common correlation coefficient.

## 9.1 Scatter Diagrams

When we collect measures on two variables for the purpose of examining the relationship between these variables, one of the most useful techniques for gaining insight into this relationship is a **scatterplot** (also called a **scatter diagram** or

**scattergram**). In a scatterplot every experimental subject or unit or observation in the study is represented by a point in two-dimensional space. The coordinates of this point $(X_i, Y_i)$ are the individual's (or object's) scores on variables X and Y, respectively. Examples of three such plots appear in Figures 9.1–9.3.

Definition    **Scatterplot (scatter diagram, scattergram):** A figure in which the individual data points are plotted in two-dimensional space.

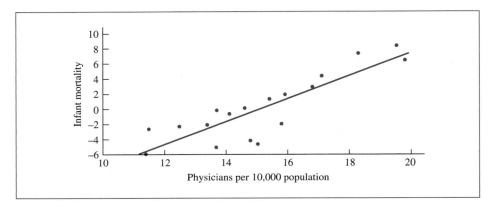

**Figure 9.1**
Infant mortality and physicians

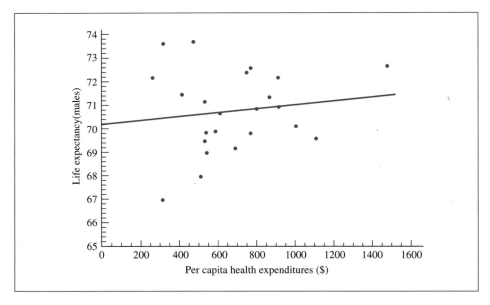

**Figure 9.2**
Life expectancy as a function of health care expenditures

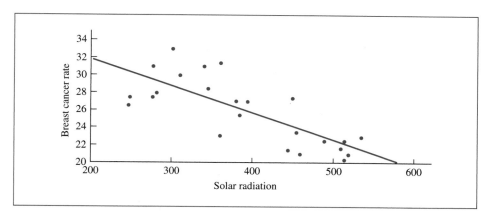

**Figure 9.3**
Cancer rate and solar radiation

In preparing a scatter diagram the **predictor variable**, or independent variable, is traditionally presented on the abscissa, or X axis, and the **criterion variable**, or dependent variable, on the ordinate, or Y axis. If the eventual purpose of the study is to predict one variable from knowledge of the other, the distinction is obvious: The criterion variable is the one to be predicted, whereas the predictor variable is the one from which the prediction is made. If the problem is simply one of obtaining a correlation coefficient, the distinction may be obvious (incidence of cancer would be dependent on amount smoked rather than the reverse, and thus incidence would appear on the ordinate), or it may not (neither running speed nor number of correct choices—common dependent variables in an animal learning study—is obviously in a dependent position relative to the other). Where the distinction is not obvious, it is irrelevant which variable is labeled X and which Y.

Definition | **Predictor variable:** The variable from which a prediction is made.
**Criterion variable:** The variable to be predicted.

Consider the three scatter diagrams in Figures 9.1–9.3. These all represent real data—they have not been contrived. Figure 9.1 is plotted from data reported by St. Leger, Cochrane, and Moore (1978) on the relationship between infant mortality, adjusted for gross national product, and the number of physicians per 10,000 population. (The adjustment for gross national product is what leaves some infant mortality scores negative. That is not a problem.) Notice the fascinating result that infant mortality increases with the number of physicians. That is clearly an unexpected result, but it is almost certainly not due to chance. (As you look at these data and read the rest of the chapter you might think about possible explanations for this surprising result.)

If you aren't quite sure how to plot a scatter diagram, you can see an illustration at

http://www.uvm.edu/~dhowell/fundamentals/More_Stuff/ PlotScatter.html

The lines superimposed on these figures represent those straight lines that "best fit the data." How we determine that line will be the subject of much of the next chapter. I have included the lines in each of these figures because they help to clarify the relationships. These lines are what we will call the **regression lines** of $Y$ predicted on $X$ (abbreviated "$Y$ on $X$"), and they represent our best prediction of $Y_i$ for a given value of $X_i$, where $i$ represents the $i$th value of $X$ or $Y$. Given any specified value of $X$, the corresponding height of the regression line represents our best prediction of $Y$ (designated $\hat{Y}$ and read "$Y$ hat"). In other words, we can draw a vertical line from $X_i$ to the regression line and then move horizontally to the $Y$ axis and read off $\hat{Y}_i$. Again, regression is covered in the next chapter.

---

**Definition**    **Regression line:** The "line of best fit" that represents a straight line drawn through the data points.

---

The degree to which the points cluster around the regression line (in other words, the degree to which the actual values of $Y$ agree with the predicted values) is related to the correlation ($r$) between $X$ and $Y$. Correlation coefficients range between 1 and $-1$. For Figure 9.1 the points cluster very closely about the line, indicating that there is a strong linear relationship between our two variables. If the points fell exactly on the line, the correlation would be $+1.00$. As it is, the correlation is actually .81, which represents a high degree of relationship for real variables. The complete data file for Figure 9.1 can be found at

http://www.uvm.edu/~dhowell/fundamentals/DataFiles/Fig9-1.dat

In Figure 9.2 I have plotted data on the relationship between life expectancy (for males) and per capita expenditure on health care for 23 developed (mostly European) countries. At a time when there is considerable discussion nationally about the cost of health care, these data give us pause. If we were to measure the health of a nation by life expectancy (certainly not the only and admittedly not the best measure), it would appear that the total amount of money we spend on health care bears no relationship to the resultant quality of health (assuming that different countries apportion their expenditures in similar ways). (Several hundred thousand dollars spent on transplanting an organ from a non-human primate into a 57-year-old male may increase his life expectancy by a few years, but it is not going to make a dent in the nation's life expectancy. A similar amount of money spent on the prevention of malaria in young children in sub-Saharan Africa, however, has the potential to have a very substantial effect—hence the inclusion of this example in a text primarily aimed at psychologists.) Notice that the two countries in Figure 9.2 with the longest life expectancy (Iceland and Japan) spend nearly the same amount of money on health care as the country with the shortest life expectancy (Portugal). The United States has the second highest rate of expenditure but ranks near the bottom in life expectancy. Figure 9.2 represents a situation in which there is no apparent relationship between the two variables under consideration. If there were absolutely no relationship between the variables, the correlation would be .0. As it is, the correlation is only .14, and even that can be shown not to be reliably different from .0. The complete data file for Figure 9.2 can be found at

 http://www.uvm.edu/~dhowell/fundamentals/DataFiles/Fig9-2.dat

Finally, Figure 9.3 presents data from a 1991 article in *Newsweek* on the relationship between breast cancer and sunshine. For people like myself who love the sun, it is encouraging to find that there may be at least some benefit from additional sunlight—though that is probably a short-sighted interpretation of the data. Notice that as the amount of solar radiation increases, the incidence of deaths from breast cancer decreases. (There has been considerable research on this topic in recent years, and the reduction in rates of certain kinds of cancer is thought to be related to the body's production of vitamin D, which is increased by sunlight.) This is a good illustration of a negative relationship, and the correlation here is −.76. The complete data file for Figure 9.3 can be found at

 http://www.uvm.edu/~dhowell/fundamentals/DataFiles/Fig9-3.dat

It is important to note that the sign of the correlation coefficient has no meaning other than to denote the direction of the relationship. The correlations of .75 and −.75 signify exactly the same *degree* of relationship. It is only the *direction* of that relationship that is different. For this reason the relationships shown in Figure 9.1 and Figure 9.3 are approximately equally strong, though of the opposite sign.

We will look a little more closely at what produces a high or low correlation by examining one further example. This example is presented in Figure 9.4, and shows the relationship between the incidence of death due to heart attacks in various European countries and the consumption of wine.

There are several things that I can point out with respect to this example that are important in your understanding of correlation and regression.

- Notice that on the X axis I have plotted the log of consumption, rather than consumption itself. This was because consumption was heavily skewed to the right, and taking logs helps to correct this. (The data file on the Web contains both Wine and Logwine, so you can plot either way.)

- Notice that for this example deaths due to heart disease actually decline with an increase in consumption of wine. This was originally a controversial finding, but there is now general

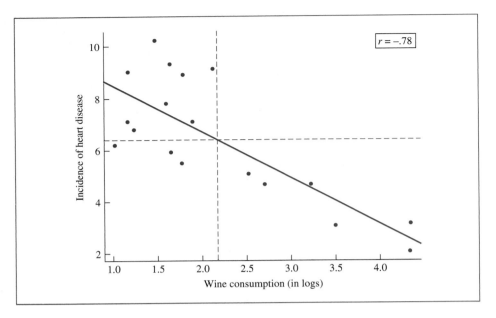

**Figure 9.4**
Relationship between death rate due to heart disease and consumption of wine (on log scale). The dashed lines are at $\overline{X}$ and $\overline{Y}$

agreement that it is a real (though not necessarily causal) effect. This might be taken by some as a license for university students to drink even more. However, heart disease is only rarely a problem for younger people, and no protection is needed. In addition alcohol has many negative effects that are not examined here. It doesn't seem sensible to increase the very real danger of alcohol abuse to ward off a problem that is highly unlikely to arise. Killing yourself by driving into a tree or developing liver problems is not a good way to reduce your risk of dying of heart disease.

- A third point to be made is that in this figure, and the previous figures, the data points represent countries rather than individuals. That just happens to be a characteristic of the data sets that I chose to use. We could, in theory, select a large sample of people, record each person's age at death (admittedly not the same as incidence of heart disease) and then plot each person's age at death against his or her level of wine consumption. It would not be an easy study to run (We would have to call each person up monthly and ask, "Are you dead yet?") but it could be done. But, whereas individuals' age at death varies all over the place (as does wine consumption), a *country's* mean age at death and a *country's* mean wine consumption are quite stable. So we need very many fewer points when each point refers to a country than when each point refers to a person.

- In Figure 9.4 I have drawn vertical and horizontal (dashed) lines corresponding to $\overline{X}$ and $\overline{Y}$. Notice in the upper left quadrant there are 9 observations with an $X$ value less than $\overline{X}$ and a $Y$ value more than $\overline{Y}$. Similarly in the lower right quadrant there are 6 instances where the value is greater than $\overline{X}$ and less than $\overline{Y}$. There are only 3 cases that break this pattern by being above the mean on both variables or below the mean on both variables.

- An interesting discussion of studies relating wine consumption and heart disease can be found at the Chance News site, which always offers an entertaining way to spend your time and frequently teaches me something. The link is

 http://chance.dartmouth.edu/chancewiki/index.php/Chance_News_16

If there were a strong negative relationship between wine drinking and heart disease, we would expect that most of the countries that were high (above the mean) on one variable would be below the mean on the other. Such an idea can be represented by a simple table in which we count the number of observations that were above the mean on both variables, the number below the mean on both variables, and the number above the mean on one and below the mean on the other. Such a table is shown in Table 9.1 for the data in Figure 9.4.

With a strong negative relationship between the two variables, we would expect most of the data points in Table 9.1 to fall into the "Above–Below" and "Below–Above" cells, with only a smattering in the "Above–Above" and "Below–Below" cells. Conversely, if the two variables are not related to each other, we would expect to see approximately equal numbers of data points in the four cells of the table (or quadrants of the scatter diagram). And for a large positive relationship we would expect a preponderance of observations falling into the "Above-Above" and "Below-Below" cells. From Table 9.1 we see that for the relationship between wine consumption and heart disease, 15 out of the 18 participants fall into the cells associated with a negative relationship between the variables. In other words, if a country is below the mean on one variable it is most likely to be above the mean on the other, and vice versa. Only three countries break this pattern. This example,

**Table 9.1**

Examining Scatterplots by Division into Quadrants in Relation to the Means

|  |  | Heart Disease | |
| --- | --- | --- | --- |
|  |  | Above | Below |
| Wine Consumption | Above | 0 | 6 |
|  | Below | 9 | 3 |

then, illustrates in a simple way the interpretation of scatterplots and the relationship between variables.[1] For Figure 9.4 the correlation is $-.78$.

## 9.2 An Example: The Relationship Between the Pace of Life and Heart Disease

The examples that we have seen in the previous pages have either been examples of very strong relationships (positive or negative) or of variables that are nearly independent of each other. Now we will turn to an example in which the correlation is not nearly as high, but is still significantly different from .00.

There is a common belief that people who lead faster-paced lives are more susceptible to heart disease and other forms of fatal illness. Levine (1990) published data on the "pace of life" and age-adjusted death rates from ischemic heart disease. In his case he collected data from 36 cities, varying in size and geographical location. To measure the "pace of life" he recorded the time that it took a bank clerk to make change for a $20 bill, the time it took an average person to walk 60 feet, and the speed at which people spoke. In each case the people being measured were not aware of the measurement. Levine also recorded the age-adjusted death rate from ischemic heart disease for each city. The data are given in Table 9.2, where "pace" is taken as the average of the three measures. (The units of

**Table 9.2**
Pace of Life and Death Rate Due to Heart Disease in 36 U.S. Cities

| Pace (X) | 27.67 | 25.33 | 23.67 | 26.33 | 26.33 | 25.00 | 26.67 | 26.33 | 24.33 | 25.67 |
|---|---|---|---|---|---|---|---|---|---|---|
| Heart (Y) | 24 | 29 | 31 | 26 | 26 | 20 | 17 | 19 | 26 | 24 |
| Pace (X) | 22.67 | 25.00 | 26.00 | 24.00 | 26.33 | 20.00 | 24.67 | 24.00 | 24.00 | 20.67 |
| Heart (Y) | 26 | 25 | 14 | 11 | 19 | 24 | 20 | 13 | 20 | 18 |
| Pace (X) | 22.33 | 22.00 | 19.33 | 19.67 | 23.33 | 22.33 | 20.33 | 23.33 | 20.33 | 22.67 |
| Heart (Y) | 16 | 19 | 23 | 11 | 27 | 18 | 15 | 20 | 18 | 21 |
| Pace (X) | 20.33 | 22.00 | 20.00 | 18.00 | 16.67 | 15.00 | | | | |
| Heart (Y) | 11 | 14 | 19 | 15 | 18 | 16 | | | | |

| | | |
|---|---|---|
| $\Sigma X = 822.333$ | $\Sigma Y = 713$ | $\Sigma XY = 16{,}487.67$ |
| $\Sigma X^2 = 19{,}102.33$ | $\Sigma Y^2 = 15{,}073$ | $N = 36$ |
| $\overline{X} = 723.74$ | $\overline{Y} = 5.351$ | |
| $s_X = 3.015$ | $s_Y = 5.214$ | |

---

[1] It is interesting to note that in the days before computers and electronic calculators, many textbooks showed how to estimate the correlation coefficient by breaking the scatterplot into squares and counting the number of observations in each square. The breakdown was finer than the four quadrants used here, but the idea was the same. Fortunately, we no longer need to compute correlations that way, though the approach is instructive.

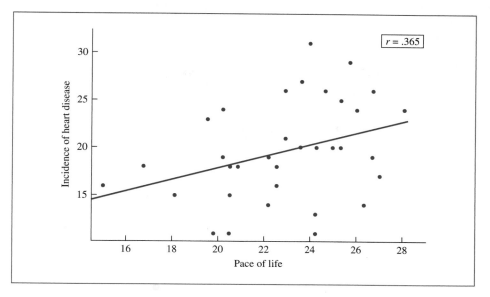

**Figure 9.5**

Relationship between pace of life and age-adjusted rate of heart disease

measurement are arbitrary. The data on all pace variables are included in the data set on the Web.) The data are plotted in Figure 9.5.

As you can see from this figure, there is a tendency for the age-adjusted incidence of heart disease to be higher in cities where the pace of life is faster—where people speak more quickly, walk faster, and carry out simple tasks at a faster rate.

From an inspection of Figure 9.5, you can see a strong positive relationship between the pace of life and heart disease—as pace increases, deaths from heart disease also increase, and vice versa. It is a **linear relationship** because the best-fitting line is straight. (We say that a relationship is linear if the criterion variable increases in a straight-line fashion with increases in the predictor variable. This is the same as saying that a relationship is linear if the best (or nearly best) fit to the data comes from a straight line. If the best-fitting line were not straight, we would refer to it as a **curvilinear relationship**.) I have drawn in this line to make the relationship clearer. Look at the scatterplot in Figure 9.5. If you just look at the people with the highest- and lowest-paced scores, you will see that the death rate is nearly twice as high in the former group.

---

Definition     **Linear relationship:** A situation in which the best-fitting regression line is a straight line.

**Curvilinear relationship:** A situation that is best represented by something other than a straight line.

---

## 9.3 The Covariance

The correlation coefficient that we want to compute on these data is itself based on a statistic called the **covariance**. The covariance is basically a number that reflects the degree to which two variables vary together. If, for example, high scores on one variable tend to be paired with high scores on the other, the covariance will be large and positive. When high scores on one variable are paired about equally often with both high and low scores on the other, the covariance will be near zero.

---

Definition    **Covariance:** A statistic representing the degree to which two variables vary together.

**Deviation score:** The difference between a score and the mean $(X - \overline{X})$.

---

To define the covariance mathematically we can write

$$cov_{XY} = \frac{\Sigma(X - \overline{X})(Y - \overline{Y})}{N - 1}$$

From this equation it is apparent that the covariance is similar in form to the variance. If we changed each $Y$ in the equation to $X$, we would have $s_X^2$. It is also apparent that the covariance is based on how an observation deviates from the mean on each variable, which is the point that was illustrated in Figure 9.4 and Table 9.1. (An expression of the form $(X - \overline{X})$ is called a **deviation score** because it measures the degree to which $X$ deviates from the mean, $(\overline{X})$. In Figure 9.4 the deviations would be the horizontal and vertical distance between each point and the dashed lines. You can see from the formula that the numerator for the covariance is the product of two deviation scores.) You can gain some insight into the meaning of the covariance by considering what we would expect to find in the case of a high negative correlation, such as the data in Table 9.2. In that situation high Pace scores will be paired with low Heart scores. Thus for a city with a high Pace score, $(X - \overline{X})$ will be positive, $(Y - \overline{Y})$ will be negative, and their product will be negative. For a city with a low Pace score, $(X - \overline{X})$ will be negative, $(Y - \overline{Y})$ will be positive, and the product will again be negative. Thus we will find that the sum of $[(X - \overline{X})(Y - \overline{Y})]$ will be large and negative, giving a large negative covariance. (To help you see this, take a few of the data points from Figure 9.4 or Table 9.2 and work out their contribution to the covariance.)

Next, consider the case of a strong positive relationship. Here large positive values of $(X - \overline{X})$ will be paired with large positive values of $(Y - \overline{Y})$ and vice versa. The sum of products of the deviations will be large and positive, indicating a high positive relationship. Such a situation was illustrated in Figure 9.3, where we saw the relationships between infant mortality and the number of physicians.

Finally, consider a situation in which there is no relationship between X and Y. In that case a positive value of $(X - \overline{X})$ will sometimes be paired with a positive value of $(Y - \overline{Y})$ and sometimes with a negative value. The result is that the products of the deviations will be positive about half the time and negative about half the time, producing a near-zero sum and indicating no relationship between the variables. A slightly less extreme instance of this case was illustrated in Figure 9.2.

It is possible to show that the covariance will be at its positive maximum whenever X and Y are perfectly positively correlated ($r = +1.00$), and at its negative maximum whenever they are perfectly negatively correlated ($r = -1$). When there is no relationship ($r = 0$), the covariance will be zero.

For computational purposes a simple expression for the covariance is given by

$$\text{cov}_{XY} = \frac{\Sigma(X - \overline{X})(Y - \overline{Y})}{N - 1} = \frac{\Sigma XY - \dfrac{\Sigma X \Sigma Y}{N}}{N - 1}$$

As you should remember from Chapter 2, $\Sigma XY$ is calculated by multiplying each participant's X score by his or her Y score and then summing the results across participants. For the data in Table 9.2, $\Sigma XY = 27.67 \times 24 + 25.33 \times 29 + 23.67 \times 31 + \cdots + 15.00 \times 16 = 16{,}487.67$. Using the results for the data in Table 9.2, the covariance is

$$\text{cov}_{XY} = \frac{\Sigma XY - \dfrac{\Sigma X \Sigma Y}{N}}{N - 1} = \frac{16{,}487.67 - \dfrac{(822.333)(713)}{36}}{35} = 5.74$$

# 9.4 The Pearson Product-Moment Correlation Coefficient (*r*)

What I have just said about the covariance might suggest that we could use the covariance as a measure of the degree of relationship between two variables. An immediate difficulty arises, however, in that the absolute value of $\text{cov}_{XY}$ is also a function of the standard deviations of X and Y. For example, $\text{cov}_{XY} = 20$ might reflect a high degree of correlation when the standard deviations are small, but a low degree of correlation when the standard deviations are large. To resolve this difficulty, we will divide the covariance by the standard deviations and make the result our estimate of correlation. (Technically, this is known as *scaling* the covariance by the standard deviations because we basically are changing the scale on which it is measured.) We will define what is known as the Pearson product-moment correlation coefficient ($r$) as[2]

$$r = \frac{cov_{XY}}{s_X s_Y}$$

The maximum value of $cov_{XY}$ turns out to be $\pm s_X s_Y$. (This can be shown mathematically, but just trust me.) Because the maximum of $cov_{XY}$ is $\pm s_X s_Y$, it follows that the limits on $r$ are $\pm 1.00$. One interpretation of $r$, then, is that it is a measure of the degree to which the covariance approaches its maximum.

An equivalent way of writing the preceding equation would be to replace the variances and covariances by their computational formulae and then simplify by cancellation. If we do this, we will arrive at

$$r = \frac{N\Sigma XY - \Sigma X \Sigma Y}{\sqrt{[N\Sigma X^2 - (\Sigma X)^2][N\Sigma Y^2 - (\Sigma Y)^2]}}$$

This formula is useful if you are calculating correlations by hand, and I am including it because several reviewers asked to have it here. But since most calculators produce the means and standard deviations automatically, it is usually much simpler to use the first formula in this section. That one at least has the advantage of making it clear what is happening. Both equations for $r$ will produce exactly the same answer; the choice is up to you. I prefer the expression in terms of the covariance and the standard deviations, but historically the second one has appeared in most texts.

Applying the first equation to the data in Table 9.2, we have

$$r = \frac{cov_{XY}}{s_X s_Y} = \frac{5.74}{(3.015)(5.214)} = .365$$

I leave the calculations using the second formula to you. You will find that it will give the same result.

The correlation coefficient must be interpreted cautiously so as not to attribute to it meaning that it does not possess. Specifically, $r = .36$ should not be interpreted to mean that there is 36% of a relationship (whatever that might mean) between Pace and Heart. The correlation coefficient is simply a point on the scale between $-1.00$ and $+1.00$, and the closer it is to either of those limits, the stronger is the relationship between the two variables. For a more specific interpretation we will prefer to speak in terms of $r^2$, which is discussed in Chapter 10.

---

[2]This coefficient is named after its creator (Karl Pearson). Deviations of the form $(X - \overline{X})$ and $(Y - \overline{Y})$ are called "moments," hence the phrase "product-moment."

## 9.5 Correlations with Ranked Data

In the previous example the data for each subject were recorded in everyday units such as the time to do three tasks and the incidence of deaths due to heart disease. Sometimes, however, we ask judges to rank items on two dimensions; we then want to correlate the two sets of ranks. For example, we might ask one judge to rank the quality of the "Statement of Purpose" found in 10 applications to graduate school in terms of clarity, specificity, and apparent sincerity. The weakest would be assigned a rank of 1, the next weakest a rank of 2, and so on. Another judge might rank the overall acceptability of these same 10 applicants based on all other available information, and we might be interested in the degree to which well-written statements of purpose are associated with highly admissible applicants. When we have such **ranked data**, we frequently use what is known as **Spearman's correlation coefficient for ranked data**, denoted $r_S$. (This is not the only coefficient that can be calculated from ranked data, nor even the best, but it is one of the simplest and most common.)

Definition | **Ranked data:** Data for which the observations have been replaced by their numerical ranks from lowest to highest.

**Spearman's correlation coefficient for ranked data ($r_S$):** A correlation coefficient on ranked data.

In the past when people obtained correlations by hand, they could save time by using special formulae. For example, if the data are ranks of $N$ objects, you can either add up all the ranks, or you can calculate $\Sigma X = N(N + 1)/2$. The answers will be the same. That was fine when we had to calculate using pencil and paper, but there is relatively little to be gained now by doing so. But that kind of formula is exactly where Spearman's formula came from. He just took Pearson's formula and made some substitutions. But if you apply Pearson's formula to those ranks instead of Spearman's, you will get the correct answer without memorizing another formula. In fact, no matter how you calculate it, Spearman's $r_S$ is a plain old Pearson product-moment correlation coefficient, only this time it is calculated on ranks rather than on measured variables. The interpretation, however, is not quite the same as the usual Pearson correlation coefficient.

### Why Rank?

It is one thing to think of Spearman's $r_S$ when the data naturally occur in the form of ranks. (For example, when the participant is asked to "Rank these cookies in terms of preference.") But why would someone want to rank values on a continuous variable? The main reason for ranking is that you either do not trust the nature of the underlying scale or you want to down-weight extreme scores. As an example of the former, we might measure a person's social isolation by the number of friends he claims to have and measure his physical attractiveness by asking an independent judge to assign a rating on a 10-point scale. Having very little faith in the underlying properties of either scale, we might then simply convert the raw data on each variable to ranks (e.g., the person reporting the fewest friends is assigned a rank of 1, and so on) and carry out our correlations with those ranks. But what about the case where you might want to down-weight extreme values? In Exercise 9.10 you will see data on the incidence of Down's syndrome as a function of age of the mother. Incidence differences due to age in younger mothers are quite small, but among older ages incidence increases sharply. Ranking will rein in those later increases and keep them at the same general level of magnitude as increases as younger ages. Whether this is a smart thing to do is a different question, and it is one you would need to consider.

### The Interpretation of $r_S$

Spearman's $r_S$ and other coefficients calculated on ranked data are slightly more difficult to interpret than Pearson's $r$, partly because of the nature of the data. In the example that I have described concerning rankings of statements of purpose, the data occurred naturally in the form of ranks because that is the task that we set our judges. In this situation, $r_S$ is a measure of the linear (straight line) relationship between one set of ranks and another set of ranks.

In cases where we convert the obtained data to a set of ranks, $r_S$ is a measure of the linearity of the relationship between the ranks, but it is a measure only of the **monotonic relationship** between the original variables. (A monotonic relationship is one that is continuously rising or continuously falling—the line does not need to be straight; it can go up for a while, level off, and then rise again. It just can't reverse direction and start falling.) This relationship should not surprise you. A correlation coefficient, regardless of whether it is a Pearson correlation or a Spearman correlation, tells us directly only about the variables on which it is computed. It cannot be expected to give very precise information about variables on which it was not computed. As discussed in Chapter 2, it is essential to keep in mind the similar distinction between the variables that you have actually measured (e.g., number of friends) and the underlying property that you want to examine (e.g., social isolation).

---

Definition  **Monotonic relationship:** A relationship represented by a line that is continually increasing (or decreasing), but perhaps not in a straight line.

---

## 9.6 Factors That Affect the Correlation

The correlation coefficient can be importantly affected by characteristics of the sample. Three of these characteristics are the restriction of the range (or variance) of $X$ and/or $Y$, nonlinearity of the relationship, and the use of heterogeneous subsamples.

## The Effect of Range Restrictions and Nonlinearity

A common problem that arises in many instances concerns restrictions on the range over which X and Y vary. The effect of such **range restrictions** is to alter the correlation between X and Y from what it would have been if the range had not been so restricted. Depending on the nature of the data, the correlation may either rise or fall as a result of such restrictions, although most commonly r is reduced.

---

Definition   **Range restrictions:** Cases wherein the range over which X or Y varies is artificially limited.

---

With the exception of very unusual circumstances, restricting the range of X will increase r only when the restriction results in eliminating some curvilinear relationship. For example, if we correlated height with age, where age ran from 0 to 70, the data would be decidedly curvilinear (rising to about 17 years of age and then leveling off or even declining), and the correlation, which measures linear relationships, would be quite low. If, however, we restricted the range of ages to 4 to 17, the correlation would be quite high, because we have eliminated those values of Y that were not varying linearly with X.

The more usual effect of restricting the range of X or Y is to reduce the correlation. This problem is especially important in the area of test construction, because in that area the criterion measure (Y) may be available for only the higher values of X. Consider the hypothetical data in Figure 9.6. *Note:* An excellent

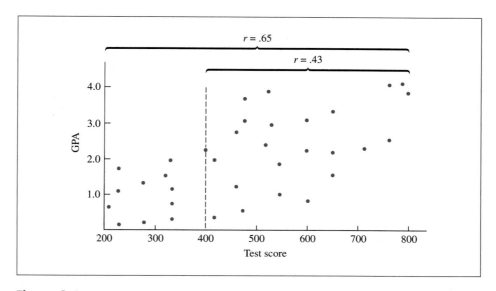

**Figure 9.6**
Hypothetical data illustrating the effect of restricted range

demonstration that you can manipulate yourself has been written by David Lane at Rice and can be found on the Connexions Web site. The URL is

 http://cnx.org/content/m11196/latest/

This figure represents the relationship between college grade point averages and scores on a standard achievement test for a sample of students. In the ideal world of the test constructor, all people who took the exam would then be sent to college and receive a grade point average, and the correlation between test scores and grade point averages would be computed. As can be seen from Figure 9.6, this correlation would be reasonably high ($r = .65$).

In the real world, however, not everyone is admitted to college. Colleges take only those who they think are the more able students, whether this ability is measured by achievement test scores, high school performance, or whatever. That means college grade point averages are available mainly for students having relatively high scores on the standardized test. This has the effect of allowing us to evaluate the relationship between $X$ and $Y$ for only those values of, say, $X$ greater than 400.

The effect of range restrictions must be taken into account whenever we see a coefficient based on a restricted sample. The coefficient might be quite inappropriate for the question at hand. Essentially what we have done is to ask how well a standardized test predicts a person's suitability for college, but we have answered that question by reference only to those people who are actually admitted to college. At the same time, it is sometimes useful to deliberately restrict the range of one of the variables. For example, if we wanted to know the way in which reading ability increases linearly with age, we probably would restrict the age range by using only subjects who are at least 5 years old and less than 20 years old (or some other reasonable limits). We presumably would never expect reading ability to continue to rise indefinitely.

## The Effect of Heterogeneous Subsamples

Another important consideration in evaluating the results of correlational analyses deals with **heterogeneous subsamples**. This point can be illustrated with a simple example involving the relationship between height and weight in male and female subjects. These variables may appear to have little to do with psychology, but considering the important role both variables play in the development of people's images of themselves, the example is not as far afield as you might expect. In addition, these relationships play a role in the debate over the appropriateness of the Body Mass Index (BMI), which is used in many studies of diet and health. The data plotted in Figure 9.7 come from sample data from the Minitab manual (Ryan et al., 1985). These are actual data from 92 college students who were asked to report height, weight, gender, and several other variables. (Keep in mind that these are self-report data, and there may be systematic reporting biases.) The complete data file can be found at

 http://www.uvm.edu/~dhowell/fundamentals/DataFiles/Fig9-7.dat

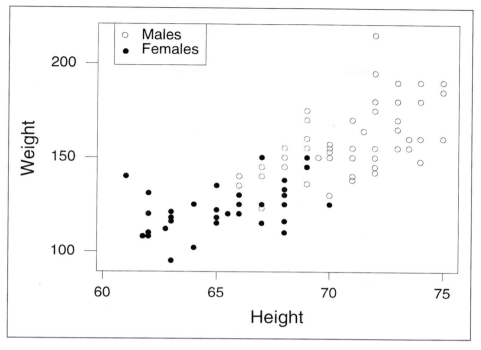

**Figure 9.7**
Relationship between height and weight for males and females combined

Definition   **Heterogeneous subsamples:** Data in which the sample of observations could be subdivided into two distinct sets on the basis of some other variable.

When we combine the data from both males and females, the relationship is strikingly good, with a correlation of .78. When you look at the data from the two genders separately, however, the correlations fall to .60 for males and .49 for females. (Males and females have been plotted using different symbols, with data from females primarily in the lower left.) The important point is that the high correlation we found when we combined genders is not due purely to the relation between height and weight. It is also due largely to the fact that men are, on average, taller and heavier than women. In fact, a little doodling on a sheet of paper will show that you could create artificial, and improbable, data where within each gender weight is negatively related to height, while the relationship is positive when you collapse across gender. (There is an example of this kind of relationship in Exercise 9.25.) The point I am making here is that experimenters must be careful when they combine data from several sources. The relationship between two variables may be obscured or enhanced by the presence of a third variable. Such a finding is important in its own right.

A second example of heterogeneous subsamples that makes a similar point is the relationship between cholesterol consumption and cardiovascular disease in men and women. If you collapse across both genders, the relationship is not impressive. But when you separate the data by male and female, there is a distinct trend for cardiovascular disease to increase with increased consumption of cholesterol. This relationship is obscured in the combined data because men, regardless of cholesterol level, have an elevated level of cardiovascular disease compared to women.

## 9.7 Beware Extreme Observations

An interesting data set on the relationship between smoking and drinking can be found at the Data and Story Library Web site (DASL). The data are from a British government survey of households in Britain on household spending on tobacco products and alcohol. The data are given in Table 9.3 for 11 regions in Great Britain, where I have recorded the average amount of household income spent on each item. These data are available at

 http://www.uvm.edu/~dhowell/fundamentals/DataFiles/Tab9-3.dat

I would expect that these two variables would tend to be related, just based on common observation. But if we compute the correlation, it is only .224, and the $p$ value is .509, meaning that we should not be surprised by a correlation at least that high from 11 pairs of observations even if the null hypothesis is true. Perhaps my intuition is wrong, or maybe there is some other explanation.

The first thing that we should do with any data, even before we jump in and calculate the correlation, is to look at the distributions. If you do, you will see that

**Table 9.3**
Household Expenditures on Tobacco and Alcohol Products in Great Britain

| Region | Alcohol | Tobacco |
|---|---|---|
| North | 6.47 | 4.03 |
| Yorkshire | 6.13 | 3.76 |
| Northeast | 6.19 | 3.77 |
| East Midlands | 4.89 | 3.34 |
| West Midlands | 5.63 | 3.47 |
| East Anglia | 4.52 | 2.92 |
| Southeast | 5.89 | 3.20 |
| Southwest | 4.79 | 2.71 |
| Wales | 5.27 | 3.53 |
| Scotland | 6.08 | 4.51 |
| Northern Ireland | 4.02 | 4.56 |

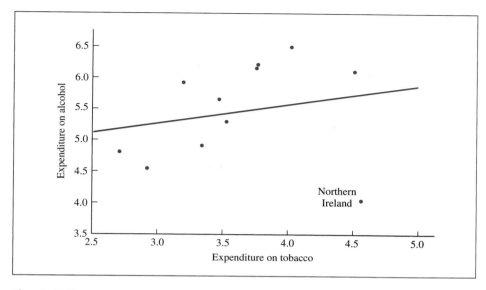

**Figure 9.8**

Scatterplot of expenditures on alcohol and tobacco

no region is particularly unusual on either variable. Expenditures in Northern Ireland on alcohol are lower than elsewhere, but not dramatically so. Similarly, the people of Northern Ireland spend a bit more on tobacco than others, but not unduly so. However, if you create a scatterplot of these data you see a problem. The plot is given in Figure 9.8.

Notice that everything looks fine except for the data point for Northern Ireland. Though it is not unusually extreme on either of the variables taken alone, the combination of the two is indeed extreme, because it is unusual to have an observation be so high on one variable *and* so low on the other. If we remove Northern Ireland from the data, we find that the remaining points show a correlation of .784, and an associated two-tailed $p$ value of .007. This is more like what I would have expected.

So, can we just toss out observations that we don't like? Not really. At least you can't just pretend they are not there. It is appropriate to leave out Northern Ireland if we make clear what we have done, and either offer a reasonable excuse for omitting that data point or else make clear to our reader that the point is aberrant for unknown reasons, and also report the result of including that point.

## 9.8 Correlation and Causation

A statement that you will find in virtually every discussion of correlation is that correlation does not imply causation. Just because two variables are correlated doesn't mean that one caused the other. In fact, I would guess that most of the time that is not the case. Textbook authors usually make this statement, give one extreme example, and move on. But I think that we need to dwell on this point a bit longer.

I have shown you several examples of correlated variables in this chapter. We began with the case of infant mortality and number of physicians in the area, and I assume everyone is willing to agree that there is no way that having more physicians causes an increase in mortality. Doctors try very hard not to kill people. Then we had the case of life expectancy and health care expenditures, and we really didn't have to even consider causation because there was clearly no relationship. (We might, however, wonder what causes our variables to appear so completely unrelated.) Then we saw the relationship between solar radiation and breast cancer, and the relationship between wine consumption and heart disease. There we have to be a great deal more careful. In both cases it would be tempting to think in terms of causation, and actually causation might be a logical explanation. Solar radiation does increase the production of vitamin D, and that might play a protective role against breast cancer. Similarly, compounds in wine might actually reduce the bodily processes that lead to heart disease. How are we to know whether we are talking about causation or something else?

Otts (2005) presents an excellent list of possible explanations of a significant correlation between two variables. In what follows, I am unabashedly following her lead. She suggested seven possible reasons for two variables to be correlated, and only one of them is causal.

1. The relationship actually could be causal. Sunlight does increase the production of vitamin D, and vitamin D might very well protect the body against breast cancer.

2. We may have the relationship backward, and the response variable could actually cause the explanatory variable. It might appear that happiness leads to better social relationships, but it is just as plausible that having good social relationships leads to people feeling happier about their lives.

3. The relationship may be only partially causal. The predictor variable may be a necessary cause, but changes in the dependent variable either only occur, or are accentuated in the presence of some other variable. Increased wealth may lead to increased happiness, but only if other conditions (e.g., a supportive family, good friends, etc.) are present.

4. There may be a third, confounding, variable present. The changing size of the population of the United States is correlated with changes in infant mortality, but no one believes that having more people around reduces the number of infants who die. Both of those variables are related to time and to the other changes in health care that have occurred over that time.

5. Both variables may be related to a third, causal, variable. Family stability and physical illness may be correlated because both are themselves a function of outside stresses on the individual.

**6.** Variables may be changing over time. Ott gives the nice example of the high correlation between divorce rate and incidence of drug offenses. Those variables are correlated mainly because they both are increasing over time.

**7.** The correlation may be due to coincidence. Your father-in-law moves in on you and your marriage goes down the tubes. It could be that your father-in-law is truly a disruptive influence, but it could also be that those two things just happened to occur at the same time. We often see causal relationships when no cause exists.

It is very difficult to establish causal relationships, and we need to be careful about any assertions of cause. One important consideration is that in order for A to cause B, A must occur before, or at the same time as B. Causation cannot work backward in time. Second, we need to rule out other variables. If we can show that A leads to B in both the presence and the absence of other possible causal factors, we have strengthened our argument. That is one reason that science is so concerned with randomization, and especially with random assignment. If we take a large group of people, *randomly* split them into three groups, expose the three groups to different conditions, and show that the three groups subsequently behave reliably differently, we have a good argument for causation. The random assignment makes it highly unlikely that there are systematic differences between the groups that were responsible for whatever differences occurred. Finally, before we declare that one variable causes another, we need to come up with some reasonable explanation of how this could be. If we can't explain why we found what we did, the best that we can say is that this is a relationship worth exploring further to see if an explanation for the correlation can be found. This leads nicely to the next section.

## 9.9 If Something Looks Too Good to Be True, Perhaps It Is

Not all statistical results mean what they seem to mean; in fact, not all results are meaningful. This is a point that will be made repeatedly throughout this book, and it is particularly appropriate when we are speaking about correlation and regression.

In Figure 9.1 we saw a plot of data collected by Cochrane, St. Leger, and Moore (1978) on the relationship between a country's infant mortality rate and the number of physicians per 10,000 population. This correlation ($r = .88$) was not only remarkably high, but positive. The data indicate that as the number of physicians increases, the infant mortality rate also increases. What are we to make of such data? Are physicians really responsible for deaths of children? In the previous section I said that I strongly doubted that the relationship was causal, and I hope that everyone would agree with that.

No one has seriously suggested that physicians actually do harm to children, and it is highly unlikely that there is a causal link between these two variables. For our purposes the data are worth studying more for what they have to say about correlation and regression than for what they have to say about infant mortality, and it is worth considering possible explanations. In doing so, we have to keep several facts in mind. First, these data are all from developed countries, primarily but not exclusively in Western Europe. In other words, we are speaking of countries with high levels of health care. Although undoubtedly there are substantial differences in infant mortality (and the number of physicians) among these countries, these differences are nowhere near as large as we would expect if we took a random sample of all countries. This suggests that at least some of the variability in infant mortality that we are trying to explain is probably more meaningless random fluctuation in the system than meaningful variability. The second thing to keep in mind is that these data are selective. Cochrane et al. did not simply take a random sample of developed countries—they chose carefully what data to include. We might, and indeed would, obtain somewhat less dramatic relationships if we looked at a more inclusive group of developed countries. A third consideration is that Cochrane et al. selected this particular relationship from among many that they looked at because it was a surprising finding. (If you look hard enough, you are likely to find something interesting in any set of data, even when there is nothing really important going on.)

In terms of explanations for the finding shown in Figure 9.1, let's consider a few possible—though not terribly good—ones. In the first place it might be argued that we have a reporting problem. With more physicians we stand a better chance of having infant deaths reported, causing the number of reported deaths to increase with increases in physicians. This would be a reasonable explanation if we were speaking of underdeveloped countries, but we are not. It is probably unlikely that many deaths would go unreported in Western Europe or North America even if there weren't so many physicians. Another possibility is that physicians go where the health problems are. This argument implies a cause-and-effect relationship, but in the opposite direction—high infant mortality causes a high number of physicians. A third possibility is that high population densities tend to lead to high infant mortality and also tend to attract physicians. In the United States both urban poverty and physicians tend to congregate in urban centers. (How would you go about testing such a hypothesis?)

## 9.10 Testing the Significance of a Correlation Coefficient

The fact that a sample correlation coefficient is not exactly zero does not necessarily mean that those variables are truly correlated in the population. For example, I wrote a simple program that drew 25 numbers from a random number generator and arbitrarily named that variable "income." I then drew another 25 random numbers and named that variable "musicality." When I paired the first number of each set with the first number of the other set, the second with the second, and so on, and calculated the correlation between the two variables, I obtained a correlation of .278. That seems pretty good. It looks as if I've shown that the more musical a person is the greater his or her income (and vice versa). But we know these data are just random numbers, and there really isn't any true correlation between two sets of random numbers. I just happened to get a reasonably large value of $r$ by chance.

The point of this example is *not* to illustrate that statistics lie. (I hear too many comments to that effect already!) The point is that correlation coefficients, like all other statistics, suffer from sampling error. They deviate from the true correlations in the population (in this case zero) by some amount. Sometimes they are too high, sometimes too low, and sometimes, but rarely, right on. If I drew a new set of data in the previous example, I might get $r = .15$, or maybe $r = .03$, or maybe even $r = -.20$. But I probably would not get $r = .95$ or $r = -.87$. Small deviations from the true value of zero are to be expected; large deviations are not.

But how large is large? When do we decide that our correlation coefficient is far enough from zero that we can no longer believe it likely that the true correlation in the population is zero? This is where we come to the issue of hypothesis testing developed in Chapter 8.

You may recall that I began Chapter 8 with an example about course evaluations and students' anticipated grades. For each of 50 courses I know the mean overall course evaluation rating and the mean anticipated grade—in both cases averaging across all students in the course. (These are actual data.) I have calculated that for this sample the correlation between evaluations and anticipated grades is .30. But I want to know whether those variables are truly correlated in the whole population of courses. In order to arrive at some decision on this question, I will set up my null hypothesis that the **population correlation coefficient rho** (denoted $\rho$) is 0 (i.e., $H_0: \rho = 0$). If I am able to reject $H_0$, I will be able to conclude that how students evaluate a course is related to how well the students expect to do in terms of grades. If I cannot reject $H_0$, I will have to conclude that I have insufficient evidence to show that these variables are related, and I will treat them as linearly independent.

---

**Definition**    **Population correlation coefficient rho ($\rho$):** The correlation coefficient for the population.

---

I prefer to use two-tailed tests, so I will choose to reject $H_0$ if the obtained correlation is too large in either a positive or a negative direction. In other words, I am testing

$$H_0: \rho = 0$$

against

$$H_0: \rho \neq 0$$

But we are still left with the question, "How big is too big?" There are at least three ways to answer, and I have chosen to discuss the two simplest ways. I'll start with the use of tables.

Table D.2 in Appendix D shows how large a sample correlation coefficient must be before we declare the null hypothesis to be rejected. To use this table, we have to know the degrees of freedom, which are directly linked to the sample size. When we are predicting one variable from one other variable, as we are in this chapter, the degrees of freedom $= N - 2$, where $N$ is the size of our sample. We are using an example where $N = 50$, so we would look up the critical value for 48 $df$, which we find to be approximately .279. (I say "approximately" because the table lists 40 and 50 $df$ but not 48, so I needed to interpolate. Since 48 is eight-tenths of the way between 40 and 50, I'll take as my critical value the value that is eight-tenths of the way between .304 and .273, which is .279.) Thus a sample correlation greater than or equal to .279 is significant at the 5% level of significance, meaning we can reject $H_0$ at $\alpha = .05$. Our sample correlation was .30, which is more extreme than .279, so we will reject $H_0$. To say this a little differently, if we take a situation in which we know the null hypothesis ($H_0$: $\rho = 0$) to be true (as, for example, the random number experiment that started this section), and if we have 50 cases with scores on the two variables, only 5% of the time will we obtain a sample correlation greater than or equal to $\pm.279$. Thus a correlation of $r = .30$ or more would occur less than 5% of the time if $H_0$ were true, so we can reject $H_0$.

I can state all this in terms of a rule. First, calculate the sample correlation and compute $df = N - 2$, where $N$ is the number of pairs of observations. Next look in Table D.2 and find the critical value of $r$. We then reject $H_0$: $\rho = 0$ whenever the absolute value of $r$ (i.e., ignore its sign) is greater than or equal to the tabled critical value.[3]

With virtually all computer programs used today, you don't even need to use a table. Most programs print out the probability (either one-tailed or two-tailed) associated with the computed value of $r$. This is the probability of obtaining that value of $r$ or one more extreme when $H_0$ is true. In our case a program would give a two-tailed probability of .0338. This means that if $H_0$ is true, the probability that we would obtain a sample correlation at least as large (positive or negative) as the one obtained is .0338. We reject $H_0$ whenever this value is less than .05. As an example, look ahead to Figure 9.10 (p. 199), where you will see that SPSS gives the correlation between life expectancy and expenditures as .138. Below this is the two-tailed significance value of .53, meaning that a correlation as extreme as this has a probability of .53 of occurring when the null hypothesis is true. We certainly have no reason to reject $H_0$.

In an extension of what I did at the start of this section, I drew five independent random variables of 20 observations each from a normally distributed population, and correlated them. By looking at the table of intercorrelations

---

[3]In the first paragraph of this section I wrote about drawing 25 pairs of random numbers and obtaining a correlation coefficient of .278. With 23 $df$ Appendix D.2 shows that at $\alpha = .05$ (two-tailed), the critical value is .396. So a correlation of .278 is well within the expected range for a sample correlation if $N = 25$ and $\rho = 0$.

(see the next section for a definition), you can get a sense of how much sample correlations vary over repeated sampling when the correlation in the population is 0. This example is contained in

 http://www.uvm.edu/~dhowell/fundamentals/More_Stuff/SampDistCorr.html

This example also illustrates what happens when you increase the sample size from $N = 20$ to $N = 200$ observations. The difference is quite dramatic.

## 9.11 Intercorrelation Matrices

So far we have largely been speaking about the relationship between two variables. Often, however, we have a whole set of variables and want to know how they relate to each other in a pairwise fashion. In Figure 9.9 I plotted, in one table, the correlations among several variables concerned with course evaluation. The raw data are available at

 http://www.uvm.edu/~dhowell/fundamentals/DataFiles/Fig9-9.dat

The variables appear in the order Overall, Teach, Exam, Knowledge, Grade, and Enroll.

| Definition | **Intercorrelation matrix:** A matrix (table) showing the pairwise correlations among all variables. |
| --- | --- |

Above the plots is a matrix of correlations among a set of variables. This is known as an **intercorrelation matrix**. These data are a sample of 50 courses from a complete set of course evaluations performed on several hundred classes in a large state university. They relate to the overall quality of the course (Overall), the rating of the skills of the teacher (Teach), the fairness of the exams (Exam), the instructor's apparent knowledge of the material (Knowledge), the student's expected grade (Grade), and class size (Enroll). The curved lines in each little box in the plots are portions of ellipses that are derived to include 95% of the data points. (The ellipses are cut off at the borders of the boxes, which is what makes them look so odd.) In these plots you can see how each variable is related to each of the other variables. (Notice that the correlation between the overall rating and the anticipated grade is given as .30, the value we used earlier.) You can see that class size and students' expected grades in the course seem less related to the overall rating of the course than are characteristics of the instructor. Notice also that students' ratings of the fairness of exams is closely related to the grades that they anticipate receiving. For our data set, pay particular

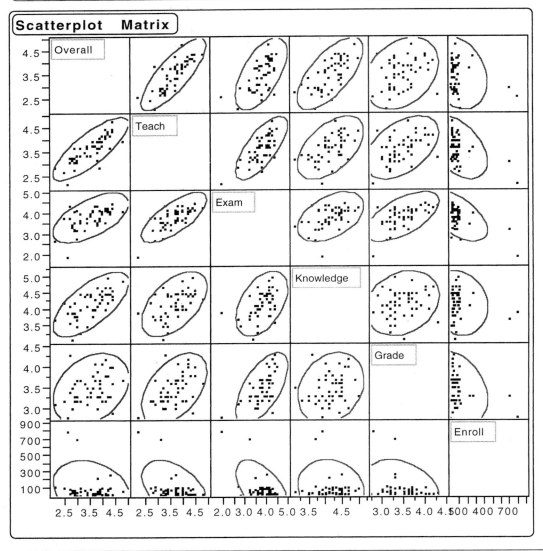

**Correlations**

| Variable | Overall | Teach | Exam | Knowledge | Grade | Enroll |
|----------|---------|-------|------|-----------|-------|--------|
| Overall | 1.0000 | .8039 | .5956 | .6818 | .3008 | −.2396 |
| Teach | .8039 | 1.0000 | .7197 | .5263 | .4691 | −.4511 |
| Exam | .5956 | .7197 | 1.0000 | .4515 | .6100 | −.5581 |
| Knowledge | .6818 | .5263 | .4515 | 1.0000 | .2242 | −.1279 |
| Grade | .3008 | .4691 | .6100 | .2242 | 1.0000 | −.3371 |
| Enroll | −.2396 | −.4511 | −.5581 | −.1279 | −.3371 | 1.0000 |

**Figure 9.9**

Matrix of intercorrelations among course evaluation variables attention to the two apparent outliers in the Enroll variable, which are clearly visible in the scatterplots.

## 9.12  Other Correlation Coefficients

The standard correlation coefficient is Pearson's $r$, which applies primarily to variables distributed more or less along interval or ratio scales of measurement. We also have seen that the same formula will produce a statistic called Spearman's $r_S$ when the variables are in the form of ranks. You should be familiar with two other correlation coefficients, although here again there is little that is new.

When we have one variable measured on a continuous scale and one variable measured as a dichotomy (i.e., that variable has only two levels), then the correlation coefficient that we produce is called the **point biserial correlation** ($r_{pb}$). For example, we might perform an analysis of test items by correlating the total score on the test ($X$) with "right/wrong" on a particular item ($Y$). (We might do this to see how well that particular item discriminates between those students who appear, from their final grade, to really know that material, and those who appear not to. What would you suggest doing when such a correlation is very low?) In this case $X$ values might run from roughly 60 to 100, but $Y$ values would be either 0 (wrong) or 1 (right). Although special formulae exist for calculating $r_{pb}$, you can accomplish exactly the same thing more easily by computing $r$. The only difference is that we call the answer $r_{pb}$ instead of $r$ to point out the nature of the data on which it was computed. Don't let the point about the calculation of $r_{pb}$ pass by too quickly. I belong to several electronic mail discussion groups dealing with statistics and computing, and once every few weeks someone asks if a particular statistical package will calculate the point biserial correlation. And every time the answer is, "Yes it will, just use the standard Pearson $r$ procedure." In fact, this is such a frequently asked question that people are beginning to be less patient with their answers.

---

Definition    **Point biserial correlation ($r_{pb}$):** The correlation coefficient when one of the variables is measured as a dichotomy.

**Dichotomous variables:** Variables that can have only two different values.

---

A point is in order here about **dichotomous variables**. In the preceding example I scored "wrong" as 0 and "right" as 1 to make the arithmetic simple for those who are doing hand calculations. I could just as easily score them as 1 and 2 or even as 87 and 213—just as long as all the "right" scores receive the same number and all the "wrong" scores receive the same (but different) number. The correlation coefficient itself will be exactly the same no matter what pair of numbers we use, with the possible exception of its sign.

**Table 9.4**
Various Correlation Coefficients

|  |  | Continuous | Variable X<br>Dichotomous | Ranked |
|---|---|---|---|---|
| **Variable Y** | **Continuous** | Pearson | Point Biserial | |
|  | **Dichotomous** | Point Biserial | Phi | |
|  | **Ranked** | | | Spearman |

A slightly different correlation coefficient, $\phi$ **(phi)**, arises when both variables are measured as dichotomies. For example, in studying the relationship between gender and religiosity we might correlate gender (coded Male = 1, Female = 2) with regular church attendance (No = 0, Yes = 1). Again it makes no difference what two values we use to code the dichotomous variables. Although phi has a special formula, it is just as easy and correct to use Pearson's formula but label the answer phi.

Definition | Phi ($\phi$): The correlation coefficient when both of the variables are measured as dichotomies.

A number of other correlation coefficients exist, but the ones given here are the most common. All those in this text are special cases of Pearson's $r$, and all can be obtained by using the formulae discussed in this chapter. These coefficients are the ones that are usually generated when a large set of data is entered into a computer data file and a correlation or regression program is run. Table 9.4 shows a diagram that illustrates the relationships among these coefficients. The empty spaces of the table reflect the fact that we do not have a good correlation coefficient to use when we have one ranked variable and one continuous or dichotomous variable. In each case you could use the standard Pearson correlation coefficient, but remember the kinds of variables you have when it comes to interpreting the result. Keep in mind that all the correlations shown in this table can be obtained by using the standard Pearson formula.

## 9.13 Using SPSS to Obtain Correlation Coefficients

Figure 9.9 showed the computer printouts of correlational analyses produced by JMP. I used JMP because of the quality of its printout for this purpose. Figure 9.10 extends this to SPSS.

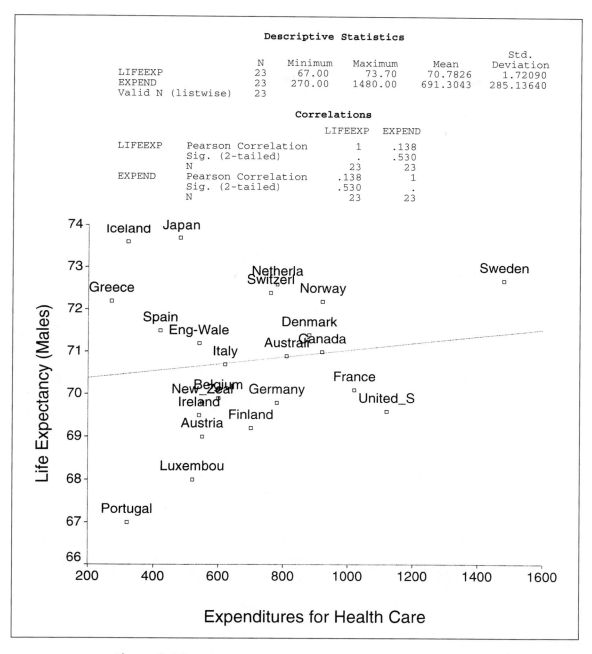

**Figure 9.10**
SPSS analysis of the relationship between life expectancy and health expenditures

## 9.14 Seeing Statistics

A number of applets will help you to see the important concepts that were developed in this chapter. These are found on the book's Web site at

www.uvm.edu/~dhowell/fundamentals/SeeingStatisticsApplets/Applets.html

The first applet allows you to enter individual data points by clicking with your mouse; it then displays the resulting correlation. The following graphic shows sample output.

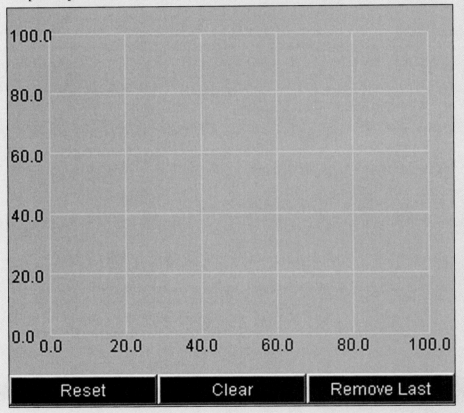

Start the Seeing Statistics applets from the Web site, and click on the first applet in Chapter 9, which is labeled Correlation Points. Now add points to the plot to see what happens to the correlation. Try to produce data with very low, low, medium, and high correlations, and then reverse those to produce negative correlations.

The next applet draws a scatterplot of a set of data and allows you to examine the correlation as you remove or replace a data point. This is illustrated in the following printout, using the data on Alcohol and Tobacco consumption in Britain that we saw in Table 9.3.

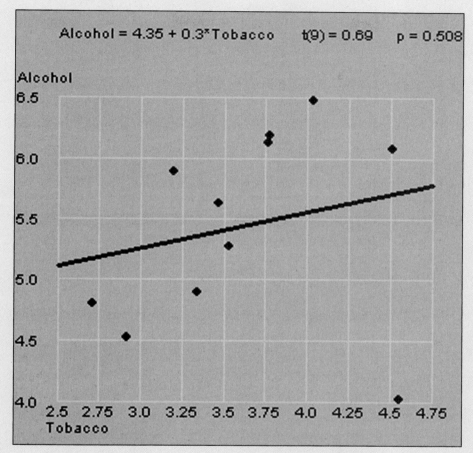

The purpose of the data in Table 9.3 was to illustrate the dramatic influence that a single data point can have. If you click on the point for Northern Ireland, in the lower right, you will remove that point from the calculation, and will see a dramatic change in the correlation coefficient. Next try clicking on other points to see what effect they have.

Another way to illustrate the relationship between a scatterplot and a correlation is shown in the applet named Correlation Picture. This applet allows you to move a slider to vary the correlation coefficient, and then see associated changes in the scatterplot. Two scatterplots are shown, one with the regression line (to be discussed in Chapter 10) superimposed. The line often makes it easier to see the relationship between the variables, especially for low correlation. An example of the output of the applet follows.

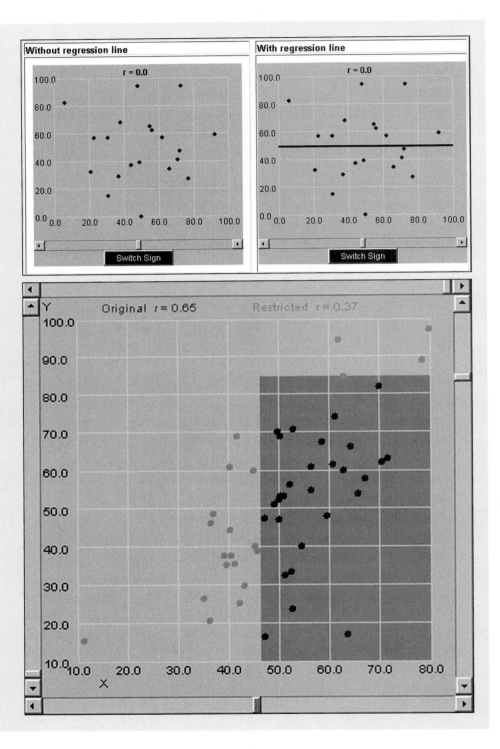

Practice moving the slider to vary the correlation coefficient. Then click on the button labeled "Switch Sign" to see the same degree of correlation in a negative relationship.

One of the important points made in this chapter was the influence of the range of values on the correlation coefficient. The applet labeled RangeRestrict allows you to move sliders to restrict the range of either variable, and then see the resulting effect on the correlation coefficient. This is illustrated above.

One final applet, called Heterogeneous Samples, illustrates some dramatic effects that you can see with heterogeneous subsamples of data. An illustration follows.

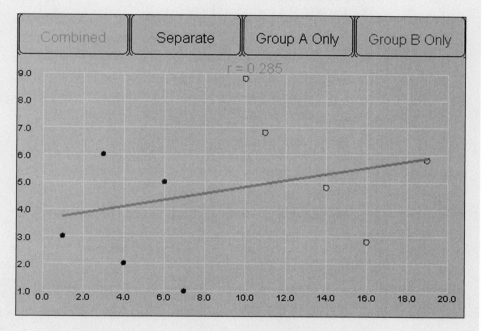

By clicking on the buttons at the top of the display, you can plot the data for all cases combined, for the combined data but with separate regression lines, or for each group alone. The applets on the Web site also allow you to investigate the data plotted in Figure 9.7 in similar ways.

## 9.15 A Final Worked Example

We have used an example in this chapter of the relationship between course evaluations and students' anticipated grades, but we never actually saw data or the calculation of the correlation. The following set of observations represents actual data on 50 courses taken from a large data set on the evaluation of several hundred courses. (I have shown only the first 15 cases on two variables to save space, but have given the results below using the data calculated on for all 50 cases.) The raw data are available at

http://www.uvm.edu/~dhowell/fundamentals/DataFiles/Fig9-9.dat

All six variables appear there, in the order Overall, Teach, Exam, Knowledge, Grade, and Enroll.

| Expected Grade (X) | Overall Quality (Y) | Expected Grade (X) | Overall Quality (Y) |
|---|---|---|---|
| 3.5 | 3.4 | 3.0 | 3.8 |
| 3.2 | 2.9 | 3.1 | 3.4 |
| 2.8 | 2.6 | 3.0 | 2.8 |
| 3.3 | 3.8 | 3.3 | 2.9 |
| 3.2 | 3.0 | 3.2 | 4.1 |
| 3.2 | 2.5 | 3.4 | 2.7 |
| 3.6 | 3.9 | 3.7 | 3.9 |
| 4.0 | 4.3 | | |

Results Based on All 50 Cases

$$\Sigma X = 174.3$$
$$\Sigma X^2 = 613.65$$
$$\Sigma Y = 177.5$$
$$\Sigma Y^2 = 648.57$$
$$\Sigma XY = 621.94$$

Our first step is to calculate the mean and the standard deviation of each variable, as follows:

$$\overline{X} = \frac{174.3}{50} = 3.486$$

$$s_X = \sqrt{\frac{613.65 - \dfrac{174.3^2}{50}}{49}} = .3511$$

$$\overline{Y} = \frac{177.5}{50} = 3.550$$

$$s_Y = \sqrt{\frac{648.57 - \dfrac{177.5^2}{50}}{49}} = .6135$$

The covariance is given by

$$cov_{XY} = \cfrac{621.94 - \cfrac{(174.3)(177.5)}{50}}{49} = .0648$$

Finally, the correlation is given by

$$r = \frac{cov_{XY}}{s_X s_Y} = \frac{.0648}{(.3511)(.6135)} = .3008$$

This is a moderate correlation, one that would lend support to the proposition that courses that have higher mean grades also have higher mean ratings. As we saw in Section 9.9, this correlation is significant. You should realize that this correlation does not necessarily mean higher grades cause higher ratings. It is just as plausible that more advanced courses are rated more highly, and it is often in these courses that students do their best work.

---

I have pulled together a few additional examples and useful material at

 http://www.uvm.edu/~dhowell/fundamentals/More_Stuff/ CorrReg.html

These are more complex examples than we have seen to date, involving several different statistical procedures for each data set. However, you can get a good idea of how correlation is used in practice by looking at these examples, and can just ignore the other material that you don't recognize. Keep in mind that even with the simple correlational material, there may be more advanced ways of dealing with data that we have not covered here—for example, a *t* test on the significance of the correlation coefficient, rather than the approach we took here using Appendix D.

---

## Writing Up the Results of a Correlational Study

If you were asked to write up the study on course evaluations concisely but accurately, how would you do it? Presumably you would want to say something about the research hypothesis that you were testing, the way you collected your data, the statistical results that followed, and the conclusions you would draw. The two paragraphs that follow are an abbreviated form of such a report. A regular report would include a review of the background literature and considerably more information on data collection. It might also speculate on future research.

 It is often thought by course instructors that the way in which students evaluate a course will be related, in part, to the grades that are given in that course. In an attempt to test this hypothesis we collected data on 50 courses in a large state university located in the Northeast, asking students to rate the overall quality of the course (on a five-point scale)

and report their anticipated grade (A = 4, B = 3, etc.) in that course. For each of the 50 courses we calculated the overall mean rating and the mean anticipated grade. Those means were the observations used in the analysis. A Pearson correlation between mean rating and mean anticipated grade produced a correlation of $r = .30$, and this correlation, though small, was significant at $\alpha = .05$ ($r(48) = .30, p < .05$). From this result we can conclude that course ratings do vary with anticipated grades, with courses giving higher grades having higher overall ratings. The interpretation of this effect is unclear. It may be that students who expect to receive good grades have a tendency to "reward" their instructors with higher ratings. But it is equally likely that students learn more in better courses and rate those courses accordingly.

## 9.16 Summary

In this chapter we dealt with the correlation coefficient as a measure of the relationship between two variables. You saw how to draw a scatterplot of the variables and how to compute the correlation coefficient. We followed this up with a discussion of how to test for the significance of a correlation coefficient. We also considered the correlation of ranked data and saw that Pearson's original formula is appropriate for this purpose. Finally, we considered factors that affect the magnitude of the correlation, some cautions concerning interpretation, and the treatment of dichotomous variables.

Some important terms in this chapter are

Correlation, *171*

Correlation coefficient, *171*

Pearson product-moment correlation coefficient (*r*), *171*

Scatterplot (scatter diagram, scattergram), *172*

Predictor variable, *173*

Criterion variable, *173*

Regression lines, *174*

Linear relationship, *179*

Curvilinear relationship, *179*

Covariance, *180*

Deviation score, *180*

Ranked data, *183*

Spearman's correlation coefficient for ranked data ($r_S$), *183*

Monotonic relationship, *184*

Range restrictions, *185*

Heterogeneous subsamples, *187*

Population correlation coefficient rho ($\rho$), *193*

Intercorrelation matrix, *195*

Point biserial correlation ($r_{pb}$), *197*

Dichotomous variables, *197*

Phi ($\phi$), *198*

# 9.17 Exercises

**9.1** In Sub-Saharan Africa, more than half of mothers lose at least one child before the child's first birthday. Below are data on 36 countries in the region, giving country, infant mortality, per capita income (in U.S. dollars), percentage of births to mothers under 20, percentage of births to mothers over 40, percentage of births less than 2 years apart, percentage of married women using contraception, and percentage of women with unmet family planning need. The data are available at

 http://www.uvm.edu/~dhowell/fundamentals/DataFiles/Ex9-1.dat

The original source of the data and a description of the results is available at

 http://www.guttmacher.org/pubs/ib_2-02.html

| Country | InfMort | Income | % Mom < 20 | % Mom > 40 | <2 Years Apart | Using Contraception | Need Family Planning |
|---|---|---|---|---|---|---|---|
| Benin Rep | 104 | 933 | 16 | 5 | 17 | 3 | 26 |
| Burkina Faso | 109 | 965 | 17 | 5 | 17 | 5 | 26 |
| Cameroon | 80 | 1,573 | 21 | 4 | 25 | 7 | 20 |
| Central African Rep | 102 | 1,166 | 22 | 5 | 26 | 3 | 16 |
| Chad Rep | 110 | 850 | 21 | 3 | 24 | 1 | missing |
| Côte d'Ivoire | 91 | 1,654 | 21 | 6 | 16 | 4 | 28 |
| Eritrea | 76 | 880 | 15 | 7 | 26 | 4 | 28 |
| Ethiopia | 113 | 628 | 14 | 6 | 20 | 6 | 23 |
| Gabon | 61 | 6,024 | 22 | 4 | 22 | 12 | 28 |
| Ghana | 61 | 1,881 | 15 | 5 | 13 | 13 | 23 |
| Guinea | 107 | 1,934 | 22 | 5 | 17 | 4 | 24 |
| Kenya | 71 | 1,022 | 18 | 3 | 23 | 32 | 24 |
| Madagascar | 99 | 799 | 21 | 5 | 31 | 10 | 26 |
| Malawi | 113 | 586 | 21 | 6 | 17 | 26 | 30 |
| Mali | 134 | 753 | 21 | 4 | 26 | 5 | 26 |
| Mozambique | 147 | 861 | 24 | 6 | 19 | 5 | 7 |
| Namibia | 62 | 5,468 | 15 | 7 | 22 | 26 | 22 |
| Niger | 136 | 753 | 23 | 5 | 25 | 5 | 17 |
| Nigeria | 71 | 853 | 17 | 5 | 27 | 9 | 18 |
| Rwanda | 90 | 885 | 9 | 7 | 21 | 13 | 36 |
| Senegal | 69 | 1,419 | 14 | 7 | 18 | 8 | 35 |
| Tanzania | 108 | 501 | 19 | 5 | 17 | 17 | 22 |
| Togo | 80 | 1,410 | 13 | 6 | 14 | 7 | 32 |
| Uganda | 86 | 650 | 23 | 4 | 28 | 8 | 35 |
| Zambia | 108 | 756 | 30 | 4 | 19 | 14 | 27 |
| Zimbabwe | 60 | 2,876 | 32 | 4 | 12 | 50 | 13 |

(a) Make a scatter diagram of InfMort and income.
(b) Draw (by eye) the line that appears to best fit the data.
(c) What effect do you suppose that the two outliers on income have?

**9.2** Calculate the correlations among all numeric variables in Exercise 9.1 using SPSS.

**9.3** Using Table D.2 in Appendix D, how large a correlation would you need for the relationships shown in Exercise 9.2 to be significant?

**9.4** What are the strongest predictors of infant mortality in Exercise 9.2?

**9.5** What can we conclude from the data on infant mortality?

**9.6** In Exercise 9.1 the percentage of mothers over 40 does not appear to be important, and yet it is a risk factor in other societies. Why do you think that this might be?

**9.7** Two predictors of infant mortality seem to be significant. If you could find a way to use both of them as predictors simultaneously, what do you think you would find?

**9.8** From the previous exercises do you think that we are able to conclude that low income causes infant mortality?

**9.9** Infant mortality is a very serious problem to society. Why would psychologists be interested in this problem any more than people in other professions?

**9.10** Down's syndrome is another problem that psychologists deal with. It has been proposed that mothers who give birth at older ages are more likely to have a child with Down's syndrome. Plot the data below relating age to incidence. The data were taken from Geyer (1991) and are available at

 http://www.uvm.edu/~dhowell/fundamentals/DataFiles/Ex9-10.dat

| Age | 17.5 | 18.5 | 19.5 | 20.5 | 21.5 | 22.5 | 23.5 | 24.5 | 25.5 |
|--------|-------|-------|-------|-------|-------|-------|-------|-------|-------|
| Births | 13555 | 13675 | 18752 | 22005 | 23796 | 24667 | 24807 | 23986 | 22860 |
| Downs | 16 | 15 | 16 | 22 | 16 | 12 | 17 | 22 | 15 |

| Age | 26.5 | 27.5 | 28.5 | 29.5 | 30.5 | 31.5 | 32.5 | 33.5 | 34.5 |
|--------|-------|-------|-------|-------|-------|-------|-------|-------|-------|
| Births | 21450 | 19202 | 17450 | 15685 | 13954 | 11987 | 10983 | 9825 | 8483 |
| Downs | 15 | 27 | 14 | 9 | 12 | 12 | 18 | 13 | 11 |

| Age | 35.5 | 36.5 | 37.5 | 38.5 | 39.5 | 40.5 | 41.5 | 42.5 | 43.5 |
|--------|-------|-------|-------|-------|-------|-------|-------|-------|-------|
| Births | 7448 | 6628 | 5780 | 4834 | 3961 | 2952 | 2276 | 1589 | 1018 |
| Downs | 23 | 13 | 17 | 15 | 30 | 31 | 33 | 20 | 16 |

| Age | 44.5 | 45.5 | 46.5 |
|--------|-------|-------|-------|
| Births | 596 | 327 | 249 |
| Downs | 22 | 11 | 7 |

Plot a scatter diagram for the percentage of Downs cases (Downs/Births) as a function of age.

**9.11** Why would you not feel comfortable computing a Pearson correlation on the data in Exercise 9.10?

**9.12** One way to get around the problem you see in Exercise 9.11 would be to convert the incidence of Down's syndrome to ranked data. Replot the data using ranked incidence and calculate the correlation. Is this a Spearman's correlation?

**9.13** In the study by Katz et al. (referred to in Chapter 4) in which subjects answered questions about passages they had not read, the question arises as to whether there is a relationship between how the students performed on this test and how they had performed on the SAT-Verbal when they applied to college. Why is this a relevant question?

**9.14**  The data relevant to Exercise 9.13 are the test scores and SAT-Verbal (SAT-V) scores for the 28 people in the group who did not read the passage. These data follow and are available at

 http://www.uvm.edu/~dhowell/fundamentals/DataFiles/Ex9-14.dat

| Score | 58 | 48 | 48 | 41 | 34 | 43 | 38 | 53 | 41 | 60 | 55 | 44 | 43 | 49 |
|-------|-----|-----|-----|-----|-----|-----|-----|-----|-----|-----|-----|-----|-----|-----|
| SAT-V | 590 | 590 | 580 | 490 | 550 | 580 | 550 | 700 | 560 | 690 | 800 | 600 | 650 | 580 |
| Score | 47 | 33 | 47 | 40 | 46 | 53 | 40 | 45 | 39 | 47 | 50 | 53 | 46 | 53 |
| SAT-V | 660 | 590 | 600 | 540 | 610 | 580 | 620 | 600 | 560 | 560 | 570 | 630 | 510 | 620 |

Make a scatterplot of these data and draw the best-fitting straight line through the points by eye.

**9.15**  Compute the correlation coefficient for the data in Exercise 9.14. Is this correlation significant, and what does it mean to say that it is (or is not) significant?

**9.16**  Interpret the results from Exercises 9.11–9.13.

**9.17**  The correlation in the Katz study between Score and SAT-V for the 17 subjects in the group who did read the passage was .68. This correlation is not significantly different from the correlation you computed in Exercise 9.13, although it is significantly different from .00. What does it mean to say that the two correlations are not significantly different from each other?

**9.18**  Expand on Exercise 9.17 to interpret the conclusion that the correlations were not significantly different.

**9.19**  Do the results of the Katz study fit with your expectations, and why?

**9.20**  Plot and calculate the correlation for the relationship between ADDSC and GPA for the data in at

 http://www.uvm.edu/~dhowell/fundamentals/DataFiles/Add.dat

Is this relationship significant?

**9.21**  Assume that a set of data contains a curvilinear relationship between X and Y (the best-fitting line is slightly curved). Would it ever be appropriate to calculate $r$ on these data?

**9.22**  Several times in this chapter I referred to the fact that a correlation based on a small sample might not be reliable.
(a) What does "reliable" mean in this context?
(b) Why might a correlation based on a small sample not be reliable?

**9.23**  What reasons might explain the finding that the amount of money that a country spends on health care is not correlated with life expectancy?

**9.24**  Considering the data relating height to weight in Figure 9.7, what effect would systematic reporting biases from males and females have on our conclusions?

**9.25**    Draw a figure using a small number of data points to illustrate the argument that you could have a negative relationship between weight and height within each gender and yet still have a positive relationship for the combined data.

**9.26**    Sketch a rough diagram to illustrate the point made in the section on heterogeneous sub-samples about the relationship between cholesterol consumption and cardiovascular disease for males and females.

**9.27**    Give an example of a situation in which you would expect a high correlation between two variables, in which it is clear that neither variable is caused by the other.

**9.28**    David Lane, at Rice University has an interesting example of a study involving correlation. This can be found at

    http://www.ruf.rice.edu/~lane/case_studies/physical_strength/index.html

Work through his example and draw your own conclusions from the data. (For now, ignore the material on regression.)

**9.29**    One of the examples in this chapter dealt with the relationship between vitamin D and cancer. Do a simple Internet search to find data on that question.

# 10

# Regression

**Q U E S T I O N S** •

■ How does regression differ from correlation?

■ What can regression tell us that correlation cannot?

■ How do we create a regression line?

■ How well does the regression line fit the data?

■ What do we do about hypothesis testing, and what hypotheses are we testing?

■ How do I get a statistical package to do the work for me so I don't have to do it for myself?

If you think of all the people you know, you are aware that there are individual differences in people's mental health. Some are cheerful and outgoing, some are depressed and withdrawn, some are aggressive and even unpleasant, some have trouble sleeping and spend their nights worrying about things over which they have no control. How do we predict what any specific individual will be like?

This question is really too big and too general, so let's narrow it down. Suppose we take a standard checklist and ask a large number of students to indicate whether they have experienced a variety of psychological symptoms in the past month. Each person's score will be a weighted sum of the reported symptoms. The higher the score, the more problems he or she has; conversely, the lower the score, the better that person's state of mental health. But again, how do we predict a person's score?

If all that we have is a set of symptom scores, the best prediction we can make for any one individual is the group's mean. Since I have never met you and don't know anything about you, I will be less in error, *on average*, if I predict the mean than if I predict any other value. Obviously I won't always be right, but it's the best I can do.

But let's be a little more specific and assume that I know whether you are male or female. Here I have another variable I can use in making my prediction. In other words, I can use one variable to help me predict another. In this case what prediction do you think I should make? I hope that you will say that I should use the mean of males to make a prediction about males and the mean of females to make a prediction about females. On  average I will do better than if I just use the overall mean. Notice that my prediction is *conditional* on gender. My prediction would be of the form, "Given that you are female, I would predict that . . ." Notice that this is the same word "conditional" that we used when discussing conditional probabilities?

Now let's go one more step and instead of using a dichotomous variable, gender, we will use a continuous variable such as stress. We know that psychological health varies with stress, in that people who experience a great deal of stress tend to have more symptoms than those who do not. Therefore we can use people's stress levels to refine our prediction of symptoms. The process is more complicated and sophisticated than using a dichotomous variable such as gender, but the underlying idea is similar. We want to write an equation that explains how differences in one variable relate to differences in another and that allows us to predict a person's score on one variable from knowledge of that person's score on another variable. When we are interested in deriving an equation for predicting one variable from another, we are dealing with **regression**, the topic of this chapter.

---

**Definition**    **Regression:** The prediction of one variable from knowledge of one or more other variables.

**Linear regression:** Regression in which the relationship is linear.

---

Just as we did in our discussion of correlation, we will restrict our coverage of regression to those cases in which the best-fitting line through the scatter diagram is a straight line, or nearly so. This means that we will deal only with **linear regression**. This restriction is not as serious as you might expect because a surprisingly high percentage of sets of data turn out to be basically linear. Even in those cases in which the relationship is curvilinear (i.e., where the best-fitting line is a curve), a straight line often will provide a very good approximation, especially if we eliminate the extremes of the distribution of one or both of the variables.

# 10.1  The Relationship Between Stress and Health

Wagner, Compas, and Howell (1988) investigated the relationship between stress and mental health in first-year college students. Using a scale developed to measure the frequency, perceived importance, and desirability of recent life events, they created a measure of negative life events weighted by the reported frequency of each event and the respondent's subjective estimate of its impact. In other words, more weight was given to those events that occurred frequently and/or that the student felt had an important impact. This served as the measure of the subject's perceived social and environmental stress. The researchers also asked students to complete the Hopkins Symptom Checklist, assessing the presence or absence of 57 psychological symptoms. The stem-and-leaf displays and boxplots for the measures of stress and symptoms are shown in Table 10.1.

**Table 10.1**
Description of Data on the Relationship Between Stress and Mental Health

| Stem-and-Leaf for Stress | Stem-and-Leaf for Symptoms |
|---|---|
| 0* \| 1123334 | 5. \| 8 |
| 0. \| 5567788899999 | 6* \| 112234 |
| 1* \| 011222233333444 | 6. \| 55668 |
| 1. \| 555555566667778889 | 7* \| 00012334444 |
| 2* \| 00000112222233333444 | 7. \| 57788899 |
| 2. \| 56777899 | 8* \| 00011122233344 |
| 3* \| 0013334444 | 8. \| 5666677888899 |
| 3. \| 66778889 | 9* \| 0111223344 |
| 4* \| 334 | 9. \| 556679999 |
| 4. \| 5555 | 10* \| 0001112224 |
|  | 10. \| 567799 |
| HI   \| 58, 74 | 11* \| 112 |
|  | 11. \| 78 |
| Code:   2. \| 5 = 25 | 12* \| 11 |
|  | 12. \| 57 |
|  | 13* \| 1 |
|  | HI   \| 135, 135, 147, 186 |
|  | Code:   5. \| 8 = 58 |

**Boxplot for Stress**

0   10   20   30   40   50   60   70

**Boxplot for Symptoms**

50   60   70   80   90   100   110   120   130   140   150 ⌐√⌐ 180

Before we consider the relationship between these variables, we need to examine the variables individually. The stem-and-leaf displays for both variables show that the distributions are unimodal but slightly positively skewed. Except for a few extreme values, there is nothing about either variable that should disturb us, such as extreme skewness or bimodality. Note that there is a fair amount of variability in each variable. This variability is important, because if we want to show that different stress scores are associated with differences in symptoms, we need to have differences to explain in the first place.

The boxplots in Table 10.1 reveal the presence of outliers on both variables. (The double circles indicate the presence of two overlapping data points.) The existence of outliers should alert us to *potential* problems that these scores may cause. The first thing we could do is to check the data to see whether these few subjects were responding in unreasonable ways; for example, do they report the occurrence of all sorts of unlikely events or symptoms, making us question the legitimacy of their responses? (Difficult as it may be to believe, some subjects have been known to treat psychological experiments with something less than the respect and reverence that psychologists think that they deserve.) The second thing to check is whether the same subject produced outlying data points on both variables. That would suggest that the subject's data, although legitimate, might have a disproportionate influence on the resulting correlations. (To put this in everyday terms, think about how you form stereotypes. The person who is really "nerdy" and who does brilliantly in class has a disproportionate role in establishing in our minds the association between nerdiness and intelligence. We forget about all those people who are brilliant but not nerdy or nerdy but not intellectually outstanding.) The third thing to do is to make a scatterplot of the data, again looking for the undue influence of particular extreme data points. (Such a scatterplot will appear in Figure 10.1.) Finally, we can run our analyses including and excluding extreme points to see what differences appear in the results. If you carry out each of these four steps on the data, you will find nothing to suggest that the outliers we have identified here influenced the resulting correlation or regression equation in any important way. These steps are important precursors to any good analysis, if only because they give us greater faith in our final results.

## 10.2 The Basic Data

A portion of the data on stress and symptoms appears in Table 10.2. The full data set is available at

 http://www.uvm.edu/~dhowell/fundamentals/DataFiles/Tab10-1.dat

Since the complete data for 107 subjects would take too much space, I have given an abbreviated dataset in the table. Here you see how the data would be set up in a data file, along with the means, the standard deviations, and the covariance for the full set of 107 pairs of observations.

**Table 10.2**
First 10 Cases from Data of Wagner et al. (1988)

| Subject | Stress (X) | Symptoms (Y) |
|:---:|:---:|:---:|
| 1 | 30 | 99 |
| 2 | 27 | 94 |
| 3 | 9 | 80 |
| 4 | 20 | 70 |
| 5 | 3 | 100 |
| 6 | 15 | 109 |
| 7 | 5 | 62 |
| 8 | 10 | 81 |
| 9 | 23 | 74 |
| 10 | 34 | 121 |
| Descriptive Statistics from Complete Data Set | | |
| Mean | 21.467 | 90.701 |
| Std. Dev. | 13.096 | 20.266 |
| Covariance | 134.301 | |
| N | 107 | |

From these data you can calculate the correlation coefficient (covered in Chapter 9):

$$r = \frac{\text{cov}_{XY}}{s_X s_Y}$$

For our data the result would be

$$r = \frac{134.301}{(13.096)(20.266)} = .506$$

This correlation is fairly substantial for real data on psychological variables such as these. Using Table D.2 in Appendix D with $N = 107$ ($df = 105$) and $\alpha = .05$, two-tailed, we see that any correlation greater than about .195 would be significant. We can therefore reject $H_0$: $\rho = 0$ and conclude that there is a significant relationship between stress and symptoms. As we saw in the previous chapter, it does not tell us that stress *causes* symptoms, although that is a possibility.

## 10.3 The Regression Line

We have just seen that there is a significant relationship between stress and psychological symptoms. We can obtain a better idea of what this relationship is like by looking at a scatterplot of the two variables and the regression line for predicting Symptoms (Y) on the basis of Stress (X). The scatterplot is shown in Figure 10.1, where the best-fitting line for predicting Y on the basis of X has been superimposed. You will see shortly where this line came from, but notice first the

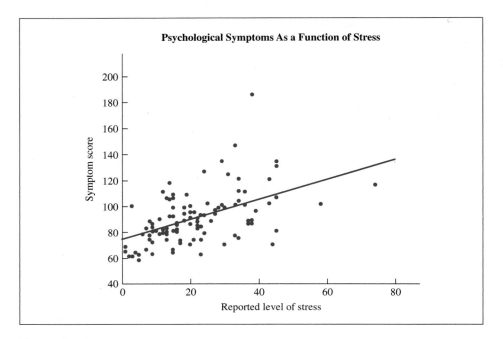

**Figure 10.1**
Scatterplot of symptoms as a function of stress

way in which the Symptom scores increase linearly with increases in Stress scores. Our correlation coefficient told us that such a relationship existed, but it is easier to appreciate just what it means when you see it presented graphically. Notice also that the degree of scatter of points about the regression line remains about the same as you move from low values of stress to high values, although with a correlation of approximately .50 the scatter is fairly wide. We will discuss scatter again in more detail when we consider the assumptions on which our procedures are based.

As you may remember from high school, the equation for a straight line is of the form $Y = bX + a$. (You may have used other letters in place of $a$ and $b$, but these are the ones used by most statisticians.) For our purposes we will write the equation as

$$\hat{Y} = bX + a$$

where

$\hat{Y} =$ the **predicted value** of $Y$
$b =$ the **slope** of the regression line (the amount of difference in $Y$ associated with a one-unit difference in $X$)
$a =$ the **intercept** (the predicted value of $Y$ when $X = 0$)

$X$ is simply the value of the predictor variable, in this case, Stress. Our task will be to solve for those values of $a$ and $b$ that will produce the best-fitting linear function. In other words, we want to use our existing data to solve for the values of $a$ and $b$

such that the line (the values of $\hat{Y}$ for different values of $X$) will come as close as possible to the actual obtained values of $Y$.

Definition

**Predicted value ($\hat{Y}$):** The value estimated from a regression equation.

**Slope:** The amount of change in $Y$ for a 1-unit change in $X$.

**Intercept:** The value of $Y$ when $X$ is 0.

**Errors of prediction:** The difference between $Y$ and $\hat{Y}$.

**Residual:** The difference between the obtained and predicted values of $Y$.

**Least squares regression:** Refers to the fact that our calculation of the regression line is based on minimizing the squared differences between $Y$ and $\hat{Y}$.

Why, you may ask, did I use the symbol $\hat{Y}$, rather than $Y$, in my equation when I defined the equation for a straight line in terms of $Y$? The reason for using $\hat{Y}$ is to indicate that the values we are searching for are *predicted* values. The symbol $Y$ represents, in this case, the actual *obtained* values for Symptoms. These are the values that our 107 different subjects reported. What we are looking for are predicted values ($\hat{Y}$) that come as close as possible to the $Y$ values actually obtained, hence the different symbol.

Having said that we are looking for the best-fitting line, we have to define what we mean by "best." A logical way would be in terms of **errors of prediction**, that is, in terms of the $(Y - \hat{Y})$ deviations. Since $\hat{Y}$ is the value of the symptom variable that our equation would predict for a given level of stress, and $Y$ is a value that we actually obtained, $(Y - \hat{Y})$ is an error of prediction, usually called the **residual**. We want to find the line (the set of $\hat{Y}$s) that minimizes such errors. We cannot just minimize the *sum* of the errors, however, because for an infinite variety of lines—any line that goes through the point $(\overline{X}, \overline{Y})$—that sum will be zero. Instead, we will look for the line that minimizes the sum of the *squared* errors, that is, that minimizes $\Sigma(Y - \hat{Y})^2$. (I said much the same thing in Chapter 5 when I discussed the variance. There I was discussing deviations from the mean, and here I am discussing deviations from the regression line—sort of a floating or changing mean. These two concepts—errors of prediction and variance—have much in common.) The fact that we are minimizing the squares of the residual gives our approach its name—"**least squares regression**."

It is not difficult to derive the equations for the optimal values for $a$ and $b$, but I will not do so here. As long as you keep in mind that they are derived in such a way as to minimize squared errors in predicting $Y$, it is sufficient to state simply

$$b = \frac{\text{cov}_{XY}}{s_X^2}$$

and

$$a = \overline{Y} - b\overline{X} = \frac{\Sigma Y - b\Sigma X}{N}$$

You should note that the equation for $a$ includes the value of $b$, so you need to solve for $b$ first. Also note that the equation for $b$ resembles the equation for $r$, except that the denominator is $s_X^2$ instead of $s_X s_Y$. Another way of writing an equation for $b$ is to write

$$b = r\frac{s_Y}{s_X}.$$

(What does that tell you about the relationship between $r$ and $b$ when $s_X = s_Y$?)

If we apply these equations (using the covariance and the variance) to the data, we obtain

$$b = \frac{\text{cov}_{XY}}{s_X^2} = \frac{134.301}{13.096^2} = .7831$$

and

$$a = \overline{Y} - b\overline{X} = 90.701 - (.7831)(21.467) = 73.891$$

We can now write

$$\hat{Y} = .7831X + 73.891$$

This equation is our **regression equation**, and the values of $a$ and $b$ are called the **regression coefficients**. The interpretation of this equation is straightforward. Consider the intercept ($a$) first. If $X = 0$ (i.e., if the participant reports no stressful events in the past month), the predicted value of $Y$ (Symptoms) is 73.891, quite a low score on the Hopkins Symptom Checklist. In other words the intercept is the predicted level of symptoms when the predictor (Stress) is .0. Next consider the slope ($b$). You may know that a slope is often referred to as the *rate of change*. In this example $b = .7831$. This means that for every 1-point difference in Stress, we predict a .7831 point difference in Symptoms. This is the rate at which predicted Symptom scores change with changes in Stress scores. Most people think of the slope as just a numerical constant in a mathematical equation, but it really makes more sense to think of it as how much different you expect $Y$ to be for a one-unit difference in $X$.

---

Definition | **Regression equation:** The equation that predicts $Y$ from $X$.

**Regression coefficients:** The general name given to the slope and the intercept; often refers only to the slope.

---

Although we rarely work with standardized data (data that have been transformed so as to have a mean of 0 and a standard deviation of 1 on each variable), it is worth considering what $b$ would represent if the data for each variable were standardized separately. In that case a difference of one unit in $X$ or $Y$ would represent a difference of one standard deviation in that variable. Thus if the slope were .75

for *standardized* data, we would be able to say that an increase of one standard deviation in X will be reflected in an increase of three-quarters of a standard deviation in Y. When speaking of the slope coefficient for standardized data, we often refer to the **standardized regression coefficient** as $\beta$ **(beta)** to differentiate it from the coefficient for nonstandardized data ($b$). We will return to the idea of standardized variables when we discuss multiple regression. (What would the intercept be if the data were standardized?)

| Definition | **Standardized regression coefficient ($\beta$):** The regression coefficient that results from data that have been standardized. |
|---|---|

The interesting thing about the standardized slope ($\beta$) is that *when we have one predictor variable* it is equivalent to $r$, the correlation coefficient. Therefore we can say that if $r = .506$, a difference of one standard deviation between two students in terms of their Stress scores would be associated with a predicted difference of about one-half a standard deviation unit in terms of Symptoms. That gives us some idea of what kind of a relationship we are speaking about. When we come to multiple regression in the next chapter $\beta$ will no longer equal the correlation, but we will find other uses for $\beta$.

A word is in order here about actually plotting the regression line. To plot the line, you can simply take any two values of X (preferably at opposite ends of the scale), calculate $\hat{Y}$ for each, mark the coordinates on the figure, and connect them with a straight line. I generally use three points, just as a check for accuracy. For the data on stress and symptoms, we have

$$\hat{Y} = .7831X + 73.891$$

When X = 0,

$$\hat{Y} = .7831 \times 0 + 73.891 = 73.891$$

When X = 50,

$$\hat{Y} = .7831 \times 50 + 73.891 = 113.046$$

The line then passes through the points (X = 0, Y = 73.891) and (X = 50, Y = 113.046), as shown in Figure 10.1. An even easier way is to pass the line through the intercept and the point ($\overline{X}, \overline{Y}$), provided that these points are far enough apart to lead to a sufficient degree of accuracy in drawing the line.

It is important to point out that we have constructed a line to predict symptoms from stress, not the other way around. Our line minimizes the sum of the squared deviations of predicted symptoms from actual symptoms. If we wanted to turn things around and predict stress ratings from symptoms, we could not use this line—it wasn't derived for that purpose. Instead we would have to find the line that minimizes the squared deviations of predicted stress from actual stress. The simplest way to do this is just to go back to the equations for *a* and *b*, reverse which variable is labeled X and which is labeled Y, and solve for the new values of *a* and *b*. You then can use the same formulae that we have already used.

## 10.4 The Accuracy of Prediction

The fact that we can fit a regression line to a set of data does not mean that our problems are solved. On the contrary, they have just begun. The important point is not whether a straight line can be drawn through the data (you can always do that), but whether that line represents a reasonable fit to the data—in other words, whether our effort was worthwhile.

Before we discuss errors of prediction, however, it is instructive to go back to the situation in which we want to predict Y without *any* knowledge of the value of X, which we considered at the very beginning of this chapter.

### The Standard Deviation as a Measure of Error

Assume that you were given the complete data set illustrated in Table 10.1 and asked to predict a particular individual's level of symptoms (Y) without being told what he or she reported in terms of stress for the past month. Your best prediction in that case would be the mean Symptom score ($\overline{Y}$). You predict the mean because it is closer, on average, to all the other scores than any other prediction would be. Think how badly you would generally do if your prediction were the smallest score or the largest one. Once in a while you would be exactly right, but most of the time you would be absurdly off. With the mean you will probably be exactly right more often (because more people actually fall in the center of the distribution), and when you are wrong you likely won't be off by as much as if you had made an extreme prediction. The error associated with your prediction will be the standard deviation of Y ($s_Y$). This is true because your prediction is the mean, and $s_Y$ deals with deviations around the mean. Examining $s_Y$, we know that it is defined as

$$s_Y = \sqrt{\frac{\Sigma(Y - \overline{Y})^2}{N - 1}}$$

and that the variance is defined as

$$s_Y^2 = \frac{\Sigma(Y - \overline{Y})^2}{N - 1}$$

The numerator is the sum of squared deviations from $\overline{Y}$ (the point you would have predicted in this particular example), which we refer to as the sum of squares of Y ($SS_Y$).

### The Standard Error of Estimate

Now suppose we want to make a prediction about the level of psychological distress (as measured by symptoms) that a person is likely to experience given that we know his or her reported level of stress. Suppose that the person's X value (Stress) is 15. In this situation we know the relevant value of X and the regression equation, and our best prediction would be $\hat{Y}$. In this case X = 15, and $\hat{Y}$ = .7831 × 15 + 73.891 = 85.64. In line with our previous measure of error (the standard deviation), the error associated with this prediction will again be a function of the deviations of Y about the predicted point; however, in this case the predicted point is $\hat{Y}$ rather than $\overline{Y}$. Specifically, a measure of error can now be defined as

$$s_{Y-\hat{Y}} = \sqrt{\frac{\Sigma(Y - \hat{Y})^2}{N - 2}}$$

and again the sum is of squared deviations about the prediction $(\hat{Y})$.[1] The statistic $s_{Y-\hat{Y}}$ is called the **standard error of estimate** and is sometimes written $s_{Y.X}$ to indicate that it is the standard deviation of Y *predicted from* X. It is the most common (though not always the best) measure of the error of prediction. Its square, $s^2_{Y-\hat{Y}}$, is called the **residual variance**, or **error variance**.

---

**Definition**

**Standard error of estimate:** The average of the squared deviations about the regression line.

**Residual variance (error variance):** The square of the standard error of estimate.

---

Table 10.3 shows how to calculate the standard error of estimate directly. The raw data for the first 10 cases are given in columns 2 and 3, and the predicted values of Y (obtained from $\hat{Y}$ = .7831X + 73.891) are given in column 4. Column 5 contains the values of $Y - \hat{Y}$ for each observation. Note that the sum of that column $(\Sigma(Y - \hat{Y}))$ is 0, because the sum of the deviations about the prediction is always 0. If we square and sum the deviations we obtain $\Sigma(Y - \hat{Y})^2$ = 32,386.048. From this sum we can calculate

$$s_{Y-\hat{Y}} = \sqrt{\frac{\Sigma(Y - \hat{Y})^2}{N - 2}} = \sqrt{\frac{32386.048}{105}} = \sqrt{308.439} = 17.562$$

Finding the standard error this way is hardly a lot of fun, and I don't recommend that you do so. I present it because it makes clear what the term represents. Fortunately, a much simpler procedure exists that not only represents a way of calculating the standard error of estimate, but also leads directly to even more

---

[1]The denominator in that equation is N − 2 because to get $\hat{Y}$ we have had to estimate two things (slope and intercept) whereas the denominator for the standard deviation was N − 1 because we had to estimate one thing (the population mean).

**Table 10.3**
First Ten Cases from Data of Wagner et al. (1988), Including $\hat{Y}$ and Residuals

| Subject | Stress(X) | Symptoms (Y) | $\hat{Y}$ | $(Y - \hat{Y})$ |
|---------|-----------|--------------|-----------|------------------|
| 1 | 30 | 99 | 97.383 | 1.617 |
| 2 | 27 | 94 | 95.034 | −1.034 |
| 3 | 9 | 80 | 80.938 | −.938 |
| 4 | 20 | 70 | 89.552 | −19.552 |
| 5 | 3 | 100 | 76.239 | 23.761 |
| 6 | 15 | 109 | 85.636 | 23.364 |
| 7 | 5 | 62 | 77.806 | −15.806 |
| 8 | 10 | 81 | 81.721 | −.721 |
| 9 | 24 | 74 | 91.901 | −17.901 |
| 10 | 34 | 121 | 100.515 | 20.485 |

| Descriptive Statistics from Complete Data Set | | | | |
|---|---|---|---|---|
| Mean | 21.467 | 90.701 | $\Sigma(Y - \hat{Y}) = .000$ | |
| Std. Dev. | 13.096 | 20.266 | $\Sigma(Y - \hat{Y})^2 = 32,386.048$ | |
| Covariance | | 134.301 | | |

important matters. But don't forget the formula we just used because it best defines what it is we are measuring.

## $r^2$ and the Standard Error of Estimate

We have defined the standard error of estimate as

$$s_{Y-\hat{Y}} = \sqrt{\frac{\Sigma(Y - \hat{Y})^2}{N - 2}}$$

From here a small amount of algebraic substitution and manipulation, which I am omitting, will bring us to

$$s_{Y-\hat{Y}} = s_Y\sqrt{(1 - r^2)\left(\frac{N - 1}{N - 2}\right)}$$

or, as it is often presented (although not quite accurately),

$$s_{Y-\hat{Y}} \approx s_Y\sqrt{(1 - r^2)}$$

We arrive at this last equation by treating the term $(N - 1)/(N - 2)$ as 1.0, which it is for all practical purposes when $N$ is large.

From our data we now can calculate $s_{Y-\hat{Y}}$ in three different ways:

**1.** $s_{Y-\hat{Y}} = \sqrt{\dfrac{\Sigma(Y-\hat{Y})^2}{N-2}} = \sqrt{\dfrac{32386.048}{105}} = 17.562$

**2.** $s_{Y-\hat{Y}} = s_Y\sqrt{(1-r^2)\left(\dfrac{N-1}{N-2}\right)}$

$\phantom{s_{Y-\hat{Y}}} = 20.266\sqrt{(1-.506^2)\left(\dfrac{106}{105}\right)} = 17.562$

**3.** $s_{Y-\hat{Y}} \approx s_Y\sqrt{(1-r^2)} = 20.266\sqrt{(1-.506^2)} = 17.480$

The third solution differs from the other two because it is based on a formula that ignores the constant $\sqrt{(N-1)/(N-2)}$. That is why the "approximately equals" sign ($\approx$) was used. For large sample sizes the difference will be minor, but not for small sample sizes.

Now that we have computed the standard error of estimate, we can interpret it as a form of standard deviation. Thus it is reasonable to say that the standard deviation of points about the regression line is 17.562. Another way of saying this is to say that $s_{Y-\hat{Y}}$ is the standard deviation of the errors that we make when using our regression equation. If all our predictions were perfect, all the errors would be zero, as would $s_{Y-\hat{Y}}$. Because the regression line represents our set of predictions, a standard deviation of approximately 18 points should make us a bit uncomfortable. Being off by 18 units, on average, is not a particularly happy state of affairs, especially given the fact that even without knowing the stress level we would have a level of inaccuracy that is only slightly greater (i.e., the standard deviation, which is 20.266).

I have a specific reason for pointing out the substantial amount of error that is left in our predictions even after taking $X$ (Stress) into account. Most people think that if we have a regression equation, we can make a prediction and that's that. Although it is true that a regression equation yields better predictions than predictions made without one, a substantial amount of error remains in the system (and in this case the correlation between the two variables was a respectable .506). However, there are many things that could lead college students to show moderate levels of depression, anxiety, and other psychological symptoms, and we can hardly expect stress to explain it all. This last set of statements might lead you to ask why I spend all this time telling you about regression and then say that it doesn't really do a whole lot better than just guessing the mean. Well, you have a point. But the major use of regression is not just to come up with a prediction for Joe Smith. The major point is to be able to describe the relationship between two variables, whether or not we actually make a prediction. And for that purpose regression works very well.

## $r^2$ as a Measure of Predictable Variability

From the preceding equation that expresses residual error in terms of $r^2$, it is possible to derive an extremely important interpretation of the correlation coefficient. To avoid having to write several convoluted sentences that you would hate, I am forced to introduce a new term: **sum of squares**, which is the sum of squared deviations from something. (You will see a similar term when we come to the analysis of variance.) Let the notation $SS_{error}$ stand for $\Sigma(Y - \hat{Y})^2$ and $SS_Y$ stand for $\Sigma(Y - \overline{Y})^2$. $SS_{error}$ represents the sum of squared deviations between actual values of Y and our predictions ($\hat{Y}$). $SS_Y$ represents the sum of squared deviations between observed values of Y and the mean ($\overline{Y}$) that would have been our prediction if we had not taken stress into account. $SS_Y$ is also called $SS_{total}$ in some contexts because it stands for the total variability in Y. It is possible to show, although I will not do so here, that

$$SS_{error} = SS_Y(1 - r^2)$$

Expanding and rearranging, we have

$$r^2 = \frac{SS_Y - SS_{error}}{SS_Y}$$

In this equation $SS_Y$ (the sum of squares of Y) represents the total of both of the following:

1. The part of the variability in Y that is related to X

2. The part of the variability in Y that is independent of X, which is $SS_{error}$

Those parts of $SS_Y$ are probably not immediately obvious. In the context of our example, we are talking about the level of symptoms related to an individual's daily stress and the level of symptoms attributable (or at least related) to other things. These concepts can be made clearer with a second example.

---

Definition

**Sum of squares:** The sum of the squared deviations around some point (usually a mean or predicted value).

**$SS_{error}$:** The sum of squared residuals or the sum of the squared deviations within each group.

**$SS_Y$:** The sum of squared deviations around the mean.

**$SS_{total}$:** The sum of squared deviations from the grand mean (the mean of all observations).

---

EXAMPLE:
Cigarette
Smoking and
Age at Death

Suppose we are interested in studying the relationship between cigarette smoking (X) and age at death (Y). As we watch people die off over time, we notice several things. First we see that not all die at precisely the same age—there is variability in age at death regardless of (i.e., ignoring) smoking behavior. This variability is measured by $SS_Y = \Sigma(Y - \overline{Y})^2$. We also notice the obvious fact that some people smoke more than others. This is variability in smoking behavior regardless of age at death and is measured by $SS_X = \Sigma(X - \overline{X})^2$. We further find that cigarette smokers die earlier than

## Table 10.4
Sources of Variance in Regression

$SS_X$ = Variability in amount smoked = $\Sigma(X - \overline{X})^2$
$SS_Y$ = Variability in life expectancy = $\Sigma(Y - \overline{Y})^2$
$SS_{\hat{Y}}$ = Variability in life expectancy directly attributable to variability in smoking
      behavior = $\Sigma(\hat{Y} - \overline{Y})^2$
$SS_{error}$ = Variability in life expectancy that cannot be attributable to variability in
      smoking behavior = $\Sigma(Y - \hat{Y})^2 = SS_Y - SS_{\hat{Y}}$

nonsmokers, and heavy smokers earlier than light smokers. Thus we write a regression equation to predict Y from X. Because people differ in their smoking behavior, they will also differ in their *predicted* life expectancy ($\hat{Y}$), and we label this variability $SS_{\hat{Y}} = \Sigma(\hat{Y} - \overline{\hat{Y}})^2 = \Sigma(\hat{Y} - \overline{Y})^2$. This last measure is variability in Y that is directly attributable to variability in X, since different values of $\hat{Y}$ arise from different values of X, and the same values of $\hat{Y}$ arise from the same value of X—that is, Y does not vary unless X varies.[2] (To see this more clearly, make predictions for two people who have stress scores of 50 and one person who has a stress score of 100. How and when do these predictions differ?)

We have one last source of variability, the variability in the life expectancy of those people who smoke exactly the same amount. It is measured by $SS_{error}$ and is variability in Y that cannot be explained by variability in X because these people did not differ in the amount they smoked. These several sources of variability (i.e., sums of squares) are summarized in Table 10.4.

If we consider the absurd extreme in which all nonsmokers die at exactly age 72 and all smokers smoke precisely the same amount and die at exactly age 68, then all the variability in life expectancy is directly predictable from variability in smoking behavior. If you smoke you will die at 68, and if you don't smoke you will die at 72.[3] Here $SS_Y = SS_{\hat{Y}}$, and $SS_{error} = 0$. ■

In a more realistic example smokers might tend to die earlier than nonsmokers, but within each group there would be a certain amount of variability in life expectancy. In this situation some of $SS_Y$ is attributable to smoking ($SS_{\hat{Y}}$) and some is not ($SS_{error}$). We want to be able to specify the *percentage* of the overall variability in life expectancy attributable to variability in smoking behavior. In other words, we want a measure that represents

$$\frac{SS_{\hat{Y}}}{SS_Y} = \frac{SS_Y - SS_{error}}{SS_Y}$$

---

[2]In the latest equation note that the mean of $\hat{Y}$ is always going to be equal to $\overline{Y}$, which is why I could make the substitution.

[3]Actually, recent data in the *British Journal of Medicine* suggest that those who continue to smoke cut 10 years (not 4) off their life expectancy (Doll, Peto, Boreham, & Sutherland, 2004).

As we have seen, that measure is $r^2$. In other words

$$r^2 = \frac{SS_{\hat{Y}}}{SS_Y}$$

This interpretation of $r^2$ is extremely useful. If, for example, the correlation between amount smoked and life expectancy were an unrealistically high .80, we could say that $.80^2 = 64\%$ of the variability in life expectancy is directly predictable from the variability in smoking behavior. Obviously, this is a substantial exaggeration of the real world. If the correlation were a more likely $r = .20$, we could say that $.20^2 = 4\%$ of the variability in life expectancy is related to smoking behavior, whereas the other 96% is related to other factors. (While 4% may seem to you to be an awfully small amount, when we are talking about how long people will live, it is far from trivial, especially for those people.)

One problem associated with focusing on the squared correlation coefficient is maintaining an appropriate sense of perspective. If it were true that smoking accounted for 4% of the variability in life expectancy, it might be tempting to dismiss smoking as a minor contributor to life expectancy. You have to keep in mind, however, that an enormous number of variables contribute to life expectancy, including such things as automobile accidents, homicide, cancer, heart disease, and stroke. Some of those are related to smoking and some are not, and one that accounts for 4% or even 1% of the variability is a fairly powerful predictor. (In fact, it has been suggested that 30% of the cancers in the United States are caused by smoking.) A variable that accounts for 4% of your grade in a course is probably minor. But something that accounts for 4% of the variability in how long you will live is not to be dismissed so easily.

Be careful in how you understand that previous paragraph. I used percentages in two quite different ways, partly to make a point. When we are speaking of $r^2$ as accounting for 4% of the variance, we are saying only that 4% of people's *variability* (i.e., differences) in life expectancy is associated with *variability* in smoking. When we say that 30% of deaths from cancer are associated with smoking, we are talking about something else.

It is important to note that phrases such as "accountable for," "attributable to," "predictable from," and "associated with" are not to be interpreted as statements of cause and effect. You could say that pains in your shoulder account for 10% of the variability in the weather without meaning to imply that sore shoulders cause rain, or even that rain itself causes sore shoulders. For example, your shoulder might hurt when it rains because carrying an umbrella aggravates your bursitis.

## 10.5 The Influence of Extreme Values

In Table 9.3 we saw a set of real data on the relationship between expenditures on alcohol and tobacco in 11 regions in Great Britain. We also saw that the inclusion of an unusual data point from Northern Ireland drastically altered the

**Table 10.5**
Regression Solutions with and without the Observation from
Northern Ireland

### (a) With Northern Ireland

Coefficients[a]

| Model | Unstandardized Coefficients | | Standardized Coefficients | | |
| | B | Std. Error | Beta | t | Sig. |
|---|---|---|---|---|---|
| 1    (Constant) | 4.351 | 1.607 | | 2.708 | .024 |
|       TOBACCO | .302 | .439 | .224 | .688 | .509 |

a. Dependent Variable: ALCOHOL

### (b) Without Northern Ireland

Coefficients[a]

| Model | Unstandardized Coefficients | | Standardized Coefficients | | |
| | B | Std. Error | Beta | t | Sig. |
|---|---|---|---|---|---|
| 1    (Constant) | 2.041 | 1.001 | | 2.038 | .076 |
|       TOBACCO | 1.006 | .281 | .784 | 3.576 | .007 |

a. Dependent Variable: ALCOHOL

correlation from what it would have been without that observation. (Inclusion of that observation caused the correlation to drop from .784 to .224.) Let's see what effect that point has on the regression equation.

In Table 10.5 I show the output for two solutions—the first with the aberrant observation, and the second without it. The regression lines are shown in parts (a) and (b) of Figure 10.2.

Notice the drastic change in the regression line. The slope went from .302 to 1.006, and the $p$ value associated with those slopes exactly mirrored the $p$ values for the corresponding correlations. This is an illustration that one unusual value can have a significant effect in pulling the regression line toward itself. This is a particularly good example because the observation in question is not particularly unusual when we look at one variable at a time. Moreover, it is a real data point, and not just an error on the part of someone who was collecting the data.

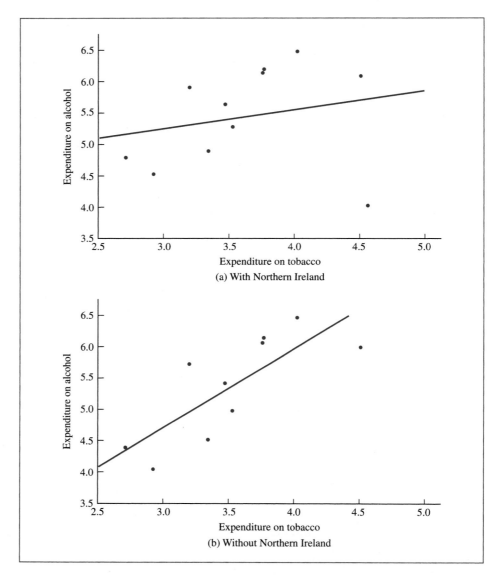

**Figure 10.2**
Scatterplots with, and without Northern Ireland

## 10.6 Hypothesis Testing in Regression

In the previous chapter we saw how to test a correlation coefficient for significance. We tested $H_0: \rho = 0$ because if $\rho = 0$, the variables are linearly independent, and if $\rho \neq 0$, the variables are related. When we come to regression problems, we have both a correlation coefficient and a slope, and it makes sense to ask if either is different from zero.[4] You know how to deal with $\rho$, but what about $b$?

The simplest approach to testing the slope is just to say that when you have only one predictor you don't need a separate test on $b$. If the *correlation* between Stress and Symptoms, for example, is significant, it means that Symptoms are related to Stress. If the *slope* is significant it means that the predicted number of symptoms increases (or decreases) with the amount of stress. But that's saying the same thing! As you will see in a moment, the test for the slope is numerically equal to the test for the correlation coefficient. The easy answer, then, is to test the correlation. If that test is significant, then both the correlation in the population and the slope in the population are nonzero. But keep in mind that this is true only when we have one predictor. When we come to multiple predictors in the next chapter that will no longer be the case.

An alternative approach is to use a test statistic we have not yet covered. I suggest that you just skim these two paragraphs and come back to them after you have read about $t$ tests in Chapter 12. What we are going to do is calculate a statistic called $t$ (using the slope, $b$) and look up $t$ in a table. If the $t$ we calculated is larger than the tabled $t$, we will reject $H_0$. Notice that this is the same kind of procedure we went through when we tested $r$. Our formula for $t$ is

$$t = \frac{b}{\dfrac{s_{Y-\hat{Y}}}{s_X \sqrt{N-1}}} = \frac{b(s_X)\sqrt{N-1}}{s_Y \sqrt{(1-r^2)\dfrac{N-1}{N-2}}}$$

I mention the $t$ test here, without elaborating on it, because you are about to see that same $t$ appear in the computer printout in the next section. (It was also in the printout in Table 10.5.) To jump ahead, if you look at Figure 10.3, the last few lines show the values for the slope (labeled "Stress") and the intercept (labeled "Constant"). To the right is a column labeled "t" and another labeled "Sig. t." The entries under "t" are the $t$ tests just referred to. (The test on the intercept is somewhat different, but it is still a $t$ test.) The entries under "Sig. t" are the probabilities associated with those $t$s under $H_0$. If the probability is less than .05, we can reject $H_0$. Here we will reject $H_0$ and conclude that the slope relating symptoms to stress is not zero. People with higher stress scores are predicted to have more symptoms.

## 10.7 Computer Solution Using SPSS

Figure 10.3 contains the printout from an SPSS analysis of the Symptoms and Stress data. The output starts by presenting the mean, the standard deviation, and the sample size of all cases, followed by the correlation coefficient matrix. Here you can see that the correlation of .506 agrees with our own calculation. For some reason SPSS chooses to report one-tailed significance probabilities, rather than the more traditional two-tailed values that they report in other procedures. You can simply double the $p$ value to have a two-tailed test. The next section presents the correlation

---

[4]You could also test the intercept, but such a test is usually not very interesting.

## Regression

**Descriptive Statistics**

|  | Mean | Std. Deviation | N |
|---|---|---|---|
| SYMPTOMS | 90.7009 | 20.2658 | 107 |
| STRESS | 21.4673 | 13.0957 | 107 |

**Correlations**

|  |  | SYMPTOMS | STRESS |
|---|---|---|---|
| Pearson Correlation | SYMPTOMS | 1.000 | .506 |
|  | STRESS | .506 | 1.000 |
| Sig. (1-tailed) | SYMPTOMS | . | .000 |
|  | STRESS | .000 | . |
| N | SYMPTOMS | 107 | 107 |
|  | STRESS | 107 | 107 |

**Model Summary**

| Model | R | R Square | Adjusted R Square | Std. Error of the Estimate |
|---|---|---|---|---|
| 1 | .506[a] | .256 | .249 | 17.5624 |

a. Predictors: (Constant), STRESS

**ANOVA[b]**

| Model |  | Sum of Squares | df | Mean Square | F | Sig. |
|---|---|---|---|---|---|---|
| 1 | Regression | 11148.382 | 1 | 11148.382 | 36.145 | .000[a] |
|  | Residual | 32386.048 | 105 | 308.439 |  |  |
|  | Total | 43534.430 | 106 |  |  |  |

a. Predictors: (Constant), STRESS

b. Dependent Variable: SYMPTOMS

**Coefficients[a]**

| Model |  | Unstandardized Coefficients | | Standardized Coefficients | t | Sig. |
|---|---|---|---|---|---|---|
|  |  | B | Std. Error | Beta |  |  |
| 1 | (Constant) | 73.890 | 3.271 |  | 22.587 | .000 |
|  | STRESS | .783 | .130 | .506 | 6.012 | .000 |

a. Dependent Variable: SYMPTOMS

**Figure 10.3**

Regression analysis of relationship between symptoms and stress coefficient again. This section also gives you the squared correlation (.256), the adjusted $r$ squared, which we will skip, and the standard error of estimate ($s_{Y-\hat{Y}}$). These values agree with those that we have calculated. The section headed "ANOVA" (Analysis of Variance) is simply a test on the significance of the correlation coefficient. The entry "Sig." is the probability, under $H_0$, of a correlation as large as .506. Since the probability is less than .05, we will reject $H_0$ and conclude that there is a significant relationship between Symptoms and Stress. Finally, in the section headed "Coefficients" we see the slope (in column B, next to the word STRESS) and the intercept directly above the slope. Skipping the next two columns we come to the $t$ tests on these coefficients and the probability of those $t$s. I have already discussed the $t$ on the slope. This is the same value you would have calculated using the formula given in Section 10.6. The $t$ test on the intercept is simply a test that the true intercept is zero. We rarely would expect it to be, so this test is not particularly useful for most purposes.

## Writing Up the Results

We might write up these results this way:

Wagner, Compas, and Howell (1988) conducted a study examining the relationship between stress and mental health in college students. They asked 107 college students to complete a checklist assessing the number and severity of negative life events that they had recently experienced. They also asked these same students to complete a checklist of psychological symptoms that they experienced in the past month. The relationship between these two variables addresses the issue of stress and mental health, and the literature would suggest that an increase in stressful events would be associated with an increase in the number of symptoms reported by the students.

The analyses of these data confirmed the prediction and produced a correlation of .506 between the two variables ($r^2 = .256$), which is significant at $\alpha = .05$ ($F (1, 105) = 36.14, p = .0000$). The regression equation has a slope = .78 ($t (105) = 6.012, p = .0000$). Higher levels of stress are associated with higher levels of psychological symptoms, and stress accounts for approximately 25% of the variation in Symptoms. The intercept was 73.89, so individuals reporting no stress would have an estimated symptom score of nearly 74, but the units of the symptom scale are somewhat arbitrary and the intercept does not provide us with much useful information in this case.

## 10.8   Seeing Statistics

The applets contained on the Web provide an excellent way for you to review what you have learned. They will also make it easier for you to recall that material on an exam, because you will have actively worked with it. In addition, the applets related to the *t* test will give you a head start on Chapters 12–14.

One of the important concepts to understand about a scatterplot with a regression line is just how the regression line helps us to predict Y. The applet entitled Predict Y, shown below, illustrates this simple principle. As you move the slider on the X axis, you vary the value of X, and can read the corresponding value of $\hat{Y}$. For this particular example, when X = 2, $\hat{Y}$ = 2.2. Additionally, by moving the sliders on the left and right, you can vary the intercept and the slope, respectively, and observe how the predictions change.

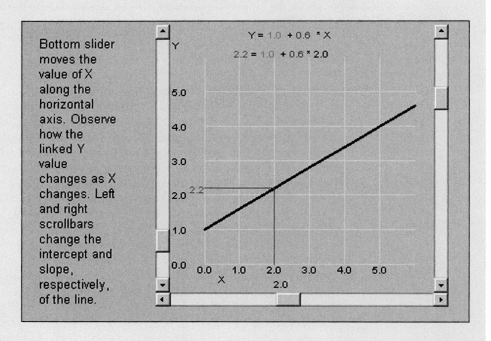

Calculate values of $\hat{Y}$ for X = 2, 3, and 4. Then make the slope steeper, by moving the slider on the right up, and again calculate $\hat{Y}$ for X = 2, 3, and 4. What has changed?

Now do the same thing, except this time change the intercept. Now how do the values of $\hat{Y}$ change as we vary X?

I have said that the regression line is the "best-fitting" line through the data points. The following applet, named FindLine, allows you to move the regression line vertically (i.e., change its intercept) and to rotate it (i.e., change its slope). The data in the following figure are taken from McClelland's original applet, and show the scores on a Statistical Knowledge Quiz (SKQ) before and after students took his statistics course.

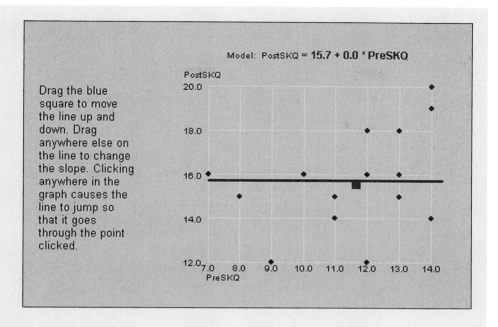

Adjust the line until you think that it is a "best fit." I happen to know that the best fitting line has an intercept of 10.9, and a slope of .42. How does the line you fit compare to that?

By clicking on the icon labeled "My Data," you can enter your own data. Enter the data on alcohol and tobacco use from Table 9.3 in Chapter 9, and see the results.

One of the applets in Chapter 9 allowed you to remove individual data points and observe the effect on the correlation between two variables. We will return to that applet here, though this time we will concentrate on the influence of extreme points on the regression line. The applet shown below is taken from the data in Figure 9.3.

By clicking on the point at approximately (2.5, 26.5) I have changed the slope of the regression line from $-3.0$ to $-3.3$. The less steep line in this figure is the line for all 24 observations, whereas the steeper line fits the data omitting the point on which I clicked.

You can click on each data point and see the effect on the slope and intercept.

One of the important points in this chapter concerned the use of Student's *t* test to test the null hypothesis that the true slope in the population is .00 (i.e., the hypothesis that there is no linear relationship between $X$ and $Y$). The applet named SlopeTest illustrates the meaning of this test with population data that support the null hypothesis. A sample screen is illustrated here.

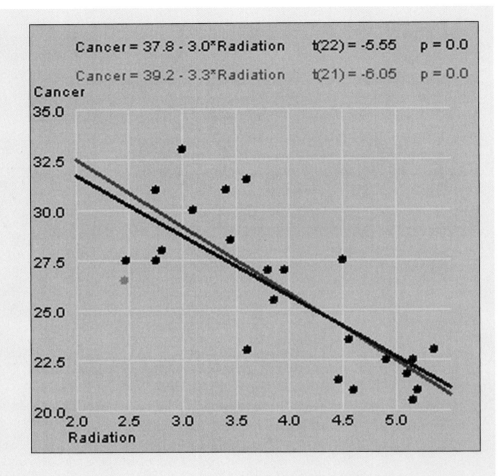

In this applet I have drawn 10 samples of 5 pairs of scores. I drew from a population where the true slope, and therefore the true correlation, is .00, so I know that the variables are not linearly related. For each slope that I obtained, I calculated a $t$ test using the formula for $t$ given in Section 10.6. The 10 $t$ values are given near the top of the display, and they range from $-2.712$ to $1.776$. The distribution of these 10 values is given at the right, and the plot of the 5 observations for my 10th set is given at the left. Each time I click the "10 sets" button, I will draw 10 new sets of observations, calculate their slopes and associated $t$ values, and add those to the plot on the right. If I click the "100 Sets" button, I will accumulate 100 $t$ values at a time.

Run this applet. First generate one set at a time and note the resulting variation in $t$ and how the regression line changes with every sample. Then accumulate 100 sets at a time and notice how the distribution of $t$

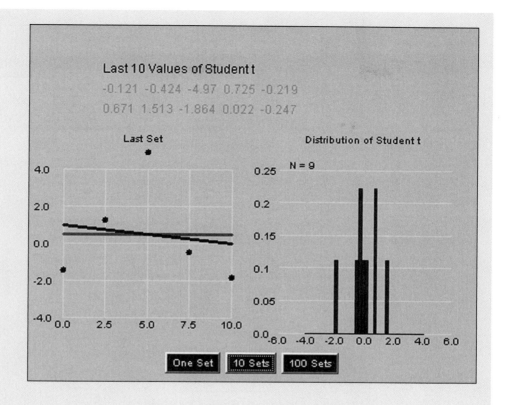

smooths out. Notice that our *t* values only rarely exceed ±3.00. (In fact, the critical value of *t* on 3 *df* is ±3.18.)

Now move to the lower applet on that page, which will sample 15 pairs per sample. Note how the *t* distribution narrows slightly with larger sample sizes.

We will use one final applet to illustrate the use of the *t* test for the slope. Several times in Chapter 9 and Chapter 10 I have focused on the data set showing the relationship between alcohol and tobacco use in Britain, and the influence of extreme data points. In Figure 10.3 I presented SPSS printout showing the slope (unstandardized) and its standard error. Along with the sample size (*N*), that is all we need for calculating *t*.

The applet Calculatet is shown next for the statistics from the complete data set (including Northern Ireland). I entered .302 as the slope, .0 as the null hypothesis to be tested (the hypothesis that the true slope is 0), and .439 as the standard error. I also entered the sample size as 11. Each time that I entered a number, I pressed the Enter key—*don't just move your mouse to another box without pressing Enter*. You can see that the resulting value of *t* is .688, and the figure at the bottom shows that the two-tailed probability is .506.

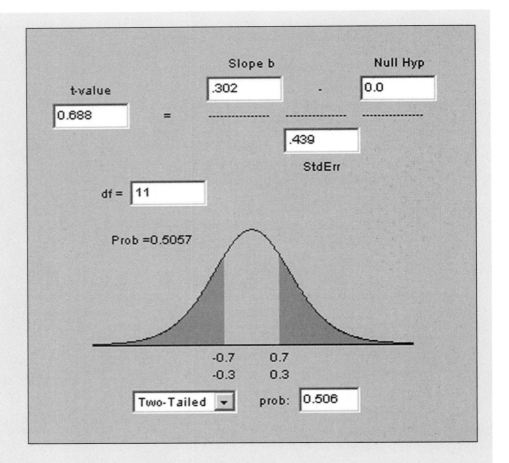

We see that the slope here is not significantly different from 0. Now enter the data from part (b) of Table 10.5, testing whether the relationship is significant once we remove the outlier.

---

## 10.9 A Final Worked Example

In Chapter 9 we obtained the correlation coefficient for the relationship between the rated quality of a course and the difficulty of that course (as reflected in the average expected grade for students taking the course). The data are repeated in Table 10.6, which shows only the first 15 cases to conserve space, but the calculations are based on all 50 cases in my sample. See

 http://www.uvm.edu/~dhowell/fundamentals/DataFiles/Tab10-6.dat

**Table 10.6**

A Worked Example of Predicting Course Quality from Grades

| Expected Grade (X) | Overall Quality (Y) | Expected Grade (X) | Overall Quality (Y) |
|---|---|---|---|
| 3.5 | 3.4 | 3.0 | 3.8 |
| 3.2 | 2.9 | 3.1 | 3.4 |
| 2.8 | 2.6 | 3.0 | 2.8 |
| 3.3 | 3.8 | 3.3 | 2.9 |
| 3.2 | 3.0 | 3.2 | 4.1 |
| 3.2 | 2.5 | 3.4 | 2.7 |
| 3.6 | 3.9 | 3.7 | 3.9 |
| 4.0 | 4.3 | | |

| Results Based on All 50 Cases |
|---|
| $\Sigma X = 174.3$ |
| $\Sigma X^2 = 613.65$ |
| $\Sigma Y = 177.5$ |
| $\Sigma Y^2 = 648.57$ |
| $\Sigma XY = 621.94$ |

Here we will solve for the regression equation for predicting rated Overall Quality ($Y$) from Expected Grade ($X$). We will then consider the interpretation of the coefficients in that equation.

Our first step is to calculate the mean and the standard deviation of each variable, as follows:

$$\overline{Y} = 177.7/50 = 3.550$$

$$s_Y = \sqrt{\frac{648.57 - 177.5^2/50}{49}} = .6135$$

$$\overline{X} = 174.3/50 = 3.486$$

$$s_X = \sqrt{\frac{613.65 - 174.3^2/50}{49}} = .3511$$

The covariance is given as

$$\text{cov}_{XY} = \frac{621.94 - \dfrac{(174.3)(177.5)}{50}}{49} = .0648$$

To calculate the slope, we have

$$b = \frac{\text{cov}_{XY}}{s_X^2} = \frac{.0648}{.3511^2} = .5257$$

We calculate the intercept as

$$a = \overline{Y} - b(\overline{X}) = 3.55 - .5257(3.486) = 1.7174$$

Our equation is then

$$\hat{Y} = .5257(X) + 1.7174$$

We can interpret the result as follows. If we had a course in which students expected a grade of 0, our best guess is that the expected course rating would be 1.7174. That is not a particularly meaningful statistic as far as interpretation is concerned because it is difficult to imagine a course in which everyone would expect to fail. In this case the intercept merely serves to anchor the regression equation.

A slope of .5257 can be interpreted to mean that if two courses differ by one point in expected grades, their overall ratings would be expected to differ by a little over one-half a point. Such a difference, then, would be expected between a course in which students anticipate a grade of C (2.0) and a course in which students anticipate a grade of B (3.0). Keep in mind, however, the earlier remarks about the fact that we are not making a causal statement here. We have no particular reason to conclude that lower expected grades *cause* lower ratings, although they are *associated* with lower ratings. Poor teaching could easily lead to both.

## 10.10 Regression Versus Correlation

We spent Chapter 9 discussing correlation and then turned around in this chapter and said some of the same things about regression. You might be forgiven for asking why we need both. I think that there are at least two answers to that question. When we have only one predictor variable, as we have had in these two chapters, the two approaches tell you many of the same things. The advantage of a correlation coefficient is that it is a single number that allows you to quickly characterize the *degree* to which two variables are related. When you can say that a specific test of manual skills is correlated .85 with performance on the job, you are saying something important. In such an example I imagine that it would be much less useful if I said that an increase of 10 points on the test is associated with a 5-point difference in job performance. On the other hand, when you are interested in speaking about the magnitude of change, a regression coefficient is useful. Suppose that I could make birth control information available to an additional 10% of a population of women at high risk of producing a child that will not live for a year. Suppose further that doing so will decrease infant mortality by 9.7 percentage points. Telling you this is probably far more useful than telling you that the correlation between contraception and infant mortality in sub-Saharan Africa is .44. Both statistics have their uses, and you can chose the one that best serves your needs.

When we come to the next chapter on multiple regression we will find that correlation and regression do not overlap so nicely. We might have a very high correlation between an outcome variable and two predictors taken together. But that might be due to either one or the other, or to both, of those predictors. The usual way of seeing which variables are important is to look at the regression coefficient. In fact, it is often the case that we will apply multiple regression in a setting where we know that the overall multiple correlation is almost certain to be significant, but we want to tease out the separate roles of the predictors.

## 10.11 Summary

In this chapter we expanded on the relationship between two variables to cover the situation in which we want to predict one variable from our knowledge of the other variable. We examined how to calculate the equation for a regression line and looked at the standard error of estimate $s_{Y - \hat{Y}}$ as a measure of the accuracy of the prediction. You saw that $r^2$ is an important index of the percentage of variability in one variable that can be accounted for by variability in the other. The use of $r^2$ instead of $r$ adds considerable meaning to the correlation coefficient, although it must be interpreted with caution. Finally, we saw an example of how extreme scores can seriously distort the regression line, and discussed the role and procedures of hypothesis testing in regression.

Some important terms in this chapter are

| | |
|---|---|
| Regression, *212* | Standardized regression coefficient, $\beta$(beta), *219* |
| Linear regression, *212* | |
| Predicted value ($\hat{Y}$), *217* | Standard error of estimate, *221* |
| Slope, *217* | Residual variance (error variance), *221* |
| Intercept, *217* | |
| Errors of prediction, *217* | Sum of squares, *224* |
| Residual, *217* | $SS_{error}$, *224* |
| Least squares regression, *217* | $SS_Y$, *224* |
| Regression equation, *218* | $SS_{total}$, *224* |
| Regression coefficients, *218* | |

## 10.12 Exercises

**10.1** The following data are from 10 Health Planning Districts in Vermont. Y is the percentage of live births $\leq 2500$ grams. $X_1$ is the fertility rate for women $\leq 17$ or $\geq 35$ years of age ($X_1$ is known as the "high-risk fertility rate"). $X_2$ is the percentage of births to unmarried women. Compute the regression equation for predicting the percentage of births of infants weighing under 2500 grams (Y) on the basis of the high-risk fertility rate.

| District | Y | $X_1$ | $X_2$ |
|---|---|---|---|
| 1 | 6.1 | 43.0 | 9.2 |
| 2 | 7.1 | 55.3 | 12.0 |
| 3 | 7.4 | 48.5 | 10.4 |
| 4 | 6.3 | 38.8 | 9.8 |
| 5 | 6.5 | 46.2 | 9.8 |
| 6 | 5.7 | 39.9 | 7.7 |
| 7 | 6.6 | 43.1 | 10.9 |
| 8 | 8.1 | 48.5 | 9.5 |
| 9 | 6.3 | 40.0 | 11.6 |
| 10 | 6.9 | 56.7 | 11.6 |

**10.2** Calculate the standard error of estimate for the regression equation in Exercise 10.1.

**10.3** If, as a result of ongoing changes in the role of women in society, we saw a change in the age of childbearing such that the high-risk fertility rate jumped to 70 in Exercise 9.1, what would we predict for the incidence of birthweight $< 2500$ grams?

**10.4** Why should you feel uncomfortable making a prediction in Exercise 10.3 for a rate of 70?

**10.5** In Exercise 9.1 we saw data on infant mortality and risk factors. Why might you feel more comfortable making a prediction based on Income for Senegal than for Ethiopia or Namibia?

**10.6** What would what you know about regression contribute to your understanding of infant health in developing countries?

**10.7** Using the data in Table 10.2, predict the Symptom score for a stress level of 45.

**10.8** The mean Stress score in Table 10.2 was 21.467. What would your prediction be for a Stress score of 21.467? How does this compare to the mean Symptom score?

**10.9** Suppose that we know that the correlation between two variables named X and Y is .56. What would you expect would happen to the *correlation* if we subtracted 10 points from every X score?

**10.10** With regard to Exercise 10.9, suppose that the mean of X was 15.6 and the mean of Y was 23.8. What would happen to the *slope* and *intercept* if we subtracted 10 points from every Y?

**10.11** Draw a diagram (or diagrams) to illustrate Exercise 10.10.

**10.12** Make up a set of 5 data points that have an intercept of 0 and a slope of 1. (There are several ways to solve this problem, so think about it a bit.)

**10.13**  Take the data that you just created in Exercise 10.11 and add 2.5 to each $Y$ value. Plot the original data and the new data. On the same graph, superimpose the regression lines.
(a) What has happened to the slope and intercept?
(b) What would happen to the correlation?

**10.14**  Generate $\hat{Y}$ and $(Y - \hat{Y})$ for the first five cases of the data in Table 10.2.

**10.15**  Using the data in

http://www.uvm.edu/~dhowell/fundamentals/DataFiles/Add.dat

compute the regression equation for predicting GPA from ADDSC.

**10.16**  Show that the two equations for $b$ (i.e., $b = \text{cov}_{XY}/s_X^2$ and $b = r\, s_Y/s_X$) are equivalent. (I couldn't resist bringing in a small amount of algebra.)

**10.17**  Within a group of 200 faculty members who have been at a small private college for less than 15 years (i.e., before the salary curve starts leveling off), the equation relating salary $(Y)$ (in thousands of dollars) to years of service $(X)$ is $Y = .9X + 31$. For administrative staff at the same college the equation is $Y = 1.5X + 18$. Assuming that all differences are significant (the slope and intercept are significantly different from zero), interpret the meaning of these two equations. How many years must pass for an administrator and a faculty member to earn roughly the same salary?

**10.18**  Why would we ever care if a slope is significantly different from 0?

**10.19**  The following data represent the actual heights and weights, referred to in Chapter 9, for male college students:

| Height | Weight | Height | Weight |
|--------|--------|--------|--------|
| 70     | 150    | 73     | 170    |
| 67     | 140    | 74     | 180    |
| 72     | 180    | 66     | 135    |
| 75     | 190    | 71     | 170    |
| 68     | 145    | 70     | 157    |
| 69     | 150    | 70     | 130    |
| 71.5   | 164    | 75     | 185    |
| 71     | 140    | 74     | 190    |
| 72     | 142    | 71     | 155    |
| 69     | 136    | 69     | 170    |
| 67     | 123    | 70     | 155    |
| 68     | 155    | 72     | 215    |
| 66     | 140    | 67     | 150    |
| 72     | 145    | 69     | 145    |
| 73.5   | 160    | 73     | 155    |
| 73     | 190    | 73     | 155    |
| 69     | 155    | 71     | 150    |
| 73     | 165    | 68     | 155    |
| 72     | 150    | 69.5   | 150    |
| 74     | 190    | 73     | 180    |

| Height | Weight | Height | Weight |
|--------|--------|--------|--------|
| 72 | 195 | 75 | 160 |
| 71 | 138 | 66 | 135 |
| 74 | 160 | 69 | 160 |
| 72 | 155 | 66 | 130 |
| 70 | 153 | 73 | 155 |
| 67 | 145 | 68 | 150 |
| 71 | 170 | 74 | 148 |
| 72 | 175 | 73.5 | 155 |
| 69 | 175 | | |

(a) Make a scatterplot of the data.
(b) Calculate the regression equation of weight predicted from height for these data. Interpret the slope and the intercept.
(c) What is the correlation coefficient for these data?
(d) Are the correlation coefficient and the slope significantly different from zero?

**10.20** The following data are the actual heights and weights, referred to in Chapter 9, for female college students:

| Height | Weight | Height | Weight |
|--------|--------|--------|--------|
| 61 | 140 | 65 | 135 |
| 66 | 120 | 66 | 125 |
| 68 | 130 | 65 | 118 |
| 68 | 138 | 65 | 122 |
| 63 | 121 | 65 | 115 |
| 70 | 125 | 64 | 102 |
| 68 | 116 | 67 | 115 |
| 69 | 145 | 69 | 150 |
| 69 | 150 | 68 | 110 |
| 67 | 150 | 63 | 116 |
| 68 | 125 | 62 | 108 |
| 66 | 130 | 63 | 95 |
| 65.5 | 120 | 64 | 125 |
| 66 | 130 | 68 | 133 |
| 62 | 131 | 62 | 110 |
| 62 | 120 | 61.75 | 108 |
| 63 | 118 | 62.75 | 112 |
| 67 | 125 | | |

(a) Make a scatterplot of the data.
(b) Calculate the regression coefficients for these data. Interpret the slope and the intercept.
(c) What is the correlation coefficient for these data?
(d) Are the correlation and the slope significantly different from zero?

**10.21** Using your own height and the appropriate regression equation from Exercise 10.19 or 10.20, predict your own weight. (If you are uncomfortable reporting your own weight, predict mine—I am 5′8″ and weigh 156 pounds—well, at least I would like to think so.)
(a) How much is your actual weight greater than or less than your predicted weight? (You have just calculated a residual.)
(b) What effect will biased reporting on the part of the students who produced the data play in your prediction of your own weight?

**10.22** Use your scatterplot of the data for students of your own gender and observe the size of the residuals. (*Hint:* You can see the residuals in the vertical distance of points from the line.) What is the largest residual for your scatterplot?

**10.23** Given a male and a female student who are both 5′6″, how much would they be expected to differ in weight? (*Hint:* Calculate a predicted weight for each of them using the regression equation specific to gender.)

**10.24** The slope (*b*) used to predict the weights of males from their heights is greater than the slope for females. What does this tell us about male weights relative to female weights?

**10.25** In Chapter 3 I presented data on the speed of deciding whether a briefly presented letter was part of a comparison set and gave data from trials on which the comparison set had contained one, three, or five letters. Eventually, I would like to compare the three conditions (using only the data from trials on which the stimulus letter had in fact been a part of that set), but I worry that the trials are not independent. If the subject (myself) was improving as the task went along, he would do better on later trials, and how he did would in some way be related to the number of the trial. If so, we would not be able to say that the responses were independent. Using only the data from the trials in which the stimulus was in the comparison set and in which there were five letters in the comparison set, obtain the regression of response on trial number. (These will be the data in the dataset for which there is a "1" in the fourth column.) Was performance improving significantly over trials? Can we assume that there is no systematic linear trend over time? These data are available for you to download from

http://www.uvm.edu/~dhowell/fundamentals/DataFiles/Tab3-1.dat

**10.26** Write a paragraph describing the results of the correlational analysis in Table 10.6. Your paragraph should be comparable to the paragraph in Chapter 9, Section 9.14 ("Summary and Conclusions of Course Evaluation Study").

**10.27** Wainer (1997) presented data on the relationship between hours of TV watching and *mean* scores on the 1990 National Assessment of Educational Progress (NAEP) for eighth-grade mathematics assessment. The data follow, separated for boys and girls.

| Hours TV Watched | 0 | 1 | 2 | 3 | 4 | 5 | 6 |
|---|---|---|---|---|---|---|---|
| Girls NAEP | 258 | 269 | 267 | 261 | 259 | 253 | 239 |
| Boys NAEP | 276 | 273 | 292 | 269 | 266 | 259 | 249 |

(a) Plot the relationship between Hours Watched and NAEP Mathematics scores separately for boys and girls (but put them on the same graph).

(b) Find and interpret the slope and intercept for these data, again keeping boys and girls separate.

(c) We know from other data that boys spend more time watching television than girls. Could this be used as an explanation of performance differences between boys and girls?

**10.28** You probably were startled to see the very neat relationships in Exercise 10.27. There was almost no variability about the regression line. I would, as a first approximation, guess that the relationship between television hours watched and standardized test performance would contain roughly as much scatter as the relationship between stress and symptoms, yet these data are far neater than the data in Figure 10.1. What might have caused this?

**10.29** Draw a scatter diagram (of 10 points) on a sheet of paper that represents a moderately positive correlation between the variables. Now drop your pencil *at random* on this scatter diagram.

(a) If you think of your pencil as a regression line, what aspect of the regression line are you changing as you move the pencil vertically on the paper?

(b) What aspect of the regression line are you changing as you twist, or rotate, your pencil?

(c) If you didn't remember any of the equations for the slope and intercept, how could you tell if your pencil was forming the optimal regression line?

**10.30** There is some really excellent material on regression at the University of Newcastle, in Australia. The address is

 http://www.anu.edu.au/nceph/surfstat/surfstat-home/surfstat.html

Go to this site and check both the links for *Statistical Inference* and for *Hotlist for Java Applets*.

The Java applets are particularly nice because they allow you to manipulate data on the screen and see what difference it makes. Write a short description of the material you found there.

# 11

# Multiple Regression

## QUESTIONS

- What if I have more than one predictor that I could use?

- What about the variability that I can't predict?

- It was easy to plot a single predictor, but how do we deal with multiple ones?

- Is this relationship that I found real, or could it have just happened by chance?

- How about some more examples?

In Chapters 9 and 10 we dealt with the case in which we were looking at the relationship between one variable and another. We wanted either to determine the degree to which the two variables were correlated or to predict one criterion (dependent) variable from one predictor (independent) variable. In that situation we have a correlation coefficient ($r$) and regression equation of the form $\hat{Y} = bX + a$. But there is no good reason why we must limit ourselves to having only one predictor. It is perfectly appropriate to ask how well some linear combination of two, three, four, or more predictors will predict the criterion. To take a greatly oversimplified example, we could ask how well I could do if I just added together the number of stressful events you report experiencing over the last month, the number of close friends you have, and your score on a measure assessing how much control you feel you have over events in your life and then used that total or composite score to predict your level of psychological symptoms. Of course you could fairly argue that it makes no sense to add together 3 stressful events, 5 friends, and a score of 50, get an answer of 58, and think that the 58 means anything sensible. The variables are measured on completely different scales.

But I can work around the objection of measuring on different scales if I give different weight to each variable. There is no reason why I should have to give equal weight to a test score and the number of close friends you have. It might make much more sense to pay more attention to some variables than to others. Perhaps your sense of personal control over events is twice as important in predicting psychological distress as is the number of stressful events, and perhaps both of those are more important than the number of your friends. Moreover, we will have to add or subtract some constant to make the mean prediction come out to equal the mean Symptom score.

If we let the letters S, F, and C represent "Stress," "Friends," and "Control," we could have a regression equation that looks like

$$\hat{Y} = 2 \times S + 1 \times F + 4 \times C + 12$$

The general form of this equation would be written as

$$\hat{Y} = b_1 S + b_2 F + b_3 C + b_0$$

where $b_1$, $b_2$, and $b_3$ are the weights for predictors S, F, and C. In other words, they are slopes, or regression coefficients. The coefficient $b_0$ is simply the intercept, with the same meaning that it has had throughout our discussion of regression (although in simple regression we denoted it as $a$).

Multiple regression solutions are usually quite cumbersome to compute by hand, especially with more than two predictors, but they can be readily computed with any of the widely available statistical programs. In this chapter we will focus exclusively on solutions generated by computer software.

## 11.1 Overview

It will be helpful to begin with an example that represents an overview of various aspects of multiple regression. Then we can go back and look specifically at each of them with some actual data at hand. I will cover a lot of ground quite quickly, but my major purpose is to give you a general understanding of where we are going, rather than to impart a lot of technical information. You will see most of this again.

How do professors in an academic department decide who will be offered admission to graduate school? Many years ago I collected data on admission to one graduate program. All faculty in that department rated several hundred graduate applications on a scale from 1 to 7, where 1 represented "reject immediately" and 7 represented "accept immediately." For a random sample of 100 applications I attempted to predict the mean rating (Rating) for each application (averaged over judgments based on all available information) on the basis of Graduate Record Exam Verbal score (GREV), a numerical rating of the combined letters of recommendation (Letters), and a numerical rating of the statements of purpose (Purpose). The obtained regression equation was

$$\hat{Y} = .009 \times \text{GREV} + .51 \times \text{Letters} + .43 \times \text{Purpose} - 1.87$$

In addition, the correlation between Rating and the three predictors considered simultaneously (the **multiple correlation coefficient, R**) was .775.[1]

---

Definition    **Multiple correlation coefficient (R):** The correlation between one variable (Y) and a set of predictors.

**Squared correlation coefficient ($R^2$):** The squared correlation coefficient between Y and a set of one or more predictor variables.

---

## Squared Multiple Correlation

We can square the correlation coefficient, just as we do in the one-predictor case, with a similar interpretation. The **squared correlation coefficient ($R^2$)** is .60. The interpretation of $R^2$ is the same as for the case of $r^2$ with one predictor. In other words, 60% of the variability in ratings can be accounted for by variability in the three predictors *considered together*. Put slightly differently, using GREV, Letters, and Purpose *simultaneously* as predictors, we can account for 60% of the variability in ratings of admissibility. (That is actually quite good, though not so good that I would be willing to substitute the regression equation for the overall ratings of the faculty.)

## Interpretation

The regression equation in multiple regression is interpreted in much the same way it was interpreted in simple regression, wherein we had only one predictor. To make a prediction, we multiply the student's GREV score by .009. In addition, we

---

[1]Note that I was predicting the rating that faculty would give, not the individual's actual success in graduate school. It is not very surprising that ratings would be related to GRE scores and what reviewers said about the candidate, though I would find if very surprising if the composite score correlated that highly with a candidate's subsequent performance once admitted.

multiply the rating of that student's letters of recommendation by .51 and the rating of the statement of purpose by .43. We then sum those results and subtract 1.87 (the intercept). For every one-unit change in GREV the predicted rating will increase by .009 unit, *assuming that Letters and Purpose remain unchanged*. Similarly, for every one-unit change in the rating of the letters of recommendation there will be a .51-unit change in the ratings, again assuming that the other two predictors are held constant. The most important words in that last sentence were "assuming that the other two predictors are held constant." We will consider this at more depth shortly, but for now keep in mind that we are looking at one variable controlling for the effects of the other variables.

## Standardized Regression Coefficients

In Chapter 10 I mentioned the standardized regression coefficient ($\beta$) and said that it represents the regression coefficient we would obtain if we standardized the variables, that is, converted the variables (separately) to $z$ scores. Here is a good place to say something meaningful about $\beta$. In the equation given for predicting ratings from GREV, Letters, and Purpose, you might at first be inclined to suggest that GREV must not be very important as a predictor because it has such a small (unstandardized) regression coefficient (.009). On the other hand, the regression coefficient for Letters is .51, which is over 5000 times greater. As we just saw, this regression equation tells us that a one-point difference in GREV would make (only) a .009 difference in our prediction, whereas a one-point difference in the rating of Letters would make a difference of about half a point in our prediction. But keep in mind that the variability of GREV is considerably greater than the variability of ratings of Letters. It is trivial to do one point better or worse on GREV. (Does anyone really care if your Verbal score was 552 instead of a 553—even ignoring the fact that the way the test is scored, values are rounded to the nearest tens' digit?) But Letters were rated on a seven-point scale, where a one-point difference is a big deal. This difference between the variances of our two measures is one major reason why we can't meaningfully compare regular (unstandardized) regression coefficients.

If I now told you that the *standardized* regression coefficient ($\beta$) for GREV was .72, while the $\beta$ for Letters was .61, you would see that, *after we take the difference in the standard deviations of the variables into account*, the weights for these variables are approximately equal. (Another way of saying that is "after we put both variables on an equal footing by standardizing them, their contributions are approximately equal.") A one standard-deviation difference in GREV will make a .72 standard-deviation difference in the prediction, while a one standard-deviation difference in Letters will make a .61 standard-deviation difference in the prediction. In this sense the two variables contribute about evenly to the prediction. But be careful of overinterpreting what I have said. Using standardized weights ($\beta$) does make it easier to keep the contributions of the variables in perspective. But this scheme is not foolproof. For reasons dealing with the intercorrelations of the predictor variables, $\beta$ weights are not perfectly related to the contribution that each variable makes to the prediction. They are a good rough guide, but don't conclude that just because the value of .72 is greater than .61, GREV is more important than Letters. In the first place it is not clear just what "more important than" means here. Additionally, some other measure of the contribution of each variable might favor Letters over GREV. The task of deciding on the relative importance of predictors is a difficult one (for predictors that are themselves highly correlated, maybe even a meaningless one). A much more extensive discussion of this problem is found in Howell (2007).

## Redundancy among Predictors

The issue of correlation among predictors in multiple regression is an important one and deserves discussion. Imagine an artificial situation wherein we have two predictor variables that are each correlated with the criterion, or dependent, variable, but are uncorrelated with each other. In this case the predictors have nothing in common, and the squared multiple correlation coefficient ($R^2$) will be equal to the sum of the squared correlations of each predictor with the dependent variable. Each predictor is bringing something new, and unique, to the prediction. That is the ideal case, but we very rarely work in a world where the predictors are not correlated with each other.

Consider the example of predicting ratings for admission to graduate school. It seems perfectly reasonable that you would likely have a better rating if you had a better GREV score. Similarly, it seems reasonable that you would have a better rating if you had stronger letters of recommendation. But GREV scores and Letters are themselves likely to be highly correlated. If you do well in your courses, you will probably do well on the GRE. In fact, I may even refer to your performance on the GRE when I write your letter of recommendation. If the reader on the other end looks at your GRE scores and then reads my letter, my letter is telling her some of what she already knew—this student knows a lot. Similarly, if the reader reads my letter and finds that you are a terrific student, she is not going to be very surprised when she turns to the GRE scores and sees that they are high. In other words, the two variables are to some extent redundant. Put another way, the total information in those two predictors is not the sum of the parts—it is something less than the sum of the parts. It is important to keep this redundancy in mind when thinking about multiple regression.

When the predictors are highly correlated with each other (a condition known as **multicollinearity**), the regression equation is very unstable from one sample of data to another. In other words, two random samples from the same population might produce regression equations that appear to be totally different from one another. I would strongly advise you to avoid using highly correlated predictors and even to avoid moderate intercorrelations when possible, though it isn't always possible.

---

Definition     Multicollinearity: A condition in which predictor variables are highly correlated among themselves.

---

## 11.2 A Different Data Set

There has been an ongoing debate in this country about what we can do to improve the quality of primary and secondary education. It is generally assumed that spending more money on education will lead to better-prepared students, but that is just an assumption. Guber (1999) addressed that question by collecting data for each of the 50 (U.S.) states. She recorded the amount spent on education, the pupil/teacher ratio, average teachers' salary, the percentage of students in that state taking the SAT exams, the SAT verbal score, the SAT math score, and the combined SAT score. The data are shown in Table 11.1 and are available at the Web site for this book.[2] We will use only three of the variables, but you might work with some of the others on your own.

**Table 11.1**

Data on Performance versus Expenditures on Education

| State | Expend | PTratio | Salary | PctSAT | Verbal | Math | Combined |
|-------|--------|---------|--------|--------|--------|------|----------|
| Alabama | 4.405 | 17.2 | 31.144 | 8 | 491 | 538 | 1029 |
| Alaska | 8.963 | 17.6 | 47.951 | 47 | 445 | 489 | 934 |
| Arizona | 4.778 | 19.3 | 32.175 | 27 | 448 | 496 | 944 |
| Arkansas | 4.459 | 7.1 | 28.934 | 6 | 482 | 523 | 1005 |
| California | 4.992 | 24.0 | 41.078 | 45 | 417 | 485 | 902 |
| Colorado | 5.443 | 18.4 | 34.571 | 29 | 462 | 518 | 980 |
| Connecticut | 8.817 | 14.4 | 50.045 | 81 | 431 | 477 | 908 |
| Delaware | 7.030 | 16.6 | 39.076 | 68 | 429 | 468 | 897 |
| Florida | 5.718 | 19.1 | 32.588 | 48 | 420 | 469 | 889 |
| Georgia | 5.193 | 16.3 | 32.291 | 65 | 406 | 448 | 854 |
| Hawaii | 6.078 | 17.9 | 38.518 | 57 | 407 | 482 | 889 |
| Idaho | 4.210 | 19.1 | 29.783 | 15 | 468 | 511 | 979 |
| Illinois | 6.136 | 17.3 | 39.431 | 13 | 488 | 560 | 1048 |
| Indiana | 5.826 | 17.5 | 36.785 | 58 | 415 | 467 | 882 |
| Iowa | 5.483 | 15.8 | 31.511 | 5 | 516 | 583 | 1099 |
| Kansas | 5.817 | 15.1 | 34.652 | 9 | 503 | 557 | 1060 |
| Kentucky | 5.217 | 17.0 | 32.257 | 11 | 477 | 522 | 999 |
| Louisiana | 4.761 | 16.8 | 26.461 | 9 | 486 | 535 | 1021 |
| Maine | 6.428 | 13.8 | 31.972 | 68 | 427 | 469 | 896 |
| Maryland | 7.245 | 17.0 | 40.661 | 64 | 430 | 479 | 909 |
| Massachusetts | 7.287 | 14.8 | 40.795 | 80 | 430 | 477 | 907 |
| Michigan | 6.994 | 20.1 | 41.895 | 11 | 484 | 549 | 1033 |
| Minnesota | 6.000 | 17.5 | 35.948 | 9 | 506 | 579 | 1085 |
| Mississippi | 4.080 | 17.5 | 26.818 | 4 | 496 | 540 | 1036 |
| Missouri | 5.383 | 15.5 | 31.189 | 9 | 495 | 550 | 1045 |
| Montana | 5.692 | 16.3 | 28.785 | 21 | 473 | 536 | 1009 |
| Nebraska | 5.935 | 14.5 | 30.922 | 9 | 494 | 556 | 1050 |

*(continued)*

[2]An abstract, and a complete copy, of this paper is available at

 http://www.amstat.org/publications/jse/v7n2_abstracts.html

**Table 11.1**

(*continued*)

| State | Expend | PTratio | Salary | PctSAT | Verbal | Math | Combined |
|---|---|---|---|---|---|---|---|
| Nevada | 5.160 | 18.7 | 34.836 | 30 | 434 | 483 | 917 |
| New Hampshire | 5.859 | 15.6 | 34.720 | 70 | 444 | 491 | 935 |
| New Jersey | 9.774 | 13.8 | 46.087 | 70 | 420 | 478 | 898 |
| New Mexico | 4.586 | 17.2 | 28.493 | 11 | 485 | 530 | 1015 |
| New York | 9.623 | 15.2 | 47.612 | 74 | 419 | 473 | 892 |
| North Carolina | 5.077 | 16.2 | 30.793 | 60 | 411 | 454 | 865 |
| North Dakota | 4.775 | 15.3 | 26.327 | 5 | 515 | 592 | 1107 |
| Ohio | 6.162 | 16.6 | 36.802 | 23 | 460 | 515 | 975 |
| Oklahoma | 4.845 | 15.5 | 28.172 | 9 | 491 | 536 | 1027 |
| Oregon | 6.436 | 19.9 | 38.555 | 51 | 448 | 499 | 947 |
| Pennsylvania | 7.109 | 17.1 | 44.510 | 70 | 419 | 461 | 880 |
| Rhode Island | 7.469 | 14.7 | 40.729 | 70 | 425 | 463 | 888 |
| South Carolina | 4.797 | 16.4 | 30.279 | 58 | 401 | 443 | 844 |
| South Dakota | 4.775 | 14.4 | 25.994 | 5 | 505 | 563 | 1068 |
| Tennessee | 4.388 | 18.6 | 32.477 | 12 | 497 | 543 | 1040 |
| Texas | 5.222 | 15.7 | 31.223 | 47 | 419 | 474 | 893 |
| Utah | 3.656 | 24.3 | 29.082 | 4 | 513 | 563 | 1076 |
| Vermont | 6.750 | 13.8 | 35.406 | 68 | 429 | 472 | 901 |
| Virginia | 5.327 | 14.6 | 33.987 | 65 | 428 | 468 | 896 |
| Washington | 5.906 | 20.2 | 36.151 | 48 | 443 | 494 | 937 |
| West Virginia | 6.107 | 14.8 | 31.944 | 17 | 448 | 484 | 932 |
| Wisconsin | 6.930 | 15.9 | 37.746 | 9 | 501 | 572 | 1073 |
| Wyoming | 6.160 | 14.9 | 31.285 | 10 | 476 | 525 | 1001 |

I have chosen to work with this particular data set because it illustrates several things. In the first place, it is a real data set that pertains to a topic of current interest. In addition, it illustrates what is, at first, a very puzzling result, and then allows us to explore that result and make sense of it. The difference between what we see with one predictor and what we see with two predictors is quite dramatic and illustrates some of the utility of multiple regression. Finally, these data illustrate well the need to think carefully about your measures, and don't simply assume that they measure what you think they measure.

From the stem-and-leaf display in Table 11.2 you can see that the expenditure variable is slightly positively skewed, whereas the combined SAT score is roughly normal. The percentage of students taking the SAT is almost a bimodal variable, and we will discuss this shortly.

## Two Variable Relationships

The most obvious thing to do with these data is to ask about the relationship between expenditure and outcome. We would presumably like to see that the more money we spend on education, the better our students do. Table 11.3 shows the Pearson correlations between some of our variables. The scatterplot in Figure 11.1 shows the relationship between Expend and PctSAT.

**Table 11.2**

Stem-and-Leaf Display for Important Variables for the Data in Table 11.1

| Expenditures | Combined SAT | Percentage Taking SAT |
|---|---|---|
| The decimal point is at the \| | The decimal point is 2 digit(s) to the right of the \| | The decimal point is 1 digit(s) to the right of the \| |
| 3 \| 7 | 8 \| 4 | 0 \| 44555689999999 |
| 4 \| 124456888888 | 8 \| 578899999 | 1 \| 01112357 |
| 5 \| 01222234457788999 | 9 \| 000000111233444 | 2 \| 1379 |
| 6 \| 0111224489 | 9 \| 5888 | 3 \| 0 |
| 7 \| 001235 | 10 \| 00112233344 | 4 \| 57788 |
| 8 \| 8 | 10 \| 55567789 | 5 \| 1788 |
| 9 \| 068 | 11 \| 01 | 6 \| 0455888 |
| | | 7 \| 00004 |
| | | 8 \| 01 |

**Table 11.3**

Correlations Between Selected Variables

| | | Correlations | | | |
|---|---|---|---|---|---|
| | | Expend | Salary | PctSAT | Combined |
| EXPEND | Pearson Correlation | 1 | .870** | .593** | −.381** |
| | Sig. (2−tailed) | . | .000 | .000 | .006 |
| | N | 50 | 50 | 50 | 50 |
| SALARY | Pearson Correlation | .870** | 1 | .617** | −.440** |
| | Sig. (2−tailed) | .000 | . | .000 | .001 |
| | N | 50 | 50 | 50 | 50 |
| PctSAT | Pearson Correlation | .593** | .617** | 1 | −.887** |
| | Sig. (2−tailed) | .000 | .000 | . | .000 |
| | N | 50 | 50 | 50 | 50 |
| COMBINED | Pearson Correlation | −.381** | −.440** | −.887** | 1 |
| | Sig. (2−tailed) | .006 | .001 | .000 | . |
| | N | 50 | 50 | 50 | 50 |

**.Correlation is significant at the .01 level (2−tailed).

Figure 11.1 is somewhat surprising, because it would suggest that the more money we spend on educating our children the worse they do. The regression line is clearly decreasing and the correlation is −.38. Although that correlation is not terribly large, it is statistically significant and cannot just be ignored. Those students who come from wealthier schools tend to do worse. Why should this be?

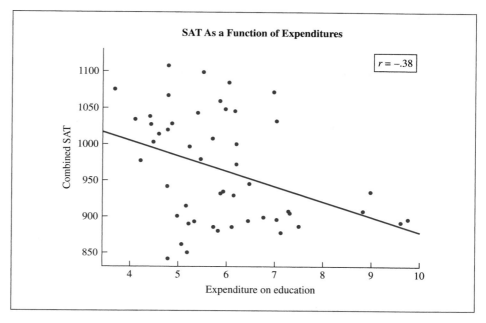

**Figure 11.1**
Relationship between Expend and PctSAT

An answer to our puzzle comes from knowing a bit about the SAT exam itself. Not all colleges and universities require that students take the SAT, and there is a tendency for those institutions that do require it to be the more prestigious ones that take only the top students. In addition, the percentage of students taking the SAT varies drastically from state to state. For example, 81% of the students in Connecticut take the test, but only 4% of the students in Utah do. The states with the lowest percentages tend to be in the Midwest, and the highest in the Northeast. In states where a small percentage of students are taking the exam, those students are most likely to be the best students—ones who have their eyes on Princeton, Harvard, Berkeley, and the like. These are students who are likely to do well. In Massachusetts and Connecticut, where most students take the SAT—the less able as well as the more able—the poorer students are going to pull the state average toward the center. If this is true, we should expect to see a negative relationship between the percentage of students taking the exam and the state's mean score. This is exactly what we find, as can be seen in Figure 11.2.

Notice the dramatic effect in Figure 11.2. The correlation coefficient is −.89, with the points clustering very close to the regression line. Notice also that you can see the effect of the bimodal distribution of PctSAT, with the bulk of the points clustering at one end or the other of the X axis.

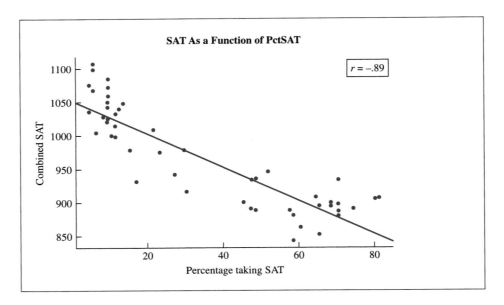

**Figure 11.2**
SAT scores as a function of the percentage of students taking the exam

## Looking at One Predictor While Controlling for Another

The question that now arises is what would happen if we used both variables simultaneously as predictors of the combined score. What this really means, though it may not be immediately obvious, is that we will look at the relationship between Expend and Combined—while *controlling for PctSAT*. When I say that we are controlling for PctSAT I mean that we are looking at the relationship while holding PctSAT constant. Imagine that we had many thousands of states instead only 50. Imagine also that we could pull out a collection of states that had exactly the same percentage of students taking the SAT—e.g., 60%. Then we could look at only the students from those states and compute the correlation and regression coefficient for predicting Combined from Expend. Then we could draw another sample of states, perhaps those with 40% of their students taking the exam. Again we could correlate Expend and Combined for only those states and compute a regression coefficient. Notice that I have calculated two correlations and two regression coefficients here, each with PctSAT held constant at a specific value (40% or 60%). Because we are only imagining that we had thousands of states, we can go further and imagine that we repeated this process many times, with PctSAT held at a specific value each time. For each of those analyses we would obtain a regression coefficient for the relationship between Expend and Combined, and an average of those many regression coefficients will be very close to the overall regression coefficient that we will shortly examine. The same is true if we averaged the correlations.

Because in our imaginary exercise each correlation is based on a sample with a fixed value of PctSAT, each correlation is independent of PctSAT. In other words, if every state included in our correlation had 35% of its students taking the SAT, then PctSAT doesn't vary, and it can't have an effect on the relationship between Expend and Combined. That means that our correlation and regression coefficient between those two variables has *controlled for* PctSAT.

Obviously we don't have thousands of states—we only have 50 and that number is not likely to get much larger. However that does not stop us from mathematically estimating what we would obtain if we could carry out the imaginary exercise that I just explained. And that is exactly what multiple regression is all about.

## The Multiple Regression Equation

There are ways to think about multiple regression other than fixing the level of one or more variables, but before I discuss those I will go ahead and run a multiple regression on these data. I used SPSS to do so, and the results are shown in Table 11.4. I have left out some of the printout to save space.

The first table that I want to discuss is labeled "Model Summary." In running this multiple regression I chose to ask SPSS to enter both Expend and PctSAT as predictors at the same time, and to use Combined as the dependent variable. From the summary you can see that the correlation for the model was .905, which is a very long way from the correlation of −.381 that we obtained with Expend alone.

A couple of things need to be said here. In multiple regression the correlations are always going to be positive, whereas in Pearson correlation they can be positive or negative. There is a good reason for this, but I don't want to elaborate on that now. (If the correlations are always positive, how do we know when the relationship is negative? We look at the sign of the regression coefficient, and I'll come to that in a minute.) You might recall that in Figure 11.2 we saw that the simple correlation between Combined and PctSAT was −.89, so perhaps we haven't gained all that much. We will discuss this in a minute, also.

In the subtable named Model Summary you will see the squared correlation. The squared correlation in multiple regression has the same meaning that it had in simple regression. Using Expend alone we were able to explain $(-.381)^2 = .145 = $ 14.5% of the variation in Combined SAT scores (not shown in table). Using both Expend and PctSAT we can explain $.905^2 = .819 = 81.9\%$ of the variability in the Combined score. To the right of these values you will see a column labeled Adjusted R square. You can ignore that column. The adjusted R square is actually a less biased estimate of the true squared correlation in the population, but we never report it. Simply use R and not adjusted R.

The third subtable in Table 11.4 is labeled ANOVA, which stands for Analysis of Variance. We will spend quite a bit of time on the analysis of variance later in the book, and I am only going to point to two parts of this table here. Notice that there is a column labeled $F$ and one labeled Sig. The $F$ is a test on whether the multiple correlation coefficient in question is significantly different from 0. We saw a test on the significance of a correlation coefficient in Chapters 9 and 10, although there we largely worked from a statistical table in the back of the book. This is the same kind of test, though it uses a different statistic. When we have only one predictor (Expend) the correlation is .38, as we saw in Table 11.3, and the probability

**Table 11.4**

Multiple Regression Predicting Combined from Expend and PctSAT

| Descriptive Statistics | | | |
|---|---|---|---|
| | Mean | Std. Deviation | N |
| COMBINED | 965.920 | 74.8206 | 50 |
| EXPEND | 5.90526 | 1.362807 | 50 |
| PctSAT | 35.2400 | 26.76242 | 50 |

| Model Summary | | | | |
|---|---|---|---|---|
| Model | R | R Square | Adjusted R Square | Std. Error of the Estimate |
| 1 | .905[a] | .819 | .812 | 32.45949 |

a. Predictors: (Constant), EXPEND, PctSAT

| ANOVA[b] | | | | | | |
|---|---|---|---|---|---|---|
| Model | | Sum of Squares | df | Mean Square | F | Sig. |
| 1 | Regression | 224787.621 | 2 | 112393.810 | 106.674 | .000[a] |
| | Residual | 49520.059 | 47 | 1053.618 | | |
| | Total | 274307.680 | 49 | | | |

a. Predictors: (Constant), PctSAT, EXPEND
b. Dependent Variable: COMBINED

| Coefficients[a] | | | | | | |
|---|---|---|---|---|---|---|
| | | Unstandardized Coefficients | | Standardized Coefficients | | |
| Model | | B | Std. Error | Beta | t | Sig. |
| 1 | (Constant) | 993.832 | 21.833 | | 45.519 | .000 |
| | EXPEND | 12.287 | 4.224 | .224 | 2.909 | .006 |
| | PctSAT | −2.851 | .215 | −1.020 | −13.253 | .000 |

a. Dependent Variable: COMBINED

of getting a correlation that high if the null hypothesis is true was .006. This is well less than .05 and we can declare that correlation to be significantly different from 0. When we move to multiple regression and include the predictor PctSAT along with Expend, we have two questions to ask. The first is whether the multiple correlation using both predictors together is significantly different from .00, and the second is whether each of the predictor variables is contributing at greater than chance levels to that relationship. From the ANOVA table we see an $F = 106.674$, with an associated probability of .000. (That does not mean that the probability is exactly zero, but it is so small that it rounds to 0 to three decimal places.) This tells us that, using both predictors, our correlation is significantly greater than 0. I will ask about the significance of the individual predictors in the next section.

Now we come to the most interesting part of the output. In the subtable labeled "Coefficients" we see the full set of regression coefficients when using both predictors at the same time. From the second column we can see that our regression equation is

$$\hat{Y} = 993.832 + 12.287(Expend) - 28.51(PctSAT)$$

The value of 993.832 is the intercept, often denoted $b_0$ and here denoted simply as "(Constant)." This is the predicted value of Combined if both Expend and PctSAT were .00, which they will never be. We need the intercept because it forces the average of our predictions to equal the average of the obtained values, but we rarely pay any real attention to it.

Just as a simple regression was of the form

$$\hat{Y} = bX + a$$

a multiple regression is written as

$$\hat{Y} = b_1X_1 + b_2X_2 + b_0$$

where $X_1$ and $X_2$ are the predictors and $b_0$ is the intercept. From the table we can see that the coefficient for Expend (call it $b_1$) is 12.287, and for PctSAT the coefficient is $-2.851$. From the sign of these coefficients we can tell whether the relationship is positive or negative. The positive coefficient for Expend tell us that *now that we have controlled PctSAT* the relationship between expenditures and performance is positive—the more the state spends, the higher their (adjusted) SAT score. That should make us feel much better. We can also see that when we control Expend, the relationship between PctSAT and Combined is negative, which makes sense. I explained earlier why increasing the percentage of a state's students taking the SAT would be expected to lower the overall mean for that state.

But you may have noticed that PctSAT itself had a correlation of $-.89$ with Combined, and perhaps Expend wasn't adding anything important to the relationship—after all, the correlation only increased to .905. If you look at the table of coefficients, you will see two columns on the right labeled $t$ and Sig. These relate to significance tests on the regression coefficients. You saw similar $t$ tests in Chapter 10. From the "Sig." column we can tell that all three coefficients are significant at $p < .05$. The intercept has no meaning because it would refer to a case in which a state spent absolutely nothing on education and had 0% of its students taking the SAT. The coefficient for Expend is meaningful because it shows that increased spending does correlate with higher scores after we control for the percentage of students taking the exam. Similarly, after we control for expenditures, SAT scores are higher for those states who have few (presumably their best) students taking the test. So although adding Expend to PctSAT as predictors didn't raise the correlation very much, it was a statistically significant contributor.

I discussed above one of the ways of interpreting what a multiple regression was—for any predictor variable the slope is the relationship between that variable and the criterion variable if we could hold all other variables constant. And by "hold constant" we mean having a collection of participants who had all the same scores on each of the other variables. But there are two other ways of thinking about regression that are useful.

## Another Interpretation of Multiple Regression

When we just correlate Expend with Combined and completely ignore PctSAT, there is a certain amount of variability in the Combined scores that is directly related to variability in PctSAT, and that was what was giving us those peculiar negative results. What we would really like to do is to examine the correlation between Expend and the Combined score when both are adjusted to be free from the influences of PctSAT. To put it another way, some of the differences in Combined are due to differences in Expend and some are due to differences in PctSAT. We want to eliminate those differences in both variables that can be attributed to PctSAT and then correlate the adjusted variables. That is actually a lot simpler than it sounds. I can't imagine anyone intentionally running a multiple regression the way that I am about to, but it does illustrate what is going on.

We know that if we ran the simple regression predicting Combined from PctSAT, the resulting set of predicted scores would represent that part of Combined that is predictable from PctSAT. If we subtract the predicted scores from the actual scores, the resulting values, call them ResidCombined, will be that part of Combined that is *not* predictable from (is independent of) PctSAT. (These new scores are called residuals, and we will have more to say about them shortly.) We can now do the same thing predicting Expend from PctSAT. We will get the predicted scores, subtract them from the obtained scores, and have a new set of scores (call them ResidExpend) that is also independent of PctSAT. So we now have two sets of residual scores—ResidCombined and ResidExpend— that are both independent of PctSAT. So PctSAT can play no role in their relationship.

If I now run the regression to predict the adjusted Combined score from the adjusted Expend score, (i.e., ResidCombined with ResidExpend) I will have

| | | Coefficients[a] | | | | |
|---|---|---|---|---|---|---|
| | | Unstandardized Coefficients | | Standardized Coefficients | | |
| Model | | B | Std. Error | Beta | t | Sig. |
| 1 | (Constant) | 5.944E-14 | 4.542 | | .000 | 1.000 |
| | Resid Expend | 12.287 | 4.180 | .391 | 2.939 | .005 |

a. Dependent Variable: Resid Combined

Notice that the regression coefficient predicting the adjusted combined score from the adjusted expend score is 12.287, which is exactly what we had (when doing things the normal way) for Expend. Notice also that the following table shows us that the correlation between these two corrected variables is .391, which is the correlation between Expend and Combined after we have removed any effects attributable to PctSAT.

Model Summary[b]

| Model | R | R Square | Adjusted R Square | Std. Error of the Estimate |
|---|---|---|---|---|
| 1 | .391[a] | .153 | .135 | 32.1195874 |

a. Predictors: (Constant), Unstandardized Residual
b. Dependent Variable: Unstandardized Residual

I hope that no one thinks that they should actually do their regression this way. The reason I went through the exercise was to make the point that when we have multiple predictor variables we are adjusting each predictor for all other predictors in the equation. And the phrases "adjusted for," "controlling," and "holding constant" all are ways of saying the same thing.

## A Final Way to Think of Multiple Regression

There is another way to think of multiple regression, and in some ways I find it the most useful. We know that in multiple regression we solve for an equation of the form

$$\hat{Y} = b_1 X_1 + b_2 X_2 + b_0$$

or, in terms of the variables we have been using,

$$\widehat{Combined} = b_1 Expend + b_2 PctSAT + b_0$$

I obtained the predicted scores from

$$\widehat{Combined} = 12.287 \times Expend - 2.851 \times PctSAT + 993.832$$

and stored the predicted scores as PredComb. (SPSS will do this for you if you use the Save button on the first dialog box under Regression.) Now if I correlate actual Combined with PredComb the resulting correlation will be .905, which is our multiple correlation. (A scatterplot of this relationship is shown in Figure 11.3, which gives the squared multiple correlation as .8195, the square root of which is .905.)

The point of this last approach is to show that you can think of a multiple correlation coefficient as the simple Pearson correlation between the criterion (Combined) and the best linear combination of the predictors. When I say "best

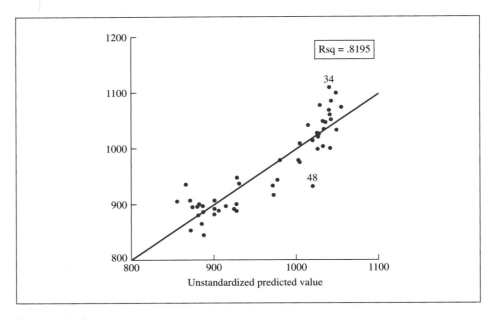

**Figure 11.3**
Scatterplot showing the relationship between the best linear combination of the predictors and Combined

linear combination" I mean that there is no set of weights (regression coefficients) that will do a better job of predicting the state's combined score from those predictors. This is actually a very important point. There are a number of advanced techniques in statistics, which we are not going to cover in this book, that really come down to creating a new variable that is some optimal weighted sum of other variables, and then using that variable in the main part of the analysis. This approach also explains why multiple correlations are always positive, even if the relationship between two variables is negative. You would certainly expect the predicted values to be positively correlated with the criterion.

## Review

We now have several ways of thinking of multiple regression, and each of them gives us a somewhat different view of what is going on. If one of them makes more sense to you than the others, you can focus on that approach.

- We can treat a regression coefficient as the coefficient we would get if we had a whole group of states that did not differ on any of the predictors except the one under consideration. In other words, all predictors but one are held constant, and we look at what varying that one predictor does.

- We can think of a regression coefficient in multiple regression as the same thing we would have in simple regression if we adjusted our two variables for any of the variables we want to control. In this example it meant adjusting both Combined and Expend for PctSAT (by computing the difference between the true score for that variable and the score predicted from the "nuisance variable" or the "to be controlled variable"). The coefficient (slope) that we obtain is the same coefficient we find in the multiple regression solution.

- We can think of the multiple correlation as the simple Pearson correlation between the criterion (call it Y) and another variable (call it $\hat{Y}$) that is the best linear combination of the predictor variables.

## 11.3 Residuals

When we make a prediction from a set of data, we don't expect to be right all the time. Sometimes our prediction will be a bit high, sometimes a bit low. And sometimes the actual data point will be far away from what we have predicted. It is worth looking briefly at these predictions and the errors of prediction, called residuals, because they tell us something more about multiple regression. Table 11.5 contains a sample of the data we saw earlier. I have added two columns—one holding the predicted values and the other the residual values. In that table you can see that some of the predictions are quite accurate (the residual is small) and other predictions are poor (the residual is large). In Figure 11.3 we saw a scatterplot of the relationship between the Combined score and our best linear prediction of that score. Notice that there are two small numbers on that figure (34 and 48). These numbers refer to the states that produced those observations. State 34 is North Dakota and State 48 is West Virginia. Notice that both states had nearly the same predicted outcome (approximately 1050), but North Dakota well exceeded that prediction (1107) while West Virginia fell short by a similar amount (932). These residuals, the difference between predicted and obtained, can either be random noise or they can be meaningful. With a difference of nearly 200 points, I would be inclined to take them seriously. I would ask what North Dakota knows about educating students that West Virginia does not. It isn't that they spend significantly more on education or have significantly fewer students taking the SAT. We can rule out those possibilities because we are looking at the residuals after controlling for PctSAT and Expend. But a close examination of these states might lead to important hypotheses about what other things are important.[3]

---

[3]See Howell (2007) for a discussion of how to evaluate the magnitude of the residuals.

**Table 11.5**
Predicted Values and Residuals for Selected States

| State | Expend | PctSAT | Combined | Predict | Residual |
|-------|--------|--------|----------|---------|----------|
| Alabama | 4.405 | 8 | 1029 | 1025.146 | 3.854 |
| Alaska | 8.963 | 47 | 934 | 969.962 | −35.962 |
| Arizona | 4.778 | 27 | 944 | 975.562 | −31.562 |
| Arkansas | 4.459 | 6 | 1005 | 1031.512 | −26.512 |
| California | 4.992 | 45 | 902 | 926.874 | −24.874 |
| Colorado | 5.443 | 29 | 980 | 978.030 | 1.970 |
| Iowa | 5.483 | 5 | 1099 | 1046.944 | 52.056 |
| . . . | . . . | . . . | . . . | . . . | . . . |
| Mississippi | 4.080 | 4 | 1036 | 032.557 | 3.443 |
| Missouri | 5.383 | 9 | 1045 | 034.311 | 10.688 |
| Montana | 5.692 | 21 | 1009 | 003.897 | 5.103 |
| . . . | . . . | . . . | . . . | . . . | . . . |
| New Hampshire | 5.859 | 70 | 935 | 866.253 | 68.747 |
| New Jersey | 9.774 | 70 | 898 | 914.355 | −16.355 |
| New Mexico | 4.586 | 11 | 1015 | 1018.817 | −3.817 |
| New York | 9.623 | 74 | 892 | 901.096 | −9.096 |
| North Carolina | 5.077 | 60 | 865 | 885.156 | −20.155 |
| North Dakota | 4.775 | 5 | 1107 | 1038.245 | 68.755 |
| Ohio | 6.162 | 23 | 975 | 1003.970 | −28.970 |
| . . . | . . . | . . . | . . . | . . . | . . . |
| Washington | 5.906 | 48 | 937 | 929.551 | 7.4489 |
| West Virginia | 6.107 | 17 | 932 | 1020.400 | −88.400 |
| Wisconsin | 6.930 | 9 | 1073 | 1053.319 | 19.681 |
| Wyoming | 6.160 | 10 | 1001 | 1041.007 | −40.007 |

## 11.4  The Visual Representation of Multiple Regression

Another way to think about multiple regression, which will perhaps give us a different view of residuals, is to plot the data with a predictor variable on each axis. When we had only two variables, plotting was relatively easy. We could plot $Y$ on the vertical axis and $X$ on the horizontal axis and make a scatterplot of the points in two dimensions. With three variables (one criterion and two predictors) we can plot in three dimensions. This is harder on paper than it is with a three-dimensional model, but it can be done. Such a plot is seen in Figure 11.4, where I have plotted Combined on the vertical axis and Expend and PctSAT on the other two axes. Each point can be thought of as a ball on the top of a flagpole, with the height of the flagpole corresponding to the state's mean Combined score, and the base of the flagpole positioned in two-dimensional space corresponding to Expend and PctSAT scores. (You can leave out the flagpoles themselves if that makes the graph easier to see.)

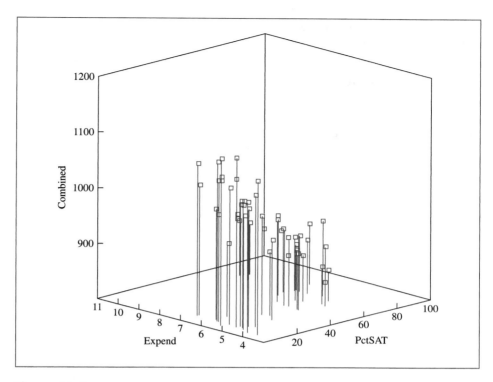

**Figure 11.4**
Three-dimensional plot of SAT performance

Now imagine that you had a sheet of glass that you could position so that it would go through most of the points. This sheet would form a plane, which is called the **regression surface**. It is analogous to the regression line that we had with one predictor. This plane would slope up from front to back, and this front-to-back slope would be the slope for Expend in an equation using these two predictors. The plane would also slope up from right to left, and this right-to-left slope would correspond to the coefficient for PctSAT in our equation. The fact that some of the points would be above this sheet of glass and some below is a statement about the residuals. In other words, the residuals are the deviations of the points from the regression surface.

Definition  **Regression surface:** The equivalent of the regression line in multidimensional space.

Another way to look at residuals is to make a simple two-dimensional plot with the predicted values on the horizontal axis and the obtained values on the vertical axis. Such a plot was shown in Figure 11.3. The advantage of this plot is that you can easily see the large residuals just by looking at the vertical deviation of each point from the regression line. You can also see that there is substantial spread among the points. I mention the spread among the points to make it clear that simply because we have a regression equation and even a substantial $R^2$ does not mean that all our predictions will be close to the mark. I have already pointed to some relatively large residuals, and I now have shown them graphically in two different ways. Two states with the same values on the two predictors, and hence the same prediction, may still differ substantially in their actual Combined score.

## 11.5 Hypothesis Testing

You saw in Chapter 10 that we can ask if the regression coefficient is significantly different from zero. In other words, we can ask if differences in one variable are related to differences in another. If the slope is not significantly different from zero, we have no reason to believe that the criterion is related to the predictor. That works very cleanly when we have only one predictor variable; in fact, I told you that a test on the correlation coefficient and a test on the regression coefficient are equivalent in the one-predictor case. But the situation is distinctly different when we have more than one predictor.

To address the problem of the significance of individual predictors, we have to stop and look a little more closely at the meaning of the regression coefficients. When we say that the regression coefficient for Expend in Table 11.4 is 12.287, we are saying that there will be a 12.287-unit change in $\hat{Y}$ for every one-unit change in Expend *if we hold PctSAT constant*. The italicized portion of the preceding sentence is very important. It says that if we have two states that have exactly the same rated PctSAT score, then a one-unit difference in Expend is associated with a 12.287-unit difference in Combined. Similarly, if we have two states with the same ratings for Expend, then a state that is one unit higher in PctSAT will have a predicted Combined rating that is 2.851 units lower.

Now we can ask if each of those coefficients is significantly different from zero. For states that are equal on PctSAT, does a difference in Expend lead to significant differences on Combined? And are states that are equivalent on Expend but different on PctSAT predicted to be significantly different on Combined? Put more directly, we want to test the null hypotheses

$$H_0: \beta_1 = 0$$
$$H_0: \beta_2 = 0$$

against the alternative hypotheses

$$H_1: \beta_1 \neq 0$$
$$H_1: \beta_2 \neq 0$$

Tests on these hypotheses were given in the column labeled $t$ in Table 11.4, along with the associated two-tailed probabilities in the next column. These tests are of the same kind we saw in the previous chapter, except that we are testing two individual slopes instead of one. Here you can see that the test for the slope for Expend is significantly different from zero because the probability value ($p = .006$) is less than .05. Similarly the slope of PctSAT is also significant ($t = -13.253, p < .000$).

One more major piece of information is given in Table 11.4 in the section "Analysis of Variance." This section is a test on the null hypothesis that there is no correlation between the set of predictors (Expend and PctSAT) taken together and the criterion. A significant effect here would mean that we reject that null hypothesis that the multiple correlation in the population is zero. In the table we see $F = 106.674$ with an associated probability of .000. Since this probability is less than $\alpha = .05$, we will reject $H_0$ and conclude that Combined is predicted at better than chance levels by these two predictors taken together. In other words, we will conclude that the true correlation in the population is not zero.

These two kinds of significance tests (tests on slopes and the test on the multiple correlation) are presented in virtually all regression analyses. I have covered them in the order they were presented in the printout, but in general if the analysis of variance test on the relationship is not significant, it usually doesn't make much sense even to worry about the significance of individual predictors. Fortunately, for most of the regression problems we see, the overall relationship is significant and the real issue is the role of individual predictors.

## 11.6 Refining the Regression Equation

In Table 11.4 we saw that Expend and PctSAT were significant predictors of Combined. We also know from correlations in Table 11.3 that teachers' Salary is significantly related to Combined. Perhaps we should add Salary to our multiple regression. But before we do that, we need to think about the relationships we have among our variables. We know that Expend, PctSAT, and Salary are *each* significantly correlated with Combined. But they are also correlated among themselves, and those correlations are not trivial. (See Table 11.4.)

Because Salary is correlated with both of the other predictors, it may not have any independent contribution to make to the prediction of Combined. This is an empirical question, however, and is best answered by actually doing the regression. The results are shown in Table 11.6, where I have only included the table of coefficients. (The overall analysis of variance on three predictors was significant.)

From Table 11.6 we see that PctSAT remains a significant predictor, but the test on the coefficient for Expend rises slightly above .05 and we can't reject the null hypothesis for that variable. We also see the Salary does not even come close to significance ($p = .853$). You might legitimately wonder why Salary does so poorly here when it was nicely correlated with Combined when treated alone. Related to this is the question of why Expend is no longer significant in the multiple regression. If you think about our variables you will realize that a great deal of the differences between states in terms of expenditures is directly related to teachers' salaries. So telling me that teachers in one state make more money than teachers in another state is nearly tantamount to telling me that the first state has

**Table 11.6**
Multiple Regression Predicting Combined from Expend, PctSAT, and Salary

| | Coefficients[a] | | | | | |
|---|---|---|---|---|---|---|
| | | Unstandardized Coefficients | | Standardized Coefficients | | |
| Model | | B | Std. Error | Beta | t | Sig. |
| 1 | (Constant) | 998.029 | 31.493 | | 31.690 | .000 |
| | EXPEND | 13.333 | 7.042 | .243 | 1.893 | .065 |
| | PctSAT | −2.840 | .225 | −1.016 | −12.635 | .000 |
| | SALARY | −.309 | 1.653 | −.025 | −.187 | .853 |

a. Dependent Variable: COMBINED

a higher score on Expend. You haven't really added much new information. Therefore I am not particularly surprised that Salary did not add anything—in fact it watered down the effect of Expend.

In this example, we have searched for a regression equation (a model of the data) that best predicts the criterion variable. But keep in mind that we had a slightly different purpose in mind—we wanted to know whether expenditures on education made a difference. In other words, we weren't just interested in any old equation that could predict Combined, but wanted to specifically address the role of Expend. We did this by starting with Expend and noticing that it was actually negatively related to outcome. We then added PctSAT because we knew that much of the variance in the outcome measure was related to how many people took the exam, which is a question that would be distinct from asking about Expend except that it is a variable that looks like it needs to be controlled. Finally we thought about adding in Salary, and found that when we did so it had nothing to contribute—in fact it seemed to do harm. I explained away this finding by noting that Salary and Expend are intimately related, and that Salary has very little *extra* to offer.

Definition   **Stepwise procedures:**   A set of rules for deriving a regression equation by adding or subtracting one variable at a time from the regression equation.

There is substantial literature on the topic of choosing an optimum regression equation. Many of the techniques are known as **stepwise procedures**. An introduction to this literature and additional references can be found in Howell (2007). The only point to be made here is that automatic computational procedures for identifying regression models can be seductive. They often produce a nice-looking model, but they also capitalize on chance differences in the data. This produces a model that fits the current data well but that might not fit a new set of data nearly as well. In trying to construct an optimal model, it is important to realize that what you know about the variables and the theoretical constructs in the field is far more important than the statistical vagaries of a set of data. A model with a strong correlation that tells you something important about the contribution of the variables involved is usually to be preferred over a model with a higher correlation that tells you little or nothing about the relationships in which you are interested. You should treat stepwise regression with considerable caution; in fact, it is sometimes referred to in the statistical literature as "unwise regression."

## 11.7 A Second Example: Height and Weight

In Section 9.6 we briefly considered a data set on the height and weight of college students. Height and weight are variables that often are used as the classic example of correlation and regression, and we usually don't take such data seriously. However, psychologists have devoted a considerable amount of effort in recent years to examining weight and body image, especially among teenage girls, and anything involving weight is potentially important. These data actually can teach us a good deal about concepts in regression; when we add sex as a variable, it makes an even better example. The data we are using were taken from data supplied with the Minitab program in a file named "Pulse." As I said in Chapter 9, these data were generated by students as a classroom exercise. Given people's attitudes toward weight in particular, and their tendency to give wishful, rather than truthful, answers, you should treat the data with caution. I have extracted the variables Height, Weight, and Sex from the data set and presented them in Table 11.7. Here males are coded 1 and females are coded 2. (These data can also be found in Exercises 10.19 and 10.20 and at

 http://www.uvm.edu/~dhowell/fundamentals/DataFiles/Tab11-7.dat

The results of the prediction of Weight on the basis of Height and Sex using SPSS are given in Table 11.8. You can see that all three variables are highly intercorrelated and that these correlations are all significant. From the ANOVA portion of the table you can see that there is a significant relationship between Weight and the two predictors ($F = 86.678, p = .000$). The multiple correlation is $\sqrt{.661} = .813$, which is a substantial correlation, accounting for 66% of the variability in weight. Finally, we can see that our regression equation is

$$\text{Predicted Weight} = 3.691 \times \text{Height} - 14.700 \times \text{Sex} - 88.199$$

The intercept in our regression equation (88.199) is meaningless, regardless of the fact that it is significant. We can not imagine an individual who is zero inches tall and neither male nor female (i.e., coded 0 for Sex), and thus it is not useful to ask what its predicted weight would be. On the other hand, the intercept is a necessary part of the regression equation, so we don't completely ignore it.

**Table 11.7**
Data on Sex, Height, and Weight for College Students

| Sex | Height | Weight | Sex | Height | Weight | Sex | Height | Weight |
|-----|--------|--------|-----|--------|--------|-----|--------|--------|
| 1 | 70 | 150 | 1 | 66 | 135 | 2 | 70 | 125 |
| 1 | 67 | 140 | 1 | 71 | 170 | 2 | 68 | 116 |
| 1 | 72 | 180 | 1 | 70 | 157 | 2 | 69 | 145 |
| 1 | 75 | 190 | 1 | 70 | 130 | 2 | 69 | 150 |
| 1 | 68 | 145 | 1 | 75 | 185 | 2 | 67 | 150 |
| 1 | 69 | 150 | 1 | 74 | 190 | 2 | 68 | 125 |
| 1 | 71.5 | 164 | 1 | 71 | 155 | 2 | 66 | 130 |
| 1 | 71 | 140 | 1 | 69 | 170 | 2 | 65.5 | 120 |
| 1 | 72 | 142 | 1 | 70 | 155 | 2 | 66 | 130 |
| 1 | 69 | 136 | 1 | 72 | 215 | 2 | 62 | 121 |
| 1 | 67 | 123 | 1 | 67 | 150 | 2 | 62 | 130 |
| 1 | 68 | 155 | 1 | 69 | 145 | 2 | 63 | 118 |
| 1 | 66 | 140 | 1 | 73 | 155 | 2 | 67 | 125 |
| 1 | 72 | 145 | 1 | 73 | 155 | 2 | 65 | 135 |
| 1 | 73.5 | 160 | 1 | 71 | 150 | 2 | 66 | 125 |
| 1 | 73 | 190 | 1 | 68 | 155 | 2 | 65 | 118 |
| 1 | 69 | 155 | 1 | 69.5 | 150 | 2 | 65 | 122 |
| 1 | 73 | 165 | 1 | 73 | 180 | 2 | 65 | 115 |
| 1 | 72 | 150 | 1 | 75 | 160 | 2 | 64 | 102 |
| 1 | 74 | 190 | 1 | 66 | 135 | 2 | 67 | 115 |
| 1 | 72 | 195 | 1 | 69 | 160 | 2 | 69 | 150 |
| 1 | 71 | 138 | 1 | 66 | 130 | 2 | 68 | 110 |
| 1 | 74 | 160 | 1 | 73 | 155 | 2 | 63 | 116 |
| 1 | 72 | 155 | 1 | 68 | 150 | 2 | 62 | 108 |
| 1 | 70 | 153 | 1 | 74 | 148 | 2 | 63 | 95 |
| 1 | 67 | 145 | 1 | 73.5 | 155 | 2 | 64 | 125 |
| 1 | 71 | 170 | 2 | 61 | 140 | 2 | 68 | 133 |
| 1 | 72 | 175 | 2 | 66 | 120 | 2 | 62 | 110 |
| 1 | 69 | 175 | 2 | 68 | 130 | 2 | 61.75 | 108 |
| 1 | 73 | 170 | 2 | 68 | 138 | 2 | 62.75 | 112 |
| 1 | 74 | 180 | 2 | 63 | 121 | 2 | | |

The regression coefficients for Height and Sex are given in the table and are readily interpretable and informative. For people who are all the same sex (e.g., for all females, or for all males), a difference of 1 inch in height is associated with a 3.691 difference in weight. Put slightly differently, our best guess is that the regression line relating weight to height for women would have a slope of 3.691. Similarly, we would expect that the line relating men's weight to their heights would also have a slope of 3.691.[4] This is what we mean by "holding sex constant." (Another phrase used in this context is "controlling for sex.") If we had completely ignored Sex and simply regressed Weight on Height, the slope would have been 5.092, which is quite different.

---

[4] It is worth noting that if we found the regression coefficients separately for males and females and then took a weighted average of those coefficients, it would be very close to the 3.691 we found here.

## Table 11.8
Prediction of Weight on the Basis of Height and Sex

### Regression

#### Descriptive Statistics

|  | Mean | Std. Deviation | N |
|---|---|---|---|
| WEIGHT | 145.1522 | 23.73940 | 92 |
| SEX | 1.38 | .488 | 92 |
| HEIGHT | 68.7174 | 3.65929 | 92 |

#### Correlations

|  |  | WEIGHT | HEIGHT | SEX |
|---|---|---|---|---|
| Pearson Correlation | WEIGHT | 1.000 | −.785 | −.709 |
|  | SEX | −.709 | −.714 | 1.000 |
|  | HEIGHT | .785 | 1.000 | −.714 |
| Sig. (1-tailed) | WEIGHT | . | .000 | .000 |
|  | SEX | .000 | .000 | . |
|  | HEIGHT | .000 | . | .000 |
| N | WEIGHT | 92 | 92 | 92 |
|  | SEX | 92 | 92 | 92 |
|  | HEIGHT | 92 | 92 | 92 |

#### Model Summary

| Model | R | R Square | Adjusted R Square | Std. Error of the Estimate |
|---|---|---|---|---|
| 1 | .813[a] | .661 | .653 | 13.98121 |

a. Predictors: (Constant), HEIGHT, SEX

#### ANOVA[b]

| Model |  | Sum of Squares | df | Mean Square | F | Sig. |
|---|---|---|---|---|---|---|
| 1 | Regression | 33886.657 | 2 | 16943.328 | 86.678 | .000[a] |
|  | Residual | 17397.213 | 89 | 195.474 |  |  |
|  | Total | 51283.870 | 91 |  |  |  |

a. Predictors: (Constant), HEIGHT, SEX
b. Dependent Variable: WEIGHT

#### Coefficients[a]

| Model |  | Unstandardized Coefficients B | Std. Error | Standardized Coefficients Beta | t | Sig. |
|---|---|---|---|---|---|---|
| 1 | (Constant) | −88.199 | 43.777 |  | −2.015 | .047 |
|  | SEX | −14.700 | 4.290 | −.302 | −3.426 | .001 |
|  | HEIGHT | 3.691 | .572 | .569 | 6.450 | .000 |

a. Dependent Variable: WEIGHT

The coefficient for Sex is $-14.700$. This means that if we hold height constant (i.e., select a large number of subjects who are all the same height), a difference of 1 unit in sex is associated with a difference of 14.7 pounds. But since males are coded 1 and females 2, this really means that if we go from males to females (with height held constant) our predicted weights will differ by 14.7 pounds. And to say it in yet a simpler way, *when we control for height*, women are 14.7 pounds lighter than men.

Let's explore this last idea just a bit further. Simple descriptive statistics will show us that the mean weight for males in our sample is 158.26 pounds, while the mean weight for females is 123.80 pounds. Thus women are, on average, 34.46 pounds lighter than men. But of course men are, on average, taller than women by about 5 inches, and some of the difference in weight is due to that height difference. Perhaps all of it, you ask? No! We have just seen that when we control for height there is still a difference of 14.7 pounds. That is a difference in weight between men and women that cannot be explained on the basis of differences in height.

In the exercises in Chapter 10 I asked you to use a regression equation to estimate your own weight using the appropriate regression equation (the one derived from subjects of your own sex). In those cases we were artificially holding sex constant by deriving separate regression equations for males and females. But now we can accomplish the same thing by using one equation, but one that includes sex as a predictor. I'll hold off asking you to do this for your own height and weight until we get to the exercises, but let's take an example of a male who happens to be 68 inches tall. We can make a prediction by inserting the appropriate values for Sex (1) and Height (68) into the equation derived earlier:

$$\text{Predicted weight} = 3.691 \times \text{Height} - 14.7 \times \text{Sex} - 88.199$$
$$= 3.691 \times 68 - 14.7 \times 1 - 88.199$$
$$= 148.089$$

For this person we would expect a weight of about 148.1 pounds. Suppose this person stepped on the scales today and weighed 145.5. Then our residual would be

$$\text{Residual} = \text{Actual weight} - \text{Predicted weight} = 145.5 - 148.1 = -2.6$$

Our prediction was too high by 2.6 pounds, which is a pretty good prediction.

## 11.8 A Third Example: Psychological Symptoms in Cancer Patients

There can be no doubt that a diagnosis of cancer is a disturbing event, and many, though not all, cancer patients show elevated levels of psychological symptoms in response to such a diagnosis. If we could understand the variables associated with psychological distress, perhaps we could implement intervention programs to prevent, or at least limit, that distress. That is the subject of this example.

Malcarne, Compas, Epping, and Howell (1995) examined 126 cancer patients soon after they were diagnosed with cancer and at a four-month follow-up. At the initial interviews (Time1) they collected data on the patients' current levels of distress (Distress1), the degree to which they attributed the blame for the cancer to the type of person they are (BlamPer), and the degree to which they attributed the cancer to the kind of behaviors in which they had engaged, such as smoking or high-fat diets (BlamBeh). At the four-month follow-up (Time2) the authors again collected data on the levels of psychological distress that the patients reported. (They also collected data on a number of other variables, which do not concern us here.)

A major purpose of this study was to test the hypothesis that psychological distress at follow-up (Distress2) was related to the degree to which the subjects blamed cancer on the type of person they are. It was hypothesized that those who blame themselves (rather than their actions) will show greater distress, in part because we do not easily change the kind of person we are, and therefore we have little control over the course, or the recurrence, of the disease.

If we want to predict distress at follow-up, one of the most important predictors is likely to be the level of distress at the initial interview. It makes sense to include this Time1 distress measure (Distress1) in the prediction along with the initial level of personal blame (BlamPer), because we want to know if personal blame contributes to distress after we control for the initial level of distress. (Notice an important point here. I am not including Distress1 because I want to maximize the accuracy of my prediction, though it will probably do that. Nor am I including it because I care greatly about the relationship between Distress1 and Distress2, though I would be very surprised if it doesn't turn out to be a strong one. I am including Distress1 because I want to ask if BlamPer can contribute to explaining Distress2 even after we hold constant (or control for) Distress1. In other words I am using multiple regression to develop or test a theory, not to make specific predictions about an individual outcome.) The dependent variable is distress at follow-up (Distress2). Because only 74 participants completed measures at follow-up, the resulting analysis is based on a sample size of 74. (You might ask yourself what might be wrong with drawing conclusions on only the 74 participants, out of an initial 126, who participated after four months of treatment.) The results of this analysis are shown in Table 11.9 and have been computed using Minitab.

The first two lines present the regression equation, with the intercept and the two slope coefficients. Immediately below that are the coefficients written out in a different form. Here the word "Constant" is used in place of the word "Intercept," and the three slopes are identified by the variable names to which they apply. Notice that we have a $t$ test on all three

## Table 11.9
Distress at Follow-up as a Function of Distress and Self-Blame at Diagnosis

```
Regression Analysis: Distres2 versus Distres1, BlamPer

The regression equation is
Distres2 = 14.2 + .642 Distres1 + 2.60 BlamPer

Predictor        Coef      SE Coef         T         P
Constant       14.209       5.716       2.49      .015
Distres1        .6424       .1024       6.27      .000
BlamPer        2.5980       .8959       2.90      .005

S = 7.610    R-Sq = 43.4%    R-Sq(adj) = 41.8%

Analysis of Variance

Source             DF         SS        MS         F         P
Regression          2     3157.0    1578.5     27.25      .000
Residual Error     71     4112.0      57.9
Total              73     7269.0

Source      DF     Seq SS
Distres1     1     2669.9
BlamPer      1      487.1

Unusual Observations
Obs   Distres1  Distres2       Fit    SE Fit    Residual   St Resid
 31       54.0    33.000    51.496     1.032     -18.496     -2.45R
 51       57.0    64.000    63.816     3.158        .184       .03 X
 52       57.0    71.000    53.424     1.055      17.576      2.33R
 59       63.0    39.000    57.278     1.333     -18.278     -2.44R
 73       80.0    69.000    68.199     2.784        .801       .11 X
 74       80.0    80.000    73.395     2.775       6.605       .93 X

R denotes an observation with a large standardized residual
X denotes an obs. whose X value gives it large influence.
```

coefficients (labeled T in the table) and that all three *t* values are significantly different from .00. This tells us that higher distress at Time2 is associated with higher distress at Time1 and with a greater tendency for patients to blame the type of person they are for the cancer. The intercept is also significantly different from .00, but this is not of interest here.

In the next portion of the table we see that the squared multiple correlation is .434 (accounting for 43.4% of the variation in Distress2) and that the squared correlation adjusted for the number of participants and the number of variables is .418.

The analysis of variance table presents a test on the null hypothesis that the true multiple correlation coefficient in the population is 0. Because we have a large value of *F* and a very small value of *p*, we can reject that hypothesis in favor of the hypothesis that there is a true correlation between Distress2 and the combination of Distress1 and BlamPer.

In the section of the table titled "Unusual Observations" are six cases that Minitab has singled out as worthy of note. These are either cases wherein the regression equation does a particularly bad job of predicting Distress2, or cases that deviate sufficiently from the rest of the participants for us to worry that they could have an undue influence on the outcome of the regression. We might want to inspect these cases closely to see if there is

## Table 11.10

### Prediction of Distress2 as a Function of Distress1, BlamPer, and BlamBeh

```
Regression Analysis: Distres2 versus Distres1, BlamPer, BlamBeh

The regression equation is
Distress2 = 14.1 + .640 Distress1 + 2.45 BlamPer + .272 BlamBeh

Predictor         Coef        Stdev      t-ratio         p
Constant        14.052        5.782        2.43       .018
Distress1         .6399        .1035        6.18       .000
BlamPer          2.451        1.048        2.34       .022
BlamBeh           .2720        .9900         .27       .784

s = 7.660     R-sq = 43.5%    R-sq(adj) = 41.1%

Analysis of Variance

SOURCE              DF          SS          MS          F          p
Regression           3      3161.4      1053.8      17.96       .000
Error               70      4107.6        58.7
Total               73      7269.0

SOURCE       DF      SEQ SS
Distress1     1      2669.9
BlamPer       1       487.1
BlamBeh       1         4.4

Unusual Observations
Obs. Distress1  Distress2      Fit    Stdev.Fit    Residual    St.Resid
31        54.0     33.000    51.599      1.104     -18.599      -2.45R
51        57.0     64.000    63.051      4.226        .949        .15 X
52        57.0     71.000    53.518      1.117      17.482       2.31R
59        63.0     39.000    57.357      1.372     -18.357      -2.44R

R denotes an obs. with a large st. resid.
X denotes an obs. whose X value gives it large influence.
```

anything unusual about them that can, perhaps, be attributed to some other variable or to erroneous data points.

You might be tempted to ask if perhaps additional predictors might improve our regression solution. For example, we also have data on the degree to which patients blame their cancer on their own behaviors (BlamBeh), and we might want to add that predictor to the ones we have already used. Although I strongly caution against throwing in additional variables just because you have them—your set of predictors should make some sort of logical sense on *a priori* grounds—I have added BlamBeh to the regression to illustrate what happens. Those results are presented in Table 11.10.

I will not discuss this table in detail because it is essentially the same as the previous table. I will point out the magnitude of $R^2$ and the probability value associated with the test on BlamPer. Notice that $R^2$ is virtually unchanged by the addition of BlamBeh, going from .434 to .435. This is our first indication that BlamBeh is not contributing noticeably to the prediction of Distress2 *over and above the predictors that were already in the equation.* This does not mean that BlamBeh is not related to Distress2, but only that it has nothing to add beyond what we can tell from the other two predictors.

Notice also that the probability value associated with the BlamPer predictor (and the associated regression coefficient) has changed somewhat. This says nothing more than that the contribution of BlamPer is somewhat, though not much, reduced when a similar variable (BlamBeh) is added to the model. This is quite common and reflects the fact that BlamPer and BlamBeh are correlated ($r = .521$) and, to some extent, account for overlapping portions of the variability in Distress2.

## Writing Up the Breast Cancer Study

The following is a brief description of the study and a summary of the results. Notice the way in which the various statistics are reported.

Malcarne, Compas, Epping, and Howell (1995) collected data on 126 breast cancer patients shortly after they were diagnosed with cancer and at a four-month follow-up. The data included, among other variables, the level of distress at each interview and an estimate of the degree to which the patients blamed their cancer on "the type of person they are." At the time of the analysis, complete data were available on only 74 participants, and these 74 participants formed the basis for subsequent analyses.

At the four-month follow-up, the level of distress was regressed on both the level of distress shortly after diagnosis, and the personal blame variable. The overall regression was significant ($F(2,71) = 27.25$, and $R^2 = .434$). Both the level of distress at Time1 ($b = .642$) and the degree of personal blame were significant predictors of distress at Time2 ($b = 2.598$). ($t = 6.27; p = .000$ and $t = 2.90; p = .005$, respectively).

When the degree to which subjects blamed their own behavior (rather than the type of person they are) was added to the equation, it did not contribute significantly to the prediction ($t = .27; p = .784$). The authors concluded that the degree to which participants blame themselves, rather than their behavior, for their cancer is an important predictor of future distress, and suggest that interventions focused on changing this self-perception might contribute toward lowering distress in breast cancer patients.

## 11.9 Summary

In this chapter we examined the prediction of one criterion variable on the basis of two or more predictor variables. We considered the interpretation of the regression equation and saw that the multiple correlation coefficient is interpreted in the same way we interpreted the simple correlation coefficient in Chapter 9. We looked at how we might plot such data and how the residuals can be interpreted with respect to such plots and investigated two forms of hypothesis testing. The important thing about almost everything in this chapter is that it is just a logical extension of the material in the preceding two chapters.

Some important terms in this chapter are

| | |
|---|---|
| Multiple correlation coefficient (R), 247 | Multicollinearity, 249 |
| | Regression surface, 263 |
| Squared correlation coefficient ($R^2$), 247 | Stepwise procedures, 266 |

## 11.10 Exercises

**11.1**  A psychologist studying perceived "quality of life" in a large number of cities ($N = 150$) came up with the following equation using mean temperature (Temp), median income in $1,000 (Income), per capita expenditure on social services (SocSer), and population density (Popul) as predictors.

$$\hat{Y} = 5.37 - .01\text{Temp} + .05\text{Income} + .003\text{SocSer} - .01\text{Popul}$$

(a) Interpret the regression equation in terms of the coefficients.
(b) Assume a city has a mean temperature of 55 degrees, a median income of $12,000, spends $500 per capita on social services, and has a population density of 200 people per block. What is its predicted Quality of Life score?
(c) What would we predict for a different city that is identical in every way except that it spends $100 per capita on social services?

**11.2**  Sethi and Seligman (1993) examined the relationship between optimism and religious conservatism by interviewing over 600 subjects from a variety of religious organizations. We can regress Optimism on three variables dealing with religiosity. These are the influence of religion on their daily lives (RelInf), their involvement with religion (RelInvol), and their degree of religious hope (belief in an after-life) (RelHope). The results are shown as SPSS printout.

Model Summary

| Model | R | R Square | Adjusted R Square | Std. Error of the Estimate |
|---|---|---|---|---|
| 1 | .321[a] | .103 | .099 | 3.0432 |

a. Predictors: (Constant), RELHOPE, RELINF, RELINVOL

$\text{ANOVA}^b$

| Model | | Sum of Squares | df | Mean Square | F | Sig. |
|---|---|---|---|---|---|---|
| 1 | Regression | 634.240 | 3 | 211.413 | 22.828 | .000[a] |
| | Residual | 5519.754 | 596 | 9.261 | | |
| | Total | 6153.993 | 599 | | | |

a. Predictors: (Constant), RELHOPE, RELINF, RELINVOL
b. Dependent Variable: OPTIMISM

Coefficients[a]

| Model | Unstandardized Coefficents | | Standardized Coefficients | | | Collinearity Statistics | |
|---|---|---|---|---|---|---|---|
| | B | Std. Error | Beta | t | Sig. | Tolerance | VIF |
| 1 (Constant) | −1.895 | .512 | | −3.702 | .000 | | |
| RELINF | .490 | .107 | .204 | 4.571 | .000 | .755 | 1.324 |
| RELINVOL | −7.938E-02 | .116 | −.033 | −.682 | .495 | .645 | 1.550 |
| RELHOPE | .428 | .102 | .199 | 4.183 | .000 | .666 | 1.502 |

a. Dependent Variable: OPTIMISM

Looking at the preceding printout,
(a) Are we looking at a reliable relationship? How can you tell?
(b) What is the degree of relationship between Optimism and the three predictors?
(c) What would most likely change in your answers to (a) and (b) if we had a much smaller number of subjects?

**11.3** In Exercise 11.2 which variables make a significant contribution to the prediction of Optimism as judged by the test on their slopes?

**11.4** In Exercise 11.2 the column headed "Tolerance" (which I have not discussed before) gives you 1 minus the squared multiple correlation of that predictor with all other *predictors*. What can you now say about the relationships among the set of predictors?

**11.5** On the basis of your answer to Exercise 11.4 speculate on one of the reasons why Religious Influence might be an important predictor of Optimism, while Religious Involvement is not.

**11.6** Substitute your own height and sex in the regression equation we computed in Section 11.7 and predict your weight. (Feel free to lie if using your actual data makes you feel uncomfortable.) How do your actual and predicted weights compare?

**11.7** Your predictions of your weight using the multiple regression equation that involves both sex and height is different from the prediction you made in Chapter 10, when you used an equation built solely on people of your own sex. Can you speculate not only why there was a difference but under what very limited set of conditions the two predictions would be equal? (*Hint:* Compare the slopes for height in the two cases.)

**11.8** The state of Vermont is divided into 10 Health Planning Districts, which correspond roughly to counties. The following data represent the percentage of live births of babies weighing under 2,500 grams ($Y$), the fertility rate for females 17 years of age or younger ($X_1$), total high-risk fertility rate for females younger than 17 or older than 35 years of age ($X_2$), percentage of mothers with fewer than 12 years of education ($X_3$), percentage of births to unmarried mothers ($X_4$), and percentage of mothers not seeking medical care until the third trimester ($X_5$). (There are too few observations for a meaningful analysis, so do not put faith in the results.)

| Y | $X_1$ | $X_2$ | $X_3$ | $X_4$ | $X_5$ |
|---|---|---|---|---|---|
| 6.1 | 22.8 | 43.0 | 23.8 | 9.2 | 6 |
| 7.1 | 28.7 | 55.3 | 24.8 | 12.0 | 10 |
| 7.4 | 29.7 | 48.5 | 23.9 | 10.4 | 5 |
| 6.3 | 18.3 | 38.8 | 16.6 | 9.8 | 4 |
| 6.5 | 21.1 | 46.2 | 19.6 | 9.8 | 5 |

(Continued)

| Y | $X_1$ | $X_2$ | $X_3$ | $X_4$ | $X_5$ |
|---|---|---|---|---|---|
| 5.7 | 21.2 | 39.9 | 21.4 | 7.7 | 6 |
| 6.6 | 22.2 | 43.1 | 20.7 | 10.9 | 7 |
| 8.1 | 22.3 | 48.5 | 21.8 | 9.5 | 5 |
| 6.3 | 21.8 | 40.0 | 20.6 | 11.6 | 7 |
| 6.9 | 31.2 | 56.7 | 25.2 | 11.6 | 9 |

Use any regression program to compute the multiple regression that predicts the percentage of births under 2,500 grams.

**11.9** Using the output from Exercise 11.8, interpret the results as if they were significant. (What is one of the reasons that this current analysis is not likely to be significant, even if those relationships are reliable in the populations?)

**11.10** Mireault (1990) studied students who had lost a parent to death during their childhood, students who came from divorced families, and students who came from intact families. Among other things she collected data on their current perceived sense of vulnerability to future loss (PVLoss), their level of social support (SuppTotl), and the age at which they lost a parent during childhood (AgeAtLos). The data can be found at

http://www.uvm.edu/~dhowell/fundamentals/DataFiles/Mireault.dat

Use the Mireault.dat dataset and any available regression program to evaluate a model that says that depression (DepressT) is a function of these three variables. (Because only subjects in Group 1 lost a parent, you will need to restrict your analysis to those cases.)

**11.11** Interpret the results of the analysis in Exercise 11.10.

**11.12** The data set Harass.dat, included on this book's Web site, contains data on 343 cases created to replicate the results of a study of sexual harassment by Brooks and Perot (1991). The variables are, in order, Age, Marital Status (1 = married, 2 = not married), Feminist Ideology, Frequency of the Behavior, Offensiveness of the Behavior, and the dependent variable, whether or not the subjects reported incidents of sexual harassment (0 = no, 1 = yes). For each variable, higher numbers represent higher levels of the variable. Technically, this is a problem that might be better approached with what is called logistic regression, because the dependent variable is a dichotomy. However we can get a very close approximation to the optimal solution by using plain old linear multiple regression instead. Use multiple regression to predict whether or not sexual harassment will be reported, based on the variables you have here. Find a model that does not have many nonsignificant predictors.

**11.13** In the previous question I was surprised that the frequency of behavior was not related to the likelihood of its being reported. Suggest why this might be.

**11.14** In the text I have recommended against the use of stepwise procedures for multiple regression, whereby we systematically hunt among the variables to predict some sort of optimal equation.
(a) Explain why I would make such a recommendation.
(b) How, then, could I justify asking you to do just that in Exercise 11.12?

**11.15** Use the table of random numbers (Table D.9 in the appendix) to generate data for 10 cases on 6 variables, and label the first variable Y and the following variables $X_1$, $X_2$, $X_3$, $X_4$, and $X_5$. Now use any regression program to predict Y from all five predictors using the complete data set with 10 cases. Are you surprised at the magnitude of $R$?

**11.16** Now restrict the data set in Exercise 11.15 to 8, then 6, then 5 cases, and record the changing values of $R$. Remember that these are only random data.

**11.17** You can find the height-weight tables of the Metropolitan Life Insurance Company on the Internet at

 http://www.med.umich.edu/1libr/primry/life15.htm

Assume that the data in Chapter 9 (Figure 9.8) came from women with a medium frame. Superimpose the tables' estimates on that figure, and compare those lines with the separate regression lines for men and women.

**11.18** From the tables referred to in Exercise 11.17, you should be able to estimate the regression coefficients for predicting weight from height and sex. How do these estimates compare with the values we found in Section 11.7?

**11.19** What kinds of things should you keep in mind in Exercises 11.17 and 11.18?

**11.20** A great source of data and an explanation to go with it is an Internet site called the Data and Story Library (DASL) maintained by Carnegie Mellon University. Go to that site and examine the example on the relationship between brain size and intelligence. Use multiple regression to predict full scale IQ from brain size (labeled MRI_Count in the file) and Gender. The address is

 http://lib.stat.cmu.edu/DASL/Datafiles/Brainsize.html

(You will have to convert Gender from Male and Female to 1 and 2. Your software probably has a recode or compute command that will do so.)

**11.21** Why would you think that it would be wise to include Sex in that regression?

**11.22** Since you have the DASL data on brain size, note that it also includes the variables of height and weight. Predict weight from height and sex and see how that compares to the results in Section 11.7. (I was pleasantly surprised, especially because there were only 40 participants and the data were not self-reported height and weight.)

**11.23** In examples like the Guber study on the funding of education, we frequently speak of variables like PctSAT as "nuisance variables." In what sense is that usage reasonable here, and in what sense is it somewhat misleading?

**11.24** In several places in the chapter I have shoved aside the intercept by saying that we really don't care about it. If we don't care about it, why do we include it?

**11.25** Using the data from Section 11.8 on the relationship between symptoms and distress in cancer patients, compute the predicted values of Distress2 using Distress1 and BlamPer. Correlate those values with the obtained values of Distress2 and show that this is equal to the multiple correlation coefficient.

**11.26** In Exercise 9.1 we saw data on infant mortality and a number of other variables. There you predicted infant mortality from income. There is reason to believe that infants of young mothers are at increased risk, and there is considerable evidence that infant mortality can be reduced by the use of contraception. Does the multiple regression using all three of those predictor variables bear out these hypotheses?

# 12

# Hypothesis Tests Applied to Means: One Sample

## QUESTIONS

- If we draw many samples from some population and calculate their means, what will the distribution of means look like?

- How could I test a null hypothesis about a mean if I knew the population variance?

- But I rarely know the population variance, so what do I do when I don't know it?

- What governs how likely it is that I will find what I'm looking for?

- I know the value of a sample mean; is that going to be close to the population mean?

In Chapter 8 we considered the general logic of hypothesis testing and ignored the specific calculations involved. In Chapters 9, 10, and 11 we looked at measures that indicate the relationship between variables and considered hypothesis testing as a way of asking whether there is a reliable nonzero correlation between variables in the population (not just in our sample) and whether the regression coefficients (slope and intercept) are reliably different from zero. In this chapter we will begin concentrating on hypothesis tests about means. In particular we will focus on testing a null hypothesis about the value of a population mean.

We will start with an example referred to in Chapter 8. There we considered the case in which we know that Total Behavior Problem scores on the Youth-Self Report form are nearly normally distributed with a mean of 50 and a standard deviation of 10. In Chapter 8 we dealt with that example in a general way. Here we will start over and deal with it more precisely. While fictitious experiments are not as interesting to study as real ones, they sometimes have the advantage of allowing us to look at the logic of what we are doing without adding other considerations. We will move to actual experiments shortly.

Because there is evidence in the psychological literature that stress in a child's life may lead to subsequent behavior problems, it might be expected that a sample of children who have been subjected to an unusual amount of stress would show an unusually high level of behavior problems. On the other hand, such children could feel that they have enough going on in their lives without complicating matters further, in which case they might show an unusually low number of behavior problems. That latter possibility does not seem terribly likely—it doesn't sound like the kids that I know—but it is worth guarding against. This means we are interested in examining a two-tailed **experimental hypothesis** that the number of behavior problems among stressed children is different from the number of behavior problems among children in general. We can't test the experimental hypothesis directly, however. Instead we will test the null hypothesis ($H_0$) that the scores of stressed children came from a population of scores with the *same* mean as the population of scores of normal children, a rejection of which would support the experimental hypothesis. More specifically, we want to decide between

$$H_0: \mu = 50$$

and

$$H_1: \mu \neq 50$$

I have chosen the two-tailed alternative form of $H_1$ because I want to reject $H_0$ if $\mu > 50$ *or* if $\mu < 50$.

---

Definition    **Experimental hypothesis:** Another name for the research hypothesis.

---

To investigate this problem, I drew a sample of five children, each of whom is under a high level of stress of one kind or another. I asked the children to complete the Youth Self-Report form and obtained the following scores:

48   62   53   66   51

This sample of five observations has a mean of 56.0 and a standard deviation of 7.65. Thus the five children have an average score six points above the mean of the population of normal children. But because this result is based on a sample of only five children, it is quite conceivable that the deviation from 50 could be due to chance (or, phrased differently, that the deviation is due to sampling error). Even if $H_0$: $\mu =$ 50 were true, we certainly would not expect our sample mean to be exactly 50.000. We probably wouldn't be particularly surprised to find a mean of 49 or 51. But what about 56? Is that surprisingly large? If so, perhaps we should not be willing to continue to entertain the idea that $\mu = 50.0$. Before we can draw any conclusions, however, we will have to know what values we reasonably could expect sample means to have if we really sampled from a population of normal children.

## 12.1 Sampling Distribution of the Mean

As I hope you will recall from Chapter 8, the sampling distribution of any statistic is the distribution of values we would expect to obtain for that statistic if we drew an infinite number of samples from the population in question and calculated the statistic on each sample. Because we are concerned here with sample *means*, we need to know something about the sampling distribution of the mean. Fortunately all the important information about the sampling distribution of the mean can be summed up in one very important theorem: the **Central Limit Theorem**. The Central Limit Theorem is a factual statement about the distribution of means. It contains several concepts:

> Given a population with mean $\mu$ and variance $\sigma^2$, the sampling distribution of the mean (the distribution of sample means) will have a mean equal to $\mu$ (i.e., $\mu_{\overline{X}} = \mu$) and a variance ($\sigma^2_{\overline{X}}$) equal to $\sigma^2/N$ (and standard deviation, $\sigma_{\overline{X}} = \sigma/\sqrt{N}$). The distribution will approach the normal distribution as $N$, the *sample size*, increases.

Definition   **Central Limit Theorem:** The theorem that specifies the nature of the sampling distribution of the mean.

The Central Limit Theorem is one of the most important theorems in statistics because it not only tells us what the mean and the variance of the sampling distribution of the sample mean must be for any given sample size but also states that as $N$ increases, the shape of this sampling distribution approaches normal, *whatever the shape of the parent population*. The importance of these facts will become clear shortly.

The rate at which the sampling distribution of the mean approaches normal is a function of the shape of the parent population. If the population itself is normal, the sampling distribution of the mean will be exactly normal regardless of $N$. If the population is symmetric but nonnormal, the sampling distribution of the mean will be nearly normal even for quite small sample sizes, especially if the population is unimodal. If the population is markedly skewed, we may require sample sizes of 30 or more before the means closely approximate a normal distribution.

To illustrate the Central Limit Theorem we will leave the behavior problem example temporarily and consider a more general example. Suppose we take an infinitely large population of random numbers evenly distributed between 0 and 100. This population will have what is called a **rectangular, or uniform, distribution**—every value between 0 and 100 being equally likely. The distribution of this population is shown in Figure 12.1, where it is evident why we describe this distribution as "rectangular" or "uniform." In this population the mean ($\mu$) is 50, the standard deviation ($\sigma$) is 28.87, and the variance ($\sigma^2$) is 833.33.

| Definition | **Rectangular (uniform) distribution:**  A distribution in which all outcomes are equally likely. |
| --- | --- |

Now suppose we draw with replacement 5,000 samples of size 5 (i.e., $N = 5$) from the population shown in Figure 12.1 and plot the resulting sample means. (Note that $N$ refers to the size of each sample, not to the number of samples, which is very large [here, 5,000].) Such sampling can be easily accomplished with the aid of a computer—the results of just such a procedure are presented in Figure 12.2(a). From Figure 12.2(a) it is apparent that the distribution of means, although not exactly normally distributed, at least peaks in the center and trails off toward the extremes. If you were to go to the effort of calculating the mean and the standard deviation of this distribution, you would find that they are extremely close to $\mu = 50$ and $\sigma_{\overline{X}} = \sigma/\sqrt{N} = 28.87/\sqrt{5} = 12.91$. (Remember that $\mu$ and $\sigma_{\overline{X}}$ refer to the mean and the standard deviation of the distribution of means.)

Suppose we repeat the entire procedure, only this time we draw 5,000 samples, each with $N = 30$ observations. The results are plotted in Figure 12.2(b). There you can see that, just as the Central Limit Theorem predicted, the distribution is

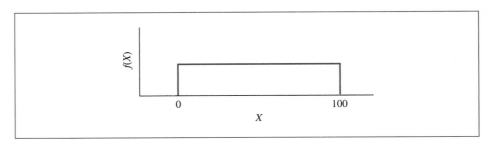

**Figure 12.1**
Rectangular distribution with $\mu = 50$ and $\sigma = 28.87$

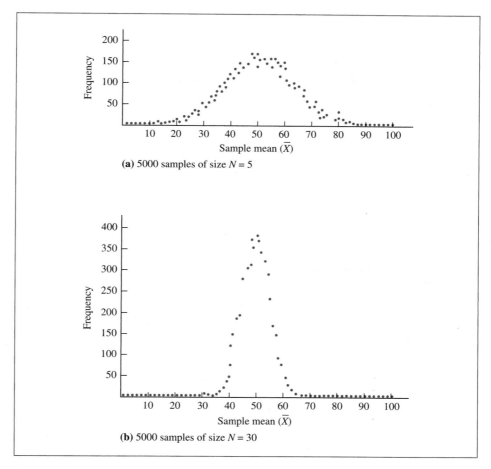

**Figure 12.2**
Computer-generated sampling distribution of the mean

approximately normal, the mean ($\mu$) is again 50, and the standard deviation has been reduced to $28.87/\sqrt{30} = 5.27$. (The first time I ran this example many years ago it took approximately 5 minutes to draw such samples. Today it took me 1.5 *seconds*. Computer simulation is not a big deal.)

## 12.2  Testing Hypotheses About Means When $\sigma$ Is Known

From the Central Limit Theorem we know all the important characteristics of the sampling distribution of the mean (its shape, its mean, and its standard deviation) even without drawing a single one of those samples. On the basis of this information we are in a position to begin testing hypotheses about means. For the sake of continuity it might be well to go back to something we discussed with respect to the normal distribution. In Chapter 8 we saw that we could test a hypothesis about the population from which a single score (in that case a finger-tapping score) was drawn by calculating

$$z = \frac{X - \mu}{\sigma}$$

and then obtaining the probability of a value of $z$ as low as or lower than the one obtained by using the tables of the standard normal distribution. Thus we ran a one-tailed test on the hypothesis that the tapping rate (70) of a single individual was drawn at random from a normally distributed population of healthy tapping rates with a mean of 100 and a standard deviation of 20. We did this by calculating

$$z = \frac{X - \mu}{\sigma} = \frac{70 - 100}{20} = \frac{-30}{20} = -1.5$$

and then using Table D.10 in Appendix D to find the area below $z = -1.5$. This value is .0668. Thus approximately 7% of the time we would expect a score this low *or lower* if we were sampling from a healthy population. Because this probability was greater than our selected significance level of $\alpha = .05$, we would not reject the null hypothesis. Instead we would conclude that we have insufficient evidence to diagnose the person's response rate as abnormal. The tapping rate for the person we examined was not an unusual rate for healthy subjects. (But what would we have concluded had the probability been calculated as .004?) Although in this example we were testing a hypothesis about a single *observation*, exactly the same logic applies to testing hypotheses about sample *means*.

In most situations in which we test a hypothesis about a population mean we don't have any knowledge about the variance of that population. (This is the primary reason that we have *t* tests, which are the main focus of this chapter.) In a limited number of situations, however, we do know $\sigma$ for some reason, and a discussion of testing a hypothesis when $\sigma$ is known provides a good transition from what we already know about the normal distribution to what we want to know about *t* tests. The example of behavior problems is useful for this purpose because we know both the mean and the standard deviation for the population of Total Behavior Problem scores from children in general ($\mu = 50$ and $\sigma = 10$). We also know that our random sample of children who were under stress had a mean score of 56.0, and we want to test the null hypothesis that these five children are a random sample from a population of normal children (i.e., normal with respect to their general level of behavior problems). In other words, we want to test $H_0$: $\mu = 50$ against the alternative $H_1$: $\mu \neq 50$, where $\mu$ represents the mean of the population from which these children were actually drawn.

Because we know the mean and standard deviation of the population of general behavior problem scores, we can use the Central Limit Theorem to obtain the sampling distribution of the mean when the null hypothesis is true. The Central Limit Theorem states that if we obtain the sampling distribution of the mean from this population, it will have a mean of 50, a variance of $\sigma^2/N = 10^2/5 = 100/5 = 20$,

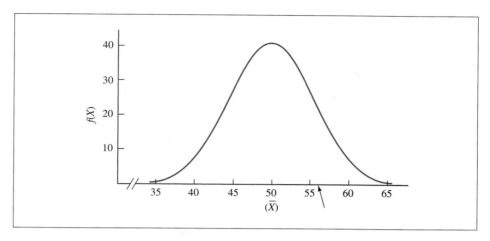

**Figure 12.3**
Sampling distribution of the mean for samples of $N = 5$ drawn from a population with $\mu = 50$ and $\sigma = 10$

and a standard deviation (usually referred to as the standard error) of $\sigma/\sqrt{N} = 4.47$. This distribution is diagrammed in Figure 12.3. The arrow in the figure points to the location of the sample mean.

A short digression about the standard error is in order here because this is a concept that runs throughout statistics. *The standard deviation of any sampling distribution is commonly referred to as the standard error of that distribution.* Thus the standard deviation of means is called the standard error of the mean (symbolized by $\sigma_{\overline{X}}$), whereas the standard deviation of differences between means, which will be discussed in Chapter 14, is called the standard error of differences between means and is symbolized $\sigma_{\overline{X}1-\overline{X}2}$. Standard errors are critically important because they tell us how much statistics, such as the mean, vary from one sample to another. If the standard error is large, that tells you that whatever sample mean you happened to find, someone else doing the same study may find quite a different one. On the other hand, if the standard error is small, another person is likely to find a value fairly similar to yours.

Because we know that the sampling distribution is normally distributed with a mean of 50 and a standard error of 4.47, we can find areas under the distribution by referring to tables of the standard normal distribution. For example, because two standard errors is $2(4.47) = 8.94$, the area to the right of $\overline{X} = 58.94$ is simply the area under the normal distribution greater than two standard deviations above the mean.

For our particular situation we first need to know the probability of a sample mean greater than or equal to 56; thus we need to find the area above $\overline{X} = 56$. We can calculate this the same way we did with individual observations, with only a minor change in the formula for $z$.

$$z = \frac{X - \mu}{\sigma}$$

becomes

$$z = \frac{\overline{X} - \mu}{\sigma_{\overline{X}}}$$

which can also be written as

$$z = \frac{\overline{X} - \mu}{\dfrac{\sigma}{\sqrt{N}}}$$

For our data this becomes

$$z = \frac{56 - 50}{4.47} = \frac{6}{4.47} = 1.34$$

Note that the equation for $z$ used here has the same form as our earlier formula for $z$. The only differences are that X has been replaced by $\overline{X}$ and $\sigma$ has been replaced by $\sigma_{\overline{X}}$. These differences occur because we now are dealing with a distribution of means rather than with single observations; thus the data points are now means, and the standard deviation in question is now the standard error of the mean (the standard deviation of means). The formula for $z$ continues to represent (1) a point on a distribution, minus (2) the mean of that distribution, all divided by (3) the standard deviation of the distribution. Now rather than being concerned specifically with the distribution of $\overline{X}$, we have reexpressed the sample mean in terms of a $z$ score and can now answer the question with regard to the standard normal distribution.

From Table D.10 in Appendix D we find that the probability of a $z$ as large as 1.34 is .0901. Because we want a two-tailed test of $H_0$, we need to double the probability to obtain the probability of a deviation as large as 1.34 standard errors in *either direction* from the mean. This is 2(.0901) = .1802. Thus with a two-tailed test (that stressed children have a mean behavior problem score that is different *in either direction* from that of normal children) at the .05 level of significance we would not reject $H_0$ because the obtained probability of such a value occurring when the null hypothesis is true is greater than .05. We would conclude that we have insufficient evidence in our small sample of five children to conclude that stressed children show more or fewer behavior problems than other children. Keep in mind that it is very possible that stressed children do indeed show behavior problems, but our data are not sufficiently convincing on that score, primarily because we have too little data. (Remember the time your mother was sure that you had broken an ornament while using the living room as a gym, and you had, but blamed your poor little dog, and she didn't have enough evidence to prove you did it? Your mother was forced to make a Type II error—she failed to reject the null hypothesis [your innocence] when it was really false. In our example, even if the true population mean for stressed children is above 50, we don't have enough evidence to build a convincing case.)

The test of one sample mean against a known population mean, which we have just performed, is based on the assumption that the sample means are normally

than not to produce a larger answer than we would have obtained if we had solved for $t$ using $\sigma^2$ itself. As a result it would not really be fair to treat the answer as a $z$ score and use the table of $z$. To do so would give us too many "significant" results, that is, we would make more than 5% Type I errors when testing the null hypothesis at significance level $\alpha = .05$. (For example, when we were calculating $z$, we rejected $H_0$ at the .05 level of significance whenever $z$ fell outside the limits of $\pm 1.96$. If we create a situation in which $H_0$ is true, repeatedly draw samples of $N = 5$, use $s^2$ in place of $\sigma^2$, and calculate $t$, we will obtain a value of $\pm 1.96$ or greater more than about 10% of the time. The cutoff point should really be 2.776, which is quite a bit larger than 1.96.)

William Gossett supplied the solution to this problem. Gossett showed that using $s^2$ in place of $\sigma^2$ would lead to a particular sampling distribution, now generally known as **Student's $t$ distribution**.[1] As a result of Gossett's work, all we have to do is substitute $s^2$, which we know, for $\sigma^2$, which we don't know, denote the answer as $t$, and evaluate $t$ with respect to its own distribution, much as we evaluated $z$ with respect to the normal distribution. The $t$ distribution is tabled in Table D.6, and examples of the actual distribution of $t$ for various sample sizes are shown graphically in Figure 12.5.

---

**Definition**   **Student's $t$ distribution:** The sampling distribution of the $t$ statistic.

---

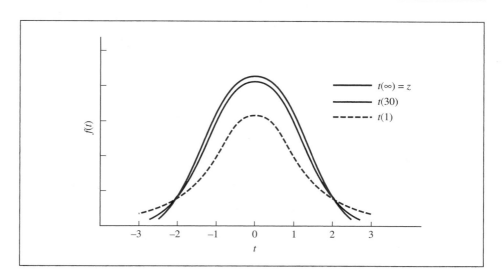

**Figure 12.5**
$t$ distribution for 1, 30, and $\infty$ degrees of freedom

---

[1]It is called "Student's $t$" because Gossett worked for the Guinness Brewing Company, which would not let him publish his results under his own name. He published under the pseudonym of "Student," hence our present-day reference to Student's $t$.

As you can see from Figure 12.5, the distribution of $t$ varies as a function of the **degrees of freedom (*df*)**, which for the moment we will define as one less than the number of observations in the sample. Because the skewness of the sampling distribution of $s^2$ disappears as the number of degrees of freedom increases, the tendency for $s$ to underestimate $\sigma$ will also disappear. Thus for an infinitely large number of degrees of freedom $t$ will become normally distributed and equivalent to $z$.

| | |
|---|---|
| Definition | **Degrees of freedom (*df*):** The number of independent pieces of information remaining after estimating one or more parameters. |

## Degrees of Freedom

I have mentioned that the $t$ distribution is dependent on its degrees of freedom. For the one-sample case, $df = N - 1$; the one degree of freedom is lost because we use the sample mean in calculating $s^2$. To be more precise, we obtain the variance ($s^2$) by calculating the deviations of the observations from their own mean ($X - \overline{X}$), rather than from the population mean ($X - \mu$). Because the sum of the deviations about the mean, $\Sigma(X - \overline{X})$, always equals 0, only $N - 1$ of the deviations are free to vary (the $N^{\text{th}}$ is determined if the sum of the deviations is to be zero). For an illustration of this point consider the case of five scores whose mean is 10. Four of these scores can be anything you want (e.g., 18, 18, 16, 2), but the fifth score cannot be chosen freely. Here it must be $-4$ if the mean is going to be 10. In other words, there are only four *free* numbers in that set of five scores once the mean has been determined; therefore, we have four degrees of freedom. This is the reason the formula for $s^2$ (defined in Chapter 5) used $N - 1$ in the denominator. Because $s^2$ is based on $N - 1$ *df*, we have $N - 1$ degrees of freedom for $t$.

| | |
|---|---|
| EXAMPLE: The Use of *t*: Do Children Always Say What They Feel? | On several occasions throughout this book I have referred to studies of children and adults under stressful situations. Often we find that stress produces negative reactions in the form of depression, anxiety, behavior problems, and so on. But in a study of the families of cancer patients, Compas and others (1994) observed that young children do not report an unusual number of symptoms of depression or anxiety. In fact they even look slightly better than average. Is it really true that young children somehow escape the negative consequences of this kind of family stressor? Can you think of an alternative hypothesis that might explain these results? |

One of the commonly used measures of anxiety in children is called the Children's Manifest Anxiety Scale (CMAS) (Reynolds and Richmond, 1978). Nine items on this scale form what is often called the "Lie Scale." These items are intended to identify children who seem to be giving socially desirable responses rather than answering honestly. (Calling it a "lie" scale is not really being fair to the children; they are just trying to tell you what they think you want to hear.) Could it be that young children under stress have low anxiety scores not because they have very little anxiety, but because the anxiety is masked by an attempt to give socially appropriate answers? One way of addressing this question is to ask if these children have unusually high scores on the Lie Scale. If so, it would be easier to defend the argument that children are just not telling us about their anxiety, not that they don't have any.

Compas et al. (1994) collected data on 36 children from families in which one parent had recently been diagnosed with cancer. Each child completed the CMAS, and their Lie Scale scores, among others, were computed. For this group of children the mean Lie Scale score was 4.39, with a standard deviation of 2.61. Reynolds and Richmond report a population mean for elementary school children of 3.87, but from their data it is not possible to determine the population variance for only this age range of children. Therefore we are required to estimate the variance from the sample variance and use the $t$ test.

We want to test the null hypothesis that the Lie Scale scores are a random sample from a population with a mean ($\mu$) of 3.87. Therefore,

$$H_0: \mu = 3.87$$

$$H_1: \mu \neq 3.87$$

We will use a two-tailed test and work at the 5% level of significance.

From the previous discussion we have

$$t = \frac{\overline{X} - \mu}{s_{\overline{X}}} = \frac{\overline{X} - \mu}{\dfrac{s}{\sqrt{N}}}$$

The numerator of the formula for $t$ represents the distance between the sample mean and the population mean given by $H_0$. The denominator represents an estimate of the standard deviation of the distribution of sample means—the standard error. This is the same thing that we had with $z$, except that the sample variance (or standard deviation) has been substituted for the population variance (or standard deviation). For our data we have

$$t = \frac{\overline{X} - \mu}{s_{\overline{X}}} = \frac{4.39 - 3.87}{\dfrac{2.61}{\sqrt{36}}} = \frac{.52}{.435} = 1.20$$

A $t$ value of 1.20 in and of itself is not particularly meaningful unless we can evaluate it against the sampling distribution of $t$ to determine whether it is a commonly expected value of $t$ when $H_0$ is true. For this purpose the critical values of $t$ are presented in Table D.6, a portion of which is shown in Table 12.1. This table differs in form from the table of the normal distribution ($z$) because, instead of giving the area above and below each specific value of $t$, which would require too much space, the table gives those values of $t$ that cut off particular critical areas, for example, the .05 and .01 levels of significance. Also, in contrast to $z$, a different $t$ distribution is defined for each

## Table 12.1
Abbreviated Version of Table D.6, Percentage Points of the *t* Distribution

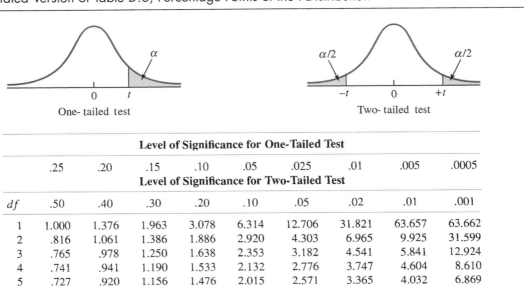

| | | | Level of Significance for One-Tailed Test | | | | | | |
|---|---|---|---|---|---|---|---|---|---|
| | .25 | .20 | .15 | .10 | .05 | .025 | .01 | .005 | .0005 |
| | | | Level of Significance for Two-Tailed Test | | | | | | |
| *df* | .50 | .40 | .30 | .20 | .10 | .05 | .02 | .01 | .001 |
| 1 | 1.000 | 1.376 | 1.963 | 3.078 | 6.314 | 12.706 | 31.821 | 63.657 | 63.662 |
| 2 | .816 | 1.061 | 1.386 | 1.886 | 2.920 | 4.303 | 6.965 | 9.925 | 31.599 |
| 3 | .765 | .978 | 1.250 | 1.638 | 2.353 | 3.182 | 4.541 | 5.841 | 12.924 |
| 4 | .741 | .941 | 1.190 | 1.533 | 2.132 | 2.776 | 3.747 | 4.604 | 8.610 |
| 5 | .727 | .920 | 1.156 | 1.476 | 2.015 | 2.571 | 3.365 | 4.032 | 6.869 |
| 6 | .718 | .906 | 1.134 | 1.440 | 1.943 | 2.447 | 3.143 | 3.707 | 5.959 |
| 7 | .711 | .896 | 1.119 | 1.415 | 1.895 | 2.365 | 2.998 | 3.499 | 5.408 |
| 8 | .706 | .889 | 1.108 | 1.397 | 1.860 | 2.306 | 2.896 | 3.355 | 5.041 |
| 9 | .703 | .883 | 1.100 | 1.383 | 1.833 | 2.262 | 2.821 | 3.250 | 4.781 |
| 10 | .700 | .879 | 1.093 | 1.372 | 1.812 | 2.228 | 2.764 | 3.169 | 4.587 |
| ... | ... | ... | ... | ... | ... | ... | ... | ... | ... |
| 30 | .683 | .854 | 1.055 | 1.310 | 1.697 | 2.042 | 2.457 | 2.750 | 3.646 |
| 40 | .681 | .851 | 1.050 | 1.303 | 1.684 | 2.021 | 2.423 | 2.704 | 3.551 |
| 50 | .679 | .849 | 1.047 | 1.299 | 1.676 | **2.009** | 2.403 | 2.678 | 3.496 |
| 100 | .677 | .845 | 1.042 | 1.290 | 1.660 | 1.984 | 2.364 | 2.626 | 3.390 |
| ∞ | .674 | .842 | 1.036 | 1.282 | 1.645 | 1.960 | 2.326 | 2.576 | 3.291 |

*Source:* The entries in this table were computed by the author.

possible number of degrees of freedom. We want to work at the two-tailed .05 level. The critical value generally is denoted $t_\alpha$ or, in this case, $t_{.05}$.[2]

To use the *t* tables, we must enter the table with the appropriate degrees of freedom. We have 36 observations in our data, so we have $N - 1 = 36 - 1 = 35$ *df* for this example. Table D.6 (or Table 12.1) tells us that the

---

[2] This is a point that can be confusing. Some texts, such as this one, will use $t_\alpha$ to refer to critical value for a two-tailed test, assuming that you know that half of $\alpha$ is located in each tail. Other texts use the notation $t_{\alpha/2}$ to make it very clear that we know that half of $\alpha$ is in each tail. In our example the critical value is $\pm2.03$. So the notational scheme used here will be $t_\alpha = t_{.05} = \pm2.03$, whereas other books could equally validly write $t_{\alpha/2} = t_{.025} = 2.03$. Just be aware that throughout this book, I always run tests at the two-tailed .05 level. (My use of $\pm$ [plus and minus] reveals that I am using a two-tailed test. You would think that statisticians could agree on something as basic as that, but it doesn't look as if that is ever going to happen.)

critical value for $t_{.05}(35)$ is $\pm 2.03$. (I obtained that value by taking the average of the critical values for 30 and 40 *df*, because the table does not contain an entry for exactly 35 *df*.)

The number in parentheses after $t_{.05}$, as in $t_{.05}(35)$, is the degrees of freedom. Our result tells us that if $H_0$ is true, only 5% of the time would a *t* computed on a sample of 36 cases lie outside $\pm 2.03$. Because the value we computed (1.20) was less than 2.03, we will not reject $H_0$. We do not have sufficient evidence to conclude that young children under stress perform any differently on the Lie Scale from a random sample of normal children. We will have to look elsewhere for an explanation of the low anxiety scores of these children. (To see if these children's *anxiety* scores really are below the population average, see Exercise 12.22.) ∎

## 12.4 Factors That Affect the Magnitude of *t* and the Decision About $H_0$

Several factors affect the magnitude of the *t* statistic and/or the likelihood of rejecting $H_0$:

**1.** The actual obtained difference $(\overline{X} - \mu)$

**2.** The magnitude of the sample variance $(s^2)$

**3.** The sample size $(N)$

**4.** The significance level $(\alpha)$

**5.** Whether the test is a one- or a two-tailed test

It should be obvious that the obtained difference between $\overline{X}$ and the mean $(\mu)$ given by $H_0$ is important. This follows directly from the fact that the larger the numerator, the larger the *t* value. But it is also important to keep in mind that the value of $\overline{X}$ is in large part a function of the mean of the population from which the sample was actually drawn. If this mean is denoted $\mu_1$ and the mean given by the null hypothesis is denoted $\mu_0$, then the likelihood of obtaining a significant result will increase as $\mu_1 - \mu_0$ increases.

When you look at the formula for *t*, it should be apparent that as $s^2$ decreases or $N$ increases, the denominator $(s/\sqrt{N})$ itself will decrease and the resulting value of *t* will increase. Because variability introduced by the experimental setting itself (caused by ambiguous instructions, poorly recorded data, distracting testing conditions, and so on) is superimposed on whatever variability there is among participants, we try to reduce *s* by controlling as many sources of variability as possible. By obtaining as many participants as possible, we also make use of the fact that increasing $N$ decreases $s_{\overline{X}}$.

Finally, it should be evident that the likelihood of rejecting $H_0$ will depend on the size of the rejection region, which in turn depends on $\alpha$ and the location of that region (whether a one-tailed or two-tailed test is used).

## 12.5  A Second Example: The Moon Illusion

It may be useful to consider a second example, this one taken from a classic paper by Kaufman and Rock (1962) on the moon illusion. You have no doubt all experienced a rising moon that looked absolutely huge, and then noticed the moon later in the night and been surprised by how small it looked. The "moon illusion" refers to this observation and is the commonly observed fact that the moon near the horizon generally appears larger than the moon at its zenith. (We examined this study in Chapter 5, p. 95.) Kaufman and Rock concluded that the moon illusion could be explained on the basis of the greater *apparent* distance of the moon when it is at the horizon. As part of a very complete series of experiments, the authors initially sought to estimate the moon illusion by asking subjects to adjust a variable "moon" appearing to be on the horizon to match the size of a standard "moon" appearing at its zenith, or vice versa. (In these measurements they did not use the actual moon, but an artificial one created with a special apparatus.) One of the first questions we might ask is whether there really is a moon illusion using their apparatus; that is, whether a larger setting is required to match a horizon moon than to match a zenith moon. (If there is no illusion, they need a different piece of apparatus for carrying out their study.) The following data for ten subjects are taken from Kaufman and Rock's paper and represent the ratio of the diameter of the variable moon and the standard moon. A ratio of 1.00 would indicate no illusion; a ratio other than 1.00 would represent an illusion. For example, a ratio of 1.5 would mean that the horizon moon appeared to have a diameter 1.5 times the diameter of the zenith moon. Evidence in support of an illusion would require that we reject $H_0$: $\mu = 1.00$ in favor of $H_1$: $\mu \neq 1.00$.

Obtained Ratio: 1.73  1.06  2.03  1.40  .95  1.13  1.41  1.73  1.63  1.56

For these data $N = 10$, $\overline{X} = 1.463$, and $s = .341$. A $t$ test on $H_0$: $\mu = 1.00$ is given by

$$t = \frac{\overline{X} - \mu}{s_{\overline{X}}} = \frac{\overline{X} - \mu}{\dfrac{s}{\sqrt{N}}} = \frac{1.463 - 1.000}{\dfrac{.341}{\sqrt{10}}} = \frac{.463}{.108} = 4.29$$

From Table D.6 in Appendix D we see that with $10 - 1 = 9$ $df$ for a two-tailed test at $\alpha = .05$ the critical value of $t_{.05}(9) = \pm 2.262$. The obtained value of $t$ (often denoted $t_{obt}$) is 4.29. Because $4.29 > 2.262$, we can reject $H_0$ at $\alpha = .05$ and conclude that the true mean ratio under these conditions is not equal to 1.00. In fact, it is greater than 1.00, which is what we would expect on the basis of our experience. (It is always comforting to see science confirm what we have all known since childhood, but the results also mean that Kaufman and Rock's experimental apparatus performs as it should.) What would we have concluded if $t$ had been equal to $-4.29$?

## 12.6  How Large Is Our Effect?

For years psychologists and others who use statistical techniques to analyze their data have been content to declare that they found a significant difference, and then consider their work done. People have suggested that this was not adequate, but their complaints largely went unheeded until not very many years ago. Those who did complain were arguing for some kind of statement by the experimenter that gave an indication that the difference was not only significant, but meaningful as well. If we use enough subjects, we can almost always find even a meaningless difference to be significant.

One of those most involved in this debate was Jacob Cohen, who insisted that we should report what he termed a measure of **effect size**. By this he meant that he wanted to see a statistic that gave a meaningful indication of how large a mean was, or how different two means were.

Definition

---

**Effect size:** The difference between two populations divided by the standard deviation of either population—sometimes presented in raw score units.

---

There are several different ways in which we could present information on the size of a difference. I will develop the concept of confidence intervals in the next section. I will also develop the concept of an effect size at greater length over the next several chapters, but at this point I want to focus only on the general idea—and the moon illusion data are ideal for this purpose. We know that we have a significant difference, but when we report this difference, we want to be able to convince the reader that he or she cares about the effect. If the moon looks just a tiny bit larger at the horizon, that may not be worth much comment.

You need to recall the nature of our dependent variable. Participants looked at the moon high in the sky and adjusted a "moon" off to one side to appear to be the same size as the real moon. Then they looked at the moon just above the horizon, and made a similar adjustment. If there were no moon illusion, the two settings would be about the same, and their ratio would be about 1.00. But in actual fact, the settings for the horizon moon were much larger than the settings for the zenith moon, and the average ratio of these two settings was 1.463. This means that, on average, the moon on the horizon appeared to be 1.463 times larger (or 46.3% larger) than the moon at its zenith. This is a huge difference—at least it appears so to me. (Notice that I am not referring to the measurement of the setting the participant made (e.g., whether it was 2 inches or 2.5 inches), but to the ratio of the settings under the two conditions. This is important because in psychology the actual measurement we make often depends on the particular way we measure and is not necessarily meaningful in its own right. But here the *ratio* of measurements is, in fact, meaningful.)

This experiment illustrates a case wherein we can convey to the reader something meaningful about the size of our effect just by reporting the mean. When you tell your readers that the moon at the horizon appears nearly half again as large as the moon at its zenith, you are telling them something more than simply that the horizon moon is significantly larger. You are certainly telling them much more than saying that the average setting for the horizon moon was 5.23 centimeters.

In this example we have a situation where the ratios that we collect are such that we can express important information simply by telling the reader what the mean ratio was. In the next few chapters you will see examples in which the magnitude of the mean is not particularly helpful, and for which we will we need to develop alternative measures.

## 12.7 Confidence Limits on the Mean

The moon illusion is also an excellent example of a case in which we are particularly interested in estimating the true value of $\mu$, in this case the true ratio of the perceived size of the horizon moon to the perceived size of the zenith moon. As we have just seen, it makes sense here to say that "people perceive a moon on the horizon to be nearly 1.5 times as large as the apparent size of the moon at its zenith." The sample mean ($\overline{X}$), as you already know, is an unbiased estimate of $\mu$. When we have one specific estimate of a parameter, we call it a **point estimate**. There are also **interval estimates**, which set limits by a procedure that has a high probability of including the true (population) value of the mean (the mean, $\mu$, of a whole population of observations). What we want, then, are **confidence limits** on $\mu$. These limits enclose what is called a **confidence interval**. In Chapter 6 we saw how to set what were called "probable limits" on an *observation*. A similar line of reasoning will apply here.

Definition

> **Point estimate:** The specific value taken as the estimate of a parameter.
>
> **Interval estimate:** A range of values estimated to include the parameter.
>
> **Confidence limits:** The limits at either end of an interval with a specified probability of including the parameter being estimated.
>
> **Confidence interval:** An interval, with limits at either end, having a specified probability of including the parameter being estimated.

If we want to set limits on $\mu$, given the data at hand, what we really want to do is to ask how large or small $\mu$ could be without causing us to reject $H_0$ if we ran a $t$ test on the obtained sample mean. In other words if $\mu$ (the true size of the illusion) is actually quite small, we would have been unlikely to obtain the sample data. The same would be true if $\mu$ is quite large. At the other extreme, our ratio of 1.46 is probably a reasonable number to expect if the true mean ratio were 1.45 or 1.50. Actually, there is a whole range of values for $\mu$ for which data such as those we obtained would not be particularly unusual. We want to calculate those values of $\mu$. In other words, we want to find those values of $\mu$ that would give us values of $t$ that are just barely significant in each tail of the distribution.

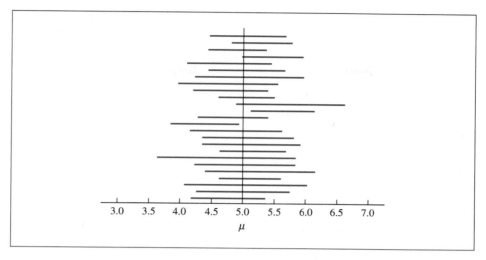

**Figure 12.6**
Confidence limits computed on 25 samples from a population with $\mu = 50$

lot of confusion over *exactly* how a confidence limit should be interpreted. I do not mean to disagree with those who hold with a precise definition of confidence intervals, but there are many worse errors you can make in statistics than erroneously thinking "I am 95% confident that the true mean is between 1.219 and 1.707."

## 12.8  Using SPSS to Run One-Sample *t* Tests

When you have large amounts of data, it is often much more convenient to use a program such as SPSS to compute *t* values. Figure 12.7 is an illustration of the use of SPSS for obtaining both a one-sample *t* test and confidence limits for the moon illusion data. Notice that the results agree, within rounding error, with those we obtained by hand. Notice also that SPSS computes the exact probability of a Type I error (the **p value**) rather than comparing *t* to a tabled value. Although we concluded that the probability of a Type I error was less than .05, SPSS reveals that the actual two-tailed probability is .002.[4] Most computer programs operate in this way.

From the output in Figure 12.7 we could conclude that the mean ratio settings for the moon illusion, based on 10 subjects, was significantly greater than 1.00, which would be the expected setting if there were, in fact, no moon illusion. This could be written as $t(9) = 4.30, p = .002$.

---

[4]We could have approximated this probability roughly by using Table D.6 in Appendix D. For 9 *df*, a *t* of 3.250 would have had a *two-tailed* probability of .01, and a value of $t = 4.781$ would have had a two-tailed probability of .001. Because the obtained *t* falls between these two values, its probability is somewhere between .01 and .001.

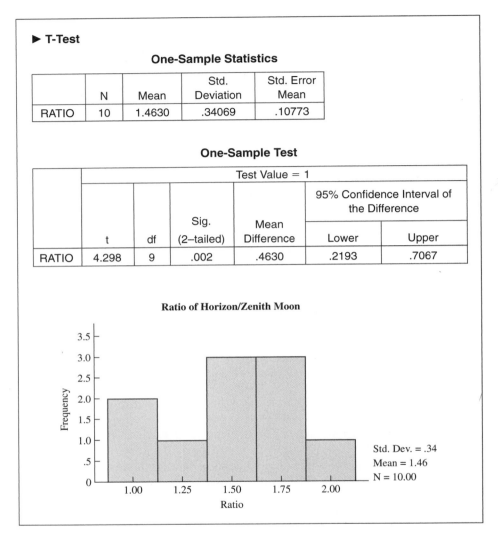

► **T-Test**

**One-Sample Statistics**

|  | N | Mean | Std. Deviation | Std. Error Mean |
|---|---|---|---|---|
| RATIO | 10 | 1.4630 | .34069 | .10773 |

**One-Sample Test**

|  | Test Value = 1 | | | | | |
|---|---|---|---|---|---|---|
|  |  |  |  |  | 95% Confidence Interval of the Difference | |
|  | t | df | Sig. (2–tailed) | Mean Difference | Lower | Upper |
| RATIO | 4.298 | 9 | .002 | .4630 | .2193 | .7067 |

**Ratio of Horizon/Zenith Moon**

Std. Dev. = .34
Mean = 1.46
N = 10.00

**Figure 12.7**
SPSS analysis for one-sample *t* tests and confidence limits

## 12.9 A Final Worked Example

We now will return to the *t* test on means and work through an example of a *t* test on a null hypothesis about a <u>single population mean</u> ($\mu$). In several places throughout this book we have worked with the study by Katz and his colleagues (1990) that analyzed student performance on an SAT-like exam wherein some of the students had not seen the passage on which the questions were based. (See Chapter 3.) The data from the 28 students in the group that had not seen the passage follow.

| ID    | 1  | 2  | 3  | 4  | 5  | 6  | 7  | 8  | 9  | 10 | 11 | 12 | 13 | 14 |
|-------|----|----|----|----|----|----|----|----|----|----|----|----|----|----|
| Score | 58 | 48 | 48 | 41 | 34 | 43 | 38 | 53 | 41 | 60 | 55 | 44 | 43 | 49 |

| ID    | 15 | 16 | 17 | 18 | 19 | 20 | 21 | 22 | 23 | 24 | 25 | 26 | 27 | 28 |
|-------|----|----|----|----|----|----|----|----|----|----|----|----|----|----|
| Score | 47 | 33 | 47 | 40 | 46 | 53 | 40 | 45 | 39 | 47 | 50 | 53 | 46 | 53 |

The mean of these observations is 46.2143, and the standard deviation is 6.7295.

If the students had really guessed blindly, without even looking at the possible answers, we would expect that they would get 20 items correct by chance, because there were 100 items with five choices per item. On the other hand, if they can guess intelligently just by looking at the choices they are given, then they should do better than chance. So we want to test $H_0$: $\mu = 20$ against $H_0$: $\mu \neq 20$.

Since we know $\overline{X}$, $s_X$, and $N$, and we know that we want to test the null hypothesis that $\mu = 20$, then we can set up a simple $t$ test.

$$t = \frac{\overline{X} - \mu}{\dfrac{s}{\sqrt{N}}} = \frac{46.21 - 20}{\dfrac{6.7295}{\sqrt{28}}}$$

$$= \frac{26.21}{1.2718} = 20.61$$

With a $t$ as large as 20.61, we don't even need to look in the appendix. If we did, we would find a two-tailed critical value of $t$, on 27 $df$ for $\alpha = .05$, of 2.052. Obviously we can reject the null hypothesis and conclude that the students were performing at better than chance levels.

I will write more about effect size calculations for one sample in the next chapter, but here I want to anticipate that discussion because it offers a nice contrast to what we said with regard to the moon illusion example. When we were looking at the moon illusion, our dependent variable was the ratio of the horizon moon to the zenith moon, and that ratio has a clear interpretation. We saw that the horizon moon appeared to be nearly half again as large as the same moon seen at its zenith. In the current example of the study by Katz et al., we don't have such a meaningful dependent variable. It probably will not satisfy you to know that participants correctly answered 46.21 questions correctly, or even to learn that they correctly answered 26.21 more questions than would be expected by chance. Is 26.21 a large number? Well, it depends on your point of reference.

To anticipate what I will say in Chapter 13, I am going to represent the effect size in terms of the number of standard deviations our mean is above or below some point, in this case above the mean that would be expected by chance. In this particular case, the size of a standard deviation was 6.73. It makes sense to me to ask how many standard deviations our mean was above a mean of 20 that we would expect with random guessing. So in this case I will divide 26.21 (the degree to which the participants' mean exceeded chance) by 6.73 and call this statistic $\hat{d}$. Then

$$\hat{d} = \frac{46.21 - 20}{6.73} = 3.89$$

On the basis of this result we can conclude that our participants scored nearly four standard deviations higher than we would have expected by chance. Four standard deviations is a lot, and I would conclude that they are doing very much better than chance responding would have predicted.

I need to stress one complicating factor in calculating $\hat{d}$. As the preceding formula shows, $\hat{d}$ is a ratio of the size of some effect (a mean or a difference in means)—and a standard deviation. But before you jump in and use just any old standard deviation, you need to think about whether that standard deviation gives us a meaningful metric. In other words, does it make sense to convey the difference in standard deviation terms? I think that most people would agree that if we are talking about the moon illusion, the mean setting itself is often sufficient, and even preferable—"the horizon moon appears to be nearly half again as large as the zenith moon." There we have just used the mean and not involved the standard deviation at all. In the most recent example, it would not be very useful to simply report how many items were correct, but it does seem meaningful to say that we are nearly four standard deviations above where we would be by chance. Just imagine a normal distribution plotted with a mean at 20 (the chance level) and imagine being four standard deviations above there. That's a big difference! However there are other situations, one of which will appear in the next chapter, where it doesn't seem to be particularly meaningful to scale a difference in standard deviation units. The task is to report some statistic that will give the reader a sense of what you have found, even if that is not statistically elegant.

## Writing Up the Results of a *One-Sample t* Test

Katz et al. (1990) presented students with exam questions similar to those on the SAT, that required them to answer 100 five-choice multiple-choice questions about a passage that they had presumably read. One of the groups (N = 28) was given the questions without being presented with the passage, but they were asked to answer them anyway. A second group was allowed to read the passage, but they are not of interest to us here.

If participants perform purely at random, those in the NoPassage condition would be expected to get 20 items correct just by chance. On the other hand, if participants read the test items carefully, they might be able to reject certain answers as unlikely regardless of what the passage said. A $t$ test on $H_0$: $\mu = 20$ produced $t(27) = 20.61$, which has an associated probability under the null hypothesis less than .05, leading us to reject $H_0$ and conclude that even without having seen the passage, students can perform at better than chance levels. Furthermore, the measure of effect ($\hat{d} = 3.89$) shows that these students were performing at nearly four standard deviations greater than we would have expected by chance, and that therefore their test-taking skills made an important contribution to their performance on this task.

## 12.10 Seeing Statistics

In this chapter we have used Student's _t_ test to test the hypothesis tha. came from a population with a specific mean, and we did this within th. of a situation in which we do not know the population standard deviation. We were required to use _t_ specifically because we did not know that population standard deviation. McClelland's applets on the Web site are excellent for illustrating exactly what is happening here, and why the _t_ distribution is more appropriate than the normal (_z_) distribution for answering our question.

### Sampling Distribution of _t_

The first applet for Chapter 12 is named Sampling Distribution of _t_. This applet is designed to allow you to draw samples from a particular population with a known mean ($\mu = 0$), calculate the mean, standard deviation, and _t_ for each sample, and plot the result. For each sample we are testing the null hypothesis that the population mean is 0, and, since we know that is true, we will have the sampling distribution of _t_ when the null is true. (This distribution is often called the **central _t_ distribution**.)

| Definition | **Central _t_ distribution:** The sampling distribution of the _t_ statistic when the null hypothesis is true. |
| --- | --- |

The opening screen, before you have done any sampling, looks like the following:

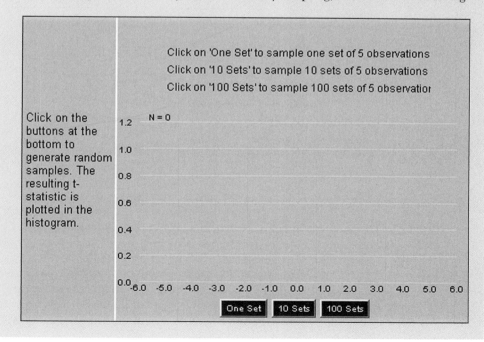

Notice that you can draw one, ten, or a hundred samples at a time, and each time you click one of the buttons you add those samples to the ones you have drawn already.

Start by drawing a number of individual samples, and note how the resulting *t* values vary from one sample to another. After you have drawn a number of individual samples, click on the button labeled "100 sets." Notice that some of the resulting *t* values are probably surprisingly large and/or small. (My first try gave me a *t* of about 4.5, and another of −4.0.) These extreme values would likely represent cases that would lead to rejection of the null hypothesis. Next, click on the "100 sets" button repeatedly until you have drawn 1,000 samples. Notice that the distribution is beginning to smooth out. Keep going until you have drawn 10,000 samples, and notice how smooth the distribution has become.

## Comparing z and t

You might be inclined to view the distribution that you have just drawn as a *normal* distribution. It looks a lot like the normal distributions we have seen. But actually, it is a bit too wide. Under a normal distribution we would expect 5% of the values to exceed ±1.96, but in our case, with only 4 *df*, 12.15% of the results would exceed ±1.96. Thus if you were to use ±1.96 as your cutoff, you would reject the null hypothesis far too often. The actual 5% cutoff (two-tailed) would be ±2.776.

Let's explore this last idea a bit further. If you go back to your browser and open the applet named "*t* versus *z*," you will see something that looks approximately like the following:

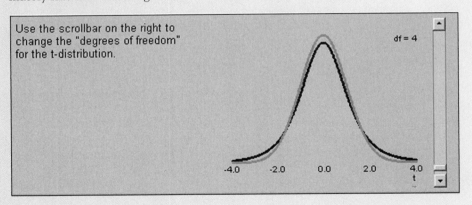

The red line and the red values (which are gray here, but red on your screen) represent the distribution of *z* (the normal distribution). The black line, with its associated values, represents the *t* distribution. Notice how the critical values for *t* are more extreme than the critical values for *z*.

On the right side of this figure you will see a slider. Moving the slider up and down varies the degrees of freedom for *t*, and allows you to see how the *t* distribution approaches the normal distribution as *df* increase. At what point would you be willing to conclude that the two distributions are "close enough?"

## Confidence Intervals

While we are looking at McClelland's applets, we will take a look at an applet that he wrote illustrating confidence limits. In Figure 12.6 I showed you the results when I drew 25 samples, with their confidence limits, computed when the null hypothesis ($\mu = 5.0$) was true. In that case there were two confidence intervals that did not enclose $\mu = 5.0$, but the rest did. What might we expect to see if the null hypothesis is actually false?

The applet entitled "Confidence Limits" illustrates this situation. It hypothesizes a population mean of 100, but actually draws samples from a population wherein $\mu = 110$. For each sample the applet calculates, and draws, a 95% confidence limit. As you might hope and expect, many of these intervals do not include $\mu = 100$, though a number of them do. I have shown one result below, where I have drawn one sample.

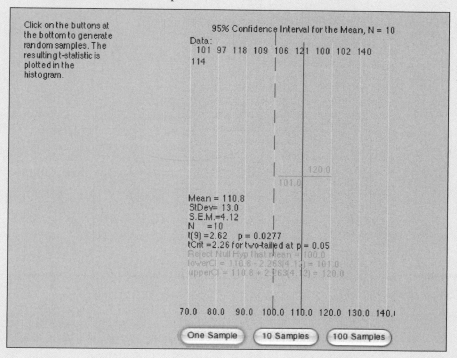

The vertical dashed line represents the null hypothesis $\mu = 100$. The solid line represents the true mean of 110. Notice that for the first sample the limits are 101.0–120.0, which do not include 100, the hypothesized mean. Your one sample example will probably be different.

First start the applet and draw one sample. Do this repeatedly, and notice how the intervals vary. Then click on the button to draw 10 samples. Here it will be clear that some intervals include 110, the true mean, while others do not. Finally, draw 100 samples. My results follow.

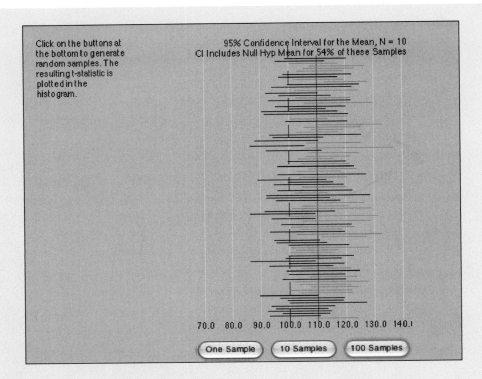

Now the second line of the heading above the graph will tell you what percentage of the intervals include the null hypothesis. (In this case it is 54%.). Repeat this several times and note how the answer varies.

## 12.11 Summary

We began this chapter by considering the sampling distribution of the mean and how the information it gives is useful in testing hypotheses. We then discussed how we could combine what we know about $z$ and what we know about the sampling distribution of the mean to produce a test of a null hypothesis concerning $\mu$. Next we examined how we could go beyond $z$ to make use of a $t$ test when the population standard deviation is not known and must be estimated by the sample standard deviation. We considered the factors that influence the magnitude of $t$ in a particular experiment and will expand on this in the next chapter. Next we considered the construction of confidence limits on the value of a population mean and calculated one measure of the size of the effect for the Katz et al. study.

Some important terms in this chapter are

| | |
|---|---|
| Experimental hypothesis, *280* | Point estimate, *296* |
| Central Limit Theorem, *281* | Interval estimate, *296* |
| Rectangular (uniform) distribution, *282* | Confidence limits, *296* |
| | Confidence interval, *296* |
| Student's *t* distribution, *289* | *p* value, *299* |
| Degrees of freedom (*df*), *290* | Central *t* distribution, *303* |
| Effect size, *295* | |

# 12.12 Exercises

**12.1** The following numbers represent 100 random numbers drawn from a rectangular population with a mean of 4.5 and a standard deviation of 2.6. Plot the distribution of these digits.

```
6 4 1 5 8 7 0 8 2 1 5 7 4 0 2 6 9 0 9 6
4 9 0 4 9 3 4 9 8 2 0 4 1 4 9 4 1 7 5 2
3 1 5 2 1 7 9 7 3 5 4 7 3 1 5 1 1 0 5 2
7 6 2 1 0 6 2 3 3 6 5 4 1 5 9 1 0 2 6 0
8 3 9 3 3 8 5 5 7 0 8 4 2 0 6 3 7 3 5 1
```

**12.2** I drew 50 samples of 5 scores each from the same population that the data in Exercise 12.1 came from, and calculated the mean of each sample. The means are shown below. Plot the distribution of these means.

```
2.8  6.2  4.4  5.0  1.0  4.6  3.8  2.6  4.0  4.8
6.6  4.6  6.2  4.6  5.6  6.4  3.4  5.4  5.2  7.2
5.4  2.6  4.4  4.2  4.4  5.2  4.0  2.6  5.2  4.0
3.6  4.6  4.4  5.0  5.6  3.4  3.2  4.4  4.8  3.8
4.4  2.8  3.8  4.6  5.4  4.6  2.4  5.8  4.6  4.8
```

**12.3** Compare the means and the standard deviations for the distribution of digits in Exercise 12.1 and the sampling distribution of the mean in Exercise 12.2.
(a) What would the Central Limit Theorem lead you to expect in this situation?
(b) Do the data correspond to what you would predict?

**12.4** In what way would the result in Exercise 12.2 differ if you had drawn more samples of size 5?

**12.5** In what way would the result in Exercise 12.2 differ if you had drawn 50 samples of size 15?

**12.6** In Table 11.1 we saw data on the state means of students who took the SAT exam. The mean Verbal SAT for North Dakota was 515. The standard deviation was not reported. Assume that 238 students took that exam.

(a) Is this result consistent with the idea that North Dakota's students are a random sample from a population of students having a mean of 500 and a standard deviation of 100?

(b) From what we learned in Chapter 11 about SAT scores, and about how, and why, they vary by state, would you feel comfortable concluding that people in North Dakota are smarter than people elsewhere?

**12.7** Why do the data in Exercise 12.6 not really speak to the issue of whether education in North Dakota is generally in good shape?

**12.8** Using the data from Table 11.1, compute the 95% confidence limits on the Pupil/Teacher ratio across the 50 states.

**12.9** You would probably be nervous about inferring a population estimate and a confidence interval for the mean U.S. SAT Combined score from the data in Table 11.1, but are probably much less worried about your confidence limits on Pupil/Teacher ratio in Exercise 12.8. Why would this be?

**12.10** In Exercise 5.21 we saw, among other things, the weight gain of each of 29 anorexic girls who received cognitive behavioral therapy. What null hypothesis would we be likely to test in this situation?

**12.11** The data referred to in Exercise 12.10 (in pounds gained) follow. Run the appropriate $t$ test and draw the appropriate conclusions.

| ID | 1 | 2 | 3 | 4 | 5 | 6 | 7 | 8 | 9 | 10 |
|------|------|------|------|------|------|------|------|------|------|------|
| Gain | 1.7 | .7 | −.1 | −.7 | −3.5 | 14.9 | 3.5 | 17.1 | −7.6 | 1.6 |
| ID | 11 | 12 | 13 | 14 | 15 | 16 | 17 | 18 | 19 | 20 |
| Gain | 11.7 | 6.1 | 1.1 | −4.0 | 20.9 | −9.1 | 2.1 | −1.4 | 1.4 | −.3 |
| ID | 21 | 22 | 23 | 24 | 25 | 26 | 27 | 28 | 29 | |
| Gain | −3.7 | −.8 | 2.4 | 12.6 | 1.9 | 3.9 | .1 | 15.4 | −.7 | |

**12.12** Compute 95% confidence limits on $\mu$ for the data in Exercise 12.11.

**12.13** Compute a measure of effect size for the data in Exercise 12.11.

**12.14** For the IQ data on females in the data on attention deficit disorder that we have referred to several times in previous chapters (data set Add.dat on the Web site), test the null hypothesis that $\mu_{female} = 100$.

**12.15** In Exercise 12.14 you probably solved for $t$ instead of $z$. Why was that necessary?

**12.16** Describe the procedures that you would go through to reproduce the results in Figure 12.4.

**12.17** In Section 12.3 we ran a $t$ test to test the hypothesis that young children under stress give more socially desirable answers on an anxiety measure than normal children. We never really tested the hypothesis that they report lower levels of anxiety. For the data on these 36 children the mean anxiety score was 11.00, with a standard deviation of 6.085. The population mean anxiety score for elementary school–aged children on this measure is reported as 14.55. Do our children show significantly lower levels of anxiety than children in the general population?

**12.18** Compute the 95% confidence limits on mean anxiety for the data in Exercise 12.17.

**12.19** Are the confidence limits that you calculated in Exercise 12.18 consistent with the results of the $t$ test in Exercise 12.17?

**12.20** Write a brief paragraph describing the research project in Exercise 12.17 and its results.

# 13

## Hypothesis Tests Applied to Means: Two Related Samples

### QUESTIONS

- What if the same people give us data on two occasions?

- This creates problems; what is the simplest way around them?

- Why would I want to use related samples?

- When would I not want to use related samples?

In Chapter 12 we considered the situation in which we had one sample mean ($\overline{X}$). We wanted to test to see if it was reasonable to believe that such a mean would have occurred if we had been sampling from a population with some specified population mean (which we denote $\mu_0$). Another way of phrasing this is to say that we were testing to determine if the mean of the population from which we sampled (call it $\mu_1$) could be equal to some particular value given by the null hypothesis ($\mu_0$).

In this chapter we will move away from the case in which we perform a test on the mean of one sample of data. Instead we will consider the case in which we have two **related samples** and we wish to perform a test on the difference between their two means. (The same analyses apply to what are variously called **repeated measures, matched samples**, paired samples, correlated samples, dependent samples, randomized blocks, or split plots, depending in part on the speaker's statistics background.) As you will see, this test is similar to the test discussed in the previous chapter.

Definition    **Related samples:** An experimental design in which the same participant is observed under more than one treatment.

**Repeated measures:** An experimental design in which the same participant is observed under more than one treatment.

**Matched samples:** An experimental design in which the participants are paired and one is assigned to each treatment.

## 13.1  Related Samples

In many (but certainly not all) situations in which we will use the form of the *t* test discussed in this chapter, we will have two sets of data from the same participants. For example, we might ask 20 people to rate their level of anxiety before and after donating blood. Or we might record ratings of level of disability made using two different rating systems for each of 20 handicapped individuals in an attempt to see whether one rating system leads to generally lower assessments than the other. In both examples we would have 20 sets of numbers, two numbers for each person, and we would expect these two sets of numbers (variables) to be correlated. We need to take this correlation into account in planning our *t* test. In the example of anxiety about donating blood, people differ widely in level of anxiety. Some seem to be anxious all the time no matter what happens, and others just take things as they come and don't worry about anything. Thus, there should be a relationship between an individual's anxiety level before donating blood and his or her anxiety level after donating blood. In other words, if we know that a person was one of the more anxious people before donation, we can make a reasonable guess that the same person was one of the more anxious people after donation. Similarly, some people are severely handicapped, whereas others are only mildly so. If we know that a particular person received a high assessment using one system, it is likely that person also received a relatively high assessment using another system. The relationship between data sets doesn't have to be perfect—in fact, it probably never will be. The fact that we can make better than chance predictions is sufficient to classify two sets of data as related or matched. (To put this another way, we have related or matched samples whenever the two variables, such as the two sets of anxiety scores, are significantly correlated, and for all practical purposes that correlation will be positive.)

In the two preceding examples I have chosen situations in which each person in the study contributed two scores. Although this is the most common way of obtaining related samples, it is not the only way. For example, a study of marital relationships might involve asking husbands and wives to rate their satisfaction with their marriage, with the goal of testing to see whether wives are, on average, more or less satisfied than husbands. Here each individual would contribute only one score, but the couple as a unit would contribute a pair of scores.

It is very probable that if the wife is very dissatisfied with the marriage, her husband isn't likely to be too happy either, and vice versa. This is a classic example of *matching* or *matched pairs*.

Many examples of experimental designs involving related samples have one thing in common, and that is the fact that knowing one member of a pair of scores tells you something—maybe not much, but something—about the other member. Whenever this is the case, we say that the samples are related. This chapter deals with *t* tests on the difference between the means of two related samples.

## 13.2 Student's *t* Applied to Difference Scores

Everitt, in Hand et al. (1994), reported on family therapy as a treatment for anorexia. There were 17 girls in this experiment, and they were weighed before and after treatment. The weights of the girls, in pounds,[1] is given in Table 13.1. The row of difference scores was obtained by subtracting the Before score from the After score, so that a negative difference represents weight *loss*, and a positive difference represents a *gain*.

One of the first things we should probably do, although it takes us away from *t* tests for a moment, is to plot the relationship between Before Treatment and After Treatment weights, looking to see if there is, in fact, a relationship, and how linear that relationship is. Such a plot is given in Figure 13.1. Notice that the relationship is basically linear, with a slope quite near 1.0. A slope of 1.00 would tell us that how much the girl weighed at the beginning of therapy did not seriously influence how much weight she gained or lost by the end of therapy. In other words, heavy and light girls each *gain* approximately the same amount.

**Table 13.1**
Data from Everitt on Weight Gain

| ID | 1 | 2 | 3 | 4 | 5 | 6 | 7 | 8 | 9 | 10 |
|---|---|---|---|---|---|---|---|---|---|---|
| Before | 83.8 | 83.3 | 86.0 | 82.5 | 86.7 | 79.6 | 76.9 | 94.2 | 73.4 | 80.5 |
| After | 95.2 | 94.3 | 91.5 | 91.9 | 100.3 | 76.7 | 76.8 | 101.6 | 94.9 | 75.2 |
| Diff | 11.4 | 11.0 | 5.5 | 9.4 | 13.6 | −2.9 | −.1 | 7.4 | 21.5 | −5.3 |

| ID | 11 | 12 | 13 | 14 | 15 | 16 | 17 | Mean | St. Dev |
|---|---|---|---|---|---|---|---|---|---|
| Before | 81.6 | 82.1 | 77.6 | 83.5 | 89.9 | 86.0 | 87.3 | 83.23 | 5.02 |
| After | 77.8 | 95.5 | 90.7 | 92.5 | 93.8 | 91.7 | 98.0 | 90.49 | 8.48 |
| Diff | −3.8 | 13.4 | 13.1 | 9.0 | 3.9 | 5.7 | 10.7 | 7.26 | 7.16 |

---

[1]Everitt reported that these weights were in kilograms, but if so he has a collection of anorexic young girls whose mean weight is about 185 pounds, and that just doesn't sound reasonable. The example is completely unaffected by the units in which we record weight.

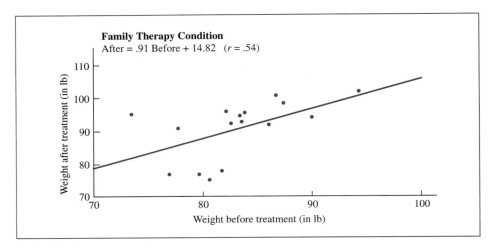

**Figure 13.1**
Relationship of weight before and after family therapy, for a group of 17 anorexic girls

The primary question we wish is ask is whether subjects gained weight as a function of the therapy sessions. We have an experimental problem here, because it is possible that weight gain resulted merely from the passage of time, and that therapy had nothing to do with it. However I know that a group that did not receive therapy did not gain weight over the same period of time, which strongly suggests that the simple passage of time was not an important variable. (We will consider this group in Chapter 14.) If you were to calculate the weight of these girls before and after therapy, the means would be 83.23 and 90.49 lbs, respectively, which translates to a gain of a little over 7 pounds. However we still need to test to see whether this difference is likely to represent a true difference in population means, or a chance difference. By this I mean that we need to test the null hypothesis that the mean *in the population* of After scores is equal to the mean *in the population* of Before scores. In other words, we are testing $H_0: \mu_A = \mu_B$.

As I suggested earlier, a problem arises when our Before and After scores are not independent, and we have such a relationship here as you can see from Figure 13.1. How much a girl weighs after therapy is clearly related to how much she weighed before therapy, which certainly sounds reasonable. This lack of independence would distort our *t* test if we couldn't find a way around it, but fortunately we do have a way around it, and so can proceed.

## Difference Scores

Although it would seem obvious to view the data as representing two samples of scores, one set obtained before the therapy program and one after, it is also possible, and very profitable, to transform the data into one set of scores—the set of differences between $X_1$ and $X_2$ for each girl. These differences are called **difference scores**, or **gain scores**, and are shown in the third row of Table 13.1. They represent the degree of weight gain between one measurement session and the next—presumably as a result of our intervention. If the therapy program actually had *no* effect (i.e., if $H_0$ is true), the average weight would not change from session to session. By chance some girls would happen to have a higher weight on $X_2$ than on $X_1$, and some would have a lower weight, but *on the average* there would be no difference.

Definition       **Difference scores (gain scores):** The set of scores representing the difference between the participant's performance on two occasions.

If we now think of our data as being the set of difference scores, the null hypothesis becomes the hypothesis that the mean of a population of difference scores (denoted $\mu_D$) equals 0. Because it can be shown that $\mu_D = \mu_1 - \mu_2$, we can write $H_0$: $\mu_D = \mu_1 - \mu_2 = 0$. But now we can see that we are testing a hypothesis using *one sample* of data (the sample of difference scores), and we already know how to do that from Chapter 12. Those of you who worked Exercise 12.17 in that chapter will probably recognize that you have done all this before, though with a different treatment condition. Yes you have. In Chapter 12 we looked at data as if they consisted solely of gain scores, whereas in this chapter we start with before-and-after data and then move to gain scores. These are just two approaches with the same end. The only difference is that in Chapter 12 we were speaking of a test that applies to one set of data regardless of whether those data are differences between two scores for each person or, as in the case of the moon illusion example, simply one set of data.

## The *t* Statistic

We are now at precisely the same place we were in the previous chapter when we had a sample of data and a null hypothesis ($\mu = 0$). The only difference is that in this case the data are difference scores, and the mean and the standard deviation are based on the differences. Recall that $t$ was defined as the difference between a sample mean and a population mean, divided by the standard error of the mean. Then we have

$$t = \frac{\overline{D} - 0}{s_{\overline{D}}} = \frac{\overline{D} - 0}{\frac{s_D}{\sqrt{N}}}$$

where and $\overline{D}$ and $s_D$ are the mean and the standard deviation of the difference scores and $N$ is the number of difference scores (i.e., the number of *pairs*, not the number of raw scores). From Table 13.1 we see that the mean difference score was

7.26, and the standard deviation of the differences was 7.16. For our data

$$t = \frac{\overline{D} - 0}{s_{\overline{D}}} = \frac{\overline{D} - 0}{\dfrac{s_D}{\sqrt{N}}} = \frac{7.26 - 0}{\dfrac{7.16}{\sqrt{17}}} = \frac{7.26}{1.74} = 4.18$$

## Degrees of Freedom

The degrees of freedom for the matched-sample case are exactly the same as they were for the one-sample case. Because we are working with the difference scores, $N$ will be equal to the number of differences (or the number of *pairs* of observations, or the number of *independent* observations—all of which amount to the same thing). Because the variance of these difference scores ($s_D^2$) is used as an estimate of the variance of a population of difference scores ($\sigma_D^2$), and because this sample variance is obtained using the sample mean ($\overline{D}$), we will lose one *df* to the mean and have $N - 1$ *df*. In other words, *df* = number of *pairs* minus 1.

We have 17 difference scores in this example, so we will have 16 degrees of freedom. From Table D.6 in Appendix D, we find that for a two-tailed test at the .05 level of significance, $t_{.05}(16) = \pm 2.12$. Our obtained value of $t(4.18)$ exceeds 2.12, so we will reject $H_0$ and conclude that the difference scores were not sampled from a population of difference scores where $\mu_D = 0$. In practical terms this means that the subjects weighed significantly more after the intervention program than before it. Although we would like to think that this means that the program was successful, keep in mind the possibility that this could just be normal growth. The fact remains, however, that for whatever reason, the weights were sufficiently higher on the second occasion to allow us to reject $H_0$: $\mu_D = \mu_1 - \mu_2 = 0$.

## 13.3 A Second Example: The Moon Illusion Again

For a second example we will return to the work by Kaufman and Rock (1962) on the moon illusion. You may recall that they postulated that we perceive the moon at the horizon to be larger than the moon at its zenith because of the greater apparent distance of the horizon. An important earlier hypothesis about the source of the moon illusion had been put forth by Holway and Boring (1940), who suggested that the illusion was due to the fact that when the moon was on the horizon, the observer looked straight at it with eyes level, whereas when it was at its zenith, the observer had to elevate his eyes as well as his head to see it. Holway and Boring proposed that this difference in the elevation of the eyes was the cause of the illusion. To test this hypothesis, Kaufman and Rock devised an apparatus that allowed them to present two artificial moons (one at the horizon and one at the zenith) and to control whether the subjects elevated their eyes or kept them level to see the zenith moon. (The horizon [comparison] moon was always viewed with eyes level.) In both cases the dependent variable was the ratio of the perceived size of the horizon moon to the perceived size of the zenith

**Table 13.2**

Magnitude of the Moon Illusion When Zenith Moon Is Viewed with Eyes Level and with Eyes Elevated

| Viewer | Eyes Elevated | Eyes Level | Difference (D) |
|--------|---------------|------------|----------------|
| 1 | 1.65 | 1.73 | −.08 |
| 2 | 1.00 | 1.06 | −.06 |
| 3 | 2.03 | 2.03 | .00 |
| 4 | 1.25 | 1.40 | −.15 |
| 5 | 1.05 | .95 | .10 |
| 6 | 1.02 | 1.13 | −.11 |
| 7 | 1.67 | 1.41 | .26 |
| 8 | 1.86 | 1.73 | .13 |
| 9 | 1.56 | 1.63 | −.07 |
| 10 | 1.73 | 1.56 | .17 |
|  |  | Mean | .019 |
|  |  | Std. Dev. | .137 |
|  |  | Std. Err. | .043 |

moon (a ratio of 1.00 would represent no illusion). If Holway and Boring were correct, there should be a greater illusion (larger ratio) in the eyes-elevated condition than in the eyes-level condition, although the "moon" was always perceived to be in the same place, the zenith. If Kaufman and Rock (with their "apparent distance" hypothesis) were correct, there should be no differences between the "eyes-level" and "eyes-elevated" conditions. The actual data for this experiment are given in Table 13.2.

In this example we want to test the *null* hypothesis that the means are equal under the two viewing conditions. Because we are dealing with related observations (each subject served under both conditions), we will work with the difference scores and test $H_0$: $\mu_D = 0$. Using a two-tailed test at $\alpha = .05$, the alternative hypothesis is $H_1$: $\mu_D \neq 0$.

From the formula for a $t$ test on related samples we have

$$t = \frac{\overline{D} - 0}{s_{\overline{D}}} = \frac{\overline{D} - 0}{\dfrac{s_D}{\sqrt{N}}} = \frac{.019 - 0}{\dfrac{.137}{\sqrt{10}}} = \frac{.019}{.043} = .44$$

From Table D.6 we find that $t_{.05}(9) = \pm 2.262$. Because our obtained $t$ ($t_{\text{obt}}$) = .44 is less than 2.262, we will fail to reject $H_0$ and decide that we have no evidence to suggest that the illusion is affected by the elevation of the eyes.[2] (These data, moreover, include a second test of Holway and Boring's hypothesis, since Holway and Boring would have predicted that

---

[2]Note: A glance at Table D.6 in Appendix D will reveal that any $t$ less than 1.96 (the critical value for $z$) will never be significant at $\alpha = .05$, regardless of the number of degrees of freedom. Moreover, unless you have at least 50 degrees of freedom, $t$ values less than 2.00 will not be significant, thus often making it unnecessary for you to even bother looking at the table of $t$.

there would not be an illusion ($\mu_D > 1.0$) if subjects viewed the zenith moon with eyes level. In fact, the data reveal a considerable illusion under this condition. A test of the significance of the illusion level can be obtained by the methods discussed in Chapter 12 and the illusion is, in fact, significant.)

## 13.4 Advantages and Disadvantages of Using Related Samples

In the next chapter we will consider experimental designs in which we use two independent groups of subjects rather than testing the same participants twice (or employ some other method of having related samples of data). In many cases independent samples are useful, but before considering that topic, it is important that we consider the strengths and weaknesses of related samples.

Probably the most important advantage of designing an experiment around related samples is that such a procedure allows us to avoid problems associated with participant-to-participant variability. Return for a moment to the data in Table 13.1 on the weights of anorexic girls. Notice that some participants (e.g., participant 9) began the study weighing considerably less than others. On the other hand, participant 8 began the study weighing well more than others. The advantage of related-samples designs is that these differences between participants do not enter into the data we analyze—the difference scores. A change from 73 pounds to 75 pounds is treated exactly the same as a change from 93 to 95. In not allowing the participant-to-participant variability in initial weight to influence the data by producing a large sample variance, related-samples designs have a considerable advantage over independent samples in terms of the ability to reject a false null hypothesis (power).

A second advantage of related samples over two independent samples is the fact that related samples allow us to control for extraneous variables. Had we measured one group of participants before they received therapy and a different group after there could have been any number of differences between the groups that had nothing to do with our intervention but that would influence the results. That was not a problem in our study because we used the same participants for both measurement sessions.

A third advantage of related-measures designs is that they require fewer participants than do independent-sample designs for the same degree of power. This is a substantial advantage, as anyone who has ever tried to recruit participants can attest. It is usually a much easier task to get 20 people to do something twice than to get 40 people to do it once.

The primary disadvantage of related-measures designs is that there may be either an **order effect** or a **carry-over effect** from one session to the next, or the first measurement may influence the treatment itself though processes such as sensitization. For example, if we plan to give a test of knowledge of current events, followed by a crash course in current events, and then follow that with a retest using the same test, it is reasonable to conclude that participants will be more familiar with the items the second time around and may even have looked up answers during the interval between the two administrations. Similarly, in drug studies the effects of the first drug may not have worn off by the next test session. A common problem with related-measures designs arises when a pretest "tips off" subjects as to the purpose of the intervention. For example, a pretest on attitudes toward breast-feeding might make you a wee bit suspicious when a stranger sits down beside you the next day and just happens to launch into a speech on the virtues of breast-feeding. Whenever you have concerns that carry-over effects could contaminate your study or that treatment effects might be influenced by pretreatment measures, a related-measures design is *not* recommended. There are techniques for controlling, though not eliminating, order and carry-over effects, but we will not discuss them here. Would you anticipate that either of these effects might influence the data on the moon illusion or the anorexia data? If so, how might we control for such effects?

Definition    **Order effect:** The effect on performance attributable to the order in which treatments were administered.

**Carry-over effect:** The effect of previous trials (conditions) on a participant's performance on subsequent trials.

## 13.5   How Large an Effect Have We Found?

In Chapter 12 I discussed the fact that there has been a trend within psychology and other disciplines to go beyond plain statistical significance  and report something about the meaningful difference of any effect that was found. As I said there, if we use enough participants, we can almost always find even a meaningless difference to be significant. I introduced Jacob Cohen's concept of effect size, by which he meant a statistic that gave a meaningful indication of how large a mean was, or how different two means were.  If you looked at the answer to Exercise 12.13 that I gave on the Web site, you will have seen that I stated that using the standard deviation of gain scores did not result in a very meaningful measure, although it is a good way to scale other kinds of outcome variables. The example we have in front of us is very similar to the study in Exercise 12.13 except that we have the pre- and postscores as well as the gains. The presence of the pretreatment scores offers us a chance to come up with more than one useful measure.

The data on treatment of anorexia offer a good example of a situation in which there are multiple ways to report on the difference in terms that people will understand. All of us step onto a scale occasionally, and we have some general idea what it means to gain or lose five or ten pounds. So for Everitt's data, we might simply report that the difference was significant ($t = 4.18$, $p < .05$) and that girls gained an average of 7.26 pounds. For girls who started out weighing, on average, 83 pounds, that is a substantial gain. In fact, it might make sense to convert pounds gained to a percentage, and say that the girls increased their weight by $7.26/83.23 = 9\%$.

An alternative measure would be to report the gain in standard deviation units. This idea goes back to Cohen, who originally formulated the problem in terms of a parameter $(d)$, where

$$d = \frac{\mu_1 - \mu_2}{\sigma}$$

In this equation, for the general case, the numerator is the difference between two population means, and the denominator is the standard deviation of either population. We can modify that slightly to let the numerator be the mean gain ($\mu_{After} - \mu_{Before}$), and the denominator the population standard deviation of the pretreatment weights. To put this in terms of statistics rather than parameters, we can substitute sample means and standard deviations instead of population values. This leaves us with

$$\hat{d} = \frac{\overline{X}_1 - \overline{X}_2}{s_{X_1}} = \frac{90.49 - 83.23}{5.02} = \frac{7.26}{5.02} = 1.45$$

I have put a "hat" over the $d$ to indicate that we are calculating an estimate of $d$, and I have put the standard deviation of the pretreatment scores in the denominator. Our estimate tells us that, on average, the girls involved in family therapy gained nearly one and a half standard deviations of pretreatment weights over the course of therapy. Often the standard deviation of the *difference scores* is not very useful because it doesn't carry much meaning. But the standard deviation of the pretest scores is meaningful because it is in the units of our original measurements. We can imagine the distribution of pretest scores (which had a mean at 83.23) and then mentally mark off 1.45 standard deviations above the mean. That is where the mean ended up for the posttest scores, and that is quite a difference. This situation is shown in the Figure 13.2.

In this particular example it might be easier to deal with the mean weight gain, rather than $d$, simply because people know something meaningful about weight. However, if this experiment had measured the girls' self-esteem, rather than weight, I would not know what to think if you said that they gained 7.26 self-esteem points. That scale means nothing to me. I would be impressed, however, if you said that they gained more than a standard deviation in self-esteem.

The preceding paragraph will probably leave you somewhat unsatisfied, because it is far more comfortable to be taught a simple rule that says "use this statistic is this situation." On the other hand, the argument put forth here is to "use whatever statistic your readers will find more meaningful." That degree of flexibility has its own kind of comfort. As a general rule of thumb, if you have one set of scores that are not a set of differences, the standard deviation of those scores is an appropriate denominator. If, however, your set of scores are gain or difference scores, the standard deviation of the pretreatment data is often a more meaningful denominator.

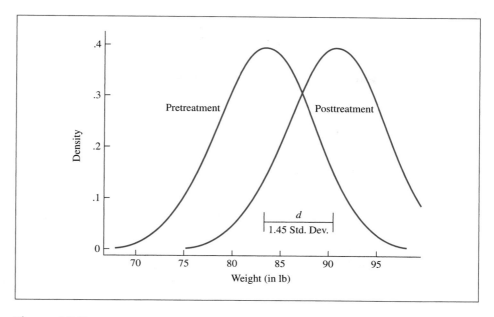

**Figure 13.2**
Schematic diagram illustrating the amount of change from pretreatment to posttreatment weights and our estimate of $d$

## 13.6 Confidence Limits on Changes

Now I am probably going to confuse the situation even more by discussing the use of confidence limits for situations in which we have two related samples. As you should recall, a confidence interval for a mean is generically written as

$$CI_{.95} = \overline{X} \pm t_{.05}(s_{\overline{X}}) = \overline{X} \pm t_{.05}(s/\sqrt{N})$$

The questions that arise concern the mean and the standard deviation that we insert in that equation to handle related samples. The general answer is that the mean is the difference between the two related means (often the difference between a pretest mean and a posttest mean). The standard deviation is the standard deviation of the *difference scores.* You are probably going to complain that this isn't what I used in estimating $d$, but I am not estimating $d$ here, I am deriving a confidence interval, and that is quite a different thing. In the former case I was trying to give you an indication of how far the girls in this study had come in putting on weight. With confidence limits I am trying to establish an interval with a known probability of bracketing the true average weight gain.

For our anorexia example the mean weight gain was 7.26 pounds. The standard deviation of that set of gain scores was 7.16. Thus the confidence limits on mean gain in the population would be

$$CI_{.95} = \overline{X} \pm t_{.05}(s/\sqrt{N}) = 7.26 \pm 2.11(7.16/\sqrt{17}) = 7.26 \pm 3.66$$

$$3.6 \leq \mu \leq 10.92$$

The probability is .95 that an interval computed in this way includes the population mean gain. That result is in line with the statistically significant $t$ test we computed earlier.

## 13.7 Using SPSS for $t$ Tests on Related Samples

Figure 13.3 is the printout of an SPSS computation of a $t$ test on two related samples. The data in this example are those we have already seen on weight gain under family therapy. The data collected in the Before and After conditions are

**Paired Samples Statistics**

| | | Mean | N | Std. Deviation | Std. Error Mean |
|---|---|---|---|---|---|
| Pair 1 | BEFORE | 83.2294 | 17 | 5.01669 | 1.21673 |
| | AFTER | 90.4941 | 17 | 8.47507 | 2.05551 |

**Paired Samples Correlations**

| | | N | Correlation | Sig. |
|---|---|---|---|---|
| Pair 1 | BEFORE & AFTER | 17 | .538 | .026 |

**Paired Samples Test**

| | Paired Differences | | | | | | | |
|---|---|---|---|---|---|---|---|---|
| | | | | 95% Confidence Interval of the Difference | | | | |
| | Mean | Std. Deviation | Std. Error Mean | Lower | Upper | $t$ | df | Sig. (2-tailed) |
| Pair 1 BEFORE -AFTER | −7.2647 | 7.15742 | 1.73593 | −10.9447 | −3.5847 | −4.185 | 16 | .001 |

**Figure 13.3**
SPSS analysis of $t$ test on related samples

entered as two separate variables, and a paired $t$ test is requested. The first part of the printout gives basic descriptive statistics. This is followed by the correlation between the two variables, and a $t$ test on the significance of the correlation. Following this is a related-samples $t$ test on the differences between the means. Notice that the $t$ value ($-4.185$) agrees with the result computed by hand, except that SPSS subtracted After from Before and came up with a negative difference, and thus a negative $t$. The sign here is irrelevant, and depends merely on how you choose to calculate the difference scores. These results agree with the results we computed by hand.

## 13.8 Writing Up the Results

To write up the results of the results of Everitt's study of family therapy for anorexia, we need to briefly describe the procedure to give a context. We then should mention the means before and after therapy and the resulting $t$ test. We also need to include some measure of effect size (perhaps more than one) and draw some conclusions.

Everitt (1994 in Hand) reported on a study of the effects of family therapy as a treatment for 17 anorexic girls. Girls were weighed before and after several weeks' involvement in family therapy. The mean pretreatment weight was 83.23 pounds and the posttreatment weight was 90.49 pounds, for a mean gain of 7.26 pounds. This difference was statistically significant ($t(16) = 4.18$, $p < .05$). Other data in this study suggest that the gain can not simply be attributed to normal growth over time. The effect size estimate ($\hat{d}$) based on the pretreatment standard deviation was 1.45, indicating a gain of nearly one and a half standard deviations from pretreatment weight. In addition, the 95% confidence interval for weight gain was $3.6 \le \mu \le 10.92$, indicating that family therapy has the potential of leading to a noticeable change in weight.

## 13.9 Summary

In this chapter we considered the analysis of data involving two related samples. You saw that the data easily can be reduced to one set of difference scores and that the standard one-sample $t$ test can be applied to those difference scores to test the null hypothesis that the mean of the differences does not deviate from zero more than would be predicted by chance. We then examined the strengths and weaknesses of experimental designs using related-measures designs, followed by a discussion of the size of an effect and the decisions to be made when computing $\hat{d}$ and confidence intervals. Finally, you saw how to use SPSS to perform *t* tests for related samples.

Some important terms in this chapter are

| | |
|---|---|
| Related samples, *310* | Order effect, *317* |
| Repeated measures, *310* | Carry-over effect, *317* |
| Matched samples, *310* | |
| Difference scores (gain scores), *313* | |

## 13.10 Exercises

**13.1** Hout, Duncan, and Sobel (1987) reported on the relative sexual satisfaction of married couples. They asked each member of 91 married couples to rate the degree to which they agreed with "Sex is fun for me and my partner" on a four-point scale ranging from "never or occasionally" to "almost always." The data appear below (I know it's a lot of data, but it's an interesting question):

```
Husband   1   1   1   1   1   1   1   1   1   1   1   1   1   1   1
Wife      1   1   1   1   1   1   1   2   2   2   2   2   2   2   3

Husband   1   1   1   1   2   2   2   2   2   2   2   2   2   2   2
Wife      3   4   4   4   1   1   2   2   2   2   2   2   2   2   3

Husband   2   2   2   2   2   2   2   2   2   3   3   3   3   3   3
Wife      3   3   4   4   4   4   4   4   4   1   2   2   2   2   2

Husband   3   3   3   3   3   3   3   3   3   3   3   3   3   4   4
Wife      3   3   3   3   4   4   4   4   4   4   4   4   4   1   1

Husband   4   4   4   4   4   4   4   4   4   4   4   4   4   4   4
Wife      2   2   2   2   2   2   2   3   3   3   3   3   3   3   3

Husband   4   4   4   4   4   4   4   4   4   4   4   4   4   4   4   4
Wife      3   3   4   4   4   4   4   4   4   4   4   4   4   4   4   4
```

Start out by running a matched-sample *t* test on these data. Why is a matched-sample test appropriate?

**13.2** In the study referred to in Exercise 13.1, what, if anything does your answer to that question tell us about whether couples are sexually compatible? What do we know from this analysis, and what don't we know?

**13.3** For the data in Exercise 13.1, create a scatterplot and calculate the correlation between husband's and wife's sexual satisfaction. How does this amplify what we have learned from the analysis in Exercise 13.1?

**13.4** Use techniques developed in Chapter 12 to construct 95% confidence limits on the true mean difference between the sexual satisfaction scores in Exercise 13.1.

**13.5** Some would object that the data in Exercise 13.1 are clearly discrete, if not ordinal, and that it is inappropriate to run a *t* test on them. Can you think of a counter argument? (This is not an easy question, and I really asked it mostly to make the point that there could be controversy here.)

**13.6** Hoaglin, Mosteller, and Tukey (1983) present data on blood levels of beta-endorphin as a function of stress. They took beta-endorphin levels for 19 patients 12 hours before surgery, and again 10 minutes before surgery. The data are presented below, in fmol/ml:

| Subject | 12 Hours Before | 10 Minutes Before |
|---------|-----------------|-------------------|
| 1 | 10.0 | 6.5 |
| 2 | 6.5 | 14.0 |
| 3 | 8.0 | 13.5 |
| 4 | 12.0 | 18.0 |
| 5 | 5.0 | 14.5 |
| 6 | 11.5 | 9.0 |
| 7 | 5.0 | 18.0 |
| 8 | 3.5 | 42.0 |
| 9 | 7.5 | 7.5 |
| 10 | 5.8 | 6.0 |
| 11 | 4.7 | 25.0 |
| 12 | 8.0 | 12.0 |
| 13 | 7.0 | 52.0 |
| 14 | 17.0 | 20.0 |
| 15 | 8.8 | 16.0 |
| 16 | 17.0 | 15.0 |
| 17 | 15.0 | 11.5 |
| 18 | 4.4 | 2.5 |
| 19 | 2.0 | 2.0 |

Based on these data, what effect does increased stress have on endorphin levels?

**13.7** Why would you use a paired *t* test in Exercise 13.6?

**13.8** Create a scatterplot of the data in Exercise 13.6, and compute the correlation between the two sets of scores. What does this say that is relevant to the answer to Exercise 13.7?

**13.9** We always need to look closely at our data. Sometimes we find things that are hard to explain. Look closely at the data in Exercise 13.6; what attracts your attention?

**13.10** Compute a measure of effect size for the data in Exercise 13.6, and indicate what this measure indicates.

**13.11** Give an example of an experiment in which using related samples would be ill-advised because of carry-over effects.

**13.12** Using the data for the first 20 subjects in the dataset on attention deficit disorder (Add.dat), test the hypothesis that English grades are generally higher than the overall GPA.

**13.13**  Assume that the mean and the standard deviation of the difference scores in Exercise 13.6 would remain the same if we added more subjects. How many subjects would we need to obtain a $t$ that is significant at $\alpha = .01$ (two-tailed)? (The difference was significant at $\alpha = .05$, but not at $\alpha = .01$.) (We will return to this general problem in Chapter 15.)

**13.14**  Modify the data in Exercise 13.6 by shifting the entries in the "12 Hour" column so as to increase the relationship between the two variables. Run a $t$ test on the modified data and notice the effect on $t$. (You could never do this with real data, because paired scores must be kept together, but doing so here reveals the important role played by the relationship between variables.)

**13.15**  Using your answer to Exercise 13.14 and your knowledge about correlation, how would you expect the degree of correlation between two variables (sets of data) to affect the magnitude of the $t$ test between them?

**13.16**  In Section 13.4 I explained that by removing subject-to-subject variability from the data, related-samples designs prevent this variability from influencing the data on which the $t$ test is run. This increases our ability to reject a false null hypothesis. Explain in your own words why this is so.

**13.17**  In Section 13.3 I discussed a second test of the Holway and Boring (1940) experiment using a one-sample $t$ test on the "eyes-level" condition. Run this $t$ test and draw the appropriate conclusions.

**13.18**  If there were reason to believe that carry-over effects could influence the data on the moon illusion referred to in Section 13.3, how might we control such effects?

**13.19**  In the anorexia example in Section 13.2 I subtracted the After scores from the Before scores. What would have happened if I had done that the other way around?

**13.20**  What would happen if we took the data from the anorexia example in Table 13.1 and reexpressed the dependent variable in kilograms instead of pounds?

**13.21**  Many mothers experience a sense of depression shortly after the birth of a child. Design a study to examine "postpartum depression" and tell how you would estimate the mean increase in depression.

# 14

## Hypothesis Tests Applied to Means: Two Independent Samples

**QUESTIONS**

- Why should it make any difference if data come from the same person or different people?

- If we have two different groups, what assumptions do I have to make before I can run a *t* test on their means?

- How do I change my *t* test to compare two independent sample means?

- What about confidence limits on differences between means?

- I hope I don't have to do all of this by hand. What about computer software?

In Chapter 13 we considered a study in which we obtained a set of weights from anorexic girls before and after a family therapy intervention. In that example the *same* participants were observed both before and after the intervention. While that was a good way to evaluate the effects of the intervention program, in a great many experiments it is either impossible or undesirable to obtain data using repeated measurements of the same participants. For example, if we want to determine if males are more socially inept than females, it clearly would be impossible to test the same people as males and then as females. Instead we would need a sample of males and a second, *independent* sample of females.

One of the most common uses of the *t* test involves testing the difference between the means of two independent groups. We might want to compare the mean number of trials needed to reach some criterion in a simple visual discrimination task for two groups of rats—one raised under normal conditions and one raised under conditions of sensory deprivation. Or in a memory study we might want to compare levels of retention for a group of college students asked to recall active declarative sentences and a group asked to recall passive negative sentences. As a final example, we might place participants in a situation in which another person needed help. We could compare the mean latency of helping behavior when participants were tested alone and when they were tested in groups.

In conducting any experiment with two independent groups, we will almost always find that the two sample means differed by at least a small amount. The important question, however, is whether that difference is sufficiently large to justify the conclusion that the two samples were drawn from different populations—for example, using the case of helping behavior, is the mean of the population of latencies from singly tested participants different from the mean of the population of latencies from group-tested participants? Before we consider a specific example, we will need to examine the sampling distribution of differences between means and the *t* test that results from that sampling distribution. What we are doing here is analogous to what we did in Chapter 12 when speaking of the mean of one sample.

## 14.1 Distribution of Differences Between Means

When we are interested in testing for a difference between the mean of one population ($\mu_1$) and the mean of a second population ($\mu_2$), we will be testing a null hypothesis of the form $H_0: \mu_1 - \mu_2 = 0$ or, equivalently, $\mu_1 = \mu_2$. Because the test of this null hypothesis involves the difference between independent sample means, it is important to digress for a moment and examine the **sampling distribution of differences between means.** Suppose we have two populations labeled $X_1$ and $X_2$ with means $\mu_1$ and $\mu_2$ and variances $\sigma_1^2$ and $\sigma_2^2$. We now draw pairs of samples of size $n_1$ from population $X_1$ and of size $n_2$ from population $X_2$ and record the means and the differences between the means for each pair of samples. (I have gone from denoting sample sizes with capital Ns to lower case ns because, when I have multiple samples, I will use N to refer to *the total number of scores in all samples*, and n with a subscript to refer to the *number of observations in that group or sample*.) Because we are sampling independently from each population, the sample means will be independent. (Means are paired only in the trivial and irrelevant sense of being drawn at the same time.) Because we are only supposing, we might as well go all the way and suppose that we repeated this procedure an infinite number of times. The results are presented schematically in Figure 14.1. In the lower portion of this figure the first two columns represent the sampling distributions of $\overline{X}_1$ and $\overline{X}_2$, and the third column represents the sampling distribution of differences in means ($\overline{X}_1 - \overline{X}_2$). It is this third column in which we are most interested, because we are concerned with testing

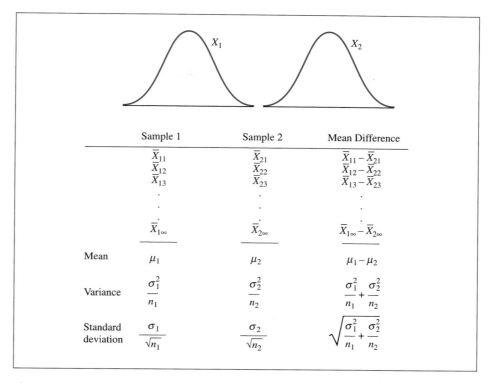

**Figure 14.1**
Hypothetical set of means and differences between means when sampling from two populations

differences between means. The mean of this distribution can be shown to equal $\mu_1 - \mu_2$. The variance of this distribution is given by what is commonly called the **Variance Sum Law**, a limited form of which states

> The variance of the sum or difference of two *independent* variables is equal to the sum of their variances.[1]

Definition    **Sampling distribution of differences between means:** The distribution of the differences between means over repeated sampling from the same population(s).

**Variance Sum Law:** The rule giving the variance of the sum (or difference) of two or more variables.

---

[1]The complete form of the law omits the restriction that the variables must be independent and states that the variance of their sum or difference is

$$\sigma^2_{X_1 \pm X_2} = \sigma^2_{X_1} + \sigma^2_{X_2} \pm 2\rho\sigma_{X_1}\sigma_{X_2}$$

where $\rho$ is the correlation coefficient in the population between $X_1$ and $X_2$. The minus signs apply when considering differences.

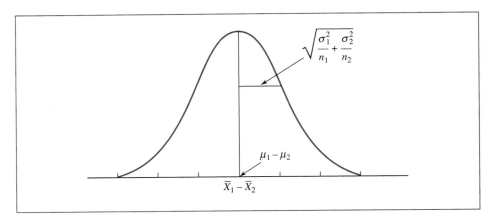

**Figure 14.2**
Sampling distribution of differences between means

We know from the Central Limit Theorem that the variance of the distribution of $\overline{X}_1$ is $\sigma_1^2/n_1$ and the variance of the distribution of $\overline{X}_2$ is $\sigma_2^2/n_2$. Because the variables (sample means) are independent, the variance of the difference of these two variables is the sum of their variances. Thus

$$\sigma^2_{\overline{X}_1 \pm \overline{X}_2} = \sigma^2_{\overline{X}_1} + \sigma^2_{\overline{X}_2} = \frac{\sigma_1^2}{n_1} + \frac{\sigma_2^2}{n_2}$$

Having found the mean and the variance of a set of differences between means, we know most of what we need to know to test a hypothesis about differences between means. The general form of the sampling distribution of mean differences is presented in Figure 14.2.

The final point to be made about this distribution concerns its shape. An important theorem in statistics states that the sum or difference of two independent normally distributed variables is itself normally distributed. Because Figure 14.2 represents the difference between two sampling distributions of means, and because we know the sampling distribution of means is at least approximately normal for reasonable sample sizes, then the distribution in Figure 14.2 must itself be at least approximately normal.

## The *t* Statistic

Given the information we now have about the sampling distribution of differences between means, we can proceed to develop the appropriate test procedure. Assume *for the moment* that knowledge of the population variances ($\sigma_1^2$ and $\sigma_2^2$) is not a problem. We have earlier defined $z$ as a statistic (a point on the distribution) minus the mean of the distribution, divided by the standard error of the distribution. Our statistic in the present case is $(\overline{X}_1 - \overline{X}_2)$, the observed difference between the sample means. The mean of the sampling distribution is $(\mu_1 - \mu_2)$, and, as we saw, the **standard error of differences between means** is

$$\sigma_{\overline{X}_1 \pm \overline{X}_2} = \sqrt{\frac{\sigma_1^2}{n_1} + \frac{\sigma_2^2}{n_2}}$$

Remember, the standard error of any statistic (in this case the difference between two sample means) is the standard deviation of the sampling distribution of that statistic. As such it is a measure of how stable we expect that statistic to be.

Given what we know, we can write

$$z = \frac{(\overline{X}_1 - \overline{X}_2) - (\mu_1 - \mu_2)}{\sigma_{\overline{X}_1 - \overline{X}_2}}$$

$$= \frac{(\overline{X}_1 - \overline{X}_2) - (\mu_1 - \mu_2)}{\sqrt{\frac{\sigma_1^2}{n_1} + \frac{\sigma_2^2}{n_2}}}$$

The critical value for $\alpha = .05$ is $z = \pm 1.96$, as it was for the one-sample tests discussed in Chapter 12.

---

Definition   **Standard error of differences between means:** The standard deviation of the sampling distribution of the differences between means.

---

The preceding formula is not particularly useful, except for the purpose of showing the origin of the appropriate $t$ test, because we rarely know the necessary population variances. (Such knowledge is so rare that it isn't even worth imagining cases in which we would have it, although a few do exist.) However, just as we did in the one-sample case, we can circumvent this problem by using the sample variances as estimates of the population variances. For the same reasons discussed earlier for the one-sample $t$, this means that the result will be distributed as $t$ rather than $z$.

$$t = \frac{(\overline{X}_1 - \overline{X}_2) - (\mu_1 - \mu_2)}{s_{\overline{X}_1 - \overline{X}_2}}$$

$$= \frac{(\overline{X}_1 - \overline{X}_2) - (\mu_1 - \mu_2)}{\sqrt{\frac{s_1^2}{n_1} + \frac{s_2^2}{n_2}}}$$

Because the null hypothesis is generally the hypothesis that $\mu_1 - \mu_2 = 0$, we usually drop that term from the equation and write

$$t = \frac{(\overline{X}_1 - \overline{X}_2)}{s_{\overline{X}_1 - \overline{X}_2}}$$

$$= \frac{(\overline{X}_1 - \overline{X}_2)}{\sqrt{\frac{s_1^2}{n_1} + \frac{s_2^2}{n_2}}}$$

## Pooling Variances

We are almost there, but just a little more elaboration. Although the equation for $t$ that we just developed is quite appropriate when the sample sizes are equal, it can be improved with some modification for unequal sample sizes. This modification is designed to provide a better estimate of the population variance. One of the assumptions required for the use of $t$ for two independent samples is that $\sigma_1^2 = \sigma_2^2$ (i.e., the samples come from populations with equal variances), regardless of the truth or falsity of $H_0$. Such an assumption is often a reasonable one and is called the assumption of **homogeneity of variance**. We often begin an experiment with two groups of participants who are equivalent and then do something to one (or both) group(s) that will raise or lower the participants' scores. In such a case it often makes sense to assume that the variances will remain unaffected. (You should recall that adding or subtracting a constant to a set of scores has no effect on its variance.) Because the population variances are assumed to be equal, this common variance can be represented by the symbol $\sigma^2$, without a subscript.

---

**Definition**

**Homogeneity of variance:** The situation in which two or more populations have equal variances.

**Weighted average:** The mean of the form $(a_1 X_1 + a_2 X_2)/(a_1 + a_2)$, where $a_1$ and $a_2$ are weighting factors and $X_1$ and $X_2$ are the values to be averaged.

**Pooled variance:** A weighted average of separate sample variances.

---

In our data we have two estimates of $\sigma^2$, namely $s_1^2$ and $s_2^2$. It seems appropriate to obtain some sort of an average of $s_1^2$ and $s_2^2$ on the grounds that this average should be a better estimate of $\sigma^2$ than either of the two separate estimates. We do not want to take the simple arithmetic mean, however, because doing so would give equal weight to the two estimates, even if one were based on considerably more observations. What we want is a **weighted average**, in which the sample variances are weighted by their degrees of freedom $(n_i - 1)$. If we call this new estimate $s_p^2$ then

$$s_p^2 = \frac{(n_1 - 1)s_1^2 + (n_2 - 1)s_2^2}{n_1 + n_2 - 2}$$

The numerator represents the sum of the variances, each weighted by its degrees of freedom, and the denominator represents the sum of the weights or, equivalently, the degrees of freedom for $s_p^2$.

The weighted average of the two sample variances is usually referred to as a **pooled variance** estimate (a rather inelegant name, but reasonably descriptive). Having defined our pooled estimate $(s_p^2)$, we can now replace $s_i^2$ with $s_p^2$ to get

$$t = \frac{\overline{X}_1 - \overline{X}_2}{s_{\overline{X}_1 - \overline{X}_2}} = \frac{\overline{X}_1 - \overline{X}_2}{\sqrt{\dfrac{s_p^2}{n_1} + \dfrac{s_p^2}{n_2}}} = \frac{\overline{X}_1 - \overline{X}_2}{\sqrt{s_p^2 \left(\dfrac{1}{n_1} + \dfrac{1}{n_2}\right)}}$$

Notice that both this formula for $t$ and the one we used in the previous section involve dividing the difference between the sample means by an estimate of the standard error of the difference between means. The only difference concerns the way in which this standard error is estimated. When sample sizes are equal, it makes absolutely no difference whether you pool variances; the resulting $t$ will be the same. When the sample sizes are unequal, however, pooling can make an important difference.

## Degrees of Freedom for $t$

$$0 \quad P = n_1 + n_2 - 2$$

You know that two sample variances ($s_1^2$ and $s_2^2$) have gone into calculating $t$. Each of these variances is based on squared deviations about their corresponding sample means; therefore, each sample variance has $n_i - 1$ $df$. Across the two samples, therefore, we will have $(n_1 - 1) + (n_2 - 1) = n_1 + n_2 - 2$ $df$. Thus the $t$ for two independent samples will be based on $n_1 + n_2 - 2$ degrees of freedom.

## Let's Stop to Review

We have just covered unusually more formulae, with somewhat more emphasis on derivation, than you have seen previously in this book. It might be smart to stop and say something about what all of that is for. It isn't as messy and cumbersome as it looks.

I started out by saying that if I want to know whether the means of two independent samples are significantly different, I need to know something about what differences between two means look like. In other words, I need to know the sampling distribution of differences between means. Such a distribution would have a mean equal to the difference between the population means and would have a standard error equal to the square root of the sum of the population variances, each divided by the corresponding sample size. Such a distribution would be at least approximately normal.

At this point I know the mean, the standard error, and the shape of the sampling distribution of differences between means. If I knew the population variances, I could now compute a $z$ score as the difference in sample means, minus the difference in population means, divided by the standard error. This is the same kind of $z$ score we have been seeing all along.

This formula is not adequate by itself because it assumes we know the population variances, which we don't. So we do the same thing we did for earlier $t$ tests—we substitute the sample variances for the population variances and call the result $t$.

Finally, when you have two sample variances, you usually want to average them to get a better estimate of the population variance. We call this averaging "pooling." We use the pooled version whenever the sample variances are in general agreement with one another, especially when sample sizes are about equal.

You should stop at this point and go back through the last few pages to see how the review I just gave you fits with the formulae we've covered so far in this chapter.

EXAMPLE:
We Haven't
Finished with
Anorexia

To illustrate the use of $t$ as a test of the difference between two independent means, let's undertake a different analysis of some of Everitt's data (Everitt, in Hand et al., 1994) on the treatment of anorexia. In Chapter 13 I pointed out that the change of means doesn't necessarily imply that the difference is due to the family therapy intervention. Perhaps the girls just gained weight because they got older and taller. One way to control for this is to look at the amount of weight gained by the Family Therapy group in contrast with the amount gained by girls in a Control group, who received no therapy. If the only reason girls are gaining weight is because they are getting older and taller, that should affect both groups equally. If weight gain is due to therapy, only the therapy group would be expected to gain. Fortunately, Everitt provided us with data on the control group as well. The data are shown in Table 14.1, although I am presenting only the amount gained, not the amounts before and after treatment.

Before we consider any statistical test—and ideally even before the data are collected—we must specify several features of the test. First, we must specify the null and alternative hypotheses:

$$H_0: \mu_{FT} = \mu_C$$
$$H_1: \mu_{FT} \neq \mu_C$$

**Table 14.1**
Weight Gain in the Family Therapy and Control Groups

| Control | Control | Family Therapy | Family Therapy |
|---|---|---|---|
| −.5 | 3.3 | 11.4 | 9.0 |
| −9.3 | 11.3 | 11.0 | 3.9 |
| −5.4 | .0 | 5.5 | 5.7 |
| 12.3 | −1.0 | 9.4 | 10.7 |
| −2.0 | −10.6 | 13.6 | |
| −10.2 | −4.6 | −2.9 | |
| −12.2 | −6.7 | −.1 | |
| 11.6 | 2.8 | 7.4 | |
| −7.1 | .3 | 21.5 | |
| 6.2 | 1.8 | −5.3 | |
| −.2 | 3.7 | −3.8 | |
| −9.2 | 15.9 | 13.4 | |
| 8.3 | −10.2 | 13.1 | |
| Mean | −.45 | | 7.26 |
| Std. Dev. | 7.99 | | 7.16 |
| Variance | 63.82 | | 51.23 |

(Here I am using the abbreviation of the group labels [FT = Family Therapy, C = Control] as the subscripts.) The alternative hypothesis is bidirectional (we will reject $H_0$ if $\mu_{FT} < \mu_C$ or if $\mu_{FT} > \mu_C$; thus we are using a two-tailed test. For the sake of consistency with other examples in this book, we will let $\alpha = .05$. It is important to keep in mind that there is nothing particularly sacred about these two decisions.[2]) Given the null hypothesis as stated, we can now calculate $t$:

$$t = \frac{\overline{X}_1 - \overline{X}_2}{s_{\overline{X}_1 - \overline{X}_2}} = \frac{\overline{X}_1 - \overline{X}_2}{\sqrt{\dfrac{s_1^2}{n_1} + \dfrac{s_2^2}{n_2}}}$$

Because we are testing $H_0$: $\mu_{FT} - \mu_C = 0$, the $\mu_{FT} - \mu_C$ term has been dropped from the equation. When we pool the variances, we obtain

$$s_p^2 = \frac{(n_1 - 1)s_1^2 + (n_2 - 1)s_2^2}{n_1 + n_2 - 2}$$

$$= \frac{25(63.82) + 16(51.23)}{26 + 17 - 2} = \frac{1595.50 + 819.68}{41} = \frac{2415.18}{41} = 58.907$$

Note that the pooled variance is somewhat closer in value to $s_1^2$ than $s_2^2$ because of the greater weight given $s_1^2$ in the formula due to the larger sample size. Then

$$t = \frac{\overline{X}_1 - \overline{X}_2}{\sqrt{\dfrac{s_p^2}{n_1} + \dfrac{s_p^2}{n_2}}} = \frac{\overline{X}_1 - \overline{X}_2}{\sqrt{s_p^2\left(\dfrac{1}{n_1} + \dfrac{1}{n_2}\right)}} = \frac{-.45 - 7.26}{\sqrt{58.907\left(\dfrac{1}{26} + \dfrac{1}{17}\right)}}$$

$$= \frac{-7.71}{\sqrt{5.731}} = \frac{-7.71}{2.394} = -3.22$$

For this example we have $(n_1 - 1) = 25$ $df$ for Group C and $(n_2 - 1) = 16$ $df$ for Group FT, making a total of $n_1 - 1 + n_2 - 1 = 41$ $df$. From the sampling distribution of $t$ in Table D.6 in Appendix D, $t_{.05}(41) = \pm 2.021$ (approximately). Because the obtained value of $t$ (i.e., $t_{obt}$) far exceeds $t_\alpha$, we will reject $H_0$ (at $\alpha = .05$, two-tailed) and conclude that there is a difference between the means of the populations from which our observations were drawn. In other words, we will conclude (statistically) that $\mu_{FT} \neq \mu_C$ and (practically) that $\mu_{FT} > \mu_C$. In terms of the experimental variables, anorexic

---

[2]If we had a good reason for testing the hypothesis that $\mu_{FT}$ was five points higher than $\mu_C$, for example, we could set $H_0$: $\mu_{FT} - \mu_C = 5$, although this type of situation is extremely rare. Similarly, we could set $\alpha$ at .01, .001, or even .10, although this last value is higher than most people would accept.

girls provided with family therapy gain significantly more weight than a control group provided with no therapy.[3]  ■

## 14.2 Heterogeneity of Variance

As we have seen, one of the assumptions behind the $t$ test for two independent samples is the assumption of homogeneity of variance ($\sigma_1^2 = \sigma_2^2$). When this assumption does not hold (i.e., when $\sigma_1^2 \neq \sigma_2^2$), we have what is called **heterogeneity of variance**. Considerable work has been done examining the practical effect of heterogeneity of variance on the $t$ test. As a result of this work we can come to some general conclusions about the kind of analysis that is appropriate with heterogeneous variances.

Definition | **Heterogeneity of variance:** A situation in which samples are drawn from populations having different variances.

The first point to keep in mind is that our homogeneity assumption refers to population variances and not to sample variances—we would expect the sample variances to be equal only rarely even if the population variances were equal. On the basis of sampling studies that have been conducted, the general rule of thumb is that if one sample variance is no more than four[4] times the other *and* if the sample sizes are equal or approximately equal, you may go ahead and compute $t$ as you would normally. Heterogeneity of variance is not likely to have a serious effect on your results under these conditions. On the other hand, if one sample variance is more than four times the other, or if the variances are quite unequal and the sample sizes are also quite unequal, then an alternative procedure may be necessary. This procedure is easy to apply, however. Simply compute $t$ using the *separate* variance estimates (i.e., do not pool). Then go to the $t$ tables using the *smaller* of $n_1 - 1$ and $n_2 - 1$ as the degrees of freedom (rather than $n_1 + n_2 - 2$). This is a conservative test, meaning that if $H_0$ is true, you are less likely to commit a Type I error than the nominal value of $\alpha$ would suggest. As an example of this procedure, suppose

---

[3]Because the Family Therapy group presumably differed from the Control group only because of the presence or absence of therapy, our conclusions can be made with respect to the effects of therapy. If the groups had also differed with regard to some other dimension, e.g., the prior weight of the participants, then the results would be unclear, and therapy would be **confounded** with prior weight.

Definition | **Confounded:** Two variables are said to be confounded when they are varied simultaneously and their effects cannot be separated.

[4]The use of the number four here is probably conservative. Some people would argue for using the standard approach when variances are considerably more different than this—as long as the sample sizes are roughly equal.

we have the following data:

$$\overline{X}_1 = 111.53 \qquad \overline{X}_2 = 108.38$$

$$s_1^2 = 19.65 \qquad s_2^2 = 3.06$$

$$n_1 = 10 \qquad n_2 = 18$$

$$t = \frac{\overline{X}_1 - \overline{X}_2}{\sqrt{\dfrac{s_1^2}{n_1} + \dfrac{s_2^2}{n_2}}} = \frac{111.53 - 108.38}{\sqrt{\dfrac{19.65}{10} + \dfrac{3.06}{18}}} = \frac{3.15}{1.461} = 2.16$$

Because the variances were very unequal (one was more than six times the other), we did not pool them. The values of $n_1 - 1$ and $n_2 - 1$ are 9 and 17, respectively, and we will evaluate $t$ by going to Table D.6 with 9 $df$ (the smaller of 9 and 17). Here we find that $t_{.05}(9) = \pm 2.262$, which is larger than the obtained value. Thus we will not reject $H_0$.[5]   $p \approx .05$

There are more accurate (less conservative) solutions to the problem of heterogeneity of variance, which rely on calculating adjusted degrees of freedom lying between the smaller of $n_1 - 1$ and $n_2 - 1$, on the one hand, and $n_1 + n_2 - 2$ on the other. Many computer programs, including SPSS, supply such an adjustment. For most purposes the conservative approach suggested here is sufficient. (A more complete discussion of the problem of heterogeneity of variance can be found in Howell, 2007.)

## 14.3 Nonnormality of Distributions

We saw earlier that another assumption required for the correct use of the $t$ test is the assumption that the population(s) from which the data are sampled is (are) normally distributed—or at least that the sampling distribution of differences between means is normal. In general, as long as the distributions of sample data are roughly mound-shaped (high in the center and tapering off on either side), the test is likely to be valid. This is especially true for large samples ($n_1$ and $n_2$ greater than 30), because then the Central Limit Theorem almost guarantees near normality of the sampling distribution of differences between means.

## 14.4 A Second Example with Two Independent Samples

Adams, Wright, and Lohr (1996) were interested in some basic psychoanalytic theories that homophobia (an irrational fear of, or aversion to, homosexuality or homosexuals) may be unconsciously related to the anxiety of being or

---

[5]Note that if we had not had a problem with heterogeneity of variance, we would have used $n_1 + n_2 - 2 = 26 \ df$, and the difference would have been significant.

becoming homosexual. They administered the Index of Homophobia to 64 heterosexual males and classed them as homophobic or nonhomophobic on the basis of their score. They then exposed homophobic and nonhomophobic heterosexual men to videotapes of sexually explicit erotic stimuli portraying heterosexual and homosexual behavior, and recorded their level of sexual arousal. Adams et al. reasoned that if homophobia were unconsciously related to anxiety about ones own sexuality, homophobic individuals would show greater arousal to the homosexual videos than would nonhomophobic individuals. A copy of the Index of Homophobia can be found at

 http://www.bgsu.edu/downloads/sa/file14259.pdf

In this example we will examine only the data from the homosexual video. (There were no group differences for the heterosexual and lesbian videos.) The data in Table 14.2 were created to have the same means and pooled variance as the data that Adams collected, so our conclusions will be the same as theirs.[6] The dependent variable is degree of arousal at the end of the four-minute video, with larger values indicating greater arousal.

Before we consider any statistical test, and ideally even before the data are collected, we must specify several features of the test. First we must specify the null and alternative hypotheses:

$$H_0: \mu_1 = \mu_2$$
$$H_1: \mu_1 \neq \mu_2$$

The alternative hypothesis is bidirectional (we will reject $H_0$ if $\mu_1 < \mu_2$ or if $\mu_1 > \mu_2$), and thus we will use a two-tailed test. For the sake of consistency

### Table 14.2
Data from Adams et al. on Level of Sexual Arousal in Homophobic and Nonhomophobic Heterosexual Males.

| Homophobic | | | | | | Nonhomophobic | | | | | |
|---|---|---|---|---|---|---|---|---|---|---|---|
| 39.1 | 38.0 | 14.9 | 20.7 | 19.5 | 32.2 | 24.0 | 17.0 | 35.8 | 18.0 | −1.7 | 11.1 |
| 11.0 | 20.7 | 26.4 | 35.7 | 26.4 | 28.8 | 10.1 | 16.1 | −.7 | 14.1 | 25.9 | 23.0 |
| 33.4 | 13.7 | 46.1 | 13.7 | 23.0 | 20.7 | 20.0 | 14.1 | −1.7 | 19.0 | 20.0 | 30.9 |
| 19.5 | 11.4 | 24.1 | 17.2 | 38.0 | 10.3 | 30.9 | 22.0 | 6.2 | 27.9 | 14.1 | 33.8 |
| 35.7 | 41.5 | 18.4 | 36.8 | 54.1 | 11.4 | 26.9 | 5.2 | 13.1 | 19.0 | −15.5 | |
| 8.7 | 23.0 | 14.3 | 5.3 | 6.3 | | | | | | | |
| **Mean** | | 24.00 | | | | **Mean** | | 16.50 | | | |
| **Variance** | | 148.87 | | | | **Variance** | | 139.16 | | | |
| *n* | | 35 | | | | *n* | | 29 | | | |

---

[6]I actually added 12 points to each mean, largely to avoid many negative scores, but it doesn't change the results or the calculations in the slightest.

with other examples in this book, we will let $\alpha = .05$. Given the null hypothesis as stated, we can now calculate $t$:

$$t = \frac{\overline{X}_1 - \overline{X}_2}{s_{\overline{X}_1 - \overline{X}_2}} = \frac{\overline{X}_1 - \overline{X}_2}{\sqrt{\dfrac{s_p^2}{n_1} + \dfrac{s_p^2}{n_2}}}$$

Because we are testing $H_0: \mu_1 - \mu_2 = 0$, the $\mu_1 - \mu_2$ term has been dropped from the equation. We should pool our sample variances because they are so similar that we do not have to worry about heterogeneity of variance. Doing so we obtain

$$s_p^2 = \frac{(n_1 - 1)s_1^2 + (n_2 - 1)s_2^2}{n_1 + n_2 - 2}$$

$$= \frac{34(148.87) + 28(139.16)}{35 + 29 - 2} = 144.48$$

Notice that the pooled variance is slightly closer in value to $s_1^2$ than to $s_2^2$ because of the greater weight given $s_1^2$ in the formula. Then

$$t = \frac{\overline{X}_1 - \overline{X}_2}{\sqrt{\dfrac{s_p^2}{n_1} + \dfrac{s_p^2}{n_2}}} = \frac{24.00 - 16.50}{\sqrt{\dfrac{144.48}{35} + \dfrac{144.48}{29}}} = \frac{7.50}{\sqrt{9.11}} = 2.48$$

For this example we have $n_1 - 1 = 34$ $df$ for the homophobic group and $n_2 - 1 = 28$ $df$ for the nonhomophobic group, making a total of $n_1 - 1 + n_2 - 1 = 62$ $df$. From the sampling distribution of $t$ in Table D.6 in Appendix D, $t_{.025}(62) = \pm 2.003$ (with linear interpolation). Since the value of $t_{obt}$ far exceeds $t_\alpha$, we will reject $H_0$ (at $\alpha = .05$) and conclude that there is a difference between the means of the populations from which our observations were drawn. In other words, we will conclude (statistically) that $\mu_1 \neq \mu_2$ and (practically) that $\mu_1 > \mu_2$. In terms of the experimental variables, homophobic participants show greater arousal to a homosexual video than do nonhomophobic participants.

## 14.5  Effect Size Again

Again we come to the issue of presenting information to our readers that conveys the magnitude of the difference between our groups, beyond the fact that the difference is statistically significant. The example from Adams et al. is a good one for this purpose, because it is a situation in which the actual value of the difference between means is not useful. None of us have any idea whether a difference of 7.5 points in sexual arousal is a large difference or a small one. We need a better measure.

In Chapters 12 and 13 we used a statistic ($\hat{d}$) that represents the size of the difference between means (in raw score units) scaled by the size of the standard deviation. In this case, however, our standard deviation will be the estimated standard deviation of either population. When we had one set of observations we used the standard deviation of those observations. When we had difference scores, we generally used the standard deviation of the pretest scores. Here we have two standard deviations to choose from (one for each group), and we have two choices. If there is a situation where one standard deviation seems to be the obvious one to use, use it. For example, if we have a true control group, its standard deviation seems like a logical choice. If we don't have an obvious control group, we will pool the variances of the two groups we have and take the square root of that (i.e., $s_p$). (If we had noticeably different variances, we would most likely use the standard deviation of one sample and note to the reader that this is what we had done.)

For our data on homophobia we have

$$\hat{d} = \frac{\overline{X}_1 - \overline{X}_2}{s_p} = \frac{24.00 - 16.50}{\sqrt{144.48}} = \frac{24.00 - 16.50}{12.02} = .62$$

This result expresses the difference between the two groups in standard deviation units, and tells us that the mean arousal for homophobic participants was nearly 2/3 of a standard deviation higher than the arousal of nonhomophobic participants. That strikes me as a big difference.

A word of caution. In the example of homophobia, the units of measurement were arbitrary, and a 7.5 difference had no intrinsic meaning to us. Thus it made more sense to express it in terms of standard deviations because we have at least some understanding of what that means. However, there are many cases wherein the original units are meaningful, and in that case it may not make much sense to standardize the measure (i.e., report it in standard deviation units). We might prefer to specify the difference between means, or the ratio of means, or some similar statistic. The earlier example of the moon illusion is a case in point. There it is far more meaningful to speak of the horizon moon appearing approximately half again as large as the zenith moon, and I see no advantage, and some obfuscation, in converting to standardized units. The important goal is to give the reader an appreciation of the size of a difference, and you should choose that measure that best expresses this difference. In one case a standardized measure such as $\hat{d}$ is best, and in other cases other measures, such as the distance between the means, is better.

## 14.6 Confidence Limits on $\mu_1 - \mu_2$

In addition to testing a null hypothesis about population means (i.e., testing $H_0: \mu_1 - \mu_2 = 0$) and stating an effect size, it is sometimes useful to set confidence limits on the difference between $\mu_1$ and $\mu_2$. The logic for setting these confidence limits is exactly the same as it was for the one-sample case in Chapter 12. The calculations are also exactly the same except that we use the *difference* between the means and the standard error of *differences* between means in place of the mean and the standard error of the mean. Thus for the 95% confidence limits on $\mu_1 - \mu_2$ we have

$$CI_{.95} = (\overline{X}_1 - \overline{X}_2) \pm t_{.05} s_{\overline{X}_1 - \overline{X}_2}$$

For the homophobia study we have

$$CI_{.95} = (\overline{X}_1 - \overline{X}_2) \pm t_{.05} s_{\overline{X}_1 - \overline{X}_2} = (24.00 - 16.5)$$
$$\pm 2.00 \sqrt{\frac{144.48}{35} + \frac{144.48}{29}} = 7.50 \pm 2.00(3.018) = 7.5 \pm 6.04$$
$$1.46 \leq (\mu_1 - \mu_2) \leq 13.54$$

The probability is .95 that an interval computed as we computed this interval (1.46, 13.54) encloses the difference in arousal to homosexual videos between homophobic and nonhomophobic participants. Although the interval is wide, it does not include 0. This is consistent with our rejection of the null hypothesis, and allows us to state that homophobic individuals are, in fact, more sexually aroused by homosexual videos than are nonhomophobic individuals.

## 14.7 Writing Up the Results

As we did in the previous chapter, we need to outline what the reader needs to know. That means we have to describe the study in very brief terms, both its purpose and its procedures, report the means and standard deviations either in the text or as a table, report *t* and our conclusion, and give some statement of the size of an effect. We then need a concluding sentence.

Adams, Wright, and Lohr (1996) investigated the relationship between homophobia and sexual arousal by homophobic participants. They theorized that homophobia might be related directly to anxiety about one's sexuality and that homophobic males would be more aroused by a homosexual video than nonhomophobic males.

The authors tested 64 participants, 24 of whom tested high on a scale of homophobia and 35 of whom were not classed as homophobic. Each participant watched a sexually explicit video of homosexual behavior, and their level of sexual arousal was assessed. Results showed that mean sexual arousal for the homophobic participants was 24.00 (sd = 12.20) while for the nonhomophobic group the mean level of arousal was 16.50 (sd = 11.80). A t test on the difference between means was statistically significant ($t(62) = 2.48, p < .05$). The 7.50 unit difference between conditions translates to $\hat{d} = .62$, indicating that the group means differed by nearly 2/3 of a standard deviation. The authors concluded that there was significant support for their theory that homophobia may result from a fear of one's own sexuality.

## 14.8 Use of Computer Programs for Analysis of Two Independent Sample Means

To illustrate how different computer programs analyze the same data set, I have chosen two programs that approach t tests on two independent groups differently. The differences in their output, and even in their answers, are of interest. There is an important difference between the way you would think of the data if you were calculating t by hand and the way we usually calculate it using computer software. By hand, we usually think of two columns of data and run a t test between the means of the two columns. The standard way to run analyses via software is to have one column of data that represents the dependent variable and another column that represents group membership (usually coded 1 and 2). You then ask the program to look at the data in the dependent variable, broken down by group.

Figure 14.3 illustrates the use of Minitab to analyze the results of the horn-honking experiment by Doob and Gross, referred to in Chapter 8. In the upper portion of the table you will see the stem-and-leaf and boxplot displays for the data for each group separately. For the stem-and-leaf display the stems are the units (and tens') digits and the leaves are the decimal digit. Minitab also adds a column to the left, which we labeled *depth* in Chapter 3. From these displays we can see that the data are symmetrically distributed with no outliers. The t test is shown in the lower portion of the table along with the 95% confidence limits on $\mu_1 - \mu_2$. This test did not pool the variances, although you can only tell that because the degrees of freedom are not equal to $n_1 + n_2 - 2$.[7]

Figure 14.4 contains output from Explore procedure in SPSS. Notice that SPSS produces a much coarser stem-and-leaf display, using the tens' digit as the stem. This display is not particularly helpful. The t test for both with and without pooling of variances is shown in the bottom half of the table. Notice that the degrees of freedom, and the resulting p values, are slightly different from those in Minitab.

---

[7]If you were to run this analysis using a statistical package other than Minitab, the adjusted *df* most likely would not be a whole integer. Minitab calculates the adjusted *df* and then rounds down to the nearest whole integer. (It really makes no difference except to the purists among us.)

```
Stem-and-leaf of Time Group = 1           Stem-and-leaf of Time Group = 2
N = 15 Leaf Unit = .10                     N = 20 Leaf Unit = .10


      1     1   6                              1     3   8
      1     2                                  2     4   4
      2     3   2                              3     5   2
      4     4   89                             4     6   8
      4     5                                  6     7   48
    (4)     6   1478                           9     8   146
      7     7   8                            (4)     9   1589
      6     8   15                             7    10   6
      4     9   04                             6    11   277
      2    10   5                              3    12   6
      1    11                                  2    13   2
      1    12   3                              1    14   0
```

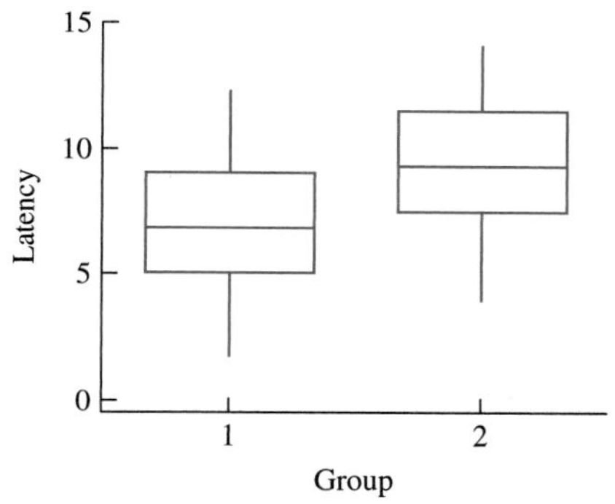

```
Two-Sample T-Test and CI: Time,Group


Two-sample T for Time


Group   N      Mean    StDev    SE Mean
1       15     7.07    2.78     0.72
2       20     9.19    2.82     0.63


Difference = mu (1) - mu (2)
Estimate for difference:  -2.11667
95% CI for difference:  (-4.06907, -0.16426)
T-Test of difference = 0 (vs not =): T-Value = -2.21  P-Value = .035  DF = 30
```

**Figure 14.3**
Minitab analysis of horn-honking data

```
LATENCY Stem-and-Leaf Plot for          LATENCY Stem-and-Leaf Plot for
CONDITIO= High status                   CONDITIO= Low status

Frequency    Stem &  Leaf               Frequency    Stem &  Leaf

    4.00      0 .  1344                      2.00      0 .  34

    9.00      0 .  666678899                11.00      0 .  56778889999

    2.00      1 .  02                        7.00      1 .  0111234

Stem width:   10.00                     Stem width:   10.00

Each leaf:    1 case(s)                  Each leaf:     1 case(s)
```

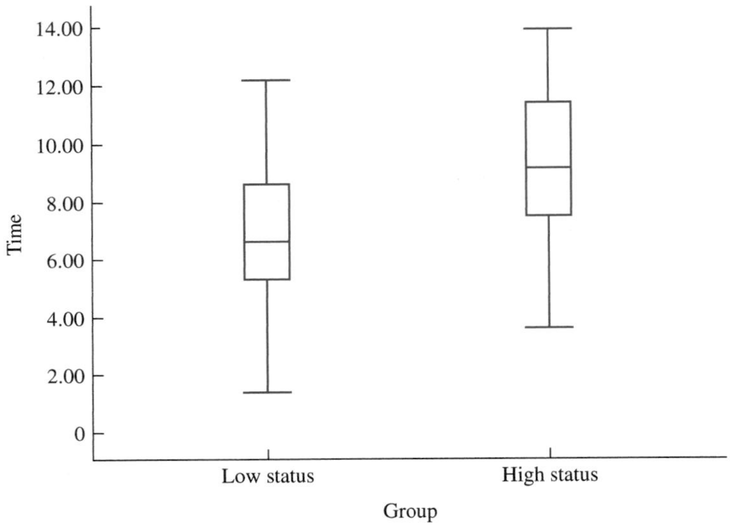

**Independent Samples Test**

| | | Leven's Test for Equality of VariaVnces | | t-test for Equality of Means | | | | | | |
| --- | --- | --- | --- | --- | --- | --- | --- | --- | --- | --- |
| | | | | | | | | | 95% Confidence Interval of the Difference | |
| | | F | Sig. | t | df | Sig. (2–tailed) | Mean Difference | Std. Error Difference | Lower | Upper |
| Time | Equal variances assumed | .022 | .882 | −2.209 | 33 | .034 | −2.11667 | .95809 | −4.06592 | −.16741 |
| | Equal variances not assumed | | | −2.214 | 30.553 | .034 | −2.11667 | .95600 | −4.06759 | −.16574 |

**Figure 14.4**
SPSS analysis of horn-honking data

## 14.9 A Final Worked Example

The following data are based on a study by Eysenck (1974) that, among other things, compared the levels of recall of older and younger participants. (We will have more to say about this study in Chapters 16 and 17.) Eysenck wanted to test the hypothesis that when participants were required to do in-depth processing of verbal information (lists of words), older participants did less processing than younger participants and therefore recalled fewer words. (In this study he also showed that there were no differences in recall between the two age groups when in-depth processing was *not* required.) The data in Table 14.3 have been constructed to have the same means and standard deviations as two of the conditions in Eysenck's study and refer to groups who were told to memorize the words so that they could be recalled later. The dependent variable is the number of items correctly recalled.

First we need to specify the null hypothesis, the significance level, and whether we will use a one- or a two-tailed test. We want to test the null hypothesis that the two age groups recall the same amount of information, so we have $H_0$: $\mu_1 = \mu_2$. We will set alpha at $\alpha = .05$, in line with what we have been using. Finally, we will choose to use a two-tailed test because it is reasonably possible for either group to show superior recall.

Next we calculate the means and the variances.

$$\overline{X}_1 = \frac{193}{10} = 19.3 \qquad \overline{X}_2 = \frac{120}{10} = 12.0$$

$$s_1^2 = \frac{3789 - \frac{193^2}{10}}{9} \qquad s_2^2 = \frac{1566 - \frac{120^2}{10}}{9}$$

$$= 7.122 \qquad\qquad = 14.00$$

**Table 14.3**
Data from Eysenck (1974)

| Younger Participants | | | | | Older Participants | | | | |
|---|---|---|---|---|---|---|---|---|---|
| 21 | 19 | 17 | 15 | 22 | 10 | 19 | 14 | 5 | 10 |
| 16 | 22 | 22 | 18 | 21 | 11 | 14 | 15 | 11 | 11 |

$$\Sigma X_1 = 193$$
$$\Sigma X_1^2 = 3789$$
$$N = 10$$

$$\Sigma X_2 = 120$$
$$\Sigma X_2^2 = 1566$$
$$N = 10$$

With equal sample sizes we do not need to bother pooling the variances because the resulting $t$ would be the same in either event. However, for the sake of an example I will do so here:

$$s_p^2 = \frac{(n_1 - 1)s_1^2 + (n_2 - 1)s_2^2}{n_1 + n_2 - 2}$$

$$= \frac{9(7.122) + 9(14.00)}{10 + 10 - 2} = 10.561$$

Finally, we can calculate $t$ using the pooled variance estimate:

$$t = \frac{\overline{X}_1 - \overline{X}_2}{\sqrt{\dfrac{s_p^2}{n_1} + \dfrac{s_p^2}{n_2}}} = \frac{19.3 - 12.0}{\sqrt{\dfrac{10.561}{10} + \dfrac{10.561}{10}}}$$

$$= \frac{7.3}{\sqrt{2.112}} = 5.02$$

For this example we have $n_1 + n_2 - 2 = 18$ degrees of freedom. From Table D.6 in the Appendix D we find $t_{.05} = \pm 2.101$. Because $5.02 > 2.101$, we will reject $H_0$ and conclude that the two population means are not equal.

Effect size for this example is best calculated using Cohen's $d$. In doing so we will use the square root of the pooled variance estimate as our standard deviation because there is no obvious reason to use the standard deviation of only one of the groups. With a mean difference of 7.3 and a pooled standard deviation of 3.25 we have

$$\hat{d} = \frac{\overline{X}_1 - \overline{X}_2}{s_p} = \frac{19.3 - 12.0}{3.25} = \frac{7.3}{3.25} = 2.25$$

indicating that the groups differ by two and a quarter standard deviations, which is a very large difference.

If you calculate the confidence limits on the difference in means you will have

$$CI_{.95} = (\overline{X}_1 - \overline{X}_2) \pm t_{.05}(s_{\overline{X}_1 - \overline{X}_2}) = (19.3 - 12.0) \pm 2.101\sqrt{2.112}$$

$$= 7.3 \pm 3.05$$

$$CI_{.95} = 4.25 \leq \mu_1 - \mu_2 \leq 10.35$$

The problem with this confidence interval is simply that, *in this case*, it doesn't tell us very much. The units are the number of items recalled by the participants, and it is not particularly helpful to say that the means differ by at least approximately 4.25 units and perhaps as much as approximately 10.35. Those numbers have no real intuitive meaning to us. (If, on the other hand, the dependent variable had been something like the ratio of horizon and zenith moons, then we would have useful information. It just depends on the nature of the dependent variable.) Our estimate of $d$, which was 2.25, is a number that has at least some meaning, and that is what should be reported.

## Writing Up the Results

If you were writing up the results of this experiment, you might write something like the following:

> In an attempt to test the hypothesis that older participants process and store information less completely than younger participants, we asked two groups of 10 participants each (differing only in age) to study and then recall a list of words that required a moderate level of verbal processing. The results showed that younger participants recalled a mean of 19.3 words, while older participants recalled a mean of 12.0 words. (The two standard deviations were 2.67 and 3.74, respectively.) A $t$ test comparing the two groups was significant ($t(18) = 5.02, p < .05$). The estimate of Cohen's $d$ using the pooled estimate of the standard error was 2.24, indicating a substantial difference. The results demonstrated that younger participants recalled significantly more words than did older participants. This is not to say that older participants are not as smart as younger ones (as someone who would fall in the older group, I can assure you that we are even smarter than the other guys), but only that for some reason they did not perform as well on this task. (Well, it's kind of a dumb task!) Because other data revealed no differences on tasks that did not require in-depth processing, it would appear that processing of information is a relevant variable. It may be that older participants are not willing to process information to the same extent that younger participants are, possibly because they are less interested in the experimental task and have better things to do with their time. (If you were really writing this up, I would suggest leaving out the snide comments.)

## 14.10 Seeing Statistics

We began this chapter by looking at the sampling distribution of the differences between means. A particularly good illustration of what that distribution looks like, and how it relates to the true difference between means, the sample size, and the population standard deviations can be seen in an applet named Sampling Distribution of Mean Differences, contained on the Web site. An example of the opening screen follows.

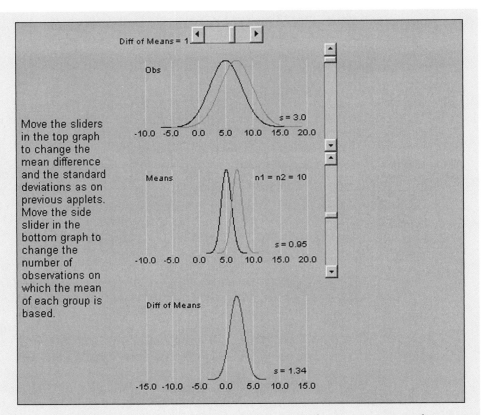

You see three sets of distributions. The pair at the top represents the populations from which we sample, while the one in the middle shows the distribution of means drawn from each population. The bottom distribution is the sampling distribution of mean differences. At the very top of the screen you see a slider that alters the difference between the population means. On the upper right is a slider that changes the standard deviations of the populations, and below that is a slider to change the sample sizes.

Move the top slider to see that as you increase the difference between population means, you also change the location of the sample distributions of means, and, more importantly for us, you change the mean of the sampling distribution of differences between means.

Move the other sliders and notice how those affect each of the distributions.

One additional applet available at the Web site (labeled *t-test on differences between means*) allows you to specify means, standard deviations, or sample sizes, and see what effect that has on both *t* and its associated probability. This applet calculates the *t* value and probability for a comparison of two means. The opening screen follows. Its use should be self-explanatory, but be sure to press the Enter or Return key after you enter each value.

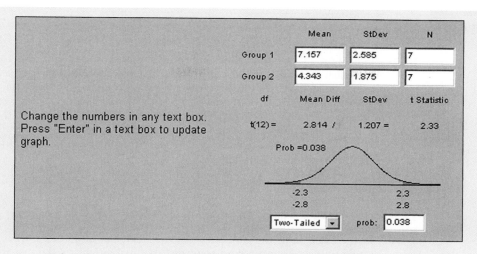

Take the data from the horn-honking example in Section 14.7, and enter the appropriate statistics. Does the answer agree with the one we obtained? Using the same example, assume that we had only 10 participants in each group. Would the result still be significant? What does that tell you about the importance of sample size? (That will be important in the next chapter.)

## 14.11 Summary

In this chapter we considered the use of the *t* test for testing the null hypothesis that two population means are equal. This test is based on sample means from two independent samples and is probably the most common form of the *t* test. We also considered the assumptions underlying the use of *t*, procedures to be applied when the assumption of homogeneity of variance is not met, the estimation of effect size, and confidence limits for mean differences.

Some important terms in this chapter are

| | |
|---|---|
| Sampling distribution of differences between means, *327* | Homogeneity of variance, *330* |
| Variance Sum Law, *327* | Weighted average, *330* |
| Standard error of differences between means, *329* | Pooled variance, *330* |
| | Heterogeneity of variance, *334* |
| | Confounded, *334* |

## 14.12 Exercises

**14.1**   In Exercise 13.1 we had paired data because we had a response from both the husband and the wife within a married couple. Suppose that instead of using married couples we just took a large group of people and asked them to what extent they endorsed the statement "Sex is fun for me and my partner" on a four-point scales ranging from "never or occasionally" to "almost always." We then sorted the data on the basis of the gender of the respondent. We could conceivably get the data we had in Exercise 13.1, though without the pairing.

Analyze the data in Exercise 13.1 as if they had been collected from independent groups. What would you conclude?

**14.2**   The $t$ value that you obtain in Exercise 14.1 will be somewhat smaller than the $t$ value from Exercise 13.1. Why should we have anticipated this?

**14.3**   Why isn't the difference between the results of Exercises 13.1 and 14.1 greater than it is?

**14.4**   In the example in this chapter about the treatment of anorexia, what basic assumption would we have to make if we compared the final weights of the two groups (rather than comparing the amount of weight gain)?

**14.5**   What is the role of random assignment in the anorexia study?

**14.6**   What is the role of random sampling in the anorexia study?

**14.7**   Why can't we use random assignment in the study of homophobia, and what effect will that have on the conclusions we are allowed to draw?

**14.8**   The Thematic Apperception Test presents participants with ambiguous pictures and asks them to tell a story about them. These stories can be scored in any number of ways. Werner, Stabenou, and Pollin (1970) asked mothers of 20 normal and 20 schizophrenic children to complete the TAT, and scored for the number of stories (out of 10) that exhibited a positive parent-child relationship. The data follow:

| Normal | 8 | 4 | 6 | 3 | 1 | 4 | 4 | 6 | 4 | 2 |
|--------|---|---|---|---|---|---|---|---|---|---|
| Schizophrenic | 2 | 1 | 1 | 3 | 2 | 7 | 2 | 1 | 3 | 1 |
| Normal | 2 | 1 | 1 | 4 | 3 | 3 | 2 | 6 | 3 | 4 |
| Schizophrenic | 0 | 2 | 4 | 2 | 3 | 3 | 0 | 1 | 2 | 2 |

(a) What would you assume to be the experimental hypothesis behind this study?
(b) What would you conclude with respect to that hypothesis?

**14.9**   In Exercise 14.8 why might it be smart to look at the variances of the two groups?

**14.10**   In Exercise 14.8 a significant difference might lead someone to suggest that poor parent-child relationships are the cause of schizophrenia. Why might this be a troublesome conclusion?

**14.11**   Much has been made of the concept of *experimenter bias*, which refers to the fact that for even the most conscientious experimenters there seems to be a tendency for the data to come out in the desired direction. Suppose we use students as experimenters. All the experimenters are told that participants will be given caffeine before the experiment, but half the experimenters are told that we expect caffeine to lead to good performance, and half are told that we expect it to lead to poor performance. The dependent variable is the number of simple arithmetic problems the participant can solve in 2 minutes. The obtained data are as follows:

| Expect Good Performance | 19 | 15 | 22 | 13 | 18 | 15 | 20 | 25 | 22 |
|---|---|---|---|---|---|---|---|---|---|
| Expect Poor Performance | 14 | 18 | 17 | 12 | 21 | 21 | 24 | 14 | |

What would you conclude?

**14.12** Calculate the 95% confidence limits on $\mu_1 - \mu_2$ for the data in Exercise 14.1.

**14.13** Calculate the 95% confidence limits on $\mu_1 - \mu_2$ for the data in Exercise 14.8.

**14.14** Using the data on attention deficit disorder (Add.dat), use a $t$ test to compare ADDSC scores of males and females.

**14.15** Using the data in Exercise 14.14, compare grade point averages for those having ADDSC scores of 65 or less with those having ADDSC scores of 66 or more.

**14.16** Calculate Cohen's $d$ for the data in Exercise 14.15.

**14.17** What do the answers to Exercises 14.15 and 14.16 tell you about the predictive utility of the ADDSC score?

**14.18** The *Roanoke Times and World News* (July 25, 1997) reported on an award-winning science project by a student named David Merrell. I'll simplify that study here, but we will see it in more detail in a later chapter. The study compared two groups of rats. Initially the two groups were allowed 10 minutes to explore a maze. Then one group was tested while listening to music by Mozart, while a second group navigated the maze without music. After nine trials through the maze, the final navigation times are shown below. (I have left out those mice who navigated to music by Anthrax, but will get to them later—I'll bet you can hardly wait.)

| Control | 444 | 219 | 347 | 327 | 431 | 333 | 310 | 341 | 206 | 203 | 999 | 267 |
|---|---|---|---|---|---|---|---|---|---|---|---|---|
| | 275 | 297 | 215 | 305 | 262 | 259 | 225 | 306 | 343 | 315 | 407 | 422 |
| Mozart | 101 | 162 | 152 | 153 | 132 | 191 | 106 | 180 | 99 | 120 | 134 | 78 |
| | 123 | 121 | 85 | 67 | 68 | 48 | 76 | 107 | 121 | 119 | 86 | 113 |

What would you conclude from these data?

**14.19** What does the experimenter have to assume about the experiment in Exercise 14.18?

**14.20** Given the definition of a weighted average (see page 330), show what the pooled variance estimate ($s_p^2$) would be if the two sample sizes were equal. (*Hint:* Replace $n_1$ and $n_2$ with $n$.)

**14.21** With respect to the previous exercise, what would happen if $s_1^2 = s_2^2$, regardless of $n_i$?

**14.22** Demonstrate that, *because we have equal sample sizes*, I would have arrived at the same answer in Section 14.8 if I had not pooled the variances, although the degrees of freedom would probably differ.

# 15

# Power

**QUESTIONS**

■ One study said that an AIDS treatment works, and a similar study said that it doesn't. So who is right? Why can't results be consistent?

■ I spent a lot of time carrying out the study. Why didn't I find anything?

■ What do I need to think about in determining how to find differences?

■ How do you measure a difference?

■ How big a sample do I need?

■ I am very confident that I am a better technical skier than my brother, but I don't expect that if a judge watched us descend through the bumps I would *always* get a better rating. What does that have to do with statistics?

■ have studiously avoided taking my examples from the sports pages, but this is a great place for one. As of the time of writing this, the New York Yankees have won 68 (59%) of the 115 games that they have played, while the Boston Red Sox have won 58 (49%) of their 119 games. If you had to bet on today's game, and if you lived in Canterbury, England or Melbourne, Australia, without any loyalty to either team, you would be well advised to bet on the Yankees because they look to be the better team. But you certainly wouldn't expect that they are a sure thing. The probabilities are in their favor, but you wouldn't stand there in astonishment if you heard they lost. It's the same thing with an experiment. Your treatment for dyslexia may be appreciably better than mine, but that doesn't mean that your subjects are *always* going to come out doing better than mine. Nor does it mean that you will find that, when compared to a control group, your treatment will always show a statistically significant difference. We have to keep in mind the fact that one team or one treatment being better than another doesn't always mean that it will win. It just means that they will win more often than they lose.

While I am not an avid reader of the sports pages, I think that this example has a great deal to say about how we think of experiments. We all seem to operate under a general belief that if we conduct an experiment to test a theory, that experiment will always come out in line with the theory: If the theory is true, the results will be statistically significant, and if the theory is wrong, they won't. But the world doesn't work that way, just as the Yankees don't always win. No one gives up on the Yankees if they lose a game, but we tend to give up on theories if the experiment doesn't come out the way the theory would predict. Maybe you just didn't look hard enough—that is, use enough observations. (Or maybe you did, and it was just not your day.)

High on the list of frequently asked questions for statisticians is the question "How many subjects do I need?" Aaarrgh!! Statisticians hate that question, because it implies that there is an answer, such as "38," that will satisfy any situation. I deeply regret that there isn't such an answer, because it would make my life very much easier, and this chapter very much shorter. The problem is that the real answer is "it depends," which is an answer people hate to hear in response to such a simple question. Their typical response is "Well, of course it depends on a lot of things, but just give me a ballpark figure." Sorry, but I can't do that either, without knowing more than you've told me.

Most applied statistical work as it is actually carried out in analyzing experimental results is concerned primarily with minimizing (or at least controlling) the probability of a Type I error ($\alpha$). When it comes to designing experiments, people generally tend to ignore that there is a probability ($\beta$) of another kind of error, a Type II error. Whereas Type I errors deal with the problem of *finding* a difference that is *not* there, Type II errors concern the serious problem of *not finding* a difference that *is* there. (In our baseball example it is analogous to the probability of the Yankees not beating the Red Sox when they really are the better team.) When we consider the substantial cost in time and money that goes into a typical experiment, it is remarkably shortsighted of experimenters not to recognize that they may, from the start, have a very small chance of finding the effect they are looking for, even if such an effect actually exists in the population and even if it is a nontrivial effect worth finding.

Investigators historically have tended to avoid concerning themselves with Type II errors. (Interestingly, people who play the horses wouldn't think of ignoring the fact that even the greatest horse sometimes loses, but we frequently ignore the fact that even the best experiments sometimes produce no significant difference.) Until recently, many textbooks ignored the problem altogether. Those books that did discuss the material discussed it in ways not easily understood by the book's intended audience. In the past 25 years, however, Jacob Cohen, a psychologist, has discussed the problem clearly and lucidly in several publications. Cohen (1988) presents a thorough and rigorous treatment of the material. In Welkowitz, Cohen, and Ewen (2006) the material is treated in a slightly simpler way, through the use of an approximation technique, which is the approach adopted in this chapter. This approximation is based on the use of the normal distribution, and differences between the level of power computed with this method and with the more exact approach are generally negligible. Cohen (1992) has written an excellent five-page paper that is quite accessible, and I hand it out to anyone who asks me about statistical power. If you become interested in this topic or need to consider power in greater depth than we do in this chapter, you should have no difficulty with the sources just mentioned or with any of the many excellent papers Cohen published on a wide variety of topics.

Speaking in terms of Type II errors is a negative way of approaching the problem, since it focuses on our mistakes. The more positive approach is to speak in terms of **power**, which is defined as the probability of *correctly* rejecting a *false* $H_0$. Put another way, power equals $1 - \beta$. When we say that the power of a particular experimental design is .65, we mean that if the null hypothesis is false *to the degree we expect*, the probability is .65 that the results of the experiment will lead us to reject $H_0$. A more powerful experiment is one that has a greater probability of rejecting a false $H_0$ than does a less powerful experiment.

---

Definition    **Power:** The probability of correctly rejecting a false $H_0$.

---

This chapter will take an approach similar to that used in Welkowitz, Cohen, and Ewen (2006) and work with an approximation to the true power of a test. This approximation is an excellent one, especially because we do not really care whether power equals .85 or .83, but rather if it is in the .80s or in the .30s. For purposes of exploring the basic material, let's assume for the moment that we are interested in using a *t* test for testing one sample mean against a specified population mean. I chose this because it is simple, but the approach immediately generalizes to the testing of other hypotheses.

## 15.1 The Basic Concept

To review briefly what we have already covered in Chapter 8, consider the two distributions in Figure 15.1. The distribution to the left (labeled $H_0$) represents the sampling distribution of the mean when the null hypothesis is true and the population mean equals $\mu_0$.[1] The right-hand tail of this distribution (the darker-shaded area) represents $\alpha$, the probability of a Type I error, assuming that we are using a one-tailed test (otherwise it represents $\alpha/2$). This area contains the values of a sample mean that would erroneously result in significant values of *t*.

---

[1]If you are not sure that you remember what a sampling distribution is, look back at Chapter 11. Briefly, a sampling distribution is the distribution that a statistic (such as the mean) will have over repeated sampling.

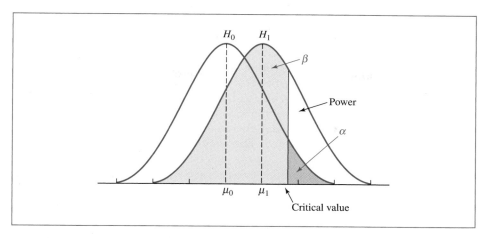

**Figure 15.1**
Sampling distributions of $\overline{X}$ under $H_0$ and $H_1$

The second distribution ($H_1$) represents the sampling distribution of the mean when $H_0$ is false and when the true mean is $\mu_1$. It is readily apparent that even when $H_0$ is false, many of the sample means (and therefore the corresponding values of $t$) will nonetheless fall to the left of the critical value, causing us to fail to reject a false $H_0$, thereby committing a Type II error. The probability of this error is indicated by the lighter-shaded area in Figure 15.1 and is labeled $\beta$.

Finally, when $H_0$ is false and the test statistic falls to the right of the critical value, we will correctly reject a false $H_0$. The probability of doing this is what we mean by power and is shown in the unshaded area of the $H_1$ distribution.

Although nothing is really new in the preceding paragraphs, putting it all together can be conceptually difficult, so we need an example. Suppose we go back to Everitt's study of anorexic girls involved in cognitive behavior therapy (Exercises 5.21 and 12.10–12.13). There are two possible situations that we care about.[2] The first would be the case where the girls really didn't gain any weight as a result of therapy. This is essentially the case of a true null hypothesis ($\mu_{\text{gain}} = 0$). If that null is true, we know that the sample mean of 29 anorexic girls will be somewhere near, but rarely exactly, 0. It has a distribution, and that is the distribution shown on the left in Figure 15.1. Once in a while the sample mean will happen to be so large that we will reject the null hypothesis, even when we shouldn't. This is a Type I error; it is shown by the dark portion of that distribution on the right, and is labeled $\alpha$. All of this represents the kind of thinking that we have been doing until now—focusing on Type I errors.

---

[2]We will stick to a one-tailed test just to avoid that additional level of complexity.

But I come from a psychology department that has a strong focus on cognitive behavior therapy, and I have been led to believe that cognitive behavior therapy is really effective. (I am an experimental psychologist, so I don't have a strong stake in the issue.) If cognitive behavior therapy is effective, and then if we could apply it to a whole population of anorexic girls, the mean gain would be some positive number—say 5 lbs (to have a number to play with). That would be $\mu_1$ in Figure 15.1. Not having access to the whole population, we would draw a sample of anorexic girls, offer them cognitive behavior therapy, and record the amount of weight they gained. The sample mean would probably be somewhere in the neighborhood of 5 lbs, but not exactly. Over repeated sampling, the sample means would have a distribution centered on 5 lbs. This is the distribution shown on the right in Figure 15.1. Sometimes the mean gain might be 7 or 8 lbs, sometimes it would only be 2 or 3 lbs, and sometimes it would even be negative. You can see each of these possibilities in the figure.

In Figure 15.1 the left edge of the darkly shaded area is that value of gain that would lead us to reject the null hypothesis. This value has been labeled as the "critical value." Anything greater than that will cause rejection, and anything less than that will cause us to retain the null. We know that if the null is true, the probability is $\alpha$ that we would exceed that critical value. You can also see that if $H_1$ is true (cognitive behavior therapy is helpful), there will be many outcomes that exceed this value—and that is a good thing. However, even when the null is false and $H_1$ is true, a large number of outcomes don't make it above the critical value, and those outcomes are going to lead us to (erroneously) retain the null—and that is a bad thing. The probability of retaining the null when $H_1$ is true is labeled $\beta$ in the figure, and is shown in the lightly shaded region. Finally, when the null is false and $H_1$ is true, those outcomes that exceed the critical value represent correct rejects. This area is what we mean by power, and it has been labeled as such.

One final point. If the null is true, we know what the distribution looks like, and where its center is located—it is located at .00. But if the null is false, we don't know how false it is, and therefore we don't know where the center of its distribution is. I picked 5 lbs because I needed a number to play with, but perhaps it is only 3 lbs, or perhaps it is 10. You should be able to see that as we slide that distribution left and right in response to different values of $\mu_1$ the size of the lightly shaded area ($\beta$) will change, as will the size of the area labeled power. All that we can do is pick a value of $\mu_1$ based on our best guess, and proceed from there.

## 15.2 Factors That Affect the Power of a Test

As you might expect, power is a function of several variables:

1. The probability of a Type I error ($\alpha$), the *a priori* level of significance, and the criterion for rejecting $H_0$

2. The true difference between the null hypothesis and an alternative hypothesis ($\mu_0 - \mu_1$)

3. The sample size ($n$) and variance ($s^2$)

4. The particular test to be employed and whether we are using a one- or a two-tailed test

We will ignore the last point, other than to say that, in general, when the assumptions behind a particular test are met, the procedures presented in this book (with the possible exception of those discussed in Chapter 20) can be shown to have more power to answer the question at hand than other available tests. Also, as we move from a one-tailed to a two-tailed test, the size of the area labeled $\alpha$ in Figure 15.1 would be halved, with corresponding changes in power.

## Power as a Function of $\alpha$

With the aid of Figure 15.1 it is easy to see why we say that power is a function of $\alpha$. If we are willing to increase $\alpha$, the cutoff point moves to the left, simultaneously decreasing $\beta$ and increasing power. Unfortunately, this is accompanied by a corresponding rise in the probability of a Type I error.

## Power as a Function of $\mu_0 - \mu_1$

The fact that power is a function of the nature of the true alternative hypothesis—more precisely, ($\mu_0 - \mu_1$)—is illustrated by a comparison of Figures 15.1 and 15.2. In Figure 15.2 the distance between $\mu_0$ and $\mu_1$ has been increased, by increasing the value of $\mu_1$, resulting in a substantial increase in power. This is not particularly surprising, since all we are saying is that the chances of finding a difference depend on how large the difference is. (It is easier to distinguish between oranges and apples than between oranges and tangerines.)

## Power as a Function of the Sample Size ($n$) and $\sigma^2$

The relationship between power and sample size (and between power and $\sigma^2$) is only a little subtler. Because we are interested in means or differences between means, we are interested, directly or indirectly, in the sampling distribution of the mean. We know that $\sigma_{\bar{X}}^2 = \sigma^2/n$. From this equation we can see that the variance of the sampling distribution of the mean decreases either as $n$ increases or as $\sigma^2$ decreases. Figure 15.3, in comparison with Figure 15.2, illustrates what happens to the two sampling distributions ($H_0$ and $H_1$) as we increase $n$ or decrease $\sigma^2$. In Figure 15.3 we see that as $\sigma_{\bar{X}}^2$ decreases, the overlap between the two distributions is reduced, with a resulting increase in power.

An experimenter concerned with the power of a test most likely will be interested in those variables governing power that she can manipulate easily. Because $n$ is more easily manipulated than either $\sigma^2$ or ($\mu_0 - \mu_1$), and because tampering with $\alpha$ produces undesirable side effects (increasing the probability of a Type I error), discussions of power are generally concerned with the effects of varying sample size.

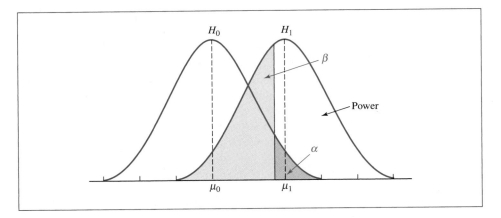

**Figure 15.2**
Effect on power of increasing distance between $\mu_0$ and $\mu_1$

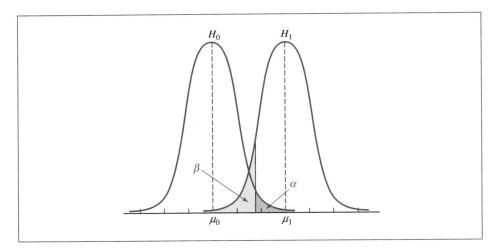

**Figure 15.3**
Effect on power of a decrease in the standard error of the mean

## 15.3 Effect Size

In several previous chapters we have discussed a measure called "the effect size." We saw several different ways of presenting it, and I suggested that in some cases simply presenting a mean or a difference in means is sufficient. However when most people use the phrase "effect size" they have something like Cohen's $d$ in mind. When it comes to discussing power we also discuss effect size, and it turns out to be the same statistic as Cohen's $d$. The only difference is that we are using it to assess how large a difference we hope to have, and then computing power, rather than using it as a measure to tell the reader how large an effect we found. So the measure stays the same; it is only the purpose that differs.

As we have seen in Figures 15.1 through 15.3, power depends on the degree of overlap between the sampling distributions under $H_0$ and $H_1$. Furthermore, this overlap is a function of *both* the distance between $\mu_0$ and $\mu_1$ (the population mean if $H_0$ is true and the population mean if $H_1$ is true) and the standard error of the mean (the standard deviation of either of these sampling distributions). One measure, then, of the degree to which $H_0$ is false would be the difference in population means under $H_0$ and $H_1$, which is $(\mu_0 - \mu_1)$, expressed in terms of the number of standard errors (i.e., $(\mu_0 - \mu_1)/\sigma_{\overline{X}}$). The problem with this measure is that the denominator ($\sigma_{\overline{X}} = \sigma/\sqrt{n}$) already includes the sample size. In practice we usually will want to keep $n$ separate from $(\mu_0 - \mu_1)$ and $\sigma$ so that we can solve for the power associated with a given value of $n$, or else for that value of $n$ required for a given level of power. For that reason we will take as our distance measure, or effect size,

$$d = \frac{\mu_1 - \mu_0}{\sigma}$$

We will ignore the sign of $d$ attending only to its absolute value.[3] It is a measure of the degree to which $\mu_1$ and $\mu_0$ differ in terms of the standard deviation of the parent population. For example, if we expect a group of children who have suffered from malnutrition to have a mean IQ 8 points below normal (where $\sigma = 16$), we are talking about an effect size of one-half a standard deviation (i.e., the malnourished group will be below average by $8/16 = 1/2$ a standard deviation). Then $d = 1/2 = .5$. From our equation we see that $d$ is estimated independently of $n$, simply by estimating $\mu_1$ and $\sigma$. We will incorporate $n$ at a later date.

## Estimating the Effect Size

The first task becomes that of estimating $d$ because it will form the basis for future calculations. We can do this in one of three ways.

**1.** *Prior research.* We often can obtain at least a rough approximation of $d$ by looking at past data. Thus we could look at sample means and variances from other studies and make an informed guess at the values we might expect for $\mu_1 - \mu_0$ and for $\sigma$. In practice this task is not as difficult as it might seem, especially when you realize that even a rough approximation is far better than no approximation at all.

**2.** *Personal assessment of what difference is important.* In many cases an investigator is able to say, "I am interested in detecting a difference of at least ten points

---

[3]In previous versions of this book I have used the symbol $\gamma$ to represent what I call $d$ here. While that is the traditional notation in discussions of power, you already know what $d$ is and I don't see any point in confusing the issue by giving it a different name.

between $\mu_1$ and $\mu_0$." The investigator is saying essentially that smaller differences have no important or useful meaning, whereas differences greater than ten points do. Here we are given the value of $\mu_1 - \mu_0$ directly, without any necessary knowledge of the particular values of $\mu_1$ and $\mu_0$. All that remains is to estimate $\sigma$ from other data. For example, the standard deviation of many standardized tests is often approximately 10. An investigator might say that he is interested in finding a study guide that will raise scores on a standardized test by four points above average. We already know that the standard deviation for this test is approximately 10. Thus $d = 4/10 = .40$. If, instead of saying that he wanted to raise scores by four points, the experimenter said he wanted to raise them by 4/10 of a standard deviation, he would have been giving us $d$ directly.

**3.** *The use of special conventions.* When we encounter a situation in which there is no way that we can estimate the required parameters, we can fall back on a set of conventions given by Cohen (1988). Cohen defined three values of $d$ that can be used when testing means. For a justification of these levels, refer to Cohen's work. Cohen's rule of thumb is

| Effect Size | $d$ |
|---|---|
| Small | .20 |
| Medium | .50 |
| Large | .80 |

Thus when all else fails, experimenters simply can decide whether they are after a small, medium, or large effect and set $d$ accordingly. Although it is common to see reference to these estimates, I must emphasize that this solution should be chosen only when the other alternatives are not feasible—but even Cohen gave up and accepted the fact that, whether he wanted them to or not, people are going to take these as firm rules, rather than rules of thumb.

You might think it is peculiar to be asked to define the difference you are looking for before the experiment is conducted. Many people would respond by claiming that if they knew how the experiment would come out, they wouldn't have needed to run it in the first place. Although many experimenters behave as if this were true, if you consider the excuse carefully you should start to question its validity. Do we really not know, at least vaguely, what will happen in our experiments, and if not, why are we running them? And even if we have no idea what to expect, we should at least consider the minimum effect we would be interested in detecting. While there is an occasional legitimate "I wonder what would happen if" experiment, "I don't know" usually translates to "I haven't thought that far ahead." Remember that most experiments are run to demonstrate to the rest of the world that a particular theory is correct, and that theory often tells us what kind of results to expect.

## Combining the Effect Size and $n$

In our discussion of the effect size ($d$), we split off the sample size from the effect size to make it easier to deal with $n$ separately. The final thing we will need is a method for combining the effect size with the sample size to determine the power of an experiment for a given $n$ and effect size $(d)$. For this we will use the symbol $\delta$ (**delta**):

$$\delta = d \times f(n)$$

where the particular function of $n$, $f(n)$, will be defined differently for each individual test.[4] In this equation the notation $f(n)$—read "$f$ of $n$"—is used as a general way of stating that $\delta$ depends not only on $d$ but also in some unspecified way on $n$. For example, you will see that in the one-sample $t$ test we will compute $\delta$ by replacing $f(n)$ with $\sqrt{n}$, whereas in the two-sample $t$ test we will replace $f(n)$ with $\sqrt{(n/2)}$. The nice thing about this system is that it allows us to use the same table of $\delta$ for power calculations for all the statistical procedures to be considered. How we will actually use $\delta$ is illustrated in the next section.

Definition | $\delta$ **(Delta):** A value used in referring to power tables that combines $d$ and the sample size.

It is probably worth restating why we have gone to all this work to define $d$ without regard to $n$ and have then put $n$ back in when it comes to defining $\delta$. When you are planning an experiment, $(\mu_1 - \mu_0)$ and $\sigma$, and therefore $d$, are more or less fixed. But the choice of $n$ is up to you. We want to be able to compute power, by way of $\delta$, for a given $d$ when $n$ is 20, for example, and then when $n$ is 50. We don't want to have to repeat a set of calculations every time we change $n$. By defining $d$ independently of $n$ and then having a simple formula to put the two together, we save ourselves a lot of work.

## 15.4   Power Calculations for the One-Sample *t* Test

For our first example we will examine the calculation of power for the one-sample $t$ test. In the previous section you saw that $\delta$ is based on $d$ and some function of $n$. For the one-sample $t$ test, that function will be $\sqrt{n}$, and $\delta$ will then be defined as

$$\delta = \hat{d}\sqrt{n}$$

In Chapter 5 (Exercise 5-21) we saw data from a study of Everitt using cognitive behavior therapy as a treatment for anorexia. Now assume a clinical psychologist

---

[4] I'm sure a lot of students out there just groaned that they had finished with their math requirement and thought they were safely away from things like $f(n)$—or else they skipped math entirely because they didn't want to worry about such stuff. Just think of $f(n)$ as a shorthand way of writing, "some value based on $n$ that I don't want to specify more precisely here."

wants to replicate that study. Needing somewhere to start, she assumes that Everitt's data are a good representation of the population parameters in question. In other words, she is willing to assume that the population mean weight gain, with cognitive behavior therapy, is $\mu_1 = 3.00$ lbs and the standard deviation ($\sigma$) is 7.31. The null hypothesis would be that the participants don't gain weight as a result of cognitive behavior therapy, and therefore $\mu_0 = .00$.

$$\hat{d} = \frac{3.00 - .00}{7.31} = .41$$

If she is going to run the same number of participants that Everitt did, then $n = 29$, and

$$\delta = \hat{d} \sqrt{n} = .41\sqrt{29} = .41(5.39) = 2.21$$

Although the experimenter expects the sample mean to be above the mean of the general population, she plans to use a two-tailed test at $\alpha = .05$ to protect against unexpected events. Given $\delta$, we immediately can determine the power of the test from Table D.5 in Appendix D. A portion of this table is reproduced in Table 15.1. To use either table, simply go down the left-hand margin until you come to the value of $\delta = 2.21$ and then read across to the column headed .05; that entry will be the power of the test. Neither table has an entry for $\delta = 2.21$, but they do have entries for $\delta = 2.20$ and $\delta = 2.30$. For $\alpha = .05$ this means that power is between .60 and .63. By linear interpolation we will say that for $\delta = 2.21$, power is equal to .60. This means that if $H_0$ is really false and $\mu_1 = 3$ lbs, only 60% of the time will the clinician obtain data that will produce a significant value of $t$ when testing the difference between her *sample* mean and that specified by $H_0$. This is a rather discouraging result because it means that if the true mean gain with cognitive behavior therapy is really 3.00 lbs, $100\% - 60\% = 40\%$ of the time the study as designed will *not* obtain a significant result.

Because the experimenter was intelligent enough to examine the question of power before she began her experiment, she still has the chance to make changes that will lead to an increase in power. She could, for example, set $\alpha$ at .10, thus increasing power to approximately .71, but this is probably unsatisfactory. (Journal reviewers, for example, generally hate to see $\alpha$ set at any value greater than .05.) Alternatively, the experimenter could make use of the fact that power increases as $n$ increases.

## Estimating Required Sample Sizes

It is fine to say that a thoughtful experimenter can increase power by increasing $n$, but how large an $n$ is needed? The answer to that question depends simply on the level of power that is acceptable. Suppose you wanted to modify the previous example to have power equal to .80. The first thing you need to do is read Table D.5 backward to find what value for $\delta$ is associated with the specified degree of power. From the table we see that for power equal to .80, $\delta$ must equal 2.80. Thus we have

**Table 15.1**
Abbreviated Version of Table D.5, Power as a Function of $\delta$ and
Significance Level

| | Alpha for Two-Tailed Test | | | |
|---|---|---|---|---|
| $\delta$ | .10 | .05 | .02 | .01 |
| 1.00 | .26 | .17 | .09 | .06 |
| 1.10 | .29 | .20 | .11 | .07 |
| 1.20 | .33 | .22 | .13 | .08 |
| 1.30 | .37 | .26 | .15 | .10 |
| 1.40 | .40 | .29 | .18 | .12 |
| 1.50 | .44 | .32 | .20 | .14 |
| 1.60 | .48 | .36 | .23 | .17 |
| 1.70 | .52 | .40 | .27 | .19 |
| 1.80 | .56 | .44 | .30 | .22 |
| 1.90 | .60 | .48 | .34 | .25 |
| 2.00 | .64 | .52 | .37 | .28 |
| 2.10 | .68 | .56 | .41 | .32 |
| 2.20 | .71 | .60 | .45 | .35 |
| 2.30 | .74 | .63 | .49 | .39 |
| 2.40 | .78 | .67 | .53 | .43 |
| 2.50 | .80 | .71 | .57 | .47 |
| 2.60 | .83 | .74 | .61 | .51 |
| 2.70 | .85 | .77 | .65 | .55 |
| 2.80 | .88 | .80 | .68 | .59 |
| 2.90 | .90 | .83 | .72 | .65 |
| 3.00 | .91 | .85 | .75 | .66 |

$\delta$ and can solve for $n$ simply by a minor algebraic manipulation:

$$\delta = d\sqrt{n}$$

$$n = \left(\frac{\delta}{d}\right)^2$$

$$= \left(\frac{2.80}{.41}\right)^2 = 6.83^2 = 46.64$$

Because clients generally come in whole units, we will round off to 47. Thus if the experimenter wants to have an 80% chance of rejecting $H_0$ when $\hat{d} = .41$(i.e., when $\mu_1 = 3.00$ or $-3.00$), she will have to provide therapy to 47 clients. Although she may feel that this is a large number of clients, there is no good alternative other than to settle for a lower level of power and increase the chance of not finding anything.

You might wonder why we selected power equal to .80 in the previous example. With this degree of power we still run a 20% chance of making a Type II error. The answer lies in the issue of practicality. Suppose, for example, that our experimenter had wanted power to equal .95. A few simple calculations will show that this would require a sample of $n = 77$; for power equal to .99 she would need approximately 105 participants. These may well be unreasonable sample sizes for a particular experimental situation or for the resources of the experimenter. While increases in power are generally bought by increases in $n$, at very high levels of power the cost can be very high. In addition, it is a case of diminishing returns because $\delta$ increases as a function of the square root of $n$. If you are taking data from files supplied by the U.S. Census Bureau, that is one thing. It is quite a different matter when you are studying identical twins reared apart.

## 15.5 Power Calculations for Differences Between Two Independent Means

The treatment of power in a situation in which we want to test the difference between two independent means is similar to our treatment of the case in which we had only one mean. In the previous section we obtained $d$ by taking the difference between $\mu$ under $H_1$ (i.e., $\mu_1$) and $\mu$ under $H_0$ (i.e., $\mu_0$) and dividing by $\sigma$. In this section we will do something similar, although this time we are going to be working with differences between means. In this case we want the difference between the two population means ($\mu_1 - \mu_2$) under $H_1$ minus the difference ($\mu_1 - \mu_2$) under $H_0$, again divided by $\sigma$. (You should recall that we assume $\sigma_1^2 = \sigma_2^2 = \sigma^2$. But ($\mu_1 - \mu_2$) under $H_0$ is zero in all usual applications, so we can drop that term from the formula. Thus

$$d = \frac{(\mu_1 - \mu_2) - 0}{\sigma} = \frac{(\mu_1 - \mu_2)}{\sigma}$$

The numerator is the difference we expect between population means under $H_1$, and the denominator is the common standard deviation of both populations.

EXAMPLE:
Equal Sample
Sizes

When we calculate power for the comparison of two groups, it makes a difference whether we have equal or unequal sample sizes. The theory isn't any different, but our choice of numbers is. We will begin with the equal sample size case, and then move quickly to the treatment of unequal sample sizes. For the sake of an example, assume that we want to test the hypothesis that rats who were food deprived in infancy hoard more food than normal rats. A somewhat similar experiment, conducted by Hunt (1941), would suggest that the mean number of food pellets hoarded by the deprived group would be approximately 35 and for the nondeprived group approximately 15. In addition, Hunt's data would suggest a value of 17 for $\sigma$. Thus, at least as a rough approximation, we expect $\mu_1 = 35$, $\mu_2 = 15$, and $\sigma = 17$. Then

$$d = \frac{(\mu_1 - \mu_2)}{\sigma} = \frac{20}{17} = 1.18$$

We are saying that we expect a difference of 1.18 standard deviations between the two means. (That is a fairly substantial difference, as you can see by comparing this value to Cohen's rule of thumb for effect sizes.)

First we will investigate the power of an experiment with 10 observations in each of two groups. We will define $\delta$ in the two-sample case as

$$\delta = d\sqrt{\frac{n}{2}}$$

where $n$ equals the number of cases *in any one sample* (there are $2n$ cases in all). Thus

$$\delta = d\sqrt{\frac{n}{2}} = 1.18\sqrt{\frac{10}{2}} = 1.18\sqrt{5} = 1.18(2.236) = 2.64$$

From Table D.5 in Appendix D we see by interpolation that for $\delta = 2.64$ with a two-tailed test at $\alpha = .05$, power equals .75. Thus if we actually run this experiment with 10 subjects in each group and if the estimate of $\delta$ is correct, then we have a 75% chance of actually rejecting $H_0$. This is a high degree of power for so few subjects, but we are dealing with a fairly large effect.

We next want to turn the question around and ask how many subjects would be needed for power equal to .90. (It is reasonable here to try to boost power to .90 [reduce $\beta$ to .10] because we already know that as few as 10 subjects per group would give us power equal to .75 with the effect size that we have.) From Table D.5 we see that this would require $\delta$ equal to 3.25.

$$\delta = d\sqrt{\frac{n}{2}}$$

Squaring for easier rearrangements of terms, we have

$$\delta^2 = \frac{d^2 n}{2}$$

Then

$$n = \frac{2\delta^2}{d^2} = \frac{2(3.25^2)}{1.18^2} = \frac{2(10.5625)}{1.3924} = 15.17$$

Because $n$ refers to the number of subjects per sample, we would need 15 subjects per group, for a total of 30 subjects, if power is to be .90. That is slightly on the large side for a typical study using laboratory rats, which must be bought, housed, and fed at considerable expense. Whether it is worth the expense depends on the importance of the research. ∎

## Unequal Sample Sizes

The case of unequal sample sizes differs from the previous example because we don't have a single number to substitute for $n$ in the formula for $\delta$. Other than that, the procedures are the same.

The simplest solution would be to use the mean of the two sample sizes. For technical reasons, instead of using the standard arithmetic mean that we are used to, we will let $n$ be the harmonic mean of the two sample sizes. In general the **harmonic mean** of $k$ numbers $(X_1, X_2, \ldots X_k)$ is defined as

$$\overline{X}_h = \frac{k}{\sum \dfrac{1}{X_i}}$$

For example, for the numbers 8, 12, and 13 the harmonic mean is

$$\overline{X}_h = \frac{3}{\dfrac{1}{8} + \dfrac{1}{12} + \dfrac{1}{13}} = 10.52$$

For the case of two sample sizes ($n_1 = 26$ and $n_2 = 29$) the formula reduces to

$$\overline{n}_h = \frac{2}{\dfrac{1}{n_1} + \dfrac{1}{n_2}} = \frac{2n_1 n_2}{n_1 + n_2}$$

We then can use the harmonic mean of $n$ in place of $n$ itself in calculating $\delta$.

---

Definition    **Harmonic mean:** The number of elements to be averaged divided by the sum of the reciprocals of the elements.

---

EXAMPLE:
Control and
Cognitive
Behavior
Therapy

Earlier we looked at an example from Everitt that used cognitive behavior therapy to treat anorexia. We were interested in the power we would have if we replicated Everitt's experiment showing that those receiving cognitive behavior therapy gained a significant amount of weight (in other words, the mean weight gain was greater than .00 lbs.) I have mentioned elsewhere that simply showing that the group gained weight does not show that any kind of therapy caused that gain—it may just be that they have gotten older. What we would need for showing a causal effect is the comparison with another group of anorexic girls who did not receive therapy—a control group. Fortunately, Everitt had such a group. Unfortunately, when we run a $t$ test comparing Control and Cognitive Behavior Therapy, the resulting $t$ has a two-tailed probability of .10, which we will not be willing to call significant. This leaves us with a question. Is it true that cognitive behavior therapy really isn't any better than doing nothing? Or is cognitive behavior therapy really an effective treatment, but we just didn't have enough power to detect the difference that was there?

We are not going to find a definitive answer to that question, but we will move toward an answer if we ask about the power of Everitt's study given that the population means and standard deviations are exactly reflected in the sample means and standard deviations. If we find that the experiment had

**Table 15.2**
Statistics from Everitt's Study of Anorexia

| | Treatment | Mean | Std. Dev. | $n$ |
|---|---|---|---|---|
| | Cog. Beh. Ther. | −.45 | 7.9887 | 26 |
| | Control | 3.007 | 7.3085 | 29 |

very little power, we might want to rerun the experiment with larger sample sizes. It might be tempting to suggest the obverse ("if the study had a great deal of power and we did not reject the null, it must really be true"). But that is based on a false premise. It is not possible to find that the study had a great deal of power if the null was not rejected. See Howell (2005) for a discussion of this issue. What you should definitely not do is to discover that the power was very low and then declare that the difference was really there, but that we just ran a poorly designed experiment. If the study was weak, rerun the study; don't just declare success in spite of a nonsignificant difference.

The relevant statistics from Everitt's study are shown in Table 15.2. For these data the value of $d$ is defined as

$$d = \frac{\mu_1 - \mu_2}{\sigma}$$

But we don't know $\sigma$, and will have to estimate it as the pooled variance estimate, as we often do in a $t$ test on two independent samples. For our example

$$s_p^2 = \frac{(n_1 - 1)s_1^2 + (n_2 - 1)s_2^2}{n_1 + n_2 - 2} = \frac{25(7.9987)^2 + 28(7.3085)^2}{26 + 29 - 2}$$

$$= \frac{25(63.97) + 28(53.41)}{53} = \frac{3094.73}{53} = 58.39$$

$$s_p = \sqrt{58.39} = 7.64$$

Therefore

$$\hat{d} = \frac{\mu_1 - \mu_2}{s_p} = \frac{-.45 - 3.007}{7.64} = \frac{-3.457}{7.64} = -.452$$

We don't care about the sign of $\hat{d}$, so we will drop the negative sign and declare $\hat{d} = .452$.

Now we need to calculate $\delta$, but first we have to estimate the sample size $(n)$.

$$\bar{n}_h = \frac{2}{\dfrac{1}{n_1} + \dfrac{1}{n_2}} = \frac{2n_1 n_2}{n_1 + n_2} = \frac{2(26)(29)}{26 + 29} = 27.42$$

Finally,

$$\delta = d\sqrt{\frac{n}{2}} = .452\sqrt{\frac{27.42}{2}} = 1.67$$

From Appendix D.5, with $\delta = 1.67$, using a two-tailed test at $\alpha = .05$, we find that power $=.39$ (approximately). So even if Everitt did an exact job of estimating the population means and variances, which would mean that the null is false because the two estimated population means are different, he would still have only about 4 chances out of 10 of actually getting a significant difference. If you are a staunch advocate of cognitive behavior therapy, and want to show that it is an effective therapy, you will need considerably more subjects.

If you want power equal to .80, you are going to need $\delta = 2.80$. Solving the previous equation backwards for $n$ with $\delta = 2.80$, we have

$$n = \frac{2\delta^2}{d^2} = \frac{2(2.80^2)}{.452^2} = 76.75$$

This means that we are going to need about 77 participants in each group, which is well more than twice as many as Everitt had. That is a lot of participants. Perhaps we would be better off with the smaller samples, but continuing therapy for longer in hopes of getting a greater mean weight gain in the cognitive behavior therapy group. ∎

## 15.6 Power Calculations for the *t* Test for Related Samples

When we move to the situation in which we want to test the difference between two matched samples, the problem becomes somewhat more difficult, and we must take into account the correlation between the two sets of observations. In earlier editions of this book I went into detail on how to calculate power in this situation, but on reflection I believe that there is little to be gained by putting you through that.

The basic idea is the same as for the two previous tests. We would define $d$ *as*

$$d = \frac{\mu_1 - \mu_2}{\sigma_D} = \frac{\mu_D}{\sigma_D}$$

and substitute sample statistics for the parameters. If you had data from a previous study that gave you the necessary statistics, you could immediately solve for $d$. And because this really represents a test on one sample mean (the mean of the difference scores), we can calculate $\delta$ *as*

$$\delta = d\sqrt{N}$$

We then can refer to Table D.5 for the value of $\delta$.

If you don't have good estimates of the necessary parameters, you *could* calculate power as if these were two separate groups of scores. That would give you an estimate of the lower bound of power. The true power would be somewhat higher, and perhaps considerably higher.

**EXAMPLE:**
**Anorexia and**
**Family Therapy**

To use an actual example, we will go back to the data in Section 13.2 on the use of family therapy as a treatment for anorexia. There we had a set of weights at the beginning and end of therapy, and calculated a *t* on matched samples. Suppose that we would like to replicate this study to verify its conclusions, but we want to have a reasonable chance of finding a significant result. Because we know about the original study, we can make some reasonable guesses about what to expect. We know that Everitt's data found a difference of 7.26 pounds between the pre- and post-therapy weights. We also know that the standard deviation of the difference scores was 7.16, so we don't have to estimate it using the pre-post correlation of scores. With this information, and with Everitt's sample size of $N = 17$, we can calculate the power assuming that the statistics that he reported are equal to the actual population parameters.

$$d = \frac{\mu_1 - \mu_2}{\sigma_D} = \frac{7.26}{7.16} = 1.01$$

$$\delta = d\sqrt{N}$$

$$= 1.01\sqrt{17} = 4.16$$

From Appendix D we find that for a two-tailed test at $\alpha = .05$, power is approximately equal to .99. This strikes me as an unusually high degree of power, but keep in mind that Everitt reported an effect size of slightly over 1.00. That is certainly a very large effect, and I am frankly quite surprised that even the greatest therapy on earth would produce such an effect. (That isn't to say that I don't believe the data, but only that I am very surprised by them.) If the therapy works as well as Everitt's data would suggest, then we are almost certain to find a significant difference when we have 17 subjects in the replication study that we want to run.[5]   ∎

---

[5]I have come close to painting myself in a box here, and think I'm better off discussing it than hoping you won't notice. I have said that there are two kinds of effect sizes. There are measures that are designed to tell the reader how large of an effect you found, and there are effect size measures, as used in this chapter, when calculating power. I have said that they are the same thing. They are, but you may notice that in the present example I obtained $d$ using the standard error of the difference ($s_{\overline{X}_{post} - \overline{X}_{pre}}$), while in Chapter 13 I said that you should use the standard deviation of the pretreatment scores as your denominator. I am right in both cases, and only good explanation is that we are using these statistics for different things. To calculate power you do need to estimate the standard error of the differences.

**Table 15.3**
Total Sample Sizes Required for Power = .80, $\alpha$ = .05, Two-Tailed

| Effect Size | d | One-Sample t | Two-Sample t |
|---|---|---|---|
| Small | .20 | 196 | 784 |
| Medium | .50 | 32 | 126 |
| Large | .80 | 13 | 49 |

## 15.7 Power Considerations in Terms of Sample Size

Our discussion of power here illustrates that reasonably large sample sizes are generally a necessity if you are to run experiments that have a good chance of rejecting $H_0$ when it is, in fact, false, especially if the effect is small. A few minutes with a calculator will show you that if we want to have power equal to .80, and if we accept Cohen's definitions for small, medium, and large effects, our samples must be quite large. Table 15.3 presents the total sample sizes required (at power = .80, $\alpha$ = .05) for small, medium, and large effects for the tests we have been discussing. These figures indicate that power (at least a substantial amount of it) is a very expensive commodity, especially for small effects. While it could be argued that this is actually a good thing, since otherwise the literature would contain many more trivial results than it already does, most experimenters will find little comfort in knowing that their poorly designed study is protecting the field from being swamped with minor effects. The general rule is to look for big effects, to use large samples, or to employ sensitive experimental designs such as those that involve the use of repeated measurements on the same subjects, reducing experimental error and thus making small differences translate into large effect sizes.

## 15.8 You Don't Have to Do It by Hand

Those of you with a connection to the World Wide Web have a lot of resources for studying power. A simple Java program that accepts keyboard input about sample sizes, effect sizes, and estimated standard deviations, is available at

http://www.stat.uiowa.edu/~rlenth/Power/index.html

This Web page calculates power for one and two sample t tests, as well as for correlational studies. A page at

http://www.math.yorku.ca/SCS/Online/power/

does a good job with power for the analysis of variance, to be described in the next few chapters. Finally, a complete review of free-standing statistical packages for power analysis, some of which can be downloaded for free, is available at

http://www.zoology.ubc.ca/~krebs/power.html

My particular favorite among these programs is one called G*Power, which is available for PCs and Macs, and which is free. The address for that is

http://www.psycho.uni-duesseldorf.de/aap/projects/gpower/

I strongly encourage you to go to these sites, and others that they point to, because it is a great way to get a handle on power. They can also lead you to all sorts of other neat, cool stuff.

## 15.9 Seeing Statistics

The applet on this book's Web site entitled Power Applet illustrates the effect of all three major variables that control power (the true difference between means, the standard deviation, and the sample size). An example of the screen is shown.

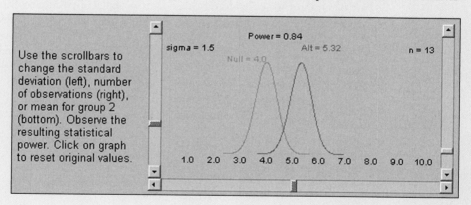

This figure differs only superficially from Figure 15.1. Whereas Figure 15.1 displays distributions corresponding to the null and alternative hypotheses, the figure in the applet shows distributions corresponding to the two populations from which we sampled. My labeling applies best to the one-group experiment, and the labeling here applies best to the two-group experiment. If you would prefer to relabel the distributions, that would not change anything else that follows.

In the top center of the display is the level of power resulting from the various settings. By dragging the slider on the bottom left and right, you can increase or decrease the distance between means. You should try dragging the slider so that the two distributions overlap exactly. This is the null case. What is the resulting power?

On the left and right are sliders that correspond to the standard deviation and sample size, respectively. We saw in this chapter that power increases as the variance decreases (it is easier to find a difference if you have less noise in your data) and as the sample size increases (large samples make it easier to pick out a difference). Move the sliders and verify these two predictions.

In Section 15.5 we looked at a study of hoarding behavior in rats. We can't apply those data exactly to this applet because we can't reproduce a difference of 20 points and a standard deviation of 17. However, it would not change the problem in any important way if I presented those data as having means of 4.0 and 6.0, and standard deviations of 1.7. There were 10 rats in each group. Set these values on the display and record the resulting power. In the chapter we found the power to be approximately .75. You won't get exactly that here, but don't worry about it. (My calculations used an approximation.) How close do you come? How many rats would you need in each group to have power = .95?

## 15.10 Summary

In this chapter we considered those factors that contribute to the power of a test. You saw that the most easily manipulated factor is the sample size, and we considered ways of calculating the power for a given sample size and, conversely, the sample size needed for a specified level of power. Finally, we considered the unwelcome conclusion that high levels of power often may require more subjects than we can reasonably expect.

Some important terms in this chapter are

| | |
|---|---|
| Power, 352 | Harmonic mean, 364 |
| Delta ($\delta$), 359 | |

## 15.11 Exercises

**15.1** I am very confident that I am a better technical skier than my brother, but I don't expect that if a judge watched us descend through the trees, I would *always* get a better rating. What does that statement have to do with statistical power?

**15.2** What is your subjective probability that the New York Yankees will win next year's World Series? What does that have to do with power?

**15.3** In Section 12.3 we looked at a set of data on whether children tend to tell us what they think we want to hear, rather than what they really feel. For those data, the test on $H_0$ was

not significant, even though the sample size was 36. Suppose that the experimenters had, in fact, actually estimated the mean and standard deviation of the population of stressed children exactly.
(a) What is the effect size in question?
(b) What is the value of $\delta$ for a sample size of 36?
(c) What is the power of the test?

**15.4** Diagram the situation described in Exercise 15.3 along the lines of Figure 15.1.

**15.5** In Exercise 15.3, what sample sizes would be needed to raise power to .70, .80, and .90?

**15.6** Following from Exercise 15.3, suppose that my colleagues were tired of having children tell us what they think we want to hear, and gave them a heart-to-heart talk on the necessity of accurate reporting. Suppose that this will reduce their population mean Lie score from 4.39 to 2.75, again with a standard deviation of 2.61. If we have 36 children for this analysis, what is the power of finding significantly fewer distortions in these children's reports than in the general population? The population of normal children still has a population mean of 3.87.

**15.7** Diagram the situation described in Exercise 15.6 along the lines of Figure 15.1.

**15.8** How many subjects would we need in Exercise 15.6 to have power = .80?

**15.9** A neuroscience laboratory run by a friend of mine has been studying avoidance behavior in rabbits for many years and has published numerous papers on the topic. It is clear from this research that the mean response latency for a particular task is 5.8 seconds with a standard deviation of 2 seconds (based on a very large number of rabbits). Now the investigators want to create lesions in certain areas of the amygdala and demonstrate poorer avoidance conditioning in those animals. (The amygdala is associated with emotion, and if you reduce an emotional response you would be expected to reduce avoidance behavior.) They expect latencies to decrease by about 1 second (i.e., rabbits will repeat the punished response sooner), and they plan to run a one-sample $t$ test (with $H_0$: $\mu_0 = 5.8$).
(a) How many subjects do the investigators need in order to have at least a 50:50 chance of success?
(b) How many subjects do they need in order to have at least an 80:20 chance of success?

**15.10** Suppose the laboratory referred to in Exercise 15.9 decided that instead of running one group and comparing it against $\mu_0 = 5.8$ they would run two groups (one with and one without lesions). They still expect the same degree of difference, however.
(a) How many subjects do they now need (overall) if they are to have power equal .60?
(b) How many subjects do they now need (overall) if they are to have power equal .90?

**15.11** As it turns out, a research assistant has just finished running the experiment described in Exercise 15.10 without having carried out any power calculations. He tried to run 20 subjects in each group, but he accidentally tipped over a rack of cages and had to void 5 subjects in the experimental group. What is the power of this experiment?

**15.12** We have just conducted a study comparing cognitive development of low-birthweight (premature) and normal-birthweight babies at one year of age. Using a score of my own devising, I found the sample means of the two groups to be 25 and 30, respectively, with a pooled standard deviation of 8. There were 20 subjects in each group. If we assume that the true means and standard deviations have been estimated exactly, what was the *a priori* probability (the probability before the experiment was conducted) that this study would find a significant difference?

**15.13** Let's modify Exercise 15.12 to have sample means of 25 and 28, with a pooled standard deviation of 8 and sample sizes of 20 and 20.
(a) What is the *a priori* power of this experiment?
(b) Run the *t* test on the data.
(c) What, if anything, does the answer to (a) have to say about the answer to (b)?

**15.14** Diagram the answer to Exercise 15.13.

**15.15** Two graduate students have recently completed their dissertations. Each used a *t* test for two independent groups. One found a barely significant *t* using 10 subjects per group. The other found a barely significant *t* using 45 subjects per group. Which result impresses you more?

**15.16** Make up a simple two-group example to demonstrate that for a total of 30 subjects power increases as the sample sizes become more nearly equal.

**15.17** A beleaguered Ph.D. candidate has the impression that he must find significant results if he wants to defend his dissertation successfully. He wants to show a difference in social awareness, as measured by his own scale, between a normal group of students and a group of ex-delinquents. He has a problem, however. He has data to suggest that the normal group has a true mean equal to 38, and he has 50 of those subjects. For the other group he has access either to 100 college students who have been classed as delinquent in the past or to 25 high school dropouts with a history of delinquency. He suspects that the scores of the college group come from a population with a mean of approximately 35, whereas the scores of the dropout group come from a population with a mean of approximately 30. He can use only one of these groups—which should it be?

**15.18** Generate a table analogous to Table 15.3 for power equal to .80, with $\alpha = .01$, two-tailed.

**15.19** Generate a table analogous to Table 15.2 for power equal to .60, with $\alpha = .05$, two-tailed.

**15.20** Assume we want to test a null hypothesis about a single mean at $\alpha = .05$, one-tailed. Further assume that all necessary assumptions are met. Is there ever a case in which we are more likely to reject a true $H_0$ than we are to reject $H_0$ if it is false? (In other words, can power ever be less than $\alpha$?)

**15.21** If $\sigma = 15$, $n = 25$, and we are testing $H_0: \mu = 100$ versus $H_1: \mu > 100$, what value of the mean under $H_1$ would result in power being equal to the probability of a Type II error? (*Hint:* This is most easily solved by sketching the two distributions. Which areas are you trying to equate?)

**15.22** Calculate the power of the anorexia experiment in Section 14.1, assuming that the parameters have been estimated correctly.

**15.23** Calculate the power of the comparison of TATs from the parents of schizophrenic and normal subjects in Exercise 14.8.

**15.24** Why would we ever want to calculate power after an experiment has been run, as we just did in Exercises 15.22 and 15.23?

**15.25** Joshua Aronson has spent considerable time studying "stereotype threat," which refers to the fact that "members of stereotyped groups often feel extra pressure in situations where their behavior can confirm the negative reputation that their group lacks a valued ability." (Aronson et al., 1998) This feeling of stereotype threat is then hypothesized to affect performance, generally lowering it from what it would have been had the participant not felt threatened. Aronson recruited two independent groups of white male college students for whom doing well in mathematics was personally important. Both groups were asked to complete a difficult math test. The Threat group was also told that the researchers were studying why Asian students typically did better in math than non-Asian students. This condition should arouse feelings of stereotype threat for these white males. The mean for the Control group was 9.64 problems correct with s = 3.17. For the Threat group the values were 6.58 and 3.03 respectively. There were 11 participants in the Control group and 12 in the Threat group. If these statistics correctly estimate population parameters, what is the power of this experiment?

# 16

# One-Way Analysis of Variance

**QUESTIONS**

■ What is the analysis of variance, and what does it do?

■ Why is it called the analysis of *variance* when it deals with *means*?

■ What do I need to know to run the calculations?

■ But what do I do when the sample sizes are unequal?

■ So I found that not all means are equal. So what? What do I know now?

■ I made some assumptions that may not be true. What effect will that have?

■ The difference is significant, but is it meaningful?

■ I'll bet there's a way to use computer software so I don't have to punch all those buttons and fit things into all those formulae.

The **analysis of variance (ANOVA)** currently enjoys the status of being probably the most used statistical technique in psychological research, with multiple regression running a close second. The popularity and usefulness of this technique can be attributed to two facts. First, the analysis of variance, like *t*, deals with differences between sample means, but unlike *t*, it has no restriction on the number of means. Instead of asking merely whether two means differ, we can ask whether two, three, four, five, or *k* means differ. Second, the analysis of variance allows us to deal with two or more independent variables simultaneously, asking not only about the individual effects of each variable separately but also about the interacting effects of two or more variables.

| Definition | **Analysis of variance (ANOVA):** A statistical technique for testing for differences in the means of several groups.<br><br>**One-way ANOVA:** An analysis of variance wherein the groups are defined on only one independent variable. |
|---|---|

This chapter will be concerned with the underlying logic of the analysis of variance (which is really quite simple) and the analysis of the results of experiments that employ only one independent variable. In addition we will deal with a few related topics that are most easily understood in the context of a one-variable analysis (**one-way ANOVA**). Subsequent chapters will deal with the analysis of experiments that involve two or more independent variables and with designs in which repeated measurements are made on each participant.

# 16.1  The General Approach

Many features of the analysis of variance can be best illustrated by a simple example, so we will begin with a study by M. W. Eysenck (1974) on recall of verbal material as a function of the level of processing. The data we will use have the same group means and standard deviations as those reported by Eysenck, but the individual observations are fictional. The importance of this study is that it illustrates a clean test of an important theory of memory, while at the same time giving clear results as an example.

Craik and Lockhart (1972) proposed as a model of memory that the degree to which verbal material is remembered by the participant is a function of the degree to which it was processed when it was initially presented. You have probably noticed that I frequently insert questions to you in the text, asking about alternative interpretations of the data, about what it would mean if the test statistic came out differently, and so on. The main purpose of these questions is to encourage you to "process" the information you have just read rather than to just let it flow past. I'm talking here about the same thing that Craik and Lockhart were. But to put the example in their terms, imagine that you are asked to memorize a list of words. Repeating a word to yourself (a low level of processing) would not be expected to lead to as good recall as thinking about each word and trying to form associations between that word and some other word. Eysenck (1974) was interested in testing this model and, more important, in looking to see whether it could help to explain reported differences between young and old participants in their ability to recall verbal material. An examination of Eysenck's data on age differences will be postponed until Chapter 17; we will concentrate here on differences due to the level of processing.

Eysenck randomly assigned 50 participants between the ages of 55 and 65 years to one of five groups: four incidental-learning groups and one intentional-learning group. (Incidental learning is learning in the absence of the expectation that the material will need to be recalled later.) The Counting group was asked to read through a list of words and simply count the number of letters in each word. This involved the lowest level of processing, because participants did not need to deal with each word as anything more than a collection of letters. The Rhyming group was asked to read each word and to think of a word that rhymed with it. This task involved considering the sound of each word but not its meaning. The Adjective group had to process the words to the extent of giving an adjective that could reasonably be used to modify each word on the list. The Imagery group was instructed to try to form vivid images of each word, and this condition was assumed to require the deepest level of processing. None of these four groups was told that they would later be asked to recall the items. Finally, the Intentional group was told to read through the list and to memorize the words for later recall. It is very likely that different people in this condition used different strategies to retain the words, which reduces the utility of this condition. After the participants had gone through the list of 27 items three times, they were given a sheet of paper and asked to write down all the words they could remember. If learning involves nothing more than being exposed to the material (the way most of us read a newspaper or, heaven forbid, a class assignment), then the five groups should have shown equal recall—after all, they all saw all the words. If the level of processing of the material is important, then there should have been noticeable differences among the group means. The data are presented in Table 16.1.

**Table 16.1**
Number of Words Recalled as a Function of the Level of Processing

|  | Counting | Rhyming | Adjective | Imagery | Intentional | Total |
|---|---|---|---|---|---|---|
|  | 9 | 7 | 11 | 12 | 10 |  |
|  | 8 | 9 | 13 | 11 | 19 |  |
|  | 6 | 6 | 8 | 16 | 14 |  |
|  | 8 | 6 | 6 | 11 | 5 |  |
|  | 10 | 6 | 14 | 9 | 10 |  |
|  | 4 | 11 | 11 | 23 | 11 |  |
|  | 6 | 6 | 13 | 12 | 14 |  |
|  | 5 | 3 | 13 | 10 | 15 |  |
|  | 7 | 8 | 10 | 19 | 11 |  |
|  | 7 | 7 | 11 | 11 | 11 |  |
| Mean | 7.00 | 6.90 | 11.00 | 13.40 | 12.00 | 10.06 |
| Std. Dev. | 1.83 | 2.13 | 2.49 | 4.50 | 3.74 | 4.01 |
| Variance | 3.33 | 4.54 | 6.22 | 20.27 | 14.00 | 16.06 |

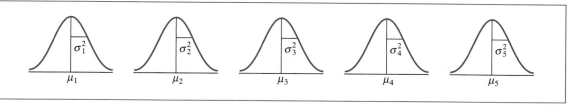

**Figure 16.1**
Graphical representation of populations of recall scores

## The Null Hypothesis

Eysenck was interested in testing the null hypothesis that the level of recall was equal under the five conditions. In other words, if $\mu_1$ represents the population mean for all participants who could potentially be tested under the Counting conditions, $\mu_2$ represents the population mean corresponding to the Rhyming condition, and so on, up to $\mu_5$ (for the Intentional condition), then the null hypothesis is

$$H_0: \mu_1 = \mu_2 = \mu_3 = \mu_4 = \mu_5$$

This is often referred to as the "**omnibus null hypothesis**" because it deals with the equality of all of the means. The alternative hypothesis will be the hypothesis that *at least* one mean is different from the others. The five hypothetical populations of recall scores are illustrated in Figure 16.1. The placement of these populations from left to right is not intended to suggest that one population mean is necessarily larger than the population mean to its left. At this point I am saying nothing about the relative magnitude of the population means.

---

Definition    **Omnibus null hypothesis:** The hypothesis that all population means are equal.

---

The analysis of variance is a technique for using differences between sample means to draw inferences about the presence or absence of differences between population means. The null hypothesis could be false in a number of ways (e.g., all means could be different from each other, or the first two could be equal to each other but different from the last three), but for now we are going to be concerned only with the problem of whether the (omnibus) null hypothesis is completely true or it is false. Later in this chapter we will deal with the problem of whether only some of the means are equal.

## The Population

One of the difficulties people frequently encounter in the study of statistics concerns the meaning of the word *population*. As mentioned in Chapter 1, a population is a collection of numbers, not a collection of rats or people or anything else. Strictly speaking, we are not trying to say that a population of people who learned a list under one condition is the same population as the population of people who learned under a different condition—obviously they are not. Rather, we want to be able to say that a population of *scores* obtained under one condition has a mean greater than or less than the mean of a population of scores obtained under another condition. This may appear to be a rather trivial point, but it isn't. If you were to compare people of different ages, for example, as we will in the next chapter, the populations of people certainly would differ in a variety of ways. However, it is not obvious beforehand that the recall scores will be different between the populations.

## The Assumption of Normality

For reasons dealing with our final test of significance, we will make the assumption that recall scores in each population are normally distributed around the population mean ($\mu_j$). This is no more than the assumption that the observations in Figure 16.1 are normally distributed. We made this same assumption for the *t* test for independent groups, but in that case there were only two populations. As with *t*, the assumption of normality deals primarily with the normality of the sampling distribution of the mean rather than the distribution of individual observations. Moreover, even substantial departures from normality may, under certain conditions, have remarkably little influence on the final result.

## The Assumption of Homogeneity of Variance

A second major assumption that we will make is that each population of scores has the same variance, specifically

$$\sigma_1^2 = \sigma_2^2 = \sigma_3^2 = \sigma_4^2 = \sigma_5^2 = \sigma_e^2$$

Here the notation $\sigma_e^2$ indicates the common value held by the five variances. The subscript *e* is an abbreviation for error, since this variance is error variance; that is, variance unrelated to any group differences.[1] Homogeneity of variance would be expected to occur if the effect of a treatment is to add a constant to everyone's score—if, for example, everyone who thought of adjectives in Eysenck's study recalled five more words than they otherwise would have recalled. As you will see later, under certain conditions this assumption also can be relaxed without doing too much damage to the final result. In other words, the analysis of variance is robust with respect to violations of the assumptions of normality and homogeneity of variance.

## The Assumption of Independence of Observations

Our third important assumption is that the observations are all independent of one another. For any two observations in an experimental treatment, we assume that knowing how one observation stands relative to the treatment (or population)

---

[1] In terms of the discussion in Chapter 10, this is error variance in the sense that it is variability that cannot be predicted from group membership, since people in the same group (population) obviously don't differ on the grouping variable.

mean tells us nothing about the other observation. (This assumption would be violated if, for example, participants cheated and copied off their neighbors or overheard each other's answers.) This assumption is one of the important reasons why participants are usually randomly assigned to groups. Violation of the independence assumption can have serious consequences for an analysis.

## 16.2   The Logic of the Analysis of Variance

The logic underlying the analysis of variance is really very simple—once you understand it, the rest of the discussion will make considerably more sense. (I don't expect that every student will have the logic down pat after reading this section once, but you should get the general idea. I recommend coming back to this section once again after you have read the whole chapter, and then probably coming back to it again the next day—but I guess I'm naive.) In this section I will simplify the presentation slightly by assuming that all groups have the same number of observations, though that is not a requirement of the analysis of variance. Consider for a moment the effect of our three major assumptions: normality, homogeneity of variance, and the independence of observations. By making the first two of these assumptions, we have said that the five populations represented in Figure 16.1 have the same shape and the same dispersion. As a result, the only way left for them to differ is in terms of their means.

We will begin by making no assumption about $H_0$—it may be true or false. For any one treatment, the variance of the 10 scores in that group would be an estimate of the variance of the population from which the scores were drawn. Because we have assumed that all populations have the same variance, it is also one estimate of the common population variance $\sigma_e^2$. If you prefer, you can think of

$$\sigma_1^2 \doteq s_1^2 \quad \sigma_2^2 \doteq s_2^2 \quad \cdots \quad \sigma_5^2 \doteq s_5^2$$

where $\doteq$ is read "is estimated by." Because of our homogeneity assumption, all of these are estimates of $\sigma_e^2$. For the sake of increased reliability, we can pool the five estimates by taking their mean, if $n_1 = n_2 = \cdots = n_5 = n$, and thus

$$\sigma_e^2 \doteq \bar{s}_j^2 = \frac{s_1^2 + s_2^2 + s_3^2 + s_4^2 + s_5^2}{5}$$

This is our best estimate of $\sigma_e^2$. Pooling of variances is exactly equivalent to what we did when we pooled variances in the $t$ test (although here we have more than two variances). This average value of the five sample variances ($s_j^2$) is one estimate of the population variance ($\sigma_e^2$) and is what we will later refer to as $\text{MS}_{\text{within}}$ or $\text{MS}_{\text{error}}$ (read "mean square within" or "mean square error"). It is important to note that this estimate does *not* depend on the truth or falsity of $H_0$, because $s_j^2$ is calculated on each sample separately. For the data from Eysenck's study, our pooled estimate of $\sigma_e^2$ will be

$$s_j^2 = \frac{(3.33 + 4.54 + 6.22 + 20.27 + 14.00)}{5} = 9.67$$

Now let us assume that $H_0$ *is true*. If that is the case, then the five samples of 10 cases can be thought of as five independent samples from the same population. We can examine the variance of means to obtain another estimate of $\sigma_e^2$. Remember from earlier discussions that means are not as variable as observations. (Why should this be?) In fact, the Central Limit Theorem states that the variance of *means* drawn from the same population equals the variance of the population divided by the sample size. If $H_0$ is true, the sample means have been drawn from the same population (or identical populations, which amounts to the same thing), and therefore

$$\frac{\sigma_e^2}{n} \doteq s_{\overline{X}}^2$$

*where n is the size of each sample.* Here all samples will have the same size. We can reverse the usual order of things and, instead of estimating the variance of means from the variance of the population, we can estimate the variance of the population(s) from the variance of the sample means ($s_{\overline{X}}^2$). If we simply clear fractions in the previous formula, we have

$$\sigma_e^2 \doteq n s_{\overline{X}}^2$$

This term is commonly known as $\mathbf{MS_{between\ groups}}$ or more simply $\mathbf{MS_{groups}}$ or $\mathbf{MS_{treatment}}$.

These few steps can be illustrated easily, as has been done for five equal-sized groups in Figure 16.2. This figure emphasizes that the average of the sample variances is $MS_{error}$ and the variance of the sample means *multiplied by the sample size* is $MS_{group}$.

We now have two estimates of the population variance ($\sigma_e^2$). One of these estimates, $MS_{error}$, is independent of the truth or falsity of $H_0$. It is *always* an estimate of the population variance. The other, $MS_{group}$, is an estimate of $\sigma_e^2$ *only as long as $H_0$ is true* (only as long as the conditions assumed by the Central Limit Theorem are met, namely that the samples are drawn from one population). Otherwise, $MS_{group}$ would estimate the variability of group means in addition to $\sigma_e^2$. If the two estimates ($MS_{error}$ and $MS_{group}$) are roughly in agreement, we will have support for the truth of $H_0$; and if they disagree substantially, we will have support for the falsity

$$s_1^2 \leftarrow \text{Sample 1} \rightarrow \overline{X}_1$$
$$s_2^2 \leftarrow \text{Sample 2} \rightarrow \overline{X}_2$$
$$s_3^2 \leftarrow \text{Sample 3} \rightarrow \overline{X}_3 \qquad \text{Variance of } \overline{X}_i = s_{\overline{X}}^2$$
$$s_4^2 \leftarrow \text{Sample 4} \rightarrow \overline{X}_4$$
$$s_5^2 \leftarrow \text{Sample 5} \rightarrow \overline{X}_5$$
$$\overline{\text{Average of } s_j^2 = \text{MS}_{\text{error}}} \qquad n(s_{\overline{X}}^2) = \text{MS}_{\text{group}}$$

**Figure 16.2**

Illustration of the meaning of $\text{MS}_{\text{error}}$ and $\text{MS}_{\text{group}}$ when sample sizes are equal

of $H_0$. I can illustrate the logic just described by way of two very simple examples that have been deliberately constructed to represent more or less ideal results under the conditions $H_0$ true and $H_0$ false. Never in practice will data be as neat and tidy as in these examples.

EXAMPLE:
The Case of a
True $H_0$

Assume that we have an experiment involving three groups. As we saw earlier, when $H_0$ is true, $\mu_1 = \mu_2 = \mu_3$, and any samples drawn from these three populations can be thought of as coming from just one population. In the first example three samples of $n = 9$ have been chosen to resemble data that might be drawn from the same normally distributed population with a mean of 5 and a variance of 10. For example, these data might represent the number of information-seeking comments uttered by nine participants in each of three groups prior to the onset of a socialization-training experiment. Because the experiment has not yet begun, we hope not to find group differences. The data are presented in Table 16.2 for the $k = 3$ groups. From this table we can see that the average variance in each group is 9.250, a respectable estimate of $\sigma_e^2 = 10$. The variance of the group means is 1.000, and because we know $H_0$ to be true,

$$s_{\overline{X}}^2 \doteq \frac{\sigma_e^2}{n}$$

$$\sigma_e^2 \doteq n s_{\overline{X}}^2 = 9(1.000) = 9$$

This is our value for $\text{MS}_{\text{group}}$. This value is also reasonably in agreement with $\sigma_e^2$ and with our other estimate based on the variability within treatments. Because these two estimates agree, we would conclude that we have no reason to doubt the truth of $H_0$. Put another way, the three sample means do not vary more than we would expect if $H_0$ were true.  ∎

**Table 16.2**
Representative Data for the Case in Which $H_0$ Is True

| Group 1 | Group 2 | Group 3 |
|---|---|---|
| 3 | 1 | 5 |
| 6 | 4 | 2 |
| 9 | 7 | 8 |
| 6 | 4 | 8 |
| 3 | 1 | 2 |
| 12 | 10 | 8 |
| 6 | 4 | 5 |
| 3 | 1 | 2 |
| 9 | 7 | 8 |
| $\overline{X} = 6.3333$ | 4.3333 | 5.3333 |
| $s_j^2 = 10.0000$ | 10.0000 | 7.7500 |

Grand mean $(\overline{X}_{..}) = 5.3333^2$

$$s_{\overline{X}}^2 = \frac{\Sigma(\overline{X}_j - \overline{X}_{..})^2}{k - 1} = 1.000$$

$$\bar{s}_j^2 = \frac{10.00 + 10.00 + 7.75}{3} = 9.250$$

$$MS_{error} = \bar{s}_j^2 = 9.25$$

$$MS_{group} = ns_{\overline{X}}^2 = 9(1.000) = 9$$

EXAMPLE:
The Case of a
False $H_0$

Next consider an example in which I know $H_0$ to be false because I made it false. The data in Table 16.3 have been obtained by adding or subtracting constants to or from the data in Table 16.2. These data might represent the number of information-seeking comments uttered by people in three different groups at the *end* of our socialization-training sessions. We now have data that might have been produced by sampling from three normally distributed populations, all with variance equal to 10. However, Group 1 scores might have come from a population with $\mu = 8$, whereas scores for Groups 2 and 3 might have come from a population, or populations, with $\mu = 4$. This represents a substantial departure from $H_0$, which stated that all population means were equal to each other.

In Table 16.3 you will note that the variance within each treatment remains unchanged, since adding or subtracting a constant has no effect on the variance within groups. This illustrates the earlier statement that the variance within groups ($MS_{error}$) is independent of the truth or falsity of the

---

[2] The symbol $\overline{X}_{..}$ is used to represent the grand mean of the observations ($X_{ij}$). The ".." indicates that we have averaged across both the rows ($i$) and the groups ($j$).

**Table 16.3**
Representative Data for the Case in Which $H_0$ Is False

| Group 1 | Group 2 | Group 3 |
|---|---|---|
| 5 | 0 | 5 |
| 8 | 3 | 2 |
| 11 | 6 | 8 |
| 8 | 3 | 8 |
| 5 | 0 | 2 |
| 14 | 9 | 8 |
| 8 | 3 | 5 |
| 5 | 0 | 2 |
| 11 | 6 | 8 |
| $\overline{X} =$  8.3333 | 3.3333 | 5.3333 |
| $s_j^2 = 10.0000$ | 10.0000 | 7.7500 |

$$\text{Grandmean}(\overline{X}_{..}) = 5.6667$$

$$s_{\overline{X}}^2 = \frac{\Sigma(\overline{X}_j - \overline{X}_{..})^2}{k-1} = 6.333$$

$$\overline{s}_j^2 = \frac{10.00 + 10.00 + 7.75}{3} = 9.250$$

$$MS_{\text{error}} = \overline{s}_j^2 = 9.25$$

$$MS_{\text{group}} = ns_{\overline{X}}^2 = 9(6.333) = 57$$

null hypothesis. The variance among the group means, however, has increased substantially, reflecting the differences among the population means. In this case the estimate of $\sigma_e^2$ based on sample means is $ns_{\overline{X}}^2 = 9(6.333) = 57$, a value that is way out of line with the estimate of 9.25 given by the variance within groups ($MS_{\text{error}}$). The most logical conclusion would be that $ns_{\overline{X}}^2$ is not estimating merely population variance ($\sigma_e^2$), but is estimating $\sigma_e^2$ *plus* the variance of the population means themselves. In other words, the scores differ not only because of random error but also because we have been successful in teaching some of our participants to ask information-seeking questions. ∎

## Summary of the Logic of the Analysis of Variance

From the preceding discussion we can state the logic of the analysis of variance concisely. To test $H_0$ we calculate two estimates of the population variance; one ($MS_{\text{error}}$) is independent of the truth or falsity of $H_0$, while the other ($MS_{\text{group}}$) is dependent on $H_0$. If the two are in approximate agreement, we have no reason to reject $H_0$. The means differ only to the extent that the sampling distribution of the mean leads us to expect when $H_0$ is true. If $MS_{group}$ is much larger than $MS_{error}$, we conclude that underlying differences in treatment means must have contributed to the second estimate, inflating it and causing it to differ from the first. We therefore reject $H_0$. This illustrates how an analysis of *variance* allows us to draw inferences about *means*.

## 16.3 Calculations for the Analysis of Variance

The calculations for the analysis of variance are quite simple and straightforward. The formulae appear to be different from the kinds of formulae you saw for *t* tests, but this difference is really a function of the fact that here we are going to emphasize the use of sums of squares instead of means and variances.

### Sums of Squares

In the analysis of variance most of our computations deal with the **sum of squares (SS)**, which, in this context, is merely the sum of squared deviations about the mean $\Sigma(X - \overline{X}..)^2$ or some multiple of that. The advantage of sums of squares and the reason that we begin by calculating them is that they can be added and subtracted, whereas mean squares usually cannot. We will take the total sum of squares ($SS_{total}$) and partition or decompose it into that part that is due to variation between groups ($SS_{group}$) and that part that is due to variation within groups ($SS_{error}$). The additive nature of sums of squares makes this possible.

Definition  **Sum of squares (SS):** The sum of the squared deviations around some point (usually around a mean or predicted value).

### The Calculations

At this point we will return to the example from Eysenck on recall of verbal material. The data have been reproduced in Table 16.4 along with the resulting computations, which we will discuss in detail.

In part (a) of Table 16.4 you can see the data, the individual observations ($X_{ij}$), the individual group means ($\overline{X}_j$), and the grand mean ($\overline{X}..$). We will use the notation $\overline{X}_j$ to represent the mean of the *j*th group throughout our discussion of the analysis of variance. In analyses in which there is more than one independent variable (factor), $\overline{X}_j$ can be extended to $\overline{X}_{row\,i}$ and $\overline{X}_{col\,j}$ without any loss of clarity.

The means and the variances are exactly those found by Eysenck, but since the data points are fictitious, there is little to be gained by examining the distribution of observations within individual groups—the data were actually drawn from normally distributed populations and then rounded to whole numbers. With real data it is important to examine these distributions first to make sure they are not seriously skewed, bimodal, or, even more important, skewed in different directions.

**Table 16.4**

Calculations of Analysis of Variance for Data in Table 16.1

**(a) Data**

| | Counting | Rhyming | Adjective | Imagery | Intentional | Total |
|---|---|---|---|---|---|---|
| | 9 | 7 | 11 | 12 | 10 | |
| | 8 | 9 | 13 | 11 | 19 | |
| | 6 | 6 | 8 | 16 | 14 | |
| | 8 | 6 | 6 | 11 | 5 | |
| | 10 | 6 | 14 | 9 | 10 | |
| | 4 | 11 | 11 | 23 | 11 | |
| | 6 | 6 | 13 | 12 | 14 | |
| | 5 | 3 | 13 | 10 | 15 | |
| | 7 | 8 | 10 | 19 | 11 | |
| | 7 | 7 | 11 | 11 | 11 | |
| Mean | 7.00 | 6.90 | 11.00 | 13.40 | 12.00 | 10.06 |
| Std. Dev. | 1.83 | 2.13 | 2.49 | 4.50 | 3.74 | 4.01 |
| Variance | 3.33 | 4.54 | 6.22 | 20.27 | 14.00 | 16.058 |

**(b) Calculations**

$$SS_{total} = \Sigma(X_{ij} - \overline{X}_{..})^2 = \Sigma X^2 - \frac{(\Sigma X)^2}{N} = (9^2 + 8^2 + \cdots + 11^2) - \frac{503^2}{50}$$

$$= 5847 - 5060.18 = 786.82$$

$$SS_{group} = n\Sigma(\overline{X}_j - \overline{X}_{..})^2$$

$$= 10[(7.00 - 10.06)^2 + (6.90 - 10.06)^2 + \cdots + (12.00 - 10.06)^2]$$

$$= 351.52$$

$$SS_{error} = SS_{total} - SS_{group} = 786.82 - 351.52 = 435.30$$

**(c) Summary Table**

total variation

| Source | df | SS | MS | F |
|---|---|---|---|---|
| Group | 4 | 351.52 | 87.88 | 9.08 |
| Error | 45 | 435.30 | 9.67 | |
| Total | 49 | 786.82 | | |

Even for this example it is useful to examine the individual group variances as a check on the assumption of homogeneity of variance. Although the variances are not as similar as we might like (the variance for Imagery is noticeably larger than for the others), they do not appear to be so drastically different as to cause concern. As you will see later, the analysis of variance is robust against violations of assumptions, especially when we have the same number of observations in each group.

SS$_{TOTAL}$   The **SS$_{total}$** (read "total sum of squares") represents the sum of the squared deviations of all the observations from the grand mean, regardless of which treatment produced them. It is also equal to the sum of all the squared observations minus the grand mean squared divided by $N$.[3]

$$SS_{total} = \Sigma(X_{ij} - \overline{X}_{..})^2 = \Sigma X^2 - \frac{(\Sigma X)^2}{N}$$

Definition
SS$_{total}$: The sum of squared deviations of all of the scores, regardless of group membership.

SS$_{group}$: The sum of squared deviations of the group means from the grand mean, multiplied by the number of observations.

SS$_{error}$: The sum of the squared residuals or the sum of the squared deviations within each group.

SS$_{GROUP}$   The **SS$_{group}$** term is a measure of differences due to groups (in effect, differences between group means) and is directly related to the variance of the group means. To calculate SS$_{group}$, we simply square and then sum the deviations of the group means from the grand mean. This is then multiplied by the sample size to produce our second estimate of the population variance ($\sigma_e^2$) if $H_0$ is true:

$$SS_{group} = n\Sigma(\overline{X}_j - \overline{X}_{..})^2$$

(Remember, in the analysis of variance we use lowercase $n$ to stand for the number of observations in a group and uppercase $N$ to stand for the total number of observations.)

SS$_{ERROR}$   In practice **SS$_{error}$** is usually obtained by subtraction. Because it can be shown easily that

$$SS_{total} = SS_{group} + SS_{error}$$

then it must also be true that

$$SS_{error} = SS_{total} - SS_{group}$$

This calculation of SS$_{error}$ is the procedure presented in Table 16.4. An alternative method of calculation is also available. As you will recall from earlier discussions, we seek a term that is not influenced by differences among treatments and therefore

---

[3]Here we come back to using a capital N, which refers to the number of all observations, regardless of group membership. When we speak of the number of observations in a single group, we will use n, often with a subscript.

a term that represents the variability within each of the five treatments separately. To that end we could calculate a sum of squares within Treatment 1 ($SS_{error1}$) and a similar term for the SS within each of the other treatments.

$$SS_{\text{within Counting}} = \Sigma(X_{i1} - \overline{X}_1)^2 = (9 - 7.00)^2 + \cdots + (7 - 7.00)^2 \quad = 30.00$$

$$SS_{\text{within Rhyming}} = \Sigma(X_{i2} - \overline{X}_2)^2 = (7 - 6.90)^2 + \cdots + (7 - 6.90)^2 \quad = 40.90$$

$$SS_{\text{within Adjective}} = \Sigma(X_{i3} - \overline{X}_3)^2 = (11 - 11.00)^2 + \cdots + (11 - 11.00)^2 = 56.00$$

$$SS_{\text{within Imagery}} = \Sigma(X_{i4} - \overline{X}_4)^2 = (12 - 13.40)^2 + \cdots + (11 - 13.40)^2 = 182.40$$

$$SS_{\text{within Intentional}} = \Sigma(X_{i5} - \overline{X}_5)^2 = (10 - 12.00)^2 + \cdots + (11 - 12.00)^2 = 126.00$$

$$SS_{error} = \overline{435.30}$$

The sum of these individual terms is 435.30, which agrees exactly with the answer we obtained in Table 16.4. This simply goes to show that $SS_{error}$ is a measure of the variability within each group.

## The Summary Table

Part (c) of Table 16.4 is the summary table for the analysis of variance. It is called a summary table for the rather obvious reason that it summarizes a series of calculations, making it possible to tell at a glance what the data have to offer.

SOURCES OF VARIATION   The first column of the summary table, labeled "Source," contains the sources of variation—I use the word "variation" as being synonymous with the phrase "sum of squares." As you can see from the table, there are three sources of variation: the total variation, the variation due to groups (variation between group means), and the variation due to error (variation within groups). These sources reflect the fact that we have partitioned the total sum of squares into two portions, one portion representing variability between the several groups and the other representing variability within the individual groups.

DEGREES OF FREEDOM   The degrees of freedom column shows the allocation of the degrees of freedom between the two sources of variation. The calculation of $df$ is probably the easiest part of our task. The total degrees of freedom ($df_{total}$) are always $N - 1$, where $N$ is the total number of observations. The degrees of freedom between groups ($df_{group}$) always equal $k - 1$, where $k$ is the number of groups. The degrees of freedom for error ($df_{error}$) are most easily thought of as what is left over, although they can be calculated more directly as the sum of the degrees of freedom within each treatment. In our example $df_{total} = 50 - 1 = 49$. Of these 49 $df$, 4 are associated with differences among the five groups, and the remaining 45 are associated with variability within groups.

---

$df_{total}$: Degrees of freedom associated with $SS_{total}$; equal to $N - 1$.

$df_{group}$: Degrees of freedom associated with $SS_{group}$; equal to $k - 1$.

$df_{error}$: Degrees of freedom associated with $SS_{error}$; equal to $k(n - 1)$.

**F statistic:** The ratio of $MS_{group}$ to $MS_{error}$.

---

A useful way to think of degrees of freedom is in terms of the number of deviations we have squared. $SS_{total}$ is the sum of $N$ squared deviations around one point—the grand mean. The fact that we have taken deviations around this one (estimated) point has cost us 1 $df$, leaving $N - 1$ $df$. $SS_{group}$ is the sum of deviations of the $k$ group means around one point (again the grand mean), and again we have lost 1 $df$ in estimating this point, leaving us with $k - 1$ $df$. $SS_{error}$ represents $k$ sets of $n$ deviations about one point (the relevant group mean), losing us 1 $df$ for each group and leaving $k(n - 1) = N - k$ $df$.

SUMS OF SQUARES    There is little to be said about the column labeled SS. It simply contains the sums of squares obtained in part (b) of the table.

MEAN SQUARES    The column of mean squares contains the two estimates of $\sigma_e^2$. These values are obtained by dividing the sums of squares by their corresponding $df$. Thus $351.52/4 = 87.88$ and $435.30/45 = 9.67$. We typically do not calculate a $MS_{total}$, because we have no use for it. If we did, it would represent the variance of all $N$ observations.

Although it is true that mean squares are variances, it is important to keep in mind what these terms are variances of. Thus $MS_{error}$ is the (average) variance of the observations within each treatment. However, $MS_{group}$ is not the variance of group means, but rather the variance of those means corrected by $n$ to produce an estimate of the population variance ($\sigma_e^2$); in other words it is an estimate of $\sigma_e^2$ based on the variance of group means.

THE F STATISTIC    The last column, headed $F$, is the most important one in terms of testing the null hypothesis. The **F statistic** is obtained by dividing $MS_{group}$ by $MS_{error}$. As noted earlier, $MS_{error}$ is an estimate of the population variance ($\sigma_e^2$). $MS_{group}$ is also an estimate of population variance ($\sigma_e^2$) if $H_0$ is true, but not if $H_0$ is false. If $H_0$ is true, then both $MS_{error}$ and $MS_{group}$ are estimating the same thing, and as such they should be approximately equal. If that is the case, the ratio of one to the other will be approximately 1, give or take a fair amount for sampling error. All we have to do is compute the ratio and determine whether it is close enough to 1 to indicate support for the null hypothesis.

When we spoke about a $t$ test, it was pretty clear what a one-tailed test meant. It meant that we would reject $H_0$ if the difference between the means were in the predicted direction. It also meant that we would reject $H_0$ if the value of $t$ were of the correct sign, in both cases assuming that the difference (or $t$) was large enough. When we have multiple groups, however, the use of the label "one-tailed" is less clear. In one sense we are running a one-tailed test because we will reject $H_0$ only if the computed value of $F$ is significantly *greater* than 1.0. On the other hand, we could obtain a large value of $F$ for a variety of reasons. In the analysis of variance we reject $H_0$ when the means are sufficiently far apart, without regard to which one(s) is (are) larger than others. Thus we have a one-tailed test of a nondirectional $H_0$.

The question remains as to how much larger than 1.0 our value of $F$ needs to be before we decide that there are differences among the population means and thus reject $H_0$.[4] The answer to this lies in the fact that if $H_0$ is true, the ratio

$$F = \frac{MS_{group}}{MS_{error}}$$

is distributed as the $F$ distribution in Table D.3 in Appendix D. It will have $df_{group}$ and $df_{error}$ degrees of freedom. A portion of Table D.3 is reproduced as Table 16.5. Because the shape of the $F$ distribution, and thus areas under it, depend on the degrees of freedom for the two mean squares, this table looks somewhat different from other tables you have seen. In this case we select the column that corresponds to the degrees of freedom for the mean square in the numerator of $F$ (i.e., $k - 1$) and the row that corresponds to the degrees of freedom for the mean square in the denominator (i.e., $k(n - 1)$). The intersection of the row and the column gives us the critical value of $F$ at the level of $\alpha$ shown at the top of the table.

To use the table of the critical values of the $F$ distribution, we first have to select the particular table corresponding to our level of $\alpha$ (in Table D.3 $\alpha = .05$, and in Table D.4 $\alpha = .01$). Then, because we have 4 $df$ for the numerator ($MS_{group}$) and 45 $df$ for the denominator ($MS_{error}$), we move down the fourth column to the row labeled 45. But there is no row that corresponds to exactly 45 $df$, so we will average the entries for the rows corresponding to 40 $df$ and 50 $df$. The intersections of those rows and column 4 contain the entries 2.61 and 2.56, the average of which rounds to 2.58. This is the critical value of $F$. We would expect to exceed an $F$ of 2.58 only 5% of the time if $H_0$ were true. Because our obtained $F = 9.08$ exceeds $F_{.05} = 2.58$, we will reject $H_0$ and conclude that the groups were sampled from populations with different means. Had we chosen to work at $\alpha = .01$, Table D.4 in Appendix D shows that $F_{.01}(4,45) = 3.78$, and we would still reject $H_0$. (Notice the format for reporting the significance level and the degrees of freedom for $F$ in the preceding sentence. That is the standard way of writing them.)

---

[4]If $H_0$ is true, the expected value of $F$ is not exactly 1, but it is so close that it doesn't make any difference to the point being made here. Also, there is usually no meaning to be assigned to an $F$ very much less than 1, though in such a case we might be puzzled that our group means were much *closer* to each other than we would expect.

**Table 16.5**
Abbreviated Version of Table D.3, Critical Values of the $F$ Distribution Where $\alpha = .05$

| df denom. | Degrees of Freedom for Numerator | | | | | | | | | |
|---|---|---|---|---|---|---|---|---|---|---|
| | 1 | 2 | 3 | 4 | 5 | 6 | 7 | 8 | 9 | 10 |
| 1 | 161.4 | 199.5 | 215.8 | 224.8 | 230.0 | 233.8 | 236.5 | 238.6 | 240.1 | 242.1 |
| 2 | 18.51 | 19.00 | 19.16 | 19.25 | 19.30 | 19.33 | 19.35 | 19.37 | 19.38 | 19.40 |
| 3 | 10.13 | 9.55 | 9.28 | 9.12 | 9.01 | 8.94 | 8.89 | 8.85 | 8.81 | 8.79 |
| 4 | 7.71 | 6.94 | 6.59 | 6.39 | 6.26 | 6.16 | 6.09 | 6.04 | 6.00 | 5.96 |
| 5 | 6.61 | 5.79 | 5.41 | 5.19 | 5.05 | 4.95 | 4.88 | 4.82 | 4.77 | 4.74 |
| 6 | 5.99 | 5.14 | 4.76 | 4.53 | 4.39 | 4.28 | 4.21 | 4.15 | 4.10 | 4.06 |
| 7 | 5.59 | 4.74 | 4.35 | 4.12 | 3.97 | 3.87 | 3.79 | 3.73 | 3.68 | 3.64 |
| 8 | 5.32 | 4.46 | 4.07 | 3.84 | 3.69 | 3.58 | 3.50 | 3.44 | 3.39 | 3.35 |
| 9 | 5.12 | 4.26 | 3.86 | 3.63 | 3.48 | 3.37 | 3.29 | 3.23 | 3.18 | 3.14 |
| 10 | 4.96 | 4.10 | 3.71 | 3.48 | 3.33 | 3.22 | 3.14 | 3.07 | 3.02 | 2.98 |
| 11 | 4.84 | 3.98 | 3.59 | 3.36 | 3.20 | 3.09 | 3.01 | 2.95 | 2.90 | 2.85 |
| 12 | 4.75 | 3.89 | 3.49 | 3.26 | 3.11 | 3.00 | 2.91 | 2.85 | 2.80 | 2.75 |
| 13 | 4.67 | 3.81 | 3.41 | 3.18 | 3.03 | 2.92 | 2.83 | 2.77 | 2.71 | 2.67 |
| 14 | 4.60 | 3.74 | 3.34 | 3.11 | 2.96 | 2.85 | 2.76 | 2.70 | 2.65 | 2.60 |
| 15 | 4.54 | 3.68 | 3.29 | 3.06 | 2.90 | 2.79 | 2.71 | 2.64 | 2.59 | 2.54 |
| 16 | 4.49 | 3.63 | 3.24 | 3.01 | 2.85 | 2.74 | 2.66 | 2.59 | 2.54 | 2.49 |
| 17 | 4.45 | 3.59 | 3.20 | 2.96 | 2.81 | 2.70 | 2.61 | 2.55 | 2.49 | 2.45 |
| 18 | 4.41 | 3.55 | 3.16 | 2.93 | 2.77 | 2.66 | 2.58 | 2.51 | 2.46 | 2.41 |
| 19 | 4.38 | 3.52 | 3.13 | 2.90 | 2.74 | 2.63 | 2.54 | 2.48 | 2.42 | 2.38 |
| 20 | 4.35 | 3.49 | 3.10 | 2.87 | 2.71 | 2.60 | 2.51 | 2.45 | 2.39 | 2.35 |
| 22 | 4.30 | 3.44 | 3.05 | 2.82 | 2.66 | 2.55 | 2.46 | 2.40 | 2.34 | 2.30 |
| 24 | 4.26 | 3.40 | 3.01 | 2.78 | 2.62 | 2.51 | 2.42 | 2.36 | 2.30 | 2.25 |
| 26 | 4.23 | 3.37 | 2.98 | 2.74 | 2.59 | 2.47 | 2.39 | 2.32 | 2.27 | 2.22 |
| 28 | 4.20 | 3.34 | 2.95 | 2.71 | 2.56 | 2.45 | 2.36 | 2.29 | 2.24 | 2.19 |
| 30 | 4.17 | 3.32 | 2.92 | 2.69 | 2.53 | 2.42 | 2.33 | 2.27 | 2.21 | 2.16 |
| 40 | 4.08 | 3.23 | 2.84 | 2.61 | 2.45 | 2.34 | 2.25 | 2.18 | 2.12 | 2.08 |
| 50 | 4.03 | 3.18 | 2.79 | 2.56 | 2.40 | 2.29 | 2.20 | 2.13 | 2.07 | 2.03 |
| 60 | 4.00 | 3.15 | 2.76 | 2.53 | 2.37 | 2.25 | 2.17 | 2.10 | 2.04 | 1.99 |
| 120 | 3.92 | 3.07 | 2.68 | 2.45 | 2.29 | 2.18 | 2.09 | 2.02 | 1.96 | 1.91 |
| 200 | 3.89 | 3.04 | 2.65 | 2.42 | 2.26 | 2.14 | 2.06 | 1.98 | 1.93 | 1.88 |
| 500 | 3.86 | 3.01 | 2.62 | 2.39 | 2.23 | 2.12 | 2.03 | 1.96 | 1.90 | 1.85 |
| 1000 | 3.85 | 3.01 | 2.61 | 2.38 | 2.22 | 2.11 | 2.02 | 1.95 | 1.89 | 1.84 |

## Conclusions

On the basis of a significant value of $F$, we have rejected the null hypothesis that the treatment means in the population are equal. Strictly speaking, this conclusion indicates that at least one of the population means is different from at least one other mean, but we don't know exactly which means are different from which other means. We will pursue this question shortly with a different example. For the moment I'm going to take some liberties and speak about individual group differences as if I had already shown that they are significantly different.

It is evident from an examination of the data in Table 16.4 that increased processing of the material is associated with increased levels of recall. For example, a strategy that involves associating images with items to be recalled leads to nearly twice as good recall as does merely counting the letters in the items. Results such as these give us important hints about how to go about learning any material and point out the poor recall to be expected from passive studying. Good recall, whether it be of lists of words or complex statistical concepts, requires active and "deep" processing of the material, which in turn is facilitated by noting associations between to-be-learned material and other material that you already know. You have probably noticed that sitting in class and dutifully recording everything that the instructor says doesn't usually lead to the grades that you think such effort deserves. Now you know a bit about why. (You'll do much better if you tell yourself silly little stories about the material. Writing down that the Congress of Vienna ended in 1815 probably will not help you much at exam time. Imagining your instructor dressed up in an 1800s wig with knee-high stockings, looking 15 years old, just might.)

## Writing Up the Results

There is more to an analysis of variance than we have yet covered. Before we can thoroughly report on our results we need to examine differences between specific sets of means and measures of effect size. However, based on just what you know at this point, if you were writing up the results of this study, you might say something like the following:

> In an attempt to investigate the role of the processing of verbal material on recall, five groups of participants were asked to study lists of words. The instructions to the participants differed in the amount of processing of the material that they were required to do. The dependent variable was the level of recall, and an analysis of variance was run to compare group means. As the level of processing increased from counting of letters to creating mental images, the mean level of recall increased from 7.00 to 13.40, with a common standard deviation of 3.11. A group that was simply instructed to memorize the words had a mean recall of 12.00 words. The analysis of variance revealed a significant difference in the means of the groups ($F(4,45) = 9.08$, $p < .05$) with groups instructed to do higher levels of processing showing better recall.

## 16.4 Unequal Sample Sizes

Most experiments are designed originally with the idea of having the same number of observations in each treatment. Frequently, however, things do not work out that way. Participants in an experiment are often remarkably unreliable, and many fail to arrive for testing or are eliminated for failure to follow instructions. My favorite example is a report in the literature in which an experimental animal was eliminated from the study for repeatedly biting the experimenter (Sgro & Weinstock, 1963). Moreover, in studies conducted on intact groups, such as school classes, groups are nearly always unequal in size for reasons that, again, have nothing to do with the experiment.

If the sample sizes are not equal, the analysis discussed earlier is not appropriate without modification. For the case of one independent variable, however, this modification is relatively minor.

For the case of equal sample sizes we have defined

$$SS_{group} = n\Sigma(\overline{X}_j - \overline{X}..)^2$$

where $n$ is the number of observations in each group. We were able to multiply the sum of the squared deviations by $n$ because $n$ was common to all treatments. If the sample sizes differ, however, and we define $n_j$ as the number of participants in the $j$th treatment ($\Sigma n_j = N$), we can rewrite the equation as

$$SS_{group} = \Sigma n_j(\overline{X}_j - \overline{X}..)^2$$

which, when all $n_j$ are equal, reduces to the original form. All we are doing here is multiplying each squared deviation by its own sample size as we go along.

**AN ADDITIONAL EXAMPLE: Adaptation to Maternal Roles**

An additional example of a one-way analysis of variance will illustrate the treatment of unequal sample sizes. In a study of the development of low-birthweight (LBW) infants (Nurcombe, Howell, Rauh, Teti, Ruoff, & Brennan, 1984), three groups of newborn infants differed in terms of birthweight and whether their mothers had participated in a training program about the special needs of low-birthweight infants. The mothers were then interviewed when the infants were 6 months old. There were three groups in the experiment—an LBW-Experimental group, an LBW-Control group, and a Full-Term-Control group. The two control groups received no special training, and so served as reference points against which to compare the performance of the trained (experimental) group. The LBW-Experimental group was part of the intervention program, and we hoped to show that those mothers would adapt to their new role as well as the mothers of full-term infants did. On the other hand, we expected that mothers of low-birthweight infants who did not receive the intervention program would have some trouble adapting. (Being a parent of a low-birthweight baby is not an easy task, especially for the first few months. For the rather dramatic results from tracking these children for nine years, see Achenbach, Howell, Aoki, and Rauh, 1993.) Actual data from that experiment are presented in Table 16.6.

**Table 16.6**
Adaptation to Maternal Role in Three Groups of Mothers (Low Scores Are Associated with Better Adaptation.)

**(a) Data**

| | Group 1 LBW-Experimental | | | Group 2 LBW-Control | | | Group 3 Full-Term | | |
|---|---|---|---|---|---|---|---|---|---|
| | 24 | 10 | 16 | 21 | 17 | 13 | 12 | 12 | 12 |
| | 13 | 11 | 15 | 19 | 18 | 25 | 25 | 17 | 20 |
| | 29 | 13 | 12 | 10 | 18 | 16 | 14 | 18 | 14 |
| | 12 | 19 | 16 | 24 | 13 | 18 | 16 | 18 | 14 |
| | 14 | 11 | 12 | 17 | 21 | 11 | 13 | 18 | 12 |
| | 11 | 11 | 12 | 25 | 27 | 16 | 10 | 15 | 20 |
| | 12 | 27 | 22 | 16 | 29 | 11 | 13 | 13 | 12 |
| | 13 | 13 | 16 | 26 | 14 | 21 | 11 | 15 | 17 |
| | 13 | 13 | 17 | 19 | 17 | 13 | 20 | 13 | 15 |
| | 13 | 14 | | | | | 23 | 13 | 11 |
| | | | | | | | 16 | 10 | 13 |
| | | | | | | | 20 | 12 | 11 |
| | | | | | | | 11 | | |

| | | | | | | |
|---|---|---|---|---|---|---|
| $n_j$ | 29 | | 27 | | 37 | $N = 93$ |
| Mean$_j$ | 14.97 | | 18.33 | | 14.84 | $\overline{X}.. = 15.89$ |

**(b) Calculations**

$$SS_{total} = \Sigma(X_{ij} - \overline{X}..)^2 = \Sigma X^2 - \frac{(\Sigma X)^2}{N}$$

$$= 24^2 + 10^2 + \cdots + 11^2 - \frac{1478^2}{93}$$

$$= 25,562 - 23,489.075 = 2072.925$$

$$SS_{group} = \Sigma n_j(\overline{X}_j - \overline{X}..)^2$$

$$= 29(14.97 - 15.89)^2 + 27(18.33 - 15.89)^2 + 37(14.84 - 15.89)^2$$

$$= 226.932$$

$$SS_{error} = SS_{total} - SS_{group} = 2072.925 - 226.932 = 1845.993$$

**(c) Summary Table**

| Source | df | SS | MS | F |
|---|---|---|---|---|
| Group | 2 | 226.932 | 113.466 | 5.53 |
| Error | 90 | 1845.993 | 20.511 | |
| Total | 92 | 2072.925 | | |

The actual data from this study are presented in part (a) of the table. Part (b) shows the calculations for the analysis of variance, and part (c) contains the summary table. The dependent variable is the score on a maternal adaptation scale. Notice that the calculations are carried out just as they would be for the case of equal sample sizes except that for $SS_{group}$, each value of $(\overline{X}_j - \overline{X}..)^2$ is multiplied by the corresponding sample size as we progress.

From the summary table we can see that the obtained $F$ value is 5.53 and that it is based on 2 and 90 degrees of freedom. From Table D.3 in Appendix D we get, through interpolation, $F_{.05}(2,90) = 3.11$. (Here 90 degrees of freedom is halfway between 60 and 120 $df$, so we take as our critical value the value halfway between 3.15 and 3.07, which is 3.11.) Because $5.53 > 3.11$, we will reject $H_0$ and conclude that not all the scores were drawn from populations with equal means. In fact, it looks as if the first and third groups are about equal, whereas the second (the LBW-Control group) has a higher mean (poorer adaptation). However, the $F$ tells us only that we can reject $H_0$: $\mu_1 = \mu_2 = \mu_3$. It does *not* tell us which groups are different from which other groups. To draw those kinds of conclusions, we will need to use special techniques known as multiple comparison procedures. ∎

## 16.5 Multiple Comparison Procedures

When we run an analysis of variance and obtain a significant $F$ value, we have shown simply that the overall null hypothesis is false. We do not know which of a number of possible alternative hypotheses (e.g., $H_1$: $\mu \neq \mu_2 \neq \mu_3 \neq \mu_4 \neq \mu_5$; $H_2$: $\mu_1 \neq \mu_2 = \mu_3 = \mu_4 = \mu_5$) is true. **Multiple comparison techniques** allow us to investigate hypotheses that involve means of individual groups or sets of groups. For example, we might be interested in whether Group 1 is different from Group 2 or whether the combination of Groups 1 and 2 is different from Group 3.

Definition | **Multiple comparison techniques:** Techniques for making comparisons between two or more group means subsequent to an analysis of variance.

One of the major problems with making comparisons among groups is that unrestricted use of these comparisons can lead to an excessively high probability of a Type I error. For example, if we have 10 groups in which the complete null hypothesis is true ($H_0$: $\mu_1 = \mu_2 = \mu_3 = \cdots = \mu_{10}$), $t$ tests between all pairs of means will lead to making *at least* one Type I error 57.8% of the time. In other words, the experimenter who thinks she is working at the $\alpha = .05$ level of significance is actually working at $\alpha = .578$. Figure 16.3 shows how the probability of making at least one Type I error increases as we increase the number of *independent t* tests we make between pairs of means. While it is nice to find significant differences, it is

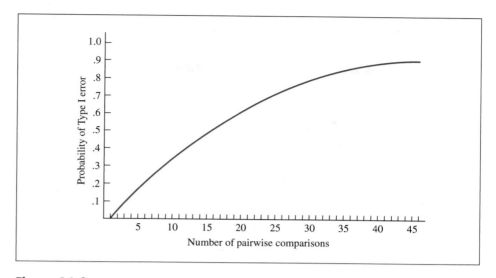

**Figure 16.3**
Probability of a Type I error as a function of the number of pairwise comparisons where $\alpha = .05$ for any one comparison

not nice to find ones that are not really there. Psychologists have enough trouble explaining all the real differences that we find without having to worry about spurious differences as well. We need to find some way to make the comparisons we need but keep the probability of incorrect rejections of $H_0$ under control.

In an attempt to control the likelihood of Type I errors, statisticians have developed a large number of procedures for comparing individual means. (For a discussion of many of these techniques see Howell, 2007.) Fortunately, two relatively simple techniques provide reasonable control of the probability of Type I errors and are applicable to most multiple comparison problems you are likely to encounter.

## Fisher's Least Significant Difference Test

The first procedure is often referred to as the **protected $t$** or **Fisher's least significant difference (LSD) test**. (If your instructor looks a little pale at the suggestion to use Fisher's least significant difference test, just wait a bit and I'll defend that suggestion. It is not as outrageous as people may think, though it has had a bad rap historically.) Fisher's procedure is one of the most liberal multiple comparison tests we have. Following the discussion of that test I present the Bonferroni procedure, which is particularly useful when you use any standard statistical computer package to solve your problem. We will look at Fisher's LSD test first.

---

Definition | **Protected $t$:** Another name for Fisher's LSD test.

**Fisher's least significant difference (LSD) test:** A technique in which we run $t$ tests between pairs of means only if the analysis of variance was significant.

---

The procedures for using a protected $t$, or LSD test, are really very simple. *The first requirement for a protected $t$ is that the F for the overall analysis of variance must be significant.* If the $F$ was not significant, no comparisons between pairs of means are allowed. You simply declare that there are no group differences and stop right there. On the other hand, if the overall $F$ is significant, you can proceed to make any (or all) pairwise comparisons between individual means by the use of a modified $t$ test. The modification is simply to replace the pooled variance estimate ($s_p^2$) in the standard $t$ formula with $MS_{error}$ from the overall analysis of variance. (We generally do not make this replacement if the variances of the groups are very different from one another.) This replacement is a perfectly reasonable thing to do. Because $MS_{error}$ is defined as the average of the variances within each group, if there were only two groups in the experiment, the $MS_{error}$ from the analysis of variance would be the same as the $s_p^2$ from the two-sample $t$ test on those group means. In comparing among several groups we use $MS_{error}$ instead of $s_p^2$ because it is based on variability within *all* the groups rather than within just the two groups we are comparing at the moment. As such it is presumably a better estimate of $\sigma_e^2$. Along with the use of this error term comes the advantage that the resulting $t$ will have $df_{error}$ degrees of freedom rather than just the $n_1 + n_2 - 2$ degrees of freedom it would have had otherwise.

When we replace $s_p^2$ with $MS_{error}$, the formula for $t$ becomes

$$t = \frac{\overline{X}_i - \overline{X}_j}{\sqrt{\dfrac{MS_{error}}{n_i} + \dfrac{MS_{error}}{n_j}}} = \frac{\overline{X}_i - \overline{X}_j}{\sqrt{MS_{error}\left(\dfrac{1}{n_i} + \dfrac{1}{n_j}\right)}}$$

To illustrate the use of the protected $t$, let's take the data on maternal adaptation from the previous example. In that case we did find a significant overall $F$, which will allow us to look further in our analysis. Given the nature of that study, we would be interested in asking two questions:

1. Are there differences between the mean of mothers in the LBW-Control group and the mean of mothers in the Full-Term group?

2. Are there differences between the mean of mothers in the LBW-Control group and the mean of mothers in the Experimental group?

The first question asks whether mothers of low-birthweight infants have more difficulty adapting than do mothers of full-term infants. Neither group received intervention, so intervention is not a confounding variable. The second question asks whether the intervention program makes a difference in adaptation for mothers of low-birthweight infants. Here both groups are composed of mothers of low-birthweight infants, so birthweight is not a confounding variable. Note that it makes little sense to compare the LBW-Experimental group with the Full-Term group because if we did find a difference we could not tell whether it was due to intervention effects or to birthweight effects. In such a comparison, intervention and birthweight are confounded.

**Table 16.7**
Fisher's Least Significant Difference Test Applied
to Low-Birthweight and Full-Term Groups

|  | Group 1 LBW-Experimental | Group 2 LBW-Control | Group 3 Full-Term |
|---|---|---|---|
| $\overline{X}_j =$ | 14.97 | 18.33 | 14.84 |
| $n_j =$ | 29 | 27 | 37 |
| $MS_{error} =$ | 20.511 | | |
| $df_{error} =$ | 90 | | |

(a) $\mu_1$ versus $\mu_2$

$$t = \frac{\overline{X}_1 - \overline{X}_2}{\sqrt{MS_{error}\left(\frac{1}{n_1} + \frac{1}{n_2}\right)}}$$

$$= \frac{14.97 - 18.33}{\sqrt{20.511\left(\frac{1}{29} + \frac{1}{27}\right)}}$$

$$= \frac{-3.36}{\sqrt{1.467}} = \frac{-3.36}{1.21} = -2.77$$

(b) $\mu_2$ versus $\mu_3$

$$t = \frac{\overline{X}_2 - \overline{X}_3}{\sqrt{MS_{error}\left(\frac{1}{n_2} + \frac{1}{n_3}\right)}}$$

$$= \frac{18.33 - 14.84}{\sqrt{20.511\left(\frac{1}{27} + \frac{1}{37}\right)}}$$

$$= \frac{3.49}{\sqrt{1.314}} = \frac{3.49}{1.15} = 3.04$$

The results on maternal adaptation are presented in Table 16.7, in which the obtained values of $t$ are $-2.77$ and $3.04$ for the two comparisons. We will use a two-tailed test at $\alpha = .05$, and we have 90 degrees of freedom for our error term. From Table D.3 we find that $t_{.05}(90) = \pm 1.99$ by interpolation. Thus for both comparisons we can reject the null hypothesis, because both values of the obtained $t$ ($t_{obt}$) are more extreme (further from 0) than $\pm 1.99$. We will therefore conclude that there is a difference in adaptation between mothers of low-birthweight babies and those of full-term infants, with the full-term mothers showing better adaptation. We will also conclude that the intervention program is effective for mothers of low-birthweight infants.

You might ask why we call this particular multiple comparison procedure a "protected *t*." Or you may have heard somewhere that it is a bad idea to run all sorts of *t* tests between pairs of means, and it often is. This is a good place to address both these concerns at the same time.

One of the primary considerations in running a set of multiple comparisons is to hold down the probability of making *at least* one Type I error. In other words, if we ran an analysis of variance and then three comparisons, we would want to ensure that the probability that we have made a Type I error *anywhere*, either in the original *F* or in any of the three comparisons, is low. The probability of making such an error is called the **familywise error rate** because it deals with the probability that the *family* of comparisons contains *at least one* Type I error. When we are talking about the familywise error rate, making ten Type I errors is treated as no worse than making one. (Or perhaps I should phrase that in reverse—making one Type I error is as bad as making ten.) If we just ran *t* tests between all pairs of means, the familywise error rate would become unacceptably high, especially if there were many means to compare. We need to impose some conditions to prevent that from happening, which is what a protected *t* test does, in part, by the simple expedient of requiring that no tests may be run unless the overall *F* from the analysis of variance is significant. To see why this simple step works, consider the following examples.

| Definition | **Familywise error rate:** The probability that a family of comparisons contains at least one Type I error. |
|---|---|

Suppose we have only two means and *the null hypothesis is true*. The probability of making a Type I error would be the probability that the original *F* was significant by chance, which is .05. If that *F* was significant, we have already made our Type I error, and even if we went on and ran a *t* test, we couldn't make the situation worse. If the *F* was not significant, we cannot run the protected *t* and so do not increase the error rate.[5] Thus with two means the familywise error rate is .05.

Now suppose we have three means. First, assume that the complete null hypothesis is true—that is, suppose that $\mu_1 = \mu_2 = \mu_3$. Next we run the overall *F*. The probability of finding a significant difference (which would be a Type I error because $H_0$ is true) is .05, and if we reported a significant difference, that represents our first Type I error out of the "at least one" that the familywise error rate protects against. If the *F* is not significant, we stop right there and have no further chances of making a Type I error. In other words, when the *complete* null hypothesis is true, the probability of making *at least one* Type I error is limited by our rule to .05, which is what we want. Next, suppose that the complete null hypothesis is false and that one mean is different from the other two (e.g., $\mu_1 = \mu_2 \neq \mu_3$). Then, because the complete null hypothesis is not true, it is impossible to make a Type I error with our

---

[5]With only two means, the *t* and the analysis of variance are equivalent tests, but that is not important here. The point is that if there is a Type I error on the *F*, we already have at least one error, and if *F* is not significant, we cannot test further.

overall $F$ test. If we have a significant $F$, which we would hope to be the case, we can go on and test, for example, each pair of means—Group 1 versus Group 2, Group 1 versus Group 3, and Group 2 versus Group 3. But there is only one of those tests for which the null hypothesis is true ($\mu_1 = \mu_2$), and therefore there is only one chance of making a Type I error. Here again the probability of at least one Type I error is only .05. Finally, suppose that all means are different from each other. Here we have no possibility of making a Type I error, because there is no true null hypothesis to erroneously declare false. From examination of these possibilities we can conclude that *with three means* the familywise error rate is also at most .05.

So we have seen that with either two or three groups, Fisher's LSD test guarantees that the probability of making at least one Type I error will not exceed .05. That's great—it is just what we want. But suppose we had four groups. In that case it is possible that there is more than one true null hypothesis. For example, Groups 1 and 2 could be equal and Groups 3 and 4 could be equal. If $\mu_1 = \mu_2$ and $\mu_3 = \mu_4$, you have two chances of making a Type I error, and the true familywise error rate is nearly .10. But I would submit that this is not an outrageous error rate, given four means, and I would not cringe at using such a test, although it is not my favorite. Now if you want to talk about ten means, that's a different story, and anyone who would use Fisher's test with ten groups is asking for trouble. This is the complaint that is often raised against Fisher, but it's not really fair. If you look through the psychological literature (and I suspect it's true for all the behavioral sciences), you'll have a hard time finding experiments with even four groups. Ten-group experiments are almost unheard of, so why reject a test on the grounds that it doesn't work well for experiments that we have no intention of running anyway? Simply demanding a significant overall $F$ before running multiple comparisons (which is where the protection comes from) is surprisingly effective in controlling familywise error rates when we have only a few groups. That is the reason I have stressed the protected $t$ in this chapter. It does a good job of controlling the familywise error rate if you have a relatively small number of groups while at the same time being a test that you can easily apply and that has a reasonable degree of power.

## The Bonferroni Procedure

| Definition | **Bonferroni procedure:** A multiple comparisons procedure in which the familywise error rate is divided by the number of comparisons. |
| --- | --- |

A second procedure that is simple to apply and that has been growing in popularity is known as the **Bonferroni procedure**, after a mathematician of that name who discovered the inequality on which the procedure is based. The basic idea behind this procedure is that if you run several tests (say $c$ tests) at a significance level represented by $\alpha'$, the probability of at least one Type I error can never exceed $c\alpha'$. Thus, for example, if you ran 5 tests, each at $\alpha' = .05$, the familywise error rate would be at most $5(.05) = .25$. But that is too high an error rate to make anyone happy. But suppose that you ran each of those 5 tests at the $\alpha' = .01$. Then the maximum familywise error rate would be $5(.01) = .05$, which is certainly acceptable. To put this in a way that is slightly more useful to us, if you want the overall familywise error rate to be no more than .05, and you want to run 3 tests, then run each of them at $\alpha' = .05/3 = .0167$. To run these tests, you do exactly what you did in Fisher's LSD test, though you omit any requirement about the significance of overall $F$. The only difference is that you change the significance level for each individual test from $\alpha$ to $\alpha/c$, where $c$ is the number of comparisons.

The original difficulty with this approach was that we didn't have tables of significance at, for example, the .0167 level. However, most people today use standard computer software to run statistical analyses, and every package I have seen presents both the $t$ or $F$ value, and its associated probability level. For example, if I used SPSS on the low-birthweight data, using the same comparisons I used with Fisher's test, I have two choices. The sloppy way would be to just run a $t$ test between Group 1 and Group 2, and between Group 2 and Group 3. This is sloppy because such a test will not pool the variances across all three groups. If I did it anyway, I would get the results shown in the following table.

Notice that SPSS gives you the result of running a $t$ test with pooled variances ("Equal variances assumed") and without pooling (Equal variances not assumed). The section of the table labeled Levene's Test represents a test on the assumption that the population variances are equal; in both cases, we retain that hypothesis. We are justified in pooling variances.

We want to run these tests with an overall familywise error rate of .05, which, with 2 tests, means that each must have a probability lower than $\alpha = .05/2 = .025$ to be declared significant. Notice that both of these $t$ tests met that criterion, with $p = .015$ and .002, respectively.

The problem with this last procedure is that SPSS didn't pool the variances over all *three* groups.[6] We can get around this by running the two tests by hand with a pooled error term, just as we did with Fisher's test. This will lead to $t$ values of $-2.77$ and 3.04, both on 90 $df$. From Appendix D, Table D.6 you can see that for $\alpha = .025$, two-tailed, both of these are significant. If you want to know their exact probabilities, go to

 http://statpages.org/pdfs.html

and enter $t$ and $df$. The probabilities are .0068 and .0031, which are both well below .025.

All Bonferroni tests can be carried out this way. We simply decide how many tests we intend to run, divide the desired familywise error rate (usually $\alpha = .05$) by that number, and reject the null hypothesis whenever the probability of our test statistic is less than our computed critical value. However, be careful if you are using software to analyze your results. Most software programs will have an option for the Bonferroni test, but that will assume that you want to test all possible pairs of means. Because there are sometimes many means, that approach can be very conservative. Instead, simply ask for only those comparisons that you really care about.

---

[6]It is possible to get around this difficulty with SPSS, but I do not show that here because I would have to go into more explanation than you probably want.

## T-Test (Groups 1 vs. 2)

### Group Statistics

| | GROUP | N | Mean | Std. Deviation | Std. Error Mean |
|---|---|---|---|---|---|
| ADAPT | LBW-exp | 29 | 14.966 | 4.844 | .899 |
| | LBW-Control | 27 | 18.333 | 5.166 | .994 |

### Independent Samples Test

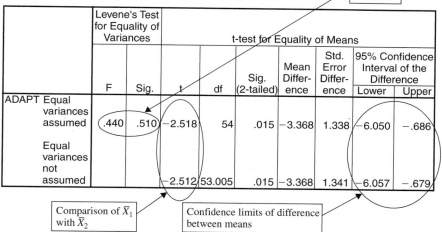

| | | Levene's Test for Equality of Variances | | t-test for Equality of Means | | | | | 95% Confidence Interval of the Difference | |
|---|---|---|---|---|---|---|---|---|---|---|
| | | F | Sig. | t | df | Sig. (2-tailed) | Mean Difference | Std. Error Difference | Lower | Upper |
| ADAPT | Equal variances assumed | .440 | .510 | −2.518 | 54 | .015 | −3.368 | 1.338 | −6.050 | −.686 |
| | Equal variances not assumed | | | −2.512 | 53.005 | .015 | −3.368 | 1.341 | −6.057 | −.679 |

Test on variances

Comparison of $\bar{X}_1$ with $\bar{X}_2$

Confidence limits of difference between means

## T-Test (Groups 2 vs. 3)

### Group Statistics

| | GROUP | N | Mean | Std. Deviation | Std. Error Mean |
|---|---|---|---|---|---|
| ADAPT | LBW-Control | 27 | 18.333 | 5.166 | .994 |
| | Full-Term | 37 | 14.838 | 3.708 | .610 |

### Independent Samples Test

| | | Levene's Test for Equality of Variances | | t-test for Equality of Means | | | | | 95% Confidence Interval of the Difference | |
|---|---|---|---|---|---|---|---|---|---|---|
| | | F | Sig. | t | df | Sig. (2-tailed) | Mean Difference | Std. Error Difference | Lower | Upper |
| ADAPT | Equal variances assumed | 2.885 | .094 | 3.154 | 62 | .002 | 3.495 | 1.108 | 1.280 | 5.711 |
| | Equal variances not assumed | | | 2.997 | 44.66 | .004 | 3.495 | 1.166 | 1.146 | 5.845 |

## Other Multiple Comparison Procedures

Many other procedures have been developed for sorting out differences among groups. The interesting thing is that they are all based roughly on the same kinds of considerations that we have seen in Fisher's LSD and the Bonferroni tests. They attempt to hold the familywise error rate to some maximum (usually .05), and they do this by taking into account the number of groups (or, more often, the number of pairwise comparisons among groups). The best known of these is the **Tukey procedure**. I won't go into it here, because it relies on a slightly different test statistic than we are used to. However I should note that it compares every mean with every other mean, and does so in a way that keeps the maximum familywise error rate at .05 (or some other percentage if you prefer). Every piece of statistical software that I know will produce a Tukey test on demand.

Definition    **Tukey procedure:** A multiple comparison procedure designed to hold the familywise error rate at $\alpha$ for a set of comparisons.

## 16.6 Violations of Assumptions

As we have seen, the analysis of variance is based on the assumptions of normality and homogeneity of variance. In practice, however, the analysis of variance is a robust statistical procedure, and the assumptions can frequently be violated with relatively minor effects.

In general, if the populations can be assumed to be either symmetric or at least similar in shape (e.g., all negatively skewed) and if the largest variance is no more than four or five times the smallest, the analysis of variance is most likely to be valid. (Some argue that it would be valid for even greater differences between the variances.) It is important to note, however, that serious heterogeneity of variance and unequal sample sizes do not mix. If you have reason to anticipate noticeably unequal variances, make every effort to keep your sample sizes as nearly equal as possible. This is particularly true when you plan to run a series of multiple comparisons.

For those situations in which the assumptions underlying the analysis of variance are seriously violated, there are alternative procedures for handling the analysis. Some of these procedures involve transforming the data (e.g., converting $X$ to $\log(X)$) and then performing standard statistical tests on the transformed data. Other procedures involve using quite different tests, which are discussed in Chapter 20. (Also see the discussion of the Behrens-Fisher problem and the use of trimmed means and Winsorized variances in Howell, 2007.)

## 16.7 The Size of the Effects

Simply because we obtain a significant difference among our treatment means does not mean that the differences are large or important. There are many real differences that are trivial. No statistic can tell us whether a difference, no matter how large, is of any practical importance to the rest of the world. However, there are procedures that give us some help in this direction.

Rosenthal (1994) made a distinction between **d-family** measures and **r-family** measures. The former are based on differences between means, while the latter are based on some sort of correlation between the dependent variable and the levels of the independent variable. I have avoided speaking about r-family measures until now, because when we have only two groups I don't think they add to our understanding. On the other hand, d-family measures (such as Cohen's d) are hard to interpret when you have multiple groups unless you restrict the measure to differences between two groups or sets of groups. I will start with the r-family measures.

Definition

---

**d-family measures:** Measures of the size of an effect that depend directly on differences between means.

**r-family measures:** Measures of the size of an effect that resemble the correlation between the dependent and the independent variable.

**Magnitude of effect:** A measure of the degree to which variability among observations can be attributed to treatments.

**Eta squared ($\eta^2$):** A measure of the magnitude of effect.

---

## r-family (Correlational) Measures

One of the simplest measures of the **magnitude of effect** is $\eta^2$ (**eta squared**). While $\eta^2$ is a biased measure (in the sense that it tends to overestimate the value we would obtain if we were able to measure whole populations of scores), its calculation is so simple and it is so useful as a first approximation that it is worth discussing. In this book I will restrict the discussion of $\eta^2$, and $\omega^2$ which follows, to measuring the effect among several groups.

In any analysis of variance, $SS_{total}$ tells us how much overall variability there is in the data. Some of that variability is due to the fact that different groups of participants are treated differently and have different scores as a result, and some of it is just due to random error—differences among people who are treated alike. The differences of importance are the differences among scores that can be attributed to our treatment, or group, effects, and they are measured by $SS_{group}$. If we form the ratio

$$\eta^2 = \frac{SS_{group}}{SS_{total}}$$

we can say what percentage of the variability among observations can be attributed to group effects.[7] For our maternal adaptation data

---

[7]If you had *two* groups and created a variable (X) by entering 1 for all participants in Group 1 and 2 for all participants in Group 2, and if you let Y be the dependent variable (e.g., maternal adaptation), then the squared correlation ($r^2$) between X and Y would be equivalent to $\eta^2$. This relationship does not work in the same way for more than two groups.

$$\eta^2 = \frac{SS_{group}}{SS_{total}} = \frac{226.932}{2072.925} = .11$$

Thus we can conclude that 11% of the variability in adaptation scores can be attributed to group membership. Although that might appear at first to be a small percentage, if you stop and think about the high level of variability among mothers you have known, explaining even 11% of it is a noteworthy accomplishment.

| Definition | **Omega squared ($\omega^2$):** A less biased measure of the magnitude of effect than eta squared. |
|---|---|

Although $\eta^2$ is a quick and easy measure to calculate, one you can even estimate in your head when reading research reports, it is a biased statistic. It will tend to overestimate the true value in the population. A much less biased estimate is afforded by another statistic, $\omega^2$ **(omega squared)**. For the analysis of variance discussed in this chapter, we can define

$$\omega^2 = \frac{SS_{group} - (k - 1)MS_{error}}{SS_{total} + MS_{error}}$$

where $k$ stands for the number of groups. For our example

$$\omega^2 = \frac{SS_{group} - (k - 1)MS_{error}}{SS_{total} + MS_{error}} = \frac{226.932 - (3 - 1)20.511}{2072.925 + 20.511} = .089$$

This value is somewhat lower than the value we obtained for $\eta^2$. However, it still suggests that we are accounting for approximately 9% of the variability.

## $d$-family Measures (Effect Size)

An alternative measure of our effect size that is becoming much more common is the measure of effect size based on Cohen's $d$. We saw such effect size measures in earlier chapters, and the one that will be most useful to us here is the measure that we used when we had two independent groups. With two groups, we defined an estimate of $d$ as

$$\hat{d} = \frac{\overline{X}_1 - \overline{X}_2}{s}$$

where $s$ is the square root of the pooled variance estimate, or, with equal sample sizes, the square root of the average of the two variances (or sometimes the standard deviation of a control group).

Although it would be possible to algebraically extend this idea to more than two groups, to obtain a measure of the multiple differences between groups, it is difficult to know how to interpret such a result. For most situations, I think it makes much more sense to restrict ourselves to two-group comparisons and to speak about the difference between specific groups or sets of groups, rather than to make a global statement about differences among all groups simultaneously. (In fact, I believe that for most analyses of variance the overall $F$ is nowhere near as important as comparisons among specific groups.)

The data on maternal adaptation for mothers with low-birthweight infants provides an excellent example of what I mean. The group means are reproduced in the following table.

|  | LBW-Exp | LBW-Control | Full-Term | Overall |
|---|---|---|---|---|
| Means | 14.966 | 18.333 | 14.838 | 15.892 |
| $MS_{error}$ |  |  |  | 20.511 |

In an earlier analysis we showed that this difference among groups is statistically significant ($F(2,90) = 5.53, p < .05$). However, we should also tell our readers something about the magnitude of the differences under discussion, and that statement should be phrased in terms that have meaning to the reader. Here it makes sense to fall back on specific comparisons, just as we did earlier when we compared the LBW-Control and Full-Term groups, and again when we compared the two low-birthweight groups (LBW-Control versus LBW-Exp). You should recall that both of those differences are significant when we compare them using the Bonferroni test.

If the raw score units had particular meaning, which they might have if our dependent variable were something such as weight, IQ, age, or some other commonly understood variable, then it would make sense to simply report the difference in original units of measurement, perhaps providing an estimate of the standard deviation as a frame of reference. However, our dependent variable is the score on a measure of maternal adaptation, and it would not be very informative to simply report that the two low-birthweight groups differed by 3.367 points. Neither you nor I have any real sense of whether that is a large or a small difference. However, we could express the effect size measure as $\hat{d}$, which is a standardized measure of the difference.

Neither the LBW-Control nor the Full-Term groups received any special training, so a difference between them would reflect a difference due to birthweight. In this case

$$\hat{d} = \frac{\overline{X}_{LBW-C} - \overline{X}_{F-T}}{s} = \frac{18.333 - 14.838}{4.523} = \frac{3.495}{4.523} = .77$$

Here we see that the two groups differ by .77 standard deviation, which is a sizeable difference. There clearly is a noticeable effect due to birthweight. (The standard deviation shown here is simply the square root of $MS_{error}$, and is the average standard deviation within groups.)

If we compare the two low-birthweight groups, we find

$$\hat{d} = \frac{\overline{X}_{\text{LBW-C}} - \overline{X}_{\text{LBW-E}}}{s} = \frac{18.333 - 14.966}{4.523} = \frac{3.367}{4.523} = .74$$

This is another large effect. So we can conclude that the LBW-Control condition scores about ¾ of a standard deviation higher (worse adaptation) than either the Full-Term group or the LBW group that receives the intervention. These measures tell us that there are important effects in the results of this experiment.

## 16.8 Writing Up the Results

When I described how we would write up the results of Eyesenck's (1974) study of recall as a function of level of processing, I had not yet covered multiple comparisons and effect size measures, and so was not able to include that in the write-up. But with the study by Nurcombe et al. (1984) on maternal adaptation to low-birthweight infants we do have those results. An abbreviated version of how these data might be written up follows.

Nurcombe et al. (1984) studied the effects of an intervention program for the mothers of low-birthweight infants. A group of 37 mothers of full-term infants served as a control. A second group of 27 mothers of low-birthweight infants was also assessed, and differences between these two groups address the question of the effects of low birthweight on maternal adaptation. Finally, a third group of 29 mothers of low-birthweight infants received an intervention program designed to make them more aware of the weak behavioral signals their infants produced.

The overall analysis of variance showed that the groups exhibited significant differences in maternal adaptation ($F(2,90) = 5.53, p < .05$). Using $\omega^2$ as a correlation-based measure of effect showed that differences among the groups accounted for 8.9% of the overall variability in the dependent variable. Individual group comparisons showed that the two low-birthweight groups differed significantly ($t(90) = -2.77$), with the group receiving the intervention ($\overline{X} = 14.97$) scoring better than the low-birthweight control group ($\overline{X} = 18.33$) on the measure of maternal adaptation. Cohen's $\hat{d}$ applied to this difference was .74, indicating that the intervention group's mean was nearly three-quarters of a standard deviation below (better) than the non-intervention mean. A comparison of the low-birthweight control condition with the full-term control condition produced a significant difference ($t(90) = 3.04, p < .05$). In this case $\hat{d} = .77$, showing that giving birth to a low-birthweight infant can result in maternal adaptation scores that are three-quarters of a standard deviation above (worse than) for mothers of full term infants.

## 16.9 The Use of SPSS for a One-Way Analysis of Variance

An illustration of SPSS printout for a one-way analysis of variance is presented in Figure 16.4 for the maternal adaptation data. This was run using the **Compare Means/One-way ANOVA** procedure instead of the **General Linear Model** procedure. In this figure it is clear that the analysis reflects the answers we obtained in Section 16.4. I have used a set of contrasts, which I have not discussed in this chapter, to run the $t$ tests between the relevant groups. The first compares the two low-birthweight groups, and the second compares the low-birthweight control group with the full-term group. The $t$ values that result agree with ours within rounding error.

▼Oneway

**ANOVA**

adapt

|  | Sum of Squares | df | Mean Square | F | Sig. |
|---|---|---|---|---|---|
| Between Groups | 226.932 | 2 | 113.466 | 5.532 | .005 |
| Within Groups | 1845.993 | 90 | 20.511 | | |
| Total | 2072.925 | 92 | | | |

**Contrast Coefficients**

| | group | | |
|---|---|---|---|
| Contrast | LBW-exp | LBW-Control | Full-Term |
| 1 | 1 | −1 | 0 |
| 2 | 0 | 1 | −1 |

**Contrast Tests**

| | Contrast | | Value of Contrast | Std. Error | t | df | Sig. (2–tailed) |
|---|---|---|---|---|---|---|---|
| adapt | Assume equal variances | 1 | −3.368 | 1.2112 | −2.781 | 90 | .007 |
| | | 2 | 3.495 | 1.1463 | 3.049 | 90 | .003 |
| | Does not assume equal variances | 1 | −3.368 | 1.3408 | −2.512 | 53.005 | .015 |
| | | 2 | 3.495 | 1.1663 | 2.997 | 44.664 | .004 |

**Figure 16.4**
SPSS analysis of maternal adaptation data

## 16.10    A Final Worked Example

The following example illustrates a one-way analysis of variance with unequal sample sizes. It also illustrates the use of the Bonferroni procedure.

What does marijuana do, and how does it do it? Aside from its better-known effects, marijuana increases, or in some cases decreases, locomotor (walking around) behavior. The nucleus accumbens is a forebrain structure that has been shown to be involved in locomotor activity in rats. (It is also thought to control feelings of pleasure.) Administration of low doses of tetrahydrocannabinol (THC, the major active ingredient in marijuana) is known to increase locomotor activity, whereas high doses are known to lead to a decrease in activity. In an attempt to examine whether THC is acting within the nucleus accumbens to produce its effects on activity, Conti and Musty (1984) bilaterally injected either a placebo or .1, .5, 1, or 2 micrograms ($\mu$g) of THC directly into the nucleus accumbens of rats. The investigators recorded the *change* in the activity level of the animals after injection. It was expected that activity would increase more with smaller injections than with larger ones. The data in Table 16.8 represent the amount of change (decrease) in each animal.[8]

First we will set up the null hypothesis, which states that all of the samples were drawn from populations with the same mean. In other words,

**Table 16.8**
Data from the Study by Conti and Musty (1984)

|  | Placebo | .1 $\mu$g | .5 $\mu$g | 1 $\mu$g | 2 $\mu$g |
|---|---|---|---|---|---|
|  | 30 | 60 | 71 | 33 | 36 |
|  | 27 | 42 | 50 | 78 | 27 |
|  | 52 | 48 | 38 | 71 | 60 |
|  | 38 | 52 | 59 | 58 | 51 |
|  | 20 | 28 | 65 | 35 | 29 |
|  | 26 | 93 | 58 | 35 | 34 |
|  | 8 | 32 | 74 | 46 | 24 |
|  | 41 | 46 | 67 | 32 | 17 |
|  | 49 | 63 | 61 |  | 50 |
|  | 49 | 44 |  |  | 53 |
| $\Sigma$ | 340 | 508 | 543 | 388 | 381 $\Sigma X = 2160$ |
| Mean | 34.00 | 50.80 | 60.33 | 48.50 | 38.1 |
| $n$ | 10 | 10 | 9 | 8 | 10 $N = 47$ |

---

[8]Although THC is expected to *increase* activity, the dependent variable is measured as a *decrease* in overall activity because the animals were becoming acclimated to a new situation and were thus exploring less. Thus rather than an increase in activity, we actually are looking for less of a decrease. It's confusing!

$H_0: \mu_1 = \mu_2 = \mu_3 = \mu_4 = \mu_5$. For consistency we will test this null hypothesis with a significance level of $\alpha = .05$.

Next, we will run the overall analysis of variance, starting with the calculation of the sums of squares:

$$SS_{total} = \Sigma(X_{ij} - \overline{X}..)^2 = \Sigma X^2 - \frac{(\Sigma X^2)}{N} = (30^2 + 27^2 + \cdots + 53^2) - \frac{2,160^2}{47}$$

$$= 113,556 - 99,268.085 = 14,287.91$$

$$SS_{group} = \Sigma n_j(\overline{X}_j - \overline{X}..)^2 = 10(34 - 45.96)^2 + \cdots + 10(38.10 - 45.96)^2$$

$$= 4,193.41$$

$$SS_{error} = SS_{total} - SS_{group} = 14,287.91 - 4,193.41 = 10,094.50$$

We can now put these terms into a summary table.

| Source | df | SS | MS | F |
|--------|-----|----------|----------|------|
| Groups | 4 | 4,193.41 | 1,048.35 | 4.36 |
| Error | 42 | 10,094.50 | 240.35 | |
| Total | 46 | 14,287.91 | | |

Finally, we compare $F = 4.36$ to the critical value from Table D.3 in Appendix D. We have 4 df for Groups and 42 df for Error. The critical value from Table D.3 is 2.61 if we round off to 40 degrees of freedom for the denominator. Because our obtained value exceeds 2.61, we will reject the null hypothesis and conclude that there are differences in activity levels among the five drug groups, presumably reflecting differences due to the dosage of THC administered.

## Comparisons of Individual Groups

The experimental hypothesis had predicted that the Placebo group would show smaller increases (or greater decreases) in activity than the medium-dose group. Therefore, we might want to compare the Placebo group with the .5-$\mu$g group. It would also be interesting to compare the 2-$\mu$g group with the .5-$\mu$g group to show that a medium dose had a greater effect than a large dose. We will make both these comparisons using the Bonferroni test. As already discussed we will perform this test by first running $t$ tests between the groups, just as we did with the protected $t$.

*Comparison of Groups 3 and 1 ( .5 $\mu$g versus Placebo):*

$$t = \frac{\overline{X}_3 - \overline{X}_1}{\sqrt{MS_{error}\left(\dfrac{1}{n_3} + \dfrac{1}{n_1}\right)}}$$

$$= \frac{60.33 - 34.00}{\sqrt{240.35\left(\dfrac{1}{9} + \dfrac{1}{10}\right)}}$$

$$= \frac{26.33}{\sqrt{240.35(.2111)}} = \frac{26.33}{\sqrt{50.74}} = \frac{26.33}{7.12} = 3.70$$

*Comparison of Groups 3 and 5 (.5 $\mu$g versus 2$\mu$g):*

$$t = \frac{\overline{X}_3 - \overline{X}_5}{\sqrt{MS_{error}\left(\dfrac{1}{n_3} + \dfrac{1}{n_5}\right)}}$$

$$= \frac{60.33 - 38.10}{\sqrt{240.35\left(\dfrac{1}{9} + \dfrac{1}{10}\right)}}$$

$$= \frac{22.23}{\sqrt{240.35(.211)}} = \frac{22.23}{\sqrt{50.74}} = \frac{22.23}{7.12} = 3.12$$

Because we ran only two tests, we can evaluate those *t* values against *t* at $\alpha = .05/2 = .025$. We could use a program such as Minitab or SPSS to calculate the actual probabilities. Alternatively, we could tell from Appendix D that even at $\alpha = .02$, which is more conservative than $\alpha = .025$, the critical value on 17 *df* is 2.567, while the critical value on 18 *df* is 2.552. Both of these differences are clearly significant. The experimental hypothesis had predicted that a moderate dose of THC would produce greater increases (or smaller decreases) in activity than either no THC or a large dose of THC. Both of these hypotheses are supported by this experiment.

### Magnitude of Effect and Effect Size Measures

As we did previously, we can assess the magnitude of effect of the treatment variable with either $\eta^2$ or $\omega^2$, or we can calculate $\hat{d}$ for specific group comparisons.

$$\eta^2 = \frac{SS_{group}}{SS_{total}} = \frac{4,193.41}{14,287.91} = .29$$

$$\omega^2 = \frac{SS_{group} - (k - 1)MS_{error}}{SS_{total} + MS_{error}} = \frac{4,193.41 - (5 - 1)240.35}{14,287.91 + 240.35} = .22$$

These two measures show that group effects account for about a quarter of the variation in this study.

Effect size measures of differences between specific groups are another way of examining the magnitude of the effect of THC. Conti and Musty (1984) had expected that medium doses of THC would lead to the highest level of activity, so it makes sense to report on the difference between the means of the Control group (which received no THC) and the .5-$\mu$g group (which received a moderate dose).

$$\ddot{d} = \frac{\overline{X}_{.5\mu g} - \overline{X}_{Control}}{s} = \frac{60.33 - 34.00}{\sqrt{240.35}} = \frac{26.33}{15.503} = 1.70$$

This is a very substantial difference (nearly one and three-quarters standard deviations), reflecting the very important influence that THC has on activity in rats.[9]

## 16.11 Seeing Statistics

In Section 16.3 we discussed the $F$ distribution, and saw that it depended on (1) the number of groups ($df$ for groups), (2) the number of observations within groups ($df$ for the error term), and (3) the magnitude of $F$ (the larger the $F$, the smaller the associated probability. An applet to illustrate these characteristics is available on the Web site labeled $F$ probabilities. An example of that applet is shown.

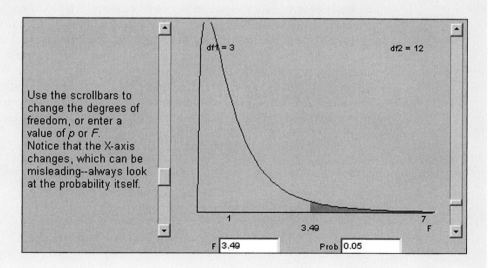

___

[9]Some people would suggest that, because the .0 $\mu$g is a true control group, its standard deviation might be better used to scale $\hat{d}$. In this case it would not make a very great difference, and I have used the square root of the pooled variance.

At the bottom of this applet you will see an $F$ value and its associated probability. You can change either of those values and the other will change accordingly. For example, if you have 3 and 12 $df$, and enter .01 into the probability box, the $F$ will change to 5.94, which is the critical value at $\alpha = .01$.

On the left and right of the display you will see sliders. If you move the one on the left, you will see the degrees of freedom for groups change. Similarly, moving the one on the right alters the degrees of freedom for error.

- What happens as you increase the $df$ for error in terms of the size of the critical value of $F$? (You have to be careful to look at the critical value, and not just at the distribution itself, because part of the reason that the distribution appears to get wider is because the scale on the $X$ axis has to change to accommodate the graphed values.)

- What happens if you increase the number of groups—and therefore the degrees of freedom for groups? (Again, notice that the scale on the $X$ axis changes.)

- What is the critical value for $F$ at $\alpha = .05$ for the Maternal Adaptation example in Table 16.6?

## 16.12 Summary

The analysis of variance is one of our most powerful statistical tools. In this chapter we began by examining the logic behind the analysis and then turned to the calculations. After considering the calculations for the case of equal sample sizes, we took up the problem of unequal sample sizes and saw that for the one-way analysis of variance we need to make only minor changes in the formulae. We then considered the problem of isolating group differences by means of multiple comparison procedures. After discussing the effects of violating the assumptions behind the test, we considered the problem of estimating the size of experimental effects.

Some important terms in the chapter are

| | |
|---|---|
| Analysis of variance (ANOVA), 375 | Sum of squares (SS), 384 |
| One-way ANOVA, 375 | $SS_{total}$, 386 |
| Omnibus null hypothesis, 377 | $SS_{group}$, 386 |
| | $SS_{error}$, 386 |
| $MS_{within}$ ($MS_{error}$), 380 | $df_{total}$, 388 |
| $MS_{between\ groups}$ ($MS_{groups}$, $MS_{treatment}$), 380 | $df_{group}$, 388 |
| | $df_{error}$, 388 |

F statistic, 388

Multiple comparison
techniques, 394

Protected *t*, 395

Fisher's least significant
difference (LSD) test, 395

Familywise error rate, 398

Bonferroni procedure, 399

Tukey procedure, 402

*d*-family measures, 403

*r*-family measures, 403

Magnitude of effect, 403

$\eta^2$ (eta squared), 403

$\omega^2$ (omega squared), 404

## 16.13 Exercises

**16.1** We began the chapter with a study by Eysenck (1974) in which he compared the recall of older participants under one of five levels of processing. Another aspect of Eysenck's study compared younger and older participants on their ability to recall material in the face of instructions telling them that they should memorize the material for later recall. (Presumably this task required a high level of processing, which older participants may not do well.) The data on 10 participants in each group follow, where the dependent variable is the number of items recalled.

| **Younger** | 21 | 19 | 17 | 15 | 22 | 16 | 22 | 22 | 18 | 21 |
| **Older** | 10 | 19 | 14 | 5 | 10 | 11 | 14 | 15 | 11 | 11 |

(a) Conduct the analysis of variance comparing the means of these two groups.
(b) Conduct a *t* test for independent groups on the data and compare the results to those you obtained in part (a).

**16.2** Another way to look at the Eysenck study mentioned in Exercise 16.1 is to compare four groups of participants. One group consisted of younger participants who were presented the words to be recalled in a condition that elicited a low level of processing. A second group consisted of younger participants who were given a task requiring the highest level of processing (as in Exercise 16.1). The two other groups were older participants who were given tasks requiring either low or high levels of processing. The data follow:

| **Younger/Low** | 8 | 6 | 4 | 6 | 7 | 6 | 5 | 7 | 9 | 7 |
| **Younger/Hi** | 21 | 19 | 17 | 15 | 22 | 16 | 22 | 22 | 18 | 21 |
| **Older/Low** | 9 | 8 | 6 | 8 | 10 | 4 | 6 | 5 | 7 | 7 |
| **Older/Hi** | 10 | 19 | 14 | 5 | 10 | 11 | 14 | 15 | 11 | 11 |

Conduct a one-way analysis of variance on these data.

**16.3** Now we will expand on the analysis of Exercise 16.2.
(a) Run a one-way analysis of variance on treatments 1 and 3 combined ($n = 20$) versus treatments 2 and 4 combined. What question are you answering?
(b) Why might your answer to part (a) be difficult to interpret?

**16.4** Refer to Exercise 16.1. Assume that we collected additional data and had two more participants in the younger group with scores of 13 and 15.
(a) Rerun the analysis of variance.
(b) Run a $t$ test for independent groups without pooling the variances.
(c) Run a $t$ test for independent groups after pooling the variances.
(d) For (b) and (c), which of these values of $t$ corresponds (after squaring) to the $F$ in (a)?

**16.5** Calculate $\eta^2$ and $\omega^2$ for the data in Exercise 16.1.

**16.6** Calculate $\eta^2$ and $\omega^2$ for the data in Exercise 16.2.

**16.7** Foa, Rothbaum, Riggs, and Murdock (1991) conducted a study evaluating four different types of therapy for rape victims. The Stress Inoculation Therapy (SIT) group received instructions on coping with stress. The Prolonged Exposure (PE) group went over the events in their minds repeatedly. The Supportive Counseling (SC) group were taught a general problem-solving technique. Finally, the Waiting List (WL) control group received no therapy. Data with the same characteristics as theirs follow, where the dependent variable was the severity rating of a series of symptoms.

| Group | $n$ | Mean | Std. Dev. |
|-------|-----|-------|-----------|
| SIT | 14 | 11.07 | 3.95 |
| PE | 10 | 15.40 | 11.12 |
| SC | 11 | 18.09 | 7.13 |
| WL | 10 | 19.50 | 7.11 |

(a) Run the analysis of variance, ignoring any problems with heterogeneity of variance, and draw whatever conclusions are warranted. (Note that you have to be a little creative here, but it is not a difficult exercise.)
(b) Draw a graph showing the means of the four groups.
(c) What does rejection of the null hypothesis mean?

**16.8** Calculate $\eta^2$ and $\omega^2$ for the data in Exercise 16.7, and interpret their meaning.

**16.9** What would happen if the sample sizes in Exercise 16.7 were twice as large as they were?

**16.10** Use protected $t$ tests for the data in Exercise 16.7 to clarify the meaning of the significant $F$.

**16.11** Calculate $\hat{d}$ for the comparisons you made in Exercise 16.10 and interpret the meaning of each.

**16.12** The data in Exercises 16.7 and 16.9 both produced a significant $F$. Do you have more or less faith in one of these effects? Why?

**16.13** For the data in the data set on attention deficit disorder (Add.dat), form three groups. Group 1 has ADDSC scores of 40 or below, Group 2 has ADDSC scores between 41 and 59, and Group 3 has ADDSC scores of 60 or above. Run an analysis of variance on the GPA scores for these three groups.

**16.14** Compute $\eta^2$ and $\omega^2$ from the results in Exercise 16.13.

**16.15**  Darley and Latané (1968) recorded the speed with which participants summoned help for a person in trouble. Some participants thought that they were alone with the person (Group 1, $n = 13$), some thought that one other person was there (Group 2, $n = 26$), and others thought that four other people were there (Group 3, $n = 13$). The dependent variable was speed ($1/\text{time} \times 100$) to call someone for help. The mean speed scores for the three groups were .87, .72, and .51, respectively. The $MS_{error}$ was .053. Reconstruct the analysis of variance. What would you conclude?

**16.16**  Using the data in Exercise 16.2, calculate $SS_{error}$ directly rather than by subtraction and show that this is the same answer you found in that exercise.

**16.17**  Use the Bonferroni test for the data in Exercise 16.2 to compare the Younger/Low with the Older/Low group, and the Younger/High with the Older/High group.

**16.18**  Use the Bonferroni test for the data in Exercise 16.7 to compare the WL group with each of the other three groups. What would you conclude? How does this compare to the answer for Exercise 16.10?

**16.19**  Calculate $\hat{d}$ for the comparison of WL with SIT in Exercise 16.18 using the standard deviation of the Control group to standardize the difference.

**16.20**  What effect does smoking have on performance? Spilich, June, and Renner (1992) asked nonsmokers (NS), smokers who had delayed smoking for three hours (DS), and smokers who were actively smoking (AS) to perform a pattern recognition task in which they had to locate a target on a screen. The dependent variable was latency (in seconds). The data are presented below. Plot the resulting means and run the analysis of variance. On the basis of these data, is there support for the hypothesis that smoking has an effect on performance?

| Non-Smokers | Delayed Smokers | Active Smokers |
|---|---|---|
| 9 | 12 | 8 |
| 8 | 7 | 8 |
| 12 | 14 | 9 |
| 10 | 4 | 1 |
| 7 | 8 | 9 |
| 10 | 11 | 7 |
| 9 | 16 | 16 |
| 11 | 17 | 19 |
| 8 | 5 | 1 |
| 10 | 6 | 1 |
| 8 | 9 | 22 |
| 10 | 6 | 12 |
| 8 | 6 | 18 |
| 11 | 7 | 8 |
| 10 | 16 | 10 |

**16.21**  In the study referred to in Exercise 16.20, Spilich et al. (1992) also investigated performance on a cognitive task that required the participant to read a passage and then to recall it later. This task has much greater information processing demands than the pattern recognition task. The independent variable was the three smoking groups referred in Exercise 16.20.

The dependent variable was the number of propositions recalled from the passage. The data follow.

| Non-Smokers | Delayed Smokers | Active Smokers |
|---|---|---|
| 27 | 48 | 34 |
| 34 | 29 | 65 |
| 19 | 34 | 55 |
| 20 | 6 | 33 |
| 56 | 18 | 42 |
| 35 | 63 | 54 |
| 23 | 9 | 21 |
| 37 | 54 | 44 |
| 4 | 28 | 61 |
| 30 | 71 | 38 |
| 4 | 60 | 75 |
| 42 | 54 | 61 |
| 34 | 51 | 51 |
| 19 | 25 | 32 |
| 49 | 49 | 47 |

Run the analysis of variance on these data and draw the appropriate conclusions.

**16.22** Use Fisher's LSD test to compare active smokers with nonsmokers and to compare the two groups of smokers on the data in Exercise 16.21. What do these data suggest about the advisability of smoking while you are studying for an exam and the advisability of smoking just before you take an exam?

**16.23** Spilich et al. (1992) ran a third experiment in which the three groups of smokers participated in a driving simulation video game. The AS group smoked immediately before the game but not during it. The data follow, where the dependent variable is an adjusted score related to the number of collisions. Run the analysis of variance and draw the appropriate conclusions.

| Non-Smokers | Delayed Smokers | Active Smokers |
|---|---|---|
| 15 | 7 | 3 |
| 2 | 0 | 2 |
| 2 | 6 | 0 |
| 14 | 0 | 0 |
| 5 | 12 | 6 |
| 0 | 17 | 2 |
| 16 | 1 | 0 |
| 14 | 11 | 6 |
| 9 | 4 | 4 |
| 17 | 4 | 1 |
| 15 | 3 | 0 |
| 9 | 5 | 0 |
| 3 | 16 | 6 |
| 15 | 5 | 2 |
| 13 | 11 | 3 |

**16.24** The three experiments by Spilich et al. (1992) on the effects of smoking on performance find conflicting results. Can you suggest why the results are different?

**16.25** Previously we saw a study by Merrell (1997) on the effects of different kinds of music on the maze performance in mice. There we looked at only the Mozart and the Control groups. Merrell also had a third group that were presented with music by Anthrax. The analysis of variance will allow us to make comparisons among all three groups. The data appear below. Run an analysis of variance on these data.

| Control | 444 | 219 | 347 | 327 | 431 | 333 | 310 | 341 | 206 | 203 | 999 | 267 |
|---|---|---|---|---|---|---|---|---|---|---|---|---|
| | 275 | 297 | 215 | 305 | 262 | 259 | 225 | 306 | 343 | 315 | 407 | 422 |

| Mozart | 101 | 162 | 152 | 153 | 132 | 191 | 106 | 180 | 99 | 120 | 134 | 78 |
|---|---|---|---|---|---|---|---|---|---|---|---|---|
| | 123 | 121 | 85 | 67 | 68 | 48 | 76 | 107 | 121 | 119 | 86 | 113 |

| Anthrax | 1729 | 1867 | 1576 | 1729 | 1849 | 1741 | 1750 | 1765 | 1764 | 1756 | 1871 | 1916 |
|---|---|---|---|---|---|---|---|---|---|---|---|---|
| | 1953 | 1735 | 1870 | 1869 | 1962 | 1826 | 1834 | 1722 | 1879 | 2050 | 1946 | 1854 |

**16.26** Use the Bonferroni test to elaborate on the results of Exercise 16.25.

**16.27** Use $\hat{d}$ to tell the reader how large a difference there was between the Control group and each of the groups that listened to music in Exercise 16.26.

**16.28** Langlois and Roggman (1990) took facial photographs of males and females. They then created five groups of composite photographs by computer-averaging the individual faces. For one group the computer averaged 32 randomly selected same-gender faces, producing a quite recognizable face with average width, height, eyes, nose length, and so on. For the other groups the composite faces were averaged over either 2, 4, 8, or 16 individual faces. Each group saw six separate photographs, all of which were computer-averaged over the appropriate number of individual photographs. Langlois and Roggman asked participants to rate the attractiveness of the faces on a 1–5 scale, where 5 represents "very attractive." The data have been constructed to have the same means and variances as those reported by Langlois and Roggman.

Data on Rated Attractiveness

| | Group 1 | Group 2 | Group 3 | Group 4 | Group 5 |
|---|---|---|---|---|---|
| | 2.201 | 1.893 | 2.906 | 3.233 | 3.200 |
| | 2.411 | 3.102 | 2.118 | 3.505 | 3.253 |
| | 2.407 | 2.355 | 3.226 | 3.192 | 3.357 |
| | 2.403 | 3.644 | 2.811 | 3.209 | 3.169 |
| | 2.826 | 2.767 | 2.857 | 2.860 | 3.291 |
| | 3.380 | 2.109 | 3.422 | 3.111 | 3.290 |
| **Mean** | 2.6047 | 2.6450 | 2.8900 | 3.1850 | 3.2600 |

(a) Specify a research hypothesis that could lie behind this study.
(b) Run the appropriate analysis of variance.
(c) What do these data tell us about how people judge attractiveness?

**16.29** Using the data from Exercise 16.28,
(a) Calculate $\eta^2$ and $\omega^2$.
(b) Why do the two estimates of the magnitude of effect in part a) differ?
(c) Calculate a measure of $\hat{d}$, using the most appropriate groups.

# 17

# Factorial Analysis of Variance

## QUESTIONS

- What if I have more than one independent variable that I want to look at?

- What do we mean by "main effects?"

- What happens if the difference between the levels of one independent variable depends on the level of the other variable that I'm looking at?

- What techniques do I have for looking at the answer to the preceding question?

- Can I deal with unequal sample sizes here as easily as I did with the one-way?

- Is it any more difficult to calculate effect size measures with a factorial design?

In Chapter 16 we dealt with a one-way analysis of variance, which is an experimental design having only one independent variable. In this chapter we will extend the analysis of variance to cover experimental designs involving two or more independent variables. For purposes of simplicity we will consider experiments involving only two independent variables, although the extension to more complex designs is not difficult (see Howell, 2007).

Why do older people often seem not to remember things as well as younger people? Do they not pay attention? Do they just not process the material as thoroughly? Do they know less? Or do they really do just as well, but are we more likely to notice when they forget than when younger people do? In Chapter 16 we considered a study by Eysenck (1974) in which he asked participants to recall lists of words to which they had been exposed under one of several different conditions. In that example we were interested in determining whether recall was related to the level at which material was processed initially. Eysenck's study was actually more complex. He was interested in whether level-of-processing notions could explain differences in recall between older and younger participants. If older participants do not process information as deeply, they might be expected to recall fewer items than would younger participants, especially in conditions that entail greater processing. This study now has two independent variables (Age and recall Condition), which we will refer to as **factors**. The experiment is an instance of what is called a **two-way factorial design**.

Definition | **Factors:** Another word for independent variables in the analysis of variance.

**Two-way factorial design:** An experimental design involving two independent variables in a way in which every level of one variable is paired with each level of the other variable.

**Factorial design:** An experimental design in which every level of each variable is paired with every level of each other variable.

To expand this experiment even further, we could classify participants additionally as male and female. We then would have what is called a *three-way factorial design*, with Age, Condition, and Gender as factors.

## 17.1 Factorial Designs

An experimental design in which every level of every factor is paired with every level of every other factor is called a factorial design. In other words a **factorial design** is one in which we include all *combinations* of the levels of the independent variables. Table 17.1 illustrates the two-way design of Eysenck's study. In the factorial designs discussed in this chapter, we will consider only the case in which different participants

**Table 17.1**
Diagrammatic Representation of Eysenck's Two-way Factorial Study

|  | Counting | Rhyming | Adjective | Imagery | Intentional |
|---|---|---|---|---|---|
| **Younger** |  |  |  |  |  |
| **Older** |  |  |  |  |  |

serve under each of the treatment combinations. For instance, in our example one group of younger participants will serve in the Counting condition, a different group of younger participants in the Rhyming condition, and so on. Since we have 10 combinations of our two factors (5 recall Conditions × 2 Ages), we will have 10 different groups of participants. When a research plan calls for the *same* participant to be included under more than one treatment combination, we speak of repeated-measures designs. Repeated-measures designs will be discussed in Chapter 18.

Factorial designs have several important advantages over one-way designs. First, they allow greater generalizability of the results. Consider Eysenck's study for a moment. If we were to run a one-way analysis of variance using the five Conditions with only older participants, as in Chapter 16, our results would apply only to older participants. When we use a factorial design with both older and younger participants, we are able to determine whether differences between Conditions apply to younger participants as well as older ones. We are also able to determine whether age differences in recall apply to all tasks, or whether younger (or older) participants excel on only certain kinds of tasks. Thus factorial designs allow for a much broader interpretation of the results and at the same time give us the ability to say something meaningful about the results for each of the independent variables.

The second important feature of factorial designs is that they allow us to look at the **interaction** of variables. We can ask whether the effect of Condition is independent of Age or whether there is some interaction between Condition and Age. I suspect that Eysenck really was not particularly interested in knowing whether recall was better if the processing of information was done at greater depth. He probably already knew that from other work. And he probably was not terribly surprised to see that younger participants did better than older ones. I'm sure you weren't surprised. But what Eysenck really cared about was whether the difference in recall between younger and older participants varied as a function of processing. If it did, he would have evidence that memory decline with age relates to the degree of processing individuals do, and that is an important and interesting finding. Interaction effects such as these are often among the most interesting results we obtain.

| Definition | **Interaction:** A situation in a factorial design in which the effects of one independent variable depend on the level of another independent variable. |
| --- | --- |

A third advantage of a factorial design is its economy. Since we are going to average the effects of one variable across the levels of the other variable, a two-variable factorial will require fewer participants than would two one-way designs for the same degree of power. Essentially, we are getting something for nothing. Suppose we had no reason to expect an interaction of Age and Condition. Then, with ten older participants and ten younger participants in each Condition, we would have 20 scores for each of the five Conditions. If we instead ran a one-way with younger participants and then another one-way with older participants, we would need twice as many participants overall for each of our experiments to have 20 participants per Condition, and we would have two experiments.

As mentioned earlier, factorial designs are labeled by the number of factors involved. A factorial design with two independent variables, or factors, is called a two-way factorial, and one with three factors is called a three-way factorial. An alternative method of labeling designs is in terms of the number of levels of each factor. Eysenck's study had two levels of Age and five levels of Condition. As such, it is a **2 × 5 factorial**. A study with three factors, two of them having three levels and one having four levels, would be called a 3 × 3 × 4 factorial. The use of such terms as "two-way" and "2 × 5" are common ways of designating designs, and both will be used in this book.

Definition

**2 × 5 factorial design:** A factorial design with one variable having two levels and the other having five levels.

**Cell:** The combination of a particular row and column; the set of observations obtained under identical treatment conditions.

In much of what follows, we will concern ourselves primarily with the two-way analysis. Higher-order analyses follow relatively easily once you understand the two-way, and many of the related problems we will discuss are most simply explained in terms of two factors.

## Notation

In this chapter I will keep the notation as simple as possible to avoid unnecessary confusion. Names of factors generally are designated by the first letter (capitalized) of the factor name, and the individual levels of each factor are indicated by that capital letter with the appropriate subscript (in Condition, for instance, Counting would be designated as $C_1$, Rhyming as $C_2$, and Intentional as $C_5$). The number of levels of the factor will be denoted by a lowercase letter corresponding to that factor. Thus Condition (C) has $c = 5$ levels, whereas Age (A) has $a = 2$ levels. Any specific combination of one level of one factor and one level of another factor (e.g., Older participants in the Rhyming condition) is called a **cell**, and the number of observations per cell will be denoted by $n$. The total number of observations is $N$, and in our example, $N = acn = 2 \times 5 \times 10 = 100$ because there are $a \times c = 10$ cells, each with 10 participants. Table 17.2 shows the factorial design of Eysenck's study.

## Table 17.2
Factorial Design of Eysenck's Study

| | | | Conditions | | | |
|---|---|---|---|---|---|---|
| Age | Counting | Rhyming | Adjective | Imagery | Intentional | Totals |
| **Younger** | $\overline{X}_{11}$ | $\overline{X}_{12}$ | $\overline{X}_{13}$ | $\overline{X}_{14}$ | $\overline{X}_{15}$ | $\overline{X}_{A1}$ |
| **Older** | $\overline{X}_{21}$ | $\overline{X}_{22}$ | $\overline{X}_{23}$ | $\overline{X}_{24}$ | $\overline{X}_{25}$ | $\overline{X}_{A2}$ |
| **Totals** | $\overline{X}_{C1}$ | $\overline{X}_{C2}$ | $\overline{X}_{C3}$ | $\overline{X}_{C4}$ | $\overline{X}_{C5}$ | $\overline{X}_{..}$ |

The subscripts $i$ and $j$ are used as general (nonspecific) notations for the level of rows and columns. Thus, cell$_{ij}$ is the cell in the $i$th row and the $j$th column. For example, cell$_{22}$ in Table 17.2 would be the Older participants (row 2) in the Rhyming Condition (column 2). The means for the individual levels of Age will be denoted as $\overline{X}_{Ai}$, and the means for the individual levels of Condition will be denoted as $\overline{X}_{Cj}$. The subscripts $A$ and $C$ refer to the variable names. Cell means are denoted as $\overline{X}_{ij}$, and the **grand mean** (the mean of all $N$ scores) is shown as $\overline{X}..$.

| Definition | **Grand mean ($\overline{X}..$):** The mean of all of the observations. |
|---|---|

The notation described here will be used throughout our discussion of the analysis of variance, and it is important that you thoroughly understand it before proceeding. The advantage of this system is that it easily generalizes to other examples. For example, if we had a Drug × Gender factorial, it should be clear that $\overline{X}_{D1}$ and $\overline{X}_{G2}$ refer to the means of the first level of the Drug variable and the second level of the Gender variable, respectively.

## 17.2 The Extension of the Eysenck Study

As we have been discussing, Eysenck actually conducted a study varying Age as well as recall Condition. The study included 50 participants 18–30 years of age and 50 participants 55–65 years of age. The data in Table 17.3 have been created to have the same means and standard deviations as those reported by Eysenck. The table contains all the calculations for the standard analysis of variance, and we will discuss each of those in turn. Before we begin the analysis, it is important to note that the data themselves are approximately normally distributed with acceptably homogeneous variances. The boxplots are not given in the table because the individual data points are artificial; for real data it would be well worth your effort to compute them. You can tell from the cell and marginal means that recall appears to increase with greater processing, and younger participants seem to recall more items than do older participants. Notice also that the difference between younger and older participants seems to depend on the task, with greater differences for those tasks that involve deeper processing. We will consider these results further after we consider the analysis itself.

| Definition | **Main effect:** The effect of one independent variable averaged across the levels of the other independent variable. |
|---|---|

It will avoid confusion later if I take the time here to define two important terms. We have two factors in this experiment—Age and Condition. If we look at the differences between older and younger participants, *ignoring the particular Conditions*, we are dealing with what is called the **main effect** of Age. Similarly, if we look at differences among the five Conditions, *ignoring the Age of participants*, we are dealing with the main effect of Conditions.

| Definition | **Simple effect:** The effect of one independent variable at one level of another independent variable. |
| --- | --- |

An alternative method of looking at the data would be to compare the means of the five Conditions for only the older participants. (This is what we did in Chapter 16.) Or we might compare older and younger participants for only the data from the Counting task, or we might compare older and younger participants on the Intentional task. In these three examples we are looking at the effect of one factor for the data at only *one* level of the other factor. When we do this, we are dealing with a **simple effect**—the effect of one factor at one level of the other factor. A main effect, on the other hand, is that of a factor *ignoring* (or averaging across) the other factor. If we say that tasks that involve more processing lead to better recall, we are speaking of a main effect. If we conclude that *for younger participants* tasks that involve more processing lead to better recall, we are speaking about a simple effect. We will have more to say about simple effects and their calculations shortly. For now it is important only that you understand the terminology.

## Calculations

The calculations for the sums of squares appear in part (b) of Table 17.3. Many of these calculations should be familiar because they resemble the procedures used with a one-way design. For example, $SS_{total}$ is computed the same way it was in Chapter 16, which is the same way it is always computed. We sum all the squared observations and subtract $(\Sigma X)^2/N$, often called the correction factor.

The sum of squares for the Age factor ($SS_A$) is nothing but the $SS_{group}$ that we would obtain if this were a one-way analysis of variance without the Condition factor. In other words, we simply sum the squared deviations of the two Age means from the grand mean and multiply by the number of observations for each mean. We use $nc$ as the multiplier here because each age has $n$ participants at each of $c$ levels. The same procedures are followed in the calculation of $SS_C$, except that here we ignore the presence of the Age variable.

You will notice that $\Sigma(\overline{X}_A - \overline{X}..)^2$ is multiplied by $nc$ and $\Sigma(\overline{X}_C - \overline{X}..)^2$ is multiplied by $na$, where A and C represent Age and Condition, respectively. Please don't try to remember these multipliers as formulae; you will be wasting your time. They represent the number of scores per means and nothing more. They are exactly analogous to the multiplier ($n$) we used in the one-way analysis when we wanted to turn a variance of means into an estimate of $\sigma_e^2$. The only difference is that in a one-way analysis, $n$ represented the number of observations per treatment, and here it represents the number of observations per cell—because $c$ cells are involved with each Age level, there must be $nc$ observations for each Age mean ($\overline{X}_A$).

**Table 17.3**
Data and Calculations for Example from Eysenck (1974)

| (a) Data | | | | | | |
|---|---|---|---|---|---|---|
| | | | Recall Conditions | | | |
| | Counting | Rhyming | Adjective | Imagery | Intentional | Mean$_i$ |
| **Old** | 9 | 7 | 11 | 12 | 10 | |
| | 8 | 9 | 13 | 11 | 19 | |
| | 6 | 6 | 8 | 16 | 14 | |
| | 8 | 6 | 6 | 11 | 5 | |
| | 10 | 6 | 14 | 9 | 10 | |
| | 4 | 11 | 11 | 23 | 11 | |
| | 6 | 6 | 13 | 12 | 14 | |
| | 5 | 3 | 13 | 10 | 15 | |
| | 7 | 8 | 10 | 19 | 11 | |
| | 7 | 7 | 11 | 11 | 11 | |
| Mean$_{1j}$ | 7.0 | 6.9 | 11.0 | 13.4 | 12.0 | 10.06 |
| **Young** | 8 | 10 | 14 | 20 | 21 | |
| | 6 | 7 | 11 | 16 | 19 | |
| | 4 | 8 | 18 | 16 | 17 | |
| | 6 | 10 | 14 | 15 | 15 | |
| | 7 | 4 | 13 | 18 | 22 | |
| | 6 | 7 | 22 | 16 | 16 | |
| | 5 | 10 | 17 | 20 | 22 | |
| | 7 | 6 | 16 | 22 | 22 | |
| | 9 | 7 | 12 | 14 | 18 | |
| | 7 | 7 | 11 | 19 | 21 | |
| Mean$_{2j}$ | 6.5 | 7.6 | 14.8 | 17.6 | 19.3 | 13.16 |
| Mean$_j$ | 6.75 | 7.25 | 12.9 | 15.5 | 15.65 | 11.61 |

(*continued*)

Definition   SS$_{cells}$: The sum of squares assessing differences among the cell means.

Having obtained SS$_{total}$, SS$_A$, and SS$_C$, we come to an unfamiliar term, SS$_{cells}$. This term represents the variability of the individual cell means and is, in fact, only a dummy term; it will not appear in the summary table. It is calculated just like any other sum of squares. We take the deviations of the cell means from the grand mean, square and sum them, and multiply by $n$, the number of observations per mean. Although it might not be readily apparent why we want this term, its usefulness will become clear when we calculate a sum of squares for the interaction of Age and Condition. (It may be easier to understand the calculation of SS$_{cells}$ if you think of it as what you would have if you viewed this as a study with 10 "groups" and calculated as SS$_{group}$.)

**Table 17.3**
(*continued*)

**(b) Calculations**

$$SS_{total} = \Sigma (X - \overline{X}..)^2 = \Sigma X^2 - \frac{(\Sigma X)^2}{N}$$

$$= 16,147 - \frac{1161^2}{100} = 16,147 - 13,479.21$$

$$= 2,667.79$$

$$SS_A = nc\Sigma(\overline{X}_A - \overline{X}..)^2$$
$$= 10 \times 5[(10.06 - 11.61)^2 + (13.16 - 11.61)^2]$$
$$= 240.25$$

$$SS_C = na\Sigma(\overline{X}_C - \overline{X}..)^2$$
$$= 10 \times 2[(6.75 - 11.61)^2 + (7.25 - 11.61)^2 + \cdots + (15.65 - 11.61)^2]$$
$$= 1,514.94$$

$$SS_{cells} = n\Sigma(\overline{X}_{AC} - \overline{X}..)^2$$
$$= 10[(7.0 - 11.61)^2 + (6.9 - 11.61)^2 + \cdots + (19.3 - 11.61)^2]$$
$$= 1,945.49$$

$$SS_{AC} = SS_{cells} - SS_A - SS_C = 1,945.49 - 240.25 - 1,514.94 = 190.30$$

$$SS_{error} = SS_{total} - SS_{cells} = 2,667.79 - 1,945.49 = 722.30$$

**(c) Summary table**

| Source | df | SS | MS | F |
|---|---|---|---|---|
| A (Age) | 1 | 240.25 | 240.250 | 29.94* |
| C (Condition) | 4 | 1,514.94 | 378.735 | 47.19* |
| AC | 4 | 190.30 | 47.575 | 5.93* |
| Error | 90 | 722.30 | 8.026 | |
| Total | 99 | 2,667.79 | | |

\*$p < .05$

SS$_{cells}$ is a measure of how much the cell means differ. Two cell means may differ for any of three reasons, other than sampling error: (1) because they come from different levels of A (Age); (2) because they come from different levels of C (Condition); or (3) because of an interaction between A and C. We already have a measure of how much the cells differ, since we know SS$_{cells}$. SS$_A$ tells us how much of this difference can be attributed to differences in Age, and SS$_C$ tells us how much can be attributed to differences in Condition. Whatever cannot be attributed to Age or Condition must be attributable to the interaction between Age and Condition (SS$_{AC}$). Thus SS$_{cells}$ has been partitioned into its three constituent parts—SS$_A$, SS$_C$, and SS$_{AC}$. To obtain SS$_{AC}$, we simply subtract SS$_A$ and SS$_C$ from

$SS_{cells}$. Whatever is left over is $SS_{AC}$. In our example

$$SS_{AC} = SS_{cells} - SS_A - SS_C$$
$$= 1,945.49 - 240.25 - 1,514.94 = 190.30$$

All that we have left to calculate is the sum of squares due to error. Just as in the one-way analysis, we will obtain this by subtraction. The total variation is represented by $SS_{total}$. Of this total, we know how much can be attributed to A, C, and AC. What is left over represents unaccountable variation or error. Thus

$$SS_{error} = SS_{total} - (SS_A + SS_C + SS_{AC})$$

However, since $SS_A + SS_C + SS_{AC} = SS_{cells}$, it is simpler to write

$$SS_{error} = SS_{total} - SS_{cells}$$

This provides us with our sum of squares for error, and we now have all of the necessary sums of squares for our analysis.

Part (c) of Table 17.3 is the summary table for the analysis of variance. The source column and the sum of squares column are fairly obvious from what has already been said. The degrees of freedom column should also be familiar from what you know about the one-way. The total degrees of freedom ($df_{total}$) are always equal to $N - 1$. The degrees of freedom for Age and Condition are the number of levels of the variable minus 1. Thus, $df_A = a - 1 = 1$ and $df_C = c - 1 = 4$. The number of degrees of freedom for any interaction is simply the product of the degrees of freedom for the components of that interaction. Thus, $df_{AC} = df_A \times df_C = (a - 1)(c - 1) = 1 \times 4 = 4$. Finally, the degrees of freedom for error can be obtained by subtraction. Thus $df_{error} = df_{total} - df_A - df_C - df_{AC}$. Alternatively, because $MS_{error}$ is the average of the AC cell variances, and because each cell variance has $n - 1$ $df$, $MS_{error}$ has $ac(n - 1)$ degrees of freedom. These rules for degrees of freedom apply to any factorial analysis of variance, no matter how complex.

Just as with the one-way analysis of variance, the mean squares are obtained by dividing the sums of squares by the corresponding degrees of freedom. This is the same procedure we will use in any analysis.

Finally, to calculate F, we divide each MS by $MS_{error}$. Thus, for Age, $F_A = MS_A/MS_{error}$; for Condition, $F_C = MS_C/MS_{error}$; and for AC, $F_{AC} = MS_{AC}/MS_{error}$. Each F is based on the number of degrees of freedom for the term in question and the $df_{error}$. Thus the F for Age is on 1 and 90 $df$, and the F for Condition and the F for the Age $\times$ Condition interaction are based on 4 and 90 $df$. From Table D.3 in the Appendix D, we find that the critical values of F are $F_{.05}(1,90) = 3.96$ (by interpolation) and $F_{.05}(4,90) = 2.49$ (again by interpolation).

## Interpretation

From part (c) of Table 17.3, the summary table, you can see that there were significant effects for Age, Condition, and their interaction. In conjunction with the cell means, it is clear that younger participants recall more items overall than do older participants. It is also clear that those tasks that involve greater depth of processing lead to better recall overall than do tasks that involve less processing, which is in line with the differences we found in Chapter 16. The significant interaction tells us that the effect of one variable depends on the level of the other variable. For example, differences between older and younger participants on the easier tasks, such as counting and Rhyming, are less than the differences between younger and older participants on those tasks that involve greater depths of processing, such as Imagery and Intentional. Another view is that differences among the five Conditions are less extreme for the older participants than they are for the younger ones.

The results support Eysenck's hypothesis that older participants do not perform as well as younger participants on tasks that involve a greater depth of processing of information but do perform about equally with younger participants when the tasks do not involve much processing. These results do not mean that older participants are not *capable* of processing information as deeply. Older participants simply may not make the effort that younger participants do. Whatever the reason, they do not perform as well on those tasks.

## 17.3  Interactions

A major benefit of factorial designs is that they allow us to examine the interaction of variables. Indeed in many cases the interaction term may be of greater interest than are the main effects (the effects of factors taken individually). Consider, for example, the study by Eysenck. The means are plotted in Figure 17.1 for each age group separately. Here you can see clearly what I referred to in the interpretation of the results when I said that the differences due to Conditions were greater for younger participants than for older ones. The fact that the two lines are not parallel is what we mean when we speak of an interaction. If Condition differences were

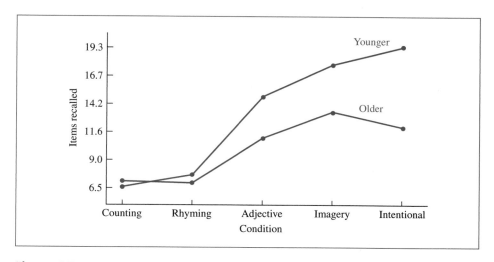

**Figure 17.1**
Cell means for data in Table 17.3

the same for the two Age groups, the lines would be parallel—whatever differences between Conditions existed for younger participants would be equally present for older participants. This would be true regardless of whether younger participants were generally superior to older participants or whether the two groups were comparable. Raising or lowering the entire line for younger participants would change the main effect of Age, but it would have no effect on the interaction.

The situation may become clearer if you consider several plots of cell means that represent the presence or absence of an interaction. In Figure 17.2 the first three plots represent the case in which there is no interaction. In all three cases the lines are parallel, even when they are not straight. Another way of looking at this is to say that the difference between $B_1$ and $B_2$ (the effect of factor B) at $A_1$ is the same as it is at $A_2$ and at $A_3$. In the second set of three plots the lines clearly are not parallel. In the first plot one line is flat and the other rises. In the second plot the lines actually cross. In the third plot the lines do not cross, but they move in opposite directions. In every case the effect of B is *not* the same at the different levels of A. Whenever the lines are (significantly) nonparallel, we say that we have an interaction.

Many people will argue that if you find a significant interaction, the main effects should be ignored. It is not reasonable, however, to automatically exclude interpretation of main effects in the presence of *any* significant interaction. In the Eysenck study we had a significant interaction, but for both younger and older

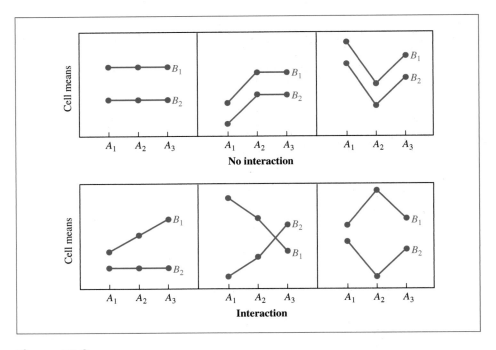

**Figure 17.2**
Illustration of possible noninteractions and interactions

participants the tasks that involved greater processing led to greater recall. The fact that this effect was more pronounced in the younger group does not negate the fact that it was also clearly present in the older participants. Here it is perfectly legitimate to speak about the main effect of Condition, even in the presence of an interaction. Had the younger group shown better recall with more demanding tasks while the older group showed poorer recall, it might not actually be of interest whether the main effect of Condition was significant or not, and we would instead concentrate on discussing the simple effects of differences among Conditions for the younger and older participants separately. In general the interpretation depends on common sense. If the main effects are clearly meaningful, it makes sense to interpret them regardless of the presence or absence of an interaction. If the main effect does not really have any meaning, it should be ignored. That's not a hard rule to remember, though it might take some thought to implement.

## 17.4 Simple Effects

I earlier defined a simple effect as the effect of one factor (independent variable) at one level of the other factor; for example, differences among Conditions for the younger participants. The analysis of simple effects can be an important technique for analyzing data that contain significant interactions. In a very real sense such analysis allows us to "tease apart" interactions.

I will use the Eysenck data to illustrate how to calculate and interpret simple effects. Table 17.4 reproduces the cell means and the summary table from Table 17.3 and contains the calculations involved in obtaining all the simple effects. As a general rule, I do not recommend running *all* simple effects. Testing all possible effects drastically increases the probability of a Type I error. Run only those that are particularly relevant to your purposes. I have run them all here simply to illustrate the procedure.

The first summary table in part (c) of Table 17.4 reveals significant effects due to Age, Condition, and their interaction. We discussed these results earlier in conjunction with the original analysis. As I said there, the presence of an interaction means that there are different Condition effects for the two Ages and different Age effects for the five Conditions. It thus becomes important to ask whether our general Condition effect really applies for older as well as younger participants and whether there really are Age differences under all Conditions. The analysis of these simple effects is found in part (b) of Table 17.4 and in the second summary in part (c). Remember I have shown all possible simple effects for the sake of completeness. In practice you should examine only those effects in which you are interested.

### Calculation

In part (b) of Table 17.4 you can see that $SS_{C \text{ at Old}}$ is calculated in the same way as any sum of squares. We simply calculate $SS_C$ using only the data for the older participants. If we consider only those data, the five Condition means are 7.0, 6.9,

## Table 17.4
Calculation of Simple Effects for Data from Table 17.3

### (a) Cell means ($n = 10$)

|  | Counting | Rhyming | Adjective | Imagery | Intentional | Mean |
|---|---|---|---|---|---|---|
| Older | 7.0 | 6.9 | 11.0 | 13.4 | 12.0 | 10.06 |
| Younger | 6.5 | 7.6 | 14.8 | 17.6 | 19.3 | 13.16 |
| Mean | 6.75 | 7.25 | 12.90 | 15.50 | 15.65 | 11.61 |

### (b) Calculations

**Conditions at Each Age**

$$SS_{C \text{ at Old}} = 10 \times [(7.0 - 10.06)^2 + (6.9 - 10.06)^2 + \cdots + (12 - 10.06)^2] = 351.52$$
$$SS_{C \text{ at Young}} = 10 \times [(6.5 - 13.16)^2 + (7.6 - 13.16)^2 + \cdots + (19.3 - 13.16)^2] = 1,353.72$$

**Age at Each Condition**

$$SS_{A \text{ at Counting}} = 10 \times [(7.0 - 6.75)^2 + (6.5 - 6.75)^2] = 1.25$$

$$SS_{A \text{ at Rhyming}} = 10 \times [(6.9 - 7.25)^2 + (7.6 - 7.25)^2] = 2.45$$

$$SS_{A \text{ at Adjective}} = 10 \times [(11.0 - 12.9)^2 + (14.8 - 12.9)^2] = 72.20$$

$$SS_{A \text{ at Imagery}} = 10 \times [(13.4 - 15.5)^2 + (17.6 - 15.5)^2] = 88.20$$

$$SS_{A \text{ at Intentional}} = 10 \times [(12.0 - 15.65)^2 + (19.3 - 15.65)^2] = 266.45$$

### (c) Summary Tables

**Overall Analysis**

| Source | df | SS | MS | F |
|---|---|---|---|---|
| A (Age) | 1 | 240.25 | 240.250 | 29.94* |
| C (Condition) | 4 | 1,514.94 | 378.735 | 47.19* |
| AC | 4 | 190.30 | 47.575 | 5.93* |
| Error | 90 | 722.30 | 8.026 | |
| Total | 99 | 2,667.79 | | |

*$p < .05$

**Simple Effects**

| Source | df | SS | MS | F |
|---|---|---|---|---|
| **Conditions** | | | | |
| C at Old | 4 | 351.52 | 87.88 | 10.95* |
| C at Young | 4 | 1,353.72 | 338.43 | 42.17* |
| **Age** | | | | |
| A at Counting | 1 | 1.25 | 1.25 | <1 |
| A at Rhyming | 1 | 2.45 | 2.45 | <1 |
| A at Adjective | 1 | 72.20 | 72.20 | 9.00* |
| A at Imagery | 1 | 88.20 | 88.20 | 10.99* |
| A at Intentional | 1 | 266.45 | 266.45 | 33.20* |
| Error | 90 | 722.30 | 8.026 | |

*$p < .05$

11.0, 13.4, and 12.0. Thus the sum of squares will be

$$SS_{C \text{ at Old}} = n\Sigma(\overline{X}_{C_{j \text{ at Old}}} - \overline{X}_{\text{Old}})^2$$
$$= 10 \times [(7 - 10.06)^2 + (6.9 - 10.06)^2 + \cdots + (12 - 10.06)^2]$$
$$= 351.52$$

The other simple effects are calculated in the same way, by ignoring all data in which you are not interested at the moment. Notice that the sum of squares for the simple effect of Condition for older participants (351.52) is the same value as that we obtained in Chapter 16 when we ran a one-way analysis of variance on only the data from older participants.

The degrees of freedom for the numerator of simple effects are calculated in the same way as for the corresponding main effects. This makes sense because the number of means we are comparing remains the same—there are five Condition means. Whether we use all the participants or only part of them, we still are comparing five Conditions and have $5 - 1 = 4$ $df$ for Conditions.

To test the simple effects, we generally use the error term from the overall analysis of variance ($MS_{\text{error}}$). This produces the $F$s shown in Table 17.4. Note that the denominator had 90 $df$ because we used $MS_{\text{error}}$ from the overall analysis.

### Interpretation

From the column labeled $F$ in the simple effects summary table in Table 17.4, it is evident that differences due to Conditions occur for both ages, although the sum of squares for the older participants is only about one-quarter of what it is for the younger ones. With regard to the Age effects, however, no differences occur on the lower-level tasks of counting and rhyming, but differences do occur on the higher-level tasks. In other words, differences between age groups show up only for those tasks involving higher levels of processing. This result is basically what Eysenck set out to demonstrate.

## 17.5 Measures of Association and Effect Size

We can look at the magnitude of an effect in two different ways, just as we did with the one-way analysis. We can either calculate a measure of association, such as $\hat{\eta}^2$ or $\hat{\omega}^2$, or we can calculate Cohen's $\hat{d}$, a very useful measure of effect size. Normally, when we are examining an omnibus $F$, we use a measure of association, an $r$-family measure. However, when we are looking at a difference between means, it is usually more meaningful to calculate an effect size estimate ($\hat{d}$), a $d$-family measure.

### $r$-family Measures

As with the one-way design, it is both possible and often desirable to calculate the magnitude of effect associated with each independent variable. The most easily computed measure is again $\hat{\eta}^2$ (eta squared) although it is still a biased estimate of the value that we would get if we obtained observations on whole populations. For each effect (main effects and interactions) in the factorial design we compute $\hat{\eta}^2$ by dividing the sum of squares for that effect by $SS_{total}$. For our example

$$\hat{\eta}^2_A = \frac{SS_A}{SS_{total}} = \frac{240.25}{2,667.79} = .09$$

$$\hat{\eta}^2_C = \frac{SS_C}{SS_{total}} = \frac{1,514.94}{2,667.79} = .57$$

$$\hat{\eta}^2_{AC} = \frac{SS_{AC}}{SS_{total}} = \frac{190.30}{2,667.79} = .07$$

Thus within this experiment differences due to Age account for 9% of the overall variability, differences due to Condition account for 57% of the variability, and differences due to the Age $\times$ Condition interaction account for 7% of the variability. The remaining 27% of the variability in this experiment is assigned to error variance.

As with the one-way analysis, $\hat{\eta}^2$ is handy for making rough estimates of the contribution of variables, but a considerably less biased estimate is given by $\hat{\omega}^2$ (omega squared). The calculations, though somewhat more cumbersome, are straightforward.

$$\hat{\omega}^2_A = \frac{SS_A - (a-1)MS_{error}}{SS_{total} + MS_{error}} = \frac{240.25 - (1)8.026}{2,667.79 + 8.026} = .087$$

$$\hat{\omega}^2_C = \frac{SS_C - (c-1)MS_{error}}{SS_{total} + MS_{error}} = \frac{1,514.94 - (4)8.026}{2,667.79 + 8.026} = .554$$

$$\hat{\omega}^2_{AC} = \frac{SS_{AC} - (a-1)(c-1)MS_{error}}{SS_{total} + MS_{error}} = \frac{190.30 - (4)8.026}{2,667.79 + 8.026} = .059$$

Notice that these values are slightly smaller than the values for $\hat{\eta}^2$, although their interpretation is basically the same.

When it comes to calculating $\hat{d}$, the procedure that we will use is essentially the same as it was for the one-way. Because we are most interested in an effect size for the comparison of two groups, or subsets of groups, we simply take the difference between the groups and divide that by our estimate of the standard deviation within groups. We can do this for either of the two main effects (Age and Condition) or for any of the simple effects, although this is more difficult when we have more than two groups. To use Age as an example,

$$\hat{d} = \frac{\overline{X}_{Younger} - \overline{X}_{Older}}{s} = \frac{13.16 - 10.06}{\sqrt{8.026}} = \frac{3.10}{2.833} = 1.09$$

The difference in recall between older and younger participants is a bit over one standard deviation, which is quite a big difference.

To look at Condition, we need to select a pair (or pairs) of means. For this example we will take the older participants, whom we expect to profit less from cognitive processing of information. (I chose this because I anticipate that an effect for younger participants would be even greater.) The Counting condition clearly represents the bare minimum of cognitive processing, while the Image condition is probably at the high end. For the older participants we have

$$\hat{d} = \frac{\overline{X}_{\text{Imagery}} - \overline{X}_{\text{Count}}}{s} = \frac{13.40 - 7.00}{\sqrt{8.026}} = \frac{6.40}{2.833} = 2.26$$

Here the two groups differ by about two and a quarter standard deviations—again, a very large effect. Clearly, the level of processing plays an important role in the amount of material people are able to recall. The methods for estimating the magnitude of effect for variables in a factorial design are simple extensions of the methods used with a one-way design. Again, we have the measures that are analogous to squared correlations ($\hat{\eta}^2$ and $\hat{\omega}^2$), and the effect size measure, $\hat{d}$.

## A Complication

Throughout this book I have avoided the common practice of putting asterisks next to section headings that are more difficult and that might be skipped. However this section is just such a section, and I am inserting it so that you have a flavor of what the issues are. I am not expecting everyone to clap their forehead and exclaim "oh, of course." Refer to Howell (2007) or Kline (2004) for a more thorough discussion of these issues.

As was the case with $t$ tests and the one-way analysis of variance, we will define our effect size as

$$\hat{d} = \frac{\overline{X}_1 - \overline{X}_2}{\hat{s}}$$

where the "hats" indicate that we are using estimates based on sample data. There is no real difficulty in estimating the numerator, because it is just the difference between two means (or the means of sets of means). On the other hand, our estimate of the appropriate standard deviation will depend on our variables. Some variables normally vary in the population (e.g., amount of caffeine a person drinks in a day, gender, intelligence) and are, at least potentially, what Glass, McGraw, and Smith (1981) call a "variable of theoretical interest." Age, extraversion, metabolic rate, and hours of sleep are other examples. On the other hand, many experimental variables, such as the number of presentations of a stimulus, area of cranial stimulation, size of a test stimulus, and presence or absence of a cue during recall do not normally vary in the population, and are of less theoretical interest (though they may be very important to that particular experiment). I am very aware that the distinction is a slippery one, and if a manipulated variable is not of theoretical interest, why are we manipulating it?

It might make more sense if we look at the problem slightly differently. Suppose that I ran a study to investigate differences among three kinds of psychotherapy. If I just ran that as a one-way design, my error term would include variability due to all sorts of things, one of which would be variability between men and women in how they respond to different kinds of therapy. Now suppose that I ran the same study but included gender as an independent variable. In effect, I am controlling for gender, and the regular $MS_{\text{error}}$ term would not include gender differences because I have "pulled them out" in my analysis. So $MS_{error}$ would be smaller here than in the one-way. That's a good thing in terms of power, but it may not be a good thing if I use the square root of $MS_{error}$ in calculating the effect size. If I did, I would have a different-sized effect due to psychotherapy in the one-way experiment than I have in the factorial experiment. That doesn't seem right. The effect of therapy ought to be pretty much the same in the two cases. (Sex happens! So it should be involved in our measure.) So what I will do instead is to put that gender variability, and the interaction of gender with therapy, back into error when it comes to computing an effect size.

But suppose that I ran a slightly different (and slightly weird) study where I examined the same three different therapies, but also included, as a second independent variable, whether or not the patient sat in a cold tub of water during therapy. Now patients don't normally sit in a cold tub of water, but it would certainly be likely to add variability to the results. That variability would not be there in the one-way design because we can't imagine some patients bringing in a tub of water and sitting in it. And it is variability that I wouldn't want to add back into the error term because it is in many ways artificial. The point is that I would like the effect size for types of therapy to be the same whether I used a one-way or a factorial design. To accomplish that, I would add effects due to Gender and the Gender X Therapy interaction back into the error term in the first study, and withhold the effects of Water and its interaction with Therapy in the second example.

As I said at the start, this is a slippery area and there is plenty of room for argument about when you should, and should not, adjust that error term. Different people might reasonably choose different approaches. Those are some of the fun issues in statistics, though I don't expect students to welcome all the fun.

I am not going to show you exactly how we can manipulate our error term, because it is not something that I think that you are likely to want to do in the near future. But I can hint at the solution, and you can find an extended discussion in Howell (2007). If we want to add the effect of Gender and its interaction with Therapy back into the error term, all we need to do is to combine $SS_{error}$, $SS_{Gender}$, and $SS_{Interaction}$ into a new $SS_{error}$ term, combine their degrees of freedom, and then divide one by the other. The square root of this *adjusted* standard deviation will serve as the denominator for $\hat{d}$. In the case of the cold bathtub, we don't want that variability added back in, so we just use the $MS_{error}$ from our overall analysis as our denominator.

## 17.6 Writing Up the Results

We have carried out a number of calculations to make various points, and I would certainly not report all them when writing up the results. What follows is the basic information that I think needs to be presented:

In an investigation of the effects of different levels of information processing on the retention of verbal material, participants were instructed to process verbal material in one of four ways, ranging from the simple counting of letters in words to the formation of a visual image of each word. Participants in a fifth condition were not given any instructions about what to do with the items except to memorize them for later recall. A second dimension of the experiment compared younger and older participants on recall, thus forming a $2 \times 5$ factorial design.

The dependent variable was the number of items recalled after three presentations. There was a significant Age effect ($F(1,90) = 29.94, p < .05, \hat{\omega}^2 = .087$), with younger participants recalling more items than did older participants. There was also a significant effect due to Condition ($F(4,90) = 47.19, p < .05, \hat{\omega}^2 = .554$), and visual inspection of the means shows that there was greater recall for conditions in which there was a greater degree of processing. Finally, the Age by Condition interaction was significant ($F(4,90) = 5.93, p < .05, \hat{\omega}^2 = .059$), with a stronger effect of Condition for the younger participants.

When we look at differences in recall between younger and older participants, $\hat{d}$ is equal to 1.09, indicating a difference of over a standard deviation. (However this difference is considerably greater for conditions involving greater processing, and is negligible for conditions involving minor processing.) For older participants the difference between a condition with minimal processing and one with maximal processing had $\hat{d} = 2.26$. The effect size would be even greater if computed on younger participants.

This study has clearly shown that the common observation that older people do not recall information as well as younger people is tied to the level of processing. In tasks requiring little possessing, there are no Age effects, whereas there are substantial age effects for tasks involving greater processing.

## 17.7 Unequal Sample Sizes

When we were dealing with a one-way analysis of variance, unequal sample sizes did not present a serious problem—we simply adjusted our formula accordingly. That is definitely *not* the case with factorial designs. Whenever we have a factorial design with unequal cell sizes, the calculations become considerably more difficult, and the interpretation can be very unclear. The best solution is not to have unequal ns in the first place. Unfortunately the world is not always cooperative, and unequal ns are often the result. Standard statistical software usually provides the results that are most likely to be meaningful as the default. However there are situations in which the standard solution is less than optimal. An extensive discussion of this problem is contained in Howell (2007).

## 17.8 A Second Example: Maternal Adaptation Revisited

In Chapter 16 we considered an example of actual data on maternal adaptation for mothers of LBW (low-birthweight) infants. Mothers were separated into Experimental and Control groups. Additionally there was a group of mothers who gave birth to full-ferm infants (Nurcombe et al., 1984). We saw there that mothers in the Experimental (Intervention) and Full-Term treatment groups adapted better than those in the LBW-Control group. A more complete analysis of those data involves breaking down the treatment groups by Maternal Education (High School or Less versus More Than High School). The authors of the study thought that the mothers with less education might benefit more from the experimental program than would more highly educated mothers. If this were true, the LBW-Control versus LBW-Experimental differences would be larger for the Low Education group than for the High Education group, giving us a significant interaction. The data and calculations for this analysis are presented in Table 17.5.

**Table 17.5**
Maternal Adaptation as a Function of Group and Education

| (a) Data | | | | |
| --- | --- | --- | --- | --- |
| | | Group | | |
| Education | Group 1 LBW-Experimental | Group 2 LBW-Control | Group 3 Full-Term | Age Means |
| High School Education or Less | 14 | 25 | 18 | |
| | 20 | 19 | 14 | |
| | 22 | 21 | 18 | |
| | 13 | 20 | 20 | |
| | 13 | 20 | 12 | |
| | 18 | 14 | 14 | |
| | 13 | 25 | 17 | |
| | 14 | 18 | 17 | |
| Mean | 15.875 | 20.250 | 16.250 | 17.458 |
| More Than High School Education | 11 | 18 | 16 | |
| | 11 | 16 | 20 | |
| | 16 | 13 | 12 | |
| | 12 | 21 | 14 | |
| | 12 | 17 | 18 | |
| | 13 | 10 | 20 | |
| | 17 | 16 | 12 | |
| | 13 | 21 | 13 | |
| Mean | 13.125 | 16.500 | 15.625 | 15.083 |
| Group Means | 14.500 | 18.375 | 15.938 | 16.271 |

*(continued)*

## Table 17.5
### (continued)

(b) Calculations

$$SS_{total} = \Sigma(X - \overline{X}..)^2 = \Sigma X^2 - \frac{(\Sigma X)^2}{N} = 13{,}363 - \frac{781^2}{48} = 13{,}363 - 12{,}707.52$$
$$= 655.48$$

$$SS_{Educ} = ng\Sigma(\overline{X}_E - \overline{X}..)^2 = (8)(3)[(17.485 - 16.271)^2 + (15.083 - 16.271)^2] = 67.69$$

$$SS_{Group} = ne\Sigma(\overline{X}_G - \overline{X}..)^2 = (8)(2)[(14.500 - 16.271)^2 + \cdots + (15.938 - 16.271)^2]$$
$$= 122.79$$

$$SS_{cells} = n\Sigma(\overline{X}_{EG} - \overline{X}..)^2 = 8[(15.875 - 16.271)^2 + \cdots + (15.625 - 16.271)^2]$$
$$= 210.86$$

$$SS_{EG} = SS_{cells} - SS_E - SS_G = 210.86 - 67.69 - 122.79 = 20.38$$

$$SS_{error} = SS_{total} - SS_{cells} = 655.48 - 210.86 = 444.62$$

(c) Summary Table

| Source | df | SS | MS | F |
|---|---|---|---|---|
| E (Education) | 1 | 67.69 | 67.69 | 6.39* |
| G (Group) | 2 | 122.79 | 61.40 | 5.80* |
| EG | 2 | 20.38 | 10.19 | <1 |
| Error | 42 | 444.62 | 10.59 | |
| Total | 47 | 655.48 | | |

*$p < .05$

These data are a subset of the real data, from which only the first eight observations in each cell have been selected. (The results agree with the results of the full data set.) You will note that there are both a statistically significant Group (G) effect and an Education (E) effect (as indicated by the asterisks following the F values), but that there is no interaction. (When F is less than 1, we normally report "$F < 1$" rather than giving the actual value.) The lack of an interaction means that group differences do not depend on education level, which runs counter to our experimental hypothesis. We would conclude from this analysis that both the amount of education and the presence or absence of the intervention program had an effect on maternal adaptation. However, differences in adaptation observed among the groups did not depend on the level of education of the mother, with both groups deriving about equal value from the program.

# 17.9 Using SPSS for Factorial Analysis of Variance

The printout from an SPSS analysis of the data in the previous example is shown in Figure 17.3. The first variable in the data set is coded 1 or 2, and indicates whether the participant had a high school education or less (1) or more than a high

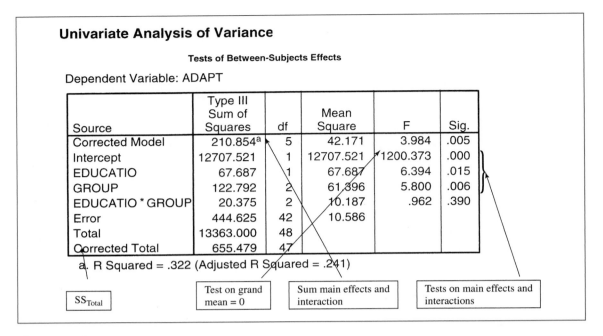

**Figure 17.3**
SPSS analysis of maternal adaptation data

school education (2). The second column indicates whether the participant was in the LBW-Experimental (1), the LBW-Control (2), or the Full-Term group (3). The third column contains the dependent variable.

The SPSS summary table is somewhat different from the ones you are used to seeing. SPSS first tells you how much of the variability can be attributed to all effects. For the equal sample size case this value is simply the sum of the sums of squares for the individual main effects and the interaction. Then it tests whether the grand mean is significantly different from .00, which is something you rarely care about. After that you see the effects you expect to see, but ignore the (uncorrected) total. (Can you find these extra sums of squares in Table 17.5?) Notice that, within rounding, the answers on this printout agree completely with the answers in Table 17.5.

## 17.10 Seeing Statistics

On the Web site you will find an interesting applet that allows you to look at, and manipulate, main effects and interactions. An example of this display follows.

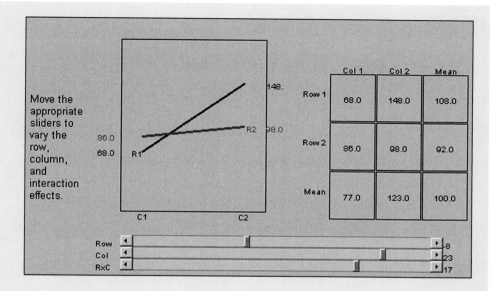

The best way to understand what this applet does is to play with it. At the bottom of the display you will see a slider for the row effect. If you move that left and right, you will alter the row effect that shows in your graph. Basically, you will move the two lines apart vertically. If you then use the slider labeled "Col," you will manipulate the column effect, which will have the result of rotating the lines by raising or lowering the right-hand ends of the lines. Finally, by manipulating the bottom slider you can increase or decrease the interaction, which has the effect of changing the degree to which the lines run nonparallel to each other.

- Use the data from Table 17.3 on recall as a function of Age and Condition. Ignore the three middle conditions, and focus on the Counting and Intentional conditions. By using all three sliders, you should be able to build the appropriate main and interaction effects. You can't exactly replicate what the data show, but you can come reasonably close.

- Now increase or decrease either the row effect of the column effect. You should see what we mean when we say that those effects are independent when we have equal sample sizes. In other words, the column (and the interaction) effect do not change just because we have increased the magnitude of the row effect.

- Now create a display that has a substantial Row effect, but absolutely no column or interaction effect.

## 17.11 Summary

In this chapter we extended the discussion of the analysis of variance to include designs involving two independent variables. In the factorial analysis we assumed that there are still different participants in the different cells. We considered some of the advantages of factorial designs, especially that they allow us to look at the interaction effects of two variables. We also considered briefly the topic of simple effects (the effect of one variable at *one* level of the other variable), the problems posed by unequal sample sizes, and procedures for estimating the magnitude of experimental effects.

Some important terms in this chapter are

| | |
|---|---|
| Factors, *419* | Cell, *421* |
| Two-way factorial design, *419* | Grand mean ($\overline{X}..$), *422* |
| Factorial design, *419* | Main effect, *422* |
| Interaction, *420* | Simple effect, *423* |
| $2 \times 5$ factorial design, *421* | $SS_{cells}$, *424* |

## 17.12 Exercises

**17.1** Thomas and Wang (1996) looked at the effects of memory on the learning of foreign vocabulary. Most of you have probably read that a good strategy for memorizing words in a foreign language is to think of mnemonic keywords. For example, in Tagalog (the official language of the Philippines), the word for eyeglasses is salamin. That word sounds much like our "salmon," so a possible strategy would be to imagine a picture of a salmon wearing glasses. This type of encoding strategy has been recommended for years, and people who try it generally report good immediate recall of foreign vocabulary. This fits nicely with dual-coding theories, in which the word is viewed as being stored both lexically and visually.

However, the studies that have looked at this phenomenon have generally asked the same participants to recall items at several different times. Since each recall session means an additional practice session, practice and time effects are confounded. To get around this problem, Thomas and Wang used different participants at the two recall intervals. Data with very nearly the same means and variances as theirs are presented below.

Thomas and Wang divided participants into one of three "Strategy" groups, and then tested them at one of two times (5 minutes or 2 days). The strategies were

**Key Word Generated** Participants generated their own key words to help them to remember 24 Tagalog words.

**Key Word Provided** The experimenters provided the key words to help them to remember 24 Tagalog words.

**Rote Learning** Participants were simply instructed to memorize the meaning of the Tagalog words.

The dependent variable was the number of English words recalled at either 5 minutes or 2 days.

| | | | | | | | | | | | | | |
|---|---|---|---|---|---|---|---|---|---|---|---|---|---|
| Generated/5 m | 18 | 9 | 22 | 21 | 11 | 10 | 16 | 13 | 4 | 15 | 21 | 17 | 17 |
| Provided/5 m | 24 | 19 | 19 | 23 | 21 | 23 | 19 | 22 | 20 | 21 | 18 | 18 | 20 |
| Rote/5 m | 7 | 21 | 14 | 18 | 12 | 24 | 15 | 11 | 16 | 11 | 18 | 24 | 9 |
| Generated/2 d | 7 | 8 | 7 | 2 | 6 | 4 | 4 | 4 | 5 | 2 | 2 | 1 | 0 |
| Provided/2d | 2 | 1 | 2 | 4 | 0 | 2 | 2 | 4 | 0 | 3 | 0 | 2 | 4 |
| Rote/2d | 15 | 23 | 9 | 18 | 13 | 7 | 7 | 3 | 5 | 12 | 26 | 15 | 13 |

(a) How would you characterize this design?
(b) What would be a reasonable *a priori* research hypothesis?
(c) Calculate the cell means and standard deviations.

**17.2** Plot the means for the data in Exercise 17.1 to show what the data have to say.

**17.3** Run the analysis of variance for the data in Exercise 17.1 and draw the appropriate conclusions.

**17.4** The interaction in the analysis for Exercise 17.3 suggests that it would be profitable to examine simple effects. Compute the simple effects for the differences due to Strategy within each time interval and interpret the results.

**17.5** Use the Bonferroni test to elaborate on the results of Exercise 17.4

**17.6** The results in Exercises 17.1–17.4 are certainly extreme, and the statistics look unusual. What might trouble you about these data?

**17.7** With respect to the previous exercises, what have you learned about how you might study for your next Spanish exam?

**17.8** In a study of mother-infant interaction, mothers are rated by trained observers on the quality of their interactions with their infants. Mothers were classified on the basis of whether this was their first child (primiparous versus multiparous) and whether the infant was low-birthweight (LBW) or full-term (FT). The data represent a score on a 12-point scale, on which a higher score represents better mother-infant interaction.

| | | | | | | | | | | |
|---|---|---|---|---|---|---|---|---|---|---|
| **Primip/LBW** | 6 | 5 | 5 | 4 | 9 | 6 | 2 | 6 | 5 | 5 |
| **Primip/FT** | 8 | 7 | 7 | 6 | 7 | 2 | 5 | 8 | 7 | 7 |
| **Multip/LBW** | 7 | 8 | 8 | 9 | 8 | 2 | 1 | 9 | 9 | 8 |
| **Multip/FT** | 9 | 8 | 9 | 9 | 3 | 10 | 9 | 8 | 7 | 10 |

Run and interpret the appropriate analysis of variance.

**17.9** Referring to Exercise 17.8, it seems obvious that the sample sizes do not reflect the relative frequency of these characteristics in the population. Would you expect the mean for all these primiparous mothers to be a good estimate of the population of primiparous mothers? Why or why not?

**17.10** Use simple effect procedures to compare low-birthweight and normal-birthweight conditions for multiparous mothers. (Do this by recalculating the error term rather than using $MS_{error}$ from the complete experiment.)

**17.11** In Exercise 17.10 you used traditional simple effect procedures.
(a) What would happen if you simply ran a $t$ test between LBW and normal-birthweight means for multiparous mothers using $MS_{error}$ as the pooled error term?
(b) What would be different if you used the pooled variances of only the two groups being compared?

**17.12** In Chapter 16 we had three different examples in which we compared three groups on the basis of smoking behavior. We can set this design up as a $3 \times 3$ factorial by using Task as one variable and Smoking group as the other. The dependent variable was the number of errors the participant made on that task. These data are repeated below.

| Pattern Recognition | | | Recall Task | | | Driving Simulation | | |
|---|---|---|---|---|---|---|---|---|
| Non-Smoke | Delay Smoke | Active Smoke | Non-Smoke | Delay Smoke | Active Smoke | Non-Smoke | Delay Smoke | Active Smoke |
| 9 | 12 | 8 | 27 | 48 | 34 | 15 | 7 | 3 |
| 8 | 7 | 8 | 34 | 29 | 65 | 2 | 0 | 2 |
| 12 | 14 | 9 | 19 | 34 | 55 | 2 | 6 | 0 |
| 10 | 4 | 1 | 20 | 6 | 33 | 14 | 0 | 0 |
| 7 | 8 | 9 | 56 | 18 | 42 | 5 | 12 | 6 |
| 10 | 11 | 7 | 35 | 63 | 54 | 0 | 17 | 2 |
| 9 | 16 | 16 | 23 | 9 | 21 | 16 | 1 | 0 |
| 11 | 17 | 19 | 37 | 54 | 44 | 14 | 11 | 6 |
| 8 | 5 | 1 | 4 | 28 | 61 | 9 | 4 | 4 |
| 10 | 6 | 1 | 30 | 71 | 38 | 17 | 4 | 1 |
| 8 | 9 | 22 | 4 | 60 | 75 | 15 | 3 | 0 |
| 10 | 6 | 12 | 42 | 54 | 61 | 9 | 5 | 0 |
| 8 | 6 | 18 | 34 | 51 | 51 | 3 | 16 | 6 |
| 11 | 7 | 8 | 19 | 25 | 32 | 15 | 5 | 2 |
| 10 | 16 | 10 | 49 | 49 | 47 | 13 | 11 | 3 |

Plot the cell means for this design.

**17.13** Run the analysis of variance on the data in Exercise 17.12 and draw the relevant conclusions.

**17.14** Even without picking up your pencil you can probably determine at least one conclusion about the data in Exercise 17.13. What is that conclusion, and why is it of no interest?

**17.15** Compute the necessary simple effects to explain the results of Exercise 17.13. What do these results tell you about the effects of smoking?

**17.16** For Exercise 17.15 use the protected $t$ test to compare the Nonsmoking group to the other two groups in the Driving Simulation condition.

**17.17** If you go back to Exercise 16.2, you will see that it really forms a $2 \times 2$ factorial. Run the factorial analysis and interpret the results. (The data are reproduced here.)

| | | | | | | | | | | |
|---|---|---|---|---|---|---|---|---|---|---|
| **Younger/Low** | 8 | 6 | 4 | 6 | 7 | 6 | 5 | 7 | 9 | 7 |
| **Younger/Hi** | 21 | 19 | 17 | 15 | 22 | 16 | 22 | 22 | 18 | 21 |
| **Older/Low** | 9 | 8 | 6 | 8 | 10 | 4 | 6 | 5 | 7 | 7 |
| **Older/Hi** | 10 | 19 | 14 | 5 | 10 | 11 | 14 | 15 | 11 | 11 |

**17.18**  In Exercise 16.3 you ran a test between Groups 1 and 3 combined versus Groups 2 and 4 combined. How does that test compare to testing the main effect of Location in Exercise 17.16? Is there any difference?

**17.19**  Calculate $\eta^2$ and $\omega^2$ for the Maternal Adaptation data in Section 17.7.

**17.20**  Calculate $\hat{d}$ for the main effect of level of processing in the data in Exercise 17.17.

**17.21**  Make up a set of data for a $2 \times 2$ design that has two main effects but no interaction.

**17.22**  Make up a set of data for a $2 \times 2$ design that has no main effects but does have an interaction.

**17.23**  Describe a reasonable experiment in which the primary interest would be in the interaction effect.

**17.24**  Calculate $\eta^2$ and $\omega^2$ for the data in Exercise 17.1.

**17.25**  Calculate $\hat{d}$ for the two main effects for the data in Exercise 17.1. (Choose two groups to compare that seem reasonable from what you understand about the design of the experiment.)

**17.26**  Calculate $\eta^2$ and $\omega^2$ for the data in Exercise 17.13.

**17.27**  Calculate $\hat{d}$ for the two main effects for the data in Exercise 17.13, choosing suitable groups for comparison.

**17.28**  By comparing the formulae for $\eta^2$ and $\omega^2$, tell when these two different statistics would be in close agreement and when they would disagree noticeably.

**17.29**  In the Eysenck (1974) study analyzed in Section 17.1, the real test of Eysenck's hypothesis about changes with age is found in the interaction. Why?

**17.30**  In the discussion of the results in Table 17.4, I stated that you should not routinely calculate every possible simple effect, but should look at only those in which you are interested. Explain why you think I said this, with reference to the discussion of familywise error rate in Chapter 16.

**17.31**  Becky Liddle at Auburn University published a study in 1997 on disclosing sexual orientation in class. She taught four sections of the same class, and at the week of the final lecture she disclosed her lesbian identity to two of the classes, and withheld it from two others. She was concerned with the issue of whether disclosure would influence student evaluations of the course. The means and average variance for the two conditions, further broken down by gender of the students, are presented below. There were 15 students in each cell. Perform a two-way analysis of variance and draw the appropriate conclusions. (The means are the same that Liddle found, but because I could not control for difference in *midterm* evaluations, as she did, the effect of gender is different from the effect she found. The other effects lead to similar conclusions.)

Sexual Identification:

|         | Disclose | Not Disclose | Mean  |
|---------|----------|--------------|-------|
| **Female** | 37.15 | 36.56 | 36.86 |
| **Male**   | 33.00 | 33.00 | 33.00 |
| **Means**  | 35.08 | 34.78 | 34.93 |

Average within-cell variance = 20.74

# 18

# Repeated-Measures Analysis of Variance

**QUESTIONS**

■ What do we do when each person gives us several scores?

■ Why is it important that repeated measurements are not independent?

■ Can we make multiple comparisons between treatment means?

■ What are the advantages and disadvantages of repeated measures?

In the previous two chapters we have been concerned with experimental designs in which there are different subjects in each group or cell. These designs are called **between-subjects designs** because they involve comparisons between different groups of subjects. However, many experimental designs involve having the same subject serve under more than one treatment condition. For example, we might take a baseline measurement of some behavior (i.e., a measurement before any treatment program begins), take another measurement at the end of a treatment program, and take yet a third measurement at the end of a six-month follow-up period. Designs such as this one, in which subjects are measured repeatedly, are called **repeated-measures designs** and are the subject of this chapter. You may recognize that what I have just described as a repeated-measures analysis of variance is very much like what I earlier called a *t* test for related samples, although we are not restricted to only two measurements. In fact this is just the general case of that test. In the same vein, everything I said about the *t* test for related samples applies here. If two or more samples are related in any way—not only by being multiple measures on the same subjects—then this design applies. By far the most common use of this design is in cases in which the same set of subjects are measured repeatedly on the same dependent variable, and that is the model followed in this chapter.

Definition

---

**Between-subjects designs:** Designs in which different subjects serve under the different treatment levels.

**Repeated-measures designs:** Experimental designs in which each subject receives all levels of at least one independent variable.

---

There are a wide variety of repeated-measures designs, depending on whether each subject[1] serves under all levels of all variables or whether some independent variables involve different groups of subjects while others involve the same subjects. In this chapter we will be concerned only with the simplest case, in which there is one independent variable and each subject serves under all levels of that variable. For analysis of more complex designs you can refer to Howell (2007) or Winer, Brown, and Michels (1991).

## 18.1 An Example: Depression as a Response to an Earthquake

Nolen-Hoeksema and Morrow (1991) had the good fortune to have administered a measure of depression to college students three weeks before the Loma Prieta earthquake in California in 1989. This was a major earthquake that would be expected to have measurable effects on students. Having collected these data, they went out and collected repeated data to track adjustment. The data that follow are modeled loosely on their findings. Our measurements are taken every three weeks, starting two weeks before the earthquake The data are shown in Table 18.1.

Look first at part (a) in Table 18.1. You will notice that there is a great deal of variability in the data, but much of that variability comes from the fact that some people exhibit more depression than others, which really has very little to do with the effects of the earthquake. The fact that you are more depressed in *general* than I am does not speak at all to the issue of whether the earthquake had the effect of increasing depression in those who experienced it. These are just individual differences in severity of depression. They lead to

---

[1]Standard APA format calls for identifying human subjects as "participants," or a similar term. However, the word "subject" is still used with statistical analyses, and is used throughout this chapter because that is the standard way to refer to these experimental designs.

**Table 18.1**
Depression Scores Before and After an Earthquake.

**(a) Data**

| | Week 0 | Week 3 | Week 6 | Week 9 | Week 12 | Subject Mean |
|---|---|---|---|---|---|---|
| | 6 | 10 | 8 | 4 | 5 | 6.6 |
| | 2 | 4 | 8 | 5 | 6 | 5.0 |
| | 2 | 4 | 8 | 5 | 5 | 4.8 |
| | 4 | 5 | 8 | 10 | 7 | 6.8 |
| | 4 | 7 | 9 | 7 | 11 | 7.6 |
| | 5 | 7 | 9 | 7 | 7 | 7.0 |
| | 2 | 9 | 11 | 8 | 7 | 7.4 |
| | 6 | 9 | 11 | 8 | 8 | 8.4 |
| | 13 | 10 | 11 | 8 | 8 | 10.0 |
| | 7 | 3 | 11 | 8 | 11 | 8.0 |
| | 7 | 12 | 8 | 8 | 10 | 9.0 |
| | 7 | 10 | 11 | 9 | 11 | 9.6 |
| | 9 | 10 | 13 | 10 | 10 | 10.4 |
| | 9 | 11 | 12 | 6 | 12 | 10.0 |
| | 11 | 11 | 12 | 19 | 6 | 11.8 |
| | 11 | 12 | 12 | 12 | 19 | 13.2 |
| | 12 | 12 | 12 | 13 | 15 | 12.8 |
| | 12 | 12 | 13 | 13 | 15 | 13.0 |
| | 7 | 12 | 13 | 13 | 14 | 11.8 |
| | 13 | 10 | 13 | 14 | 15 | 13.0 |
| | 13 | 14 | 11 | 15 | 15 | 13.6 |
| | 13 | 14 | 14 | 17 | 16 | 14.8 |
| | 13 | 14 | 15 | 11 | 16 | 13.8 |
| | 14 | 14 | 15 | 20 | 14 | 15.4 |
| | 15 | 17 | 16 | 21 | 18 | 17.4 |
| **Weekly Mean** | 8.68 | 10.12 | 11.36 | 10.84 | 11.24 | 10.448 |

Grand mean = 10.448    $\Sigma X$ = 1,306.00    $\Sigma X^2$ = 15,596.00
$N$ = 125    $w$ = # weeks = 5    $n$ = # of subjects = 25

(*continued*)

a correlation between the observations at one time and the observations at another time, and factoring this correlation out of the overall earthquake effect is what makes this design so powerful. What we are able to do with a repeated-measures design that we were not able to do with between-subjects designs is to remove this variability in people's *general* level of depression from $SS_{total}$. This has the effect of removing subject differences from the error term and producing a smaller $MS_{error}$ than we would have otherwise. We do this by calculating a term called $SS_{subjects}$, which measures differences among people

## Table 18.1
(*continued*)

**(b) Calculations**

$$SS_{total} = \Sigma(X - \overline{X}..)^2 = \Sigma X^2 - \frac{(\Sigma X)^2}{N} = 15{,}596.00 - \frac{1{,}306^2}{125} = 1{,}950.912$$

$$SS_{subjects} = w\Sigma(\overline{X}_{subj} - \overline{X}..)^2 = 5[(6.80 - 10.448)^2 + \cdots + (17.40 - 10.448)^2]$$

$$= 1375.712$$

$$SS_{weeks} = n\Sigma(\overline{X}_{week} - \overline{X}..)^2 = 25[(8.68 - 10.448)^2 + \cdots + (11.24 - 10.448)^2]$$

$$= 121.152$$

$$SS_{error} = SS_{total} - SS_{subjects} - SS_{weeks} = 1{,}950.912 - 1{,}375.712 - 121.152 = 454.048$$

**(c) Summary Table**

| Source | df | SS | MS | F |
|--------|-----|----------|--------|-------|
| Subjects | 24 | 1,375.712 | | |
| Weeks | 4 | 121.152 | 30.288 | 6.40* |
| Error | 96 | 454.048 | 4.730 | |
| Total | 124 | 1,950.912 | | |

*Source:* Based on Nolan-Hoeksema and Morrow (1991).
* $p < .05$

in terms of their reported depression. The $SS_{subjects}$ term is then subtracted from $SS_{total}$, along with $SS_{weeks}$, when we calculate $SS_{error}$. (In the between-subject designs, in which every score represented a different subject, if we had calculated $SS_{subjects}$ it would have been the same thing as $SS_{total}$.)

From part (b) in Table 18.1 you can see that $SS_{total}$ is calculated in the usual manner. Similarly $SS_{subjects}$ and $SS_{weeks}$ are calculated just as main effects always are (square the deviations of the group means from the grand mean, then sum, and finally, multiply by the number of observations per mean). Finally, the error term is obtained by subtracting $SS_{subjects}$ and $SS_{weeks}$ from $SS_{total}$.

The summary table, part (c) of Table 18.1, shows that I have computed an F for Weeks but not for Subjects. The reason is that $MS_{error}$ is not an appropriate denominator for an F on subjects, nor do we have a term that would be. Therefore we cannot test the Subjects variable. This is not a great loss, however, because we rarely are concerned with determining whether subjects are different from one another—they generally are. We computed $SS_{subjects}$ only to allow us to remove those differences from the error term and thus compute an appropriate error term to test Weeks.

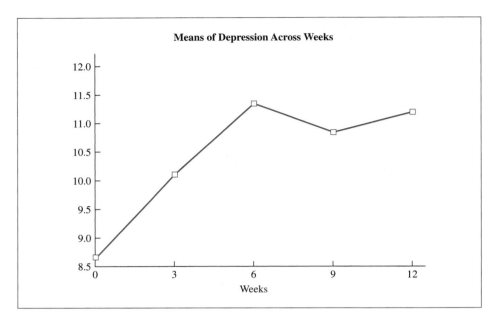

**Figure 18.1**
Plot of mean depression scores across weeks

You may have noticed that no Subjects × Weeks interaction is shown in the summary table. With only one score per cell, the interaction term *is* the error term; in fact some people prefer to write $S \times W$ instead of error. No matter whether you think of it as error or as the $S \times W$ interaction, this term is still the appropriate denominator for the $F$ on Weeks.

The $F$ value for Weeks is 6.40, based on 4 and 96 degrees of freedom. The critical value of $F$ on 4 and 96 $df$ is $F_{.05}(4,96) = 2.49$. We can therefore reject $H_0$: $\mu_1 = \mu_2 = \cdots = \mu_5$ and conclude that the earthquake was associated with a statistically significant increase in depression scores. It will be easier to see what has happened if we look at the means across weeks, plotted in Figure 18.1.

From Figure 18.1 we can see that depression increased for the first two measurements following the earthquake and then began to level off. It had not, however, begun to fall even after 12 weeks.

## 18.2 Multiple Comparisons

If we wanted to carry the analysis further and make comparisons among means, we could use the protected $t$ procedure discussed in Chapter 16. (Alternatively, we could use a Bonferroni test by dividing the selected significance level by the number of tests. The arithmetic for both tests would be exactly the same.) The $MS_{error}$ in this analysis would be the appropriate term to use in the protected $t$. For our data the results are clear-cut, and there is little or nothing to be gained by making multiple comparisons. However I will illustrate the procedure by comparing the mean depression score before the earthquake with the mean of all of the depression scores after the earthquake. Because the overall $F$ was significant, we can use the protected $t$ (Fisher's LSD test) to make this comparison.

The mean depression score before the earthquake can be read from Table 18.1 as 8.68. We can then average the postearthquake means as

$$\overline{X}_{post} = \frac{10.12 + 11.36 + 10.84 + 11.24}{4} = 10.89$$

To compare depression pre- and postearthquake we have

$$t = \frac{\overline{X}_i - \overline{X}_j}{\sqrt{MS_{error}\left(\dfrac{1}{n_i} + \dfrac{1}{n_j}\right)}} = \frac{\overline{X}_1 - \overline{X}_2}{\sqrt{MS_{error}\left(\dfrac{1}{n_1} + \dfrac{1}{n_2}\right)}}$$

$$= \frac{8.68 - 10.89}{\sqrt{4.74\left(\dfrac{1}{25} + \dfrac{1}{100}\right)}} = \frac{-2.21}{\sqrt{.237}} = -4.54$$

This $t$ has $df_{error}$ degrees of freedom because $MS_{error}$ was used in place of the pooled variance. A $t$ of $-4.54$ clearly is significant at $\alpha = .05$. Thus we can conclude that depression scores are significantly higher, on average, after the earthquake. Note that we were able to run the protected $t$ test *as if* the means were from two independent samples because the error term has been adjusted accordingly in the calculation of the error term.

You might wonder how we can apply what *appears* to be a standard independent group's $t$ test when we know that the data are not independent. You will recall that in Chapter 13 we handled dependent observations by forming differences and then taking the standard deviation of the differences. In footnote 1 in Chapter 14 (p. 327) you could infer that the reason why we work with difference scores is because we could not calculate the variances of differences of nonindependent samples directly from variables $X_1$ and $X_2$ unless we knew the correlations between $X_1$ and $X_2$. In other words, we do it to obtain a correct error term. However, for a repeated-measures analysis of variance, $MS_{error}$ is, in fact, a correct estimate of the standard error of the differences, even though we don't use difference scores to calculate it. You can easily demonstrate this to yourself by running a repeated-measures analysis of variance and a $t$ test for two related samples on the same set of data (e.g., use Week0 and Week3 from this study) and noting the similarities among the terms you calculate. (With one $df$ in the numerator, $F = t^2$.)

I chose the comparison that I just tested for specific reasons, even though no particular comparison was required for us to see what was going on in the data. The first reason for choosing this comparison is that it represents a reasonable thing to test—are scores after the earthquake higher than those collected before the earth-quake? The second reason for choosing this comparison is that it illustrates how we can compare one mean with a combination of other means. All we have to do is to average the postearthquake means and compare that result with the preearthquake means. Notice that I kept track of the number of scores going into each mean (25 and 100).

## 18.3 Effect Size

The example involving depression offers a meaningful example of the use of effect size measures. First, we are dealing with a problem that affects a many people, especially those living in earthquake zones. It is important not only to know that depression scores rise following an earthquake, but to have a measure on just how large a difference there is. Because depression scores do not have direct meaning to people, saying that depression increased by 2.2 points is not particularly informative. This is an ideal case wherein we might wish to scale and report the difference in terms of standard deviation units.

Before the earthquake the mean depression score was 8.68. After the earthquake depression rose to 10.89. We could either scale this increase by the size of the standard deviation for the prequake scores (4.14) or by the pooled overall standard deviation (2.18), which is the square root of $MS_{error}$. I will do it both ways to make a point.

We will again use $\hat{d}$ as our measure of effect size, and we will calculate $\hat{d}$ as

$$\hat{d} = \frac{\overline{X}_{pre-quake} - \overline{X}_{post-quake}}{s} = \frac{8.68 - 10.89}{4.14} = \frac{-2.21}{4.14} = -.53$$

This tells us that postquake scores are about half a standard deviation higher than they were before the quake. That is a substantial difference.

If we use the square root of $MS_{error} = \sqrt{4.74} = 2.18$, we will have a measure of effect size that is

$$\hat{d} = \frac{\overline{X}_{pre-quake} - \overline{X}_{post-quake}}{s} = \frac{8.68 - 10.89}{2.18} = \frac{-2.21}{2.18} = -1.01$$

and this result is nearly double the result we found using the prequake standard deviation. The reason that we find such a difference is that when using $\sqrt{MS_{error}}$ we are factoring out the correlation among scores, and therefore we are factoring out individual differences in depression. Since differences between people in terms of depression is a normal part of life, it seems reasonable to leave it in when we calculate an effect size measure. (See the discussion in Chapter 13, where I talk about this issue.) I realize that the distinction is not an easy one to see, and that it is not always easy to choose the correct approach. My general suggestion would be to use the standard deviation of a control condition (e.g., pretest scores) if you have one.

## 18.4   Assumptions Involved in Repeated-Measures Designs

Repeated-measures designs involve the same assumptions of normality and homogeneity of variance required for any analysis of variance. In addition, they require (for most practical purposes) the assumption that the correlations among pairs of levels of the repeated variable are constant.[2] In the case of our example this would mean that we assume that (in the population) the correlation between Week 0 and Week 3 is the same as the correlation between Weeks 3 and 6, and so on. For example, if the correlation between depression at Week 0 and depression at Week 3 is .50, then the correlation between depression scores for any other pairs of weeks should also be about .50. This is a rather stringent assumption and one that probably is violated at least as often as it is met. The test is not seriously affected unless this assumption is seriously violated. If it is seriously violated, there are two things you can do to ease the situation. The first thing you can do is to limit the levels of the independent variable to those that have a chance of meeting the assumption. For example, if you are running a learning study in which *everyone* starts out knowing nothing and ends up knowing everything, the correlation between early and late trials will be near zero, whereas the correlations between pairs of intermediate trials probably will be high. In that case do not include the earliest and latest trials in your analysis. (They wouldn't tell you much anyway.)

The second thing you can do is to use a procedure proposed by Greenhouse and Geisser (1959). For our example we had $(w - 1)$ and $(w - 1) \times (n - 1)$ $df$ for our $F$. It has been shown that if you took the same $F$ but evaluated it on 1 and $(n - 1)df$, you would have a conservative test no matter how serious the violation. For our example this would mean evaluating our obtained $F$ against $F(1,8) = 5.32$. We would still reject our null hypothesis even using this conservative test. Greenhouse and Geisser (and later Huynh and Feldt, 1976) derived less conservative corrections to the degrees of freedom. We will see a reference to this shortly. For a further discussion of these corrections, see Howell (2007).

## 18.5   Advantages and Disadvantages of Repeated-Measures Designs

The major advantage of repeated-measures designs has already been discussed. Where there are large individual differences among subjects, these differences lead to large variability in the data. When subjects are measured only once, we cannot

---

[2]The assumption isn't actually about the correlations, but about the pattern of covariances, but it is much easier to comprehend, and not very far wrong, to think in terms of the correlations.

separate subject differences from random error, and everything goes into the error term. (That is what happened when we used the standard deviation of prequake scores to calculate $\hat{d}$.) When we measure subjects repeatedly, however, we can assess subject differences and separate them from error. This produces a more powerful experimental design and thus makes it easier to reject $H_0$.

The disadvantages of repeated-measures designs are similar to the disadvantages we discussed with respect to related-sample $t$ tests (which are just special cases of repeated-measures designs). When subjects are used repeatedly, there is always the risk of carry-over effects from one trial to the next. For example, the drug you administer on Trial 1 may not have worn off by Trial 2. Similarly, a subject may learn something in early trials that will help her in later trials. In some situations this problem can be reduced by **counterbalancing** the order in which treatments are administered. Thus half the subjects might have Treatment A followed by Treatment B, and the other half might receive Treatment B followed by Treatment A. This counterbalancing will not make carry-over effects disappear, but it may make them affect both treatments equally. Although there are disadvantages associated with repeated-measures designs, in most situations the advantages outweigh the disadvantages, and such designs are popular and extremely useful in experimental work.

---

Definition | **Counterbalancing:** An arrangement of treatment conditions designed to balance practice effects.

---

## 18.6 Using SPSS to Analyze Data in a Repeated-Measures Design

Repeated-measures analyses can be a problem with some statistical software. SPSS will run the analysis fairly easily, although the printout is not what you might expect. I will present an abbreviated version of that printout in Figure 18.2. I will also show how the data need to be entered into a data file (one row per subject) and what choices to make in the various dialog boxes. I only show the data for the first ten subjects to save space.

Notice that each line represents the data for a single participant. We then use the SPSS **Analyze/General Linear Model/Repeated Measures . . .** command to specify the design of our analysis. Because the way you set up the analysis is unusual, I have shown in Figure 18.3(a) and (b) the two important dialog boxes.

At this point you would click on the **Add** button to move the information to the window, and then click on the **Define** button, which would bring you to the next dialog box.

In the dialog box shown in Figure 18.3 (b) I have specified that the scores for the five Weeks are the within-subject variables. I don't have any between-subjects variables (or covariates), so those boxes are left blank.

| | week0 | week3 | week6 | week9 | week12 |
|---|---|---|---|---|---|
| 1 | 6.0 | 10.0 | 8.0 | 4.0 | 5.0 |
| 2 | 2.0 | 4.0 | 8.0 | 5.0 | 6.0 |
| 3 | 2.0 | 4.0 | 8.0 | 5.0 | 5.0 |
| 4 | 4.0 | 5.0 | 8.0 | 10.0 | 7.0 |
| 5 | 4.0 | 7.0 | 9.0 | 7.0 | 11.0 |
| 6 | 5.0 | 7.0 | 9.0 | 7.0 | 7.0 |
| 7 | 2.0 | 9.0 | 11.0 | 8.0 | 7.0 |
| 8 | 6.0 | 9.0 | 11.0 | 8.0 | 8.0 |
| 9 | 13.0 | 10.0 | 11.0 | 8.0 | 8.0 |
| 10 | 7.0 | 3.0 | 11.0 | 8.0 | 11.0 |

**Figure 18.2**
SPSS analysis of the earthquake data

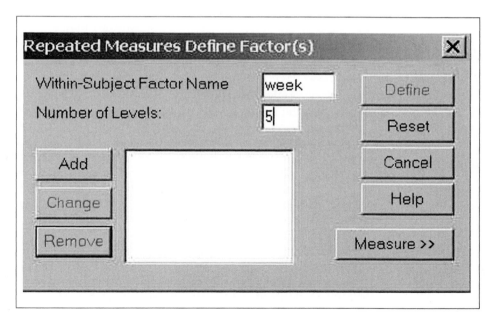

**Figure 18.3a**
Dialog boxes showing how to specify the repeated measures analysis using SPSS
(a) Specify a name for the repeated measures, and the number of levels

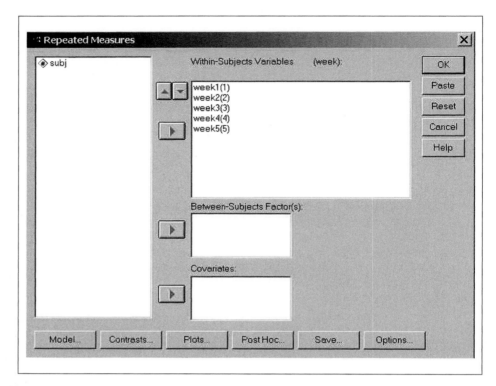

**Figure 18.3b**
(b) Specify the design

The most relevant part of the analysis of variance is shown in Figure 18.4. You can see that the results in this figure are the same as the results we obtained in Table 18.1.

Although many of the numerical values in Figure 18.4 can be found in Table 18.1, there are many that are new. This requires some explanation.

When SPSS runs a repeated-measures analysis of variance, it breaks the summary table into that part that deals with repeated measures (Within-Subjects effects) and that part that deals with measures that are not repeated across the same subjects (Between-Subjects effects). In the output dealing with Within-Subjects effects, you see the test on Weeks, which is the effect that we particularly care about. This $F$ (6.404) is the same $F$ that we obtained before. However in that same table you see references to Greenhouse-Geisser, Huyhn-Feldt, and Lower-Bound. These are just corrections that can be applied when we violate the assumption that correlations between pairs of weeks are equal. See Howell (2007) for a more extensive discussion of this.

In the Between-Subjects part of the output you normally see tests related to differences between subjects. Here we don't have a between subjects variable (as we would if we broke the data down by males and females, who obviously must

**Tests of Within-Subjects Effects**

Measure: MEASURE_1

| Source | | Type III Sum of Squares | df | Mean Square | F | Sig. |
|---|---|---|---|---|---|---|
| WEEK | Sphericity Assumed | 1934.533 | 4 | 483.633 | 21.463 | .000 |
| | Greenhouse-Geisser | 1934.533 | 1.687 | 1146.534 | 21.463 | .000 |
| | Huynh-Feldt | 1934.533 | 2.089 | 926.174 | 21.463 | .000 |
| | Lower-bound | 1934.533 | 1.000 | 1934.533 | 21.463 | .002 |
| Error(WEEK) | Sphericity Assumed | 721.067 | 32 | 22.533 | | |
| | Greenhouse-Geisser | 721.067 | 13.498 | 53.419 | | |
| | Huynh-Feldt | 721.067 | 16.710 | 43.152 | | |
| | Lower-bound | 721.067 | 8.000 | 90.133 | | |

Corrections for violation of assumptions

Error term to test differences due to weeks

*F* for differences over time

**Tests of Between-Subjects Effects**

Measure: MEASURE_1

Transformed Variable: Average

| Source | Type III Sum of Squares | df | Mean Square | F | Sig. |
|---|---|---|---|---|---|
| Intercept | 6993.800 | 1 | 6993.800 | 67.119 | .000 |
| Error | 833.600 | 8 | 104.200 | | |

*F* on $H_0$: grand mean = 0

**Figure 18.4**
Selected output from SPSS

be based on different subjects), and so the only test here is a test on the null hypothesis that the grand mean is 0. Such a test is only rarely of interest, and we usually ignore it.

## 18.7 Writing Up the Results

If I were writing up the results of this study I would give a short introduction to why the study was run, and I would most likely plot the means over time. (Following I have indicated, in standard APA format, where the figure should be included. The figure would actually appear at the end of the manuscript and would be what was shown earlier as Figure 18.1.) I would give both the *F* from the overall analysis and the results of any subsequent tests that I ran, and an effect size for those subsequent tests. My write-up would look as follows.

Nolen-Hoeksema and Morrow (1991) collected data on depression from a large group of students as part of a different study. Because the Loma Prieto earthquake occurred shortly after their data collection, they tracked these same participants and collected a depression score every three weeks through Week 12. The weekly means are shown in Figure 1 below and show that depression scores increased for several weeks after the earthquake and then began to level off.

---

Insert Figure 1 about here

---

A repeated measures analysis of variance on these data produced a significant result ($F(4,96) = 6.404$, $p < .05$). A subsequent comparison of the prequake measure with the mean of the postquake measures was statistically significant ($t(96) = -4.54$), indicating that depression scores increased significantly in the weeks after the earthquake. A measure of effect size, using the prequake standard deviation as the basis for standardization, yielded $\hat{d} = -.53$, indicating an increase in depression scores of just over half a standard deviation. As is apparent in Figure 1, by week 12 the depression scores appear to be leveling off, but have not started to return to baseline levels.

## 18.8 A Final Worked Example

As a final example I will adapt an example from Chapter 16 to illustrate the differences and similarities between the repeated-measures design and the more traditional between-subjects design. In Chapter 16 we used the data from Eysenck (1974) on recall as a function of depth of processing and examined the effect of recall Condition on older subjects. In Table 18.2 I use the same set of numbers for the sake of continuity. However, I have rearranged the data points to look like what we would expect if the data came from 10 subjects who served under each of the five recall Conditions, rather than from 50 subjects who each served under only one Condition.[3] I have merely shifted scores up and down in a column so that an individual who was one of the poor performers under one condition is also a poor performer under the other Conditions, and similarly for the subjects showing good recall. The numbers in each Condition are still the same. (If you moved these new data back into Chapter 16, you would obtain exactly the same results that we found there.) The data follow, with an additional column on the right for the subject means.

---

[3]We would *never* cavalierly rearrange real data like this. I did it here only to show the differences and similarities between the two experimental situations.

**Table 18.2**
Repeated-Measures Analysis Applied to the Eysenck Example

| | Condition | | | | | |
| --- | --- | --- | --- | --- | --- | --- |
| Subject | Count | Rhyming | Adjective | Imagery | Intentional | Subject Mean |
| 1 | 4 | 3 | 6 | 9 | 5 | 5.40 |
| 2 | 5 | 6 | 8 | 12 | 10 | 8.20 |
| 3 | 6 | 6 | 10 | 11 | 15 | 9.60 |
| 4 | 6 | 8 | 11 | 11 | 11 | 9.40 |
| 5 | 7 | 6 | 14 | 11 | 11 | 9.80 |
| 6 | 7 | 7 | 11 | 10 | 11 | 9.20 |
| 7 | 8 | 7 | 13 | 19 | 14 | 12.20 |
| 8 | 8 | 6 | 13 | 16 | 14 | 11.40 |
| 9 | 9 | 9 | 13 | 12 | 10 | 10.60 |
| 10 | 10 | 11 | 11 | 23 | 19 | 14.80 |
| **Means** | 7.00 | 6.90 | 11.00 | 13.40 | 12.00 | 10.06 |

First we will calculate the $SS_{total}$:

$$SS_{total} = \Sigma(X - \overline{X}..)^2 - \Sigma X^2 - \frac{(\Sigma X)^2}{N} = 4^2 + 5^2 + \cdots + 19^2 - \frac{503^2}{50}$$

$$= 5,847 - 5,060.18 = 786.82$$

We now have two main effects to calculate, one based on the Condition totals and one based on the Subject totals:

$$SS_{Conditions} = n\Sigma(\overline{X}_C - \overline{X}..)^2 = 10[(7.00 - 10.06)^2 + \cdots + (12.00 - 10.06)^2]$$

$$= 351.52$$

$$SS_{Subjects} = c\Sigma(\overline{X}_S - \overline{X}..)^2 = 5[(5.40 - 10.06)^2 + \cdots + (14.80 - 10.06)^2]$$

$$= 278.82$$

The error term can now be obtained by subtraction:

$$SS_{error} = SS_{total} - SS_{Conditions} - SS_{Subjects}$$

$$= 786.82 - 351.52 - 278.82 = 156.48$$

This error term is also equivalent to the Conditions $\times$ Subjects interaction, as described earlier.

We now set up the summary table:

| Source | df | SS | MS | F |
|---|---|---|---|---|
| Subjects | 9 | 278.82 | | |
| Conditions | 4 | 351.52 | 87.88 | 20.22 |
| Error | 36 | 156.48 | 4.35 | |
| Total | 49 | 786.82 | | |

To test the $F$ for the Conditions effect, we go to the $F$ table with 4 and 36 degrees of freedom. From Table D.3 in the appendix we find through interpolation that the critical value of $F$ is 2.65. Because $20.22 > 2.65$, we will reject the null hypothesis and conclude that recall of verbal material varies with the conditions under which that material is learned.

If you go back to Section 16.3, you will see that when I analyzed the same basic data set as a between-subjects design I obtained an $F$ of 9.08 instead of 20.22. The difference is that in this analysis I have treated the data as if they were repeated measures and thus subtracted out differences due to subjects from the error term. Notice two things. In the earlier analysis the $SS_{Conditions}$ was 351.52, which is exactly what it is here. $SS_{error}$ in the earlier analysis was 435.30. If you were to subtract from that the $SS_{subjects}$ (278.82) that we have here, you would get 156.48, which is the present $SS_{error}$. So you can see that we literally have subtracted out the sum of squares due to individual differences from our error term to make a more powerful test.

It is important to keep in mind that, for the sake of an example, I have moved the data around slightly to produce subjects who were consistently poor or consistently good. But this is nothing more than you would expect to find if you used the same subjects under all conditions. From a comparison of the $F$ here and the one in Chapter 16, you can see that you generally increase the power of an experiment (on within-subject terms) and therefore the probability of finding a significant difference by using a repeated-measures design, if it is practical and appropriate.

## 18.9 Summary

In this chapter you saw how to handle data in which individual subjects served under all levels of one or more independent variables. We examined a simple case of a repeated-measures design and saw that such designs remove differences among subjects from the error term. By eliminating individual differences from $MS_{error}$, repeated-measures designs generally are more powerful than comparable between-subjects designs for tests on within-subject terms. We also saw that it is quite simple to report relevant effect sizes for such designs. For effect sizes we generally use the standard deviation of baseline data or a control condition if such exist in the data. Alternatively we can use the square root of $MS_{error}$.

Some important terms in this chapter are

# 18.10  Exercises

**18.1**  Migraine headaches are a problem for many people, and one way of treating them involves relaxation therapy. A study of the effectiveness of relaxation techniques in the treatment of migraines was conducted by Blanchard, Theobald, Williamson, Silver, and Brown (1978). The data that follow are in agreement with those found by Blanchard et al. (Their study was more complex than the one examined here.) I have calculated $\Sigma X^2$ to save you work.

| Subject | Baseline Week 1 | Week 2 | Training Week 3 | Week 4 | Week 5 | Subject Mean |
|---------|------|------|------|------|------|------|
| 1 | 21 | 22 | 8 | 6 | 6 | 12.6 |
| 2 | 20 | 19 | 10 | 4 | 9 | 12.4 |
| 3 | 7 | 5 | 5 | 4 | 5 | 5.2 |
| 4 | 25 | 30 | 13 | 12 | 4 | 16.8 |
| 5 | 30 | 33 | 10 | 8 | 6 | 17.4 |
| 6 | 19 | 27 | 8 | 7 | 4 | 13.0 |
| 7 | 26 | 16 | 5 | 2 | 5 | 10.8 |
| 8 | 13 | 4 | 8 | 1 | 5 | 6.2 |
| 9 | 26 | 24 | 14 | 8 | 17 | 17.8 |
| **Weekly Means** | 20.78 | 20.00 | 9.00 | 5.78 | 6.78 | 12.47 |

Grand Mean = 12.47   $\Sigma X = 561$   $\Sigma X^2 = 10.483$

Calculate and plot the appropriate column means

**18.2**  Run a repeated measures analysis of variance on the data in Exercise 18.1 and explain your results.

**18.3**  If you were designing the study referred to in Exercise 18.1, what else would you like to have collected to clarify the meaning of your results?

**18.4**  Using the data from Week 2 and Week 3 of Exercise 18.1, run a matched-sample *t* test to test the hypothesis that migraines decreased from before to after relaxation therapy.

**18.5**  Run a repeated measures analysis of variance on the same data that you used in Exercise 18.4 and draw the appropriate conclusions.

**18.6**  For Exercise 18.5 compare the results you had in the two analyses.

**18.7**  Calculate $\hat{d}$ as an effect size estimate to elaborate on the results in Exercise 18.4.

**18.8** Use the protected $t$ tests with the data in Exercise 18.1 to help you interpret the results. However this time compare the mean of the two baseline measures with the mean of the three training measures. (*Hint:* As I pointed out, you can calculate the $t$ test as if these were independent samples because $MS_{error}$ has been adjusted appropriately by removing subject differences.)

**18.9** Calculate an estimate of $d$ for the comparison you made in Exercise 18.8.

**18.10** St. Lawrence, Brasfield, Shirley, Jefferson, Alleyne, and O'Brannon (1995) investigated the effects of an 8-week Behavioral Skills Training (BST) program aimed at reducing the risk of HIV infection among African-American adolescents. The study followed males and females from a pretest to a 12-month follow-up, recording the frequency of condom-protected sex. (They also had a control condition, but I am going to look only at the males in the BST condition for this exercise.) The actual dependent variable is one thousand times the natural logarithm of the frequency of protected sex. (I multiplied the log by 1,000 to eliminate decimal values.) The data for males follow.

| Pretest | Posttest | Follow-up 6 Months | Follow-up 12 Months |
|---|---|---|---|
| 07 | 22 | 13 | 14 |
| 25 | 10 | 17 | 24 |
| 50 | 36 | 49 | 23 |
| 16 | 38 | 34 | 24 |
| 33 | 25 | 24 | 25 |
| 10 | 07 | 23 | 26 |
| 13 | 33 | 27 | 24 |
| 22 | 20 | 21 | 11 |
| 04 | 00 | 12 | 00 |
| 17 | 16 | 20 | 10 |

(a) Calculate and plot the means.
(b) Use the analysis of variance to draw the appropriate conclusions.

**18.11** What null hypothesis did you test in Exercise 18.10?

**18.12** In the study discussed in Exercise 18.10, the authors also ran a control group under the same conditions, but without the BST intervention. Those data (for males) follow.

| Pretest | Posttest | Follow-up 6 Months | Follow-up 12 Months |
|---|---|---|---|
| 00 | 00 | 00 | 00 |
| 69 | 56 | 14 | 36 |
| 05 | 00 | 00 | 05 |
| 04 | 24 | 00 | 00 |
| 35 | 08 | 00 | 00 |
| 07 | 00 | 09 | 37 |
| 51 | 53 | 08 | 26 |
| 25 | 00 | 00 | 15 |
| 59 | 45 | 11 | 16 |
| 40 | 02 | 33 | 16 |

(a) Calculate the means for these data and plot them on the same graph used in Exercise 18.10
(b) Run the analysis of variance on these data.

**18.13**   What would you conclude from the comparison of the answers to Exercises 18.10 and 18.12? (You do not know how to run the appropriate analysis of variance, though you might be able to figure it out if you have the appropriate software, but the analysis itself is not the issue.)

**18.14**   In Exercise 18.10 why did we treat time as a repeated measure rather than as a between-subjects measure?

**18.15**   Use Bonferroni *t* tests with the data in Table 18.1 to compare performance at the following points:
(a)   Week 0 and Week 6
(b)   Week 0 and Week 12
(c)   Week 3 and Week 12
(*Hint:* See the hint in Exercise 18.8. I would not recommend all of those comparisons for an actual study unless you have a very good reason for doing so.)

**18.16**   Write a short paragraph describing the results of the analysis of the data in Exercise 18.1.

# 19

# Chi-Square

In Saint-Exupery's *The Little Prince* (1943), the narrator, remarking that he believes the prince came from an asteroid known as B-612, explains his attention to such a trivial detail as the precise number of the asteroid with the following comment:

> Grown-ups love figures. When you tell them you have made a new friend, they never ask you any questions about essential matters. They never say to you, "What does his voice sound like? What games does he love best? Does he collect butterflies?" Instead they demand: "How

old is he? How many brothers has he? How much does he weigh? How much does his father make?" Only from these figures do they think they have learned anything about him.

In some ways the first chapters of this book have concentrated on dealing with the kinds of numbers Saint-Exupery's grown-ups like so much. This chapter will be devoted to the analysis of largely nonnumerical data.

In Chapter 1 I drew a distinction between measurement data (sometimes called quantitative data) and categorical data (sometimes called frequency data). When we deal with measurement data, each observation represents a score along some continuum, and the most common statistics are the mean and the standard deviation. When we deal with categorical data, on the other hand, the data consist of the frequencies of observations that fall into each of two or more categories ("Does your friend have a gravelly voice or a high-pitched voice?" or "Is he a collector of butterflies, coins, or baseball cards?").

As an example, we could ask 100 participants to classify a vaguely worded newspaper editorial as to whether it favored or opposed unrestricted dissemination of birth control information (no neutral or undecided response is allowed). The results might look as follows:

Editorial View Seen as

| In Favor | Opposed | Total |
|----------|---------|-------|
| 58       | 42      | 100   |

Here the data are the numbers of observations that fall into each of the two categories. Given such data, we might be interested in asking whether significantly more people view the editorial as in favor of the issue than view it as opposed or whether the editorial is really neutral and the frequencies just represent a chance deviation from a 50:50 split. (Recall that participants were forced to choose between "*in favor of*" and "*opposed*.")

A differently designed study might collect the same data on the newspaper editorial but try to relate those data to the individual's own views on the topic. Thus we might also classify respondents with respect to their views about the dissemination of birth control information. This study might arrive at the following data:

Editorial View Seen as

| Respondent's View | In Favor | Opposed | Total |
|-------------------|----------|---------|-------|
| In Favor          | 46       | 24      | 70    |
| Opposed           | 12       | 18      | 30    |
| Total             | 58       | 42      | 100   |

Here we see that people's judgments of the editorial depend on their own point of view, with the majority (46/70) of those in favor of the unrestricted dissemination of birth control information viewing the editorial as being on their side, and those opposed generally seeing the editorial as siding with them (18/30). In other words, respondents' personal opinions and their judgments about the editorial are not independent of one another. (In the words of Chapter 17, they interact.)

Although these two examples appear somewhat different in terms of the way the data are arranged and in terms of the experimental questions being asked, the same statistical technique—the **chi-square test**—is applicable to both. However, because the research questions we are asking and the way that we apply the test are different in the two situations, we will deal with them separately.

Definition | **Chi-square test:** A statistical test often used for categorical data.

# 19.1 One Classification Variable: The Chi-Square Goodness-of-Fit Test

The following example is based on one of the most famous early experiments in animal learning, conducted by Tolman, Ritchie, and Kalish (1946). Although the study took place over 60 years ago, it was fundamental to a long standing argument in learning theory that continues, at a less vocal level, today. At the time of the original study Tolman was engaged in a theoretical debate with Clark Hull and the latter's students on whether a rat in a maze learns a discrete set of motor responses (Hull) or forms some sort of cognitive map of the maze and responds on the basis of that map (Tolman). At issue was the fundamental question of whether animals learn by stimulus-response conceptions or whether there is room for a cognitive interpretation of animal behavior. (To put this in less academic language, "Do animals think?") The statistical test in question is called a **goodness-of-fit test** because it asks whether there is a "good fit" between the data (observed frequencies) and the theory (expected frequencies).

Definition | **Goodness-of-fit test:** A test for comparing observed frequencies with theoretically predicted frequencies.

In a simple and ingenious experiment, Tolman and his colleagues first taught rats to run down a starting alley of a maze into a large circular area. From the circular area another alley exited straight across from the entrance but then turned and ended up in a goal box containing food, which was actually to the right of the circular area. After the rats had learned the task ("go to the circular area and exit straight across"), Tolman changed the task by making the original exit alley a dead end and by adding several new alleys, one of which pointed in the direction of the original goal box. Thus the rat had several choices, one of which included the original alley, which now dead-ended, and one of which included a new alley that pointed directly toward the goal.

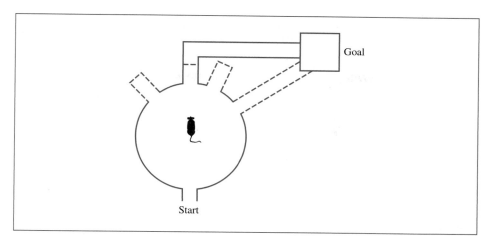

**Figure 19.1**
Schematic view of Tolman's maze

The maze is shown in Figure 19.1, with the original exit alley drawn with solid lines and the new alleys drawn with dashed lines. If Hull was correct, the rat would learn a stimulus-response sequence during the first part of the experiment and would therefore continue to make the same set of responses, thus entering the now dead-end alley. If Tolman was right and the rat learned a cognitive map of the situation, then the rat would enter the alley on the *right* because it knew that the food was "over there to the right." Since Tolman was the one who published the study, you can probably guess how it came out—the rats were more likely to choose the alley on the right. But we still need some way of testing whether the preference for the alley on the right was due to chance (the rats entered the alleys at random) or whether the data support a general preference for the right alley. Do the data represent a "good fit" to the model?

For the sake of this example I have modified the study slightly to include only two alleys in the second part of the experiment (Tolman et al. used 18). The choices for the 32 rats in the study are as follows (these are not Tolman's original data, which showed an even more dramatic difference):

| | Alley Chosen | | |
|---|---|---|---|
| | Original | Right | Total |
| Observed | 9 | 23 | 32 |
| Expected | 16 | 16 | 32 |

The first line of this table shows the number of rats observed entering each alley in the second part of the experiment. This row sums to 32 because there were 32 rats in the experiment. We will take as our null hypothesis ($H_0$) for this test the hypothesis that the rats showed no preference for either of the two alleys. (Hull predicted that the rats would favor Alley A, whereas Tolman predicted that they would favor Alley B. We are testing the null hypothesis that they do not favor either alley.) In other words $H_0$ states that there is no difference between $p$ (the probability of choosing Alley A) and $q$ (the probability of choosing Alley B) and therefore that $p = q = .50$. In terms of **expected frequencies** this means that under $H_0$ we would expect half of the 32 rats to choose Alley A and half to choose Alley B. These expected frequencies are shown in the second row of the table. Since Tolman et al. used 32 *different* rats, the observations should be independent; there is no reason to expect that one rat's behavior would influence another rat's behavior. (If the study used eight rats four times each, we would have strong reservations about the independence of the observation. We would have similar reservations if the animals left odor cures in the maze.)

---

Definition    **Expected frequencies:** The expected value for the number of observations in a cell if $H_0$ is true.

---

## The Chi-Square ($\chi^2$) Statistic

We will approach this problem by use of the chi-square ($\chi^2$) statistic, which is defined as

$$\chi^2 = \Sigma \frac{(O - E)^2}{E}$$

where

   $O$ = the observed frequency in each category

   $E$ = the expected frequency in each category

and the summation is taken over all categories.

Examination of this equation will make it clear why it is applicable to the question we want to ask. In the numerator we are directly measuring how far the observed frequencies deviate from the expected frequencies. (For the Original alley the null expected 16, but we had only 9 entries. For the Right alley the null expected 16 entries, and we had 23.) The greater the deviations, the larger the value of $\chi^2$. We square the numerator for the same reason we square the numerator in calculating a variance—the sum of (unsquared) deviations will always be 0. The denominator plays a useful role in terms of keeping the deviations in perspective. If we had expected 5 observations in a given category and obtained 15, that 10-point difference is substantial. On the other hand, if we had expected 500 and obtained 510, that 10-point difference would likely be brushed aside as inconsequential. When we divide by $E$, we are weighting the size of the squared deviations by the size of the expected frequency. Again, that seems like a reasonable thing to do.

From our formula for the chi-square test, we can calculate

$$\chi^2 = \Sigma \frac{(O - E)^2}{E}$$
$$= \frac{(9 - 16)^2}{16} + \frac{(23 - 16)^2}{16}$$
$$= 6.125$$

## The Chi-Square Distribution

Throughout this book, whenever we have calculated a statistic, such as $t$ or $F$, we have evaluated it against a value in the appropriate appendix. The value in the table tells us how large a value we might expect for the statistic if the null hypothesis were true; and if we exceed that value, we reject the null hypothesis. The same holds with the chi-square test. To test the null hypothesis that the probabilities of choosing the two alleys are equal, we need to evaluate the obtained $\chi^2$ against the sampling distribution of chi-square in Table D.1 in Appendix D. A portion of that table is presented in Table 19.1.

The chi-square distribution, like other distributions we have seen, depends on the degrees of freedom. For the goodness-of-fit test the degrees of freedom are defined as $k - 1$, where $k$ is the number of categories (in our example, 2). Examples of the chi-square distribution for four different degrees of freedom are shown in Figure 19.2, along with the critical values and shaded rejection regions for $\alpha = .05$. You can see that the critical value for a specified level of $\alpha$ (e.g., $\alpha = .05$) will be larger for larger degrees of freedom. For our example we have $k - 1 = 2 - 1 = 1$ $df$. From Table D.1 (or Table 19.1) you will see that, at $\alpha = .05$, $\chi^2_{.05}(1) = 3.84$. Thus when $H_0$ is true, only 5% of the time would we obtain a value of $\chi^2 \geq 3.84$. Because our obtained value is 6.125, we will reject $H_0$ and conclude that the two alleys are not equally likely to be chosen. Tolman's rats chose Alley B at greater than chance levels.

I should note that here, as in the analysis of variance, we are using a one-tailed test of a nondirectional null hypothesis. By that I mean that we reject only

**Table 19.1**
Abbreviated Version of Table D.1, Upper Percentage Points of the $\chi^2$ Distribution

| df | .995 | .990 | .975 | .950 | .900 | .750 | .500 | .250 | .100 | .050 | .025 | .010 | .005 |
|----|------|------|------|------|------|------|------|------|------|------|------|------|------|
| 1 | 0.00 | 0.00 | 0.00 | 0.00 | 0.02 | 0.10 | 0.45 | 1.32 | 2.71 | 3.84 | 5.02 | 6.63 | 7.88 |
| 2 | 0.01 | 0.02 | 0.05 | 0.10 | 0.21 | 0.58 | 1.39 | 2.77 | 4.61 | 5.99 | 7.38 | 9.21 | 10.60 |
| 3 | 0.07 | 0.11 | 0.22 | 0.35 | 0.58 | 1.21 | 2.37 | 4.11 | 6.25 | 7.82 | 9.35 | 11.35 | 12.84 |
| 4 | 0.21 | 0.30 | 0.48 | 0.71 | 1.06 | 1.92 | 3.36 | 5.39 | 7.78 | 9.49 | 11.14 | 13.28 | 14.86 |
| 5 | 0.41 | 0.55 | 0.83 | 1.15 | 1.61 | 2.67 | 4.35 | 6.63 | 9.24 | 11.07 | 12.83 | 15.09 | 16.75 |
| 6 | 0.68 | 0.87 | 1.24 | 1.64 | 2.20 | 3.45 | 5.35 | 7.84 | 10.64 | 12.59 | 14.45 | 16.81 | 18.55 |
| 7 | 0.99 | 1.24 | 1.69 | 2.17 | 2.83 | 4.25 | 6.35 | 9.04 | 12.02 | 14.07 | 16.01 | 18.48 | 20.28 |
| 8 | 1.34 | 1.65 | 2.18 | 2.73 | 3.49 | 5.07 | 7.34 | 10.22 | 13.36 | 15.51 | 17.54 | 20.09 | 21.96 |
| 9 | 1.73 | 2.09 | 2.70 | 3.33 | 4.17 | 5.90 | 8.34 | 11.39 | 14.68 | 16.92 | 19.02 | 21.66 | 23.59 |
| ⋮ | ⋮ | ⋮ | ⋮ | ⋮ | ⋮ | ⋮ | ⋮ | ⋮ | ⋮ | ⋮ | ⋮ | ⋮ | ⋮ |

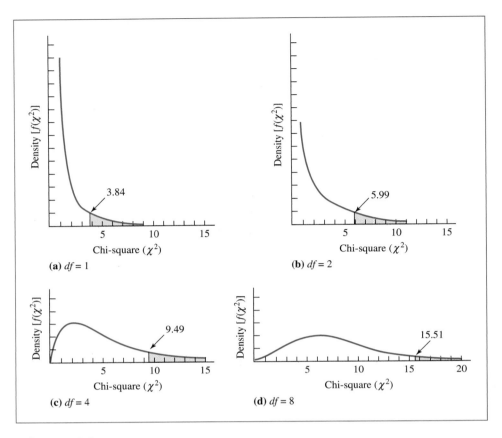

**Figure 19.2**
Chi-square distribution for $df = 1, 2, 4$, and 8 with critical values for $\alpha = .05$

for large values of $\chi^2$, not for small ones. In that sense the test is one-tailed. However, we will obtain large values of $\chi^2$, in the two-category case, regardless of which category has the larger obtained frequency. In that sense the test is two-tailed. Multiple categories have a wide variety of patterns of differences that would lead to rejection, and the test could be thought of as multitailed or nondirectional.

## Extension to the Multicategory Case

In the example of place learning in rats we had a situation in which the data fell into one of two categories. We can easily extend this example to the **multicategory case**, in which data can be classified into three or more categories, the number being signified by $k$.

Definition    **Multicategory case:** A situation in which data can be sorted into more than two categories.

As an example, we can expand the place-learning problem to allow for multiple alleys running off the circular area. (Remember, Tolman used 18.) We will let Alley A be the one that was originally correct and now has a dead end. Alley D will be the one on the right, which rats would be expected to choose if they were trying to go to the place where the goal box previously had been. Alleys B and C are located on either side of the originally correct alley. The data follow:

| | A | B | C | D | Total |
|---|---|---|---|---|---|
| | | | Alley Chosen | | |
| Observed | 4 | 5 | 8 | 15 | 32 |
| Expected | 8 | 8 | 8 | 8 | 32 |

You can see that approximately half the rats chose the alley that Tolman would have predicted they would choose, whereas only four animals chose Alley A, the one that Hull's "response-learning" hypothesis would have predicted.

As in the first example, we have 32 animals. But this time we have four alleys. If the rats were responding at random—that is, if our null hypothesis were true—we would expect one-quarter of them to choose each alley. This leads to the expected frequency of eight for each alley. Our calculations for the chi-square test are the same as those followed in the earlier example, except that this time we will sum over four categories instead of two.

$$\chi^2 = \Sigma \frac{(O - E)^2}{E}$$

$$= \frac{(4 - 8)^2}{8} + \frac{(5 - 8)^2}{8} + \frac{(8 - 8)^2}{8} + \frac{(15 - 8)^2}{8}$$

$$= 9.25$$

From Table D.1 we see that for $k - 1 = 3$ $df$, $\chi^2_{.05} (3) = 7.82$. Our value of 9.25 is greater than 7.82, so once again we will reject $H_0$. Again, we have shown that our rats are not choosing at random. They are choosing the alley that leads in the correct direction at greater than chance levels, supporting Tolman's cognitive learning theory over Hull's response-learning model.

The thoughtful reader might ask why we analyzed the data this way rather than lumping Alleys A, B, and C together into one category labeled "wrong alley." There is no particularly convincing statistical answer to this question other than to say that it depends on what you know about the behavior of your animals and what you expect the data to look like. In our example the fact that about as many rats chose one of the three wrong alleys as chose the right one does not seem as relevant as the fact that about three times as many rats chose Alley D as chose any of the other alleys. (If you were to collapse back to "right" and "wrong," the *expected* frequency for "wrong" would be 24, because there are three wrong alleys, each with an expectancy of 8.)

## 19.2 Two Classification Variables: Analysis of Contingency Tables

In the two previous examples we considered the case in which data are categorized along only one dimension (classification variable). Often, however, data are categorized with respect to two (or more) independent variables, and we are interested in asking whether those variables are independent of one another. To put this in the reverse, we often are interested in asking whether the distribution of one variable is *contingent* or *conditional* on a second variable. In this situation we will construct a **contingency table** showing the distribution of one variable at each level of the other. We saw one example of this kind of question when we wondered if the choices people made about the orientation of a newspaper editorial on birth control information depended on (was contingent on) the individual's own personal beliefs. Another example is offered in a study by Walsh et al. (2006) on the use of an antidepressant in the treatment of anorexia.

Definition

**Contingency table:** A two-dimensional table in which each observation is classified on the basis of two variables simultaneously.

It has long been hypothesized that depression is one reason that girls who have been successfully treated for anorexia nervosa tend to relapse after treatment. (Even after returning to normal weight, 30% to 50% of patients are back in the hospital within one year.) A very common approach is to prescribe Prozac, or a related drug, to newly recovered patients with the idea that the drug will reduce depression, which will in turn reduce relapse.

Walsh et al. sampled 93 patients who had been successfully restored to an acceptable body mass. Forty-nine of these patients were then prescribed Prozac for one year, while 44 of them were given a placebo. This was a double-blind study in which neither the patient nor the study coordinators knew whether the drug or the placebo was being administered. The dependent variable was the number of patients in each group who successfully maintained their weight over one year. The data follow in the form of a contingency table. (Expected frequencies are shown in parentheses.)

| Treatment | Outcome | | Total |
|---|---|---|---|
| | Success | Relapse | |
| Drug | 13 (14.226) | 36 (34.774) | 49 |
| Placebo | 14 (12.774) | 30 (31.226) | 44 |
| Total | 27 | 66 | 93 |

This table is not encouraging. It shows that not only did the Drug group not outperform the Placebo group, they actually underperformed that group (26.5% versus 31.5%). We still want to know if the underperformance is statistically significant or is simply a chance result. (It is possible that Prozac actually decreases a girl's ability to maintain weight, in which case it would actually be harmful to prescribe it to this population.)

## Expected Frequencies for Contingency Tables

For a contingency table the expected frequency for a given cell is obtained by multiplying together the totals for the row and column in which the cell is located and dividing by the total sample size ($N$). (These totals are known as **marginal totals** because they sit at the margins of the table.) If $E_{ij}$ is the expected frequency for the cell in row $i$ and column $j$, $R_i$ and $C_j$ are the corresponding row and column totals, and $N$ is the total number of observations, we have the following formula[1]:

$$E_{ij} = \frac{R_i C_j}{N}$$

For our example

$$E_{11} = \frac{49 \times 27}{93} = 14.226$$

$$E_{12} = \frac{49 \times 66}{93} = 34.774$$

$$E_{21} = \frac{44 \times 27}{93} = 12.774$$

$$E_{22} = \frac{44 \times 66}{93} = 31.226$$

---

**Definition**    **Marginal total:** Totals for the levels of one variable summed across the levels of the other variable.

---

## Calculation of Chi-Square

Now that we have the observed and expected frequencies in each cell, the calculation of $\chi^2$ is straightforward. We simply use the same formula that we have been using all along, although we sum our calculations over all cells in the table.

$$\chi^2 = \Sigma \frac{(O - E)^2}{E}$$

$$= \frac{(13 - 14.226)^2}{14.226} + \frac{(36 - 34.774)^2}{34.774} + \frac{(14 - 12.774)^2}{12.774}$$

$$+ \frac{(30 - 31.226)^2}{31.226} = .315$$

---

[1] This formula for the expected values is derived directly from the formula for the probability of the joint occurrence of two *independent* events given in Chapter 7 on probability. For this reason the expected values that result are those that would be expected if $H_0$ were true and the variables were independent. A large discrepancy in the fit between expected and observed would reflect a large departure from independence, which is what we want to test.

## Degrees of Freedom

Before we can compare our value of $\chi^2$ to the value in Table D.1, we must know the degrees of freedom. For the analysis of contingency tables, the degrees of freedom are given by

$$df = (R - 1)(C - 1)$$

where

$R$ = the number of rows in the table

and

$C$ = the number of columns in the table

For our example we have $R = 2$ and $C = 2$; therefore we have $(2 - 1)$ $(2 - 1) = 1$ $df$. It may seem strange to have only 1 $df$ when we have four cells, but you can see that once you know the row and column totals, you need to know only one cell frequency to be able to determine the rest.

## Evaluation of $\chi^2$

With 1 $df$ the critical value of $\chi^2$, as found in Table D.1, is 3.84. Because our value of .315 falls below the critical value, we will not reject the null hypothesis that the variables are independent of each other. In this case we will conclude that we have no evidence to suggest that whether a girl does or does not relapse is dependent on whether she was provided with Prozac or a placebo. Notice that I have not said that we have proven that the two variables are independent, but only that we have not shown that they are related. However, given the fact that the difference actually favored the placebo and that the probability under the null was so large (the probability of chi-square $\geq$ .315 = .57), we certainly would be justified in acting as if we have shown that Prozac did not have the desired effect.

# 19.3 Possible Improvements on Standard Chi-Square

The result of a chi-square test when the data contain few observations can be very discontinuous. For example, if we simply took the first row of the table and changed the entries from 13 and 36 to 12 and 37, the resulting chi-square would change from .315 to .618, which is a huge change. When we try to evaluate our obtained chi-square against tables that assume an underlying continuous distribution of chi-square, the fit is poor.

Some books advocate that for 2 × 2 tables you apply what is called a correction for continuity (also known as Yates's correction), which simply amounts to reducing each numerator by one-half unit before squaring. This correction was once quite common, but it has lost favor as we have learned more about the analysis of contingency tables. The ready availability of Fisher's Exact Test, to be discussed next, makes the correction superfluous. For more extensive coverage see Howell (2007), who generally doesn't recommend it either.

## Fisher's Exact Test

Fisher introduced what is called Fisher's Exact Test in 1934 at a meeting of the Royal Statistical Society. (Good [2001] has pointed out that one of the speakers who followed Fisher referred to Fisher's presentation as "the braying of the Golden Ass." Statistical debates at that time were far from boring, and no doubt Fisher had something equally kind to say about his critic.)

Without going into details, Fisher's proposal was to take all possible $2 \times 2$ tables that could be formed from the fixed set of marginal totals (i.e., without changing the totals on the right and bottom margins of the contingency table). For example, the following three tables all have the same marginal totals but different cell frequencies.

|  | Outcome | | | Outcome | | | Outcome | | |
|--|---------|-------|-------|---------|-------|-------|---------|-------|-------|
|  | Success | Relapse | Total | Success | Relapse | Total | Success | Relapse | Total |
| Drug | 13 | 36 | 49 | 12 | 37 | 49 | 11 | 36 | 49 |
| Placebo | 14 | 30 | 44 | 14 | 30 | 44 | 16 | 30 | 44 |
| **Total** | 27 | 66 | 93 | 27 | 66 | 93 | 27 | 66 | 93 |

Fisher could, for example, calculate a statistic like chi-square for all possible tables. He could then determine the proportion of those tables whose results (chi-square values) are as extreme, or more so, than the table we obtained from our data. If this proportion is less than $\alpha$, we reject the null hypothesis that the two variables are independent and conclude that there is a statistically significant relationship between the two variables that make up our contingency table. (This would be a great deal of work, but it could be done in theory.) Instead of doing all possible calculations, I have assumed that you would run the test directly using statistical software. I will show the use of SPSS for these analyses shortly, but here I will only say that SPSS gives the exact two-sided probability for Fisher's Exact Test as .650, which again leads us to retain the null hypothesis.

## Fisher's Exact Test versus Pearson's Chi Square

We now have at least two statistical tests for $2 \times 2$ contingency tables—which one should we use? Probably the most common solution is to go with Pearson's chi-square; perhaps because "that is what we have always done." In previous editions of this book I recommended against Fisher's Exact Test, primarily because of its reliance on fixed marginal totals. However, in recent years there has been an important growth of interest in permutation and randomization tests, of which Fisher's Exact Test is an example. I am extremely impressed with the logic and simplicity of such tests and have come to side with Fisher's Exact Test. In most cases, the conclusion you will draw will be the same for the two approaches, though this is not always the case. When we come to tables larger than $2 \times 2$, Fisher's approach does not apply, without modification, and there we almost always use the Pearson chi-square. (But see Howell & Gordon, 1976.)

## 19.4 Chi-Square for Larger Contingency Tables

The previous example involved two variables (Drug and Outcome), each of which had two levels. This particular design is referred to as a $2 \times 2$ contingency analysis and is a special case of more general $R \times C$ designs (where $R$ and $C$ represent the number of rows and columns). For an example of the analysis of a larger contingency table we can analyze data collected by Darley and Latané (1968) on bystander intervention. Why is it that bystanders who witness attacks and other negative events seem reluctant to intervene even in life-threatening situations? Are there any variables that can be shown to play a role in governing such bystander behavior? (There was a reference to this study earlier in Exercise 16.15, but in that instance the dependent variable was "time to respond," whereas here it is the dichotomy "yes/no.")

Darley and Latané asked participants to engage in a discussion carried on over an intercom system (supposedly to preserve confidentiality). One group of participants was led to believe that they were speaking with only the discussion leader (later termed the victim); a second group of participants thought one other person was involved in the discussion; and a third group thought that four other people were involved. In fact, the participant was alone in all cases. Part way through the discussion the victim on the other end of the line pretended to have a seizure and began asking for help. He even stated that he was afraid that he might die without help. One of the dependent variables was the number of participants in each condition who tried to obtain help for the victim. The results are hardly encouraging for those of us who like to believe in the kindness of our fellow creatures. For the group of participants each of whom thought he or she was alone with the victim, 85% tried to obtain help (the other 15% apparently decided to let nature take its course). For those participants who thought one other person was listening, the response rate dropped to 62%. Worst of all, when the participants thought there were four other listeners, the response rate was a meager 31%. Although it is conceivable that these differences were due to chance, that doesn't seem likely. We can use chi-square to test the null hypothesis that helping behavior is independent of the number of bystanders. The data are presented in Table 19.2. The expected frequencies were obtained the same way they were obtained in the $2 \times 2$ case. In other words, the expected frequency in the upper left cell is $(13 \times 31)/52 = 7.75$.

In this example we have $(3 - 1)(2 - 1) = 2$ $df$, and the critical value of $\chi^2$ is 5.99. Because the obtained value of $\chi^2$ (7.90) is greater than the critical value,

**Table 19.2**
Observed and Expected Frequencies for Helping Behavior as a Function of the Number of Bystanders

| | Observed | | | Expected | | |
| | Sought Assistance | | | Sought Assistance | | |
| Number Bystanders | Yes | No | Total | Yes | No | Total |
|---|---|---|---|---|---|---|
| 0 | 11 | 2 | 13 | 7.75 | 5.25 | 13 |
| 1 | 16 | 10 | 26 | 15.50 | 10.50 | 26 |
| 4 | 4 | 9 | 13 | 7.75 | 5.25 | 13 |
| Total | 31 | 21 | 52 | 31 | 21 | 52 |

$$\chi^2 = \Sigma \frac{(O - E)^2}{E}$$

$$= \frac{(11 - 7.75)^2}{7.75} + \frac{(2 - 5.25)^2}{5.25} + \frac{(16 - 15.50)^2}{15.50} + \frac{(10 - 10.50)^2}{10.50}$$

$$+ \frac{(4 - 7.75)^2}{7.75} + \frac{(9 - 5.25)^2}{5.25}$$

$$= 1.36 + 2.01 + 0.02 + 0.02 + 1.81 + 2.68$$

$$= 7.90$$

we will reject $H_0$. If you expect something unpleasant to happen to you, be sure there are not too many people around—one person is about right.

## 19.5  The Problem of Small Expected Frequencies

Chi-square is an important and valid test for examining either goodness of fit or the independence of variables (contingency tables). However, the test is not as good as we would like when the *expected* frequencies are too small. The chi-square test is based in part on the assumption that if an experiment were repeated an infinite number of times with the same number of participants, the obtained frequencies in any given cell would be normally distributed around the expected frequency. But if the expected frequency is small (e.g., 1.0), there is no way that the observed frequencies *could* be normally distributed around it. (The frequencies must be integers and you can't have frequencies less than zero.) In cases in which the expected frequencies are too small, chi-square may not be a valid statistical test. The problem, however, is how we define "too small." There are almost as many definitions as there are statistics textbooks, and the issue still is being debated in the journals. Here I take the admittedly conservative position that for small contingency tables (nine or fewer cells) all expected frequencies should be at least 5. For larger tables this restriction can be relaxed somewhat. There are people who argue that the test is conservative and produces few Type I errors, even with much smaller expected frequencies, but even these people are forced to admit that when the total sample size is very small—as is frequently the case when the expected frequencies are small—the test has remarkably little power to detect false null hypotheses. (See Camilli and Hopkins,1978, for a more complete discussion of this issue.)

## 19.6  The Use of Chi-Square as a Test on Proportions

The chi-square test can be used as a test on proportions or differences between two independent proportions. This is the same test we have been using all along. We simply change the way we conceive of our proportions (i.e., we change proportions to frequencies).

The most common question to ask with respect to proportions concerns whether one proportion is significantly higher or lower than another. A good example of this is found in another study of helping behavior by Latané and Dabbs (1975). In that study experimenters were instructed to walk into elevators and, just after the elevator started, drop a handful of pencils or coins on the floor. The dependent variable was whether bystanders helped pick up the pencils. One of the independent variables was the gender of the bystanders. The study was conducted in three cities (Columbus, Seattle, and Atlanta), but we will concentrate on the data from Columbus, where gender differences were least. We will also ignore any effect of the gender of the experimenter. Basically Latané and Dabbs found that 23% of the female bystanders and 28% of the male bystanders helped pick up the dropped items. (It is interesting that about three-quarters of the bystanders just stood there staring at the ceiling as if nothing had happened. Latané's work has had a depressing effect on my belief in human goodness.) The question of interest is whether the difference between 23% and 28% is statistically significant. To answer this question, we must know the total sample sizes. In this case there were 1,303 female bystanders and 1,320 males. (Notice the large sample sizes that are easily obtained in this type of experiment.) Because we know the sample sizes, we can convert the cell proportions to cell frequencies easily.

Proportional Data

|         | Sex of Bystander | |
|---------|--------|-------|
|         | Female | Male  |
| Help    | 23%    | 28%   |
| No Help | 77%    | 72%   |
| Number  | 1,303  | 1,320 |

Frequency Data

| | Sex of Bystander | | |
| --- | --- | --- | --- |
| | Female | Male | Total |
| **Help** | 300 | 370 | 670 |
| | (332.83) | (337.17) | |
| **No Help** | 1,003 | 950 | 1,953 |
| | (970.17) | (982.83) | |
| **Total** | 1,303 | 1,320 | 2,623 |

The entry of 300 in the upper left corner of the table was obtained by taking 23% of 1,303 females. The other entries were obtained in an analogous way. The values in parentheses are the expected frequencies, computed in the normal way. We calculate $\chi^2$ as follows:

$$\chi^2 = \Sigma \frac{(O - E)^2}{E}$$

$$= \frac{(300 - 332.83)^2}{332.83} + \frac{(370 - 337.17)^2}{337.17} + \frac{(1,003 - 970.17)^2}{970.17}$$

$$+ \frac{(950 - 982.83)^2}{982.83} = 8.64$$

The critical value on 1 $df$ at $\alpha = .05$ is 3.84, so I will reject $H_0$ and conclude that the proportions are significantly different. We can conclude that under the conditions of this study males are more willing to help than females. (This study was conducted over 30 years ago. Do you think that we would obtain similar results today?)

A word of warning when using proportions. You will have noticed that we converted proportions to frequencies and then ran the chi-square test on the frequencies. This is the *only* correct way to do that. I sometimes see people form a contingency table with the proportions themselves as cell entries and then go ahead and compute $\chi^2$ as if nothing were wrong. But something is *very* wrong. They will not have a legitimate value of $\chi^2$, and their test will be incorrect. Proportions, even if you throw away the decimal point and pretend that they are whole numbers, are not legitimate data for a chi-square test. You must use frequencies.

## 19.7 **Nonindependent Observations**

Aside from questions about small expected frequencies, the chi-square test also is based on the assumption that observations are independent of one another. In practical terms what this means is that participants must contribute one, *and only one*, observation to the data. If in their bystander study Darley and Latané had decided to use each participant two or three times to save the effort of recruiting more participants, a chi-square analysis of the data would not have been appropriate. Fortunately they knew better, but this problem has a habit of sneaking into analyses carried out by even experienced investigators. The simplest rule is that N (the total of the row or column totals) must be equal to the number of *participants* (not observations) in the experiment. If it is too large, you are probably using more than one observation from each participant. If it is too small, you have omitted some data (such as counting only how many participants sought help for the victim and forgetting about counting those who did not seek help). A similar kind of problem arises in the Latané and Dabbs example. If there are 10 people in an elevator and one of them jumps in to help, the others may feel so guilty that they help too. If so, the observations are not independent.

## 19.8 SPSS Analysis of Contingency Tables

SPSS has more than one way of computing chi-square. I will use **Analyze/ Nonparametric Tests/Chi-square** to obtain a goodness-of-fit (i.e., one dimensional) test on Tolman's study of animal learning and **Descriptive statistics/ Crosstabs** for the contingency table analysis of the study of treatment for anorexia. I have combined the data for both goodness-of-fit test (using Tolman's data) and the contingency table test (using Walsh's data) into one spreadsheet to save space. This is shown in Figure 19.3. The data from Tolman's study is shown in the two columns on the left, and the data for Walsh's study is shown in the three columns to the right.

Notice that for the Tolman study the first column indicates whether the rat ran to the original alley or the (now correct) alley on the right. The column headed Freq1 is the frequency for each of those choices. For the Walsh study of anorexia the Drug column indicates whether the participant received Prozac or the Placebo, the Outcome column indicates whether the participant relapsed or maintained their weight, and the column headed Freq2 gives the frequencies of each Drug/Outcome combination.

To use a table like this we need to tell SPSS to weight the alleys (or the Drug/Outcome combinations) by the values in Freq1 (or Freq2). This is done by selecting **Data/Weight Cases** and then specifying which variable is the weighting variable. This is shown in Figure 19.4 for the goodness-of-fit analysis.

|   | Alley | Freq1 | Drug | Outcome | Freq2 |   |
|---|-------|-------|------|---------|-------|---|
| 1 | 1.00  | 9.00  | 1.00 | 1.00    | 13.00 |   |
| 2 | 2.00  | 23.00 | 1.00 | 2.00    | 36.00 |   |
| 3 | .     | .     | 2.00 | 1.00    | 14.00 |   |
| 4 | .     | .     | 2.00 | 2.00    | 30.00 |   |
| 5 |       |       |      |         |       |   |

**Figure 19.3**
Data for the goodness-of-fit and contingency table analysis

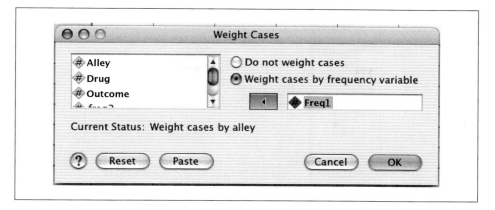

**Figure 19.4**
Weighting of cases

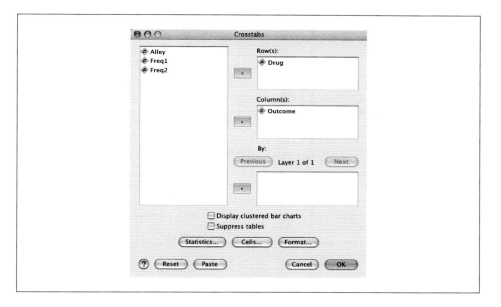

**Figure 19.5**
Selection of variables for analysis of contingency tables

To run the goodness-of-fit test we choose **Analyze/Nonparametric tests/Chi-Square** and specify that Alley is the independent variable—having already instructed SPSS to weight the cases by Freq1. For the contingency table test we use **Data/Weight Cases** to set Freq2 as the weighting variable, select **Descriptive statistics/Crosstabs** to specify the independent variables, and then select Drug and Outcome. The second of these steps is shown in Figure 19.5 for the case of the contingency table analysis.

Finally, the following display shows the output for the two analyses. You should be able to see that the results agree with what we found earlier.

▶ **Output for goodness of fit test:**

**Frequencies**

ALLEY

|  | Observed N | Expected N | Residual |
|---|---|---|---|
| Original | 9 | 16.0 | −7.0 |
| Right | 23 | 16.0 | 7.0 |
| Total | 32 | | |

Test Statistics

|  | Alley |
|---|---|
| Chi-Square[a] | 6.125 |
| df | 1 |
| Asymp. Sig. | .013 |

a. 0 cells (.0%) have expected frequencies less than
   5. The minimum expected cell frequency is 16.0.

▶ **Output for analysis of anorexia data:**

**DRUG * OUTCOME Crosstabulation**

|  |  |  | Outcome | | Total |
|---|---|---|---|---|---|
|  |  |  | No relapse | Relapse |  |
| DRUG | Prozac | Count | 13 | 36 | 49 |
|  |  | Expected Count | 14.2 | 34.8 | 49.0 |
|  |  | Residual | −1.2 | 1.2 | |
|  | Placebo | Count | 14 | 30 | 44 |
|  |  | Expected Count | 12.8 | 31.2 | 44.0 |
|  |  | Residual | 1.2 | −1.2 | |
| Total |  | Count | 27 | 66 | 93 |
|  |  | Expected Count | 27.0 | 66.0 | 93.0 |

**Chi-Square Tests**

|  | Value | df | Asymp. Sig. (2-sided) | Exact Sig. (2-sided) | Exact Sig. (1-sided) |
|---|---|---|---|---|---|
| Pearson Chi-Square | .315[b] | 1 | .575 | | |
| Continuity Correction[a] | .110 | 1 | .740 | | |
| Likelihood Ratio | .314 | 1 | .575 | | |
| Fisher's Exact Test | | | | .650 | .370 |
| Linear-by-Linear Association | .311 | 1 | .577 | | |
| N of Valid Cases | 93 | | | | |

a. Computed only for a 2 × 2 table
b. 0 cells (.0%) have expected count less than 5. The minimum expected count is 12.77

You will see several statistics here that you have not seen before, but the two that we care about are the Pearson chi-square and the Fisher's Exact Test. You can ignore the others.

## 19.9 Measures of Effect Size

The fact that a relationship is "statistically significant" doesn't tell us very much about whether it is of practical significance. The fact that two independent variables are not statistically independent does not mean that the lack of independence is important or worthy of our attention. In fact, if you allow the sample size to grow large enough, almost any two variables would likely show a statistically significant lack of independence.

What we need, then, are ways to go beyond a simple test of significance to present one or more statistics that reflect the size of the effect we are looking at. As we have seen elsewhere in this book, there are two different types of measures designed to represent the size of an effect. One type, called the *d*-family by Rosenthal (1994), is based on one or more measures of the *differences* between groups or levels of the independent variable. The other type of measure, called the *r*-family, represents some sort of correlation coefficient between the two independent variables. I will not cover the *r*-family measures here because they rarely give us a good intuitively appealing measure. (Essentially you could simply score a person as 1 or 2 depending on whether they received the drug or the placebo, again score them 1 or 2 depending on whether they relapsed, and then correlate those two variables.)

### The Effect of Aspirin on Reducing Heart Attacks

An important study of the beneficial effects of small daily doses of aspirin on reducing heart attacks in men was reported in 1988. More than 22,000 physicians were administered aspirin or a placebo, and the incidence of later heart attacks was recorded. The data are shown in Table 19.3. Notice that this design is a

**Table 19.3**
The Effect of Aspirin on the Incidence of Heart Attacks

|  | Outcome | | |
| --- | --- | --- | --- |
|  | Heart Attack | No Heart Attack | |
| **Aspirin** | 104 | 10,933 | 11,037 |
| **Placebo** | 189 | 10,845 | 11,034 |
|  | 293 | 21,778 | 22,071 |

prospective study because the treatments (aspirin versus no aspirin) were applied and then future outcome was determined. (A **retrospective study** would select people who had, or had not, experienced a heart attack and then look backward in time to see whether they had been in the habit of taking aspirin in the past.)

Definition   **Prospective study:** A study in which a treatment is administered and we look for its effects in the future.

**Retrospective study:** A study in which we selected participants on the basis of some condition and then look retrospectively at their behavior in the past.

For these data, $\chi^2 = 25.014$ on one degree of freedom, which is statistically significant at $\alpha = .05$, indicating that there is a relationship between whether or not one takes aspirin daily and whether one later has a heart attack.[2]

## d-family: Risks and Odds

Two important concepts with regard to categorical data, especially for $2 \times 2$ tables, are the concepts of risks and odds. These concepts are closely related, and often confused, but they are basically very simple.

For the aspirin data, .94% (104/11,037) of people in the aspirin group and 1.71% (189/11,034) of those in the control group suffered a heart attack during the study. (Unless you are a middle-aged male worrying about your health, the numbers look rather small. But they are important.) These two statistics are commonly referred to as **risk** estimates because they describe the risk that someone with, or without, aspirin will suffer a heart attack. Risk measures offer a useful way of looking at the size of an effect.

Definition   **Risk:** The number of people or objects experiencing an event divided by the total number of people or objects. For example, the frequency of success divided by the total number of observations.

**Risk difference:** The difference in the risks for two groups.

The **risk difference** is simply the difference between the two proportions. In our example, the difference is 1.71% − .94% = .77%. Thus, there is about three-quarters of a percentage point difference between the two conditions. Put another way, the difference in risk between a male taking aspirin and one not taking aspirin is about three quarters of 1%. This may not appear to be very large, but keep in mind that we are talking about heart attacks, which are serious events.

---

[2]It is important to note that, although taking aspirin daily is associated with a lower rate of heart attack, more recent data have shown that there are important negative side effects. Current literature suggests that Omega-3 fish oil may be at least as effective with fewer side effects.

One problem with a risk difference is that its magnitude depends on the overall level of risk. Heart attacks are quite low-risk events, so we would not expect a huge difference between the two conditions. (In contrast, Pugh (1983) studied conviction for rape depending on whether the *victim* was portrayed as being at fault. The probability of being convicted in either event was quite high, so there was a lot of room for the two conditions to differ. He found 30 percentage point difference in favor of conviction when the victim was not portrayed as at fault. Does that mean that Pugh's study found a much larger effect size than the aspirin study? Well, it depends—it certainly did with respect to risk difference.)

Another way to compare the risks is to form a **risk ratio**, also called **relative risk**, which is just the ratio of the two risks. For the heart attack data the risk ratio is

$$RR = Risk_{\text{no aspirin}}/Risk_{\text{aspirin}} = 1.71\%/.94\% = 1.819$$

Thus the risk of having a heart attack if you do not take aspirin is 1.8 times higher than if you do take aspirin. That strikes me as quite a difference.

We must consider a third measure of effect size, and that is the odds ratio. At first glance, odds and odds ratios look like risk and risk ratios, and they are often confused, even by people who know better. (Although I knew better, in a previous edition I referred to odds, but described them as risks, much to my chagrin.) Recall that we defined the risk of a heart attack in the aspirin group as the number having a heart attack divided by the *total number of people in that group*. (e.g., 104/11,037 = .0094 = .94%.) The **odds** of having a heart attack for a member of the aspirin group is the number having a heart attack divided by the number *not having a heart attack*. (e.g., 104/10,933 = .0095.) The difference (though very slight) comes in what we use as the denominator—risk uses the total sample size and is thus the proportion of people in that condition who experience a heart attack. Odds uses as a denominator the number *not* having a heart attack and is thus the ratio of the number having an attack versus the number not having an attack. Because the denominators are so much alike in this example, the results are almost indistinguishable. That is certainly not always the case. In Pugh's example, the *risk* of being convicted of rape in the low-fault condition is 153/177 = .864 (86% of the cases are convicted), whereas the *odds* of being convicted in the low-fault condition are 153/24 = 6.375 (the number of people being convicted is 6.4 times the number of people being found innocent).

---

Definition | **Risk ratio (relative risk):** The ratio of two estimates of risk.

**Odds:** The frequency of occurrence of one event divided by the frequency of occurrence of the other event. For example, the frequency of success divided by the frequency of failure.

**Odds ratio:** The ratio of two odds.

---

Just as we can form a risk ratio by dividing the two risks, we can form an **odds ratio** by dividing the two odds. For the aspirin example the odds of heart attack given that you did not take aspirin were 189/10,845 = .0174. The odds of a heart attack given that you did take aspirin were 104/10,933 = .0095. The odds ratio is simply the ratio of these two odds and is

$$OR = \frac{Odds \mid No \; Aspirin}{Odds \mid Aspirin} = \frac{.0174}{.0095} = 1.83$$

Thus, the odds of a heart attack without aspirin are 1.83 times higher than the odds of a heart attack with aspirin.[3]

Why do we have to complicate things by having both odds ratios and risk ratios? That is a very good question, and it has some good answers. Risk is something that I think most of us understand. When we say the risk of having a heart attack in the No Aspirin condition is .0171, we are saying that 1.7% of the participants in that condition had a heart attack, and that is pretty straightforward. When we say that the odds of a heart attack in that condition are .0174, we are saying that the number of people having a heart attack is 1.7% of the number of people not having a heart attack. That may be a popular way of setting bets on race horses, but it leaves me dissatisfied. So why have an odds ratio in the first place?

The odds ratio has an important point in its favor. In the first place, it can be calculated in situations in which a true risk ratio cannot be. In a retrospective study, where we find a group of people with heart attacks and another group of people without heart attacks-and then look back to see if they took aspirin, we can't really calculate *risk*. Risk is future oriented. On the other hand, if we give 1,000 people aspirin and withhold it from 1,000 others, we can look at these people 10 years down the road and calculate the risk (and risk ratio) of heart attacks. But if we take 1,000 people with (and without) heart attacks and look backward, we can't really calculate risk because we have sampled heart attack patients at far greater than their normal rate in the population (50% of our sample has had a heart attack, but certainly 50% of the population does not suffer from heart attacks). But we can always calculate odds ratios. And, when we are talking about low- probability events, such as having a heart attack, the odds ratio is usually a very good estimate of what the risk ratio would be. The odds ratio is equally valid for prospective, retrospective, and cross-sectional sampling designs. That is important.

## 19.10 A Final Worked Example

We will take as our final example a study by Geller, Witmer, and Orebaugh (1976). These authors were studying littering behavior and were interested in, among other things, whether a message about not littering would be effective if placed on the handbills often given out in supermarkets advertising the

---

[3]In computing an odds ratio, there is no rule about which odds go in the numerator and which in the denominator. It depends on convenience. Where reasonable, I prefer to put the larger value in the numerator to make the ratio come out greater than 1.0, simply because I find it easier to talk about that way. If we reversed them in this example, we would find OR = .546, and conclude that your odds of having a heart attack in the aspirin condition are about half of what they are in the No Aspirin condition. That is simply the inverse of the original OR (.546 = 1/1.83).

**Table 19.4**
Data from Study by Geller, Witmer, and Orebaugh (1976)

|          | Trashcan | Litter   | Removed  | Total |
|----------|----------|----------|----------|-------|
| Control  | 41       | 385      | 477      | 903   |
|          | (61.66)  | (343.98) | (497.36) |       |
| Message  | 80       | 290      | 499      | 869   |
|          | (59.34)  | (331.02) | (478.64) |       |
| Total    | 121      | 675      | 976      | 1,772 |

daily specials. (This experiment was used in Chapter 7 to illustrate probability concepts.) To simplify a more complex study, two of Geller's conditions involved passing out handbills in a supermarket. Under one condition (Control) the handbills contained only a listing of the daily specials. In the other condition (Message), the handbills also included the notation, "Please don't litter. Please dispose of this properly." At the end of the day Geller and his students searched the store for handbills. They recorded the number found in trashcans; the number left in shopping carts, on the floor, and in various other places where they didn't belong (denoted Litter); and the number that could not be found and were apparently removed from the premises. The data obtained under the two conditions are shown in Table 19.4 and are taken from a larger table reported by Geller et al. Would you expect that such a notice on a handbill would have much effect on what *you* did with that handbill when you were finished with it?

We can analyze this contingency table appropriately by using the chi-square test because we have 1,772 independent observations falling into six mutually exclusive cells. We will test the null hypothesis that the location of the fliers at the end of the day is independent of the instructions on the flier, and we will set $\alpha = .05$.

We calculate the expected frequencies by the same procedure we have used before. Namely, for a contingency table the expected frequencies are given by $E = RT \times CT/GT$, where $RT$, $CT$, and $GT$ stand for row, column, and grand totals, respectively. Therefore, if $H_0$ were true, the expected number of fliers found in the trashcan from the Control group (the fliers without the message) would be $E_{11} = (903)(121)/1,772 = 61.66$. Similarly, the number of people who received the anti-littering message and removed their fliers would be expected to be $E_{23} = (869)(976)/1,772 = 478.64$.

The calculation of $\chi^2$ is based on the same formula we have been using all along:

$$\chi^2 = \Sigma \frac{(O - E)^2}{E}$$
$$= \frac{(41 - 61.66)^2}{61.66} + \frac{(385 - 343.98)^2}{343.98} + \cdots + \frac{(499 - 478.64)^2}{478.64}$$
$$= 25.79$$

There are 2 *df* for this analysis because $(R - 1)(C - 1) = (2 - 1)(3 - 1) = 2$. The critical value of $\chi^2_{.05}(2) = 5.99$, so we are led to reject $H_0$ and to conclude that the location in which handbills were left depended on the instructions given. In other words, Instruction and Location are not independent. From the data it is evident that when subjects were asked not to litter, a higher percentage of handbills were thrown into the trashcan or taken out of the store, and fewer were left lying in the shopping carts or on the floors and shelves.

## Writing Up the Results of the Littering Behavior Study

If you were writing up these results, you would probably want to say something like the following:

> In an attempt to investigate whether people respond to anti-littering messages on handbills, 1,772 shoppers at a local supermarket were given handbills advertising daily specials. Approximately half of these fliers contained a message asking people not to litter and to dispose of the handbill in an appropriate place, while the other half did not contain such a message. At the end of the day a count was made of the number of messages found in the trash, the number that were found as litter, and the number that were removed from the store. These were classified by the presence or absence of the message on the flier, and a chi-square test was applied to the results. For these data $\chi^2(2) = 25.79, p < .05$. Examination of the results indicated that a smaller percentage of the handbills containing the anti-littering message were found as litter, and a higher percentage were placed in the trash or removed from the store.

## 19.11 Writing Up the Results

We will take as a second example of how to write up results our example of Pugh's study of rape convictions (1983). It is a good example because the question is timely and the statistics are straightforward. If you were writing up those results, you would probably want to say something like the following:

> In examining the question of whether a defense lawyer's attempt to place blame on the victim of rape would influence a jury's decision in a rape case, jury participants were presented with a situation in which the victim was characterized by the defense as either partly responsible for the rape or not responsible. The jurors were then asked to make a judgment about whether the defendant was guilty or not guilty of the crime. When the victim was portrayed as low in fault, 86% of the time the defendant was judged to be guilty. When the victim was portrayed as high in fault, the defendant was judged guilty only 58% of the time. A chi-square test of

the relationship between Fault and Guilt produced $\chi^2(1) = 35.93$, which is statistically significant at $p < .05$. This is associated with an odds ratio of 4.61, indicating that the odds of being found guilty of rape are more than four and a half times higher in the condition in which the victim is portrayed as not bearing fault for the rape. The odds ratio would indicate that we are speaking of a meaningful difference between the two conditions.

## 19.12  Seeing Statistics

The applet entitled Mosaic Two-Way, which can be found on the Web site, illustrates the meaning of chi-square in a 2 × 2 contingency table. The display that follows was taken from data that McClelland originally produced, although the variable names have been changed. In this display, the bluer the rectangle, the greater the number of observations in that cell over what would be expected if the null hypothesis were true. On the other hand, the redder the rectangle the more the observations fall below expectation. (For the printed book, you can translate blue and red to darker and lighter, respectively.)

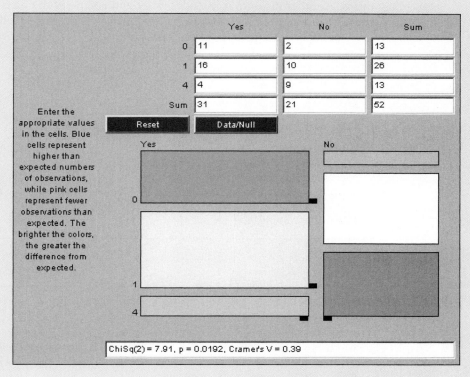

Enter the appropriate values in the cells. Blue cells represent higher than expected numbers of observations, while pink cells represent fewer observations than expected. The brighter the colors, the greater the difference from expected.

You can substitute the data from the study by Walsh on depression and anorexia. Which cells are over- and underrepresented?

You can also enter the data from Latané and Dabbs (see Section 19.6). Now which cells are over represented?

Finally, using the Latané and Dabbs example again, assume that you could add 10 observations to any one cell. Where should you add those observations to produce the greatest increase in chi-square?

## 19.13 Summary

This chapter discussed the use of the chi-square test for the analysis of frequency data. We first considered the test for goodness of fit for the situation in which there is only one variable of classification. We then dealt with the use of chi-square for testing the independence of two variables, which is the way the test is most commonly used. Next, we considered the problem of small expected frequencies and the need for the independence of observations. Finally we looked at several different kinds of measures of how large an effect we have, with special focus on risk ratios. Another measure is the odds ratio, and compares the odds of one event to the odds of the other. Odds ratios are very intuitive measures of effect size.

Some important terms in this chapter are

| | |
|---|---|
| Chi-square test, 464 | Retrospective study, 482 |
| Goodness-of-fit test, 464 | Risk, 482 |
| Expected frequencies, 466 | Risk difference, 482 |
| Multicategory case, 468 | Risk ratio (relative risk), 483 |
| Contingency table, 470 | Odds, 483 |
| Marginal totals, 471 | Odds ratio, 483 |
| Prospective study, 482 | |

## 19.14 Exercises

**19.1** The chair of a psychology department suspects that some of his faculty are more popular than others. There are three sections of Introductory Psychology (taught at 10:00 A.M, 11:00 A.M., and noon) by Professors Anderson, Klansky, and Kamm. The number of students who enroll for each section are given.

| Professor Anderson | Professor Klansky | Professor Kamm |
|---|---|---|
| 25 | 32 | 10 |

Run the appropriate chi-square test and interpret the results.

**19.2**   From the point of view of designing a valid experiment, an important difference exists between Exercise 19.1 and a similar example used in this chapter. The data in Exercise 19.1 will not really answer the question that the chair wants answered. What is the problem, and how could the experiment be improved?

**19.3**   I have a theory that if you ask participants to sort one-sentence characteristics of people (e.g., "I eat too fast") into five piles ranging from *not at all like me* to *very much like me*, the percentage of items placed in each pile will be approximately 10%, 20%, 40%, 20%, and 10% for the five piles. I have one of my children sort 50 statements and obtain the following data:

8   10   20   8   4

Do these data support my hypothesis?

**19.4**   To what population does the answer to Exercise 19.3 generalize?

**19.5**   In an old study by Clark and Clark (1939) black children were shown black dolls and white dolls and were asked to select one to play with. Out of 252 children, 169 chose the white doll and 83 chose the black doll. What can we conclude about the behavior of these children?

**19.6**   Following up the study referred to in Exercise 19.5, Hraba and Grant (1970) repeated the Clark and Clark study. The studies were not exactly equivalent, but they were close enough and the results are interesting. They found that out of 89 black children, 28 chose the white doll and 61 chose the black doll. Run the appropriate chi-square test on their data and interpret the results.

**19.7**   Combine the data from Exercises 19.5 and 19.6 into a two-way contingency table and run the appropriate test. How does the question addressed by the two-way classification differ from the questions addressed by Exercises 19.5 and 19.6?

**19.8**   We know that smoking has all sorts of ill effects on people, and among other things there is evidence that it affects fertility. Weinberg and Gladen (1986) examined the effects of smoking on the ease with which women become pregnant. They took 586 women who had planned pregnancies, and asked them how many menstrual cycles it had taken for them to become pregnant after discontinuing contraception. They also sorted the women into whether they were smokers or nonsmokers. The data follow.

|  | 1 Cycle | 2 Cycles | 3+ Cycles | Total |
|---|---|---|---|---|
| **Smokers** | 29 | 16 | 55 | 100 |
| **Nonsmokers** | 198 | 107 | 181 | 486 |
| **Total** | 227 | 123 | 236 | 586 |

Does smoking affect the ease with which women become pregnant? (I do not recommend smoking as a birth-control device.)

**19.9** How would you modify the analysis of the data in Exercise 19.8 if you also had the data on smoking behavior of the partners of these women?

**19.10** Use the data in Exercise 19.8 to demonstrate how chi-square varies as a function of sample size.
(a) Double each cell entry and recompute chi-square.
(b) What does this have to say about the role of the sample size in hypothesis testing?

**19.11** Howell and Huessy (1985) used a rating scale to classify children as to whether or not they showed Attention Deficit Disorder (ADD)-like behavior in the second grade. They then classified these same children again in the fourth and fifth grades. At the end of the ninth grade they examined school records and noted which children were enrolled in remedial English. In the following data all children who were ever classified as ADD have been combined into one group (labeled ADD):

| Classification | Remedial English | Nonremedial English | Total |
|---|---|---|---|
| Normal | 22 | 187 | 209 |
| ADD | 19 | 74 | 93 |
| Total | 41 | 261 | 302 |

Does ADD classification in elementary school predict high school enrollment in remedial and nonremedial English?

**19.12** In Exercise 19.11 children were classified as those who never showed ADD-like behavior and those who showed ADD behavior at least once in the second, fourth, or fifth grade. If we do not collapse across categories, we obtain the following data:

| Exhibition of ADD-Like Behaviors | Remedial English | Nonremedial English |
|---|---|---|
| Never | 22 | 187 |
| Grade 2 | 2 | 17 |
| Grade 4 | 1 | 11 |
| Grades 2 & 4 | 3 | 16 |
| Grade 5 | 2 | 9 |
| Grades 2 & 5 | 4 | 7 |
| Grades 4 & 5 | 3 | 8 |
| Grade 2, 4, & 5 | 4 | 6 |

(a) Run the chi-square test.
(b) What would you conclude, ignoring the small expected frequencies?
(c) How comfortable do you feel with these small expected frequencies? How might you handle the problem?

**19.13** It would be possible to calculate a one-way chi-square test on the data in column 1 of Exercise 19.12. What hypothesis would you be testing if you did that? How would that hypothesis differ from the one you tested in Exercise 19.12?

**19.14** In a study of eating disorders in female adolescents, Gross (1985) asked each of her participants whether they would prefer to gain weight, lose weight, or maintain their current weight. (*Note:* Only 12% of the girls in Gross's sample were actually more than 15% above what normative tables say they should weigh, a common cutoff for a label of "overweight.") When she broke down the data for girls by race (African-American versus white), she obtained the following results. (Other races have been omitted because of small sample sizes.)

|  | Reducers | Maintainers | Gainers | Total |
|---|---|---|---|---|
| White | 352 | 152 | 31 | 535 |
| African–American | 47 | 28 | 24 | 99 |
| Total | 399 | 180 | 55 | 634 |

(a) What conclusions can you draw from these data?

(b) Ignoring race, what conclusions can you draw about adolescent girls' attitudes toward their own weight?

**19.15** Stress has long been known to influence physical health. Visintainer, Volpicelli, and Seligman (1982) investigated the hypothesis that rats given 60 trials of inescapable shock would be less likely to later reject an implanted tumor than would rats who had received 60 trials of escapable shock or 60 no-shock trials. They obtained the following data:

|  | Inescapable Shock | Escapable Shock | No Shock | Total |
|---|---|---|---|---|
| Reject | 8 | 19 | 18 | 45 |
| No Reject | 22 | 11 | 15 | 48 |
| Total | 30 | 30 | 33 | 93 |

What would you conclude from these data?

**19.16** Suppose that in the study by Latané and Dabbs (1975) (referred to in Section 19.6), only 100 males and 100 females were involved. Compute $\chi^2$.

**19.17** What does the answer to Exercise 19.16 say about the effects of sample size on the power of an experiment?

**19.18** Dabbs and Morris (1990) examined archival data from military records to study the relationship between high testosterone levels and antisocial behavior in males. Out of the 4,016 men in the Normal testosterone group, 10.0% had a record of adult delinquency. Out of the 446 men in the High testosterone group, 22.6% had a record of adult delinquency.

(a) Create a contingency table of *frequencies,* classifying men by High and Normal testosterone levels and by Delinquency and Nondelinquency.

(b) Compute $\chi^2$ for this table.

(c) Draw the appropriate conclusions.

**19.19** In the study described in Exercise 19.18, 11.5% of the Normal testosterone group and 17.9% of the High testosterone group had a history of childhood Delinquency.

(a) Is there a significant relationship between these two variables?

(b) Interpret this relationship.

(c) How does this result expand on what we already know from Exercise 19.18?

**19.20** Let's see how students and faculty compare on a basic statistical question. Zuckerman, Hodgins, Zuckerman, and Rosenthal (1993) surveyed 550 people and asked a number of questions on statistical issues. In one question a reviewer warned a researcher that she had a high probability of a Type I error because she had a small sample size. The researcher disagreed. Participants were asked, "Was the researcher correct?" The proportions of respondents, partitioned among students, assistant professors, associate professors, and full professors, who sided with the researcher, and the total number of respondents in each category, were as follows:

|  | Students | Assistant Professors | Associate Professors | Full Professors |
|---|---|---|---|---|
| **Proportion** | .59 | .34 | .43 | .51 |
| **Sample Size** | 17 | 175 | 134 | 182 |

(*Note:* These data mean that 59% of the 17 students who responded sided with the researcher. When you calculate the actual *obtained* frequencies, round to the nearest whole person.)
(a) Who do you think was correct?
(b) What do these data tell you about differences among groups of respondents? (*Note:* The *researcher* was correct. Our tests are specifically designed to hold the probability of a Type I error at $\alpha$, regardless of the sample size. It is the probability of a Type II error that generally increases as sample size decreases.)

**19.21** The Zuckerman et al. paper referred to in the previous question hypothesized that faculty were less accurate than students because they have a tendency to give negative responses to such questions. ("There must be a trick.") How would you test such a hypothesis?

**19.22** Calculate the odds ratio for the 2 × 2 table from Exercise 19.7 that combines the data of Clark and Clark (1939) and Hraba and Grant (1970).

**19.23** Combine the data in Exercise 19.14 by adding together the Maintainers and Gainers categories. Then compute an odds ratio to say something about racial differences in high school girls' perceptions of weight.

**19.24** Use an odds ratio to clarify the results of the Dabbs and Morris study of testosterone in Exercise 19.18.

# 20

# Nonparametric and Distribution-Free Statistical Tests

## QUESTIONS

■ What's so different about a distribution-free test?

■ Is there an underlying principle to most distribution-free tests?

■ When would I prefer a distribution-free test over a parametric test?

■ Does this mean that all of the analyses I have learned so far are irrelevant?

■ What kinds of things can I do with distribution-free tests?

**M**ost of the statistical procedures we have discussed in the preceding chapters have involved the estimation of one or more parameters of the distribution of scores in the population(s) from which the data were sampled, and assumptions concerning the shape of that distribution. For example, the $t$ test makes use of the sample variance ($s^2$) as an estimate of the population variance ($\sigma^2$) and also requires the assumption that the population from which we sampled is normal (or at least that the sampling distribution of the mean is normal). Tests, such as the $t$ test, that involve assumptions either about specific parameters or about the distribution of the population are referred to as **parametric tests**.

**Parametric tests:** Statistical tests that involve assumptions about, or estimation of, population parameters.

**Nonparametric tests:** Statistical tests that do not rely on parameter estimation or precise distributional assumptions.

**Distribution-free tests:** Another name for nonparametric tests.

One class of tests, however, places less reliance on parameter estimation and/or distribution assumptions. Such tests usually are referred to as **nonparametric tests** or **distribution-free tests**. By and large if a test is nonparametric, it is also distribution-free; in fact, it is the distribution-free nature of the test that is most valuable to us. Although the two names often are used interchangeably, these tests will be referred to here as distribution-free tests.

The argument over the value of distribution-free tests has gone on for many years, and it certainly cannot be resolved in this chapter. Many experimenters feel that, for the vast majority of cases, parametric tests are sufficiently robust (unaffected by violations of assumptions) to make distribution-free tests unnecessary. Others, however, believe just as strongly in the unsuitability of parametric tests and the overwhelming superiority of the distribution-free approach. (Bradley, 1968, is a forceful and articulate spokesman for the latter group, even though his book on the subject is nearly 40 years old.) Regardless of the position you take on this issue, it is important that you are familiar with the most common distribution-free procedures and their underlying rationale. These tests are too prevalent in the experimental literature simply to be ignored.

The major advantage generally attributed to distribution-free tests is also the most obvious—they do not rely on any seriously restrictive assumptions concerning the shape of the sampled population(s). This is not to say that distribution-free tests do not make *any* distribution assumptions, only that the assumptions they do require are far more general than those required for the parametric tests. The exact null hypothesis being tested may depend, for example, on whether two populations are symmetric or have a similar shape. None of these tests, however, makes an *a priori* assumption about the specific shape of the distribution; that is, the validity of the test is not affected by whether the distribution of the variable in the population is normal. A parametric test, on the other hand, usually includes some type of normality assumption; if that assumption is false, the conclusions drawn from the test may be inaccurate. Another characteristic of distribution-free tests that often acts as an advantage is that many of them, especially the ones discussed in this chapter, are more sensitive to medians than to means. Thus if the nature of your data is such that you are interested primarily in medians, the tests presented here may be particularly useful to you.

Those who favor using parametric tests in every case do not deny that the distribution-free tests are more liberal in the assumptions they require. They do argue, however, that the assumptions normally cited as being required of parametric tests are overly restrictive in practice and that the parametric tests are remarkably unaffected by violations of distribution assumptions.

The major disadvantage generally attributed to distribution-free tests is their lower power relative to the corresponding parametric test. In general, *when the assumptions of the parametric test are met*, the distribution-free test requires more observations than the comparable parametric test for the same level of power. Thus for a given set of data the parametric test is more likely to lead to rejection of a false null hypothesis than is the corresponding distribution-free test. Moreover, even when the distribution assumptions are violated to a moderate degree, the parametric tests are thought to maintain their advantage.

It often is claimed that the distribution-free procedures are particularly useful because of the simplicity of their calculations. However, for an experimenter who has just invested six months collecting data, a difference of five minutes in computation time hardly justifies the use of a less desirable test. Moreover, since most people run their analyses using computer software, the difference in ease of use disappears completely.

There is one other advantage of distribution-free tests. Because many of them rank the raw scores and operate on those ranks, they offer a test of differences in central tendency that are not affected by one or a few very extreme scores (outliers). An extreme score in a set of data actually can make the parametric test *less* powerful because it inflates the variance and hence the error term, as well as biasing the mean by shifting it toward the outlier (the latter may increase or decrease the difference between means).

In this chapter we will be concerned with four of the most important distribution-free methods. The first two are analogues of the *t* test, one for independent samples and one for matched samples. The next two tests are distribution-free analogues of the analysis of variance, the first for *k* independent groups and the second for *k* repeated measures. All these tests are members of a class known as **rank-randomization tests** because they deal with ranked data and take as the distribution of their test statistic, when the null hypothesis is true, the theoretical distribution of randomly distributed ranks. I'll come back to this idea shortly. Because these tests convert raw data to ranks, the shape of the underlying distribution of scores in the population becomes less important. Thus both the sets

11   14   15   16   17   22
(data that might have come from a normal distribution)

and

11   12   13   30   31   32
(data that might have come from a bimodal distribution)

reduce to the ranks

1   2   3   4   5   6

---

Definition   **Rank-randomization tests:** A class of nonparametric tests based on the theoretical distribution of randomly assigned ranks.

---

The use of methods based on ranks is not the only approach when we are concerned about nonnormality, though it is the most common. Wilcox (2003) has an extensive discussion of newer alternative methods (often relying on the trimming of samples), though there is not space to discuss those methods here.

## 20.1 The Mann–Whitney Test

One of the most common and best known of the distribution-free tests is the **Mann–Whitney test** for two independent samples. This test often is thought of as the distribution-free analogue of the $t$ test for two independent samples, although it tests a slightly different, and broader, null hypothesis. Its null hypothesis is the hypothesis that the two samples were drawn at random from identical populations (not just populations with the same mean), but it is especially sensitive to population differences in central tendency. Thus rejection of $H_0$ generally is interpreted to mean that the two distributions had different central tendencies, but it is possible that rejection actually resulted from some other difference between the populations. Notice that when we gain one thing (freedom from assumptions), we pay for it with something else (loss of specificity).

Definition
| **Mann–Whitney test:** A nonparametric test for comparing the central tendency of two independent samples. |
| --- |

The Mann–Whitney test is a variation on a test originally devised by Wilcoxon called the Rank-Sum test. Because Wilcoxon also devised another test, to be discussed in the next section, we will refer to this version as the Mann–Whitney test to avoid confusion. Although the test as devised by Mann and Whitney used a slightly different test statistic, the statistic used in this chapter (the sum of the ranks of the scores in one of the groups) is often advocated because it is much easier to calculate. Either test statistic would lead to exactly the same conclusion when applied to the same set of data.

The logical basis of the Mann–Whitney test is particularly easy to understand. Assume that we have two independent treatment groups, with $n_1$ observations in Group 1 and $n_2$ observations in Group 2. To make it concrete, assume that there are eight observations in each group. Further assume that we don't know whether or not the null hypothesis is true, but we happen to obtain the following data:

**Raw Scores**

| Group 1 | 18 | 16 | 17 | 21 | 15 | 13 | 24 | 20 |
| --- | --- | --- | --- | --- | --- | --- | --- | --- |
| Group 2 | 35 | 38 | 31 | 27 | 37 | 26 | 28 | 25 |

Well, it looks as if Group 2 outscored Group 1 by a substantial margin. Now suppose that we rank the data from lowest to highest, without regard to group membership.

**Ranked Scores**

| Group 1 | 5 | 3 | 4 | 7 | 2 | 1 | 8 | 6 | Σ Ranks = 36 |
|---------|----|----|----|----|----|----|----|----|--------------|
| Group 2 | 14 | 16 | 13 | 11 | 15 | 10 | 12 | 9 | Σ Ranks = 100 |

Look at that! The lowest 8 ranks ended up in Group 1 and the highest 8 ranks ended up in Group 2. That doesn't look like a very likely event if the two populations don't differ.

We could calculate how often such a result would happen if we really need to, and if you are very patient. Although it could be done mathematically, we could do it empirically by taking 16 balls and writing the numbers 1 through 16 on them, corresponding to the 16 ranks. (We don't have to worry about actual scores, because we are going to replace scores with ranks anyway.) Now we will toss all of the balls into a bucket, shake the bucket thoroughly, pull out 8 balls (as if we were looking at the ranks for Group 1), record the sum of the numbers on those balls, toss them back into the bucket, shake and draw again, record the sum of the numbers, and continue that process all night. By the next morning we will have drawn an awful lot of samples, and we can look at the values we recorded and make a frequency distribution of them. This will tell us how often we had a sum of the ranks of only 36, how often the sum was 37, how often it was 50, or 60, or 90, or whatever. Now we really are finished. We know that if we just draw ranks out at random, only very rarely will we get a sum as small as 36. (A simple calculation shows that an outcome as extreme as ours would be expected to occur only one time out of 12,870, for a probability of .00008.) If the null hypothesis is really true, then there should be no *systematic* reason for the first group to have only the lowest ranks. It should have ranks that are about like those of the second group. If the ranks in Group 1 are improbably low, that is evidence against the null hypothesis.

I mentioned above that this is a "rank randomization" test, and what we have just done illustrates where the name comes from. We run the test by looking at what would happen if we randomly assigned scores (or actually ranks) to groups, even if we don't actually go through the process of doing the random assignment ourselves. (We have tables that do that for us.)

Now consider the case in which the null hypothesis is true and the scores for the two groups were sampled from identical populations. In this situation if we were to rank all $N$ scores without regard to group membership, we would expect some low ranks and some high ranks in each group, and the sum of the ranks assigned to Group 1 would be roughly equal to the sum of the ranks assigned to Group 2. Reasonable results for the situation with a true null hypothesis are illustrated.

**Raw Scores**

| Group 1 | 31 | 16 | 17 | 28 | 15 | 38 | 24 | 20 |
|---------|----|----|----|----|----|----|----|----|
| Group 2 | 35 | 13 | 18 | 27 | 37 | 26 | 21 | 25 |

Now it looks as if Group 2 scores are not a lot different from Group 1 scores. We can rank the data across both groups.

**Ranked Scores**

Group 1    13  3  4  12    2  16  8  6    $\Sigma$ Ranks = 64

Group 2    14  1  5  11  15  10  7  9    $\Sigma$ Ranks = 72

Here the sum of the ranks in Group 1 is not much different from the sum of the ranks in Group 2, and a sum like that would occur quite often if we just drew ranks at random.

Mann and Whitney (and Wilcoxon) based their tests on the logic just described, using the sum of the ranks in one of the groups as the test statistic. If that sum is too small relative to the other sum, we will reject the null hypothesis. More specifically, we will take as our test statistic the sum of the ranks assigned to the *smaller* group, or if $n_1 = n_2$, the *smaller* of the two sums. Given this value, we can use tables of the Mann–Whitney statistic ($W_S$) to test the null hypothesis. (They needed only one of the sums, because with a fixed set of numbers [ranks], the sum of the ranks in one group is directly related to the sum of the ranks in the other group. If one sum is high, the other must be low.)

To take a specific example, consider the data in Table 20.1 on the number of recent stressful life events reported by a group of cardiac patients in a local hospital and a control group of orthopedic patients in the same hospital. It is well known that stressful life events (marriage, new job, death of a spouse, etc.) are associated with illness, and it is reasonable to expect that many cardiac patients would have experienced more recent stressful events than orthopedic patients (who just happened to break an ankle while tearing down a building or a collarbone while skiing). It would appear from the data that this expectation is borne out. Because we have some reason to suspect that life stress scores probably are not symmetrically distributed in the population (especially for cardiac patients if our research hypothesis is true), we will choose to use a distribution-free test. In this case we will use the Mann–Whitney test because we have two independent groups.

To apply the Mann–Whitney test, we first rank all 11 scores from lowest to highest, *assigning tied ranks to tied scores*. The orthopedic group is the smaller of the two, and if those patients generally have had fewer recent stressful life events, then the sum of the ranks assigned to that group would be relatively low. Letting

## Table 20.1
Stressful Life Events Reported by Cardiac and Orthopedic Patients

|  | Cardiac Patients | | | | | | Orthopedic Patients | | | | |
|---|---|---|---|---|---|---|---|---|---|---|---|
| **Data** | 32 | 8 | 7 | 29 | 5 | 0 | 1 | 2 | 2 | 3 | 6 |
| **Ranks** | 11 | 9 | 8 | 10 | 6 | 1 | 2 | 3.5 | 3.5 | 5 | 7 |

$W_S$ stand for the sum of the ranks in the smaller group (the orthopedic group), we find

$$W_S = 2 + 3.5 + 3.5 + 5 + 7 = 21$$

We can evaluate the obtained value of $W_S$ by using Table D.8 in the Appendix D, which gives the *smallest* value of $W_S$ we would expect to obtain by chance if the null hypothesis were true. From Table D.8 we find that for $n_1 = 5$ subjects in the smaller group and $n_2 = 6$ subjects in the larger group ($n_1$ is *always* used to represent the number of subjects in the smaller group) the entry for $\alpha = .025$ (one-tailed) is 18. This means that for a difference between groups to be significant at the two-tailed .05 level (or the one-tailed .025 level), $W_S$ must be less than or equal to 18. Because we found $W_S$ to be 21, we cannot reject $H_0$. (By way of comparison, if we ran a $t$ test on these data, ignoring the fact that one sample variance is almost 50 times the other and that the data suggest that our prediction of the shape of the distribution of cardiac scores may be correct, $t$ would be 1.52 on 9 $df$, which is also a nonsignificant result.)

As an aside, I should point out that we would have rejected $H_0$ if our value of $W_S$ was *smaller* than the tabled value. Until now you have been rejecting $H_0$ when the obtained test statistic was *larger* than the corresponding tabled value. When we work with nonparametric tests the tables are usually set up to lead to rejection for small obtained values. If I were redesigning statistical procedures, I would set the tables up differently, but nobody asked me. Just get used to the fact that parametric tables are set up such that you reject $H_0$ for *large* obtained values, and nonparametric tables are often set up so that you reject for *small* values. That's just the way it is.

The entries in Table D.8 are for a one-tailed test and will lead to rejection of the null hypothesis only if the sum of the ranks for the smaller group is sufficiently *small*. It is possible, however, that the larger ranks could be congregated in the smaller group, in which case if $H_0$ is false, the sum of the ranks would be larger than chance expectation rather than smaller. One rather awkward way around this problem would be to rank the data all over again, this time ranking from high to low, rather than from low to high. If we did that, the smaller ranks would appear in the smaller group, and we could proceed as before. We do not have to go through the process of reranking data, however. We can accomplish the same thing by making use of the symmetric properties of the distribution of the rank sum by calculating a statistic called $W_S'$. $W_S'$ is the sum of the ranks for the smaller group *that we would have found if we had reversed our ranking* and ranked from highest to lowest:

$$W_S' = 2\overline{W} - W_S$$

where $2\overline{W} = n_1(n_1 + n_2 + 1)$ and is tabled in Table D.8 in Appendix D. We then can evaluate $W_S$ against the tabled value and have a one-tailed test on the *upper* tail of the distribution. For a two-tailed test of $H_0$ (which is what we normally want) we calculate both $W_S$ and $W_S'$, enter the table with whichever is smaller, and double the listed value of $\alpha$.

For an illustration of $W_S$ and $W_S'$, consider the following two sets of data:

**Set 1**

| | Group 1 | | | | Group 2 | | | | |
|---|---|---|---|---|---|---|---|---|---|
| $X$ | 2 | 15 | 16 | 19 | 18 | 23 | 25 | 37 | 82 |
| Ranks | 1 | 2 | 3 | 5 | 4 | 6 | 7 | 8 | 9 |

$W_S = 11 \quad W_S' = 29$

**Set 2**

| | Group 1 | | | | Group 2 | | | | |
|---|---|---|---|---|---|---|---|---|---|
| $X$ | 60 | 40 | 24 | 21 | 23 | 18 | 15 | 14 | 4 |
| Ranks | 9 | 8 | 7 | 5 | 6 | 4 | 3 | 2 | 1 |

$W_S = 29 \quad W_S' = 11$

Notice that the two data sets exhibit the same degree of *extremeness*, in the sense that for the first set four of the five lowest ranks are in Group 1, and in the second set four of the five highest ranks are in Group 1. Moreover, $W_S$ for Set 1 is equal to $W_S'$ for Set 2 and vice versa. Thus if we establish the rule that we will calculate both $W_S$ and $W_S'$ for the *smaller* group and refer the *smaller* of $W_S$ and $W_S'$ to the tables, we will have a two-tailed test and will come to the same conclusion with respect to the two data sets.

## The Normal Approximation

Table D.8 in Appendix D is suitable for all cases in which $n_1$ and $n_2$ are less than or equal to 25. For larger values of $n_1$ and/or $n_2$ we can make use of the fact that the distribution of $W_S$ approaches a normal distribution as sample sizes increase. This distribution has

$$\text{Mean} = \frac{n_1(n_1 + n_2 + 1)}{2}$$

and

$$\text{Standard error} = \sqrt{\frac{n_1 n_2(n_1 + n_2 + 1)}{12}}$$

Because the distribution is normal and we know its mean and its standard deviation (the standard error), we can calculate $z$:

$$z = \frac{\text{Statistic} - \text{Mean}}{\text{Standard error}} = \frac{W_S - \dfrac{n_1(n_1 + n_2 + 1)}{2}}{\sqrt{\dfrac{n_1 n_2(n_1 + n_2 + 1)}{12}}}$$

and obtain from the tables of the normal distribution an approximation of the true probability of a value of $W_S$ at least as low as the one obtained.

To illustrate the computations for the case in which the larger ranks fall into the smaller group and to illustrate the use of the normal approximation (although we don't really need to use an approximation for such small sample sizes), consider the data in Table 20.2. These data are hypothetical (but reasonable) data on the birthweights (in grams) of children born to mothers who did not seek prenatal care until the third trimester, and of children born to mothers who received prenatal care starting in the first trimester.

For the data in Table 20.2 the sum of the ranks in the smaller group equals 100. From Table D.8 in Appendix D we find $2\overline{W} = 152$; thus $W_S' = 2\overline{W} - W_S = 52$. Because 52 is smaller than 100, we go to Table D.8 with $W_S = 52$, $n_1 = 8$, and $n_2 = 10$. (Remember, $n_1$ is defined as the smaller sample size.) Because we want a two-tailed test, we will double the column headings for $\alpha$. The critical value of $W_S$ (or $W_S'$) for a two-tailed test at $\alpha = .05$ is 53, meaning that only 5% of the time would we expect a value of $W_S$ or $W_S'$ less than or equal to 53 when $H_0$ is true. Our obtained value of $W_S$ is 52, which falls into the rejection region, so we will reject $H_0$. We will conclude that mothers who do not receive prenatal care until the third trimester tend to give birth to smaller babies. This probably does not mean that not having care until the third trimester causes smaller babies, but only that variables associated with delayed care (e.g., young mothers, poor nutrition, and poverty) also are associated with lower birthweight.

The use of the normal approximation for evaluating $W_S$ is illustrated in the lower section of Table 20.2. Here we find that $z = 2.13$. From Table D.10 in Appendix D we find that the probability of $W_S$ or $W_S'$ at least as small as 52 (a $z$ at least as extreme as $\pm 2.13$) is $2(.0166) = .033$. Because this value is smaller than our traditional cutoff of $\alpha = .05$, we will reject $H_0$ and again conclude that there is sufficient evidence to say that failing to seek early prenatal care is related to lower birthweight. Note that both the exact solution and the normal approximation lead to the same conclusion with respect to $H_0$. (With the normal approximation it is not necessary to calculate and use $W_S'$ because use of $W_S$ will lead to the same value of $z$ except for the reversal of its sign. It would be instructive for you to calculate Student's $t$ test for the same set of data.)

## The Treatment of Ties

When the data contain tied scores, any test that relies on ranks is likely to be somewhat distorted. There are several different ways of dealing with ties. You can assign tied ranks to tied scores (as we have been doing), you can flip a coin and assign

**Table 20.2**
Data on Birthweight of Infants Born to Mothers with Different Levels of Prenatal Care

| Beginning of Care | | | |
|---|---|---|---|
| Third Trimester | | First Trimester | |
| Birthweight | Rank | Birthweight | Rank |
| 1,680 | 2 | 2,940 | 10 |
| 3,830 | 17 | 3,380 | 16 |
| 3,110 | 14 | 4,900 | 18 |
| 2,760 | 5 | 2,810 | 9 |
| 1,700 | 3 | 2,800 | 8 |
| 2,790 | 7 | 3,210 | 15 |
| 3,050 | 12 | 3,080 | 13 |
| 2,660 | 4 | 2,950 | 11 |
| 1,400 | 1 | | |
| 2,775 | 6 | | |

$$W_S = \Sigma \text{ (ranks in Group 2)} = 100$$

$$W_S' = 2\overline{W} - W_S = 152 - 100 = 52$$

$$z = \frac{W_S - \dfrac{n_1(n_1 + n_2 + 1)}{2}}{\sqrt{\dfrac{n_1 n_2(n_1 + n_2 + 1)}{12}}}$$

$$= \frac{100 - \dfrac{8(8 + 10 + 1)}{2}}{\sqrt{\dfrac{8(10)(8 + 10 + 1)}{12}}}$$

$$= \frac{100 - 76}{\sqrt{126.6667}} = 2.13$$

consecutive ranks to tied scores, or you can assign untied ranks in whatever way will make it hardest to reject $H_0$. In actual practice most people simply assign tied ranks. Although that may not be the statistically best way to proceed, it is the most common and the method we will use here.

## The Null Hypothesis

The Mann–Whitney test evaluates the null hypothesis that the two sets of scores were sampled from identical populations. This is broader than the null hypothesis tested by the corresponding $t$ test, which dealt specifically with means (primarily as a result of the underlying assumptions that ruled out other sources of difference). If the two populations are assumed to have the same shape and dispersion, then the null hypothesis tested by the Mann–Whitney test would actually deal with the central tendency (in this case the medians) of the two populations; if the populations are also symmetric, the test will be a test of means. In any event the Mann–Whitney test is particularly sensitive to differences in central tendency.

## 20.2 Wilcoxon's Matched-Pairs Signed-Ranks Test

Wilcoxon is credited with developing the most popular distribution-free test for independent groups, which I referred to as the Mann–Whitney test to avoid confusion and because of their work on it. He also developed the most popular test for matched groups (or paired scores). This test is the distribution-free analogue of the *t* test for related samples. It tests the null hypothesis that two related (matched) samples were drawn either from identical populations or from symmetric populations with the same mean. More specifically it tests the null hypothesis that the distribution of difference scores (in the population) is symmetric about zero. This is the same hypothesis tested by the corresponding *t* test when that test's normality assumption is met.

The logic behind **Wilcoxon's matched-pairs signed-ranks test** is straightforward and can be illustrated with an example of a study of schizophrenia and subcortical structures by Suddath, Christison, Torrey, Casanova, and Weinberger (1990). Bleuler (1911) originally described schizophrenia has being characterized by a lack of connections between associations in memory. The hippocampus has been suggested as playing an important role in memory storage and retrieval, and it is reasonable to ask if differences in hippocampal structures (particularly size) could play a role in schizophrenia. Suddath et al. obtained MRI scans on the brains of 15 schizophrenic individuals and their monozygotic (identical) twins. They measured the volume of each brain's left hippocampus. Because there are many things that control the volume of cortical and subcortical structures, Suddath used monozygotic twin pairs in an effort to control as many of these as possible and to reduce the amount of variance to be explained. The results appear in Table 20.3 as taken from Ramsey and Schafer (1997).

Definition    **Wilcoxon's matched-pairs signed-ranks test:** A nonparametric test for comparing the central tendency of two matched (related) samples.

If you plot the difference scores shown in Figure 20.1 for these 15 twin pairs, you will note that the distribution is far from normal. With so few observations it is not feasible to make a definitive statement about normality, but I would not like to have to defend that idea that these are normally distributed observations. For that reason I would prefer to rely on a distribution-free test for paired observations, and that test is the Wilcoxon matched-pairs signed-ranks test, which is based, as its name suggests, on the ranks of the differences rather than their numerical values.

If schizophrenia is associated with lower (or higher) volume for the left hippocampus. we would expect most of the twin pairs to show a lower (or higher) volume for the schizophrenic twin and thus a predominantly positive (or negative)

**Table 20.3**
Data on Volume (in cm³) of Left Hippocampus in Schizophrenic and Nonschizophrenic Twin Pairs

| Pair | Normal | Schizophrenic | Difference | Rank | Signed Rank |
|------|--------|---------------|------------|------|-------------|
| 1 | 1.94 | 1.27 | .67 | 15 | 15 |
| 2 | 1.44 | 1.63 | −.19 | 9 | −9 |
| 3 | 1.56 | 1.47 | .09 | 5 | 5 |
| 4 | 1.58 | 1.39 | .19 | 10 | 10 |
| 5 | 2.06 | 1.93 | .13 | 8 | 8 |
| 6 | 1.66 | 1.26 | .40 | 12 | 12 |
| 7 | 1.75 | 1.71 | .04 | 3 | 3 |
| 8 | 1.77 | 1.67 | .10 | 6 | 6 |
| 9 | 1.78 | 1.28 | .50 | 13 | 13 |
| 10 | 1.92 | 1.85 | .07 | 4 | 4 |
| 11 | 1.25 | 1.02 | .23 | 11 | 11 |
| 12 | 1.93 | 1.34 | .59 | 14 | 14 |
| 13 | 2.04 | 2.02 | .02 | 1 | 1 |
| 14 | 1.62 | 1.59 | .03 | 2 | 2 |
| 15 | 2.08 | 1.97 | .11 | 7 | 7 |

$T+ = \Sigma \text{ (Positive ranks)} = 111$
$T- = \Sigma \text{ (Negative ranks)} = -9$

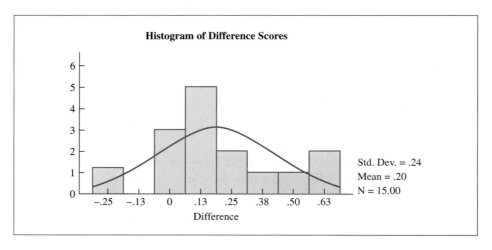

**Figure 20.1**
Distribution of differences between schizophrenic and normal twins.

difference. We also would expect twin pairs who broke this pattern to differ only slightly in the opposite direction from the trend. On the other hand, if schizio-phrenia has nothing to do with volume, we would expect about one-half of the difference scores to be positive and one-half to be negative, with the positive differences about as large as the negative ones. In other words, if $H_0$ is really true, we would no longer expect most changes to be in the predicted direction with only small changes in the unpredicted direction. Notice that I have deliberately phrased this paragraph for a two-tailed (nondirectional) test. For a directional test you would simply remove the phrases in parentheses.

In carrying out the Wilcoxon matched-pairs signed-ranks test we first calculate the difference score for each pair of measurements. We then rank all difference scores without regard to the sign of the difference, give the algebraic sign of the differences to the ranks themselves, and finally sum the positive and negative ranks separately. The data in Table 20.3 present the numerical scores (in $cm^3$) for the 15 schizophrenic participants and their twins in columns two and three. The fourth column shows the differences between the twins, with these differences ranked (without regard to sign) in the fifth column. Although the difference for pair 2 is the smallest number in column four ($-.19$), and would normally be ranked 1, when we drop its sign and look only at the size of the difference (.19), and not its direction, it is the  ninth-smallest difference. The last column shows the ranks found in column five with the sign of the difference applied. The test statistic ($T$) is taken as the smaller of the absolute values (i.e., dropping the sign) of the two sums and is evaluated against Table D.7 in Appendix D. (It is important to note that in calculating $T$ we attach algebraic signs to the ranks only for convenience. We could just as easily, for example, circle those ranks that went with lower volume for the normal twin and underline those that went with higher volume for the normal twin. We are merely trying to differentiate between the two cases.)

For the data in Table 20.3 only one of the pairs had the normal twin with a smaller volume than the schizophrenic twin. Although that was the ninth-largest difference, it was still only one case. All other pairs showed a difference in the other direction. The sum of the positive ranks ($T+$) = 111 and the sum of the negative ranks ($T-$) = $-9$. Because $T$ is defined as the smaller absolute value of $T+$ and $T-$, $T = 9$.

To evaluate $T$, we refer to Table D.7, a portion of which is shown in Table 20.4. The format of this table is somewhat different from that of the other tables we have seen. The easiest way to understand what the entries in the table represent is by way of an analogy. Suppose that to test the fairness of a coin, you were going to flip it eight times and reject the null hypothesis, at $\alpha = .05$ (one-tailed), if there were too few heads. Out of eight flips of a coin there is no set of outcomes that has a probability of exactly .05 under $H_0$. The probability of one or fewer heads is .0352, and the probability of two or fewer heads is .1445. Thus if we want to work at $\alpha = .05$, we can either reject for one or fewer heads, in which case the probability of a Type I error is actually .0352 (less than .05), or we can reject for two or fewer heads, in which case the probability of a Type I error is actually .1445 (much greater than .05). Do you see where we are going? The same kind of problem arises with $T$ because it is a discrete distribution. No value has a probability of exactly the desired $\alpha$.

**Table 20.4**
Critical Lower-Tail Values of *T* and Their Associated Probabilities
(Abbreviated Version of Table D.7)

| | Nominal $\alpha$ (One-Tailed) | | | | | | | |
|---|---|---|---|---|---|---|---|---|
| | .05 | | .025 | | .01 | | .005 | |
| *N* | *T* | $\alpha$ | *T* | $\alpha$ | *T* | $\alpha$ | *T* | $\alpha$ |
| 5 | 0 | .0313 | | | | | | |
| | 1 | .0625 | | | | | | |
| 6 | 2 | .0469 | 0 | .0156 | | | | |
| | 3 | .0781 | 1 | .0313 | | | | |
| 7 | 3 | .0391 | 2 | .0234 | 0 | .0078 | | |
| | 4 | .0547 | 3 | .0391 | 1 | .0156 | | |
| 8 | 5 | .0391 | 3 | .0195 | 1 | .0078 | 0 | .0039 |
| | 6 | .0547 | 4 | .0273 | 2 | .0117 | 1 | .0078 |
| 9 | 8 | .0488 | 5 | .0195 | 3 | .0098 | 1 | .0039 |
| | 9 | .0645 | 6 | .0273 | 4 | .0137 | 2 | .0059 |
| 10 | 10 | .0420 | 8 | .0244 | 5 | .0098 | 3 | .0049 |
| | 11 | .0527 | 9 | .0322 | 6 | .0137 | 4 | .0068 |
| ... | ... | ... | ... | ... | ... | ... | ... | ... |
| 15 | 30 | .0473 | 25 | .0240 | 19 | .0090 | 15 | .0042 |
| | 31 | .0535 | 26 | .0277 | 20 | .0108 | 16 | .0051 |

In Table D.7 we find that for a one-tailed test at $\alpha = .025$ (or a two-tailed test at $\alpha = .05$) with $n = 15$ the entries are 25 [.0240] and 26 [.0277]. This tells us that if we want to work at a (one-tailed) $\alpha = .025$ (and thus a two-tailed test at $\alpha = .05$), we can reject $H_0$ either for $T \leq 25$ (in which case $\alpha$ actually equals .0240) or for $T \leq 26$ (in which case the true value of $\alpha$ is .0277). Because we want a two-tailed test, the probabilities should be doubled to 25 [.0480] and 26 [.0554]. We obtained a *T* value of 9, so we would reject $H_0$, whichever cutoff we choose. We will conclude, therefore, that we reject the null hypothesis of equal volumes for the left hippocampus for both schizophrenic and normal participants. We can see from the data that the left hippocampus is generally smaller in those suffering from schizophrenia. This is a very important finding if only in that it demonstrates that there is a physical basis underlying schizophrenia, and not simply "mistaken ways of living."

## Ties

Ties can occur in the data in two different ways. One way would be for a twin pair to have the same scores for both the normal and schizophrenic twin, leading to a difference score of zero, which has no sign. In that case we normally eliminate that pair from consideration and reduce the sample size accordingly, although this leads to some bias in the test.

We could have tied difference scores that lead to tied rankings. If both tied scores have the same sign, we can break the tie in any way we want (or assign tied ranks) without affecting the final outcome. If the scores have opposite signs, we normally assign tied ranks and proceed as usual.

## The Normal Approximation

Just as with the Mann–Whitney test, when the sample size is too large (in this case, larger than 50, which is the limit for Table D.7), a normal approximation is available to evaluate $T$. For larger sample sizes we know that the sampling distribution is approximately normally distributed with

$$\text{Mean} = \frac{n(n + 1)}{4}$$

and

$$\text{Standard error} = \sqrt{\frac{n(n + 1)(2n + 1)}{24}}$$

Thus we can calculate $z$ as

$$z = \frac{T - \dfrac{n(n + 1)}{4}}{\sqrt{\dfrac{n(n + 1)(2n + 1)}{24}}}$$

and evaluate $z$ using Table D.10. The procedure is directly analogous to that used with the Mann–Whitney test and will not be repeated here.

## 20.3  Kruskal–Wallis One-Way Analysis of Variance

The **Kruskal–Wallis one-way analysis of variance** is a direct generalization of the Mann–Whitney test to the case in which we have three or more independent groups. As such it is the distribution-free analogue of the one-way analysis of variance discussed in Chapter 16. It tests the hypothesis that all samples were drawn from identical populations and is particularly sensitive to differences in central tendency.

Definition | **Kruskal–Wallis one-way analysis of variance:** A nonparametric test analogous to a standard one-way analysis of variance.

To perform the Kruskal–Wallis test, we simply rank all scores without regard to group membership and then compute the sum of the ranks for each group. The sums are denoted by $R_j$. If the null hypothesis were true, we would expect the $R_j$s to be more or less equal (aside from differences due to the size of the samples). A measure of the degree to which the $R_j$s differ from one another is provided by

$$H = \frac{12}{N(N+1)} \sum \frac{R_j^2}{n_j} - 3(N+1)$$

where

$n_j$ = the number of observations in the $j$th group
$R_j$ = the sum of the ranks in the $j$th group
$N = \Sigma n_j$ = total sample size

and the summation is taken over all $k$ groups. $H$ is then evaluated against the $\chi^2$ distribution on $k - 1$ df. (Students frequently have problems with a statement such as "$H$ is then evaluated against the $\chi^2$ distribution on $k - 1$ df." All that it really means is that we treat $H$ as if it were a value of $\chi^2$, and look it up in the chi-square tables on $k - 1$ df.)

For an example assume that the data in Table 20.5 represent the number of simple arithmetic problems (out of 85) solved (correctly or incorrectly) in one hour

**Table 20.5**
Kruskal–Wallis Test Applied to Data on Problem Solving

| Depressant | | Stimulant | | Placebo | |
|---|---|---|---|---|---|
| Score | Rank | Score | Rank | Score | Rank |
| 55 | 9 | 73 | 15 | 61 | 11 |
| 0 | 1.5 | 85 | 18 | 54 | 8 |
| 1 | 3 | 51 | 7 | 80 | 16 |
| 0 | 1.5 | 63 | 12 | 47 | 5 |
| 50 | 6 | 85 | 18 | | |
| 60 | 10 | 85 | 18 | | |
| 44 | 4 | 66 | 13 | | |
| | | 69 | 14 | | |
| $R_i$ | 35 | | 115 | | 40 |

$$H = \frac{12}{N(N+1)} \sum_{i=1}^{k} \frac{R_i^2}{n_i} - 3(N+1)$$

$$= \frac{12}{19(20)} \left( \frac{35^2}{7} + \frac{115^2}{8} + \frac{40^2}{4} \right) - 3(19+1)$$

$$= \frac{12}{380}(2228.125) - 60$$

$$= 70.36 - 60$$

$$= 10.36$$

$$\chi_{.05}^2(2) = 5.99$$

by participants given a depressant drug, a stimulant drug, or a placebo. Notice that in the Depressant group three of the participants were too depressed to do much of anything and in the Stimulant group three of the participants ran up against the limit of 85 available problems. These data are decidedly nonnormal, and we will convert the data to ranks and use the Kruskal–Wallis test. The calculations are shown in the lower part of the table. The obtained value of $H$ is 10.36, which can be treated as a $\chi^2$ on $3 - 1 = 2$ $df$. The critical value of $\chi^2_{.05}(2)$ is found in Table D.1 in Appendix D to be 5.99. Because $10.36 > 5.99$, we can reject $H_0$ and conclude that the three drugs lead to different rates of performance. (Like other chi-square tests, this test rejects $H_0$ for *large* values of $H$. It is nonetheless a nondirectional test.)

## 20.4 Friedman's Rank Test for *k* Correlated Samples

The last test to be discussed in this chapter is the distribution-free analogue of the one-way repeated-measures analysis of variance, **Friedman's rank test for k correlated samples**. It was developed by the well-known economist Milton Friedman—in the days before he was a well-known economist. This test is closely related to a standard repeated-measures analysis of variance applied to ranks instead of raw scores. It is a test on the null hypothesis that the scores for each treatment were drawn from identical populations, and it is especially sensitive to population differences in central tendency.

Definition

> **Friedman's rank test for k correlated samples:** A nonparametric test analogous to a standard one-way repeated-measures analysis of variance.

We will base our example on a study by Foertsch and Gernsbacher (1997), who investigated the substitution of the genderless word "they" for "he" or "she." With the decrease in the acceptance of the word "he" as a gender-neutral pronoun, many writers are using the grammatically incorrect "they" in its place. (You may have noticed that in this text I have very deliberately used the less-expected pronoun, such as "he" for nurse and "she" for professor, to make the point that profession and gender are not linked. You may also have noticed that you sometimes stumbled over some of those sentences, taking longer to read them. That is what Foertsch and Gernsbacher's study was all about.) Foertsch and Gernsbacher asked participants to read sentences like "A truck driver should never drive when sleepy, even if (*he*/*she*/*they*) may be struggling to make a delivery on time, because many accidents are caused by drivers who fall asleep at the wheel." In some trials the words in parentheses were replaced by the gender-stereotypic expected pronoun, sometimes by the gender-stereotypic unexpected pronoun, and sometimes by "they." For our purposes the dependent variable will be taken as the difference in reading time between sentences with unexpected pronouns and sentences with "they." There were three kinds of sentences in this study, those in which the

### Table 20.6
Data on Reading Times as a Function of Pronoun

| Participant | 1 | 2 | 3 | 4 | 5 | 6 | 7 | 8 | 9 | 10 | 11 |
|---|---|---|---|---|---|---|---|---|---|---|---|
| Expect He/See She | 50 | 54 | 56 | 55 | 48 | 50 | 72 | 68 | 55 | 57 | 68 |
| Expect She/See He | 53 | 53 | 55 | 58 | 52 | 53 | 75 | 70 | 67 | 58 | 67 |
| Neutral/See They | 52 | 50 | 52 | 51 | 46 | 49 | 68 | 60 | 60 | 59 | 60 |

expected pronoun was male, those in which it was female, and those in which it could equally be male or female. There are several dependent variables I could use from this study, but I have chosen the effect of seeing "she" when expecting "he," the effect of seeing "he" when expecting "she," and effect of seeing "they" when the expectation is neutral. (The original study is more complete than this.) The dependent variable is the reading time/character (in milliseconds). The data in Table 20.6 have been created to have roughly the same medians as the authors' report.

Here we have repeated measures on each participant, because each participant was presented with each kind of sentence. Some people read anything more slowly than others, which is reflected in the raw data. The data are far from normally distributed, which is why I am applying a distribution-free test.

For Friedman's test the data are ranked *within each subject* from low to high. If it is easier to read neutral sentences with "they" than sentences with an unexpected pronoun, then the lowest ranks for each participant should pile up in the Neutral category. The ranked data follow.

**Raw Data**

| Participant | 1 | 2 | 3 | 4 | 5 | 6 | 7 | 8 | 9 | 10 | 11 | Sum |
|---|---|---|---|---|---|---|---|---|---|---|---|---|
| Expect He/See She | 1 | 3 | 3 | 2 | 2 | 2 | 2 | 2 | 1 | 1 | 3 | 22 |
| Expect She/See He | 3 | 2 | 2 | 3 | 3 | 3 | 3 | 3 | 3 | 2 | 2 | 29 |
| Neutral/See They | 2 | 1 | 1 | 1 | 1 | 1 | 1 | 1 | 2 | 3 | 1 | 15 |

If the null hypothesis were true, we would expect the rankings to be randomly distributed within each subject. Thus one participant might do best on sentences with an expected "he," another might do best with an expected "she," and a third might do best with an expected "they." If this were the case, the sum of the rankings in each condition (row) would be approximately equal. On the other hand, if neutral sentences with "they" are easiest, then most participants would have their lowest ranking under that condition, and the sum of the rankings for the three conditions would be decidedly unequal.

To apply Friedman's test, we rank the raw scores for each participant separately and then sum the rankings for each condition. We then evaluate the variability of the sums by computing

$$\chi_F^2 = \frac{12}{Nk(k + 1)} \sum R_j^2 - 3N(k + 1)$$

where

$R_j$ = the sum of the ranks for the $j$th condition
$N$ = the number of subjects
$k$ = the number of conditions

and the summation is taken over all $k$ conditions. This value of $\chi^2$ can be evaluated with respect to the standard $\chi^2$ distribution on $k - 1$ $df$.

For the data in Table 20.6 we have

$$\chi_F^2 = \frac{12}{Nk(k + 1)} \sum R_j^2 - 3N(k + 1)$$

$$= \frac{12}{11(3)(4)}(22^2 + 29^2 + 15^2) - 3(11)(4)$$

$$= \frac{12}{11(3)(4)}(1550) - 3(11)(4) = 140.9 - 132 = 8.9$$

The critical value of $\chi^2$ on $3 - 1 = 2$ $df$ is 5.99, so we can reject $H_0$ and conclude that reading times are not independent of conditions. People can read a neutral sentence with "they" much faster than they can read sentences wherein the gender of the pronoun conflicts with the expected gender. From additional data that Foertsch and Gernsbacher present, it is clear that "they" is easier to read than the "wrong" gender, but harder than the expected gender.

## 20.5 Measures of Effect Size

Measures of effect size are difficult to find with distribution-free statistical tests.[1] An important reason for this is because many of our effect size measures are based on the size of the standard deviation, and if the data are very badly (nonnormally) distributed, a standard deviation loses much of its meaning for this purpose. If we know that data are normally distributed, and we know that the mean for one group is a standard deviation above the mean for another group, we can estimate that about two-thirds of the participants in the second group outscore the mean of the

---

[1]Conover (1980) discusses the use of confidence intervals for nonparametric procedures.

first group. But if our data are badly skewed we lose that kind of interpretation of the effect size. Similarly, even if we don't standardize the difference between means on the basis of a standard deviation, with badly skewed data we still do not have a good understanding of what it means to say that the median of group 1 is 15 points above the median of group 2.

One effect size measure that you could use is to directly count, in your sample, the number, or better yet the percentage, of one group that outscored those in another group. For example, for the data in Table 20.2 we see that the median birthweight for those who received prenatal care in the first trimester was 3,245 grams. For those who did not receive it until the third trimester, the median weight was 2,765.5 grams. This difference was statistically significant, and all mothers in the first trimester group had infants that weighed more than the median of the third trimester mothers. (Or, to put it in the reverse, only one mother in the third trimester group gave birth to an infant that was over the median weight of the first trimester group.) Reporting an effect size in this way may not be as satisfying as reporting effect sizes using $\hat{d}$ or a related statistic, but it is certainly more informative than simply reporting that the difference was significant.

## 20.6 Writing Up the Results

I will give an example of writing up the results for the study by Suddath et al. (1990). In writing those results we want to mention briefly what the study was about and how it was conducted. Then we want to explain why we would use a distribution-free test in this situation and then go on to report the results of that test. Finally, we want to give the reader some sense of how large an effect we found.

Suddath et al. (1990) examined the size of cortical structures in schizophrenic patients and their monozygotic twins. To control for possibly confounding variables, they chose 15 pairs of monozygotic twins. Because schizophrenic patients often cannot seem to form appropriate connections between items stored in memory, the investigators were particularly interested in the hippocampus due to its role in memory storage and retrieval. The measures used in this example were the volume of the left hippocampus taken from MRI scans of the brains of the participants. Because the data were far from normally distributed—particularly the set of differences between the normal and schizophrenic siblings in each pair—the Wilcoxon matched-pairs signed-ranks test was used.

The results showed that the median difference in left hippocampus volume between normal and schizophrenic twins was 10.5 cm³, with the schizophrenic twins having the lower volume. This difference was statistically significant ($T = 9$, $p < .05$), and in all but one case out of 15 (93%) the normal twin had the larger volume, indicating a robust finding. These results strongly support the belief that there is a clear structural difference between schizophrenic and normal participants in terms of the size of at least one subcortical structure.

## 20.7 Summary

This chapter summarized briefly a set of procedures that require far less restrictive assumptions concerning the populations from which our data have been sampled. We first examined the Mann–Whitney test, which is the distribution-free analogue of the independent sample $t$ test. To perform the test we simply ranked the data and asked if the distribution of ranks resembled the distribution we would expect if the null hypothesis were true. The same general logic applies to the Wilcoxon matched-pairs signed-ranks test, which is the distribution-free test corresponding to the matched-sample $t$ test. We then discussed two distribution-free tests that are analogous to an analysis of variance on independent measures (the Kruskal–Wallis one-way analysis of variance) and repeated measures (Friedman's rank test for $k$ correlated samples). Although it is important to be familiar with these four tests simply because they are commonly used, the advantages we gain by limiting our assumptions may not be worth the loss in power that often accompanies the use of distribution-free tests. Whatever one's stand on this question, the general principle remains that the overriding concern in the use and interpretation of any statistical procedure is not statistical sophistication but common sense.

Some important terms in this chapter are

| | |
|---|---|
| Parametric tests, *494* | Kruskal–Wallis one-way analysis of variance, *507* |
| Nonparametric tests (distribution-free tests), *494* | Friedman's rank test for *k* correlated samples, *509* |
| Rank-randomization tests, *495* | |
| Mann–Whitney test, *496* | |
| Wilcoxon's matched-pairs signed-ranks test, *503* | |

## 20.8 Exercises

**20.1** McConaughy (1980) has argued that younger children organize stories in terms of simple descriptive ("and then . . .") models, whereas older children incorporate causal statements and social inferences. Suppose we asked two groups of children differing in age to summarize a story they just read. We then counted the number of statements in the summary that can be classed as inferences. The data are shown.

| Younger Children | Older Children |
|---|---|
| 0 | 4 |
| 1 | 7 |
| 0 | 6 |
| 3 | 4 |
| 2 | 8 |
| 5 | 7 |
| 2 | |

(a) Analyze these data using the two-tailed rank-sum test.
(b) What would you conclude?

**20.2** Kapp, Frysinger, Gallagher, and Hazelton (1979) have demonstrated that lesions in the amygdala can reduce certain responses commonly associated with fear (e.g., *decreases* in heart rate). If fear is really reduced by the lesion, it should be more difficult to train an avoidance response in those animals because the aversiveness of the stimulus will consequently be reduced. Assume two groups of rabbits: One group has lesions in the amygdala, and the other is an untreated control group. The following data represent the number of trials needed for each animal to learn an avoidance response.

| Group with Lesions | Control Group |
|---|---|
| 15 | 9 |
| 14 | 4 |
| 8 | 10 |
| 7 | 6 |
| 22 | 6 |
| 36 | 4 |
| 19 | 5 |
| 14 | 9 |
| 18 | 9 |
| 17 | |
| 15 | |

(a) Analyze the data using the Mann–Whitney test (two-tailed).
(b) What would you conclude?

**20.3** Repeat the analysis in Exercise 20.2 using the normal approximation.

**20.4** Repeat the analysis in Exercise 20.2 using the appropriate one-tailed test.

**20.5** Nurcombe and Fitzhenry-Coor (1979) have argued that training in diagnostic techniques should lead a clinician to generate and test more hypotheses in the process of coming to a decision about a case. Suppose we take 10 psychiatric residents who are just beginning their residency and use them as participants. We ask them to watch a videotape of an interview and to record their thoughts on the case every few minutes. We then count the number of hypotheses each resident includes in his or her written remarks. The experiment is repeated with the same residents at the end of the residency with a comparable videotape. The data are given.

Participant

|        | 1 | 2 | 3 | 4 | 5 | 6 | 7 | 8 | 9 | 10 |
|--------|---|---|---|---|---|---|---|---|---|----|
| Before | 8 | 4 | 2 | 2 | 4 | 8 | 3 | 1 | 3 | 9  |
| After  | 7 | 9 | 3 | 6 | 3 | 10| 6 | 7 | 8 | 7  |

(a) Analyze the data using Wilcoxon's matched-pairs signed-ranks test.
(b) What would you conclude?

**20.6** Referring to Exercise 20.5,
(a) Repeat the analysis using the normal approximation.
(b) How well do the two answers agree? Why don't they agree exactly?

**20.7** It has been argued that firstborn children tend to be more independent than later-born children. Suppose we develop a 25-point scale of independence and rate each of 20 firstborn children and their second-born siblings using our scale. We do this when both siblings are adults, thus eliminating obvious age effects. The data on independence are as follows (a higher score means that the person is more independent):

| Sibling Pair | First-Born | Second-Born | Sibling Pair | First-Born | Second-Born |
|---|---|---|---|---|---|
| 1 | 12 | 10 | 11 | 13 | 8 |
| 2 | 18 | 12 | 12 | 5 | 9 |
| 3 | 13 | 15 | 13 | 14 | 8 |
| 4 | 17 | 13 | 14 | 20 | 10 |
| 5 | 8 | 9 | 15 | 19 | 14 |
| 6 | 15 | 12 | 16 | 17 | 11 |
| 7 | 16 | 13 | 17 | 2 | 7 |
| 8 | 5 | 8 | 18 | 5 | 7 |
| 9 | 8 | 10 | 19 | 15 | 13 |
| 10 | 12 | 8 | 20 | 18 | 12 |

(a) Analyze the data using Wilcoxon's matched-pairs signed-ranks test.
(b) What would you conclude?

**20.8** Rerun the analysis in Exercise 20.7 using the normal approximation.

**20.9** The results in Exercise 20.7 are not quite as clear-cut as we might like. Plot the differences as a function of the firstborn's score. What does this figure suggest?

**20.10**  What is the difference between the null hypothesis tested by the Mann–Whitney test and the corresponding $t$ test?

**20.11**  What is the difference between the null hypothesis tested by Wilcoxon's matched-pairs signed-ranks test and the corresponding $t$ test?

**20.12**  One of the arguments in favor of distribution-free tests is that they are more appropriate for ordinal scale data. (This issue was addressed earlier in the book in a different context.) Give a reason why this argument is not a good one.

**20.13**  Why is rejection of the null hypothesis using a $t$ test a more specific statement than rejection of the null hypothesis using the appropriate distribution-free test?

**20.14**  Three rival professors teaching English 1 all claim the honor of having the best students. To settle the issue eight students are randomly drawn from each class and given the same exam. The exams are graded by a neutral professor who does not know which class the students came from. The data are shown.

| Professor Li | Professor Kessler | Professor Bright |
|---|---|---|
| 82 | 55 | 65 |
| 71 | 88 | 54 |
| 56 | 85 | 66 |
| 58 | 83 | 68 |
| 63 | 71 | 72 |
| 64 | 70 | 78 |
| 62 | 68 | 65 |
| 53 | 72 | 73 |

Run the appropriate test and draw the appropriate conclusions.

**20.15**  A psychologist operating a group home for delinquent adolescents needs to show that the home is successful at reducing delinquency. He samples 10 adolescents living in their own homes who have been identified by the police as having problems, 10 similar adolescents living in foster homes, and 10 adolescents living in the group home. As an indicator variable he uses truancy (number of days truant in the past semester), which is readily obtained from school records. On the basis of the following data, draw the appropriate conclusions:

| Natural Home | Foster Home | Group Home |
|---|---|---|
| 15 | 16 | 10 |
| 18 | 14 | 13 |
| 19 | 20 | 14 |
| 14 | 22 | 11 |
| 5 | 19 | 7 |
| 8 | 5 | 3 |
| 12 | 17 | 4 |
| 13 | 18 | 18 |
| 7 | 12 | 2 |

**20.16** As an alternative method of evaluating a group home, suppose we take 12 adolescents who have been declared delinquent. We take the number of days truant during each of three time periods: (1) the month before they are placed in the home, (2) the month they live in the home, and (3) the month after they leave the home. The data are as follows:

| Adolescent | Before | During | After |
|---|---|---|---|
| 1 | 10 | 5 | 8 |
| 2 | 12 | 8 | 7 |
| 3 | 12 | 13 | 10 |
| 4 | 19 | 10 | 12 |
| 5 | 5 | 10 | 8 |
| 6 | 13 | 8 | 7 |
| 7 | 20 | 16 | 12 |
| 8 | 8 | 4 | 5 |
| 9 | 12 | 14 | 9 |
| 10 | 10 | 3 | 5 |
| 11 | 8 | 3 | 3 |
| 12 | 18 | 16 | 2 |

Apply Friedman's test. What do you conclude?

**20.17** What advantage does the study described in Exercise 20.16 have over the study described in Exercise 20.15?

**20.18** It would be possible to apply Friedman's test to the data in Exercise 20.5. What would we lose if we did?

**20.19** For the data in Exercise 20.5 we could say that 3 out of 10 residents used fewer hypotheses the second time and 7 used more. We could test this with $\chi^2$. How would this differ from Friedman's test applied to those data?

**20.20** Compute a reasonable effect size measure for the data in Exercise 20.2. There are probably several different measures that you could come up with, so you should chose one that will give your reader a real sense of the role played by lesions with regard to the fear-response of the amygdala.

**20.21** The history of statistical hypothesis testing really began with a tea-tasting experiment (Fisher, 1935), so it seems fitting to use a similar example near the end of this book. The owner of a small tearoom doesn't think people really can tell the difference between the first cup made with a given tea bag and the second and third cups made with the same bag (which is why it is still a *small* tearoom). He chooses eight different brands of tea bags, makes three cups of tea with each, and then has a group of customers rate each cup on a 20-point scale (without knowing which cup is which). The data are shown here, with higher ratings indicating better tea:

| Tea Brands | Cup | | |
|---|---|---|---|
| | First | Second | Third |
| 1 | 8 | 3 | 2 |
| 2 | 15 | 14 | 4 |
| 3 | 16 | 17 | 12 |
| 4 | 7 | 5 | 4 |
| 5 | 9 | 3 | 6 |
| 6 | 8 | 9 | 4 |
| 7 | 10 | 3 | 4 |
| 8 | 12 | 10 | 2 |

Using Friedman's test, draw the appropriate conclusions.

# 21

## Choosing the Appropriate Analysis

**QUESTIONS**

- I have learned about a whole range of analyses, but what do I use where?

- Is there some sort of procedure that will get me to the right analysis?

- Is there only one correct analysis?

**M**ost of this book has been concerned with presenting and explaining procedures commonly used to describe and analyze experimental data. As important as it is for you to know *how to* apply those procedures, it is equally important for you to know *when to* apply them. One of the greatest difficulties students face when presented with real data is to know which of the many procedures they have learned is applicable to that set of data.

In Chapter 1 I presented a brief discussion of the tree diagram found on the inside cover of this book. That diagram is designed to help you consider the relevant issues involved in selecting a statistical test (the issues of the type of data, the question of relationships versus differences, the number of groups, and whether variables are independent or dependent). The tree diagram is largely self-explanatory, and it is worth your time to go over it and make sure you understand the distinctions it makes. At the same time it is difficult to use something like that diagram effectively unless you have had practice in doing so. The exercises in this chapter are designed to give you that practice.

The exercises and examples in this chapter cite research studies drawn from the published literature. Each study is an actual one that resulted in data that someone had to analyze. Your task is to identify the appropriate statistical procedure to be used in each case. In some cases several procedures could be properly applied, and in other cases there may be room for disagreement over just what procedure would be best. In some cases the appropriate procedure may simply be the calculation of one or more descriptive statistics, whereas in others—the majority—some sort of hypothesis testing is called for. You should assume that the assumptions required by the standard parametric tests have been met unless you are told otherwise. For some of the examples I have noted what the experimenter found. This is simply for your interest and is not intended to be part of the question.

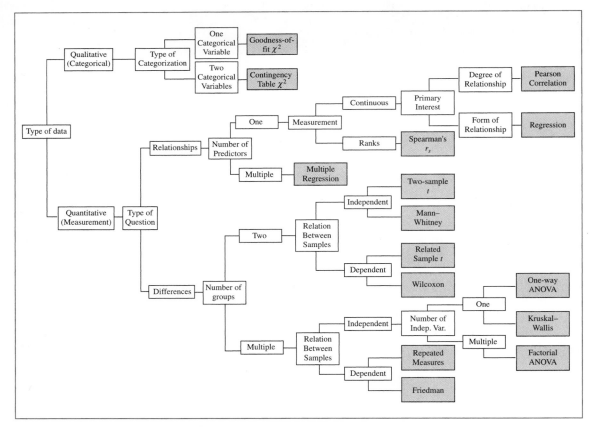

**Figure 21.1**
Decision tree

In selecting these examples I have occasionally simplified the actual experiment in minor ways, usually by omitting either independent or dependent variables. I have tried not to change the nature of the experiment in any important way. Should you be interested in following up any of these studies, they are all listed in the references. If you would like even more practice, the summaries of studies found in *PsychInfo* are excellent sources of examples.

I have supplied my answers to half of these examples in the answer section at the end of the book. As I said, there is occasionally room for disagreement over the appropriate analysis. My approach may differ from that of the original experimenter, who would have had a better grasp of the data. If your answer differs from mine, be sure you understand why I gave the answer I did and consider whether yours is just a different way of answering the same question, whether it answers an entirely different question, or whether you have failed to take something into account. The order of the questions does not correspond to the order in which various procedures were discussed in the text. This was done deliberately.

## 21.1 Exercises and Examples

**21.1** Klahr and Nigam (2004) studied the question of whether learning by "discovery" is better than direct instruction. Two groups of third- and fourth-grade children were asked to learn how to create simple experiments in which the explanatory variables were not confounded. One group designed two experiments and then received direct instruction as to the differences between good and bad experiments. A second group was allowed to explore on their own and come up with their own ways of designing unconfounded experiments. In an assessment phase children were graded as "masters" or "nonmasters" of design skills. The results showed that 77% of the 52 children receiving direct instruction became masters, whereas only 23% of the 52 discovery children did so. How would you analyze these data?

**21.2** Hygge, Evans, and Bullinger (2002) recruited four groups of children. Two of the groups lived near an airport that was just about to open, and the other two lived near an airport that was about to close. Those groups were further divided into children who were tested when there was aircraft noise present, and children who were tested when there was no aircraft noise present. The children read lists of difficult words, and the number of errors was recorded. (When the children lived near an existing airport, they performed much more poorly when noise was present. The same was not true of children who did not live near an existing airport.)

**21.3** Seligman, Nolen-Hoeksema, Thornton, and Thornton (1990) administered an optimism/pessimism scale to the members of a university swim team. They then had everyone swim their best event, and falsely reported that each person had done somewhat worse than they usually did. Half an hour later they had each person swim the same event again, and took as their dependent measure the ratio of the first time to the second. They hypothesized that more optimistic swimmers would maintain or better their (true) first time, whereas pessimists would feel there was little they could do and would do more poorly the second time around. (Their hypothesis was confirmed.)

**21.4** Do people pay any attention to the pictures included in introductory psychology textbooks? Goldstein, Bailis, and Chance (1983) presented 47 participants with a large number of pictures and asked them to pick out the ones they recognized. Many of the pictures were taken from the introductory psychology textbook the students were using. The experimenters also presented the same pictures to 56 students who were using a different text. For each participant they recorded the percentage of pictures correctly identified. In addition, they asked participants in the first group to indicate the degree to which they used textbook pictures in general as study aids. How would you analyze the data on recognition and the data on reported use of pictures?

**21.5** Franklin, Janoff-Bulman, and Roberts (1990) looked at the long-term impact of divorce on college students' levels of optimism and trust. They compared students from divorced families and students from intact families. (*Note:* They found no differences on generalized trust, but children of divorced families showed less optimism about the future of their own marriages.)

**21.6** Zaragoza and Mitchell (1996) showed participants a video tape of a burglary, and then asked them many questions about what happened. Some of the questions were deliberately misleading, such as saying "At the beginning of the scene, a young man dressed in jeans, a T-shirt, and gloves entered the house. Did he enter through the door?" In fact, the young man did *not* wear gloves. Every participant heard some misleading statements zero times, other misleading statements once, and still other misleading statements three times. The experimenters examined how often participants later reported that the video actually included those incorrect observations. (As you might expect, the more often the statements were repeated, the more often they were reported as actually occurring.)

**21.7** Suppose that we take the Seligman, et al. (1990) data from Exercise 21.3 and split the participants into three groups on the basis of their performance on the optimism scale (i.e., Optimists, Neutrals, and Pessimists). Now how would we analyze the data?

**21.8** Carli (1990) compared males and females on their use of language and their influence on their listeners. They compared male and female speakers who spoke either tentatively or assertively. They also took into account the gender of the listener. Separate groups of speakers were used for each sex of listener, and each listener heard only one speaker. The dependent variable was the perceived influence of the speaker. (*Note:* Female speakers who spoke tentatively were more influential than assertive female speakers when speaking to men, but less influential when speaking to women. Male speakers were equally influential when speaking to either group.)

**21.9** Lundberg (1983) studied the origins of what is usually called Type A behavior. He administered a questionnaire to 15 children aged 3 to 6 and scored the children with respect to the competitiveness, impatience/anger, and aggressiveness components of Type A behavior. Those above the median were classed as Type A, and those below the median were classed as Type B. (This is called a "median split.") He then measured heart rate and blood pressure during an emotional event. How should he analyze these data for each of the dependent variables? (*Note:* There were differences, but only in systolic blood pressure. Note also that using a median split is general not considered good experimental practice—though it is frequently done.)

**21.10** Pihl, Lau, and Assaad (1997) classified participants as being generally aggressive or not aggressive. These participants were randomly assigned to a drunk or sober condition, given significant amounts of alcohol or juice, and were then run in a study in which they both administered and received electrical shock from a fictitious opponent. When sober, participants in the high aggressive group administered higher shock levels than participants in the low aggressive group. When intoxicated and highly provoked, both high and low aggressive participants administered equal amounts of shock. It was the low aggressive participants who increased the aggressiveness of their behavior when they had been drinking.

**21.11**  Blair, Judd, and Chapleau (2004) studied the influence of Afrocentric facial features in criminal sentencing. After studying 216 randomly selected cases, they found that black and white inmates received roughly equal sentences after controlling for the severity of the crime. However within each group those with more predominant Afrocentric features received harsher sentences. (Interestingly, after controlling for severity of offence *and degree of Afrocentric features*, white inmates received longer sentences.)

**21.12**  Pope and Yurgelun-Todd (1996) gave a battery of standard neuropsychological tests to light and heavy users of marijuana after both had abstained from marijuana and other drugs for at least 19 hours. What analysis could they use to compare the performance of the two groups? (The results showed that "heavy users displayed significantly greater impairment than light users on attentional/executive functions.")

**21.13**  Obrzut, Hansen, and Heath (1982) identified 153 children as poor visual processors on the basis of the Matching Familiar Figures Test (MFFT). They then assigned the children to one of three treatment groups. One group received tutoring in visual information processing, another group received small-group instruction with regular classroom materials, and the third group was a control group receiving no special treatment. The dependent variable was the child's score on a second administration of the MFFT. What analysis is appropriate?

**21.14**  Many foods and beverages, such as coffee and scotch, are frequently termed "acquired tastes." Pliner (1982) was interested in investigating whether familiarity with a flavor leads to greater approval—the "acquired-taste" phenomenon. She had 24 undergraduates taste each of four unfamiliar tropical fruit juices 0, 5, 10, or 20 times. (For each participant she randomized which juice would be tasted how many times.) Participants were then asked to rate the degree to which they liked the taste of the juice. What statistical procedures are suitable for analyzing these data? What test would she use if she wanted a distribution-free test? (*Note:* She found the effect that she had expected—greater familiarity led to greater approval.)

**21.15**  Cohn, Mehl, & Pennebaker (2004) collected online diaries of over 1,000 people for the period two months prior to September 11, 2001 and two months after. Entries for each person were computer-scored for Emotional Positivity, Cognitive Processing, Social Orientation, Psychological Distancing, and Preoccupation with September 11.

**21.16**  Fagerström (1982) studied the effect of using nicotine gum as an adjunct to a standard program for giving up smoking. One group received the standard psychological treatment program normally employed by Fagerström's clinic. A second group received the same program but was also supplied with gum containing nicotine, which they were instructed to chew when they felt the need to smoke. Each group contained 50 participants, and participants were classified as abstinent or not at one month and at six months. How should he analyze his data? What problem arises from the fact that there was not a group given plain-old-candy-store gum? (*Note:* The experimental [gum] group had abstinence rates of 90% and 64% at one and six months, respectively, and the control group had rates of 60% and 45%.)

**21.17**  Payne (1982) asked male and female participants to rank 10 common job characteristics (e.g., salary, workload) for the characteristics' personal importance to the participant and their perceived importance to a member of the opposite sex. The data were collected from 92 participants in 1973 and from 145 participants in 1981. How should she analyze these data?

**21.18** Most people are basically happy. Diener and Diener (1996) reported data on subjective well-being from residents of 43 countries around the world. The mean was 6.33 on a scale from 0 (most unhappy) to 10 (most happy). What would you do with data such as these?

**21.19** Vasta, Rosenburg, Knott, and Gaze (1997) compared the performance of four groups of male and female participants to Piaget's water-level task, in which a participant looks at a partially full glass of water and then draws where the water level would be if the glass were tilted to the side. The four groups were bartenders, servers, clerical workers, and salespersons. (Contrary to previous research, bartenders and servers were best. Females were generally better than males.)

**21.20** Cochran and Urbanczyk (1982) were concerned with the effect of the height of a room on the desired personal space of participants. They tested 48 participants in both a high-ceiling (10 ft) and a low-ceiling (7 ft) room. Participants stood with their backs to a wall while a stranger approached. Participants were told to say "stop" when the approaching stranger's nearness made them feel uncomfortable. The dependent variable was the distance at which the participant said "stop." What should the experimenters do with their data? What should they do instead if they are unwilling to use a parametric test? (*Note:* The distance was greater with a lower ceiling, which suggests that interpersonal space is not dependent on just horizontal distance.)

**21.21** Robinson, Barrett, and Skeen (1983) compared scores on a scale of locus of control for 20 unwed adolescent fathers and 20 unwed adolescent males who were not fathers. How could they analyze these data if they were unwilling to make parametric assumptions? (*Note:* They found no difference.)

**21.22** Hosch and Cooper (1982) looked at the role that being a victim rather than just a bystander had on eyewitness identification. In the control condition a confederate of the experimenter entered the experimental room with a participant, completed a few forms, and left. In another condition the confederate did the same thing, but as she was leaving she stole the experimenter's calculator. In the third condition the confederate stole the *participant's* watch, which the participant had been instructed to leave on the table. There were two dependent variables. The first was whether the participant was able to correctly identify the confederate from a set of six photographs, and the second was the participant's subjective rating on a 9-point scale of his or her confidence in the identification. The experimenter was most interested in seeing whether being a victim of a theft led to better and more confident identification than just observing a theft. How can these data be analyzed? (*Note:* The two theft conditions did not differ, and there was no relationship between accuracy and confidence.)

**21.23** Bradley and Kjungja (1982) experimented with the perception of subjective triangles. When you look at three points that form a triangle, there is a subjective impression of lines connecting those points to form the contours of the triangle. Bradley and Kjungja asked participants to view the subjective triangle while it was stationary and again while it was rotating in a circle. The participant was instructed to say whether the subjective contours were stronger while the triangle was stationary or while it was rotating. Out of 37 participants, 35 said that the contours were stronger when the triangle was rotating. How could they test whether this difference was significant (although here a formal test isn't really needed)?

**21.24** Lobel, Dunkel-Schetter, and Scrimshaw (1992) examined medical risk factors, gestational age, and the mother's emotional stress as predictors of low birthweight. How could they assess the relationship between these factors and low birthweight? (*Note:* Gestational age and stress predicted birthweight but not medical risks. Women who experienced daily anxiety were most likely to deliver low-birthweight babies.)

**21.25** Brown, Lewis, Brown, Horn, and Bowes (1982) investigated drug-induced amnesia as a way of shedding light on organically produced amnesia. They first presented participants with a list of words to learn and then injected the participants with either lorazepam (which produces amnesia) or saline. After 1.5 hours they asked all participants to recall the words they had learned. They also asked the same participants to learn a list after the drug had been injected and to recall it after 1.5 hours. If lorazepam interferes with the *storage* of material in memory, then recall only of the second list should be affected. If lorazepam interferes with *retrieval* rather than storage, then recall of both lists should be disrupted. What statistical test would be appropriate for analyzing these data? This is a case in which you do not know how to perform the analysis, but you should be able to describe the design. (*Note:* Recall of the list learned before the injection was unaffected, but the list studied after the administration of the drug was poorly recalled.)

**21.26** Hicks and Guista (1982) asked seven participants who habitually had less than 6.5 hours of sleep per night and nine participants who habitually had more than 8.5 hours of sleep per night to complete the Stanford Sleepiness Scale (SSS) at two-hour intervals for 30 days. The SSS is a measure of alertness and simply requires the participant to rate his or her level of alertness by responding with a number between 1 (very alert) and 7 (struggling to stay awake). The authors actually broke the data into seven different times of day, but for purposes of this example assume that the dependent variable is each participant's mean SSS score over the 30-day period. What is the appropriate analysis of these data?

**21.27** Hunt, Streissguth, Kerr, and Olson (1995) asked 14-year-olds to perform a spatial-visual reasoning task in which it was possible to evaluate the amount of time each person viewed a figure before responding, and the accuracy of that response. They also obtained the amount of alcohol the child's mother reported consuming during pregnancy (14 years earlier). (Both study time and number correct were negatively correlated with alcohol consumption during pregnancy, though, as expected, the correlations were not very high.)

**21.28** It has been known for some time that men with older brothers are more likely to be homosexual than men without older brothers. One explanation for this effect has been that this is a phenomenon of socialization related to the environment in which males are raised. Bogaert and Bocklandt (2006) investigated this possibility by studying 944 people and looking at the number of older brothers and sisters an individual had and whether those were biological siblings or step-siblings. With older biological brothers the probability of homosexuality increased from 3% to around 5%, but there was no similar increase with older stepbrothers or with biological sisters or stepsisters. How should the authors analyze these data?

# Appendix A
# Arithmetic Review

| | |
|---|---|
| Standard Symbols and Basic Information | Parentheses |
| | Fractions |
| Addition and Subtraction | Algebraic Operations |
| Multiplication and Division | |

The following is intended as a quick refresher of some of the simple arithmetic operations you learned in high school but probably have not used since. Although some of what follows will seem so obvious that you wonder why it is included, people sometimes forget the most obvious things. A more complete review is found on the book companion Web site at http://www.thomsonedu.com/psychology/howell.

One of the things that students never seem to learn is that it is easy to figure out most of these principles for yourself. For example, if you can't remember whether

$$\frac{18.1}{28.6 + 32.7} \quad \text{can be reduced to} \quad \frac{18.1}{28.6} + \frac{18.1}{32.7}$$

(it cannot, but it is one of the foolish things that I can never keep in my head), try it out with very simple numbers. Thus,

$$\frac{2}{1 + 4} = \frac{2}{5} = .4$$

is obviously not the same as

$$\frac{2}{1} + \frac{2}{4} = 2.5$$

It is often quicker to check on a procedure by using small numbers than by looking it up.

## Standard Symbols and Basic Information

| | |
|---|---|
| **Numerator** | The thing on the top |
| **Denominator** | The thing on the bottom |
| *a/b* | $a$ = Numerator; $b$ = Denominator |
| **+, −, ×, ÷ (or /)** | Symbols for addition, subtraction, multiplication, and division; called *operators* |
| $X = Y$ | $X$ equals $Y$ |
| $X \approx Y$ or $X \simeq Y$ | $X$ approximately equal to $Y$ |
| $X \neq Y$ | $X$ unequal to $Y$ |
| $X < Y$ | $X$ less than $Y$ (*Hint:* The smaller end points to the smaller number.) |
| $X \leq Y$ | $X$ less than or equal to $Y$ |
| $X > Y$ | $X$ greater than $Y$ |
| $X \geq Y$ | $X$ greater than or equal to $Y$ |
| $X < Y < Z$ | $X$ less than $Y$ less than $Z$ (i.e., $Y$ is between $X$ and $Z$) |
| $X \pm Y$ | $X$ plus or minus $Y$ |
| $\lvert X \rvert$ | Absolute value of $X$—ignore the sign of $X$ |
| $\dfrac{1}{X}$ | The reciprocal of $X$ |
| $X^2$ | $X$ squared |
| $X^n$ | $X$ raised to the $n$th power |
| $\sqrt{X} = X^{1/2}$ | Square root of $X$ |

## Addition and Subtraction

| | |
|---|---|
| $8 - 12 = -4$ | To subtract a larger number from a smaller one, subtract the smaller from the larger and make the result negative. |
| $-8 + 12$ <br> $= 12 - 8 = 4$ | The order of operations is not important. |

## Multiplication and Division

2(3)(6)
= 2 × 3 × 6

If no operator appears before a set of parentheses, multiplication is implied.

2 × 3 × 6
= 2 × 6 × 3

Numbers can be multiplied in any order.

$$\frac{2 \times 8}{4}$$

$$= \frac{2}{4} \times 8$$

$$= 2 \times \frac{8}{4}$$

$$= \frac{16}{4} = 4$$

Division can take place in any order.

7 × 3 + 6
= 21 + 6 = 27

Multiply or divide *before* you add or subtract the result. But for the same operators, work from left to right [e.g., 8 ÷ 2 ÷ 4 = (8 ÷ 2) ÷ 4, not 8 ÷ (2 ÷ 4)].

2 × 3 = 6

(−2)(−3) = 6

$$\frac{6}{3} = 2$$

$$\frac{-6}{-3} = 2$$

Multiplication or division of numbers with the *same* sign produces a positive answer.

(−2)3 = −6

$$\frac{-6}{3} = -2$$

Multiplication or division of numbers with *opposite* signs produces a negative answer.

(−2)(3)(−6)(−4)
= (−6)(24)
= −144

With several numbers having different signs, work in pairs to get the correct sign.

## Parentheses

2(7 − 6 + 3) =
2(4) = 8

When multiplying, either perform the operations inside parentheses before multiplying, or multiply *each* element within the parentheses and then sum.

or

$2(7) + 2(-6) + 2(3)$
$\quad = 14 - 12 + 6 = 8$

$2(7 - 6 + 3)^2$
$\quad = 2(4)^2 = 2(16)$
$\quad = 32$

When the parenthetical term is raised to a power, perform the operations inside the parentheses, raise the result to the appropriate power, and then carry out the other operations.

# Fractions

$\dfrac{1}{5} = .20$

To convert to a decimal, divide the numerator by the denominator.

$\dfrac{4}{3}$

The reciprocal of $\frac{3}{4}$. To take the reciprocal of a fraction, stand it on its head.

$3 \times \dfrac{6}{5} = \dfrac{3 \times 6}{5}$

$\quad = \dfrac{18}{5} = 3.6$

To multiply a fraction by a whole number, multiply the numerator by that number.

$\dfrac{3}{5} \times \dfrac{6}{7} \times \dfrac{1}{2}$

$\quad = \dfrac{3 \times 6 \times 1}{5 \times 7 \times 2}$

$\quad = \dfrac{18}{70} = .26$

To multiply a series of fractions, multiply numerators together and multiply denominators together.

$\dfrac{1}{3} + \dfrac{4}{3} = \dfrac{5}{3} = 1.67$

To add fractions with the *same* denominator, add the numerators and divide by the common denominator.

$\dfrac{1}{6} + \dfrac{4}{3} = \dfrac{1}{6} + \dfrac{8}{6} = \dfrac{9}{6}$

$\quad = 1.5$

To add fractions with *different* denominators, multiply the numerator and the denominator by a constant to equate the denominators and follow the previous rule.

$\dfrac{8}{13} + \dfrac{12}{25}$

This is a more elaborate example of the same rule.

$= \left(\dfrac{25}{25} \times \dfrac{8}{13}\right) + \left(\dfrac{13}{13} \times \dfrac{12}{25}\right)$

$$= \frac{200}{325} + \frac{156}{325}$$

$$= \frac{356}{325} = 1.095$$

$$\frac{8}{1/3} = 8\left(\frac{3}{1}\right) = 24$$  To divide by a fraction, multiply by the reciprocal of that fraction.

## Algebraic Operations

Most algebraic operations boil down to moving things from one side of the equation to the other. Mathematically, the rule is that whatever you do to one side of the equation you must do to the other side.

Solve the following equation for $X$:

$$3 + X = 8$$

We want $X$ on one side and the answer on the other. All we have to do is to subtract 3 from both sides to get

$$3 + X - 3 = 8 - 3$$
$$X = 5$$

If the equation had been

$$X - 3 = 8$$

we would have added 3 to both sides:

$$X - 3 + 3 = 8 + 3$$
$$X = 11$$

For equations involving multiplication or division, we follow the same principle:

$$2X = 21$$

Dividing both sides by 2, we have

$$\frac{2X}{2} = \frac{21}{2}$$

$$X = 10.5$$

and

$$\frac{X}{7} = 13$$

$$\frac{7X}{7} = 7(13)$$

$$X = 91$$

Personally, I prefer to think of things in a different, but perfectly equivalent, way. When you want to get rid of something that has been added (or subtracted) to (or from) one side of the equation, move it to the other side and reverse the sign:

$$3 + X = 12 \qquad \text{or} \qquad X - 7 = 19$$

$$X = 12 - 3 \qquad\qquad X = 19 + 7$$

When the thing you want to get rid of is in the numerator, move it to the other side and put it in the denominator:

$$7.6X = 12$$

$$X = \frac{12}{7.6}$$

When the thing you want to get rid of is in the denominator, move it to the numerator on the other side and multiply:

$$\frac{X}{8.9} = 14.6$$

$$X = 14.6(8.9)$$

Notice that with more complex expressions, you must multiply (or divide) everything on the other side of the equation. Thus,

$$7.6X = 12 + 8$$

$$X = \frac{12 + 8}{7.6}$$

For complex equations, just work one step at a time:

$$7.6(X + 8) = \frac{14}{7} - 5$$

First, get rid of the 7.6:

$$X + 8 = \frac{14/7 - 5}{7.6}$$

Now get rid of the 8:

$$X = \frac{14/7 - 5}{7.6} - 8$$

Now clean up the messy fraction:

$$X = \frac{2 - 5}{7.6} - 8 = \frac{-3}{7.6} - 8 = -.395 - 8 = -8.395$$

# Appendix B
# Symbols and Notation

## Greek Letter Symbols

| | |
|---|---|
| $\alpha$ | Level of significance—probability of a Type I error (alpha) |
| $\beta$ | Probability of a Type II error (beta); standardized regression coefficient |
| $\delta$ | Effect size combined with sample size to compute power (delta) |
| $\eta^2$ | Eta squared |
| $\mu$ | Population mean (mu) |
| $\mu_{\bar{X}}$ | Mean of the sampling distribution of the mean |
| $\rho$ | Population correlation coefficient (rho) |
| $\sigma$ | Population standard deviation (sigma) |
| $\sigma^2$ | Population variance |
| $\Sigma$ | Summation notation (uppercase sigma) |
| $\phi$ | Phi coefficient |
| $\chi^2$ | Chi-square |
| $\chi^2_F$ | Friedman's chi-square |
| $\omega^2$ | Omega squared |

## English Letter Symbols

| | |
|---|---|
| $a$ | Intercept; number of levels of variable A in analysis of variance |
| $b$ | Slope (also called regression coefficient) |
| CI | Confidence interval |
| $\text{cov}_{XY}$ | Covariance of $X$ and $Y$ |

| | |
|---|---|
| $\hat{d}$ | Effect size estimate |
| $df$ | Degrees of freedom |
| $E$ | Expected frequency; expected value |
| $F$ | $F$ statistic |
| $H$ | Kruskal–Wallis statistic |
| $H_0; H_1$ | Null hypothesis; alternative hypothesis |
| $MS$ | Mean square |
| $MS_{error}$ | Mean square error |
| $n, n_i, N_i$ | Number of cases in a sample |
| $N(0, 1)$ | Read "normally distributed with $\mu = 0$, $\sigma^2 = 1$" |
| $O$ | Observed frequency |
| $p$ | General symbol for probability |
| $r, r_{XY}$ | Pearson's correlation coefficient |
| $r_{pb}$ | Point biserial correlation coefficient |
| $r_S$ | Spearman's rank-order correlation coefficient |
| $R$ | Multiple correlation coefficient |
| $s^2, s_X^2$ | Sample variance |
| $s_p^2$ | Pooled variance |
| $s, s_X$ | Sample standard deviation |
| $s_D$ | Standard deviation of difference scores |
| $s_{\overline{D}}$ | Standard error of the mean of difference scores |
| $s_{\overline{X}}, s_{\overline{X}_1 - \overline{X}_2}$ | Standard error of the mean; standard error of differences between means |
| $s_{Y - \hat{Y}}$ | Standard error of estimate |
| $SS_A$ | Sum of squares for variable $A$ |
| $SS_{AB}$ | Interaction sum of squares |
| $SS_{error}$ | Error sum of squares |
| $SS_Y$ | Sum of squares for variable $Y$ |
| $SS_{\hat{Y}}$ | Sum of squares of predicted values of $Y$ |
| $SS_{Y - \hat{Y}}$ | Error sum of squares $= SS_{error}$ |

| | |
|---|---|
| $t$ | Student's $t$ statistic |
| $t_{.025}$ | Critical value of $t$ |
| $T$ | Wilcoxon's matched-pairs signed-ranks statistic |
| $T_j$ | Total for group $j$ |
| $W_S, W'_S$ | Mann–Whitney statistic |
| $X$ or $X_{ij}$ | Individual observation |
| $\overline{X}$ or $\overline{X}..$ | Grand mean |
| $\overline{X}, \overline{X}_i, \overline{X}_{A_i}$ | Sample mean |
| $\overline{X}_h$ | Harmonic mean |
| $\hat{Y}, \hat{Y}_i,$ | Predicted value of $Y$ |
| $z$ | Normal deviate (also called standard score) |

# Appendix C
# Basic Statistical Formulae

## Descriptive Statistics

| | |
|---|---|
| **Variance ($s^2$)** | $s^2 = \dfrac{\Sigma(X - \overline{X})^2}{N - 1} = \dfrac{\Sigma X^2 - (\Sigma X)^2/N}{N - 1}$ |
| **Standard deviation ($s$)** | $s = \sqrt{s^2}$ |
| **Median location** | $\dfrac{(N + 1)}{2}$ |
| **Hinge location** | $\dfrac{\text{Median location} + 1}{2}$ |
| **General formula for $z$ score** | $\dfrac{\text{Score} - \text{Mean}}{\text{Std. deviation}}$ or $\dfrac{\text{Statistic} - \text{Parameter}}{\text{Std. error of statistic}}$ |
| **$z$ score for an observation** | $z = \dfrac{X - \overline{X}}{s}$ |

## Tests on Sample Means

| | |
|---|---|
| **Standard error of the mean ($s_{\overline{X}}$)** | $\dfrac{s_X}{\sqrt{N}}$ |
| **$z$ for $\overline{X}$ given $\sigma$** | $z = \dfrac{\overline{X} - \mu}{\sigma_{\overline{X}}}$ |
| **$t$ for one sample** | $t = \dfrac{\overline{X} - \mu}{s_{\overline{X}}} = \dfrac{\overline{X} - \mu}{\dfrac{s}{\sqrt{N}}}$ |

| | |
|---|---|
| Confidence interval on $\mu$ | $\text{CI} = \overline{X} \pm t_{.05}(s_{\overline{X}})$ |
| $t$ for two related samples | $t = \dfrac{\overline{D}}{s_{\overline{D}}} = \dfrac{\overline{D}}{s_D/\sqrt{N}}$ |
| $t$ for two independent samples (unpooled) | $t = \dfrac{\overline{X}_1 - \overline{X}_2}{s_{\overline{X}_1 - \overline{X}_2}} = \dfrac{\overline{X}_1 - \overline{X}_2}{\sqrt{\dfrac{s_1^2}{N_1} + \dfrac{s_2^2}{N_2}}}$ |
| Pooled variance ($s_p^2$) | $s_p^2 = \dfrac{(N_1 - 1)s_1^2 + (N_2 - 1)s_2^2}{N_1 + N_2 - 2}$ |
| $t$ for two independent samples (pooled) | $t = \dfrac{\overline{X}_1 - \overline{X}_2}{s_{\overline{X}_1 - \overline{X}_2}} = \dfrac{\overline{X}_1 - \overline{X}_2}{\sqrt{\dfrac{s_p^2}{N_1} + \dfrac{s_p^2}{N_2}}} = \dfrac{\overline{X}_1 - \overline{X}_2}{\sqrt{s_p^2\left(\dfrac{1}{N_1} + \dfrac{1}{N_2}\right)}}$ |
| Confidence interval on $\mu_1 - \mu_2$ | $\text{CI} = (\overline{X}_1 - \overline{X}_2) \pm t_{.05}s_{(\overline{X}_1 - \overline{X}_2)}$ |

## Power

| | |
|---|---|
| Effect size (one sample) | $d = (\mu_1 - \mu_0)/\sigma$ |
| Effect size (two sample) | $d = (\mu_1 - \mu_2)/\sigma$ |
| Delta (one-sample $t$) | $\delta = d\sqrt{N}$ |
| Delta (two-sample $t$) | $\delta = d\sqrt{\dfrac{N}{2}}$ |

## Correlation and Regression

| | |
|---|---|
| Sum of squares | $SS_X = \Sigma(X - \overline{X})^2 = \Sigma X^2 - \dfrac{(\Sigma X)^2}{N}$ |
| Sum of products | $\Sigma(X - \overline{X})(Y - \overline{Y}) = \Sigma XY - \dfrac{(\Sigma X \Sigma Y)}{N}$ |
| Covariance | $\text{cov}_{XY} = \dfrac{\Sigma(X - \overline{X})(Y - \overline{Y})}{N - 1} = \dfrac{\Sigma XY - \dfrac{\Sigma X \Sigma Y}{N}}{N - 1}$ |

| | |
|---|---|
| Correlation (Pearson) | $r = \dfrac{\text{cov}_{XY}}{s_X s_Y}$ |
| Slope | $b = \dfrac{\text{cov}_{XY}}{s_X^2}$ |
| Intercept | $a = \dfrac{\Sigma Y - b\Sigma X}{N} = \overline{Y} - b\overline{X}$ |
| Standard error of estimate | $s_{Y-\hat{Y}} = \sqrt{\dfrac{\Sigma(Y - \hat{Y})^2}{N-2}} = \sqrt{\dfrac{SS_{error}}{N-2}}$ |
| | $= s_Y\sqrt{(1 - r^2)\dfrac{N-1}{N-2}}$ |
| $SS_Y$ | $\Sigma Y^2 - \dfrac{(\Sigma Y)^2}{N}$ |
| $SS_{\hat{Y}}$ | $\Sigma \hat{Y}^2 - \dfrac{(\Sigma \hat{Y})^2}{N}$ |
| $SS_{Y-\hat{Y}}$ | $SS_Y - SS_{\hat{Y}} = SS_{error}$ |
| $SS_{error}$ | $SS_Y(1 - r^2)$ |
| $SS_{total}$ | $\Sigma(X - \overline{X})^2 = \Sigma X^2 - \dfrac{(\Sigma X)^2}{N}$ |
| $SS_{group}$ (one-way) | $n\Sigma(\overline{X}_j - \overline{X}..)^2$ |
| $SS_{error}$ (one-way) | $SS_{total} - SS_{group}$ |
| $SS_{rows}$ (two-way) | $nc\Sigma(\overline{X}_{r_i} - \overline{X}..)^2$ |
| $SS_{col}$ (two-way) | $nr\Sigma(\overline{X}_{c_j} - \overline{X}..)^2$ |
| $SS_{cells}$ (two-way) | $n\Sigma(\overline{X}_{ij} - \overline{X}..)^2$ |
| $SS_{R \times C}$ (two-way) | $SS_{cells} - SS_{rows} - SS_{col}$ |
| $SS_{error}$ (two-way) | $SS_{total} - SS_{rows} - SS_{col} - SS_{R \times C}$ or $SS_{total} - SS_{cells}$ |
| Protected $t$ (Use only if $F$ is significant.) | $t = \dfrac{\overline{X}_i - \overline{X}_j}{\sqrt{\dfrac{MS_{error}}{n_i} + \dfrac{MS_{error}}{n_j}}}$ |
| Eta squared | $\eta^2 = \dfrac{SS_{group}}{SS_{total}}$ |

Omega squared (one-way)

$$\omega^2 = \frac{SS_{group} - (k-1)MS_{error}}{SS_{total} + MS_{error}}$$

## Chi-Square

Chi-square

$$\chi^2 = \Sigma\frac{(O-E)^2}{E}$$

## Distribution-Free Statistics

Mean and standard deviation
(large sample) for
Mann–Whitney statistic

$$\text{Mean} = \frac{n_1(n_1 + n_2 + 1)}{2}; \quad s = \sqrt{\frac{n_1 n_2(n_1 + n_2 + 1)}{12}}$$

Mean and standard deviation (large
sample) for Wilcoxon statistic

$$\text{Mean} = \frac{n(n+1)}{4}; \quad s = \sqrt{\frac{n(n+1)(2n+1)}{24}}$$

Kruskal–Wallis $H$ statistic

$$H = \frac{12}{N(N+1)}\Sigma\frac{R_j^2}{n_j} - 3(N+1)$$

Friedman's chi-square statistic

$$\chi_F^2 = \frac{12}{Nk(k+1)}\Sigma R_j^2 - 3N(k+1)$$

# Appendix D
# Statistical Tables

## Table D.1
Upper Percentage Points of the $\chi^2$ Distribution

| df | .995 | .990 | .975 | .950 | .900 | .750 | .500 | .250 | .100 | .050 | .025 | .010 | .005 |
|---|---|---|---|---|---|---|---|---|---|---|---|---|---|
| 1 | .00 | .00 | .00 | .00 | .02 | .10 | .45 | 1.32 | 2.71 | 3.84 | 5.02 | 6.63 | 7.88 |
| 2 | .01 | .02 | .05 | .10 | .21 | .58 | 1.39 | 2.77 | 4.61 | 5.99 | 7.38 | 9.21 | 10.60 |
| 3 | .07 | .11 | .22 | .35 | .58 | 1.21 | 2.37 | 4.11 | 6.25 | 7.82 | 9.35 | 11.35 | 12.84 |
| 4 | .21 | .30 | .48 | .71 | 1.06 | 1.92 | 3.36 | 5.39 | 7.78 | 9.49 | 11.14 | 13.28 | 14.86 |
| 5 | .41 | .55 | .83 | 1.15 | 1.61 | 2.67 | 4.35 | 6.63 | 9.24 | 11.07 | 12.83 | 15.09 | 16.75 |
| 6 | .68 | .87 | 1.24 | 1.64 | 2.20 | 3.45 | 5.35 | 7.84 | 10.64 | 12.59 | 14.45 | 16.81 | 18.55 |
| 7 | .99 | 1.24 | 1.69 | 2.17 | 2.83 | 4.25 | 6.35 | 9.04 | 12.02 | 14.07 | 16.01 | 18.48 | 20.28 |
| 8 | 1.34 | 1.65 | 2.18 | 2.73 | 3.49 | 5.07 | 7.34 | 10.22 | 13.36 | 15.51 | 17.54 | 20.09 | 21.96 |
| 9 | 1.73 | 2.09 | 2.70 | 3.33 | 4.17 | 5.90 | 8.34 | 11.39 | 14.68 | 16.92 | 19.02 | 21.66 | 23.59 |
| 10 | 2.15 | 2.56 | 3.25 | 3.94 | 4.87 | 6.74 | 9.34 | 12.55 | 15.99 | 18.31 | 20.48 | 23.21 | 25.19 |
| 11 | 2.60 | 3.05 | 3.82 | 4.57 | 5.58 | 7.58 | 10.34 | 13.70 | 17.28 | 19.68 | 21.92 | 24.72 | 26.75 |
| 12 | 3.07 | 3.57 | 4.40 | 5.23 | 6.30 | 8.44 | 11.34 | 14.85 | 18.55 | 21.03 | 23.34 | 26.21 | 28.30 |
| 13 | 3.56 | 4.11 | 5.01 | 5.89 | 7.04 | 9.30 | 12.34 | 15.98 | 19.81 | 22.36 | 24.74 | 27.69 | 29.82 |
| 14 | 4.07 | 4.66 | 5.63 | 6.57 | 7.79 | 10.17 | 13.34 | 17.12 | 21.06 | 23.69 | 26.12 | 29.14 | 31.31 |
| 15 | 4.60 | 5.23 | 6.26 | 7.26 | 8.55 | 11.04 | 14.34 | 18.25 | 22.31 | 25.00 | 27.49 | 30.58 | 32.80 |
| 16 | 5.14 | 5.81 | 6.91 | 7.96 | 9.31 | 11.91 | 15.34 | 19.37 | 23.54 | 26.30 | 28.85 | 32.00 | 34.27 |
| 17 | 5.70 | 6.41 | 7.56 | 8.67 | 10.09 | 12.79 | 16.34 | 20.49 | 24.77 | 27.59 | 30.19 | 33.41 | 35.72 |
| 18 | 6.26 | 7.01 | 8.23 | 9.39 | 10.86 | 13.68 | 17.34 | 21.60 | 25.99 | 28.87 | 31.53 | 34.81 | 37.15 |
| 19 | 6.84 | 7.63 | 8.91 | 10.12 | 11.65 | 14.56 | 18.34 | 22.72 | 27.20 | 30.14 | 32.85 | 36.19 | 38.58 |
| 20 | 7.43 | 8.26 | 9.59 | 10.85 | 12.44 | 15.45 | 19.34 | 23.83 | 28.41 | 31.41 | 34.17 | 37.56 | 40.00 |
| 21 | 8.03 | 8.90 | 10.28 | 11.59 | 13.24 | 16.34 | 20.34 | 24.93 | 29.62 | 32.67 | 35.48 | 38.93 | 41.40 |
| 22 | 8.64 | 9.54 | 10.98 | 12.34 | 14.04 | 17.24 | 21.34 | 26.04 | 30.81 | 33.93 | 36.78 | 40.29 | 42.80 |
| 23 | 9.26 | 10.19 | 11.69 | 13.09 | 14.85 | 18.14 | 22.34 | 27.14 | 32.01 | 35.17 | 38.08 | 41.64 | 44.18 |
| 24 | 9.88 | 10.86 | 12.40 | 13.85 | 15.66 | 19.04 | 23.34 | 28.24 | 33.20 | 36.42 | 39.37 | 42.98 | 45.56 |
| 25 | 10.52 | 11.52 | 13.12 | 14.61 | 16.47 | 19.94 | 24.34 | 29.34 | 34.38 | 37.65 | 40.65 | 44.32 | 46.93 |
| 26 | 11.16 | 12.20 | 13.84 | 15.38 | 17.29 | 20.84 | 25.34 | 30.43 | 35.56 | 38.89 | 41.92 | 45.64 | 48.29 |
| 27 | 11.80 | 12.88 | 14.57 | 16.15 | 18.11 | 21.75 | 26.34 | 31.53 | 36.74 | 40.11 | 43.20 | 46.96 | 49.64 |
| 28 | 12.46 | 13.56 | 15.31 | 16.93 | 18.94 | 22.66 | 27.34 | 32.62 | 37.92 | 41.34 | 44.46 | 48.28 | 50.99 |
| 29 | 13.12 | 14.26 | 16.05 | 17.71 | 19.77 | 23.57 | 28.34 | 33.71 | 39.09 | 42.56 | 45.72 | 49.59 | 52.34 |
| 30 | 13.78 | 14.95 | 16.79 | 18.49 | 20.60 | 24.48 | 29.34 | 34.80 | 40.26 | 43.77 | 46.98 | 50.89 | 53.67 |
| 40 | 20.67 | 22.14 | 24.42 | 26.51 | 29.06 | 33.67 | 39.34 | 45.61 | 51.80 | 55.75 | 59.34 | 63.71 | 66.80 |
| 50 | 27.96 | 29.68 | 32.35 | 34.76 | 37.69 | 42.95 | 49.34 | 56.33 | 63.16 | 67.50 | 71.42 | 76.17 | 79.52 |
| 60 | 35.50 | 37.46 | 40.47 | 43.19 | 46.46 | 52.30 | 59.34 | 66.98 | 74.39 | 79.08 | 83.30 | 88.40 | 91.98 |
| 70 | 43.25 | 45.42 | 48.75 | 51.74 | 55.33 | 61.70 | 69.34 | 77.57 | 85.52 | 90.53 | 95.03 | 100.44 | 104.24 |
| 80 | 51.14 | 53.52 | 57.15 | 60.39 | 64.28 | 71.15 | 79.34 | 88.13 | 96.57 | 101.88 | 106.63 | 112.34 | 116.35 |
| 90 | 59.17 | 61.74 | 65.64 | 69.13 | 73.29 | 80.63 | 89.33 | 98.65 | 107.56 | 113.14 | 118.14 | 124.13 | 128.32 |
| 100 | 67.30 | 70.05 | 74.22 | 77.93 | 82.36 | 90.14 | 99.33 | 109.14 | 118.49 | 124.34 | 129.56 | 135.82 | 140.19 |

(*Source:*   The entries in this table were computed by the author.)

**Table D.2**
Significant Values of the Correlation Coefficient

| df | Two-Tailed Tests | | | |
|---|---|---|---|---|
| | $p = .10$ | $p = .05$ | $p = .025$ | $p = .01$ |
| 3 | .805 | .878 | .924 | .959 |
| 4 | .729 | .811 | .868 | .917 |
| 5 | .669 | .755 | .817 | .875 |
| 6 | .622 | .707 | .771 | .834 |
| 7 | .582 | .666 | .732 | .798 |
| 8 | .549 | .632 | .697 | .765 |
| 9 | .521 | .602 | .667 | .735 |
| 10 | .498 | .576 | .640 | .708 |
| 11 | .476 | .553 | .616 | .684 |
| 12 | .458 | .533 | .594 | .661 |
| 13 | .441 | .514 | .575 | .641 |
| 14 | .426 | .497 | .557 | .623 |
| 15 | .412 | .482 | .541 | .605 |
| 16 | .400 | .468 | .526 | .590 |
| 17 | .389 | .455 | .512 | .575 |
| 18 | .379 | .444 | .499 | .562 |
| 19 | .369 | .433 | .487 | .549 |
| 20 | .360 | .423 | .476 | .537 |
| 21 | .351 | .413 | .466 | .526 |
| 22 | .344 | .404 | .456 | .515 |
| 23 | .337 | .396 | .447 | .505 |
| 24 | .330 | .388 | .439 | .496 |
| 25 | .323 | .381 | .431 | .487 |
| 26 | .317 | .374 | .423 | .478 |
| 27 | .311 | .367 | .415 | .471 |
| 28 | .306 | .361 | .409 | .463 |
| 29 | .301 | .355 | .402 | .456 |
| 30 | .296 | .349 | .396 | .449 |
| 40 | .257 | .304 | .345 | .393 |
| 50 | .231 | .273 | .311 | .354 |
| 60 | .211 | .250 | .285 | .325 |
| 120 | .150 | .178 | .203 | .232 |
| 200 | .116 | .138 | .158 | .181 |
| 500 | .073 | .088 | .100 | .115 |
| 1000 | .052 | .062 | .071 | .081 |

(*Source:*   The entries in this table were computed by the author.)

**Table D.3**

Critical Values of the *F* Distribution: Alpha = .05

| | Degrees of Freedom for Numerator | | | | | | | | | | | | | | | |
|---|---|---|---|---|---|---|---|---|---|---|---|---|---|---|---|---|
| **Degrees of Freedom for Denominator** | **1** | **2** | **3** | **4** | **5** | **6** | **7** | **8** | **9** | **10** | **15** | **20** | **25** | **30** | **40** | **50** |
| **1** | 161.4 | 199.5 | 215.8 | 224.8 | 230.0 | 233.8 | 236.5 | 238.6 | 240.1 | 242.1 | 245.2 | 248.4 | 248.9 | 250.5 | 250.8 | 252.6 |
| **2** | 18.51 | 19.00 | 19.16 | 19.25 | 19.30 | 19.33 | 19.35 | 19.37 | 19.38 | 19.40 | 19.43 | 19.44 | 19.46 | 19.47 | 19.48 | 19.48 |
| **3** | 10.13 | 9.55 | 9.28 | 9.12 | 9.01 | 8.94 | 8.89 | 8.85 | 8.81 | 8.79 | 8.70 | 8.66 | 8.63 | 8.62 | 8.59 | 8.58 |
| **4** | 7.71 | 6.94 | 6.59 | 6.39 | 6.26 | 6.16 | 6.09 | 6.04 | 6.00 | 5.96 | 5.86 | 5.80 | 5.77 | 5.75 | 5.72 | 5.70 |
| **5** | 6.61 | 5.79 | 5.41 | 5.19 | 5.05 | 4.95 | 4.88 | 4.82 | 4.77 | 4.74 | 4.62 | 4.56 | 4.52 | 4.50 | 4.46 | 4.44 |
| **6** | 5.99 | 5.14 | 4.76 | 4.53 | 4.39 | 4.28 | 4.21 | 4.15 | 4.10 | 4.06 | 3.94 | 3.87 | 3.83 | 3.81 | 3.77 | 3.75 |
| **7** | 5.59 | 4.74 | 4.35 | 4.12 | 3.97 | 3.87 | 3.79 | 3.73 | 3.68 | 3.64 | 3.51 | 3.44 | 3.40 | 3.38 | 3.34 | 3.32 |
| **8** | 5.32 | 4.46 | 4.07 | 3.84 | 3.69 | 3.58 | 3.50 | 3.44 | 3.39 | 3.35 | 3.22 | 3.15 | 3.11 | 3.08 | 3.04 | 3.02 |
| **9** | 5.12 | 4.26 | 3.86 | 3.63 | 3.48 | 3.37 | 3.29 | 3.23 | 3.18 | 3.14 | 3.01 | 2.94 | 2.89 | 2.86 | 2.83 | 2.80 |
| **10** | 4.96 | 4.10 | 3.71 | 3.48 | 3.33 | 3.22 | 3.14 | 3.07 | 3.02 | 2.98 | 2.85 | 2.77 | 2.73 | 2.70 | 2.66 | 2.64 |
| **11** | 4.84 | 3.98 | 3.59 | 3.36 | 3.20 | 3.09 | 3.01 | 2.95 | 2.90 | 2.85 | 2.72 | 2.65 | 2.60 | 2.57 | 2.53 | 2.51 |
| **12** | 4.75 | 3.89 | 3.49 | 3.26 | 3.11 | 3.00 | 2.91 | 2.85 | 2.80 | 2.75 | 2.62 | 2.54 | 2.50 | 2.47 | 2.43 | 2.40 |
| **13** | 4.67 | 3.81 | 3.41 | 3.18 | 3.03 | 2.92 | 2.83 | 2.77 | 2.71 | 2.67 | 2.53 | 2.46 | 2.41 | 2.38 | 2.34 | 2.31 |
| **14** | 4.60 | 3.74 | 3.34 | 3.11 | 2.96 | 2.85 | 2.76 | 2.70 | 2.65 | 2.60 | 2.46 | 2.39 | 2.34 | 2.31 | 2.27 | 2.24 |
| **15** | 4.54 | 3.68 | 3.29 | 3.06 | 2.90 | 2.79 | 2.71 | 2.64 | 2.59 | 2.54 | 2.40 | 2.33 | 2.28 | 2.25 | 2.20 | 2.18 |
| **16** | 4.49 | 3.63 | 3.24 | 3.01 | 2.85 | 2.74 | 2.66 | 2.59 | 2.54 | 2.49 | 2.35 | 2.28 | 2.23 | 2.19 | 2.15 | 2.12 |
| **17** | 4.45 | 3.59 | 3.20 | 2.96 | 2.81 | 2.70 | 2.61 | 2.55 | 2.49 | 2.45 | 2.31 | 2.23 | 2.18 | 2.15 | 2.10 | 2.08 |
| **18** | 4.41 | 3.55 | 3.16 | 2.93 | 2.77 | 2.66 | 2.58 | 2.51 | 2.46 | 2.41 | 2.27 | 2.19 | 2.14 | 2.11 | 2.06 | 2.04 |
| **19** | 4.38 | 3.52 | 3.13 | 2.90 | 2.74 | 2.63 | 2.54 | 2.48 | 2.42 | 2.38 | 2.23 | 2.16 | 2.11 | 2.07 | 2.03 | 2.00 |
| **20** | 4.35 | 3.49 | 3.10 | 2.87 | 2.71 | 2.60 | 2.51 | 2.45 | 2.39 | 2.35 | 2.20 | 2.12 | 2.07 | 2.04 | 1.99 | 1.97 |
| **22** | 4.30 | 3.44 | 3.05 | 2.82 | 2.66 | 2.55 | 2.46 | 2.40 | 2.34 | 2.30 | 2.15 | 2.07 | 2.02 | 1.98 | 1.94 | 1.91 |
| **24** | 4.26 | 3.40 | 3.01 | 2.78 | 2.62 | 2.51 | 2.42 | 2.36 | 2.30 | 2.25 | 2.11 | 2.03 | 1.97 | 1.94 | 1.89 | 1.86 |
| **26** | 4.23 | 3.37 | 2.98 | 2.74 | 2.59 | 2.47 | 2.39 | 2.32 | 2.27 | 2.22 | 2.07 | 1.99 | 1.94 | 1.90 | 1.85 | 1.82 |
| **28** | 4.20 | 3.34 | 2.95 | 2.71 | 2.56 | 2.45 | 2.36 | 2.29 | 2.24 | 2.19 | 2.04 | 1.96 | 1.91 | 1.87 | 1.82 | 1.79 |
| **30** | 4.17 | 3.32 | 2.92 | 2.69 | 2.53 | 2.42 | 2.33 | 2.27 | 2.21 | 2.16 | 2.01 | 1.93 | 1.88 | 1.84 | 1.79 | 1.76 |
| **40** | 4.08 | 3.23 | 2.84 | 2.61 | 2.45 | 2.34 | 2.25 | 2.18 | 2.12 | 2.08 | 1.92 | 1.84 | 1.78 | 1.74 | 1.69 | 1.66 |
| **50** | 4.03 | 3.18 | 2.79 | 2.56 | 2.40 | 2.29 | 2.20 | 2.13 | 2.07 | 2.03 | 1.87 | 1.78 | 1.73 | 1.69 | 1.63 | 1.60 |
| **60** | 4.00 | 3.15 | 2.76 | 2.53 | 2.37 | 2.25 | 2.17 | 2.10 | 2.04 | 1.99 | 1.84 | 1.75 | 1.69 | 1.65 | 1.59 | 1.56 |
| **120** | 3.92 | 3.07 | 2.68 | 2.45 | 2.29 | 2.18 | 2.09 | 2.02 | 1.96 | 1.91 | 1.75 | 1.66 | 1.60 | 1.55 | 1.50 | 1.46 |
| **200** | 3.89 | 3.04 | 2.65 | 2.42 | 2.26 | 2.14 | 2.06 | 1.98 | 1.93 | 1.88 | 1.72 | 1.62 | 1.56 | 1.52 | 1.46 | 1.41 |
| **500** | 3.86 | 3.01 | 2.62 | 2.39 | 2.23 | 2.12 | 2.03 | 1.96 | 1.90 | 1.85 | 1.69 | 1.59 | 1.53 | 1.48 | 1.42 | 1.38 |
| **1000** | 3.85 | 3.01 | 2.61 | 2.38 | 2.22 | 2.11 | 2.02 | 1.95 | 1.89 | 1.84 | 1.68 | 1.58 | 1.52 | 1.47 | 1.41 | 1.36 |

(*Source:* The entries in this table were computed by the author.)

## Table D.4
Critical Values of the $F$ Distribution: Alpha = .01

| | | | | | | Degrees of Freedom for Numerator | | | | | | | | | | |
|---|---|---|---|---|---|---|---|---|---|---|---|---|---|---|---|---|
| | **1** | **2** | **3** | **4** | **5** | **6** | **7** | **8** | **9** | **10** | **15** | **20** | **25** | **30** | **40** | **50** |
| **1** | 4052 | 5000 | 5403 | 5624 | 5764 | 5859 | 5928 | 5981 | 6022 | 6056 | 6151 | 6209 | 6240 | 6260 | 6287 | 6303 |
| **2** | 98.50 | 99.00 | 99.17 | 99.25 | 99.30 | 99.33 | 99.36 | 99.37 | 99.39 | 99.40 | 99.43 | 99.45 | 99.47 | 99.48 | 99.48 | 99.59 |
| **3** | 34.12 | 30.82 | 29.46 | 28.71 | 28.24 | 27.91 | 27.67 | 27.49 | 27.34 | 27.23 | 26.87 | 26.69 | 26.58 | 26.51 | 26.41 | 26.36 |
| **4** | 21.20 | 18.00 | 16.69 | 15.98 | 15.52 | 15.21 | 14.98 | 14.80 | 14.66 | 14.55 | 14.20 | 14.02 | 13.91 | 13.84 | 13.75 | 13.69 |
| **5** | 16.26 | 13.27 | 12.06 | 11.39 | 10.97 | 10.67 | 10.46 | 10.29 | 10.16 | 10.05 | 9.72 | 9.55 | 9.45 | 9.38 | 9.29 | 9.24 |
| **6** | 13.75 | 10.92 | 9.78 | 9.15 | 8.75 | 8.47 | 8.26 | 8.10 | 7.98 | 7.87 | 7.56 | 7.40 | 7.30 | 7.23 | 7.14 | 7.09 |
| **7** | 12.25 | 9.55 | 8.45 | 7.85 | 7.46 | 7.19 | 6.99 | 6.84 | 6.72 | 6.62 | 6.31 | 6.16 | 6.06 | 5.99 | 5.91 | 5.86 |
| **8** | 11.26 | 8.65 | 7.59 | 7.01 | 6.63 | 6.37 | 6.18 | 6.03 | 5.91 | 5.81 | 5.52 | 5.36 | 5.26 | 5.20 | 5.12 | 5.07 |
| **9** | 10.56 | 8.02 | 6.99 | 6.42 | 6.06 | 5.80 | 5.61 | 5.47 | 5.35 | 5.26 | 4.96 | 4.81 | 4.71 | 4.65 | 4.57 | 4.52 |
| **10** | 10.04 | 7.56 | 6.55 | 5.99 | 5.64 | 5.39 | 5.20 | 5.06 | 4.94 | 4.85 | 4.56 | 4.41 | 4.31 | 4.25 | 4.17 | 4.12 |
| **11** | 9.65 | 7.21 | 6.22 | 5.67 | 5.32 | 5.07 | 4.89 | 4.74 | 4.63 | 4.54 | 4.25 | 4.10 | 4.01 | 3.94 | 3.86 | 3.81 |
| **12** | 9.33 | 6.93 | 5.95 | 5.41 | 5.06 | 4.82 | 4.64 | 4.50 | 4.39 | 4.30 | 4.01 | 3.86 | 3.76 | 3.70 | 3.62 | 3.57 |
| **13** | 9.07 | 6.70 | 5.74 | 5.21 | 4.86 | 4.62 | 4.44 | 4.30 | 4.19 | 4.10 | 3.82 | 3.66 | 3.57 | 3.51 | 3.43 | 3.38 |
| **14** | 8.86 | 6.51 | 5.56 | 5.04 | 4.69 | 4.46 | 4.28 | 4.14 | 4.03 | 3.94 | 3.66 | 3.51 | 3.41 | 3.35 | 3.27 | 3.22 |
| **15** | 8.68 | 6.36 | 5.42 | 4.89 | 4.56 | 4.32 | 4.14 | 4.00 | 3.89 | 3.80 | 3.52 | 3.37 | 3.28 | 3.21 | 3.13 | 3.08 |
| **16** | 8.53 | 6.23 | 5.29 | 4.77 | 4.44 | 4.20 | 4.03 | 3.89 | 3.78 | 3.69 | 3.41 | 3.26 | 3.16 | 3.10 | 3.02 | 2.97 |
| **17** | 8.40 | 6.11 | 5.18 | 4.67 | 4.34 | 4.10 | 3.93 | 3.79 | 3.68 | 3.59 | 3.31 | 3.16 | 3.07 | 3.00 | 2.92 | 2.87 |
| **18** | 8.29 | 6.01 | 5.09 | 4.58 | 4.25 | 4.01 | 3.84 | 3.71 | 3.60 | 3.51 | 3.23 | 3.08 | 2.98 | 2.92 | 2.84 | 2.78 |
| **19** | 8.18 | 5.93 | 5.01 | 4.50 | 4.17 | 3.94 | 3.77 | 3.63 | 3.52 | 3.43 | 3.15 | 3.00 | 2.91 | 2.84 | 2.76 | 2.71 |
| **20** | 8.10 | 5.85 | 4.94 | 4.43 | 4.10 | 3.87 | 3.70 | 3.56 | 3.46 | 3.37 | 3.09 | 2.94 | 2.84 | 2.78 | 2.69 | 2.64 |
| **22** | 7.95 | 5.72 | 4.82 | 4.31 | 3.99 | 3.76 | 3.59 | 3.45 | 3.35 | 3.26 | 2.98 | 2.83 | 2.73 | 2.67 | 2.58 | 2.53 |
| **24** | 7.82 | 5.61 | 4.72 | 4.22 | 3.90 | 3.67 | 3.50 | 3.36 | 3.26 | 3.17 | 2.89 | 2.74 | 2.64 | 2.58 | 2.49 | 2.44 |
| **26** | 7.72 | 5.53 | 4.64 | 4.14 | 3.82 | 3.59 | 3.42 | 3.29 | 3.18 | 3.09 | 2.81 | 2.66 | 2.57 | 2.50 | 2.42 | 2.36 |
| **28** | 7.64 | 5.45 | 4.57 | 4.07 | 3.75 | 3.53 | 3.36 | 3.23 | 3.12 | 3.03 | 2.75 | 2.60 | 2.51 | 2.44 | 2.35 | 2.30 |
| **30** | 7.56 | 5.39 | 4.51 | 4.02 | 3.70 | 3.47 | 3.30 | 3.17 | 3.07 | 2.98 | 2.70 | 2.55 | 2.45 | 2.39 | 2.30 | 2.25 |
| **40** | 7.31 | 5.18 | 4.31 | 3.83 | 3.51 | 3.29 | 3.12 | 2.99 | 2.89 | 2.80 | 2.52 | 2.37 | 2.27 | 2.20 | 2.11 | 2.06 |
| **50** | 7.17 | 5.06 | 4.20 | 3.72 | 3.41 | 3.19 | 3.02 | 2.89 | 2.78 | 2.70 | 2.42 | 2.27 | 2.17 | 2.10 | 2.01 | 1.95 |
| **60** | 7.08 | 4.98 | 4.13 | 3.65 | 3.34 | 3.12 | 2.95 | 2.82 | 2.72 | 2.63 | 2.35 | 2.20 | 2.10 | 2.03 | 1.94 | 1.88 |
| **120** | 6.85 | 4.79 | 3.95 | 3.48 | 3.17 | 2.96 | 2.79 | 2.66 | 2.56 | 2.47 | 2.19 | 2.03 | 1.93 | 1.86 | 1.76 | 1.70 |
| **200** | 6.76 | 4.71 | 3.88 | 3.41 | 3.11 | 2.89 | 2.73 | 2.60 | 2.50 | 2.41 | 2.13 | 1.97 | 1.87 | 1.79 | 1.69 | 1.63 |
| **500** | 6.69 | 4.65 | 3.82 | 3.36 | 3.05 | 2.84 | 2.68 | 2.55 | 2.44 | 2.36 | 2.07 | 1.92 | 1.81 | 1.74 | 1.63 | 1.57 |
| **1000** | 6.67 | 4.63 | 3.80 | 3.34 | 3.04 | 2.82 | 2.66 | 2.53 | 2.43 | 2.34 | 2.06 | 1.90 | 1.79 | 1.72 | 1.61 | 1.54 |

*Degrees of Freedom for Denominator* (row labels)

(*Source:*  The entries in this table were computed by the author.)

**Table D.5**
Power as a Function of $\delta$ and Significance Level ($\alpha$)

| $\delta$ | Alpha for Two-Tailed Test | | | |
|---|---|---|---|---|
| | **.10** | **.05** | **.02** | **.01** |
| 1.00 | .26 | .17 | .09 | .06 |
| 1.10 | .29 | .20 | .11 | .07 |
| 1.20 | .33 | .22 | .13 | .08 |
| 1.30 | .37 | .26 | .15 | .10 |
| 1.40 | .40 | .29 | .18 | .12 |
| 1.50 | .44 | .32 | .20 | .14 |
| 1.60 | .48 | .36 | .23 | .17 |
| 1.70 | .52 | .40 | .27 | .19 |
| 1.80 | .56 | .44 | .30 | .22 |
| 1.90 | .60 | .48 | .34 | .25 |
| 2.00 | .64 | .52 | .37 | .28 |
| 2.10 | .68 | .56 | .41 | .32 |
| 2.20 | .71 | .60 | .45 | .35 |
| 2.30 | .74 | .63 | .49 | .39 |
| 2.40 | .78 | .67 | .53 | .43 |
| 2.50 | .80 | .71 | .57 | .47 |
| 2.60 | .83 | .74 | .61 | .51 |
| 2.70 | .85 | .77 | .65 | .55 |
| 2.80 | .88 | .80 | .68 | .59 |
| 2.90 | .90 | .83 | .72 | .63 |
| 3.00 | .91 | .85 | .75 | .66 |
| 3.10 | .93 | .87 | .78 | .70 |
| 3.20 | .94 | .89 | .81 | .73 |
| 3.30 | .95 | .91 | .84 | .77 |
| 3.40 | .96 | .93 | .86 | .80 |
| 3.50 | .97 | .94 | .88 | .82 |
| 3.60 | .98 | .95 | .90 | .85 |
| 3.70 | .98 | .96 | .92 | .87 |
| 3.80 | .98 | .97 | .93 | .89 |
| 3.90 | .99 | .97 | .94 | .91 |
| 4.00 | .99 | .98 | .95 | .92 |
| 4.10 | .99 | .98 | .96 | .94 |
| 4.20 | ... | .99 | .97 | .95 |
| 4.30 | ... | .99 | .98 | .96 |
| 4.40 | ... | .99 | .98 | .97 |
| 4.50 | ... | .99 | .99 | .97 |
| 4.60 | ... | ... | .99 | .98 |
| 4.70 | ... | ... | .99 | .98 |
| 4.80 | ... | ... | .99 | .99 |
| 4.90 | ... | ... | ... | .99 |
| 5.00 | ... | ... | ... | .99 |

(*Source:*   The entries in this table were computed by the author.)

## Table D.6
Percentage Points of the *t* Distribution

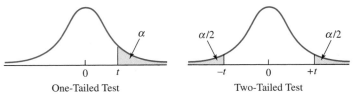

One-Tailed Test          Two-Tailed Test

| | Level of Significance for One-Tailed Test | | | | | | | | |
|---|---|---|---|---|---|---|---|---|---|
| | .25 | .20 | .15 | .10 | .05 | .025 | .01 | .005 | .0005 |
| | Level of Significance for Two-Tailed Test | | | | | | | | |
| *df* | .50 | .40 | .30 | .20 | .10 | .05 | .02 | .01 | .001 |
| 1 | 1.000 | 1.376 | 1.963 | 3.078 | 6.314 | 12.706 | 31.821 | 63.657 | 63.662 |
| 2 | .816 | 1.061 | 1.386 | 1.886 | 2.920 | 4.303 | 6.965 | 9.925 | 31.599 |
| 3 | .765 | .978 | 1.250 | 1.638 | 2.353 | 3.182 | 4.541 | 5.841 | 12.924 |
| 4 | .741 | .941 | 1.190 | 1.533 | 2.132 | 2.776 | 3.747 | 4.604 | 8.610 |
| 5 | .727 | .920 | 1.156 | 1.476 | 2.015 | 2.571 | 3.365 | 4.032 | 6.869 |
| 6 | .718 | .906 | 1.134 | 1.440 | 1.943 | 2.447 | 3.143 | 3.707 | 5.959 |
| 7 | .711 | .896 | 1.119 | 1.415 | 1.895 | 2.365 | 2.998 | 3.499 | 5.408 |
| 8 | .706 | .889 | 1.108 | 1.397 | 1.860 | 2.306 | 2.896 | 3.355 | 5.041 |
| 9 | .703 | .883 | 1.100 | 1.383 | 1.833 | 2.262 | 2.821 | 3.250 | 4.781 |
| 10 | .700 | .879 | 1.093 | 1.372 | 1.812 | 2.228 | 2.764 | 3.169 | 4.587 |
| 11 | .697 | .876 | 1.088 | 1.363 | 1.796 | 2.201 | 2.718 | 3.106 | 4.437 |
| 12 | .695 | .873 | 1.083 | 1.356 | 1.782 | 2.179 | 2.681 | 3.055 | 4.318 |
| 13 | .694 | .870 | 1.079 | 1.350 | 1.771 | 2.160 | 2.650 | 3.012 | 4.221 |
| 14 | .692 | .868 | 1.076 | 1.345 | 1.761 | 2.145 | 2.624 | 2.977 | 4.140 |
| 15 | .691 | .866 | 1.074 | 1.341 | 1.753 | 2.131 | 2.602 | 2.947 | 4.073 |
| 16 | .690 | .865 | 1.071 | 1.337 | 1.746 | 2.120 | 2.583 | 2.921 | 4.015 |
| 17 | .689 | .863 | 1.069 | 1.333 | 1.740 | 2.110 | 2.567 | 2.898 | 3.965 |
| 18 | .688 | .862 | 1.067 | 1.330 | 1.734 | 2.101 | 2.552 | 2.878 | 3.922 |
| 19 | .688 | .861 | 1.066 | 1.328 | 1.729 | 2.093 | 2.539 | 2.861 | 3.883 |
| 20 | .687 | .860 | 1.064 | 1.325 | 1.725 | 2.086 | 2.528 | 2.845 | 3.850 |
| 21 | .686 | .859 | 1.063 | 1.323 | 1.721 | 2.080 | 2.518 | 2.831 | 3.819 |
| 22 | .686 | .858 | 1.061 | 1.321 | 1.717 | 2.074 | 2.508 | 2.819 | 3.792 |
| 23 | .685 | .858 | 1.060 | 1.319 | 1.714 | 2.069 | 2.500 | 2.807 | 3.768 |
| 24 | .685 | .857 | 1.059 | 1.318 | 1.711 | 2.064 | 2.492 | 2.797 | 3.745 |
| 25 | .684 | .856 | 1.058 | 1.316 | 1.708 | 2.060 | 2.485 | 2.787 | 3.725 |
| 26 | .684 | .856 | 1.058 | 1.315 | 1.706 | 2.056 | 2.479 | 2.779 | 3.707 |
| 27 | .684 | .855 | 1.057 | 1.314 | 1.703 | 2.052 | 2.473 | 2.771 | 3.690 |
| 28 | .683 | .855 | 1.056 | 1.313 | 1.701 | 2.048 | 2.467 | 2.763 | 3.674 |
| 29 | .683 | .854 | 1.055 | 1.311 | 1.699 | 2.045 | 2.462 | 2.756 | 3.659 |
| 30 | .683 | .854 | 1.055 | 1.310 | 1.697 | 2.042 | 2.457 | 2.750 | 3.646 |
| 40 | .681 | .851 | 1.050 | 1.303 | 1.684 | 2.021 | 2.423 | 2.704 | 3.551 |
| 50 | .679 | .849 | 1.047 | 1.299 | 1.676 | 2.009 | 2.403 | 2.678 | 3.496 |
| 100 | .677 | .845 | 1.042 | 1.290 | 1.660 | 1.984 | 2.364 | 2.626 | 3.390 |
| ∞ | .674 | .842 | 1.036 | 1.282 | 1.645 | 1.960 | 2.326 | 2.576 | 3.291 |

(*Source:*   The entries in this table were computed by the author.)

## Table D.7
Critical Lower-Tail Values of *T* (and Their Associated Probabilities) for Wilcoxon's Matched-Pairs Signed-Ranks Test

| | Nominal Alpha (One-Tailed) | | | | | | | | Nominal Alpha (One-Tailed) | | | | | | | |
|---|---|---|---|---|---|---|---|---|---|---|---|---|---|---|---|---|
| | .05 | | .025 | | .01 | | .005 | | | .05 | | .025 | | .01 | | .005 |
| n | T | α | T | α | T | α | T | α | n | T | α | T | α | T | α | T | α |
| 5 | 0 | .0313 | | | | | | | 28 | 130 | .0496 | 116 | .0239 | 101 | .0096 | 91 | .0048 |
| | 1 | .0625 | | | | | | | | 131 | .0521 | 117 | .0252 | 102 | .0102 | 92 | .0051 |
| 6 | 2 | .0469 | 0 | .0156 | | | | | 29 | 140 | .0482 | 126 | .0240 | 110 | .0095 | 100 | .0049 |
| | 3 | .0781 | 1 | .0313 | | | | | | 141 | .0504 | 127 | .0253 | 111 | .0101 | 101 | .0053 |
| 7 | 3 | .0391 | 2 | .0234 | 0 | .0078 | | | 30 | 151 | .0481 | 137 | .0249 | 120 | .0098 | 109 | .0050 |
| | 4 | .0547 | 3 | .0391 | 1 | .0156 | | | | 152 | .0502 | 138 | .0261 | 121 | .0104 | 110 | .0053 |
| 8 | 5 | .0391 | 3 | .0195 | 1 | .0078 | 0 | .0039 | 31 | 163 | .0491 | 147 | .0239 | 130 | .0099 | 118 | .0049 |
| | 6 | .0547 | 4 | .0273 | 2 | .0117 | 1 | .0078 | | 164 | .0512 | 148 | .0251 | 131 | .0105 | 119 | .0052 |
| 9 | 8 | .0488 | 5 | .0195 | 3 | .0098 | 1 | .0039 | 32 | 175 | .0492 | 159 | .0249 | 140 | .0097 | 128 | .0050 |
| | 9 | .0645 | 6 | .0273 | 4 | .0137 | 2 | .0059 | | 176 | .0512 | 160 | .0260 | 141 | .0103 | 129 | .0053 |
| 10 | 10 | .0420 | 8 | .0244 | 5 | .0098 | 3 | .0049 | 33 | 187 | .0485 | 170 | .0242 | 151 | .0099 | 138 | .0049 |
| | 11 | .0527 | 9 | .0322 | 6 | .0137 | 4 | .0068 | | 188 | .0503 | 171 | .0253 | 152 | .0104 | 139 | .0052 |
| 11 | 13 | .0415 | 10 | .0210 | 7 | .0093 | 5 | .0049 | 34 | 200 | .0488 | 182 | .0242 | 162 | .0098 | 148 | .0048 |
| | 14 | .0508 | 11 | .0269 | 8 | .0122 | 6 | .0068 | | 201 | .0506 | 183 | .0252 | 163 | .0103 | 149 | .0051 |
| 12 | 17 | .0461 | 13 | .0212 | 9 | .0081 | 7 | .0046 | 35 | 213 | .0484 | 195 | .0247 | 173 | .0096 | 159 | .0048 |
| | 18 | .0549 | 14 | .0261 | 10 | .0105 | 8 | .0061 | | 214 | .0501 | 196 | .0257 | 174 | .0100 | 160 | .0051 |
| 13 | 21 | .0471 | 17 | .0239 | 12 | .0085 | 9 | .0040 | 36 | 227 | .0489 | 208 | .0248 | 185 | .0096 | 171 | .0050 |
| | 22 | .0549 | 18 | .0287 | 13 | .0107 | 10 | .0052 | | 228 | .0505 | 209 | .0258 | 186 | .0100 | 172 | .0052 |
| 14 | 25 | .0453 | 21 | .0247 | 15 | .0083 | 12 | .0043 | 37 | 241 | .0487 | 221 | .0245 | 198 | .0099 | 182 | .0048 |
| | 26 | .0520 | 22 | .0290 | 16 | .0101 | 13 | .0054 | | 242 | .0503 | 222 | .0254 | 199 | .0103 | 183 | .0050 |
| 15 | 30 | .0473 | 25 | .0240 | 19 | .0090 | 15 | .0042 | 38 | 256 | .0493 | 235 | .0247 | 211 | .0099 | 194 | .0048 |
| | 31 | .0535 | 26 | .0277 | 20 | .0108 | 16 | .0051 | | 257 | .0509 | 236 | .0256 | 212 | .0104 | 195 | .0050 |
| 16 | 35 | .0467 | 29 | .0222 | 23 | .0091 | 19 | .0046 | 39 | 271 | .0492 | 249 | .0246 | 224 | .0099 | 207 | .0049 |
| | 36 | .0523 | 30 | .0253 | 24 | .0107 | 20 | .0055 | | 272 | .0507 | 250 | .0254 | 225 | .0103 | 208 | .0051 |
| 17 | 41 | .0492 | 34 | .0224 | 27 | .0087 | 23 | .0047 | 40 | 286 | .0486 | 264 | .0249 | 238 | .0100 | 220 | .0049 |
| | 42 | .0544 | 35 | .0253 | 28 | .0101 | 24 | .0055 | | 287 | .0500 | 265 | .0257 | 239 | .0104 | 221 | .0051 |
| 18 | 47 | .0494 | 40 | .0241 | 32 | .0091 | 27 | .0045 | 41 | 302 | .0488 | 279 | .0248 | 252 | .0100 | 233 | .0048 |
| | 48 | .0542 | 41 | .0269 | 33 | .0104 | 28 | .0052 | | 303 | .0501 | 280 | .0256 | 253 | .0103 | 234 | .0050 |
| 19 | 53 | .0478 | 46 | .0247 | 37 | .0090 | 32 | .0047 | 42 | 319 | .0496 | 294 | .0245 | 266 | .0098 | 247 | .0049 |
| | 54 | .0521 | 47 | .0273 | 38 | .0102 | 33 | .0054 | | 320 | .0509 | 295 | .0252 | 267 | .0102 | 248 | .0051 |
| 20 | 60 | .0487 | 52 | .0242 | 43 | .0096 | 37 | .0047 | 43 | 336 | .0498 | 310 | .0245 | 281 | .0098 | 261 | .0048 |
| | 61 | .0527 | 53 | .0266 | 44 | .0107 | 38 | .0053 | | 337 | .0511 | 311 | .0252 | 282 | .0102 | 262 | .0050 |
| 21 | 67 | .0479 | 58 | .0230 | 49 | .0097 | 42 | .0045 | 44 | 353 | .0495 | 327 | .0250 | 296 | .0097 | 276 | .0049 |
| | 68 | .0516 | 59 | .0251 | 50 | .0108 | 43 | .0051 | | 354 | .0507 | 328 | .0257 | 297 | .0101 | 277 | .0051 |
| 22 | 75 | .0492 | 65 | .0231 | 55 | .0095 | 48 | .0046 | 45 | 371 | .0498 | 343 | .0244 | 312 | .0098 | 291 | .0049 |
| | 76 | .0527 | 66 | .0250 | 56 | .0104 | 49 | .0052 | | 372 | .0510 | 344 | .0251 | 313 | .0101 | 292 | .0051 |
| 23 | 83 | .0490 | 73 | .0242 | 62 | .0098 | 54 | .0046 | 46 | 389 | .0497 | 361 | .0249 | 328 | .0098 | 307 | .0050 |
| | 84 | .0523 | 74 | .0261 | 63 | .0107 | 55 | .0051 | | 390 | .0508 | 362 | .0256 | 329 | .0101 | 308 | .0052 |
| 24 | 91 | .0475 | 81 | .0245 | 69 | .0097 | 61 | .0048 | 47 | 407 | .0490 | 378 | .0245 | 345 | .0099 | 322 | .0048 |
| | 92 | .0505 | 82 | .0263 | 70 | .0106 | 62 | .0053 | | 408 | .0501 | 379 | .0251 | 346 | .0102 | 323 | .0050 |
| 25 | 100 | .0479 | 89 | .0241 | 76 | .0094 | 68 | .0048 | 48 | 426 | .0490 | 396 | .0244 | 362 | .0099 | 339 | .0050 |
| | 101 | .0507 | 90 | .0258 | 77 | .0101 | 69 | .0053 | | 427 | .0500 | 397 | .0251 | 363 | .0102 | 340 | .0051 |
| 26 | 110 | .0497 | 98 | .0247 | 84 | .0095 | 75 | .0047 | 49 | 446 | .0495 | 415 | .0247 | 379 | .0098 | 355 | .0049 |
| | 111 | .0524 | 99 | .0263 | 85 | .0102 | 76 | .0051 | | 447 | .0505 | 416 | .0253 | 380 | .0100 | 356 | .0051 |
| 27 | 119 | .0477 | 107 | .0246 | 92 | .0093 | 83 | .0048 | 50 | 466 | .0495 | 434 | .0247 | 397 | .0098 | 373 | .0050 |
| | 120 | .0502 | 108 | .0260 | 93 | .0100 | 84 | .0052 | | 467 | .0506 | 435 | .0253 | 398 | .0101 | 374 | .0051 |

(*Source:* The entries in this table were computed by the author.)

## Table D.8

Critical Lower-Tail Values of $W_S$ for the Mann–Whitney Test for Two Independent Samples $(N_1 \leq N_2)$

| | $n_1 = 1$ | | | | | | | $n_1 = 2$ | | | | | | | |
|---|---|---|---|---|---|---|---|---|---|---|---|---|---|---|---|
| $n_2$ | .001 | .005 | .010 | .025 | .05 | .10 | $2\overline{W}$ | .001 | .005 | .010 | .025 | .05 | .10 | $2\overline{W}$ | $n_2$ |
| 2 | | | | | | | 4 | | | | | | ⋮ | 10 | 2 |
| 3 | | | | | | | 5 | | | | | | 3 | 12 | 3 |
| 4 | | | | | | | 6 | | | | | ⋮ | 3 | 14 | 4 |
| 5 | | | | | | | 7 | | | | | 3 | 4 | 16 | 5 |
| 6 | | | | | | | 8 | | | | | 3 | 4 | 18 | 6 |
| 7 | | | | | | | 9 | | | | ⋮ | 3 | 4 | 20 | 7 |
| 8 | | | | | | ⋮ | 10 | | | | 3 | 4 | 5 | 22 | 8 |
| 9 | | | | | | 1 | 11 | | | | 3 | 4 | 5 | 24 | 9 |
| 10 | | | | | | 1 | 12 | | | | 3 | 4 | 6 | 26 | 10 |
| 11 | | | | | | 1 | 13 | | | | 3 | 4 | 6 | 28 | 11 |
| 12 | | | | | | 1 | 14 | | | ⋮ | 4 | 5 | 7 | 30 | 12 |
| 13 | | | | | | 1 | 15 | | | 3 | 4 | 5 | 7 | 32 | 13 |
| 14 | | | | | | 1 | 16 | | | 3 | 4 | 6 | 8 | 34 | 14 |
| 15 | | | | | | 1 | 17 | | | 3 | 4 | 6 | 8 | 36 | 15 |
| 16 | | | | | | 1 | 18 | | | 3 | 4 | 6 | 8 | 38 | 16 |
| 17 | | | | | | 1 | 19 | | | 3 | 5 | 6 | 9 | 40 | 17 |
| 18 | | | | | ⋮ | 1 | 20 | | ⋮ | 3 | 5 | 7 | 9 | 42 | 18 |
| 19 | | | | | 1 | 2 | 21 | | 3 | 4 | 5 | 7 | 10 | 44 | 19 |
| 20 | | | | | 1 | 2 | 22 | | 3 | 4 | 5 | 7 | 10 | 46 | 20 |
| 21 | | | | | 1 | 2 | 23 | | 3 | 4 | 6 | 8 | 11 | 48 | 21 |
| 22 | | | | | 1 | 2 | 24 | | 3 | 4 | 6 | 8 | 11 | 50 | 22 |
| 23 | | | | | 1 | 2 | 25 | | 3 | 4 | 6 | 8 | 12 | 52 | 23 |
| 24 | | | | | 1 | 2 | 26 | | 3 | 4 | 6 | 9 | 12 | 54 | 24 |
| 25 | ⋮ | ⋮ | ⋮ | ⋮ | 1 | 2 | 27 | ⋮ | 3 | 4 | 6 | 9 | 12 | 56 | 25 |

| | $n_1 = 3$ | | | | | | | $n_1 = 4$ | | | | | | | |
|---|---|---|---|---|---|---|---|---|---|---|---|---|---|---|---|
| $n_2$ | .001 | .005 | .010 | .025 | .05 | .10 | $2\overline{W}$ | .001 | .005 | .010 | .025 | .05 | .10 | $2\overline{W}$ | $n_2$ |
| 3 | | | | | 6 | 7 | 21 | | | | | | | | |
| 4 | | | | ⋮ | 6 | 7 | 24 | | | ⋮ | 10 | 11 | 13 | 36 | 4 |
| 5 | | | | 6 | 7 | 8 | 27 | | ⋮ | 10 | 11 | 12 | 14 | 40 | 5 |
| 6 | | | ⋮ | 7 | 8 | 9 | 30 | | 10 | 11 | 12 | 13 | 15 | 44 | 6 |
| 7 | | | 6 | 7 | 8 | 10 | 33 | | 10 | 11 | 13 | 14 | 16 | 48 | 7 |
| 8 | | ⋮ | 6 | 8 | 9 | 11 | 36 | | 11 | 12 | 14 | 15 | 17 | 52 | 8 |
| 9 | | 6 | 7 | 8 | 10 | 11 | 39 | ⋮ | 11 | 13 | 14 | 16 | 19 | 56 | 9 |
| 10 | | 6 | 7 | 9 | 10 | 12 | 42 | 10 | 12 | 13 | 15 | 17 | 20 | 60 | 10 |
| 11 | | 6 | 7 | 9 | 11 | 13 | 45 | 10 | 12 | 14 | 16 | 18 | 21 | 64 | 11 |
| 12 | | 7 | 8 | 10 | 11 | 14 | 48 | 10 | 13 | 15 | 17 | 19 | 22 | 68 | 12 |
| 13 | | 7 | 8 | 10 | 12 | 15 | 51 | 11 | 13 | 15 | 18 | 20 | 23 | 72 | 13 |
| 14 | | 7 | 8 | 11 | 13 | 16 | 54 | 11 | 14 | 16 | 19 | 21 | 25 | 76 | 14 |
| 15 | | 8 | 9 | 11 | 13 | 16 | 57 | 11 | 15 | 17 | 20 | 22 | 26 | 80 | 15 |
| 16 | ⋮ | 8 | 9 | 12 | 14 | 17 | 60 | 12 | 15 | 17 | 21 | 24 | 27 | 84 | 16 |
| 17 | 6 | 8 | 10 | 12 | 15 | 18 | 63 | 12 | 16 | 18 | 21 | 25 | 28 | 88 | 17 |
| 18 | 6 | 8 | 10 | 13 | 15 | 19 | 66 | 13 | 16 | 19 | 22 | 26 | 30 | 92 | 18 |
| 19 | 6 | 9 | 10 | 13 | 16 | 20 | 69 | 13 | 17 | 19 | 23 | 27 | 31 | 96 | 19 |
| 20 | 6 | 9 | 11 | 14 | 17 | 21 | 72 | 13 | 18 | 20 | 24 | 28 | 32 | 100 | 20 |
| 21 | 7 | 9 | 11 | 14 | 17 | 21 | 75 | 14 | 18 | 21 | 25 | 29 | 33 | 104 | 21 |
| 22 | 7 | 10 | 12 | 15 | 18 | 22 | 78 | 14 | 19 | 21 | 26 | 30 | 35 | 108 | 22 |
| 23 | 7 | 10 | 12 | 15 | 19 | 23 | 81 | 14 | 19 | 22 | 27 | 31 | 36 | 112 | 23 |
| 24 | 7 | 10 | 12 | 16 | 19 | 24 | 84 | 15 | 20 | 23 | 27 | 32 | 38 | 116 | 24 |
| 25 | 7 | 11 | 13 | 16 | 20 | 25 | 87 | 15 | 20 | 23 | 28 | 33 | 38 | 120 | 25 |

(*Source:*  Table 1 in L. R. Verdooren, Extended tables of critical values for Wilcoxon's test statistic, *Biometrika*, 1963, 50, 177–186, with permission of the author and editor.)

**Table D.8**
*Continued*

| | | | $n_1 = 5$ | | | | | | | | $n_1 = 6$ | | | |
|---|---|---|---|---|---|---|---|---|---|---|---|---|---|---|
| $n_2$ | .001 | .005 | .010 | .025 | .05 | .10 | $2\overline{W}$ | .001 | .005 | .010 | .025 | .05 | .10 | $2\overline{W}$ | $n_2$ |
| 5 | | 15 | 16 | 17 | 19 | 20 | 55 | | | | | | | | 5 |
| 6 | | 16 | 17 | 18 | 20 | 22 | 60 | ... | 23 | 24 | 26 | 28 | 30 | 78 | 6 |
| 7 | ... | 16 | 18 | 20 | 21 | 23 | 65 | 21 | 24 | 25 | 27 | 29 | 32 | 84 | 7 |
| 8 | 15 | 17 | 19 | 21 | 23 | 25 | 70 | 22 | 25 | 27 | 29 | 31 | 34 | 90 | 8 |
| 9 | 16 | 18 | 20 | 22 | 24 | 27 | 75 | 23 | 26 | 28 | 31 | 33 | 36 | 96 | 9 |
| 10 | 16 | 19 | 21 | 23 | 26 | 28 | 80 | 24 | 27 | 29 | 32 | 35 | 38 | 102 | 10 |
| 11 | 17 | 20 | 22 | 24 | 27 | 30 | 85 | 25 | 28 | 30 | 34 | 37 | 40 | 108 | 11 |
| 12 | 17 | 21 | 23 | 26 | 28 | 32 | 90 | 25 | 30 | 32 | 35 | 38 | 42 | 114 | 12 |
| 13 | 18 | 22 | 24 | 27 | 30 | 33 | 95 | 26 | 31 | 33 | 37 | 40 | 44 | 120 | 13 |
| 14 | 18 | 22 | 25 | 28 | 31 | 35 | 100 | 27 | 32 | 34 | 38 | 42 | 46 | 126 | 14 |
| 15 | 19 | 23 | 26 | 29 | 33 | 37 | 105 | 28 | 33 | 36 | 40 | 44 | 48 | 132 | 15 |
| 16 | 20 | 24 | 27 | 30 | 34 | 38 | 110 | 29 | 34 | 37 | 42 | 46 | 50 | 138 | 16 |
| 17 | 20 | 25 | 28 | 32 | 35 | 40 | 115 | 30 | 36 | 39 | 43 | 47 | 52 | 144 | 17 |
| 18 | 21 | 26 | 29 | 33 | 37 | 42 | 120 | 31 | 37 | 40 | 45 | 49 | 55 | 150 | 18 |
| 19 | 22 | 27 | 30 | 34 | 38 | 43 | 125 | 32 | 38 | 41 | 46 | 51 | 57 | 156 | 19 |
| 20 | 22 | 28 | 31 | 35 | 40 | 45 | 130 | 33 | 39 | 43 | 48 | 53 | 59 | 162 | 20 |
| 21 | 23 | 29 | 32 | 37 | 41 | 47 | 135 | 33 | 40 | 44 | 50 | 55 | 61 | 168 | 21 |
| 22 | 23 | 29 | 33 | 38 | 43 | 48 | 140 | 34 | 42 | 45 | 51 | 57 | 63 | 174 | 22 |
| 23 | 24 | 30 | 34 | 39 | 44 | 50 | 145 | 35 | 43 | 47 | 53 | 58 | 65 | 180 | 23 |
| 24 | 25 | 31 | 35 | 40 | 45 | 51 | 150 | 36 | 44 | 48 | 54 | 60 | 67 | 186 | 24 |
| 25 | 25 | 32 | 36 | 42 | 47 | 53 | 155 | 37 | 45 | 50 | 56 | 62 | 69 | 192 | 25 |

| | | | $n_1 = 7$ | | | | | | | | $n_1 = 8$ | | | |
|---|---|---|---|---|---|---|---|---|---|---|---|---|---|---|
| $n_2$ | .001 | .005 | .010 | .025 | .05 | .10 | $2\overline{W}$ | .001 | .005 | .010 | .025 | .05 | .10 | $2\overline{W}$ | $n_2$ |
| 7 | 29 | 32 | 34 | 36 | 39 | 41 | 105 | | | | | | | | 7 |
| 8 | 30 | 34 | 35 | 38 | 41 | 44 | 112 | 40 | 43 | 45 | 49 | 51 | 55 | 136 | 8 |
| 9 | 31 | 35 | 37 | 40 | 43 | 46 | 119 | 41 | 45 | 47 | 51 | 54 | 58 | 144 | 9 |
| 10 | 33 | 37 | 39 | 42 | 45 | 49 | 126 | 42 | 47 | 49 | 53 | 56 | 60 | 152 | 10 |
| 11 | 34 | 38 | 40 | 44 | 47 | 51 | 133 | 44 | 49 | 51 | 55 | 59 | 63 | 160 | 11 |
| 12 | 35 | 40 | 42 | 46 | 49 | 54 | 140 | 45 | 51 | 53 | 58 | 62 | 66 | 168 | 12 |
| 13 | 36 | 41 | 44 | 48 | 52 | 56 | 147 | 47 | 53 | 56 | 60 | 64 | 69 | 176 | 13 |
| 14 | 37 | 43 | 45 | 50 | 54 | 59 | 154 | 48 | 54 | 58 | 62 | 67 | 72 | 184 | 14 |
| 15 | 38 | 44 | 47 | 52 | 56 | 61 | 161 | 50 | 56 | 60 | 65 | 69 | 75 | 192 | 15 |
| 16 | 39 | 46 | 49 | 54 | 58 | 64 | 168 | 51 | 58 | 62 | 67 | 72 | 78 | 200 | 16 |
| 17 | 41 | 47 | 51 | 56 | 61 | 66 | 175 | 53 | 60 | 64 | 70 | 75 | 81 | 208 | 17 |
| 18 | 42 | 49 | 52 | 58 | 63 | 69 | 182 | 54 | 62 | 66 | 72 | 77 | 84 | 216 | 18 |
| 19 | 43 | 50 | 54 | 60 | 65 | 71 | 189 | 56 | 64 | 68 | 74 | 80 | 87 | 224 | 19 |
| 20 | 44 | 52 | 56 | 62 | 67 | 74 | 196 | 57 | 66 | 70 | 77 | 83 | 90 | 232 | 20 |
| 21 | 46 | 53 | 58 | 64 | 69 | 76 | 203 | 59 | 68 | 72 | 79 | 85 | 92 | 240 | 21 |
| 22 | 47 | 55 | 59 | 66 | 72 | 79 | 210 | 60 | 70 | 74 | 81 | 88 | 95 | 248 | 22 |
| 23 | 48 | 57 | 61 | 68 | 74 | 81 | 217 | 62 | 71 | 76 | 84 | 90 | 98 | 256 | 23 |
| 24 | 49 | 58 | 63 | 70 | 76 | 84 | 224 | 64 | 73 | 78 | 86 | 93 | 101 | 264 | 24 |
| 25 | 50 | 60 | 64 | 72 | 78 | 86 | 231 | 65 | 75 | 81 | 89 | 96 | 104 | 272 | 25 |

*continued*

## Table D.8
*Continued*

| | $n_1 = 9$ | | | | | | | | $n_1 = 10$ | | | | | | | |
|---|---|---|---|---|---|---|---|---|---|---|---|---|---|---|---|---|
| $n_2$ | .001 | .005 | .010 | .025 | .05 | .10 | $2\bar{W}$ | .001 | .005 | .010 | .025 | .05 | .10 | $2\bar{W}$ | $n_2$ |
| 9 | 52 | 56 | 59 | 62 | 66 | 70 | 171 | | | | | | | | |
| 10 | 53 | 58 | 61 | 65 | 69 | 73 | 180 | 65 | 71 | 74 | 78 | 82 | 87 | 210 | 10 |
| 11 | 55 | 61 | 63 | 68 | 72 | 76 | 189 | 67 | 73 | 77 | .81 | 86 | 91 | 220 | 11 |
| 12 | 57 | 63 | 66 | 71 | 75 | 80 | 198 | 69 | 76 | 79 | 84 | 89 | 94 | 230 | 12 |
| 13 | 59 | 65 | 68 | 73 | 78 | 83 | 207 | 72 | 79 | 82 | 88 | 92 | 98 | 240 | 13 |
| 14 | 60 | 67 | 71 | 76 | 81 | 86 | 216 | 74 | 81 | 85 | 91 | 96 | 102 | 250 | 14 |
| 15 | 62 | 69 | 73 | 79 | 84 | 90 | 225 | 76 | 84 | 88 | 94 | 99 | 106 | 260 | 15 |
| 16 | 64 | 72 | 76 | 82 | 87 | 93 | 234 | 78 | 86 | 91 | 97 | 103 | 109 | 270 | 16 |
| 17 | 66 | 74 | 78 | 84 | 90 | 97 | 243 | 80 | 89 | 93 | 100 | 106 | 113 | 280 | 17 |
| 18 | 68 | 76 | 81 | 87 | 93 | 100 | 252 | 82 | 92 | 96 | 103 | 110 | 117 | 290 | 18 |
| 19 | 70 | 78 | 83 | 90 | 96 | 103 | 261 | 84 | 94 | 99 | 107 | 113 | 121 | 300 | 19 |
| 20 | 71 | 81 | 85 | 93 | 99 | 107 | 270 | 87 | 97 | 102 | 110 | 117 | 125 | 310 | 20 |
| 21 | 73 | 83 | 88 | 95 | 102 | 110 | 279 | 89 | 99 | 105 | 113 | 120 | 128 | 320 | 21 |
| 22 | 75 | 85 | 90 | 98 | 105 | 113 | 288 | 91 | 102 | 108 | 116 | 123 | 132 | 330 | 22 |
| 23 | 77 | 88 | 93 | 101 | 108 | 117 | 297 | 93 | 105 | 110 | 119 | 127 | 136 | 340 | 23 |
| 24 | 79 | 90 | 95 | 104 | 111 | 120 | 306 | 95 | 107 | 113 | 122 | 130 | 140 | 350 | 24 |
| 25 | 81 | 92 | 98 | 107 | 114 | 123 | 315 | 98 | 110 | 116 | 126 | 134 | 144 | 360 | 25 |

| | $n_1 = 11$ | | | | | | | | $n_1 = 12$ | | | | | | | |
|---|---|---|---|---|---|---|---|---|---|---|---|---|---|---|---|---|
| $n_2$ | .001 | .005 | .010 | .025 | .05 | .10 | $2\bar{W}$ | .001 | .005 | .010 | .025 | .05 | .10 | $2\bar{W}$ | $n_2$ |
| 11 | 81 | 87 | 91 | 96 | 100 | 106 | 253 | | | | | | | | |
| 12 | 83 | 90 | 94 | 99 | 104 | 110 | 264 | 98 | 105 | 109 | 115 | 120 | 127 | 300 | 12 |
| 13 | 86 | 93 | 97 | 103 | 108 | 114 | 275 | 101 | 109 | 113 | 119 | 125 | 131 | 312 | 13 |
| 14 | 88 | 96 | 100 | 106 | 112 | 118 | 286 | 103 | 112 | 116 | 123 | 129 | 136 | 324 | 14 |
| 15 | 90 | 99 | 103 | 110 | 116 | 123 | 297 | 106 | 115 | 120 | 127 | 133 | 141 | 336 | 15 |
| 16 | 93 | 102 | 107 | 113 | 120 | 127 | 308 | 109 | 119 | 124 | 131 | 138 | 145 | 348 | 16 |
| 17 | 95 | 105 | 110 | 117 | 123 | 131 | 319 | 112 | 122 | 127 | 135 | 142 | 150 | 360 | 17 |
| 18 | 98 | 108 | 113 | 121 | 127 | 135 | 330 | 115 | 125 | 131 | 139 | 146 | 155 | 372 | 18 |
| 19 | 100 | 111 | 116 | 124 | 131 | 139 | 341 | 118 | 129 | 134 | 143 | 150 | 159 | 384 | 19 |
| 20 | 103 | 114 | 119 | 128 | 135 | 144 | 352 | 120 | 132 | 138 | 147 | 155 | 164 | 396 | 20 |
| 21 | 106 | 117 | 123 | 131 | 139 | 148 | 363 | 123 | 136 | 142 | 151 | 159 | 169 | 408 | 21 |
| 22 | 108 | 120 | 126 | 135 | 143 | 152 | 374 | 126 | 139 | 145 | 155 | 163 | 173 | 420 | 22 |
| 23 | 111 | 123 | 129 | 139 | 147 | 156 | 385 | 129 | 142 | 149 | 159 | 168 | 178 | 432 | 23 |
| 24 | 113 | 126 | 132 | 142 | 151 | 161 | 396 | 132 | 146 | 153 | 163 | 172 | 183 | 444 | 24 |
| 25 | 116 | 129 | 136 | 146 | 155 | 165 | 407 | 135 | 149 | 156 | 167 | 176 | 187 | 456 | 25 |

| | $n_1 = 13$ | | | | | | | | $n_1 = 14$ | | | | | | | |
|---|---|---|---|---|---|---|---|---|---|---|---|---|---|---|---|---|
| $n_2$ | .001 | .005 | .010 | .025 | .05 | .10 | $2\bar{W}$ | .001 | .005 | .010 | .025 | .05 | .10 | $2\bar{W}$ | $n_2$ |
| 13 | 117 | 125 | 130 | 136 | 142 | 149 | 351 | | | | | | | | |
| 14 | 120 | 129 | 134 | 141 | 147 | 154 | 364 | 137 | 147 | 152 | 160 | 166 | 174 | 406 | 14 |
| 15 | 123 | 133 | 138 | 145 | 152 | 159 | 377 | 141 | 151 | 156 | 164 | 171 | 179 | 420 | 15 |
| 16 | 126 | 136 | 142 | 150 | 156 | 165 | 390 | 144 | 155 | 161 | 169 | 176 | 185 | 434 | 16 |
| 17 | 129 | 140 | 146 | 154 | 161 | 170 | 403 | 148 | 159 | 165 | 174 | 182 | 190 | 448 | 17 |
| 18 | 133 | 144 | 150 | 158 | 166 | 175 | 416 | 151 | 163 | 170 | 179 | 187 | 196 | 462 | 18 |
| 19 | 136 | 148 | 154 | 163 | 171 | 180 | 429 | 155 | 168 | 174 | 183 | 192 | 202 | 476 | 19 |
| 20 | 139 | 151 | 158 | 167 | 175 | 185 | 442 | 159 | 172 | 178 | 188 | 197 | 207 | 490 | 20 |
| 21 | 142 | 155 | 162 | 171 | 180 | 190 | 455 | 162 | 176 | 183 | 193 | 202 | 213 | 504 | 21 |
| 22 | 145 | 159 | 166 | 176 | 185 | 195 | 468 | 166 | 180 | 187 | 198 | 207 | 218 | 518 | 22 |
| 23 | 149 | 163 | 170 | 180 | 189 | 200 | 481 | 169 | 184 | 192 | 203 | 212 | 224 | 532 | 23 |
| 24 | 152 | 166 | 174 | 185 | 194 | 205 | 494 | 173 | 188 | 196 | 207 | 218 | 229 | 546 | 24 |
| 25 | 155 | 170 | 178 | 189 | 199 | 211 | 507 | 177 | 192 | 200 | 212 | 223 | 235 | 560 | 25 |

## Table D.8
*Continued*

| $n_2$ | .001 | .005 | .010 | .025 | .05 | .10 | $2\bar{W}$ | .001 | .005 | .010 | .025 | .05 | .10 | $2\bar{W}$ | $n_2$ |
|---|---|---|---|---|---|---|---|---|---|---|---|---|---|---|---|
| | | | | $n_1 = 15$ | | | | | | | $n_1 = 16$ | | | | |
| 15 | 160 | 171 | 176 | 184 | 192 | 200 | 465 | | | | | | | | |
| 16 | 163 | 175 | 181 | 190 | 197 | 206 | 480 | 184 | 196 | 202 | 211 | 219 | 229 | 528 | 16 |
| 17 | 167 | 180 | 186 | 195 | 203 | 212 | 495 | 188 | 201 | 207 | 217 | 225 | 235 | 544 | 17 |
| 18 | 171 | 184 | 190 | 200 | 208 | 218 | 510 | 192 | 206 | 212 | 222 | 231 | 242 | 560 | 18 |
| 19 | 175 | 189 | 195 | 205 | 214 | 224 | 525 | 196 | 210 | 218 | 228 | 237 | 248 | 576 | 19 |
| 20 | 179 | 193 | 200 | 210 | 220 | 230 | 540 | 201 | 215 | 223 | 234 | 243 | 255 | 592 | 20 |
| 21 | 183 | 198 | 205 | 216 | 225 | 236 | 555 | 205 | 220 | 228 | 239 | 249 | 261 | 608 | 21 |
| 22 | 187 | 202 | 210 | 221 | 231 | 242 | 570 | 209 | 225 | 233 | 245 | 255 | 267 | 624 | 22 |
| 23 | 191 | 207 | 214 | 226 | 236 | 248 | 585 | 214 | 230 | 238 | 251 | 261 | 274 | 640 | 23 |
| 24 | 195 | 211 | 219 | 231 | 242 | 254 | 600 | 218 | 235 | 244 | 256 | 267 | 280 | 656 | 24 |
| 25 | 199 | 216 | 224 | 237 | 248 | 260 | 615 | 222 | 240 | 249 | 262 | 273 | 287 | 672 | 25 |

| $n_2$ | .001 | .005 | .010 | .025 | .05 | .10 | $2\bar{W}$ | .001 | .005 | .010 | .025 | .05 | .10 | $2\bar{W}$ | $n_2$ |
|---|---|---|---|---|---|---|---|---|---|---|---|---|---|---|---|
| | | | | $n_1 = 17$ | | | | | | | $n_1 = 18$ | | | | |
| 17 | 210 | 223 | 230 | 240 | 249 | 259 | 595 | | | | | | | | |
| 18 | 214 | 228 | 235 | 246 | 255 | 266 | 612 | 237 | 252 | 259 | 270 | 280 | 291 | 666 | 18 |
| 19 | 219 | 234 | 241 | 252 | 262 | 273 | 629 | 242 | 258 | 265 | 277 | 287 | 299 | 684 | 19 |
| 20 | 223 | 239 | 246 | 258 | 268 | 280 | 646 | 247 | 263 | 271 | 283 | 294 | 306 | 702 | 20 |
| 21 | 228 | 244 | 252 | 264 | 274 | 287 | 663 | 252 | 269 | 277 | 290 | 301 | 313 | 720 | 21 |
| 22 | 233 | 249 | 258 | 270 | 281 | 294 | 680 | 257 | 275 | 283 | 296 | 307 | 321 | 738 | 22 |
| 23 | 238 | 255 | 263 | 276 | 287 | 300 | 697 | 262 | 280 | 289 | 303 | 314 | 328 | 756 | 23 |
| 24 | 242 | 260 | 269 | 282 | 294 | 307 | 714 | 267 | 286 | 295 | 309 | 321 | 335 | 774 | 24 |
| 25 | 247 | 265 | 275 | 288 | 300 | 314 | 731 | 273 | 292 | 301 | 316 | 328 | 343 | 792 | 25 |

| $n_2$ | .001 | .005 | .010 | .025 | .05 | .10 | $2\bar{W}$ | .001 | .005 | .010 | .025 | .05 | .10 | $2\bar{W}$ | $n_2$ |
|---|---|---|---|---|---|---|---|---|---|---|---|---|---|---|---|
| | | | | $n_1 = 19$ | | | | | | | $n_1 = 20$ | | | | |
| 19 | 267 | 283 | 291 | 303 | 313 | 325 | 741 | | | | | | | | |
| 20 | 272 | 289 | 297 | 309 | 320 | 333 | 760 | 298 | 315 | 324 | 337 | 348 | 361 | 820 | 20 |
| 21 | 277 | 295 | 303 | 316 | 328 | 341 | 779 | 304 | 322 | 331 | 344 | 356 | 370 | 840 | 21 |
| 22 | 283 | 301 | 310 | 323 | 335 | 349 | 798 | 309 | 328 | 337 | 351 | 364 | 378 | 860 | 22 |
| 23 | 288 | 307 | 316 | 330 | 342 | 357 | 817 | 315 | 335 | 344 | 359 | 371 | 386 | 880 | 23 |
| 24 | 294 | 313 | 323 | 337 | 350 | 364 | 836 | 321 | 341 | 351 | 366 | 379 | 394 | 900 | 24 |
| 25 | 299 | 319 | 329 | 344 | 357 | 372 | 855 | 327 | 348 | 358 | 373 | 387 | 403 | 920 | 25 |

| $n_2$ | .001 | .005 | .010 | .025 | .05 | .10 | $2\bar{W}$ | .001 | .005 | .010 | .025 | .05 | .10 | $2\bar{W}$ | $n_2$ |
|---|---|---|---|---|---|---|---|---|---|---|---|---|---|---|---|
| | | | | $n_1 = 21$ | | | | | | | $n_1 = 22$ | | | | |
| 21 | 331 | 349 | 359 | 373 | 385 | 399 | 903 | | | | | | | | |
| 22 | 337 | 356 | 366 | 381 | 393 | 408 | 924 | 365 | 386 | 396 | 411 | 424 | 439 | 990 | 22 |
| 23 | 343 | 363 | 373 | 388 | 401 | 417 | 945 | 372 | 393 | 403 | 419 | 432 | 448 | 1012 | 23 |
| 24 | 349 | 370 | 381 | 396 | 410 | 425 | 966 | 379 | 400 | 411 | 427 | 441 | 457 | 1034 | 24 |
| 25 | 356 | 377 | 388 | 404 | 418 | 434 | 987 | 385 | 408 | 419 | 435 | 450 | 467 | 1056 | 25 |

| $n_2$ | .001 | .005 | .010 | .025 | .05 | .10 | $2\bar{W}$ | .001 | .005 | .010 | .025 | .05 | .10 | $2\bar{W}$ | $n_2$ |
|---|---|---|---|---|---|---|---|---|---|---|---|---|---|---|---|
| | | | | $n_1 = 23$ | | | | | | | $n_1 = 24$ | | | | |
| 23 | 402 | 424 | 434 | 451 | 465 | 481 | 1081 | | | | | | | | |
| 24 | 409 | 431 | 443 | 459 | 474 | 491 | 1104 | 440 | 464 | 475 | 492 | 507 | 525 | 1176 | 24 |
| 25 | 416 | 439 | 451 | 468 | 483 | 500 | 1127 | 448 | 472 | 484 | 501 | 517 | 535 | 1200 | 25 |

| $n_2$ | .001 | .005 | .010 | .025 | .05 | .10 | $2\bar{W}$ |
|---|---|---|---|---|---|---|---|
| | | | | $n_1 = 25$ | | | |
| 25 | 480 | 505 | 517 | 536 | 552 | 570 | 1275 |

## Table D.9
### Table of Uniform Random Numbers

| | | | | | | | | |
|---|---|---|---|---|---|---|---|---|
| 68204 | 38787 | 73304 | 44886 | 92836 | 43877 | 61049 | 49249 | 66105 |
| 61010 | 78345 | 75444 | 91680 | 33003 | 24128 | 97817 | 77562 | 62045 |
| 04604 | 93468 | 78459 | 27541 | 19672 | 14220 | 25102 | 42021 | 19252 |
| 36021 | 25507 | 64060 | 72923 | 58848 | 10374 | 63102 | 41534 | 92884 |
| 28129 | 43470 | 94097 | 16753 | 56425 | 75299 | 93688 | 75569 | 52067 |
| 09406 | 06584 | 46324 | 13981 | 06449 | 42604 | 13372 | 69040 | 95955 |
| 86423 | 81835 | 64226 | 20398 | 65772 | 91052 | 73496 | 14451 | 95967 |
| 13249 | 58525 | 81893 | 32894 | 68627 | 75644 | 45848 | 61511 | 90232 |
| 75454 | 17352 | 56548 | 39618 | 86705 | 50783 | 48388 | 82047 | 14660 |
| 06260 | 46176 | 99237 | 69874 | 84180 | 32005 | 66130 | 18055 | 99748 |
| 38507 | 92795 | 80672 | 00102 | 22980 | 69115 | 95653 | 05231 | 94996 |
| 03917 | 26795 | 59832 | 19014 | 96206 | 45413 | 76624 | 71219 | 65855 |
| 17927 | 32368 | 08!77 | 31236 | 45401 | 26731 | 92256 | 99530 | 43998 |
| 26811 | 88937 | 37187 | 39762 | 29942 | 40091 | 65731 | 95955 | 23368 |
| 18480 | 28160 | 81908 | 30456 | 22462 | 15677 | 55642 | 67383 | 86884 |
| 37589 | 91842 | 76351 | 90585 | 45588 | 42858 | 37806 | 67969 | 50621 |
| 79903 | 34187 | 26952 | 75820 | 96335 | 90281 | 04269 | 85202 | 94965 |
| 46155 | 30200 | 75000 | 28570 | 47516 | 06744 | 72193 | 01258 | 85047 |
| 60916 | 73212 | 15853 | 28398 | 04721 | 69363 | 47071 | 65568 | 88519 |
| 34419 | 82840 | 88235 | 61966 | 86517 | 23966 | 45764 | 42177 | 17269 |
| 08692 | 26667 | 12941 | 14813 | 30815 | 26633 | 68184 | 80721 | 80505 |
| 92851 | 44185 | 90848 | 18341 | 77915 | 00177 | 64014 | 35490 | 02937 |
| 97909 | 07280 | 72167 | 10002 | 27374 | 92880 | 60055 | 94168 | 30742 |
| 28437 | 22027 | 07739 | 30905 | 33151 | 73567 | 82960 | 50104 | 67005 |
| 48165 | 28174 | 17909 | 11230 | 00929 | 54604 | 32435 | 54120 | 85199 |
| 99891 | 30913 | 06315 | 30201 | 72073 | 39589 | 62868 | 66339 | 15850 |
| 98022 | 13010 | 67970 | 99203 | 12536 | 88149 | 44387 | 20250 | 50798 |
| 91292 | 54688 | 47029 | 38970 | 77880 | 77295 | 11887 | 17628 | 93802 |
| 89081 | 34643 | 12988 | 12971 | 87742 | 57720 | 24438 | 64088 | 49496 |
| 32527 | 74239 | 20056 | 46668 | 94561 | 70111 | 92537 | 83562 | 11306 |
| 01870 | 21584 | 48574 | 09871 | 74453 | 24812 | 45770 | 95667 | 52377 |
| 84011 | 87542 | 96564 | 64256 | 64653 | 90025 | 61613 | 94168 | 83254 |
| 01568 | 29682 | 67489 | 62984 | 51901 | 30716 | 24513 | 46678 | 67991 |
| 40360 | 19206 | 40321 | 16004 | 64481 | 16130 | 03904 | 15811 | 19369 |
| 09392 | 39926 | 79590 | 23991 | 82492 | 13032 | 67337 | 54322 | 06058 |
| 77323 | 20500 | 52466 | 33008 | 84211 | 26357 | 79006 | 41178 | 35169 |
| 47590 | 01007 | 65376 | 18189 | 84040 | 39476 | 25383 | 45398 | 64917 |
| 29321 | 65783 | 71403 | 32894 | 32627 | 39067 | 47985 | 51485 | 27415 |
| 09530 | 05358 | 58722 | 31912 | 73356 | 65884 | 12883 | 36242 | 29646 |
| 65612 | 06843 | 72233 | 73352 | 66600 | 23237 | 71759 | 76881 | 19652 |
| 40355 | 85067 | 40788 | 40148 | 46099 | 48056 | 27858 | 58365 | 30202 |
| 24963 | 49571 | 82377 | 08687 | 73448 | 95484 | 15155 | 41780 | 71951 |
| 87273 | 44050 | 71961 | 48464 | 84084 | 65225 | 62846 | 11634 | 04853 |
| 31643 | 44756 | 12493 | 09024 | 74204 | 69949 | 67842 | 36141 | 08477 |
| 58326 | 55342 | 31419 | 80776 | 64028 | 59957 | 52969 | 71997 | 71477 |
| 02327 | 00460 | 39178 | 09511 | 92688 | 88585 | 99257 | 98752 | 39623 |
| 19377 | 49122 | 60591 | 79773 | 66289 | 89650 | 49298 | 13499 | 53623 |
| 95046 | 30203 | 47493 | 74395 | 45213 | 66739 | 45097 | 91670 | 62152 |
| 65013 | 71958 | 48360 | 70885 | 60313 | 44241 | 18740 | 05705 | 07488 |
| 86032 | 89018 | 97117 | 35656 | 20401 | 86438 | 87250 | 04717 | 67726 |
| 11799 | 15777 | 11548 | 45918 | 45706 | 88554 | 75315 | 70233 | 72575 |
| 17843 | 64809 | 00390 | 11980 | 66129 | 07197 | 36712 | 55062 | 61191 |
| 42770 | 65397 | 45010 | 06463 | 86242 | 06361 | 14293 | 36343 | 97628 |
| 02410 | 96933 | 57864 | 93197 | 88227 | 57139 | 66382 | 95768 | 60660 |
| 70939 | 20457 | 62468 | 68698 | 74875 | 61111 | 59083 | 09152 | 93625 |
| 85616 | 15100 | 26242 | 28677 | 74655 | 05679 | 56676 | 67224 | 75318 |
| 85515 | 33174 | 05496 | 78789 | 81297 | 73985 | 82120 | 94070 | 20529 |

(*Source:* The entries in this table were computed by the author.)

**Table D.9**
*Continued*

| | | | | | | | | |
|---|---|---|---|---|---|---|---|---|
| 73466 | 06254 | 88113 | 98367 | 22018 | 99372 | 70171 | 52705 | 61202 |
| 72255 | 50729 | 05681 | 37216 | 09363 | 02385 | 93098 | 09502 | 92589 |
| 08121 | 48330 | 86725 | 52922 | 90349 | 81934 | 14849 | 68005 | 06791 |
| 94005 | 85164 | 22994 | 58921 | 85943 | 67506 | 79730 | 85382 | 61568 |
| 09108 | 52299 | 25991 | 00940 | 22493 | 60987 | 93573 | 79469 | 97147 |
| 85687 | 31723 | 67907 | 55306 | 71748 | 85048 | 17690 | 04784 | 98470 |
| 26190 | 02164 | 95889 | 89712 | 89795 | 73001 | 82210 | 39357 | 23867 |
| 34208 | 07539 | 60907 | 60693 | 01965 | 43492 | 46688 | 28891 | 23410 |
| 13032 | 78798 | 21733 | 35703 | 71707 | 11931 | 93513 | 78339 | 74754 |
| 16801 | 05582 | 47975 | 25046 | 59220 | 08275 | 67901 | 94954 | 36662 |
| 88735 | 91500 | 41654 | 97225 | 61188 | 24527 | 35220 | 99794 | 56097 |
| 82127 | 17594 | 94217 | 55324 | 06134 | 25207 | 26758 | 08687 | 06929 |
| 29284 | 42271 | 45833 | 19481 | 56972 | 99042 | 45304 | 39832 | 40188 |
| 56300 | 60964 | 13751 | 72385 | 91180 | 42371 | 55924 | 95783 | 33096 |
| 33132 | 33229 | 39955 | 16779 | 99286 | 23392 | 24255 | 90856 | 60004 |
| 65296 | 94444 | 32091 | 90681 | 95823 | 73091 | 92912 | 85979 | 30232 |
| 11069 | 52931 | 26381 | 71830 | 50467 | 47783 | 25223 | 81796 | 97745 |
| 06720 | 69637 | 99670 | 58392 | 57943 | 75965 | 14740 | 74814 | 75598 |
| 62719 | 14295 | 16605 | 13146 | 36992 | 50560 | 50121 | 90278 | 98283 |
| 95556 | 36672 | 87202 | 92730 | 81961 | 38894 | 61358 | 44519 | 71529 |
| 12490 | 12304 | 28804 | 42772 | 27104 | 35518 | 67361 | 84159 | 52442 |
| 29865 | 28847 | 70904 | 96638 | 54226 | 44701 | 67589 | 27352 | 81078 |
| 74486 | 63507 | 92193 | 65022 | 09583 | 43615 | 59910 | 05301 | 69347 |
| 01878 | 56351 | 68618 | 84432 | 30948 | 65180 | 75446 | 95963 | 75619 |
| 65405 | 25720 | 09364 | 51333 | 03752 | 65756 | 51967 | 92469 | 47296 |
| 31711 | 35173 | 45290 | 49326 | 50368 | 63829 | 05640 | 26675 | 27367 |
| 41028 | 50367 | 01904 | 68068 | 02324 | 58723 | 96333 | 77032 | 47878 |
| 76916 | 55336 | 48767 | 76915 | 79711 | 05182 | 70489 | 10244 | 45078 |
| 16404 | 93068 | 91519 | 85895 | 34872 | 24701 | 60932 | 91141 | 33252 |
| 06776 | 51133 | 76482 | 14812 | 19777 | 19614 | 51100 | 52943 | 04068 |
| 76818 | 05839 | 26058 | 80972 | 43337 | 24203 | 72345 | 37967 | 88138 |
| 16916 | 64028 | 38968 | 02783 | 63049 | 12261 | 89587 | 88988 | 88834 |
| 33696 | 41621 | 16648 | 11837 | 08094 | 38217 | 32919 | 16625 | 91567 |
| 00143 | 56431 | 90537 | 95332 | 29879 | 29363 | 48055 | 86410 | 10594 |
| 15932 | 59628 | 00086 | 74633 | 81208 | 05470 | 56385 | 23601 | 70545 |
| 86111 | 14530 | 39958 | 36155 | 60613 | 73849 | 74842 | 31030 | 30448 |
| 46218 | 36313 | 62063 | 59326 | 93522 | 48983 | 50335 | 30178 | 42755 |
| 84153 | 32199 | 77166 | 63912 | 07984 | 55369 | 56520 | 14633 | 00252 |
| 81439 | 35471 | 29742 | 57110 | 13710 | 21351 | 29816 | 32783 | 69004 |
| 92339 | 82043 | 80136 | 97269 | 28858 | 03036 | 01304 | 51363 | 40412 |
| 78421 | 33809 | 92792 | 96106 | 95191 | 43514 | 08320 | 25690 | 76117 |
| 44265 | 86707 | 80637 | 44879 | 81457 | 06781 | 11411 | 88804 | 62551 |
| 89430 | 51314 | 76126 | 62672 | 31815 | 12947 | 76533 | 19761 | 93373 |
| 36462 | 19901 | 02919 | 29311 | 31275 | 83593 | 34933 | 95758 | 63944 |
| 55996 | 59605 | 51680 | 27755 | 06077 | 12797 | 67082 | 12536 | 64069 |
| 69338 | 43838 | 06320 | 63988 | 16549 | 27931 | 27270 | 94711 | 47834 |
| 40276 | 17751 | 72508 | 23027 | 70257 | 42812 | 87319 | 09160 | 02913 |
| 67834 | 93014 | 07816 | 93085 | 14552 | 10115 | 87740 | 44125 | 51227 |

## Table D.10
The Normal Distribution ($z$)

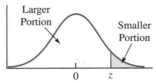

| $z$ | Mean to $z$ | Larger Portion | Smaller Portion | $z$ | Mean to $z$ | Larger Portion | Smaller Portion |
|-----|-------------|----------------|-----------------|-----|-------------|----------------|-----------------|
| .00 | .0000 | .5000 | .5000 | .40 | .1554 | .6554 | .3446 |
| .01 | .0040 | .5040 | .4960 | .41 | .1591 | .6591 | .3409 |
| .02 | .0080 | .5080 | .4920 | .42 | .1628 | .6628 | .3372 |
| .03 | .0120 | .5120 | .4880 | .43 | .1664 | .6664 | .3336 |
| .04 | .0160 | .5160 | .4840 | .44 | .1700 | .6700 | .3300 |
| .05 | .0199 | .5199 | .4801 | .45 | .1736 | .6736 | .3264 |
| .06 | .0239 | .5239 | .4761 | .46 | .1772 | .6772 | .3228 |
| .07 | .0279 | .5279 | .4721 | .47 | .1808 | .6808 | .3192 |
| .08 | .0319 | .5319 | .4681 | .48 | .1844 | .6844 | .3156 |
| .09 | .0359 | .5359 | .4641 | .49 | .1879 | .6879 | .3121 |
| .10 | .0398 | .5398 | .4602 | .50 | .1915 | .6915 | .3085 |
| .11 | .0438 | .5438 | .4562 | .51 | .1950 | .6950 | .3050 |
| .12 | .0478 | .5478 | .4522 | .52 | .1985 | .6985 | .3015 |
| .13 | .0517 | .5517 | .4483 | .53 | .2019 | .7019 | .2981 |
| .14 | .0557 | .5557 | .4443 | .54 | .2054 | .7054 | .2946 |
| .15 | .0596 | .5596 | .4404 | .55 | .2088 | .7088 | .2912 |
| .16 | .0636 | .5636 | .4364 | .56 | .2123 | .7123 | .2877 |
| .17 | .0675 | .5675 | .4325 | .57 | .2157 | .7157 | .2843 |
| .18 | .0714 | .5714 | .4286 | .58 | .2190 | .7190 | .2810 |
| .19 | .0753 | .5753 | .4247 | .59 | .2224 | .7224 | .2776 |
| .20 | .0793 | .5793 | .4207 | .60 | .2257 | .7257 | .2743 |
| .21 | .0832 | .5832 | .4168 | .61 | .2291 | .7291 | .2709 |
| .22 | .0871 | .5871 | .4129 | .62 | .2324 | .7324 | .2676 |
| .23 | .0910 | .5910 | .4090 | .63 | .2357 | .7357 | .2643 |
| .24 | .0948 | .5948 | .4052 | .64 | .2389 | .7389 | .2611 |
| .25 | .0987 | .5987 | .4013 | .65 | .2422 | .7422 | .2578 |
| .26 | .1026 | .6026 | .3974 | .66 | .2454 | .7454 | .2546 |
| .27 | .1064 | .6064 | .3936 | .67 | .2486 | .7486 | .2514 |
| .28 | .1103 | .6103 | .3897 | .68 | .2517 | .7517 | .2483 |
| .29 | .1141 | .6141 | .3859 | .69 | .2549 | .7549 | .2451 |
| .30 | .1179 | .6179 | .3821 | .70 | .2580 | .7580 | .2420 |
| .31 | .1217 | .6217 | .3783 | .71 | .2611 | .7611 | .2389 |
| .32 | .1255 | .6255 | .3745 | .72 | .2642 | .7642 | .2358 |
| .33 | .1293 | .6293 | .3707 | .73 | .2673 | .7673 | .2327 |
| .34 | .1331 | .6331 | .3669 | .74 | .2704 | .7704 | .2296 |
| .35 | .1368 | .6368 | .3632 | .75 | .2734 | .7734 | .2266 |
| .36 | .1406 | .6406 | .3594 | .76 | .2764 | .7764 | .2236 |
| .37 | .1443 | .6443 | .3557 | .77 | .2794 | .7794 | .2206 |
| .38 | .1480 | .6480 | .3520 | .78 | .2823 | .7823 | .2177 |
| .39 | .1517 | .6517 | .3483 | .79 | .2852 | .7852 | .2148 |

(*Source:*   The entries in this table were computed by the author.)

**Table D.10**
*Continued*

| z | Mean to z | Larger Portion | Smaller Portion | z | Mean to z | Larger Portion | Smaller Portion |
|---|-----------|----------------|-----------------|---|-----------|----------------|-----------------|
| .80 | .2881 | .7881 | .2119 | 1.29 | .4015 | .9015 | .0985 |
| .81 | .2910 | .7910 | .2090 | 1.30 | .4032 | .9032 | .0968 |
| .82 | .2939 | .7939 | .2061 | 1.31 | .4049 | .9049 | .0951 |
| .83 | .2967 | .7967 | .2033 | 1.32 | .4066 | .9066 | .0934 |
| .84 | .2995 | .7995 | .2005 | 1.33 | .4082 | .9082 | .0918 |
| .85 | .3023 | .8023 | .1977 | 1.34 | .4099 | .9099 | .0901 |
| .86 | .3051 | .8051 | .1949 | 1.35 | .4115 | .9115 | .0885 |
| .87 | .3078 | .8078 | .1922 | 1.36 | .4131 | .9131 | .0869 |
| .88 | .3106 | .8106 | .1894 | 1.37 | .4147 | .9147 | .0853 |
| .89 | .3133 | .8133 | .1867 | 1.38 | .4162 | .9162 | .0838 |
| .90 | .3159 | .8159 | .1841 | 1.39 | .4177 | .9177 | .0823 |
| .91 | .3186 | .8186 | .1814 | 1.40 | .4192 | .9192 | .0808 |
| .92 | .3212 | .8212 | .1788 | 1.41 | .4207 | .9207 | .0793 |
| .93 | .3238 | .8238 | .1762 | 1.42 | .4222 | .9222 | .0778 |
| .94 | .3264 | .8264 | .1736 | 1.43 | .4236 | .9236 | .0764 |
| .95 | .3289 | .8289 | .1711 | 1.44 | .4251 | .9251 | .0749 |
| .96 | .3315 | .8315 | .1685 | 1.45 | .4265 | .9265 | .0735 |
| .97 | .3340 | .8340 | .1660 | 1.46 | .4279 | .9279 | .0721 |
| .98 | .3365 | .8365 | .1635 | 1.47 | .4292 | .9292 | .0708 |
| .99 | .3389 | .8389 | .1611 | 1.48 | .4306 | .9306 | .0694 |
| 1.00 | .3413 | .8413 | .1587 | 1.49 | .4319 | .9319 | .0681 |
| 1.01 | .3438 | .8438 | .1562 | 1.50 | .4332 | .9332 | .0668 |
| 1.02 | .3461 | .8461 | .1539 | 1.51 | .4345 | .9345 | .0655 |
| 1.03 | .3485 | .8485 | .1515 | 1.52 | .4357 | .9357 | .0643 |
| 1.04 | .3508 | .8508 | .1492 | 1.53 | .4370 | .9370 | .0630 |
| 1.05 | .3531 | .8531 | .1469 | 1.54 | .4382 | .9382 | .0618 |
| 1.06 | .3554 | .8554 | .1446 | 1.55 | .4394 | .9394 | .0606 |
| 1.07 | .3577 | .8577 | .1423 | 1.56 | .4406 | .9406 | .0594 |
| 1.08 | .3599 | .8599 | .1401 | 1.57 | .4418 | .9418 | .0582 |
| 1.09 | .3621 | .8621 | .1379 | 1.58 | .4429 | .9429 | .0571 |
| 1.10 | .3643 | .8643 | .1357 | 1.59 | .4441 | .9441 | .0559 |
| 1.11 | .3665 | .8665 | .1335 | 1.60 | .4452 | .9452 | .0548 |
| 1.12 | .3686 | .8686 | .1314 | 1.61 | .4463 | .9463 | .0537 |
| 1.13 | .3708 | .8708 | .1292 | 1.62 | .4474 | .9474 | .0526 |
| 1.14 | .3729 | .8729 | .1271 | 1.63 | .4484 | .9484 | .0516 |
| 1.15 | .3749 | .8749 | .1251 | 1.64 | .4495 | .9495 | .0505 |
| 1.16 | .3770 | .8770 | .1230 | 1.65 | .4505 | .9505 | .0495 |
| 1.17 | .3790 | .8790 | .1210 | 1.66 | .4515 | .9515 | .0485 |
| 1.18 | .3810 | .8810 | .1190 | 1.67 | .4525 | .9525 | .0475 |
| 1.19 | .3830 | .8830 | .1170 | 1.68 | .4535 | .9535 | .0465 |
| 1.20 | .3849 | .8849 | .1151 | 1.69 | .4545 | .9545 | .0455 |
| 1.21 | .3869 | .8869 | .1131 | 1.70 | .4554 | .9554 | .0446 |
| 1.22 | .3888 | .8888 | .1112 | 1.71 | .4564 | .9564 | .0436 |
| 1.23 | .3907 | .8907 | .1093 | 1.72 | .4573 | .9573 | .0427 |
| 1.24 | .3925 | .8925 | .1075 | 1.73 | .4582 | .9582 | .0418 |
| 1.25 | .3944 | .8944 | .1056 | 1.74 | .4591 | .9591 | .0409 |
| 1.26 | .3962 | .8962 | .1038 | 1.75 | .4599 | .9599 | .0401 |
| 1.27 | .3980 | .8980 | .1020 | 1.76 | .4608 | .9608 | .0392 |
| 1.28 | .3997 | .8997 | .1003 | 1.77 | .4616 | .9616 | .0384 |

*continued*

## Table D.10
*Continued*

| z | Mean to z | Larger Portion | Smaller Portion | z | Mean to z | Larger Portion | Smaller Portion |
|---|---|---|---|---|---|---|---|
| 1.78 | .4625 | .9625 | .0375 | 2.28 | .4887 | .9887 | .0113 |
| 1.79 | .4633 | .9633 | .0367 | 2.29 | .4890 | .9890 | .0110 |
| 1.80 | .4641 | .9641 | .0359 | 2.30 | .4893 | .9893 | .0107 |
| 1.81 | .4649 | .9649 | .0351 | 2.31 | .4896 | .9896 | .0104 |
| 1.82 | .4656 | .9656 | .0344 | 2.32 | .4898 | .9898 | .0102 |
| 1.83 | .4664 | .9664 | .0336 | 2.33 | .4901 | .9901 | .0099 |
| 1.84 | .4671 | .9671 | .0329 | 2.34 | .4904 | .9904 | .0096 |
| 1.85 | .4678 | .9678 | .0322 | 2.35 | .4906 | .9906 | .0094 |
| 1.86 | .4686 | .9686 | .0314 | 2.36 | .4909 | .9909 | .0091 |
| 1.87 | .4693 | .9693 | .0307 | 2.37 | .4911 | .9911 | .0089 |
| 1.88 | .4699 | .9699 | .0301 | 2.38 | .4913 | .9913 | .0087 |
| 1.89 | .4706 | .9706 | .0294 | 2.39 | .4916 | .9916 | .0084 |
| 1.90 | .4713 | .9713 | .0287 | 2.40 | .4918 | .9918 | .0082 |
| 1.91 | .4719 | .9719 | .0281 | 2.41 | .4920 | .9920 | .0080 |
| 1.92 | .4726 | .9726 | .0274 | 2.42 | .4922 | .9922 | .0078 |
| 1.93 | .4732 | .9732 | .0268 | 2.43 | .4925 | .9925 | .0075 |
| 1.94 | .4738 | .9738 | .0262 | 2.44 | .4927 | .9927 | .0073 |
| 1.95 | .4744 | .9744 | .0256 | 2.45 | .4929 | .9929 | .0071 |
| 1.96 | .4750 | .9750 | .0250 | 2.46 | .4931 | .9931 | .0069 |
| 1.97 | .4756 | .9756 | .0244 | 2.47 | .4932 | .9932 | .0068 |
| 1.98 | .4761 | .9761 | .0239 | 2.48 | .4934 | .9934 | .0066 |
| 1.99 | .4767 | .9767 | .0233 | 2.49 | .4936 | .9936 | .0064 |
| 2.00 | .4772 | .9772 | .0228 | 2.50 | .4938 | .9938 | .0062 |
| 2.01 | .4778 | .9778 | .0222 | 2.51 | .4940 | .9940 | .0060 |
| 2.02 | .4783 | .9783 | .0217 | 2.52 | .4941 | .9941 | .0059 |
| 2.03 | .4788 | .9788 | .0212 | 2.53 | .4943 | .9943 | .0057 |
| 2.04 | .4793 | .9793 | .0207 | 2.54 | .4945 | .9945 | .0055 |
| 2.05 | .4798 | .9798 | .0202 | 2.55 | .4946 | .9946 | .0054 |
| 2.06 | .4803 | .9803 | .0197 | 2.56 | .4948 | .9948 | .0052 |
| 2.07 | .4808 | .9808 | .0192 | 2.57 | .4949 | .9949 | .0051 |
| 2.08 | .4812 | .9812 | .0188 | 2.58 | .4951 | .9951 | .0049 |
| 2.09 | .4817 | .9817 | .0183 | 2.59 | .4952 | .9952 | .0048 |
| 2.10 | .4821 | .9821 | .0179 | 2.60 | .4953 | .9953 | .0047 |
| 2.11 | .4826 | .9826 | .0174 | 2.61 | .4955 | .9955 | .0045 |
| 2.12 | .4830 | .9830 | .0170 | 2.62 | .4956 | .9956 | .0044 |
| 2.13 | .4834 | .9834 | .0166 | 2.63 | .4957 | .9957 | .0043 |
| 2.14 | .4838 | .9838 | .0162 | 2.64 | .4959 | .9959 | .0041 |
| 2.15 | .4842 | .9842 | .0158 | 2.65 | .4960 | .9960 | .0040 |
| 2.16 | .4846 | .9846 | .0154 | 2.66 | .4961 | .9961 | .0039 |
| 2.17 | .4850 | .9850 | .0150 | 2.67 | .4962 | .9962 | .0038 |
| 2.18 | .4854 | .9854 | .0146 | 2.68 | .4963 | .9963 | .0037 |
| 2.19 | .4857 | .9857 | .0143 | 2.69 | .4964 | .9964 | .0036 |
| 2.20 | .4861 | .9861 | .0139 | 2.70 | .4965 | .9965 | .0035 |
| 2.21 | .4864 | .9864 | .0136 | 2.71 | .4966 | .9966 | .0034 |
| 2.22 | .4868 | .9868 | .0132 | 2.72 | .4967 | .9967 | .0033 |
| 2.23 | .4871 | .9871 | .0129 | 2.73 | .4968 | .9968 | .0032 |
| 2.24 | .4875 | .9875 | .0125 | 2.74 | .4969 | .9969 | .0031 |
| 2.25 | .4878 | .9878 | .0122 | 2.75 | .4970 | .9970 | .0030 |
| 2.26 | .4881 | .9881 | .0119 | 2.76 | .4971 | .9971 | .0029 |
| 2.27 | .4884 | .9884 | .0116 | 2.77 | .4972 | .9972 | .0028 |

**Table D.10**

*Continued*

| z | Mean to z | Larger Portion | Smaller Portion | z | Mean to z | Larger Portion | Smaller Portion |
|---|---|---|---|---|---|---|---|
| 2.78 | .4973 | .9973 | .0027 | 2.94 | .4984 | .9984 | .0016 |
| 2.79 | .4974 | .9974 | .0026 | 2.95 | .4984 | .9984 | .0016 |
| 2.80 | .4974 | .9974 | .0026 | 2.96 | .4985 | .9985 | .0015 |
| 2.81 | .4975 | .9975 | .0025 | 2.97 | .4985 | .9985 | .0015 |
| 2.82 | .4976 | .9976 | .0024 | 2.98 | .4986 | .9986 | .0014 |
| 2.83 | .4977 | .9977 | .0023 | 2.99 | .4986 | .9986 | .0014 |
| 2.84 | .4977 | .9977 | .0023 | 3.00 | .4987 | .9987 | .0013 |
| 2.85 | .4978 | .9978 | .0022 | ⋮ | ⋮ | ⋮ | ⋮ |
| 2.86 | .4979 | .9979 | .0021 | 3.25 | .4994 | .9994 | .0006 |
| 2.87 | .4979 | .9979 | .0021 | ⋮ | ⋮ | ⋮ | ⋮ |
| 2.88 | .4980 | .9980 | .0020 | 3.50 | .4998 | .9998 | .0002 |
| 2.89 | .4981 | .9981 | .0019 | ⋮ | ⋮ | ⋮ | ⋮ |
| 2.90 | .4981 | .9981 | .0019 | 3.75 | .4999 | .9999 | .0001 |
| 2.91 | .4982 | .9982 | .0018 | ⋮ | ⋮ | ⋮ | ⋮ |
| 2.92 | .4982 | .9982 | .0018 | 4.00 | .5000 | 1.0000 | .0000 |
| 2.93 | .4983 | .9983 | .0017 | | | | |

# Glossary

**2 × 5 factorial design**   A factorial design with one variable having two levels and the other having five levels

**Abscissa**   Horizontal axis

**Additive law of probability**   The rule giving the probability of the occurrence of one or more mutually exclusive events

**α (Alpha)**   The probability of a Type I error

**Alternative hypothesis ($H_1$)**   The hypothesis that is adopted when $H_0$ is rejected; usually the same as the research hypothesis

**Analysis of variance (ANOVA)**   A statistical technique for testing for differences in the means of several groups

**Analytic view**   Definition of probability in terms of analysis of possible outcomes

**Bar graph**   A graph in which the frequency of occurrence of different values of $X$ is represented by the height of a bar

**β (Beta)**   The probability of a Type II error

**Between-subjects designs**   Designs in which different subjects serve under the different treatment levels

**Bias**   A property of a statistic whose long-range average is not equal to the parameter it estimates

**Bimodal**   A distribution having two distinct peaks

**Bonferroni procedure**   A multiple comparisons procedure in which the per-comparison error rate is divided by the number of comparisons

**Box-and-whisker plot**   A graphical representation of the dispersion of a sample

**Boxplot**   A graphical representation of the dispersion of a sample

**Carry-over effect**   The effect of previous trials (conditions) on a subject's performance on subsequent trials

**Categorical data (frequency data, count data)**   Data representing counts or number of observations in each category

**Cell**   The combination of a particular row and column; the set of observations obtained under identical treatment conditions

**Central Limit Theorem**   The theorem that specifies the nature of the sampling distribution of the mean

**Central $t$ distribution**   The sampling distribution of the $t$ statistic when the null hypothesis is true

**Chi-square test**   A statistical test often used for analyzing categorical data

**Conditional probability**   The probability of one event *given* the occurrence of some other event

**Confidence interval**   An interval, with limits at either end, with a specified probability of including the parameter being estimated

**Confidence limits**   The limits at either end of a confidence interval with a specified probability of including the parameter being estimated

**Confounded**   Two variables are said to be confounded when they are varied simultaneously and their effects cannot be separated

**Constant**   A number that does not change in value in a given situation

**Contingency table**   A two-dimensional table in which each observation is classified on the basis of two variables simultaneously

**Continuous variables**   Variables that take on *any* value

**Correlation**   Relationship between variables

**Correlation coefficient**   A measure of the relationship between variables

**Counterbalancing**   An arrangement of treatment conditions designed to balance practice effects

**Covariance**   A statistic representing the degree to which two variables vary together

**Cramér's phi ($\phi_c$)**   A measure of the magnitude of effect in a contingency table

**Criterion variable**   The variable to be predicted

**Critical value**   The value of a test statistic at or beyond which we will reject $H_0$

**Curvilinear relationship**   A situation that is best represented by something other than a straight line

**$\hat{d}$**   A standardized $d$-family measure of effect size

**Decision making**   A procedure for making logical decisions on the basis of sample data

**Decision tree** Graphical representation of decisions involved in the choice of statistical procedures

**Degrees of freedom ($df$)** The number of independent pieces of information remaining after estimating one or more parameters

**$\delta$ (Delta)** A value used in referring to power tables that combines $\hat{d}$ and the sample size

**Density** Height of the curve for a given value of $X$; closely related to the probability of an observation in an interval around $X$

**Dependent variables** The variables being measured; the data or score

**Descriptive statistics** Statistics that describe the sample data without drawing inferences about the larger population

**Deviation score** The difference between a score and the mean

**$df_{error}$** Degrees of freedom associated with $SS_{error}$; equal to $k(n - 1)$

**$df_{group}$** Degrees of freedom associated with $SS_{group}$; equal to $k - 1$

**$df_{total}$** Degrees of freedom associated with $SS_{total}$; equal to $N - 1$

**Dichotomous variables** Variables that can have only two different values

**Difference scores (gain scores)** The set of scores representing the difference between the subjects' performance on two occasions

**Directional test** A test that rejects extreme outcomes in only one specified tail of the distribution

**Discrete variables** Variables that take on a small set of possible values

**Dispersion (variability)** The degree to which individual data points are distributed around the mean

**Distribution-free tests** Statistical tests that do not rely on parameter estimation or precise distributional assumptions

**Effect size** The difference between two population means divided by the standard deviation of either population—sometimes presented in raw score units

**Error variance** The square of the standard error of estimate

**Errors of prediction** The differences between $Y$ and $\hat{Y}$

**Eta squared ($\eta^2$)** An $r$-family measure of the magnitude of effect

**Event** The outcome of a trial

**Exhaustive** A set of events that represents all possible outcomes

**Expected frequencies** The expected value for the number of observations in a cell if $H_0$ is true

**Expected value** The long-range average of a statistic over repeated samples

**Experimental hypothesis** Another name for the research hypothesis

**Exploratory data analysis (EDA)** A set of techniques developed by Tukey for presenting data in visually meaningful ways

**$F$ statistic** The ratio of $MS_{group}$ to $MS_{error}$

**Factorial design** An experimental design in which every level of each variable is paired with every level of each other variable

**Factors** Another word for independent variables in the analysis of variance

**Familywise error rate** The probability that a family of comparisons contains at least one Type I error

**Fisher's least significant difference (LSD) test** A multiple comparison technique that requires a significant overall $F$, and that involves standard $t$ tests between pairs of means; also known as the "protected $t$ test"

**Frequency data** Data representing counts or number of observations in each category

**Frequency distribution** A distribution in which the values of the dependent variable are tabled or plotted against their frequency of occurrence

**Friedman's rank test for $k$ correlated samples** A nonparametric test analogous to a standard one-way repeated-measures analysis of variance

**Goodness-of-fit test** A test for comparing observed frequencies with theoretically predicted frequencies

**Grand mean ($\overline{X}..$)** The mean of all of the observations

**H-spread** The range between the two hinges

**Harmonic mean** The number of elements to be averaged divided by the sum of the reciprocals of the elements

**Heterogeneity of variance** A situation in which samples are drawn from populations having different variances

**Heterogeneous subsamples** Data in which the sample of observations could be subdivided into two distinct sets on the basis of some other variable

**Hinges (quartiles)** Those points that cut off the bottom and top quarter of a distribution

**Histogram** Graph in which rectangles are used to represent frequencies of observations within each interval

**Homogeneity of variance**   The situation in which two or more populations have equal variances

**Hypothesis testing**   A process by which decisions are made concerning the values of parameters

**Independent events**   Events are independent when the occurrence of one has no effect on the probability of the occurrence of the other

**Independent variables**   Those variables controlled by the experimenter

**Inferential statistics**   That branch of statistics that involves drawing inferences about parameters of the population(s) from which you have sampled

**Interaction**   A situation in a factorial design in which the effects of one independent variable depend on the level of another independent variable

**Intercept**   The value of $Y$ when $X$ is 0

**Intercorrelation matrix**   A matrix (table) showing the pairwise correlations among all variables

**Interquartile range**   The range of the middle 50% of the observations

**Interval estimate**   A range of values estimated to include the parameter

**Interval scale**   Scale on which equal intervals between objects represent equal differences—differences are meaningful

**Joint probability**   The probability of the co-occurrence of two or more events

**Kruskal–Wallis one-way analysis of variance**   A nonparametric test analogous to a standard one-way analysis of variance

**Leading digits (most significant digits)**   Leftmost digits of a number

**Least significant difference (LSD) test**   A technique in which we run $t$ tests between pairs of means only if the analysis of variance was significant

**Leaves**   Horizontal axis of display containing the trailing digits

**Line graph**   A graph in which the $Y$ values corresponding to different values of $X$ are connected by a line

**Linear regression**   Regression in which the relationship is linear

**Linear relationship**   A situation in which the best-fitting regression line is a straight line

**Linear transformation**   A transformation involving addition, subtraction, multiplication, or division of or by a constant

**Magnitude of effect**   A measure of the degree to which variability among observations can be attributed to treatments

**Main effect**   The effect of one independent variable averaged across the levels of the other independent variable(s)

**Mann–Whitney test**   A nonparametric test for comparing the central tendency of two independent samples

**Marginal probability**   The probability of falling into a particular row or a particular column

**Marginal totals**   Totals for the levels of one variable summed across the levels of the other variable

**Matched samples**   An experimental design in which the subjects are paired and one is assigned to each treatment

**Matched-samples $t$ test**   A $t$ test comparing the means of matched (or repeated) samples

**Mean ($\overline{X}$)**   The sum of the scores divided by the number of scores

**Measurement**   The assignment of numbers to objects

**Measurement data (quantitative data)**   Data obtained by measuring objects or events

**Measures of central tendency**   Numerical values that refer to the center of the distribution

**Median (Med)**   The score corresponding to the point having 50% of the observations below it when observations are arranged in numerical order

**Median location**   The location of the median in an ordered series

**Midpoint**   Center of the interval; average of the upper and lower limits

**Modality**   The number of meaningful peaks in a frequency distribution of data

**Mode (Mo)**   The most commonly occurring score

**Monotonic relationship**   A relationship represented by a line that is continually increasing (or decreasing), but perhaps not in a straight line

**$MS_{\text{between groups}}$ ($MS_{\text{groups}}$)**   Variability among group means

**$MS_{\text{within}}$ ($MS_{\text{error}}$)**   Variability among subjects in the same treatment group

**Multicategory case**   A situation in which data can be sorted into more than two categories

**Multicollinearity**   A condition in which predictor variables are highly correlated among themselves

**Multiple comparison techniques**   Techniques for making comparisons between two or more group means subsequent to an analysis of variance

**Multiple correlation coefficient (R)**   The correlation between one variable ($Y$) and a set of predictors

**Multiple regression**   Regression with two or more independent variables

**Multiplicative law of probability**   The rule giving the probability of the joint occurrence of independent events

**Mutually exclusive**   Two events are mutually exclusive when the occurrence of one precludes the occurrence of the other

**Negative relationship**   A relationship in which increases in one variable are associated with decreases in the other

**Negatively skewed**   A distribution that trails off to the left

**Nominal scale**   Numbers used only to distinguish among objects

**Nondirectional test**   A test that rejects extreme outcomes in either tail of the distribution

**Nonparametric tests**   Statistical tests that do not rely on parameter estimation or precise distributional assumptions

**Normal distribution**   A specific distribution having a characteristic bell-shaped form

**Null hypothesis ($H_0$)**   The statistical hypothesis tested by the statistical procedure; usually a hypothesis of no difference or no relationship

**Observed frequencies**   The cell frequencies that were actually observed—as distinguished from expected frequencies

**Odds**   The frequency of occurrence of one event divided by the frequency of occurrence of another event. For example, the frequency of success divided by the frequency of failure

**Odds ratio**   The ratio of the odds of success in one condition divided by the odds of success in another condition, where "success" is an arbitrary label

**Omega squared ($\omega^2$)**   A less biased measure of the magnitude of effect

**One-tailed test**   A test that rejects extreme outcomes in one specified tail of the distribution

**One-way ANOVA**   An analysis of variance wherein the groups are defined on only one independent variable

**Order effect**   The effect on performance attributable to the order in which treatments were administered

**Ordinal scale**   Numbers used only to place objects in order

**Ordinate**   Vertical axis

**Outlier**   An extreme point that stands out from the rest of the distribution

**$p$ value**   The probability that a particular result would occur by chance if $H_0$ is true; the exact probability of a Type I error

**Parameters**   Numerical values summarizing population data

**Parametric tests**   Statistical tests that involve assumptions about, or estimation of, population parameters

**Pearson product-moment correlation coefficient ($r$)**   The most common correlation coefficient

**Percentile**   The point below which a specified percentage of the observations fall

**Phi ($\phi$)**   The correlation coefficient when both of the variables are measured as dichotomies

**Point biserial correlation ($r_{pb}$)**   The correlation coefficient when one of the variables is measured as a dichotomy

**Point estimate**   The specific value taken as the estimate of a parameter

**Pooled variance**   A weighted average of the separate sample variances

**Population**   Complete set of events in which you are interested

**Population correlation coefficient rho ($\rho$)**   The correlation coefficient for the population

**Population variance ($\sigma^2$)**   Variance of the population; usually estimated, rarely computed

**Positively skewed**   A distribution that trails off to the right

**Power**   The probability of correctly rejecting a false $H_0$

**Predicted value ($\hat{Y}$)**   The value estimated from a regression equation

**Predictor variable**   The variable from which a prediction is made

**Protected $t$**   A technique in which we run $t$ tests between pairs of means only if the analysis of variance was significant

**Quartile location**   The location of a quartile in an ordered series

**Quartiles**   The points which break the distribution into fourths

**Random assignment**   The allocation or assignment of participants to groups by a random process

**Random sample**   A sample in which each member of the population has an equal chance of inclusion

**Range**   The distance from the lowest to the highest score

**Range restrictions**   Cases wherein the range over which $X$ or $Y$ varies is artificially limited

**Ranked data** Data for which the observations have been replaced by their numerical ranks from lowest to highest

**Rank-randomization tests** A class of nonparametric tests based on the theoretical distribution of randomly assigned ranks

**Ratio scale** A scale with a true zero point—ratios are meaningful

**Real lower limit** The point halfway between the bottom of one interval and the top of the one below it

**Real upper limit** The point halfway between the top of one interval and the bottom of the one above it

**Rectangular distribution** A distribution in which all outcomes are equally likely

**Regression** The prediction of one variable from the knowledge of one or more other variables

**Regression coefficients** The general name given to the slope and the intercept; often refers only to the slope

**Regression equation** The equation that predicts $Y$ from $X$

**Regression line** The "line of best fit" that represents a straight line drawn through the data points

**Regression surface** The equivalent of the regression line in multidimensional space

**Rejection level** The probability with which we are willing to reject $H_0$ when it is, in fact, correct

**Rejection region** The set of outcomes of an experiment that will lead to rejection of $H_0$

**Related samples** An experimental design in which the same subject is observed under more than one treatment

**Relative frequency view** Definition of probability in terms of past performance

**Repeated measures** An experimental design in which the same subject is observed under more than one treatment

**Repeated-measures designs** Experimental designs in which each subject receives all levels of at least one independent variable

**Research hypothesis** The hypothesis that the experiment was designed to investigate

**Residual** The difference between the obtained and predicted values of $Y$

**Residual variance (error variance)** The square of the standard error of estimate

**Rho ($\rho$)** Correlation coefficient on the population. Also occasionally used for Spearman's rank-order correlation

**Sample** Set of actual observations; subset of the population

**Sample statistics** Statistics calculated from a sample and used primarily to describe the sample

**Sample variance ($s^2$)** Sum of the squared deviations about the mean divided by $N - 1$

**Sample with replacement** Sampling in which the item drawn on trial $N$ is replaced before the drawing on trial $N + 1$

**Sampling distribution** The distribution of a statistic over repeated sampling from a specified population

**Sampling distribution of differences between means** The distribution of the differences between means over repeated sampling from the same population(s)

**Sampling distribution of the mean** The distribution of sample means over repeated sampling from one population

**Sampling error** Variability of a statistic from sample to sample due to chance

**Scales of measurement** Characteristics of relations among numbers assigned to objects

**Scatterplot (scatter diagram, scattergram)** A figure in which the individual data points are plotted in two-dimensional space

**Sigma ($\Sigma$)** Symbol indicating summation

**Significance level** The probability with which we are willing to reject $H_0$ when it is, in fact, correct

**Simple effect** The effect of one independent variable at one level of another independent variable

**Skewness** A measure of the degree to which a distribution is asymmetrical

**Slope** The amount of change in $Y$ for a 1-unit change in $X$

**Spearman's correlation coefficient for ranked data ($r_S$)** A correlation coefficient on ranked data

**Squared correlation coefficient ($R^2$)** The squared correlation coefficient between $Y$ and a set of one or more predictor variables

**$SS_{cells}$** The sum of squares assessing differences among cell means

**$SS_{error}$** The sum of the squared residuals or the sum of the squared deviations within each group

**$SS_{group}$** The sum of squared deviations of the group means from the grand mean, multiplied by the number of observations

**$SS_{total}$** The sum of squares of all of the scores, regardless of group membership

**Standard deviation ($s$ or $\sigma$)** Square root of the variance

**Standard error** The standard deviation of a sampling distribution

**Standard error of differences between means** The standard deviation of the sampling distribution of the differences between means

**Standard error of estimate** The average of the squared deviations around the regression line

**Standard normal distribution** A normal distribution with a mean equal to 0 and variance equal to 1; denoted as $N(0, 1)$

**Standard scores** Scores with a predetermined mean and standard deviation

**Standardized regression coefficient ($\beta$)** The regression coefficient that results from data that have been standardized

**Statistics** Numerical values summarizing sample data

**Stem** Vertical axis of display containing the leading digits

**Stem-and-leaf display** Graphical display presenting original data arranged into a histogram

**Stepwise procedures** A set of rules for deriving a regression equation by adding or subtracting one variable at a time from the regression equation

**Student's $t$ distribution** The sampling distribution of the $t$ statistic

**Subjective probability** Definition of probability in terms of personal subjective belief in the likelihood of an outcome

**Sum of squares** The sum of the squared deviations around some point (usually a mean or predicted value)

**Symmetric** Having the same shape on both sides of the center

**T scores** A set of scores with a mean of 50 and a standard deviation of 10

**Test statistics** The results of a statistical test

**Trailing digits (least significant digits)** Digits to the right of the leading digits

**Trimmed samples** Samples with a percentage of extreme scores removed

**Trimmed statistics** Statistics calculated on trimmed samples

**Tukey procedure** A multiple comparison procedure designed to hold the familywise error rate at $\alpha$ for a set of comparisons

**Two-tailed test** A test that rejects extreme outcomes in either tail of the distribution

**Two-way factorial design** An experimental design involving two independent variables in which every level of one variable is paired with each level of the other variable

**Type I error** The error of rejecting $H_0$ when it is true

**Type II error** The error of not rejecting $H_0$ when it is false

**Unconditional probability** The probability of one event *ignoring* the occurrence or nonoccurrence of some other event

**Uniform distribution** A distribution in which all possible outcomes have an equal chance of occurring; also known as a rectangular distribution

**Unimodal** A distribution having one distinct peak

**Variables** Properties of objects or events that can take on different values

**Variance** The sum of the squared deviations from the mean, divided by the degrees of freedom ($N - 1$)

**Variance sum law** The rule giving the variance of the sum (or difference) of two or more variables

**Weighted average** The mean of the form $(a_1X_1 + a_2X_2)/(a_1 + a_2)$, where $a_1$ and $a_2$ are weighting factors, and $X_1$ and $X_2$ are the values to be averaged

**Whisker** Line from each side of the box to the farthest point no more than 1.5 times the $H$-spread from the box

**Wilcoxon's matched-pairs signed-ranks test** A nonparametric test for comparing the central tendency of two matched (related) samples

**Wilcoxon's rank-sum test** A nonparametric test for comparing two independent groups; functionally equivalent to the Mann–Whitney $U$ test

**Winsorized samples** Samples in which extreme values have been trimmed and replaced by the most extreme value(s) remaining in the distribution

**$z$ score** Number of standard deviations above or below the mean

# References

Achenbach, T. M. (1991). *Integrative Guide for the 1991 CBCL/4-18, YSR, and TRF Profiles*. Burlington, VT: University of Vermont Department of Psychiatry.

Achenbach, T. M., Howell, C. T., Aoki, M. F., & Rauh, V. A. (1993). Nine-year outcome of the Vermont Intervention Program for low-birthweight infants. *Pediatrics, 91,* 45–55.

Adams, H. E., Wright, L. W., Jr., & Lohr, B. A. (1996). Is homophobia associated with homosexual arousal? *Journal of Abnormal Psychology, 195,* 440–445.

Aronson, J., Lustina, M. J., Good, C., Keough, K., Steele, C. M., & Brown, J. (1998). When white men can't do math: Necessary and sufficient factors in stereotype threat. *Journal of Experimental Social Psychology, 35,* 29–46.

Associated Press. (Dec. 13, 2001). Study: American kids getting fatter at alarming rate.

Beck, A. T., Ward, C. H., Mendelson, M., Mock, J., & Erbaugh, J. (1961). An inventory for measuring depression. Archives of General Psychiatry 4, 561–571.

Benson, J. B. (1993). Season of birth and onset of locomotion: Theoretical and methodological implications. *Infant Behavior and Development, 16,* 69–81.

Blair, I. V., Judd, C. M., & Chapleau, K. M. (2004). The influence of Afrocentric facial features in criminal sentencing. *Psychological Science, 15,* 674–679.

Blanchard, E. B., Theobald, D. E., Williamson, D. A., Silver, B. V., & Brown, D. A. (1978). Temperature biofeedback in the treatment of migraine headaches. *Archives of General Psychiatry, 35,* 581–588.

Bleuler, E. (1950). *Dementia Praecox or the Group of Schizophrenias* (H. Zinkin, Trans.). New York: International Universities Press. (Original work published 1911).

Bogaert, A. F., & Bocklandt, X. (2006). Biological versus nonbiological older brothers and sexual orientation in men. *Proceedings of the National Academy of Sciences, 103,* 10771–10774.

Bradley, D. R., & Kjungja, L. (1982). Animated subjective contours. *Perception and Psychophysics, 32,* 393–395.

Bradley, J. V. (1963, March). *Studies in Research Methodology: IV. A Sampling Study of the Central Limit Theorem and the Robustness of One-Sample Parametric Tests.* AMRL Technical Documentary Report 63–29, 650th Aerospace Medical Research Laboratories, Wright-Patterson Air Force Base, OH.

Bradley, J. V. (1968). *Distribution-Free Statistical Tests.* Englewood Cliffs, NJ: Prentice-Hall.

Brooks, L., & Perot, A. R. (1991). Reporting sexual harassment. *Psychology of Women Quarterly, 15,* 31–47.

Brown, J., Lewis, V., Brown, M., Horn, G., & Bowes, J. B. (1982). A comparison between transient amnesias induced by two drugs (diazepam and lorazepam) and amnesia of organic origin. *NeuropsychoLogia, 20,* 55–70.

Camilli, G., & Hopkins, K. D. (1978). Applicability of chi-square to 2 × 2 contingency tables with small expected frequencies. *Psychological Bulletin, 85,* 163–167.

Campbell, A., Converse, P. E., & Rodgers, W. L. (1976). *The Quality of American Life.* New York: Russell Sage Foundation.

Carli, L. L. (1990). Gender, language, and influence. *Journal of Personality and Social Psychology, 59,* 941–951.

Chicago Tribune ( July 21, 1995). Girl finds salary gap could begin at home.

Clark, K. B., & Clark, M. K. (1947). Racial identification and preference in Negro children. In E. E. Maccoby, T. M. Newcomb, & E. L. Hartley (Eds), *Readings in Social Psychology* (pp. 602–611). New York: Holt, Rinehart, and Winston.

Cochran, C. D., & Urbanczyk, S. (1982). The effect of availability of vertical space on personal space. *Journal of Psychology, 111,* 137–140.

Cochrane, A. L., St. Leger, A. S., & Moore, F. (1978). Health service "input" and mortality "output" in developed countries. *Journal of Epidemiology and Community Health, 32,* 200–205.

Cohen, J. (1988). *Statistical Power Analysis for the Behavioral Sciences* (2nd ed.). Hillsdale, NJ: Lawrence Erlbaum Associates.

Cohen, J. (1992). A power primer. *Psychological Bulletin*, *112*, 155–159.

Cohen, S., Kaplan, J. R., Cunnick, J. E., Manuck, S. B., & Rabin, B. S. (1992). Chronic social stress, affiliation, and cellular immune response in nonhuman primates. *Psychological Science*, *3*, 301–304.

Cohn, M. A., Mehl, M. R., & Pennebaker, J. W. (2004). Linguistic markers of psychological change surrounding September 11, 2001. *Psychological Science*, *15*, 687–693.

Compas, B. E., Worsham, N. S., Grant, K., Mireault, G., Howell, D. C., & Malcarne, V. L. (1994). When mom or dad has cancer: I. Symptoms of depression and anxiety in cancer patients, spouses, and children. *Health Psychology*, *13*, 507–515.

Conover, W. J. (1980). *Practical Nonparametric Statistics* (2nd ed.). New York: John Wiley & Sons.

Conti, L., & Musty, R. E. (1984). The effects of delta9-tetrahydrocannabinol injections to the nucleus accumbens on the locomotor activity of rats. In S. Aquell et al. (Eds.), *The Cannabinoids: Chemical, Pharmacologic, and Therapeutic Aspects*. New York: Academic Press.

Cowley, G. (1991). Can sunshine save your life? *Newsweek*, December 30, 1991, p. 56.

Craik, F. I. M., & Lockhart, R. S. (1972). Levels of processing: A framework for memory research. *Journal of Verbal Learning and Verbal Behavior*, *11*, 671–684.

Dabbs, J. M., Jr., & Morris, R. (1990). Testosterone, social class, and antisocial behavior in a sample of 4462 men. *Psychological Science*, *1*, 209–211.

Darley, J. M., and Latané, B. (1968). Bystander intervention in emergencies: Diffusion of responsibility. *Journal of Personality and Social Psychology*, *8*, 377–383.

Diener, E., & Diener, C. (1996). Most people are happy. *Psychological Science*, *7*, 181–185.

Dieter, R. C. (1998). The death penalty in black and white: Who lives, who dies, who decides. Retrieved June 6, 2006, from http://www.deathpenaltyinfo.org/article.php?scid=45&did=539

Doll R., Peto R., Boreham J., & Sutherland I. (2004). Mortality in relation to smoking: 50 years' observations on male British doctors. *British Journal of Medicine*, *328*, 1519–1528.

Doob, A. N., & Gross, A. E. (1968). Status of frustration as an inhibitor of horn-honking responses. *Journal of Social Psychology*, *76*, 213–218.

Epping-Jordan, J. E., Compas, B. E., & Howell, D. C. (1994). Predictors of cancer progression in young adult men and women: Avoidance, intrusive thoughts, and psychological symptoms. *Health Psychology*, *13*, 539–547.

Everitt, B. (1994). Cited in Hand et al. (1994), p. 229.

Eysenck, M. W. (1974). Age differences in incidental learning. *Developmental Psychology*, *10*, 936–941.

Fagerström, K. (1982). A comparison of psychological and pharmacological treatment of smoking cessation. *Journal of Behavioral Medicine*, *5*, 343–351.

Fell, J. C. (1995). What's new in alcohol, drugs, and traffic safety in the U.S. (Paper presented at the 13th International Conference on Alcohol, Drugs, and Traffic Safety, Adelaide, Australia.)

Fisher, R. A. (1935). *The Design of Experiments*. Edinburgh: Oliver & Boyd.

Foa, E. B., Rothbaum, B. O., Riggs, D. S., & Murdock, T. B. (1991). Treatment of posttraumatic stress disorder in rape victims: A comparison between cognitive-behavioral procedures and counseling. *Journal of Consulting and Clinical Psychology*, *59*, 715–723.

Foertsch, J., & Gernsbacher, M. A. (1997). In search of gender neutrality: Is singular *they* a cognitively efficient substitute for generic *he*? *Psychological Science*, *8*, 106–111.

Fombonne, E. (1989). Season of birth and childhood psychosis. *British Journal of Psychiatry*, *155*, 655–661.

Franklin, K. M., Janoff-Bulman, R., & Roberts, J. E. (1990). Long-term impact of parental divorce on optimism and trust: Changes in general assumptions or narrow beliefs? *Journal of Personality and Social Psychology*, *59*, 743–755.

Geller, E. S., Witmer, J. F., & Orebaugh, A. L. (1976). Instructions as a determinant of paper disposal behaviors. *Environment and Behavior*, *8*, 417–439.

Geyer, C. J. (1991). Constrained maximum likelihood exemplified by isotonic convex logistic regression. *Journal of the American Statistical Association*, *86*, 717–724.

Glass, G. V., McGaw, B., & Smith, M. L. (1981). *Meta-Analysis in Social Research*. Newbury Park, CA: Sage.

Goldstein, A. G., Bailis, K., & Chance, J. E. (1983). Do students remember pictures in psychology textbooks? *Teaching of Psychology*, *10*, 23–26.

Good, P. I. (1999). *Resampling Methods: A Practical Guide to Data Analysis*. Boston: Birkhäuser.

Greenhouse, S. W., & Geisser, S. (1959). On methods in the analysis of profile data. *Psychometrika*, *24*, 95–112.

Gross, J. S. (1985). Weight modification and eating disorders in adolescent boys and girls. (Unpublished doctoral dissertation, University of Vermont, Burlington.)

Guber, D. L. (1999). Getting what you pay for: The debate over equity in public school expenditures. *Journal of Statistics Education, 7,* (2).

Hand, D. J., Daly, F., Lunn, A. D., McConway, K. J., & Oserowski, E. (1994). *A Handbook of Small Data Sets.* London: Chapman & Hall.

Hicks, R. A., & Guista, M. (1982). The energy level of habitual long and short sleepers. *Bulletin of the Psychonomic Society, 19,* 131–132.

Hoaglin, D. C., Mosteller, F., & Tukey, J. W. (1983). *Understanding Robust and Exploratory Data Analysis.* New York: John Wiley & Sons.

Holmes, T. A., & Rahe, T. H. (1967). The social readjustment rating scale. *Journal of Psychosomatic Research, 11,* 213.

Holway, A. H., & Boring, E. G. (1940). The moon illusion and the angle of regard. *American Journal of Psychology, 53,* 509–516.

Hosch, H. M., & Cooper, D. S. (1982). Victimization as a determinant of eyewitness accuracy. *Journal of Applied Psychology, 67,* 649–652.

Hout, M., Duncan, O. D., & Sobel, M. E. (1987). Association and heterogeneity: Structural models of similarities and differences. In C. C. Clogg (Ed.), *Sociological Methodology, 17,* 145ff.

Howell (2005). Power. In B. S. Everitt, & D. C. Howell (Eds.), *Encyclopedia of Statistics in Behavioral Science.* Chichester, England: John Wiley & Sons.

Howell, D. C. (2007). *Statistical Methods for Psychology* (6th ed.). Thomson Wadsworth, A Wadsworth Imprint.

Howell, D. C., & Gordon, L. R. (1976). Computing the exact probability of an R X C contingency table with fixed marginal totals. *Behavior Research Methods and Instrumentation, 8,* 317.

Howell, D. C., & Huessy, H. R. (1985 ). A fifteen year follow-up of a behavioral history of Attention Deficit Syndrome (ADD). *Pediatrics, 76,* 185–190.

Hraba, J., & Grant, G. (1970). Black is beautiful: A reexamination of racial preference and identification. *Journal of Personality and Social Psychology, 16,* 398–402.

Hunt, E., Streissguth, A. P., Kerr, B., & Olson, H. C. (1995). Mothers' alcohol consumption during pregnancy: Effects on spatial-visual reasoning in 14-year-old children. *Psychological Science, 6,* 339–342.

Hunt, J. McV. (1941). The effects of infant feeding frustration upon adult hoarding behavior. *Journal of Abnormal and Social Psychology, 36,* 338–360.

Huynh, H., & Feldt, L. S. (1976). Estimation of the Box correction for degrees of freedom for sample data in the randomized block and split plot designs. *Journal of Educational Statistics, 1,* 69–82.

Hygge, S., Evans, G. W., & Bullinger, M. (2002). A prospective study of some effects of aircraft noise on cognitive performance in school children. *Psychological Science, 13,* 469–479.

Jones, L. V., & Tukey, J. W. (2000). A sensible formulation of the significance test. *Psychological Methods, 5,* 411–414.

Kapp, B., Frysinger, R., Gallagher, M., & Hazelton, J. (1979). Amygdala central nucleus lesions: Effects on heart rate conditioning in the rabbit. *Physiology and Behavior, 23,* 1109–1117.

Katz, S., Lautenschlager, G. J., Blackburn, A. B., & Harris, F. H. (1990). Answering reading comprehension items without passages on the SAT. *Psychological Science, 1,* 122–127.

Kaufman, L., & Rock, I. (1962). The moon Illusion. I. *Science, 136,* 953–961.

Klahr, D., & Nigam, M. (2004). The equivalence of learning paths in early science instruction. *Psychological Science, 15,* 661–667.

Kline, R. B. (2004). *Beyond significance testing.* Washington, D.C.: American Psychological Association.

Landwehr, J. M., & Watkins, A. E. (1987). *Exploring Data: Teacher's Edition.* Palo Alto, CA: Dale Seymour Publications.

Lane, D. (2003, July 14). *Restriction of Range Simulation.* Retrieved May 10, 2006, from the Connexions Web site: http://cnx.org/content/m11196/1.4/

Langlois, J. H., & Roggman, L. A. (1990). Attractive faces are only average. *Psychological Science, 1,* 115–121.

Latané, B., & Dabbs, J. M., Jr. (1975). Sex, group size, and helping in three cities. *Sociometry, 38,* 180–194.

Levine, R. (1990). The pace of life and coronary heart disease. *American Scientist, 78,* 450–459.

Liddle, B. J. (1997). Coming out in class: Disclosure of sexual orientation and teaching evaluations. *Teaching of Psychology, 24,* 32–35.

Lobel, M., Dunkel-Schetter, C., & Scrimshaw, C. M. (1992). Prenatal maternal stress and prematurity: A prospective study of disadvantaged women. *Health Psychology, 11,* 32–40.

Lord, F. M. (1953). On the statistical treatment of football numbers. *American Psychologist, 8,* 750–751.

Lundberg, U. (1983 ). Note on Type A behavior and cardiovascular responses to challenge in 3- to 6-year-old children. *Journal of Psychosomatic Research, 27,* 39–42.

Malcarne, V., Compas, B. E., Epping, J., & Howell, D. C. (1995). Cognitive factors in adjustment to cancer: Attributions of self-blame and perceptions of control. *Journal of Behavioral Medicine, 18*, 401–417.

Mann-Joes, J. M., Ettinger, R. H., Baisden, J., & Baisden, K. (under review). Dextromethorphan modulation of context-dependent morphine tolerance. Retrieved November 20, 2006, from www.eou.edu/psych/re/morphinetolerance.doc

McConaughy, S. H. (1980). Cognitive structures for reading comprehension: Judging the relative importance of ideas in short stories. (Unpublished doctoral dissertation, University of Vermont, Burlington.)

Mireault, G. C. (1990). Parent death in childhood, perceived vulnerability, and adult depression and anxiety. (Unpublished master's thesis, University of Vermont, Burlington.)

Moran, P. A. P. (1974). Are there two maternal age groups in Down's syndrome? *British Journal of Psychiatry, 124*, 453–455.

Nolen-Hoeksema, S., & Morrow, J. (1991). A prospective study of depression and posttraumatic stress symptoms after a natural disaster: The 1989 Loma Prieta earthquake. *Journal of Personality and Social Psychology, 61*, 115–121.

Nurcombe, B., & Fitzhenry-Coor, I. (1979). Decision making in the mental health interview: I. An introduction to an education and research program. (Paper delivered at the Conference on Problem Solving in Medicine, Smuggler's Notch, VT.)

Nurcombe, B., Howell, D. C., Rauh, V. A., Teti, D. M., Ruoff, P., & Brennan, J. (1984). An intervention program for mothers of low-birthweight infants: Preliminary results. *Journal of the American Academy of Child Psychiatry, 23*, 319–325.

Obrzut, J. E., Hansen, R. L., & Heath, C. P. (1982). The effectiveness of visual information processing training with Hispanic children. *Journal of General Psychology, 107*, 165–174.

Payne, S. L. (1982). Job-orientation stereotyping: Is it changing? *Journal of Psychology, 111*, 51–55.

Pihl, R. O., Lau, M. L., & Assaad, J. (1997). Aggressive disposition, alcohol, and aggression. *Aggressive Behavior, 23*, 11–18.

Pliner, P. (1982). The effects of mere exposure on liking for edible substances. *Appetite, 3*, 283–290.

Pliner, P., & Chaiken, S. (1990). Eating, social motives, and self-presentation in women and men. *Journal of Experimental Social Psychology, 26*, 240–254.

Pope, H. G., & Yurgelun-Todd, D. (1996). The residual cognitive effects of heavy marijuana use in college students. *Journal of the American Medical Association, 275*, 560–561.

Pugh, M. D. (1983). Contributory fault and rape conviction: Loglinear models for blaming the victim. *Social Psychology Quarterly, 46*, 233–242.

Radelet, M. L., & Pierce, G. L. (1991). Choosing those who will die: Race and the death penalty in Florida. *Florida Law Review, 43*, 1–34.

Ramsey, F. L., & Schaffer, D. W. (1996). *The Statistical Sleuth*. Belmont, CA: Duxbury Press.

Ramsey, F. L., & Schafer, D. W. (1997). *The statistical sleuth: A course in data analysis*. Belmont, CA: Duxbury Press.

Reynolds, C. R., & Richmond, B. O. (1978). What I think and feel: A revised measure of children's manifest anxiety. *Journal of Abnormal Child Psychology, 6*, 271–280.

Roanoke Times. (July 25, 1997). Rock 'n' roll rodents mazed and confused: Of mice and music.

Robinson, B. E., Barrett, R. L., & Skeen, P. (1983). Locus of control of unwed adolescent fathers versus adolescent nonfathers. *Perceptual and Motor Skills, 56*, 397–398.

Rogers, R. W., & Prentice-Dunn, S. (1981). Deindividuation and anger-mediated aggression: Unmasking regressive racism. *Journal of Personality and Social Psychology, 41*, 63–73.

Rosenthal, R. (1994). Parametric measures of effect size. In H. Cooper, & L. Hedges (Eds), *The handbook of research synthesis*. New York, Russell Sage Foundation.

Ruback, R. B., & Juieng, D. (1997). Territorial defense in parking lots: Retaliation against waiting drivers. *Journal of Applied Social Psychology, 27*, 821–834.

Ryan, T., Joiner, B., & Ryan, B. (1985). *Minitab Student Handbook*. Boston: Duxbury Press.

Saint-Exupery, A. de (1943). *The Little Prince* (K. Woods, Trans.). New York: Harcourt Brace Jovanovich. (Original work published in 1943.)

Seligman, M. E. P., Nolen-Hoeksema, S., Thornton, N., & Thornton, C. M. (1990). Explanatory style as a mechanism of disappointing athletic performance. *Psychological Science, 1*, 143–146.

Sethi, S., & Seligman, M. E. P. (1993). Optimism and fundamentalism. *Psychological Science, 4*, 256–259.

Sgro, J. A., & Weinstock, S. (1963). Effects of delay on subsequent running under immediate reinforcement. *Journal of Experimental Psychology, 66*, 260–263.

Siegel, S. (1975). Evidence from rats that morphine tolerance is a learned response. *Journal of Comparative and Physiological Psychology, 80,* 498–506.

Simon, J. L., & Bruce, P. (1991). Resampling: A tool for everyday statistical work. *Chance: New Directions for Statistics and Computing, 4,* 22–58.

Spilich, G. J., June, L., & Renner, J. (1992). Cigarette smoking and cognitive performance. *British Journal of Addiction, 87,* 1313–1326.

St. Lawrence, J. S., Brasfield, T. L., Shirley, A., Jefferson, K. W., Alleyne, E., & O'Brannon, R. E., III (1995). Cognitive-behavioral intervention to reduce African-American adolescents' risk for HIV infection. *Journal of Consulting & Clinical Psychology, 63,* 221–237.

St. Leger, A. S., Cochrane, A. L., & Moore, F. (1978). The anomaly that wouldn't go away. *Lancet, ii,* 1153.

Sternberg, S. (1966). High–speed scanning in human memory. *Science, 153,* 652–654.

Stevens, S. S. (1951). Mathematics, measurement, and psychophysics. In S. S. Stevens (Ed.), *Handbook of Experimental Psychology.* New York: John Wiley & Sons.

Suddath, R. L., Christison, G. W., Torrey, E. F., Casanova, M. F., Weinberger, D. R. (1990). Anatomical abnormalities in the brains of monozygotic twins discordant for schizophrenia. *New England Journal of Medicine, 322,* 789–794.

Thomas, M. H., & Wang, A. Y. (1996). Learning by the keyword mnemonic: Looking for long-term benefits. *Journal of Experimental Psychology: Applied, 2,* 330–342.

Tolman, E. C., Ritchie, B. F., & Kalish, D. (1946). Studies in spatial learning: I. Orientation and the short cut. *Journal of Experimental Psychology, 36,* 13–24.

Tufte, E. R. (1983). *The Visual Display of Quantitative Information.* Cheshire, CT: Graphics Press.

Tukey, J. W. (1977). *Exploratory Data Analysis.* Reading, MA: Addison-Wesley.

U.S. Department of Commerce. (1977). *Social Indicators, 1976.* Washington, DC: U.S. Government Printing Office.

U.S. Department of Justice, Bureau of Justice Statistics, *Prisoners in 1982.* Bulletin NCJ-87933 (Washington, D.C.: U.S. Government Printing Office, 1983.

Utts, J. M. (2005). *Seeing through statistics, 3rd edition,* Belmont, CA: Brooks Cole.

Vasta, R., Rosenberg, D., Knott, J. A., & Gaze, C. E. (1997). Experience and the water-level task revisited: Does expertise exact a price? *Psychological Science, 8,* 336–339.

Verdooren, L. R. (1963). Extended tables of critical values for Wilcoxon's test statistic. *Biometrika, 50,* 177–186.

Vermont Department of Health. (1982). *1981 Annual Report of Vital Statistics in Vermont.* Burlington, VT.

Visintainer, M. A., Volpicelli, J. R., & Seligman, M. E. P. (1982). Tumor rejection in rats after inescapable or escapable shock. *Science, 216,* 437–439.

Wagner, B. M., Compas, B. E., & Howell, D. C. (1988). Daily and major life events: A test of an integrative model of psychosocial stress. *American Journal of Community Psychology, 61,* 189–205.

Wainer, H. (1997). Some multivariate displays for NAEP results. *Psychological Methods, 2,* 34–63.

Walsh, T. B., Kaplan, A. S., Attia, E., Olmsted, M., Parides, M., Carter, J. C., Pike, K. M., Devlin, M. J., Woodside, B., Roberto, C. A., Rockert, W. (2006). Fluoxetine After Weight Restoration in Anorexia Nervosa. *Journal of the American Medical Association, 295,* 2605–2612.

Weinberg, C. R., & Gladen, B. C. (1986). The beta-geometric distribution applied to comparative fecundability studies. *Biometrics, 42,* 547–560.

Welkowitz, J., Cohen, B. M., & Ewen, R., (2006). *Introductory Statistics for the Behavioral Sciences* (6th ed.). New York: John Wiley & Sons.

Werner, M., Stabenau, J. B., & Pollin, W. (1970). TAT method for the differentiation of families of schizophrenics, delinquents, and normals. *Journal of Abnormal Psychology, 75,* 139–145.

Wilcox, R. R. (2003). *Applying Contemporary Statistical Techniques.* New York: Academic Press.

Winer, B. J., Brown, D. R., & Michels, K. M. (1991). *Statistical Principles in Experimental Design.* New York: McGraw-Hill.

Zaragoza, M. S., & Mitchell, K. J. (1996). Repeated exposure to suggestion and the creation of false memories. *Psychological Science, 7,* 294–300.

Zuckerman, M., Hodgins, H. S., Zuckerman, A., & Rosenthal, R. (1993). Contemporary issues in the analysis of data. *Psychological Science, 4,* 49–53.

Zumbo, B. D., & Zimmerman, D. W. (2000). Scales of measurement and the relation between parametric and nonparametric statistical tests. In B. Thompson (Ed.), *Advances in Social Science Methodology, Vol. 6.* Greenwich, CT: JAI Press.

# Answers to Exercises

(I have not provided graphs where those are called for because of the amount of space they require and the cost of preparation. I have also left out a few answers that would require an inordinate amount of space. These items are included in both the Instructor's Manual and the Student's Manual. The Student's manual is available at http://www.uvm.edu/~dhowell/fundamentals/. In early chapters there is often close correspondence between these answers and the answers in the Student Manual. This is much less true in later chapters, where the problems are more computational.)

## Chapter 1

**1.1** A good example is the development of tolerance to caffeine. People who do not normally drink caffeinated coffee are often startled by the effect of one or two cups of regular coffee, whereas those who normally drink regular coffee see no such effect. To test for a context effect of caffeine, you would first need to develop a dependent variable measuring the alerting effect of caffeine, which could be a vigilance task. You could test for a context effect by serving a group of users of decaffeinated coffee two cups of regular coffee every morning in their office for a month, but have them drink decaf the rest of the time. The vigilance test would be given shortly after the coffee, and tolerance would be seen by an increase in errors over days. At the end of the month they would be tested after drinking caffeinated coffee in the same and in a different setting.

**1.3** Context affects people's response to alcohol, to off-color jokes, or to observed aggressive behavior.

**1.5** The sample would be the addicts that we observe.

**1.7** Not all people in the city are listed in the phonebook. In particular, women and children are under-represented, as are those who rely mainly on cell phones.

**1.9** In the tolerance study discussed in the text we really do not care what the mean length of paw-lick latency is. No one would be excited to know that a mouse can stand on a surface at 105° for 3.2 seconds without licking its paws. But we do very much care that the population mean of paw-lick latencies for morphine-tolerant mice is longer in one context than in another.

**1.11** I would expect that my mother would continue to wander around in a daze, wondering what happened.

**1.13** Three examples of measurement data: performance on a vigilance task, typing speed, blood alcohol level.

**1.15** Relationship: the relationship between stress and susceptibility to disease, the relationship between driving speed and accident rate.

**1.17** You could have one group of mice trained and tested in the same condition, one group trained in one condition and tested in the other, and a third group given a placebo in the training context but given morphine in the testing condition.

**1.19** This is an Internet search exercise with no fixed answer.

## Chapter 2

**2.1** Nominal: names of students in the class, Ordinal: the order in which students hand in their first exam. Interval: a student's grade on that first exam. Ratio: the amount of time that a student spent taking the exam.

**2.3** If the rat lies down to sleep in the maze after performing successfully for several trials, this probably says little about what the animal has learned in the task, but more about motivation.

**2.5** We have assumed the following at the very least (and I may have left some out):

1. Mice are adequate models for human behavior.
2. Morphine tolerance effects in mice are like heroin effects in humans.
3. Time on a warm surface is in some way analogous to a human response to heroin.
4. A context shift for mice is analogous to a context shift for humans.
5. A drug overdose is analogous to pain tolerance.

**2.7** The independent variables are the gender of the subject and the gender of the other person.

**2.9** The experimenter expected to find that women would eat less in the presence of a male partner than in the presence of a female partner. Men, on the other hand, were not expected to vary the amount that they ate as a function of gender of their partner.

**2.11** Continuous variables: the grams of food that the participants ate in the previous experiment; the number of seconds it takes a mouse to lick its paws; the time that a rat spends getting from one end of a maze to another.

**2.13** When I drew 50 numbers three times I obtained 29, 26, and 19 even numbers, respectively. The last time only 38% of my numbers were even, which is probably less than I might have expected—especially if I didn't have a fair amount of experience with similar exercises.

**2.15** Eyes level condition:
(a) $X_3 = 2.03$; $X_5 = 1.05$; $X_8 = 1.86$
(b) $\Sigma X = 14.82$
(c) $\sum_{i=1}^{10} X_i = 14.82$

**2.17** Eyes level condition:
(a) $(\Sigma X)^2 = (14.82)^2 = 219.63$;
$\Sigma X^2 = 1.65^2 + \cdots + 1.73^2 = 23.22$
(b) $\Sigma X/N = 14.82/10 = 1.482$
(c) This is the mean, a type of average.

**2.19** Putting the two sets of data together:
(a) $XY = 2.854\ 1.06\ 4.121\ 1.750\ .998$
$1.153\ 2.355\ 3.218\ 2.543\ 2.699$
(b) $\Sigma XY = 22.7496$
(c) $\Sigma X \Sigma Y = (14.82)(14.63) = 216.82$

(d) $22.7496 \neq 216.82$
(e) .1187

**2.21** Show $\Sigma(X + C) = \Sigma X + NC$:

| $X$ | 5 | 7 | 3 | 6 | 3 | $\Sigma X = 24$ |
|---|---|---|---|---|---|---|
| $X + 4$ | 9 | 11 | 7 | 10 | 7 | $\Sigma(X + 4) = 44 = (24 + 5 \times 4)$ |

**2.23** In the text I spoke about room temperature as an ordinal scale of comfort (at least up to some temperature). Room temperature is a continuous physical measure, even though with respect to comfort it measures only at an ordinal level.

**2.25** Beth Peres:
(a) In the Beth Peres story the dependent variable is the weekly allowance, and the independent variable is the gender of the child.
(b) We are dealing with a selected sample—the children in her class.
(c) The age of the students would influence the overall mean. The fact that these children are classmates could easily lead to socially appropriate responses—or what the children deem to be socially appropriate in their setting.
(d) At least within her school Beth could randomly sample by taking a student roster, assigning each student a number, and matching those with the numbers drawn from a random number table. Random assignment to Gender would obviously be impossible.
(e) I don't see negative aspects of the lack of random assignment here because that is the nature of the variable under consideration. It might be better if we could randomly assign a child to a gender and see the result, but we clearly can't.
(f) The outcome of the study could be influenced by the desire of some children to exaggerate their allowance or to minimize it so as not to appear too different from their peers. I would suspect that boys would be likely to exaggerate.
(g) The descriptive features of the study are her statements that the boys in her class received $3.18 per week in allowance, on average, whereas the girls received an average of $2.73. The inferential aspects are the inferences to the population of all children, concluding that boys get more than girls.

**2.27** Even a complete random process produces data that don't correspond to our intuitive ideas of randomness.

## Chapter 3

**3.1** (b) There is too little data to say much about the shape of this distribution.

**3.3** I would use stems of 3*, 3., 4*, 4., 5*, and 5. for this display.

**3.5** Compared to those who read the passages:
(a) Almost everyone who read the passages did better than the best person who did not read them. Certainly knowing what you are talking about is a good thing (though not always practiced).
(c) It is obvious that the two groups are very different in their performance. We would be worried if they were not.
(d) This is an Internet question with no fixed answer.

**3.7** A bimodal set of data can be created by combining the two groups from the Katz et al. study. The NoPassage group's scores will be well below the Passage group's scores.

**3.9** Histogram of GPA:

**3.11** (1) Mexico has very many young people and very few old people, whereas Spain has a more even distribution. (2) The difference between males and females is more pronounced at most ages in Spain than it is in Mexico. (3) You can see the high infant mortality rate in Mexico.

**3.13** The distribution of those whose attendance is poor is far more spread out than the distribution of normal attendees. This is expected because a few very good students can score well on tests even when they don't attend, but most of the poor attendees are generally poor students who would score badly no matter what. The difference between the average grades of these two groups is obvious.

**3.15** The stem-and-leaf displays in Exercise 3.14 support the sequential processing hypothesis.

**3.17** The data points are probably not independent in that dataset. At first the subject might get better with practice, but then fatigue would start to set in. Data nearer in time should be more similar than data further apart in time.

**3.19** The amount of shock that a subject delivers to a white participant does not vary as a function of whether than subject has been insulted by the experimenter. However, black participants do suffer when the subject has been insulted.

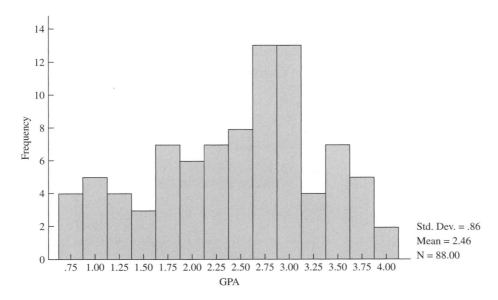

Std. Dev. = .86
Mean = 2.46
N = 88.00

**3.21** Both AIDS cases and AIDS deaths began to drop off about 1992, but the number of people living with AIDS has continued to increase substantially.

**3.23** There is a tremendous increase in Down's syndrome in children born to older mothers. This increase doesn't really take off until mothers are in their 40s, but with parents delaying having children, this is a potential problem.

**3.25** The relationship is unlikely to be a fluke because it is so consistent year after year. You can see that within each group there is very little variability.

**3.27** White females have a longer life expectancy than black females, but the difference has shrunk considerably since 1920, though recent changes have been modest.

## Chapter 4

**4.1** Mode = 72, Median = 72, Mean = 70.18

**4.3** Even without reading the passage, students are still getting about twice as many items correct as they would by chance. This suggests than the test, which tests reading comprehension, is also testing something else.

**4.5** The mean falls above the median.

**4.7** Rats running a straight-alley maze:

$$\Sigma X = 320; \overline{X} = \frac{\Sigma X}{N} = \frac{320}{15} = 21.33;$$

Median = 21

**4.9** Multiplying by a constant (5):

Original data
  8   3   5   5   6   2    Mean = 4.833

Revised data
40  15  25  25  30  10    Mean = 24.17 = 5 × 4.833

**4.11** Measures of central tendency for ADDSC and GPA:

    ADDSC
        Mode = 50
        Median = 50
        Mean = 4629/88 = 52.6
    GPA
        Mode = 3.00
        Median = 2.635
        Mean = 216.15/88 = 2.46

**4.13** The only measure that is acceptable for nominal data is the mode because the mode is the only one that does not depend on the relationship among the points on the scale.

**4.15** The measures of central tendency in Exercise 4.14 suggest that we process information sequentially, at least within the domain of Sternberg's experimental design.

**4.17** Class attendance:

Regular attendees: Mean = 276.417; Median = 276
Poor attendees:     Mean = 248.333; Median = 256

The two groups were 20 points apart in terms of the medians, and about 25 points apart in terms of means. Clearly those students who come to class do better.

**4.19** This is an Internet activity for which there is no fixed answer.

**4.21** Trimmed means:
(a) Mean = 46.57; 10% trimmed mean = 46.67.
(b) Mean = 28.40; 10% trimmed mean = 25.00.
(c) Trimming was more effective in the second example because that distribution was quite skewed.

**4.23** The male optimists had a mean of 1.016 while the male pessimists had a mean of .945. This difference is reliable.

## Chapter 5

**5.1** Variability of NoPassage group:

Range = 57 − 34 = 23
Std. Dev. = 6.83
Variance = 46.62

**5.3** The variability of the NoPassage group is much smaller than the variability of the Passage group. If this difference turns out to be reliable, it could possibly be explained by the fact that the questions for the Passage group are asking for more than guessing and test-taking skills, and there may be greater variability due to variability in knowledge. On the other hand, it is not uncommon to find one standard deviation equal to two or three times another in small samples.

**5.5** Percentages within two standard deviations in Exercise 5.2:

$$s = 10.61$$
$$\overline{X} \pm 2(10.61) = 70.18 \pm 21.22 = 48.96 - 91.40$$

16 scores (or 94%) lie within two standard deviations of the mean.

**5.7** Multiplying or dividing by a constant:

| Original | 2 | 3 | 4 | 4 | 5 | 5 | 9 | $\overline{X}_1 = 4.57$ $s_1 = 2.23$ |
|---|---|---|---|---|---|---|---|---|
| $X \times 2$ | 4 | 6 | 8 | 8 | 10 | 10 | 18 | $\overline{X}_2 = 9.14$ $s_2 = 4.45$ |
| $X/2$ | 1 | 1.5 | 2 | 2 | 2.5 | 2.5 | 4.5 | $\overline{X}_3 = 2.29$ $s_3 = 1.11$ |

**5.9** Since adding or subtracting a constant will not change the standard deviation but will change the mean, I can subtract 3.27 from every score for $X_2$ in Exercise 5.8, making the mean 0 and keeping $s_2 = 1.0$. The new values are

$$-.889 \quad .539 \quad -1.842 \quad .539 \quad -.413 \quad 1.016 \quad 1.016$$
$$\overline{X}_1 = 0 \quad s_1 = 1.0$$

**5.11** Boxplot for Exercise 5.1:

Median location $= (N + 1)/2 = 29/2 = 14.5$
Median $= 46$
Hinge location $= $ (Median location $+ 1)/2 = $ 
    $15/2 = 7.5$
Hinges $= 43$ and $52$
H-spread $= 52 - 43 = 9$
Inner fences $= $ Hinges $\pm 1.5 \times$ H-spread $=$
    Hinges $\pm 1.5 \times 9 = $ Hinges $\pm 13.5 = 29.5$ and $65.5$
Adjacent values $= 34$ and $57$

**5.13** Boxplot for ADDSC:

Median location $= (N + 1)/2 = 89/2 = 44.5$
Median $= 50$
Hinge location $= $ (Median location $+ 1)/2 = 45/2 = $
    $22.5$
Hinges $= 44.5$ and $60.5$
H-spread $= 60.5 - 44.5 = 16$
Inner fences $= $ Hinges $\pm 1.5 \times$ H-spread $=$
    Hinges $\pm 1.5 \times 16 = $ Hinges $\pm 24 = 20.5$ and $85.5$
Adjacent values $= 26$ and $78$

**5.15** Adding a score equal to the mean will not change the numerator, but will increase the

denominator to 28. The new variance is $(1 - 1/N)$ times the old variance.

**5.17** There are too many samples to reproduce the results, but it will be clear whether you have the right answer. A more complete answer can be found in the Student Manual on the Web.

**5.19** The vertical bars lie at those points that cut off the minimum, the lowest 10%, the lowest 25%, the 50% point, the lowest 75%, the lowest 90%, and the maximum score. The diamond delineates the mean and a region around that mean that we will later identify as the 95% confidence interval. The mean is at the tallest point of the diamond. That is a lot of information for one simple graphic.

**5.21** Treatment of anorexia:
I hypothesize that the two treatment groups will show more of a weight gain that the control group, but I have no reason to predict which treatment group would do better.

| | Cognitive Behavioral | Control | Family Therapy |
|---|---|---|---|
| Mean | 3.01 | −.45 | 7.26 |
| Median | 1.40 | −.35 | 9.00 |
| Std. Dev. | 7.31 | 7.99 | 7.16 |

If we look at the changes from Before to After it appears that the Control group stayed about the same, but the two experimental groups increased their weight. This is true whether we look at means or medians. Notice that the standard deviation in the two experimental groups was noticeably higher after treatment, whereas the standard deviation of the Control actually decreased slightly. This suggests that some participants were helped more than others by the therapies.

**5.23** For data on Cognitive Behavior Therapy:

```
                Descriptive Statistics

              Min-   Max-          Std.      Vari-
           N  imum   imum   Mean   Deviation ance

COGBEHAV   29  −9.10  20.90  3.0069  7.30850  53.414
TRIM       19  −1.40  11.70  1.8000  3.04211   9.254
WINSOR     29  −1.40  11.70  2.9552  4.88851  23.898
Valid N    19
(listwise)
```

Notice that the Winsorized variance is considerably greater than the trimmed variance, as it should be. However, it is lower than the variance of the original data, reflecting the fact that the extreme values have been replaced. Cognitive behavior scores were positively skewed, with several quite high values and one or two low values. Trimming and Winsorizing reduced the influence of those values. This causes the Winsorized variance to be considerably smaller than the original variance. The trimmed mean is considerably smaller than the original mean, but the Winsorized mean is only slightly smaller.

## Chapter 6

**6.1** Distribution of original values:

For the first distribution the abscissa would take on the values of

| 1 | 2 | 3 | 4 | 5 | 6 | 7 |

For the second distribution the values would be

| −3 | −2 | −1 | 0 | 1 | 2 | 3 |

For the third distribution the values would be

| −1.90 | −1.27 | −0.63 | 0 | .63 | 1.27 | 1.90 |

**6.3** Distribution of grades:
  (a) .6826
  (b) .5000
  (c) .8413

**6.5** The Katz study:
  (a) 84.6
  (b) 80.0625
  (c) 25.65
  (d) I would conclude that they were not guessing.

**6.7** Reading scores:
  (b) 15.87%
  (c) 30.85%

**6.9** A $T$ score of 62.8 is the score that cuts off the top 10% of the distribution and is therefore a diagnostically meaningful cutoff.

**6.11** (b) The probability of $z \geq 2.57 = .0051$. This is such a small probability that we will probably conclude that the student just made up the data rather than collecting them honestly.

**6.13** (b) The easiest way to find the cutoff for the lowest 10% is to simply take the sample data and count them, empirically finding the point with 10% of the scores below it. Sometimes the simplest way is the best.

**6.15** The 75th percentile would be the value with $z = .675$. $X = 574$.

**6.17** Percentiles are critically dependent on the reference group. As a group the seniors and nonenrolled college graduates did better on the GRE than did the "combined group" of all people taking the exam. A person receiving a given score, therefore, did better (scored at a higher percentile) when compared to all people taking the exam than when compared only to seniors and nonenrolled college graduates.

**6.19** The critical cutoff is a score of 70.5.

**6.21** The statisticians were upset because, by defining "overweight" as weighing more than 95% of peers (i.e., above the 95th percentile), the article seemed to be suggesting that there were 22% of children in the top 5%. Moreover, the article says that in 1986 only 8% of children were in the top 15%. That is just silly—it is analogous to "all of the children are above average." I assume that they meant to say that 22% (etc.) were above what the 95th percentile was some years ago, but that is a different thing. Even if that is the case, the results still look too extreme to be likely.

## Chapter 7

**7.1** Views of probability:
  (a) Analytic: If two tennis players are exactly equally skillful so that the outcome of their match is random, the probability is .50 that Player A will win the upcoming match.
  (b) Relative Frequency: If in past matches Player A has beaten Player B on 13 of the 17 occasions they have played, then Player A has a probability of 13/17 = .76 of winning their upcoming match.
  (c) Subjective: Player A's coach feels that she has a probability of .90 of winning the upcoming match with Player B.

**7.3** More raffle tickets:
  (a) .001
  (b) .000001
  (c) .000001
  (d) .000002

**7.5** Part (a) of Exercise 7.3 dealt with conditional probabilities.

**7.7** An example of a conditional probability is the probability that you will go to see tonight's fireworks, given that the forecast is for rain.

**7.9** $p$(mom looking) = 2/13 = .154; $p$(baby looking) = 3/13 = .231; $p$(both looking) = 2/13 × 3/13 = .154 × .231 = .036.

**7.11** It would appear that having a message on a flyer increases the probability of proper disposal.

**7.13** A continuous variable that is routinely treated as if it were discrete is children's learning abilities, where placement in classes often assumes that the child falls within one category or another.

**7.15** The probability of admission is .02.

**7.17** The probability associated with $z = -.21$ is .5832.

**7.19** $p$(dropout | ADDSC ≥ 60) = 7/25 = .28.

**7.21** Conditional and unconditional probability of dropping out:

$p$(dropout) = 10/88 = .11
$p$(dropout | ADDSC ≥ 60) = .28

Students are much more likely to drop out of school if they score at or above ADDSC = 60 in elementary school

**7.23** If there is no discrimination in housing, then a person's race and whether or not that person is offered a particular unit of housing are independent events. We could calculate the probability that a particular unit (or a unit in a particular section of the city) will be offered to anyone in a specific income group. We can then calculate the probability of that person being shown the unit, *assuming independence,* and compare that answer against the actual proportion of times a member of an ethnic minority was offered such a unit.

**7.25** The data again would appear to show that the U.S. attorneys are more likely to request the death penalty when the victim was White than when the victim was Nonwhite. (This finding is statistically significant, though we won't address that question until Chapter 19.)

## Chapter 8

**8.1** Last night's hockey game:
(a) Null hypothesis: The game was actually an NHL hockey game.
(b) On the basis of that null hypothesis, I expected that each team would score somewhere between 0 and 6 points. I then looked at the actual points and concluded that they were way out of line with what I would expect if this were an NHL hockey game. I therefore rejected the null hypothesis.

**8.3** A Type I error would be concluding that I was shortchanged when, in fact, I was not.

**8.5** The rejection region is the set of outcomes for which we would reject the null hypothesis. The critical value would be the minimum amount of change below which I would reject the null. It is the border of the rejection region.

**8.7** For the Mode test I would draw a very large number of samples and calculate the mode, range, and their ratio (M). I would then plot the resulting values of M.

**8.9** We are constantly testing hypotheses every time we drive. We watch a driver approach a stop sign and test the hypothesis that he will stop. (We don't start up until we are satisfied that we are not going to reject that null hypothesis.)

**8.11** A sampling distribution is just a special case of a general distribution in which the thing that we are plotting is a statistic that is the result of repeated sampling.

**8.13** Hypotheses:
Research hypothesis: Children who attend kindergarten adjust to first grade faster than those who do not. Null hypothesis: First grade adjustment rates are the same for children who did, and did not, attend kindergarten.
Research hypothesis: Sex education in junior high school decreases the rate of pregnancies among unmarried girls in high school. Null hypothesis: The rate of pregnancies among unmarried girls in high school is the same regardless of the presence or absence of sex education in junior high school.

**8.15** $z = -1.33$. From Table D.10 in Appendix D we find that .9082 of the scores fall above this cutoff. Therefore $\beta = .908$.

**8.17** To determine whether there is a true relationship between grades and course evaluations, I would find a statistic that reflected the degree of relationship between two variables. (You will see such a statistic, $r$, in the next chapter). I would then calculate the sampling distribution of that statistic in a situation in which there is no relationship between two variables.

Finally, I would calculate the statistic for a representative set of students and classes and compare my sample value with the sampling distribution of that statistic.

**8.19** Allowances for fourth-grade students:
(a) The null hypothesis in this case would be the hypothesis that boys and girls receive the same allowance on average.
(b) I would use a two-tailed test because I want to reject the null hypothesis whenever there is a difference in favor of one gender over the other.
(c) I would reject the null hypothesis whenever the obtained difference between the average allowances was greater than I would be led to expect if they were paid the same in the population.
(d) I would increase the sample size and get something other than a self-report of allowances.

**8.21** Hypothesis testing and the judicial system:

The judicial system operates in ways similar to our standard logic of hypothesis testing. However, in a court we are particularly concerned with the danger of convicting an innocent person. In a trial the null hypothesis is equivalent to the assumption that the accused person is innocent. We set a very small probability of a Type I error, which is far smaller than we normally do in an experiment. Presumably the jury tries to set that probability as close to 0 as they reasonably can. By setting the probability of a Type I error so low, they knowingly allow the probability of a Type II error (releasing a guilty person) to rise, because that is thought to be the lesser evil.

## Chapter 9

**9.1** (c) The two outliers would appear to have a distorting effect on the correlation coefficient. However, if you replot the data without those points the relationship is still apparent and the correlation only drops to $-.54$.

**9.3** With 24 degrees of freedom, a two-tailed test at $\alpha = .05$ would require $r > \pm.388$.

**9.5** We can conclude that infant mortality is closely tied to both income and the availability of contraception. Infants born to people living in poverty are much more likely to die before their first birthday, and

the availability of contraception significantly reduces the number of infants put at risk in the first place.

**9.7** Because both income and contraception are related to mortality, we might expect that using them together would lead to a substantial increase in predictability. But note that they are correlated with each other, and therefore share some of the same variance.

**9.9** Psychologists have a professional interest in infant mortality because some of the variables that contribute to infant mortality are behavioral ones, and we care about understanding, and often controlling, behavior. Psychologists have an important role to play in world health that has little to do with pills and irrigation systems.

**9.11** A Pearson correlation is designed for linear relationships and this relationship is so far from linear that it would be an inappropriate statistic.

**9.13** The relationship between test scores in the Katz et al. study and SAT scores for application purposes is a relevant question because we would not be satisfied with a set of data that used SAT questions and yet gave answers that were not in line with SAT performance. We want to know that the tests are measuring at least roughly the same thing. In addition, by knowing the correlation between SATs and performance without seeing the questions we get a better understanding of some of what the SAT is measuring.

**9.15** $r = .532$. With 26 $df$ we would need a correlation of .374 for it to be significant. Because our value exceeds that, we can conclude that the relationship between test scores and the SAT is reliably different from 0.

**9.17** When we say that two correlations are not significantly different we mean that they are sufficiently close that they could both have come from samples from populations with exactly the same population correlation coefficient.

**9.19** The answer to this question depends on the student's expectations.

**9.21** It is sometimes appropriate to find the correlation between two variables even if you know that the relationship is slightly curvilinear. A straight line often does a remarkably good job of fitting a curved function provided that it is not too curved.

**9.23** The amount of money that a country spends on health care may have little to do with life expectancy because to change a country's life expectancy you would have to change the health of a great many people. Spending a great deal of money on one person, even if it were to extend her life by dozens of years, would not change the average life expectancy in any noticeable way. Often the things that make a major change in life expectancy, such as inoculations, really cost very little money.

**9.25** Extremely exaggerated data on male and female weight and height to show a negative slope within gender but a positive slope across gender:

| Height | 68 | 72 | 66 | 69 | 70 |
|--------|------|------|------|------|------|
| Weight | 185 | 175 | 190 | 180 | 180 |
| Gender | Male | Male | Male | Male | Male |

| Height | 66 | 60 | 64 | 65 | 63 |
|--------|--------|--------|--------|--------|--------|
| Weight | 135 | 155 | 145 | 140 | 150 |
| Gender | Female | Female | Female | Female | Female |

**9.27** I would expect a high correlation between performance in Intermediate French and in English Literature, but there is no reason to assume a causal relationship between them. The causal factor, common to both, would be something like general scholastic ability.

**9.29** This is an Internet question with no fixed answer.

# Chapter 10

**10.1** $\hat{Y} = .0689X + 3.53$

**10.3** The predicted percentage of LBW infants would be 8.36.

**10.5** I would be more comfortable speaking about the effects on Senegal because it is already at approximately the mean income level and we are not extrapolating for extreme values of X.

**10.7** $\hat{Y} = 109.13$

**10.9** Subtracting 10 points from every X or Y score would not change the correlation in the slightest. The relationship between X and Y would remain the same—only the intercept would change.

**10.13** Adding a constant to each Y value:
(a) Adding 2.5 to Y simply raised the regression line by 2.5 units.
(b) The correlation would be unaffected.

**10.15** $\hat{Y} = -.0426X + 4.699$

**10.17** For the faculty the starting salary would appear to be (on average) $31,000. This is the intercept, and therefore the value of salary when years of service

is 0. Salary seems to increase by $900 for every year of service. For a new faculty member this is a 3% raise, but it is considerably smaller than that for more senior faculty. Administrators average a much lower starting salary ($18,000), but it increases by $1500 for every year of service. The salaries will be equal at 21.67 years.

**10.19** Weight as a function of height for males:
(b) $\hat{Y} = 4.356 Height - 149.93$ The intercept is $-149.93$, which has no interpretable meaning with these data. The slope of 4.356 tells us that a 1-unit increase in height is associated with a 4.356 increase in weight.
(c) The correlation is .60, telling us that for females 36% of the variability in weight is associated with variability in height.
(d) Both the correlation and the slope are significantly different from zero as shown by an $F = 31.54$ and an (equivalent) $t$ of 5.616.

**10.21** $\hat{Y} = 4.356 \times 68 - 149.93 = 146.28$
(b) The residual is $Y - \hat{Y} = 156 - 146.28 = 9.72$.
(c) If students who supplied the data gave biased responses, then, to the degree that the data are biased, the coefficients are biased and the prediction will not apply accurately to me.

**10.23** The male and female students would be expected to differ by 12.28 pounds

**10.25** $\hat{Y} = -.014 \times Trial + 67.805$

The slope is only $-.014$ and it is not remotely significant. For this set of data we can conclude that there is not a linear trend for reaction times to change over time. From the scatterplot we can see no hint of a nonlinear pattern either.

**10.27** The evils of television:
(b) Boys: $\hat{Y} = -4.821X + 283.61$
Girls: $\hat{Y} = -3.460X + 268.39$

The slopes are roughly equal given the few data points we have, with a slightly greater decrease with increased time for boys. The difference in intercepts reflects the fact that the line for girls is about 9 points below that for boys.
(c) Television can not be used as an explanation for poorer scores in girls, because we see that girls score below boys even when we control for television viewing.

**10.29** Dropping pencils:

(a) As you move the pencil vertically you are changing the intercept.

(b) As you rotate the pencil you are changing the slope.

(c) You can come up with a very good line simply by rotating and raising or lowering your pencil so as to make the deviations from the line as small as possible. (We really want to minimize squared deviations, but I don't expect that anyone's eyes are good enough to notice the difference.)

## Chapter 11

**11.1** Predicting quality of life:

(a) All other variables held constant, a difference of $+1$ degree in Temperature is associated with a difference of $-.01$ in perceived Quality of Life. A difference of \$1000 in median income, again with all other variables held constant, is associated with a $+.05$ difference in perceived Quality of Life. A similar interpretation applies to $b_3$ and $b_4$. Because values of 0 cannot reasonably occur for all predictors, the intercept has no meaningful interpretation.

(b) $\hat{Y} = 5.37 - .01(55) + .05(12) + .003(500) - .01(200) = 4.92$

(c) $\hat{Y} = 5.37 - .01(55) + .05(12) + .003(100) - .01(200) = 3.72$

**11.3** Religious Influence and Religious Hope contribute significantly to the prediction, but not Religious Involvement.

**11.5** I would have speculated that Religious Involvement was not a significant predictor because of its overlap with the other predictors, but the tolerances kick a hole in that theory to some extent.

**11.7** The answer to Exercise 11.6 and the comparable result in Chapter 10 will agree only when the slopes for males and females, taken separately, are exactly the same. Basically multiple regression is substituting a common slope for the two separate slopes.

**11.9** The multiple correlation between the predictors and the percentage of births under 2500 grams is .855. The incidence of low birthweight increases when there are more mothers under 17, when mothers have fewer than 12 years of education, and when mothers are unmarried. All of the predictors are associated with

young mothers. (As the question noted, there are too few observations for there to be a meaningful analysis of the variables in question.)

**11.11** The multiple correlation between Depression and the three predictor variables was significant, with $R = .49$ [$F(3, 131) = 14.11$, $p = .0000$]. Thus approximately 25% of the variability in Depression can be accounted for by variability in these predictors. The results show us that depression among students who have lost a parent through death is positively associated with an elevated level of perceived vulnerability to future loss and negatively associated with the level of social support. The age at which the student lost his or her parent does not appear to play a role.

**11.13** The fact that the frequency of the behavior was not a factor in reporting is an interesting finding. My first thought would be that it is highly correlated with Offensiveness, and that Offensiveness is carrying the burden. But a look at the simple correlation shows that the two variables are correlated at less than $r = .20$.

**11.15** The multiple correlation for *my* data was .739, which is astonishingly high. Fortunately the $F$ test on the regression is not significant. Notice that we have only twice as many subjects as predictors.

**11.17** This is an Internet question with no fixed answer.

**11.19** In the two previous exercises we had to keep in mind that the tables apply to a cross section of the population with a "medium frame." The example in the book came from college students, and the relationship between height and weight for them may be different from that relationship in the general population.

**11.21** Gender is important to include in this relationship because women tend to be smaller than men, and thus probably have smaller (though not less effective) brains. We probably don't want that contamination in our data. However, note that Gender was not significant in the previous answer, though the sample size (and hence power) is low.

**11.23** A nuisance variable is usually a variable that confuses the relationship between other variables. It is not necessarily an unimportant variable, and the choice of name is not a good one.

**11.25** The correlation between our best estimates of Distress2 and the actual values of Distress2 is .434, which is the multiple correlation.

## Chapter 12

**12.3** Mean = 4.1, standard deviation = 2.82. These are reasonably close to the parameters of the population for which the sample was drawn. The mean of the distribution of means is 4.28, which is somewhat closer to the population mean, and the standard deviation is 1.22

> (a) The Central Limit Theorem predicts a sampling distribution of the mean with a mean of 4.5 and a standard deviation of $2.6/\sqrt{5} = 1.16$.
>
> (b) These values are close to the values that we would expect.

**12.5** If you had drawn 50 samples of size 15 the mean of the sampling distribution would still approximate the mean of the population, but the standard error of that distribution would now be only $2.6/\sqrt{15} = .689$.

**12.7** First, these students scored better than we might have predicted, not worse. Second, these students are certainly not a random sample of high school students. Finally, there is no definition of what is meant by "a terrible state," nor any idea of whether the SAT measures such a concept.

**12.9** Unlike the results in the two previous questions, this interval probably is a fair estimate of the confidence interval for P/T ratio across the country. It is not itself biased by the bias in the sampling of SAT scores.

**12.11** $t = 2.22, p < .05$. Reject the null hypothesis and conclude that the girls gained weight at better than chance levels in this experiment.

**12.13** The best measure of effect size is simply to report the result in pounds gained, which is 3.01. However for those who want a more involved measure we can calculate

$$\hat{d} = \frac{\overline{X}}{s} = \frac{3.01}{7.3} = .41.$$

The problem with this measure is that it uses the standard deviation of gain scores, which is not a very satisfying metric.

**12.15** You needed to solve for $t$ instead of $z$ because I did not know the population variance.

**12.17** $t = -3.50$. With 35 $df$ the critical value of $t$ at $\alpha = .05$ is $\pm 2.03$. We can reject $H_0$ and conclude that

children under stress show significantly lower levels of anxiety than children in the general population.

**12.19** The results in Exercise 12.18 are consistent with the $t$ test in Exercise 12.17. The $t$ test showed that these children showed lower levels of anxiety than normal population, and the confidence interval did not include the general population mean of 14.55.

## Chapter 13

**13.1** $t = -.48$. Do not reject the null hypothesis. This is a matched-sample $t$ because responses came from married couples. We would hope that there is some relationship between the sexual satisfaction of one member of the couple and the other, but perhaps that is asking too much.

**13.3** This analysis finally addresses the degree of compatibility between couples. The correlation is significant, but it is not very large.

**13.5** The most important thing about a $t$ test is the assumption that the mean (or difference between means) is normally distributed. Even though the individual values can range only over the integers $1 - 4$, the mean of 91 subjects can take on a large number of values between 1 and 4. It is a continuous variable for all practical purposes and can exhibit substantial variability.

**13.7** We used a paired $t$ test because the data were paired in the sense of coming from the same subject. Some subjects showed generally more beta-endorphins at any time than others, and we wanted to eliminate this subject-to-subject variability.

**13.9** If we look at the actual numbers given in Exercise 13.6 we would generally be led to expect that whatever was used to measure beta-endorphins was accurate only to the nearest half unit. But then where did 5.8 and 4.7 come from? If we can tell the difference to a tenth of a unit, why are most, but not all, of the scores reported to the nearest 0.5? It's a puzzlement.

**13.11** You would not want to use a repeated measures design in any situation where the first measure will "tip off" or sensitize participants to what comes next.

**13.13** How many participants do we need?
First of all, in Exercise 13.6 we had 19 participants, giving us 18 $df$. This means that for a one-tailed test at $\alpha = .01$ we will need a $t$ of at least 2.552 to be

significant. So we can substitute everything we know about the data except for the $N$ and then solve for $N$. $N = 4.481^2 = 21$ participants.

**13.15** As the correlation between the two variables increases, the standard error of the difference will decrease and the resulting $t$ will increase.

**13.17** Analysis of Holway and Boring (1940) data: $t = 4.29$. We can reject the null hypothesis and conclude that there was an illusion even in the eyes-level condition. This refutes the Holway and Boring conclusion.

**13.19** If I subtracted the Before scores from the After scores I would simply change the sign of the mean difference and the sign of $t$. There would be no other effect.

**13.21** There is no answer I can give for this question because it asks the students to design a study.

## Chapter 14

**14.1** $t = -.40$. We can conclude that we have no reason to doubt the hypothesis that males and females are equal with respect to sexual satisfaction.

**14.3** The difference between the $t$ in Exercises 13.1 and 14.1 is small because the relationship between the two variables was so small.

**14.5** Random assignment plays the role of ensuring (as much as possible) that there is no systematic difference between the subjects assigned to the two groups. Without random assignment it might be possible that those who signed up for the family therapy condition were more motivated or had more serious problems than those in the control group.

**14.7** You can not use random assignment to homophobic categories for a study such as this because the group assignment is the property of the participants themselves.

**14.9** In Exercise 14.8 it could well have been that there was much less variability in the schizophrenic group than in the normal group because the number of TATs showing that positive parent-child relationships could have had a floor effect at .0. This did not happen but it is important to check for it anyway.

**14.11** Experimenter bias effect:

$$t = .587 \ [t_{.05}(15) = \pm 2.131]$$

Do not reject the null hypothesis. We cannot conclude that our data show the experimenter bias effect.

**14.13** Ninety-five percent Confidence limits for Exercise 14.8:

Mean difference $= 1.45$

Standard error $= .545$

$t_{.05}(38) = 2.02$

$$CI(.95) = (\overline{X}_1 - \overline{X}_2) \pm t_{.05}(38)s_{\overline{X}_1 - \overline{X}_2}$$
$$= 1.45 \pm 2.02(.545) = 1.45 \pm 1.10$$
$$.35 \le \mu \le 2.55$$

**14.15** Comparing GPA for those with low and high ADDSC scores:
  $t = 3.77$. Reject $H_0$ and conclude that people with high ADDSC scores in elementary school have a lower grade point average in ninth grade than do people with lower scores.

**14.17** The answer to 14.15 tells you that ADDSC scores have significant predictability of grade point average several years later. Moreover the answer to Exercise 14.16 tells you that this difference is substantial.

**14.19** The experimenter has to assume that the two groups of mice were comparable at the start of the experiment.

**14.21** If the variances are equal they will also be equal to the pooled variance.

## Chapter 15

**15.1** The statement on skiing is intended to point out that just because two things are different doesn't mean that the larger (better, greater, etc.) one will *always* come out ahead.

**15.3** Power for socially desirable responses:
  Assume the population mean $= 4.39$ and the population standard deviation $= 2.61$.
  (a) Effect size $= .20$
  (b) Delta $= 1.20$
  (c) Power $= .22$

**15.5** Sample sizes (before rounding): 156.25, 196.00, and 264.06

**15.9** Avoidance behavior in rabbits using a one-sample $t$ test:
  (a) For power $= .50$, $N = 15.21 = 16$
  (b) For power $= .80$, $N = 31.36 = 32$

**15.11** With $\delta = 1.46$, power $= .31$.

**15.13** Modifying Exercise 15.12:
(a) Power $= .22$
(b) $t = -1.19$. Do not reject the null hypothesis.
(c) The $t$ numerically equals $\delta$, although $t$ is calculated from statistics and $\delta$ is calculated from parameters. In other words $\delta$ is equal to the $t$ we would get if the sample means and standard deviations were equal to the corresponding parameters.

**15.15** The result with the smaller sample size impresses me more because it generally takes a larger effect to find significance with a smaller sample size.

**15.17** Assuming equal standard deviations, the high school dropout group of 25 would result in a higher estimate of $\delta$ and therefore a higher level of power.

**15.19** Total Sample Sizes Required for Power $= .60$, $\alpha = .05$, Two-Tailed ($\delta = 2.20$)

| Effect Size | $\gamma$ | One-Sample $t$ | Two-Sample $t$ (per group) | Two-Sample $t$ (overall) |
|---|---|---|---|---|
| Small | .20 | 121 | 242 | 484 |
| Medium | .50 | 20 | 39 | 78 |
| Large | .80 | 8 | 16 | 32 |

**15.21** The mean under $H_1$ should fall at the critical value under $H_0$. The question implies a one-tailed test. Thus the mean is 1.645 standard errors about $\mu_0$, which is 100. Power $= \beta$ when $\mu = 104.935$.

**15.23** Power $= .75$.

**15.25** Aronson's study:
$\delta = 2.37$. Power $= .658$

# Chapter 16

**16.1** Analysis of Eysenck's data:
(a) The analysis of variance:

| Source | df | SS | MS | F |
|---|---|---|---|---|
| Treatment | 1 | 266.45 | 266.45 | 25.23* |
| Error | 18 | 190.10 | 10.56 | |
| Total | 19 | 456.55 | | |

$* p < .05$

(b) $t = 5.02$. Reject the null hypothesis.

**16.3** Expanding on Exercise 16.2:
(a) Combine the Low groups together and the High groups together:

| Source | df | SS | MS | F |
|---|---|---|---|---|
| Treatment | 1 | 792.10 | 792.10 | 59.45* |
| Error | 38 | 506.30 | 13.324 | |
| Total | 39 | 1298.40 | | |

$* p < .05$

We have compared recall under conditions of Low versus High processing and can conclude that higher levels of processing lead to significantly better recall.
(b) The answer is still a bit difficult to interpret because both groups contain both younger and older participants, and it is possible that the effect holds for one age group but not for the other.

**16.5** $\eta^2$ and $\omega^2$ for the data in Exercise 16.1:
$\eta^2 = .58$ and $\omega^2 = .55$.

**16.7** Foa et al. study:

| Source | df | SS | MS | F |
|---|---|---|---|---|
| Treatment | 3 | 507.84 | 169.28 | 3.04* |
| Error | 41 | 2279.07 | 55.59 | |
| Total | 44 | 2786.91 | | |

$* p < .05$

(c) It would appear that the more interventionist treatments lead to fewer symptoms than the less interventionist ones, although we would have to run multiple comparison tests to tell exactly which groups are different from which other groups.

**16.9** If the sample sizes in Exercise 16.7 were twice as large, that would double the $SS_{treat}$ and $MS_{treat}$. However it would have no effect on $MS_{error}$, which is simply the average of the group variances. The result would be that the $F$ value would be doubled.

**16.11** Effect size for tests in Exercise 16.10:
It only makes sense to calculate an effect size for significant comparisons in this study, so we will deal with SIT vs SC.

$$\hat{d} = \frac{\overline{X}_{SC} - \overline{X}_{SIT}}{\sqrt{MS_{error}}} = \frac{18.09 - 11.07}{\sqrt{55.579}} = \frac{7.02}{7.455} = .94$$

The SIT group is nearly a full standard deviation lower in symptoms when compared to the SC group, which is a control group.

**16.13** ANOVA for ADDSC data

| Source | df | SS | MS | F |
|---|---|---|---|---|
| Treatment | 2 | 22.50 | 11.25 | 22.74* |
| Error | 85 | 42.06 | .49 | |
| Total | 87 | 64.56 | | |

* $p < .05$

**16.15** Darley and Latané study:

| Source | df | SS | MS | F |
|---|---|---|---|---|
| Treatment | 2 | .854 | .427 | 8.06* |
| Error | 49 | 2.597 | .053 | |
| Total | 51 | 3.451 | | |

* $p < .05$

We can reject the null hypothesis and conclude that subjects are less likely to summon help quickly if there are other bystanders around.

**16.17** Bonferroni test on data in Exercise 16.2:

For Young/Low versus Old/Low $t = -.434$

For Young/High versus Old/High $t = 6.34$

There is clearly not a significant difference between young and old subjects on tasks requiring little cognitive processing, but there is a significant difference for tasks requiring substantial cognitive processing. The probability that *at least* one of these statements represents a Type I error is at most .05.

**16.19** Comparison of WL and SIT:

$\hat{d} = 1.18$. The two groups differ by over a standard deviation.

**16.21** Spilich et al. study:

| Source | df | SS | MS | F |
|---|---|---|---|---|
| Treatment | 2 | 2643.38 | 1321.69 | 4.74* |
| Error | 42 | 11700.40 | 278.58 | |
| Total | 44 | 14343.78 | | |

* $p < .05$

Here we have a task that involves more cognitive involvement, and it does show a difference due to smoking condition.

**16.23** Spilich et al. data on driving simulation:

| Source | df | SS | MS | F |
|---|---|---|---|---|
| Treatment | 2 | 437.64 | 218.82 | 9.26* |
| Error | 42 | 992.67 | 23.64 | |
| Total | 44 | 1430.31 | | |

* $p < .05$

Here we have a case in which the active smokers again performed worse than the nonsmokers, and the differences are significant.

**16.25** Analysis of Merrell's study:

$F = 1692.44$. We can clearly reject the null hypothesis.

**16.27** Effect sizes for Merrell's study:

When we compare the Control group and the Mozart group, $\hat{d} = 2.00$.

When we compare the Control group and the Anthrax group, $\hat{d} = -13.44$

Whereas the Control and Mozart groups differ by about two standard deviations (which is a lot), the Anthrax group is about 13.44 standard deviations below the Control in performance.

**16.29** Measures of effect for data in Exercise 16.28:
(a) $\eta^2 = .33$
$\omega^2 = .22$
(b) The two results differ because the first is somewhat biased, and becomes more biased as the number of treatment groups increases.
(c) It makes most sense to calculate $\hat{d}$ for the difference between the most extreme treatments, which, in this case, involves comparing groups 1 and 5. The square root of $MS_{error}$ will serve as our estimate of the standard deviation.

$$\hat{d} = \frac{\overline{X}_5 - \overline{X}_1}{\sqrt{MS_{error}}} = \frac{3.26 - 2.60}{\sqrt{.173}} = \frac{.66}{.4159} = 1.59$$

The two extreme groups differ by more than one and a half standard deviations.

# Chapter 17

**17.1** Thomas and Wang study:
(a) This design can be characterized as a $3 \times 2$ factorial, with three levels of Strategy and two levels of Delay.

(b) I expect that recall will be better when participants generate their own key words, and worse when participants are in the rote learning condition. I also expect better recall for a shorter retention interval.

(c)

| Strategy | Delay | Mean | Std. Dev. | Cases |
|----------|-------|------|-----------|-------|
| Gen. | 5 min | 14.92 | 5.33 | 13 |
| Gen. | 2 day | 4.00 | 2.52 | 13 |
| Prov. | 5 min | 20.54 | 1.98 | 13 |
| Prov. | 2 day | 2.00 | 1.47 | 13 |
| Rote | 5 min | 15.38 | 5.45 | 13 |
| Rote | 2 day | 12.77 | 6.80 | 13 |

**17.3** Analysis of variance:

| Source | df | SS | MS | F |
|--------|-----|---------|---------|---------|
| Strategy | 2 | 281.26 | 140.63 | 7.22* |
| Delay | 1 | 2229.35 | 2229.35 | 114.53* |
| S × D | 2 | 824.54 | 412.27 | 21.18* |
| Error | 72 | 1401.54 | 19.47 | |
| Total | 77 | 4736.68 | | |

*$p < .05$

There are significant differences due to both Strategy and Delay, but more importantly, there is a significant interaction.

**17.5** Bonferroni test of data in Exercise 17.4:

For data at 5-minute delay:

| Generated versus Provided $t = -3.15$ | Generated versus Rote $t = -.26$ | Provided versus Rote $t = 2.89$ |
|---|---|---|

For data at 2-day delay:

| Generated versus Provided $t = 1.19$ | Generated versus Rote $t = -5.24$ | Provided versus Rote $t = -6.43$ |
|---|---|---|

For six comparisons with 36 *df* the critical value of *t* is 2.80.

For the 5-minute delay the condition with the key words provided by the experimenter is significantly better than both the condition in which the participants generated their own key words and the rote learning condition. The latter two are not different from each other.

For the 2-day delay the rote learning condition is better than either of the other two conditions, which do not differ from each other.

We clearly see distinct patterns of differences in the two delay conditions. The most surprising result is the superiority of rote learning with a 2-day delay.

**17.7** The results in the last few exercises suggest to me that if I were studying for a Spanish exam I would fall back on rote learning, painful as it sounds and as much against common wisdom as it is.

**17.9** In this experiment we have as many primiparous mothers as multiparous ones, which certainly does not reflect the population. Similarly, we have as many LBW infants as full-term ones, which is not a reflection of reality. The mean for primiparous mothers is based on an equal number of LBW and full-term infants, which we know is not representative of the population. Comparisons between groups are still legitimate, but it makes no sense to take the mean of all primiparous moms combined as a reflection of any meaningful population value.

**17.11** Simple effects versus *t* tests for Exercise 17.10.
(a) If I had run a *t* test between those means my result would simply be the square root of the $F = 1.328$ that I obtained.
(b) If I used $MS_{error}$ for my estimated error term it would give me a *t* that is the square root of the *F* that I would have had if I had used the overall $MS_{error}$, instead of the $MS_{error}$ obtained in computing the simple effect.

**17.13** Analysis of variance for Exercise 17.12:

| Source | df | SS | MS | F |
|--------|-----|-----------|-----------|---------|
| Task | 2 | 28,661.53 | 14,330.76 | 132.90* |
| Smokegrp | 2 | 354.55 | 177.27 | 1.64 |
| T × S | 4 | 2728.65 | 682.16 | 6.33* |
| Error | 126 | 13,587.20 | 107.84 | |
| Total | 134 | 45,331.93 | | |

*$p < .05$

The main effect of Task and the interaction are significant. The main effect of Task is of no interest because there is no reason why different tasks should be equally difficult, We don't care about the main effect of Smoking either because it is created by large effects for two levels of Task and no effect for the third. What is important is the interaction.

**17.15** Simple effects to clarify the Spilich et al. example:

We have already seen these simple effects in Chapter 16, in Exercises 16.18, 16.19, and 16.21.

**17.17** Further analysis of Exercise 16.2:

| Source | df | SS | MS | F |
|--------|----|----|----|----|
| Age | 1 | 115.60 | 115.60 | 17.44* |
| HiLo | 1 | 792.10 | 792.10 | 119.51* |
| A × H | 1 | 152.10 | 152.10 | 22.95* |
| Error | 36 | 238.60 | 6.63 | |
| Total | 39 | 1298.40 | | |

\* $p < .05$

We have a significant effect due to age, with younger subjects outperforming older subjects, and a significant effect due to the level of processing, with better recall of material processed at a higher level. Most importantly, we have a significant interaction, reflecting the fact that there is no important difference between younger and older subjects for the task with low levels of processing, but there is a big difference when the task calls for a high level of processing—younger subjects seem to benefit more from that processsing (or do more of it).

**17.19** $\eta^2$ and $\omega^2$ for the data in Section 17.7:

$$\eta^2_{Educ} = \frac{SS_{Educ}}{SS_{total}} = .10$$

$$\omega^2_{Educ} = \frac{SS_{Educ} - (e - 1)MS_{error}}{SS_{total} + MS_{error}} = .086$$

$$\eta^2_{Group} = \frac{SS_{Group}}{SS_{total}} = .19$$

$$\omega^2_{Group} = \frac{SS_{Group} - (g - 1)MS_{error}}{SS_{total} + MS_{error}} = .15$$

$$\eta^2_{EG} = \frac{SS_{EG}}{SS_{total}} = .03$$

$$\omega^2_{EG} = \frac{SS_{EG} - (e - 1)(e - 1)MS_{error}}{SS_{total} + MS_{error}} = .00$$

**17.21** Two main effects but no interaction:

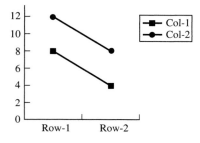

**17.23** An example would be any experiment in which one independent variable has no effect at one level of the other independent variable, but a substantial effect at another level of the second independent variable. There are many other examples that you could come up with.

**17.25** Calculation of effect size for main effects in Exercise 17.1:

$$\hat{d}_{Time} = \frac{\overline{X}_{5min} - \overline{X}_{2day}}{\sqrt{MS_{error}}} = 2.42$$

This represents a huge effect size for the Time variable.

It would be logical to compare the condition in which participants select their own keyword to the rote learning condition.

$$\hat{d}_{Condition} = \frac{\overline{X}_{generate} - \overline{X}_{rote}}{\sqrt{MS_{error}}} = 1.05$$

The two groups differ by about one standard deviation, which is still a large effect.

**17.27** There is nothing of interest in looking at the Task variable, so we will ignore it. However, so that you have an answer, the two tasks differ by 2.8 standard deviations in the number of errors.

It does make sense to compare the nonsmoking and actively smoking participants, because those are meaningful groups.

$$\hat{d}_{Smoke} = \frac{\overline{X}_{NonSmoke} - \overline{X}_{Active}}{\sqrt{MS_{error}}} - .37$$

The two conditions differ by about a third of a standard deviation.

**17.29** The important test for the Eysenck data is the interaction, because Eysenck thought that the two age groups would only differ in important ways when the tasks involved a greater amount of cognitive processing.

**17.31** Liddle's study on coming out:

| Source | df | SS | MS | F |
|--------|----|----|----|----|
| Gender | 1 | 223.49 | 223.49 | 10.78* |
| Condition | 1 | 1.35 | 1.35 | <1 |
| G × C | 1 | .69 | .69 | <1 |
| Error | 56 | 1161.44 | 20.74 | |
| Total | 59 | 1386.97 | | |

\* $p < .05$

## Chapter 18

**18.1** Study of migraines: (Results taken from SPSS)

| Descriptives Statistics | | | | | |
|---|---|---|---|---|---|
| | N | Minimum | Maximum | Mean | Std. Deviation |
| WEEK1 | 9 | 7.0 | 30.0 | 20.778 | 7.1725 |
| WEEK2 | 9 | 4.0 | 33.0 | 20.000 | 10.2225 |
| WEEK3 | 9 | 5.0 | 14.0 | 9.000 | 3.1225 |
| WEEK4 | 9 | 1.0 | 12.0 | 5.778 | 3.4197 |
| WEEK5 | 9 | 4.0 | 17.0 | 6.778 | 4.1164 |
| Valid N (listwise) | 9 | | | | |

**18.3** I would have liked to collect data from students on the use of pain killers and other ways of dealing with migraines. I might also like to have data on stress levels over time so that I could possibly rule out the effects of stress.

**18.5** Analysis of data in Exercise 18.4:

| Source | df | SS | MS | F |
|---|---|---|---|---|
| Subjects | 8 | 612.00 | | |
| Weeks | 1 | 554.50 | 554.50 | 14.42* |
| Error | 8 | 302.00 | 37.75 | |
| Total | 17 | 1159.70 | | |

\* $p < .05$

There is a significant increase in decrease in severity of headaches over time. $F = t^2 = 3.798^2 = 14.424$.

**18.7** Effect size for Exercise 18.4:

We will use the square root of $MS_{error}$ as our estimate of the standard deviation, because this is a standard deviation corrected for any differences due to subject effects.

$$\hat{d} = \frac{\overline{X}_0 - \overline{X}_3}{\sqrt{MS_{error}}} = 3.44$$

The decrease in severity from baseline to training is a reduction of approximately three and one half standard deviations.

**18.9** I would standardize the difference in means using the square root of the average of the variances of the two baseline measures. This gives us a denominator of 8.83.

$$\hat{d} = \frac{\overline{X}_{baseline} - \overline{X}_{training}}{s} = 1.49$$

On average, the severity of headaches decreased by nearly 1.50 standard deviations from baseline to training.

**18.11** Exercise 18.10 tested the null hypothesis that condom use did not change over time. We would have hoped to see that the intervention worked and that condom use increased, but that was not what we found. The increase was not significant.

**18.13** It would appear that without the intervention, condom use would actually have declined. This suggests that the intervention may have prevented that decline, in which case that nonsignificant result is actually a positive finding.

**18.15** Bonferroni tests on data in Table 18.1:

We can use a standard $t$ test because the error term has been corrected by the repeated-measures analysis of variance, which has already removed variability between subjects.

The Bonferroni alpha level would be $.05/3 = .01667$

We will reject all of the null hypotheses because each $p$ value is less than .0167.

### Paired Samples Test

| | | Paired Differences | | | | | | | |
|---|---|---|---|---|---|---|---|---|---|
| | | | | | 95% Confidence Interval of the Difference | | | | Sig. (2-tailed) |
| | | Mean | Std. Deviation | Std. Error Mean | Lower | Upper | t | df | |
| Pair 1 | WEEK0–WEEK6 | −2.680 | 2.6727 | .5345 | −3.783 | −1.577 | −5.014 | 24 | .000 |
| Pair 2 | WEEK0–WEEK12 | −3.040 | 2.9928 | .5986 | −4.275 | −1.805 | −5.079 | 24 | .000 |
| Pair 3 | WEEK3–WEEK12 | −1.600 | 2.8868 | .5774 | −2.792 | −.408 | −2.771 | 24 | .011 |

# Chapter 19

**19.1** $\chi^2 = 11.33$. We will reject the null hypothesis and conclude that students do not enroll at random.

**19.3** $\chi^2 = 2.4$. Do not reject the null hypothesis that my daughter's sorting behavior is in line with my theory.

**19.5** $\chi^2 = 29.35$. We can reject $H_0$ and conclude that the children did not choose dolls at random, but chose white dolls more often than black.

**19.7** $\chi^2 = 34.184$. Reject the null hypothesis and conclude that the distribution of choices between black and white dolls was different in the two studies. Choice is *not* independent of the study and could easily be related to the time at which the studies were run. We are no longer asking whether one color doll is preferred over the other color, but whether the *pattern* of preference is constant across studies. In analysis of variance terms we are dealing with an interaction.

**19.9** There are several ways that this study could be modified. We could simply rerun the present analysis by defining smokers and nonsmokers on the basis of the partner's smoking behavior. Alternatively, we could redefine the Smoker variable as "neither," "mother," "father," or "both."

**19.11** $\chi^2 = 5.38$. We can reject the null hypothesis and conclude that achievement level during high school varies as a function of performance during elementary school.

**19.13** A one-way chi-square test on the data in the first column of Exercise 19.12 would be asking whether the students are evenly distributed among the eight categories. What we really tested in Exercise 19.12 is whether that distribution, *however it appears*, is the same for those who later took remedial English as it is for those who later took nonremedial English.

**19.15** $\chi^2 = 8.85$. The ability to reject a tumor is affected by the shock condition.

**19.17** This is another place where we see the important relationship between sample size and power.

**19.19** Dabbs and Morris study:
(a) These results show that there is a significant relationship between the two variables.
(b) Testosterone levels in adults are related to the behavior of those individuals where they were children.

(c) This result shows that we can tie the two variables (delinquency and testosterone) together historically. I would assume that people who have high testosterone levels now also had high levels when they were children, but that is just an assumption.

**19.21** We could ask a series of similar questions, evenly split between "right" and "wrong" answers. We could then sort the replies into positive and negative categories and ask whether faculty were more likely than students to give negative responses.

**19.23** Racial differences in desired weight gain:
For white females, the odds of wishing to lose weight were $352/183 = 1.9235$, meaning that white females are nearly twice as likely to wish to lose weight as to stay the same or gain weight. For African-American females, the corresponding ratio is $47/52 = .9038$. The odds ratio is $1.9235/.9038 = 2.1281$. This means that the odds of wishing to lose weight were more than twice as high among white females than they were among African-American females.

# Chapter 20

**20.1** McConaughy study:
(a) $W_S = 23$; $W_{.025} = 27$
(b) I would reject $H_0$ and conclude that older children include more inferences in their summaries.

**20.3** Repeating 20.2 with normal approximation: $z = -3.15$; reject $H_0$ and come to the same conclusion we came to earlier.

**20.5** Nurcombe et al. study:
(a) $T = 8.5$; $T_{.025} = 8$. Do not reject $H_0$.
(b) We cannot conclude that we have evidence supporting the hypothesis that there is a reliable increase in hypothesis generation and testing over time. (This is a case in which alternative methods of breaking ties could lead to different conclusions.)

**20.7** Firstborn children's independence:
(a) $T = 46$; $T_{.025}(20) = 52$
(b) We can reject the null hypothesis and conclude that firstborn children are more independent that second-born children.

**20.9** The scatterplot shows that the difference between the pairs is heavily dependent on the score of the firstborn.

**20.11** Wilcoxon's matched-pairs signed-ranks test tests the null hypothesis that paired scores were drawn from identical populations or from symmetric populations with the same mean (and median). The corresponding $t$ test tests the null hypothesis that the paired scores were drawn from populations with the same mean and assumes normality.

**20.13** Rejection of the null hypothesis by a $t$ test is a more specific statement than rejection using the appropriate distribution-free test because, by making assumptions about normality and homogeneity of variance, the $t$ test refers specifically to the population means—although it is also dependent on those assumptions.

**20.15** $H = 6.757$. We can reject the null hypothesis and conclude that placement of these adolescents has an effect on truancy rates.

**20.17** It eliminates the influence of individual differences (differences in overall level of truancy from one person to another).

**20.19** $\chi^2 = 1.60.$ $\quad X_F^2 = 1.60.$

These are exactly equivalent tests, and we cannot reject the null hypothesis.

**20.21** $X_F^2 = 9.00$. We can reject the null hypothesis and conclude that people don't really like tea made with used tea bags.

## Chapter 21

*Note:* Please review the disclaimer concerning these answers at the beginning of Chapter 21. There are many different ways to think about a study.

**21.1** This test involves comparing two proportions, and the easiest way to do that is to set up a $2 \times 2$ contingency table with Group on one dimension and Mastery on the other.

**21.3** Probably the most appropriate approach is simply to correlate the difference in times between the two swims with the swimmer's optimism score. Alternatively you could break the subjects into groups on the basis of their optimism scores (e.g., Optimists, Neutral, Pessimists) and run an analysis of variance on the difference scores.

**21.5** This is a $t$ test for two independent groups—children of divorced families and children of intact families.

**21.7** Here is the situation that I described in the answer to Exercise 21.3, and we would have an analysis of variance with three groups, using the difference score as the dependent variable.

**21.9** Here we have two independent groups with three different dependent variables. The author could run three separate $t$ tests for independent groups, but we might want to use a more stringent level of significance, (e.g., $\alpha = .01$) to avoid a high familywise error rate.

**21.11** This could be treated as a two-way analysis of variance if we break the data down by race and by Afrocentric facial features. A problem with this is that we would presumably have more Afrocentric features for black inmates, which would lead to unequal sample sizes (i.e. an unbalanced design).

**21.13** The authors simply want to compare the performance of three groups. They could use a one-way analysis of variance on the MFFT scores for the second administration. They should probably also run it on the scores for the first administration to check the experimental hypothesis that the groups started out together.

**21.15** The most important thing to do would be to plot the data over time looking for trends. A repeated measures analysis of variance would tell you if differences are significant, but it is the direction of differences, and whether they return to baseline, that is likely to be most informative. The authors further broke down the participants in terms of their preoccupation with 9/11 and looked at differences between those groups. Interestingly, even the least preoccupied group showed changes over time.

**21.17** This is a difficult one, partly because it depends on what Payne wants to know. I assume that she wants to know how rankings of characteristics agree across gender or across years. She could first find the mean rank assigned to each characteristic separately for each gender and year. Because the raw data were originally ranks, I would probably be inclined to then rank these mean values. She could then calculate Spearman's $r_S$ between males and females for each year or between years within each gender. The correlations would be obtained for the 10 pairs of scores (one per characteristic).

**21.19** This is a $2 \times 4$ analysis of variance with two levels of gender and four levels of occupation. The major emphasis is on the occupations, so multiple comparisons of those means would be appropriate.

**21.21** There are two independent groups in this experiment. The authors should use a Mann–Whitney test to compare average locus of control scores.

**21.23** This is a situation for a chi-square goodness-of-fit test. The conditions are Rotated versus Stationary, and the count is the number of subjects nominating that condition as giving stronger contours. The expected values would be $37/2 = 18.5$.

**21.25** This is another complex repeated-measures analysis of variance. The comparison of recall of the two lists (one learned before administration of the drug and the other learned after) is a repeated measurement because the same subjects are involved. The comparison of the Drug versus Saline groups is a between-subjects effect because the groups involve different subjects.

**21.27** This is basically a correlational study where we separately correlate the two dependent variables with amount of alcohol consumed. Given the 14-year gap and all of the other factors that affect development, we should not expect very strong correlations even under the best of conditions.

# Index